What does this word mean? **Что означа́ет э́то сло́во?**

I come fro
fornia, I
Вашингт

Excuse me.

With pleasu

Yes. **Да.**

No. **Нет.**

All right. **Хорошо́.**

Where is the hotel? **Где нахо́дится гости́ница?**

What is your name? **Как вас зову́т?**

What is your surname? **Как ва́ша фами́лья?**

My name is ... **Меня́ зову́т ...**

What time is it? **Кото́рый час?** (*or*) **Ско́лько вре́мени?**

How much does this cost? **Ско́лько э́то сто́ит?**

Waiter, the check, please. **Пода́йте, пожа́луйста, счёт.**

MONTHS AND DAYS OF THE WEEK

January **янва́рь**
February **февра́ль**
March **март**
April **апре́ль**
May **май**
June **ию́нь**
July **ию́ль**
August **а́вгуст**
September **сентя́брь**
October **октя́брь**
November **ноя́брь**
December **дека́брь**

Sunday **воскресе́нье**
Monday **понеде́льник**
Tuesday **вто́рник**
Wednesday **среда́**
Thursday **четве́рг**
Friday **пя́тница**
Saturday **суббо́та**

The
Random House
Russian
Dictionary

The
Random House
Russian
DICTIONARY

RUSSIAN-ENGLISH
ENGLISH-RUSSIAN

Stefan Congrat-Butlar

RANDOM HOUSE
NEW YORK

1991 Printing

Abbreviations

abbr.	abbreviation	*det.*	determinate verb
acc.	accusative case	*dim.*	diminutive
adj.	adjective	*dir.*	direction
adv.	adverb	*eccles.*	ecclesiastic
arch.	architecture	*econ.*	economics
astr.	astronomy	*educ.*	education
athl.	athletics	*elec.*	electricity
Bibl.	Biblical	*f.*	feminine
biol.	biology	*fig.*	figurative
bot.	botany	*furn.*	furniture
cap.	capital	*gen.*	genitive case
chem.	chemistry	*geog.*	geography
coll.	collective	*geol.*	geology
colloq.	colloquial	*geom.*	geometry
conj.	conjunction	*gram.*	grammar
dat.	dative case	*hist.*	history
dept.	department	*imp.*	imperfective verb

impers.	impersonal form of verb	*ocean.*	oceanography
ind.	indeclinable	*perf.*	perfective verb
indet.	indeterminate verb	*phon.*	phonetics
instr.	instrumental case	*phot.*	photography
		pl.	plural
interj.	interjection	*polit.*	politics
intr.	intransitive verb	*prep.*	preposition; prepositional case
ling.	linguistics	*print.*	printing
lit.	literature	*pron.*	pronoun
loc.	location	*refl.*	reflexive verb
m.	masculine	*sg.*	singular
mach.	machinery	*surg.*	surgery
math.	mathematics	*swim.*	swimming
mech.	mechanics	*tech.*	technical
med.	medicine	*theat.*	theater
mus.	music	*tr.*	transitive verb
myth.	mythology	*typog.*	typography
n.	noun	*univ.*	university
naut.	nautical	*v.*	verb
nt.	neuter	*v.i.*	verb intransitive
num.	numeral	*v.t.*	verb transitive
		zool.	zoology

Alphabet *and* Concise Pronunciation Guide

The Russian alphabet consists of 32 letters: 20 consonants, 9 vowels, a semivowel, and 2 mute letters that serve to indicate the pronunciation of a preceding consonant.

	Letter	Russian Name	Corresponding English Sound
1	А а	а	calm, father
2	Б б	бэ	bad, rob
3	В в	вэ	van, love
4	Г г	гэ	get, bag
5	Д д	дэ	day, bad
6	Е е	е	yes, yet
	Ё ё[1]	ё	yawn, york
7	Ж ж	же	azure, measure

[1] ё: a graphic variant of e, used mainly in accented foreign textbooks to distinguish the sound *yo* from *ye*. It is not considered a separate letter of the alphabet. ё is accented except in some compound words.

	Letter	Russian Name	Corresponding English Sound
8	З з	зэ	zest, size
9	И и	и	eve, beat
10	Й й	и краткое	feel, realty
11	К к	ка	kind, back
12	Л л	эль	full, lead
13	М м	эм	am, man
14	Н н	эн	no, can
15	О о[2]	о	awe, fought
16	П п	пэ	spin, tops
17	Р р	эр	slightly trilled **r** (no English equivalent)
18	С с	эс	speak, less
19	Т т	тэ	step, pots
20	У у	у	fool, ooze
21	Ф ф	эф	fine, off
22	Х х	ха	as in Scot. loch (no English equivalent)
23	Ц ц	цэ	its, tsetse
24	Ч ч	че	cheap, which
25	Ш ш	ша	sharp, mash
26	Щ щ	ща	plushchair
27	Ъ ъ[3]	твёрдый знак	(not pronounced)
28	Ы ы	ы	approximates **i** in bit, still

[2]**о**: in unaccented syllables, pronounced like *o* in mother, love. In a syllable preceding an accented syllable, **o** is pronounced like Russian **a**.

[3]**ъ**: hard sign; mute

	Letter	Russian Name	Corresponding English Sound
29	Ь ь[4]	мя́гкий знак	**(not pronounced)**
30	Э э	э оборо́тное	let, set
31	Ю ю	ю	you, yule
32	Я я	я	yard, yarn

[4]ь: soft sign; softens the preceding consonant.

The accent in Russian, as in English, is mobile—it is not fixed on the same syllable in all forms of the same word. Thus, the accent in every word and in every form of a word must be memorized. In this dictionary, each word is accented in its basic form: nouns, pronouns, and adjectives in the nominative case singular, verbs in the infinitive. When a word appears in two differently accented forms, the first is the preferred or most commonly encountered.

Russian is a highly inflected language with three genders (masculine, feminine, neuter), two numbers (singular, plural), and six cases (nominative, genitive, dative, accusative, instrumental, prepositional) with inflectional forms by means of which the interrelationship of words in a sentence is indicated. The inflectional forms of nouns, pronouns, and adjectives are called cases and each case has its own ending in every gender and number.

Whereas in English the role of a word is indicated by its position in a sentence, or by word order, in Russian the role of a word is indicated mainly by its inflectional ending.

Length

inch (2.54 centimeters)	дюйм
foot (30.48 centimeters)	фут
yard (91.44 centimeters)	ярд
mile (1,609.33 meters)	ми́ля
millimeter (0.04 in.)	миллиме́тр
centimeter (0.39 in.)	сантиме́тр
meter (39.37 in.)	метр
kilometer (0.62 mile)	киломе́тр

Weight

ounce (28.35 grams)	у́нция
pound (453.59 grams)	фунт
gram (0.04 ounce)	грамм
kilogram (2.2 lbs.)	килогра́мм
ton (2,204 lbs.)	то́нна

Area

sq. foot (929 sq. centimeters)	кв. фут
sq. yard (8361.3 sq. centimeters)	кв. ярд
acre (0.4047 hectares)	акр
sq. mile (2.59 sq. kilometers)	кв. ми́ля
hectare (2.47 acres)	гекта́р

Liquid

pint (.47 liter)	пи́нта
quart (.94 liter)	ква́рта
gallon (3.78 liters)	га́ллон
liter (1.05 liquid quarts)	литр

Introduction

The Russian language is a Slavic language, belonging to the East Slavic subgroup, and is the predominant, official, and administrative language of the USSR. It is the native language of the Great Russians, the main stock of the Russian people dwelling chiefly in the northern and central parts of the Soviet Union, and as spoken in Moscow it is the standard literary language of the USSR. It is with this language that this dictionary is concerned.

The Slavic languages are a branch of the Indo-European linguistic family, which comprises the chief languages of Europe, Indo-Iranian and a few other Asiatic languages. Thus, Russian has many linguistic features in common with other European languages, including Latin and Greek: morphological structure, syntax and vocabulary; e.g.

Russian	English	German	Latin	Italian
мать	mother	Mutter	mater	madre
сестра́	sister	Schwester	——	——
брат	brother	Bruder	frater	——
дом	(domestic)	——	domus	(domestico)
мо́ре	(marine)	Meer	mare	mare
мёд	mead	Met	——	——
седло́	saddle	Sattel	——	sella
вино́	wine	Wein	vino	vino

The
Random House
Russian
Dictionary

A

a, *conj.* but; and. **а то**, otherwise, else, or. **а и́менно**, namely, that is.

абажу́р, *m.* lampshade.

аббревиату́ра, *f.* abbreviation; acronym.

аббревиа́ция, *f.* acronym.

абза́ц, *m.* paragraph.

абисси́нец *m.*, **абисси́нка** *f.*, Abyssinian.

абисси́нский, *adj.* Abyssinian.

абонеме́нт, *m.* subscription.

абоне́нт, *m.* subscriber.

абрико́с, *m.* apricot.

абсолю́тный, *adj.* absolute.

абстра́ктный, *adj.* abstract.

аванга́рд, *m.* advance guard; avant-garde.

ава́нс, *m.* advance. **-ом**, in advance.

авантю́ра, *f.* adventure.

ава́рия, *f.* wreck, crash.

а́вгуст, *m.* August. **-ский**, *adj.* August.

А́вгуст, *m.* Augustus.

Аве́ль, *m.* (*Bible.*) Abel.

авиазаво́д, *m.* aircraft plant.

авиано́сец, *m.* aircraft carrier.

авиапо́чта (*abbr. of* **авиацио́нная по́чта**), *f.* air mail.

авиацио́нный, *adj.* aviation.

авиа́ция, *f.* aviation; (*coll.*) aircraft.

аво́сь, *adv.* perhaps. **на аво́сь**, on the chance (that).

Авро́ра, *f.* Aurora.

австрали́ец *m.*, **австрали́йка** *f.*, Australian.

Австра́лия, *f.* Australia.

австри́ец *m.*, **австри́йка** *f.*, Austrian.

А́встрия, *f.* Austria.

автобиогра́фия, *f.* autobiography.

авто́бус, *m.* bus.

автома́т, *m.* automatic machine; public telephone; vending machine; (*of persons*) automaton. **-и́ческий**, *adj.* automatic.

автомоби́ль, *m.* automobile.

автоно́мный, *adj.* autonomous

а́втор, *m.* author.

авторите́т, *m.* authority. **-ный**, *adj.* authoritative.

а́вторство, *nt.* authorship.

Ага́фья (*also* **Ага́та**), *f.* Agatha.

аге́нт, *m.* agent. **-ство**, *nt.* agency. **-у́ра**, *f.* agency.

агита́тор, *m.* agitator, propagandist.

агита́ция, *f.* agitation, propaganda.

агити́ровать *v. imp.* (*perf.* **сагити́ровать**), disseminate propaganda; agitate.

агити́пункт, *m.* propaganda center.

аго́ния, *f.* agony.

агра́рный, *adj.* agrarian.

агре́ссия, *f.* aggression.

агроно́м, *m.* agronomist. **-и́ческий**, *adj.* agricultural. **-ия**, *f.* agriculture.

ад, *m.* hell; Hades.

ада́мово я́блоко, Adam's apple.

адвока́т, *m.* lawyer, attorney for the defense; advocate. **-у́ра**, *f.* legal profession.

администра́ция, *f.* administration.

адмира́л, *m.* admiral.

а́дрес, *m.* address. **-а́нт**, *m.* sender. **-а́т**, *m.* addressee. **ный**, *adj.* address.

адресова́ть, *v. imp. & perf.* address (mail).

аза́рт, *m.* excitement; passion.
-ный, *adj.* reckless; passionate.

а́збука, *f.* alphabet.

азиа́т *m.*, **-ка** *f.*, Asian, Asiatic. **-ский**, *adj.* Asiatic.

азо́т, *m.* nitrogen.

а́ист, *m.* stork.

акаде́мик, *m.* academician.

академи́ческий, *adj.* academic.

акаде́мия, *f.* academy.

акваре́ль, *f.* water color.

аккомпанеме́нт, *m.* accompaniment.

аккомпани́ровать, *v. imp. & perf.* accompany.

акко́рд, *m.* chord.

аккура́тный, *adj.* regular; accurate; punctual.

акроба́т *m.* acrobat.

акт, *m.* act; deed.

актёр, *m.* actor.

акти́в, *m.* (financial) assets; active membership.

актри́са, *f.* actress.

актуа́льный, *adj.* actual; urgent; topical.

аку́ла, *f.* shark.

акце́нт, *m.* accent.

акционе́р, *m.* shareholder, stockholder.

а́кция, *f.* share; action.

алба́нец *m.*, **алба́нка** *f.*, Albanian.

алба́нский, *adj.* Albanian.

а́лгебра, *f.* algebra. **-и́ческий**, *adj.* algebraic.

Алекса́ндр, *m.* Alexander.

Алекса́ндра, *f.* Alexandra.

Алёша, *dim. of name* Алексе́й.

алиме́нты, *pl.* alimony.

алкого́ль, *m.* alcohol.

Алла́х, *m.* Allah.

алле́я, *f.* avenue; path.

алло́! *interj.* hello.

алма́з, *m.* diamond.

алфави́т, *m.* alphabet. **-ный**, *adj.* alphabetical.

а́лчный, *adj.* greedy.

а́лый, *adj.* scarlet.

альбо́м, *m.* album.

А́льпы, *pl.* the Alps.

алюми́ний, *m.* aluminum.

амба́р, *m.* barn; silo.

амбулато́рия, *f.* dispensary;

outpatient clinic.

америка́нец *m.*, **америка́нка** *f.*, American.

амни́стия, *f.* amnesty.

ампути́ровать, *v. imp. & perf.* amputate.

ана́лиз, *m.* analysis.

анализи́ровать, *v. imp. (perf.* проанализи́ровать), analyze.

аналоги́чный, *adj.* analogous.

анало́гия, *f.* analogy.

ана́рхия, *f.* anarchy.

Анаста́сий, *m.* Anastasius.

Анаста́сия (*also* **Наста́сья**), *f.* Anastasia.

Анато́лий, *m.* Anatole.

ана́том, *m.* anatomist.

анатоми́ровать, *v. imp & perf.* anatomize.

анга́р, *m.* hangar; shed.

анги́на, *f.* tonsillitis.

англи́йский, *adj.* English. **англи́йская була́вка**, safety pin.

англича́нин, *m.* Englishman.

англича́нка, *f.* Englishwoman

А́нглия, *f.* England.

Андре́й, *m.* Andrew.

Андрю́ш(к)а, *dim. of* Андре́й.

анке́та, *f.* (printed) form; questionnaire.

анне́ксия, *f.* annexation

аннули́ровать, *v. imp. & perf.* annul; cancel.

А́ннушка, *dim. of name* А́нна.

анони́мный, *adj.* anonymous.

Антаркти́да, *f.* Antarctica.

Анта́рктика, *f.* the Antarctic.

анте́нна, *f.* antenna.

антило́па, *f.* antelope.

антипати́чный, *adj.* antipathetic.

антисанита́рный, *adj.* insanitary.

антите́за, *f.* antithesis.

анти́чный, *adj.* antique; ancient.

Анто́н, *m.* Anton.

Анто́ний, *m.* Anthony.

Анто́ша, *dim. of* Анто́н.

антра́кт, *m.* intermission.

Аню́та, *dim. of* А́нна.

А́ня, *dim. of* А́нна.

апати́чный, *adj.* apathetic.

апа́тия, *f.* apathy.

апелля́ция, *f.* appeal.

апелли́ровать, v. imp. & perf. appeal.

апельси́н, m. orange.

аплоди́ровать, v. imp. & perf. applaud.

аплодисме́нты, pl. applause.

Аполло́н, m. Apollo.

аппара́т, m. apparatus.

аппети́т, m. appetite. -ный, adj. appetizing.

апре́ль, m. April. -ский, adj. April.

апте́ка, f. pharmacy, drug store.

ара́б, m., -ка f., Arabian. -ский (also арави́йский), adj. Arabian, Arabic.

арбитра́ж, m. arbitration.

арбу́з, m. watermelon.

аргуме́нт, m. argument.

аре́на, f. arena, ring; scene (of action).

аре́нда, f. lease. -тор, m. lessee, tenant.

арендова́ть, v. imp. & perf. rent (from).

аре́ст, m. arrest; custody; attachment.

аресто́вывать, v. imp. (perf. аресто́вать), arrest.

арифме́тика, f. arithmetic.

арифмети́ческий, adj. arithmetical.

а́рия, f. aria.

а́рка, f. arch.

А́рктика, f. the Arctic.

аркти́ческий, adj. arctic.

а́рмия, f. army.

армяни́н m., армя́нка f., Armenian.

армя́нский, adj. Armenian.

арома́т, m., aroma, fragrance.

арте́ль, f. cooperative.

арте́рия, f. (anat.) artery.

арти́кль, m. (gram.) article.

арти́ст, m. artist; actor. -и́ческий, adj. artistic.

Арту́р, m. Arthur.

архи́в, m. archives.

архите́ктор, m. architect.

архитекту́ра, f. architecture.

аспира́нт, m. postgraduate student. -у́ра, f. postgraduate studies or research.

ассамбле́я, f. assembly.

ассигнова́ть, v. imp. & perf. assign, allocate.

ассисте́нт, m. assistant.

ассоциа́ция, f. association.

АССР, abbrev. of Автоно́мическая Сове́тская Социалисти́ческая Респу́блика, Autonomous Soviet Socialist Republic.

астроно́м, m. astronomer. -ия, f. astronomy.

ата́ка, f. attack.

атакова́ть, v. imp. & perf. attack.

атеи́ст, m. atheist.

Атла́нт, m. (myth.) Atlas.

атла́с, m. satin.

а́тлас, m. (myth.) Atlas.

атле́т, m. athlete. -ика, f. athletics.

атмосфе́ра, f. atmosphere.

атмосфе́рный, adj. atmospheric.

а́том, m. atom. -ный, adj. atomic.

аттеста́т, m. certificate; endorsement.

аттестова́ть, v. imp. & perf. certify; endorse; recommend.

аудито́рия, f. auditorium; audience.

аукцио́н, m. auction.

Афана́сий, m. Athanasius.

Афи́ны, pl. Athens.

афи́ша, f. placard, poster.

африка́нец m., африка́нка f., African.

Афо́нька (also Афо́нюшка, Афо́ня), dim. of Афана́сий.

а́хать, v. imp. (perf. а́хнуть), exclaim; gasp.

Ахилле́с, m. Achilles.

аэропо́рт, m. airport.

Б

б, see бы.

ба́ба, f. hag; (tech.) ram; (pastry) baba. сне́жная ба́ба, snow man.

бáбка, *f.* (*colloq.*) old woman; grandmother.

бáбочка, *f.* butterfly. ночнáя бáбочка, moth.

бáбушка, *f.* grandmother.

бáбье лéто, Indian summer.

багáж, *m.* luggage; baggage.

багрóвый, *adj.* crimson.

бáза, *f.* base; basis.

базáр, *m.* market, bazaar.

бази́ровать, *v. imp. & perf.* base; found; ground.

бáзис, *m.* basis; base.

байдáрка, *f.* canoe; kayak.

бак, *m.* tank, cistern; boiler.

бакалéйный, *adj.* grocery.

бакалéйщик, *m.* grocer.

бакалéя, *f.* (*coll.*) groceries.

бактериолóгия, *f.* bacteriology.

бактéрия, *f.* bacterium.

бал, *m.* ball, dance.

балагáн, *m.* booth; show; (*fig.*) farce.

балагýрить, *v. imp.* joke, jest.

баламýтить, *v. imp.* (*perf.* взбаламýтить) confuse; trouble; disturb.

балáнс, *m.* balance.

балдахи́н, *m.* canopy.

балери́на, *f.* ballerina.

балéт, *m.* ballet.

бáлка, *f.* beam, girder.

балкóн, *m.* balcony.

баллáда, *f.* ballad; (*mus.*) ballade.

баллáст, *m.* ballast.

баллоти́ровать, *v. imp.* vote by ballot. -ся, be a candidate, run for an office.

баллотирóвка, *f.* balloting, voting; ballot, poll.

баловáть, *v. imp.* pamper, spoil. -ся, (*colloq.*) play pranks; frolic.

бáловень, *m.* pet; favorite.

баловствó, *nt.* pampering, spoiling; mischievousness.

Балти́йское мóре, Baltic Sea.

бамбýк, *m.* bamboo. -овый, *adj.* bamboo.

банáльный, *adj.* banal, trite.

бáнда, *f.* band, gang.

бандáж, *m.* bandage; truss, belt.

бандерóль, *f.* wrapper.

банди́т, *m.* thug, bandit.

банк, *m.* bank. -и́р, *m.* banker.

бáнка, *f.* jar, pot; bank, shoal; thwart.

банкéт, *m.* banquet.

банкрóт, *m.* bankrupt. -ство, *nt.* bankruptcy.

бант, *m.* bow.

бáня, *f.* bath, bathhouse; (*fig.*) hothouse.

барабáн, *m.* drum.

барабáнить, *v. imp.* drum.

барáк, *m.* temporary wooden barrack; hut.

барáн, *m.* ram. -ина, *f.* mutton.

барáхтаться, *v. imp.* flounder; roll; wallow.

барáшек, *m.* lamb; lambskin.

барáшки, *pl.* fleecy clouds; (*naut.*) whitecaps.

барáшковый, *adj.* lambskin.

бáржа, *f.* barge.

баррикáда, *f.* barricade.

бáрхат, *m.* velvet. -истый, *adj.* velvety. -ный, *adj.* velvet.

барьéр, *m.* barrier; hurdle.

бары́ш, *m.* profit, gain. -ник, *m.* profiteer. -ничество, *nt.* profiteering.

бас, *m.* (*mus.*) bass.

баскетбóл, *m.* basketball.

баснопи́сец, *m.* fabulist.

баснослóвный, *adj.* legendary; (*fig.*) incredible.

бáсня, *f.* fable.

басóвый, *adj.* (*mus.*) bass.

бассéйн, *m.* pond, pool; basin.

бáста, *interj.* enough.

бастовáть, *v. imp.* strike, go on strike.

бастýющий, *adj.* striking. — *m.* striker.

батарéя, *f.* battery.

бати́ст, *m.* batiste, cambric.

баттерфля́й, *m.* (*swimming*) butterfly stroke.

бахвáлиться, *v. imp.* (*colloq.*) brag.

башлы́к, *m.* hood.

башмáк, *m.* shoe.

башмáчник, *m.* shoemaker.

бáшня, *f.* tower.

бая́н, *m.* accordion; bard.

бдéние, *nt.* vigil.

бди́тельный, *adj.* vigilant.

бег, *m.* race; run, running.

бега́, *pl.* races. **быть в бега́х**, (*colloq.*) be on the run.

бе́гать *v. imp. indet.* (*det.* **бежа́ть**, *perf.* **побежа́ть**), run, run about; hurry.

бегемо́т, *m.* hippopotamus.

бегле́ц, *m.* fugitive.

бе́глый, *adj.* fluent; cursory; fugitive.

бего́м, *adv.* on the double.

бе́гство, *nt.* flight; escape.

бегу́н, *m.* (*tech.*) runner.

беда́, *f.* misfortune, trouble.

бедне́ть, *v. imp.* become poor.

беднота́, *f.* (*coll.*) the poor.

бе́дный, *adj.* poor.

бедня́га, *m.* (*colloq.*) poor fellow.

бедня́к, *m.* poor man. **-и́**, *pl.* (*coll.*) the poor.

бедро́, *nt.* thigh; hip.

бе́дствие, *nt.* calamity; disaster.

бе́дствовать, *v. imp.* live in poverty.

бежа́ть, *v. imp. det.* (*indet.* **бе́гать**, *perf.* **побежа́ть**), run; escape; flee.

бе́женец *m.*, **бе́женка** *f.*, refugee.

без (**бе́зо**), *prep.* (+ *gen.*) without.

безала́берный, *adj.* disorderly.

безапелляцио́нный, *adj.* peremptory, categorical.

безбе́дный, *adj.* comfortable, well-to-do.

безбо́жие, *nt.* godlessness, atheism.

безбо́жник, *m.* atheist.

безбо́жный, *adj.* godless, atheistic.

безболе́зненный, *adj.* painless.

безбоя́зненный, *adj.* fearless.

безбра́чие, *nt.* celibacy.

безбре́жный, *adj.* boundless.

безви́нный, *adj.* innocent, guiltless.

безвку́сный, *adj.* tasteless.

безво́дный, *adj.* waterless; arid

безвозвра́тный, *adj.* irrevocable.

безвозду́шный, *adj.* airless.

безвозме́здный, *adj.* gratuitous.

безво́лие, *nt.* weakness of will.

безволо́сый, *adj.* hairless.

безво́льный, *adj.* weak-willed.

безвре́дный, *adj.* harmless, innocuous.

безвре́менный, *adj.* untimely; premature.

безвы́ходный, *adj.* hopeless, desperate.

безгла́сный, *adj.* soundless, mute.

безголо́вый, *adj.* headless; (*fig.*) brainless.

безгра́мотный, *adj.* ungrammatical; illiterate.

безграни́чный, *adj.* infinite, boundless.

безгре́шный, *adj.* sinless.

безда́рный, *adj.* untalented.

безде́йствие, *nt.* inaction, inertia, inertness.

безде́йствовать, *v. imp.* be inactive, inert, idle.

безде́лье, *nt.* idleness.

безде́льник, *m.* idler, loafer.

безде́льничать, *v. imp.* loaf.

безде́нежный, *adj.* impecunious.

безде́тный, *adj.* childless.

безде́ятельный, *adj.* inactive, inert.

бе́здна, *f.* abyss, chasm.

бездо́мный, *adj.* homeless.

безду́шный, *adj.* callous, heartless.

безжа́лостный, *adj.* pitiless, merciless.

безжи́зненный, *adj.* lifeless; lacklustre.

безрабо́тный, *adj.* carefree, unconcerned.

безза́ветный, *adj.* selfless.

беззако́нник, *m.* lawbreaker.

беззако́нность, *f.* lawlessness.

беззасте́нчивый, *adj.* shameless; impudent.

беззащи́тный, *adj.* defenceless, unprotected.

беззву́чный, *adj.* soundless, noiseless.

безземе́льный, *adj.* landless.

безли́чно, *adv.* impersonally.

безли́чный, *adj.* lacking indi-

6viduality *or* personality; (*gram.*) impersonal.

безмо́лвный, *adj.* speechless, silent, mute.

езмяте́жный, *adj.* serene, 6tranquil.

езнадёжный, *adj.* hopeless.

безнака́занно, *adv.* with impunity.

безнача́лие, *adj.* anarchy.

безнра́вственный, *adj.* immoral; dissolute.

безобра́зие, *nt.* ugliness; deformity.

безобра́зный, *adj.* ugly; deformed; formless; disgraceful, outrageous.

безоговоро́чный, *adj.* unconditional.

безопа́сность, *f.* safety.

безопа́сный, *adj.* safe.

безору́жный, *adj.* unarmed.

безостано́вочный, *adj.* ceaseless, unceasing; non-stop.

безотве́тный, *adj.* unrequited; unresponsive; meek.

безотве́тственный, *adj.* irresponsible.

безотлу́чный, *adj.* uninterrupted, continuous.

безоши́бочный, *adj.* unerring, faultless; correct.

безрабо́тица, *f.* unemployment.

безрабо́тный, *adj.* unemployed.

безразде́льный, *adj.* undivided.

безразли́чие, *nt.* indifference; nonchalance.

безразли́чно, *adv.* indifferently. **мне безразли́чно,** it makes no difference to me.

безразли́чный, *adj.* indifferent; nonchalant.

безрассу́дный, *adj.* thoughtless, foolhardy; rash, reckless.

безрезульта́тный, *adj.* futile, ineffectual; unsuccessful, vain.

безро́потность, *f.* resignation; meekness.

безро́потный, *adj.* resigned; uncomplaining.

безуда́рный, *adj.* (*gram.*) unaccented, unstressed.

безукори́зненный, *adj.* irreproachable, unimpeachable.

безу́мец, *m.* fool, idiot; madman.

безу́мие, *nt.* folly; madness.

безу́мный, *adj.* senseless, foolish; reckless; mad.

безу́мство, *nt.* madness.

безупре́чный, *adj.* irreproachable, blameless.

безусло́вный, *adj.* unconditional, absolute.

безуспе́шный, *adj.* unsuccessful.

безуча́стный, *adj.* apathetic, indifferent.

безымённый, *adj.* nameless, anonymous.

белёный, *adj.* bleached.

беле́ть, *v. imp.* (*perf.* **побеле́ть**) *intr.,* become white, whiten.

белизна́, *f.* whiteness.

бели́ть, *v. imp.* whiten, bleach.

бе́лка, *f.* squirrel.

беллетри́ст, *m.* fiction writer, novelist. **-ика,** *f.* belles-lettres; fiction.

бело́к, *m.* white of an egg.

белоку́рый, *adj.* blond, fair, fair-haired.

белоли́цый, *adj.* white-faced.

белору́с *m.,* **-ка** *f.,* Byelorussian.

белосне́жный, *adj.* snow-white.

белоте́лый, *adj.* fair-skinned, white-skinned.

бе́лый, *adj.* white. **бе́лые стихи́,** blank verse.

бельги́ец *m.,* **бельги́йка** *f.,* Belgian.

бельги́йский, *adj.* Belgian.

бельё, *nt.* linen.

бельэта́ж, *m.* first floor; (*theat.*) dress circle.

бемо́ль, *f.* (*mus.*) flat.

бенга́лец *m.,* **бенга́лка** *f.,* Bengali.

бензи́н, *m.* benzine; gasoline.

бе́рег, *m.* shore; coast. **-ово́й,** *adj.* pertaining to a shore, coast; coastal.

бережли́вый, *adj.* thrifty, economical.

берёза, *f.* birch.

берѐменеть, *v. imp. (perf.* **забѐременеть,** become pregnant), be pregnant.

берѐменная, *adj.* pregnant.

берѐчь, *v. imp.* take care of; spare; protect. **-ся,** to be careful; beware; to be on one's guard.

Бѐрингово мо́ре, Bering Sea.

берло́га, *f.* den, lair.

бес, *m.* demon.

бесѐда, *f.* conversation, talk, chat.

бесѐдка, *f.* summerhouse, pergola.

бесѐдовать, *v. imp.* talk, chat.

бескла́ссовый, *adj.* classless.

бесконѐчный, *adj.* endless, infinite; eternal.

бескоры́стный, *adj.* disinterested; unselfish.

бескро́вие, *nt.* bloodlessness, anemia.

бескро́вный, *adj.* bloodless, anemic; pallid.

бескручинный, *adj.* carefree.

бесновáтый, *adj.* raging, raving, frenzied.

бесновáться, *v. imp.* rage, rave.

беспáмятный, *adj.* forgetful.

беспáмятство, *nt.* unconsciousness.

беспардо́нный, *adj. (colloq.)* unceremonious, impudent; insolent.

беспатѐнтный, *adj.* unlicensed.

беспересáдочный билѐт, through-ticket.

беспѐчный, *adj.* careless, unconcerned, care-free.

беспла́тный, *adj.* free of charge, complimentary.

беспло́дие, *nt.* sterility, barrenness.

беспло́дный, *adj.* sterile, barren; fruitless; vain.

беспово́ротный, *adj.* irrevocable.

беспо́добный, *adj. (colloq.)* matchless, incomparable.

беспоко́ить, *v. imp.* perturb, trouble; disturb, bother. **-ся,** worry; be anxious *or* uneasy. **не беспоко́йтесь!** don't bother!

беспоко́йный, *adj.* uneasy, troubled, perturbed.

бесполѐзный, *adj.* useless.

беспо́лый, *adj.* sexless, asexual.

беспо́мощный, *adj.* helpless.

беспоря́док, *m.* disorder.

беспоря́дочный, *adj.* disorderly.

беспоса́дочный перелѐт, nonstop flight.

беспо́чвенный, *adj.* groundless.

беспо́шлинный, *adj.* duty-free.

беспоща́дный, *adj.* merciless, ruthless.

бесправие, *nt.* lawlessness; illegality.

беспра́вный, *adj.* without any rights.

беспредѐльный, *adj.* boundless, infinite.

беспредмѐтный, *adj.* pointless, aimless, purposeless.

беспрерывный, *adj.* incessant.

беспрестáнный, *adj.* continuous, incessant.

беспризо́рный, *adj.* neglected; homeless.

беспримѐрный, *adj.* unexampled; unparalleled.

беспринци́пный, *adj.* unprincipled, unscrupulous.

беспристрáстный, *adj.* impartial, unbiased.

бесприю́тный, *adj.* homeless.

беспробу́дный, *adj.* deep, heavy.

беспрово́лочный, *adj.* wireless.

беспросвѐтный, *adj.* lightless, dark; black; *(fig.)* cheerless, gloomy.

беспроцѐнтный, *adj.* bearing no interest.

бессвя́зный, *adj.* incoherent.

бессемѐйный, *adj.* without a family.

бессемя́нный, *adj.* seedless.

бессердѐчный, *adj.* heartless, callous.

бесси́лие, *nt.* impotence; debility; weakness.

бесси́льный, *adj.* impotent; feeble, weak.

бесслáвный, *adj.* infamous, ignominious.

бесслѐдно, *adv.* without a trace.

бессме́нный, *adj.* continuous, constant, permanent; uninterrupted.

бессме́ртие, *nt.* immortality.

бессме́ртный, *adj.* immortal.

бессмы́сленный, *adj.* senseless, foolish.

бессо́вестный, *adj.* unscrupulous, dishonest.

бессодержа́тельный, *adj.* empty; insipid, vapid.

бессозна́тельный, *adj.* unconscious.

бессо́нница, *f.* insomnia, sleeplessness.

бессо́нный, *adj.* sleepless.

бесспо́рный, *adj.* indisputable, unquestionable.

бессро́чный, *adj.* indefinite; having no time limit.

бесстра́стный, *adj.* impassive.

бесстра́шный, *adj.* fearless, intrepid.

бессты́дный, *adj.* shameless.

беста́ктный, *adj.* tactless.

бесхара́ктерный, *adj.* spineless, weak-willed.

бесцве́тный, *adj.* colorless, drab.

бесце́льный, *adj.* aimless.

бесце́нный, *adj.* priceless.

бесцеремо́нный, *adj.* unceremonious.

бесчелове́чный, *adj.* inhuman; brutal.

бесче́стить, *v. imp.* disgrace.

бесче́стный, *adj.* dishonorable.

бесчи́сленный, *adj.* innumerable, numberless.

бесчу́вственный, *adj.* insensible, insensitive.

бесшу́мный, *adj.* noiseless.

бето́н, *m.* concrete.

бе́шенство, *nt.* hydrophobia, rabies; fury, rage.

бе́шеный, *adj.* rabid, mad; furious, frenzied.

библе́йский, *adj.* Biblical.

библиогра́фия, *f.* bibliography.

библиоте́ка, *f.* library.

библиоте́карь *m.,* -ша *f.,* librarian.

би́блия, *f.* Bible.

бие́ние, *nt.* beating, throbbing, pulsation.

биле́т, *m.* ticket.

билья́рд, *m.* billiards.

бинт, *m.* bandage.

бинтова́ть, *v. imp.* to bandage.

биогра́фия, *f.* biography.

биоло́гия, *f.* biology.

би́ржа, *f.* exchange.

бирма́нец, *m.,* бирма́нка *f.,* Burmese.

бирюза́, *f.* turquoise.

бирюзо́вый, *adj.* turquoise.

бисси́ровать, *v. imp. & perf.* repeat; play encores.

би́тва, *f.* battle.

било́к, *m.* mallet, club; beef cutlet.

би́тый, *adj.* beaten; whipped; broken.

бить, *v. imp.* beat, hit; kill; break.

бич, *f.* whip, lash.

бичева́ть, *v. imp.* whip, lash, flaggelate; castigate.

бла́го, *nt.* blessing, boon.

благови́дный, *adj.* seemly.

благоволе́ние, *nt.* goodwill; kindness.

благовоспи́танный, *adj.* well-bred; polite, courteous, civil.

благогове́ние, *nt.* reverence; awe; veneration.

благодари́ть, *v. imp.* thank.

благода́рность, *f.* gratitude; thanks. не сто́ит благода́рности, don't mention it.

благода́рный, *adj.* grateful, thankful; gratifying.

благодаря́, *prep.* thanks to; owing to.

благоду́шный, *adj.* complacent; placid; good-natured; good-humored.

благожела́тельный, *adj.* kindly, kind; benevolent; kindly disposed.

благозву́чный, *adj.* harmonious; euphonious; melodious.

благо́й, *adj.* good, useful.

благоле́пие, *nt.* splendor, grandeur.

благонаде́жный, *adj.* trustworthy.

благонаме́ренный, *adj.* loyal.

благополу́чный, *adj.* happy; satisfactory; fortunate.

благоприя́тный, *adj.* favorable; propitious; auspicious.

благоразу́мие, *nt.* sense, wisdom, prudence.

благоразу́мный, *adj.* sensible; reasonable; judicious, wise, prudent.

благоро́дный, *adj.* noble.

благоскло́нный, *adj.* favorable.

благослове́ние, *nt.* blessing(s).

благословля́ть, *v. imp.* (*perf.* **благослови́ть**), bless, give one's blessings.

благотвори́тель, *m.* philanthropist.

благотвори́тельность, *f.* philanthropy, charity.

благоустро́енный, *adj.* well-organized; comfortable; well-built.

благоче́стие, *nt.* piety.

блаже́нство, *nt.* bliss, felicity, beatitude.

бланши́ровать, *v. imp.* (*tech.*) to blanch.

бледне́ть, *v. imp.* to pale, turn pale.

бле́дный, *adj.* pale, pallid; colorless.

блёклый, *adj.* faded.

блеск, *m.* brilliance, luster.

блесну́ть, *v. perf.* to flash.

блесте́ть, *v. imp.* to shine, glitter, sparkle.

бле́ять, *v. imp.* bleat.

ближа́йший, *adj.* nearest; next; immediate.

бли́же, *adv.* nearer; closer; more intimate.

бли́жний, *adj.* neighboring. — *m.* neighbor, fellow.

близ, *prep.* (+ *gen.*) near, close to.

бли́зиться, *v. imp.* approach, draw near.

бли́зкий, *adj.* near; imminent; like, similar; intimate.

бли́зко, *adv.* near, close.

близлежа́щий, *adj.* neighboring, nearby.

близне́ц, *m.* twin.

близору́кий, *adj.* near-sighted; (*fig.*) short-sighted.

бли́зость, *f.* nearness; proximity; propinquity.

блин, *m.* pancake.

блиста́тельный, *adj.* brilliant, resplendent, splendid.

блиста́ть, *v. imp.* shine; be conspicuous.

блок, *m.* (*tech.*) pulley.

блока́да, *f.* blockade.

блоки́ровать, *v. imp. & perf.* blockade.

блокно́т, *m.* notebook; writing pad.

блонди́н, *m.* blond. **-ка,** *f.* blonde.

блоха́, *f.* flea.

блуд, *m.* lechery. **-ли́вый,** *adj.* lascivious. **-ный,** *adj.* prodigal.

блужда́ть, *v. imp.* roam, wander.

блу́за (*also* блу́зка), *f.* blouse.

блю́до, *nt.* dish; course.

блю́дце, *nt.* saucer.

блюсти́, *v. imp.* maintain, observe; guard, protect.

блюсти́тель, *m.* observer.

бля́ха, *f.* plate, metal plate.

боб, *m.* bean. **-о́вый,** *adj.* leguminous.

бобёр, *m.* beaver.

бог, *m.* God.

богате́ть, *v. imp.* to grow rich.

бога́тство, *nt.* wealth; riches.

бога́тый, *adj.* rich; wealthy.

богаты́рь, *m.* (*epic*) hero; Hercules.

боги́ня, *f.* goddess.

богомо́лец, *m.* pilgrim.

бода́ть, *v. imp.* butt.

бо́дрый, *adj.* brisk; cheerful.

бое́ц, *m.* fighter, warrior.

боже́ственный, *adj.* divine.

божество́, *nt.* deity; idol.

бой, *m.* battle, combat. **-ня,** *f.* slaughterhouse.

бок, *m.* side; **бок-о́-бок,** side by side, shoulder to shoulder; **с бо́ку на́ бок,** from side to side. **-ово́й,** *adj.* lateral; side.

бокс, *m.* boxing. **-ёр,** *m.* boxer, pugilist.

бокси́ровать, *v. imp.* box.

болва́н, *m.* (*colloq.*) blockhead, dummy; (*cards*) dummy.

болга́рин, *m.*, болга́рка *f.*, Bulgarian.

бо́лее, *adv.* more. тем бо́лее, что, the more so, since.

боле́зненный, *adj.* ailing, sickly; unhealthy; morbid.

боле́знь, *f.* illness, disease, ailment, malady.

боле́льщик, *m.* fan, rooter.

боле́ть, *v. imp.* be ill, ailing; ache, hurt.

боло́то, *nt.* bog, swamp, marsh; mire.

болтли́вый, *adj.* talkative, garrulous.

болтовня́, *f.* chatter.

болту́нья, *f.* scrambled eggs.

боль, *f.* pain.

больни́ца, *f.* hospital.

бо́льно, *adv.* painfully, badly. — (*impers.*) it is painful.

больно́й, *adj.* sick, ill, diseased. — *m.*, больна́я *f.*, patient.

бо́льше, *adj.* bigger, larger, greater, — *adv.* more.

большеви́стский, *adj.* Bolshevik.

большинство́, *nt.* majority.

большо́й, *adj.* big, large, great. большо́й па́лец, thumb.

бо́мба, *f.* bomb.

боре́ц, *m.* champion; fighter; wrestler.

борза́я, *f.* greyhound; Russian wolfhound.

Бори́с, *m.* Boris.

бормота́ть, *v. imp.* mutter, mumble.

борода́, *f.* beard. -тый, *adj.* bearded.

борода́вка, *f.* wart.

борозда́, *f.* furrow; (*anat.*) fissure.

борозди́ть, *v. imp.* to furrow; wrinkle.

борона́, *f.* harrow.

боро́ться, *v. imp.* fight, struggle, contend.

борт, *n. m.* (*naut.*) side. на борту́, on board. за бо́ртом, overboard.

борщ, *m.* borsch.

борьба́, *f.* struggle; fight; wrestling.

Бо́рька, *dim. cf* Бори́с.

босико́м, *adv.* barefoot.

босо́й, *adj.* barefooted.

Босфо́р, проли́в, Bosporus.

бота́ник, *m.* botanist.

бота́ника, *f.* botany.

ботани́ческий, *adj.* botanical.

боти́нки, *pl.* boots.

бо́чка, *f.* barrel, cask.

боязли́вый, *adj.* timid, timorous.

боя́знь, *f.* dread, fear.

боя́ться, *v. imp.* fear, be afraid, dread.

брази́лец *m.*, брази́лья́нка *f.*, Brazilian.

брак, *m.* marriage, matrimony, wedlock.

брани́ть, *v. imp.* scold, reprove, rebuke.

бранчли́вый, *adj.* quarrelsome.

брасс, *m.* breast stroke.

брат, *m.* brother. -а́ние, *nt.* fraternization. -ский, *adj.* brotherly, fraternal. -ство, *nt.* brotherhood, fraternity.

брата́ться, *v. imp.* fraternize.

брать, *v. imp.* (*perf.* взять), take. -ся, undertake, begin.

бра́чный, *adj.* matrimonial, marital, conjugal.

бревно́, *nt.* log.

бред, *m.* delirium.

бре́дить, *v. imp.* be delirious, mad; rave.

бре́дни, *pl.* raving; nonsense.

брезгли́вый, *adj.* squeamish; fastidious.

брезе́нт, *m.* tarpaulin.

бре́мя, *nt.* burden, load.

Брета́нь, *f.* Brittany.

брешь, *f.* breach; gap.

брига́да, *f.* brigade; team, crew.

бриллиа́нт, *m.* diamond. -овый, *adj.* diamond.

брита́нец *m.*, брита́нка *f.*, Britisher.

брита́нский, *adj.* British.

бри́тва, *f.* razor.

бри́тый, *adj.* shaved, cleanshaven.

брить, *v. imp., tr.*, shave.

бритьё, *nt.* shaving.

бровь, *f.* eyebrow, brow.

брод, *m.* ford.

броди́льный, *adj.* fermenting, fermentative.

броди́ть, *v. imp.* wander, roam, rove; ramble.

бродя́га, *m.* tramp, vagrant, hobo.

бродя́чий, *adj.* vagrant; itinerant.

броже́ние, *nt.* fermentation; ferment; discontent.

бро́нза, *f.* bronze.

бронхи́т, *m.* bronchitis.

броня́, *f.* armor; quota.

броса́ть, *v. imp.* (*perf.* бро́сить) throw, hurl, fling. -ся, throw oneself; rush.

бросо́к, *m.* throw, heave.

бро́шенный, *adj.* thrown, hurled; abandoned, deserted.

брошю́ра, *f.* booklet, brochure, pamphlet.

бру́тто, *adj.* gross.

бры́згать, *v. imp.* (*perf.* бры́знуть), splash, spatter, sprinkle.

бры́зги, *pl.* spray; splash; sparks.

брыка́ть, *v. imp.* (*perf.* бры́кнуть), to kick.

брюзгли́вый, *adj.* peevish, grumbling.

брюзжа́ть, *v. imp.* grumble.

брю́ки, *pl.* trousers, pants; breeches.

брю́хо, *nt.* abdomen, belly.

брюшно́й, *adj.* abdominal.

бубны́, *pl.* (*cards*) diamonds.

буди́льник, *m.* alarm clock.

буди́ть, *v. imp.* wake, awaken; arouse, provoke.

бу́дка, *f.* box, booth, stall; cabin. соба́чья будка, doghouse.

бу́дни, *pl.* weekdays. -чный, *adj.* everyday, humdrum, prosaic, dull. бу́дничный день, weekday.

бу́дто, *adv.* as if, as though.

бу́дущее, *nt.* future.

бу́дущий, *adj.* future.

бу́дущность, *f.* future.

бу́йвол, *m.* buffalo.

бу́йный, *adj.* violent, lush, thick.

бу́йство, *nt.* uproar.

бу́йствовать, *v. imp.* behave violently.

бук, *m.* beech.

бу́ква, *f.* letter (of the alphabet).

буква́льный, *adj.* literal.

буква́рь, *m.* primer.

буке́т, *m.* bouquet.

букси́р, *m.* tug, tugboat.

була́вка, *f.* pin.

бу́лка, *f.* roll, bun.

бу́лочная, *f.* bakery.

бу́лочник, *m.* baker.

булы́жник, *m.* cobble, cobblestone.

бульва́р, *m.* boulevard, avenue.

бульо́н, *m.* broth.

бума́га, *f.* paper.

бума́жник, *m.* wallet, pocketbook.

бума́жный, *adj.* paper.

бунт, *m.* riot, mutiny, revolt.

бунтова́ть, *v. imp.* rebel, revolt.

бунтовщи́к, *m.* rebel, insurgent, mutineer, rioter.

бура́вить, *v. imp.* (*tech.*) drill, perforate.

бура́н, *m.* snowstorm.

буре́ние, *nt.* boring, drilling.

буржуази́я, *f.* bourgeoisie.

буржуа́зный, *adj.* bourgeois.

бури́ть, *v. imp.* to bore.

бу́рный, *adj.* stormy; impetuous; violent.

бу́рый, *adj.* brown.

бу́ря, *f.* storm, tempest, gale.

бу́сы, *pl.* beads.

бутербро́д *m.* sandwich.

буто́н, *m.* bud.

бутоньё́рка, *f.* boutonniere.

буты́лка, *f.* bottle.

буфе́т, *m.* sideboard, buffet; canteen, refreshment bar.

бухга́лтер, *m.* bookkeeper, accountant. -ия, *f.* bookkeeping; accounting department.

бу́хта, *f.* (*geog.*) bay; (*rope*) coil.

бушева́ть, *v. imp.* to rage, storm; create an uproar.

бы, *particle used with verbs to*

form the subjunctive or conditional mood.

быва́ть, *v. imp.* to be from time to time; frequent; happen, be held, take place.

бы́вший, *adj.* former, one-time; late.

бык, *m.* bull, ox; abutment, pier.

было́е, *nt.* the past.

было́й, *adj.* former, bygone, past.

быль, *f.* fact; true story.

быстроно́гий, *adj.* swift-footed. fleet-footed.

быстрота́, *f.* quickness, rapidity, speed.

быстрохо́дный, *adj.* high-speed.

бы́стрый, *adj.* quick, rapid, swift.

быт, *m.* mode of life.

бытие́, *nt.* being, existence.

быть, *v. imp.* be.

бюдже́т, *m.* budget.

бюллете́нь, *m.* bulletin, report. избира́тельный бюллете́нь, ballot.

бюро́, *nt. ind.* office.

бюрокра́тия, *f.* bureaucracy.

бюст, *m.* bust. -га́льтер, *m.* brassière.

В

в (во), *prep.* (+ *acc.*) in, into, to; (+ *prep.*) in, at.

ва́бить, *v. imp.* lure, decoy.

ваго́н, *m.* carriage; coach; car.

ва́жничать, *v. imp.* put on airs.

ва́жно, *adv.* with an air of importance; grandly. -сть, *f.* importance; significance.

ва́жный, *adj.* important; significant.

ва́за, *f.* vase; bowl.

вака́нсия, *f.* vacancy.

ва́кса, *f.* shoe polish.

вал, *m.* (*naut.*) billow, roller; bank, rampart.

Валенти́н, *m.* Valentine. -а, *f.* Valentina, Valentine.

вали́ть, *v. imp.* (*perf.* повали́ть), overturn, knock down, fell.

валово́й, *adj.* gross.

вальси́ровать, *v. imp.* waltz.

валю́та, *f.* currency.

Ва́ля, *dim. of* Валенти́н, Валенти́на.

вам, *dat. pl. of* вы..

ва́ми, *instr. pl. of* вы.

Ва́нечка (*also* Ва́нька, Ва́ня), *dim. of name* Ива́н.

ва́нна, *f.* bath; bathtub.

ва́нная, *f.* bathroom.

ва́рвар, *m.* barbarian. -ский, *adj.* barbaric.

Варва́ра, *f.* Barbara.

варёный, *adj.* boiled.

варе́нье, *nt.* jam.

Ва́ренька (*also* Ва́рька, Ва́ря), *dim. of* Варва́ра.

вари́ть, *v. imp.* (*perf.* свари́ть), boil, cook; brew.

Варша́ва, *f.* Warsaw.

вас, *gen., acc., prep. of* вы.

Ва́сек (*also* Ва́сенька, Ва́ська, Ва́ся), *dim. of name* Васи́лий.

василёк, *m.* cornflower.

ва́та, *f.* cotton.

ва́тный, *adj.* quilted; wadded.

ватт, *m.* watt.

ва́хта, *f.* (*naut.*) watch.

ваш, *pron.* your; yours.

вая́ть, *v. imp.* (*perf.* извая́ть), sculpture.

вбега́ть, *v. imp.* (*perf.* вбежа́ть), rush in, run in.

вбива́ть, *v. imp.* (*perf.* вбить), *tr.*, drive in.

вбира́ть, *v. imp.* (*perf.* вобра́ть), absorb; take in.

вблизи́, *prep.* (+ *gen.*) near; not far from.

вброд, *adv.:* переходи́ть вброд, to ford.

введе́ние, *nt.* introduction; preface.

ввезти́, *v. perf. of* ввози́ть.

вверх, *adv.* up, upward(s); вверх дном, upside down.

вверху́, *adv.* above; overhead.

вверя́ть, *v. imp.* (*perf.* вве́рить), entrust.

ввиду́, *prep.* (+ *gen.*) in view of.

вви́нчивать, *v. imp.* (*perf.* ввинти́ть), screw, screw in.

вводи́ть, *v. imp.* (*perf.* ввести́) introduce; lead in *or* into; bring in *or* into.

вво́дный, *adj.* introductory.

ввоз, *m.* importation; imports.

ввози́ть, *v. imp.* (*perf.* ввезти́), import.

вво́лю, *adv.* (*colloq.*) to one's heart's content.

вглубь, *adv.* deep in *or* into.

вгля́дываться, *v. imp.* (*perf.* вгляде́ться), peer at *or* into; observe closely.

вгоня́ть, *v. imp.* (*perf.* вогна́ть) *tr.,* drive in.

вдава́ться, *v. imp.* (*perf.* вда́ться), jut out.

вдалеке́ (*also* вдали́), *adv.* in the far distance; far off.

вдаль, *adv.* far; into the far distance.

вдво́е, *adv.* doubly, double; twice: вдво́е бо́льше, twice as much.

вдвоём, *adv.* together, two together.

вдвойне́, *adv.* doubly, double.

вдева́ть, *v. imp.* (*perf.* вдеть) *tr.,* put into, pass through.

вдоба́вок, *adv.* (*colloq.*) in addition; to boot; on top of everything else.

вдова́, *f.* widow.

вдове́ц, *m.* widower.

вдо́воль, *adv.* enough, plenty.

вдого́нку, *adv.* in pursuit of; after.

вдоль, (*prep.* (+ *gen.*) along. вдоль и попере́к, far and wide; thoroughly.

вдохнове́ние, *nt.* inspiration.

вдохновля́ть, *v. imp.* (*perf.* вдохнови́ть), inspire. -ся, become (*or* feel) inspired.

вдохну́ть, *v. perf. of* вдыха́ть.

вдре́безги, *adv.* to pieces, into smithereens.

вдруг, *adv.* suddenly, all of a sudden.

вду́мчивый, *adj.* thoughtful.

вдыха́ть, *v. imp.* (*perf.* вдохну́ть), inhale.

вегетариа́нец, *m.* vegetarian.

ве́дение, *nt.* authority; competence.

веде́ние, *nt.* conduct; direction; management.

ве́домо, *nt.*: без их ве́дома, without their knowledge *or* consent.

ве́домость, *f.* list; register; record.

ве́домство, *nt.* department.

ведро́, *nt.* bucket, pail.

веду́щий, *adj.* leading; chief.

ведь, *conj.* but; indeed, well.

ве́ер, *m.* fan.

ве́жливый, *adj.* polite, courteous.

везде́; *adv.* everywhere.

везти́, *v. imp. det. of* вози́ть.

век, *m.* century; age; (*colloq.*) lifetime. -ово́й, *adj.* century-old, age-old; secular.

ве́ко, *nt.* eyelid.

ве́ксель, *m.* promissory note.

веле́ть, *v. imp. & perf.* order; tell.

велика́н, *m.* giant.

вели́кий, *adj.* great.

Великобрита́ния, *f.* Great Britain.

великоду́шный, *adj.* magnanimous, generous.

великоле́пный, *adj.* magnificent; splendid; glorious.

велича́йший, *adj.* greatest; supreme.

вели́чественный, *adj.* majestic; grand; sublime.

вели́чие, *nt.* greatness; grandeur.

величина́, *f.* size; (*math.*) quantity; magnitude.

велого́нщик, (*abbr. of* велосипе́дный го́нщик) *m.* cyclist, bicycle racer.

велосипе́д, *m.* bicycle.

велоспо́рт, (abbr. of велосипе́дный спорт) m. cycling.

ве́на, f. (anat.) vein.

Ве́на, f. Vienna.

венге́рец m., венге́рка f., Hungarian.

венге́рский, adj. Hungarian.

Ве́нгрия, f. Hungary.

Вене́ра, f. Venus.

венери́ческий, adj. venereal.

венесуэ́лец m., венесуэ́лка f., Venezuelan.

вене́ц m. crown; wreath.

венециа́нский, adj. Venetian.

Вене́ция, f. Venice.

ве́нзель, m. monogram.

Вениами́н, see Веньями́н.

вено́к, m. garland; wreath.

ве́нский, adj. Viennese.

вентили́ровать, v. imp. (perf. провентили́ровать), ventilate.

вентиля́ция, f. ventilation.

венча́ние, nt. wedding (or marriage) ceremony; coronation.

венча́ть, v. imp. (perf. повенча́ть), crown; marry.

Веньями́н, (also Вениами́н), m. Benjamin.

вепрь, m. wild boar.

ве́ра, f. faith, belief; trust.

Ве́ра, f. Vera.

верблю́д, m. camel.

верблю́жий, adj. camel; camel's-hair.

вербова́ть, v. imp. (perf. завербова́ть), recruit, enlist.

верёвка, f. cord, rope; string.

ве́реск, m. heather.

веретено́, nt. spindle.

ве́рить, v. imp. (perf. пове́рить), believe; trust.

ве́рно, adv. correctly, right; faithfully. — impers. it is true.

ве́рность, f. correctness, truth; faithfulness, fidelity.

верну́ть, v. perf., tr., return, give back; recover; compel. -ся, intr., return, come back.

ве́рный, adj. correct, right; true; faithful.

вероло́мный, adj. perfidious, treacherous.

вероло́мство, nt. perfidy, treachery.

вероя́тность, f. probability.

вероя́тный, adj. probable, likely.

верте́ть, v. imp., tr., twirl, turn, twist. -ся, intr., turn, revolve, spin; (colloq.) fidget.

вертика́льный, adj. vertical.

верфь, f. shipyard; dockyard.

верх, m. top, summit; height. -ни́й, adj. upper, top.

Ве́рхнее о́зеро, Lake Superior.

верхова́я езда́, horseback riding.

верхо́вный, adj. supreme; sovereign.

верхо́м, adv. (on) horseback.

верши́на, f. summit, peak; acme; (math.) apex, vertex.

вес, m. weight; (fig.) influence.

весели́ть, v. imp. (perf. развесели́ть), cheer; amuse. -ся, enjoy oneself, have fun, have a good time.

весёлый, adj. merry, gay; cheerful, jovial.

весе́лье, nt. merriment, merry-making.

весе́нний, adj. spring.

ве́сить, v. imp. weigh.

ве́ский, adj. weighty; significant; convincing, persuasive.

весло́, nt. oar, paddle.

весна́, f. spring.

весно́й (also весно́ю), in the spring.

весну́шка, f. freckle.

весну́шчатый, adj. (colloq.) freckled.

вести́, v., imp. det. of води́ть. вести́ себя́, behave.

вести́сь, v. imp. (colloq.) be under way; progress.

весть, f. news, word.

весы́, pl. scale, scales.

весь, m., вся f., всё nt., все, pl. pron., adj.; all; the whole.

весьма́, adv. very; extraordinarily; highly.

ветвь, n. f. branch, bough.

ве́тер, m. wind; breeze.

ветера́н, m. veteran.

ветерина́р, m. veterinary.

ветеро́к, m. light breeze.

ветка, f. branch, twig.

веточка, f. twig, spring, shoot.

ветрено, adv. frivolously. — impers. pred. it's windy.

ветреный, adj. frivolous, flighty.

ветхий, adj. decrepit; dilapidated.

ветчина, f. ham.

веха, f. boundary mark; landmark.

вечер, m. evening; party. -ом, in the evening.

вечерний, adj. evening.

вечность, f. eternity.

вечный, adj. eternal, everlasting.

вешалка, f. hanger; clothes rack.

вешать, v. imp. (perf. **повесить**), tr., hang; hang up; weigh. -ся, hang oneself.

вещественность, f. materiality.

вещественный, adj. material.

вещество, nt. matter, substance.

вещь, f. thing; object; work.

веять, v. imp. winnow; blow; wave, flutter.

взад и вперёд, up and down, back and forth.

взаимный, adj. mutual, reciprocal.

взаимодействие, nt. interaction, reciprocal action.

взаимоотношение, nt. interrelation, interrelationship.

взаимопомощь, f. mutual aid.

взаймы, adv.; брать взаймы, to borrow. давать взаймы, to lend.

взамен, prep. (+ gen.) in exchange for.

взаперти, adv. under lock; locked up.

взбаламутить, v., perf. of баламутить.

взбунтоваться, v. perf. revolt, mutiny.

взвешивать, v. imp. (perf. **взвесить**), weigh oneself.

взволновать, v., perf. of волновать.

взгляд, m. glance, look; opinion, view.

взглядывать, v. imp. (perf. **взглянуть**), (на + acc.) glance at, look at.

вздор, m. nonsense. -ный, adj. quarrelsome; nonsensical.

вздох, m. sigh.

вздохнуть, v., perf. of вздыхать.

вздрагивать, v. imp. (perf. **вздрогнуть**), shudder; wince.

вздремнуть, v. perf. nap.

вздумать, v. imp. conceive; take it into one's head.

вздыхать, v. imp. (perf. вздохнуть), sigh; long (for).

взламывать, v. imp. (perf. **взломать**), break into.

взлёт, m. take-off.

взлетать, v. imp. (perf. **взлететь**), fly-up, take off.

взлом, m. burglary by breaking in.

взломать, v., perf. of взламывать.

взмах, m. stroke; movement; wave.

взмахивать, v. imp. (perf. **взмахнуть**), flap; wave.

взморье, nt. seashore, beach.

взнос, m. payment, fee.

взойти, v., perf. of всходить.

взор, m. look; gaze.

взрослый, adj. adult.

взрыв, m. explosion.

взрывать, v. imp. (perf. **взорвать**), tr., blow up; infuriate.

взрывчатый, adj. explosive.

взывать, v. imp. appeal; call.

взыскивать, v. imp. (perf. **взыскать**), exact.

взятие, nt. seizure, capture.

взятка, f. bribe; graft.

взяточничество, nt. bribery.

взять (ся), v., perf. of брать(ся).

вид, m. appearance, look; shape, form; view; sight; (gram.) aspect.

видение, nt. vision.

видеть, v. imp. (perf. **увидеть**), see.

видимо, adv. apparently, evidently.

видимый, adj. visible.

видно, impers. pred. it is obvious or clear.

ви́дный, *adj.* visible; prominent, eminent.

визг, *m.* squeal; yelp.

визжа́ть, *v. imp.* (*perf.* завизжа́ть), squeal; yelp.

Вике́нтий, *m.* Vincent.

Ви́ктор, *m.* Victor.

Викто́рия, *f.* Victoria.

ви́лка, *f.* fork; electric plug.

ви́лы, *pl.* pitchfork.

вина́, *f.* guilt; fault.

винегре́т, *m.* mixed salad.

вини́тельный, *adj.* (*gram.*) accusative.

вини́ть, *v. imp.* (*perf.* обвини́ть), blame.

вино́, *nt.* wine.

винова́т!, I'm sorry! Excuse me!

винова́тый, *adj.* guilty.

вино́вник, *m.* culprit.

вино́вный, *adj.* guilty.

виногра́д, *m.* grapes. -ник, *m.* vineyard.

винт, *m.* screw.

винто́вка, *f.* rifle.

винтово́й, *adj.* spiral.

винто́вщик, *m.* rifleman.

виолонче́ль, *f.* 'cello.

ви́селица, *f.* gallows; gibbet.

висе́ть, *v. imp.* (*perf.* пови́снуть), *intr.*, hang, be suspended.

висо́к, *m.* temple (*of the head*).

високо́сный год, leap year.

витри́на, *f.* display window.

вить, *v. imp.* (*perf.* свить), *tr.*, weave; twist. -ся, *intr.*, curl; wind.

Ви́тя, *dim. of* Ви́ктор, Викто́рия.

вихрь, *m.* whirlwind.

вишнёвый, *adj.* cherry.

ви́шня, *f.* cherry; cherry tree.

вка́тывать, *v. imp.* (*perf.* вкати́ть), *tr.*, roll in, wheel in.

вклад, *m.* investment; deposit; contribution.

вкла́дывать, *v. imp.* (*perf.* вложи́ть), put in; invest.

вкле́ивать, *v. imp.* (*perf.* вкле́ить), paste in.

включа́ть, *v. imp.* (*perf.* включи́ть), include; embrace; switch on.

включе́ние, *nt.* inclusion; insertion.

включи́тельно, *adv.* inclusive-(ly).

вкореня́ться, *v. imp.* (*perf.* вкорени́ться), take root.

вкось, *adv.* aslant.

вкра́дчивый, *adj.* insinuating.

вкра́тце, *adv.* in brief, in short; briefly.

вкруту́ю, *adv.* яйцо́ вкруту́ю, hard-boiled egg.

вкус, *m.* taste. -ный, *adj.* tasteful.

вла́га, *f.* moisture, dampness.

владе́лец, *m.* owner, proprietor.

владе́ние, *nt.* property; possession, ownership.

владе́ть, *v. imp.* (*perf.* завладе́ть), own, possess; control.

вла́жный, *adj.* humid; moist, damp.

вла́ствовать, *v. imp.* dominate, rule.

вла́стный, *adj.* commanding, dominating; imperious.

власть, *f.* power.

вле́во, *adv.* to the left.

влеза́ть, *v. imp.* (*perf.* влезть), get in, climb in, crawl in.

влета́ть, *v. imp.* (*perf.* влете́ть) fly in or into.

влече́ние, *nt.* inclination; bent.

влечь, *v. imp.* draw; attract.

влива́ть, *v. imp.* (*perf.* влить), *tr.*, pour in or into.

влия́ние, *nt.* influence.

влия́тельный, *adj.* influential.

влия́ть, *v. imp.* (*perf.* повлия́ть), influence; have influence (on, over).

вложи́ть, *v.*, *perf. of* вкла́дывать.

влюблённый, *adj.* in love.

влюбля́ться, *v. imp.* (*perf.* влюби́ться), fall in love.

вменя́ть, *v. imp.* (*perf.* вмени́ть), impute.

вме́сте, *adv.* together.

вмести́мость, *f.* capacity.

вмести́тельный, *adj.* spacious; capacious.

вмести́ть, *v.*, *perf. of* вмеща́ть

вме́сто, *prep.* (+ *gen.*) instead of, in place of.

вмеша́тельство, *f.* interference; intervention.

вме́шиваться, *v. imp.* (*perf.* **вмеша́ться**), interfere; meddle; intervene.

вмеща́ть, *v. imp.* (*perf.* **вмести́ть**), contain, hold; accomodate.

вмиг, *adv.* in an instant *or* moment.

внаём (*also* **внаймы́**), *adv.*: **брать внаём** (**внаймы́**), to hire, to rent. **отдава́ть внаём** (**внаймы́**) to let, to hire out.

внача́ле, *adv.* at first, in the beginning.

вне, *prep.* (+ *gen.*) outside, out of; beyond. **вне себя́**, beside oneself.

внедря́ть, *v. imp.* (*perf.* **внедри́ть**), inculcate.

внеза́пный, *adj.* sudden; unexpected.

внести́, *v.*, *perf. of* **вноси́ть**.

вне́шний, *adj.* external, outward.

вне́шность, *f.* exterior; external appearance.

вниз, *adv.* down, downwards. **-у**, *adv.* below; downstairs.

вника́ть, *v. imp.* (*perf.* **вни́кнуть**), delve into; try to understand.

внима́ние, *nt.* attention.

внима́тельный, *adj.* attentive.

ничью́, *adv.* in *or* to a draw.

вновь, *adv.* again, anew, once again.

вноси́ть, *v. imp.* (*perf.* **внести́**), *tr.*, carry in, bring in; enter; insert.

внук, *m.* grandson; grandchild.

вну́тренний, *adj.* inner, inside, internal.

вну́тренности, *pl.* (*anat.*) internal organs.

вну́тренность, *f.* interior.

внутри́, *adv.* in, inside. — *prep.* (+ *gen.*) within, inside.

внутрь, *adv.* in, inside. — *prep.* (+ *gen.*) in; into; inside.

вну́чка, *f.* granddaughter.

внуша́ть, *v. imp.* (*perf.* **внуши́ть**), suggest; impress; inspire.

внуше́ние, *nt.* suggestion.

вня́тный, *adj.* distinct; audible.

во, *see* **в**.

вовлека́ть, *v. imp.* (*perf.* **вовле́чь**), *tr.*, involve; draw in.

во́-время, *adv.* in time.

во́все, *adv.* (*colloq.*) quite. **во́все нет**, not at all.

всю́, *adv.* (*colloq.*) to the utmost extent.

во-вторы́х, in the second place; secondly.

вогна́ть, *v.*, *perf. of* **вгоня́ть**.

во́гнутый, *adj.* concave.

вода́, *f.* water.

водворя́ть, *v. imp.* (*perf.* **водвори́ть**), *tr.*, settle, install; establish.

води́тель, *m.* driver.

води́ть, *v. imp. indet.* (*det.* **вести́**, *perf.* **повести́**), *tr.*, conduct, lead; drive; carry on.

во́дка, *f.* vodka.

во́дный, *adj.* water.

водобоя́знь, *f.* hydrophobia.

водовмести́лище, *nt.* water reservoir.

водоворо́т, *n.* whirlpool, eddy.

водоизмеще́ние, *nt.* (water) displacement.

водола́з, *m.* diver.

водолече́бный, *adj.* hydropathic.

водолече́ние, *nt.* hydropathy.

водопа́д, *m.* waterfall.

водопо́й, *m.* watering place.

водопрово́д, *m.* water pipe. **-чик**, *m.* plumber.

водоро́д, *m.* hydrogen.

водоросль, *m.* (*bot.*) water plant; seaweed.

водоснабже́ние, *nt.* water supply.

водосто́к, *m.* water drain; gutter.

водохрани́лище, *m.* reservoir; tank.

водяни́стый, *adj.* watery.

водя́нка, *f.* dropsy.

водяно́й, *adj.* water, aquatic.

воева́ть, *v. imp.* wage war; quarrel, war with.

воединó, *adv.* together.

военноплéнный, *m.* prisoner of war.

воéнный, *adj.* military, martial.

вожáтый, *m.* guide.

вождь, *m.* leader.

вóжжи, *pl.* reins.

воз, *m.* cart; cartful.

возбуди́тель, *m.* agent; stimulus.

возбуждáть, *v. imp.* (*perf.* **возбуди́ть**), excite; arouse, stimulate.

возвещáть, *v. imp.* (*perf.* **возвести́ть**), announce; proclaim.

возврáт, *m.* return; reimbursement, repayment. **-ный,** *adj.* (*med.*) recurrent; (*gram.*) reflexive.

возвращáть, *v. imp.* (*perf.* **возврати́ть**), *tr.*, return, give back; repay. **-ся,** *v. imp.* (*perf.* **возврати́ться, верну́ться**), *intr.*, return; recur, revert.

возвышáть, *v. imp.* (*perf.* **возвы́сить**), raise.

возвышéние, *nt.* rise; elevation.

возвы́шенность, *f.* height, heights; loftiness.

возвы́шенный, *adj.* high, lofty; elevated; exalted.

возглавля́ть, *v. imp.* (*perf.* **возглáвить**), be at the head (of); head.

вóзглас, *m.* exclamation; ejaculation.

возглашáть, *v. imp.* (*perf.* **возгласи́ть**), proclaim.

возгорáемый, *adj.* flammable.

воздвигáть, *v. imp.* (*perf.* **воздви́гнуть**), erect.

воздéйствие, *nt.* influence.

воздéйствовать, *v. imp.* influence; affect.

воздержáние, *nt.* abstention; abstinence; temperance.

воздéрживаться, *v. imp.* (*perf.* **воздержáться**), refrain from; abstain from.

вóздух, *m.* air.

воздýшный, *adj.* air; aerial.

воззвáние, *nt.* appeal.

воззрéние, *nt.* view, opinion.

вози́ть *v. imp. ind.* (*det.* **везти́,** *perf.* **повезти́**), carry, convey; cart; drive.

возлагáть, *v. imp.* (*perf.* **возложи́ть**), *tr.*, lay, place, rest; entrust.

вóзле, *adv., prep.* (+ *gen.*) by, near, beside.

возлюбленный, *adj.* beloved. — *m.* (**возлюбленная** *f.*), sweetheart.

возмéздие, *nt.*, requital; retribution.

возмещáть, *v. imp.* (*perf.* **возмести́ть**), compensate; repay; make up for.

возмóжно, *adv.* it is possible. **как возмóжно скорéе,** as soon as possible.

возмóжность, *f.* possibility, opportunity.

возмóжный, *adj.* possible.

возмужáлый, *adj.* grown-up.

возмути́тельный, *adj.* scandalous; outrageous.

возмущáть, *v. imp.* (*perf.* **возмути́ть**), arouse indignation.

возмущéние, *nt.* indignation.

вознаграждáть, *v. imp.* (*perf.* **вознагради́ть**), reward; recompense.

возникáть, *v. imp.* (*perf.* **возни́кнуть**), arise; originate.

возникновéние, *nt.* rise; origin.

возня́, *f.* bustle; noise, racket.

возобновля́ть, *v. imp.* (*perf.* **возобнови́ть**), renew; resume.

возражáть, *v. imp.* (*perf.* **рази́ть**), object.

возражéние, *nt.* objection.

вóзраст, *m.* age.

возрастáть, *v. imp.* (*perf.* **возрасти́**), grow; increase rise.

возрождáть, *v. imp.* (*perf.* **возроди́ть**), revive; regenerate.

возрождéние, *nt.* revival; regeneration. **епóха Возрождéния,** Renaissance.

вóин, *m.* warrior.

вои́нственный, *adj.* warlike martial; militant.

вой, *m.* howl, wail, whine.

войлóк, *m.* felt.

войнá, *f.* war.

войскá, *pl.* forces, troops.

войти́, *v.,* perf. of входи́ть.

вокáльный, *adj.* vocal.

вокзáл, *m.* railroad station.

вокрýг, *adv.,* prep. (+ *gen.*) round, around; about.

вол, *m.* ox.

волды́рь, *m.* blister.

вóлей-невóлей, *adv.* willy-nilly.

волк, *m.* wolf.

волнá, *f.* wave; breaker.

волнéние, *nt.* agitation; alarm.

волни́стый, *adj.* wavy; corrugated.

волновáть, *v. imp.* (perf. взволновáть), agitate; alarm; disturb.

Волóд(ен)ька (*also* Волóдя), *dim.* of name Влади́мир.

волокни́стый, *adj.* fibrous.

волокнó, *nt.* fibre; filament.

вóлос, *m.* hair. -áтый, *adj.* hairy. -óк, *m.* hair; filament.

волочи́ть, *v. imp., tr.,* drag; trail.

волшéбник, *m.* magician.

волшéбный, *adj.* magic(al).

вóльно, *adv.* freely; (*mil.*) at ease! -сть, *f.* liberty; freedom.

вóльный, *adj.* free.

вольт, *m.* volt. -áж, *m.* voltage.

вóля, *f.* will; liberty; freedom.

вон! *adv.* out; there.

вонзáть, *v. imp.* (perf. вонзи́ть) *tr.,* plunge, thrust. -ся, *intr.,* pierce.

вонь, *f.* stench.

воня́ть, *v. imp.* stink.

воню́чий, *adj.* stinking; foul.

воображáть, *v. imp.* (perf. вообрази́ть), imagine.

вообщé, *adv.* in general, generally.

воодушевлéние, *nt.* enthusiasm.

воодушевля́ть, *v. imp.* (perf. воодуши́ть), inspire, make enthusiastic.

вооружáть, *v. imp.* (perf. вооружи́ть), *tr.,* arm.

вооружéние, *nt.* arms; armament.

воóчию, *adv.* with one's own eyes.

во-пéрвых, in the first place; first of all; firstly.

вопи́ть, *v. imp.* howl; wail.

вопию́щий, *adj.* crying, flagrant, scandalous.

воплощáть, *v. imp.* (perf. воплоти́ть), embody, personify; incarnate.

вопль, *m.* cry, wail.

вопреки́, *prep.* (+ *dat.*) in spite of, despite.

вопрóс, *m.* question; issue. -и́тельный, *adj.* interrogative; question. -ник, *m.* questionnaire.

вор, *m.* thief.

ворвáться, *v. perf.* of врывáться.

воробéй, *m.* sparrow.

воровáть, *v. imp.* steal.

воровствó, *nt.* thievery; stealing.

вóрон, *m.* raven.

ворóна, *f.* crow.

вóрот, *m.* collar; windlass. -ник (*also* -ничóк) *m. dim.* collar.

ворóта, *f.* gate; gates.

вóрох, *m.* pile, heap.

ворóчаться, *v. imp., intr.,* turn, toss.

ворс, *m.* nap; pile.

ворчáть, *v. imp.* growl, snarl; grumble.

восемнáдцатый, *adj.* eighteenth.

восемнáдцать, *num.* eighteen.

вóсемь, *num.* eight.

вóсемьдесят, *num.* eighty.

восемьсóт, *num.* eight hundred.

воск, *m.* wax.

восклúкнуть, *v.,* perf. of восклицáть.

восклицáние, *nt.* exclamation.

восклицáтельный, *adj.* exclamatory; exclamation.

восклицáть, *v. imp.* (perf. восклúкнуть), exclaim.

воскресéнье, *nt.* Sunday.

воскрéсный, *adj.* Sunday.

воспале́ние, nt. inflammation.
воспале́ние лёгких, pneumonia.

воспева́ть, v. imp. (perf. воспе́ть), glorify, celebrate.

воспита́ние, nt. education, training, rearing.

воспита́нник, m., воспита́нница f., pupil.

воспита́тель, m. teacher, tutor.

воспи́тывать, v. imp. (perf. воспита́ть), rear, bring up; teach, educate.

воспламеня́ть, v. imp. (perf. воспламени́ть), inflame; ignite.

воспо́льзоваться, v. perf. (+ instr.) make use of; use; take advantage of.

воспомина́ние, nt. recollection. reminiscence.

воспреща́ть, v. imp. (perf. воспрети́ть), forbid, prohibit.

воспреще́ние, nt. prohibition.

восприе́мник m. godfather.

восприе́мница f. godmother.

восприи́мчивый, adj. susceptible.

воспринима́ть, v. imp. (perf. восприня́ть), perceive; assimilate.

восприня́тие, nt. perception.

воспроизводи́ть, v. imp. (perf. воспроизвести́), reproduce; reprint.

воспроти́виться, v. imp. (perf. воспроти́виться), oppose; resist.

воспря́нуть, v. perf.: воспря́нуть ду́хом, to cheer up.

восстава́ть, v. imp. (perf. восста́ть), про́тив + dat., rise; revolt; rebel.

восстана́вливать, v. imp. (perf. восстанови́ть), restore, re-establish; rehabilitate.

восста́ние, nt. revolt, insurrection, uprising.

восстановле́ние, nt. restoration, reconstruction, rehabilitation.

восто́к, m. east.

восто́рг, m. rapture; enthusiasm.

восторга́ть, v. imp. to entrance enrapture; delight.

восто́чный, adj. east, easterly, eastern; oriental.

востре́бование, nt. claim, claiming. до востре́бования, general delivery; poste restante.

восхвале́ние, nt. praise, praising; praises.

восхваля́ть, v. imp. (perf. восхвали́ть), praise, laud; eulogize.

восхити́тельный, adj. delightful, charming; exquisite.

восхища́ть, v. imp. (perf. восхити́ть), charm, delight. -ся, + instr., admire; be delighted (with); be charmed (by).

восхище́ние, nt. admiration; delight.

восхо́д, m. rise, rising.

восхожде́ние, nt. ascent.

восьмёрка, f. (cards) eight.

восьмидеся́тый, adj. eightieth.

восьмисо́тый, adj. eight hundreth.

восьмиуго́льный, adj. octaganol.

восьмо́й, adj. eighth.

вот, particle there; there is.

воткну́ть, v. perf. of втыка́ть.

вошь, f. louse.

вою́ющий, adj. warring, belligerent.

впада́ть, v. imp. (perf. впасть), в + acc., fall in or into.

впаде́ние, nt. confluence.

впа́дина, f. hollow; cavity.

впа́лый, adj. hollow; caved in.

впасть, v., perf. of впада́ть.

впервы́е, adv. the first time; first.

вперёд, adv. forward; in the future, henceforth. идти вперёд, (of timepieces) be fast.

впереди́, adv. in front, before, ahead.

впереме́жку, adv. alternately.

впереме́шку, adv. pell-mell.

впечатли́тельный, adj. impressionable.

впечатле́ние, nt. impression.

впива́ть, v. imp. (perf. впить), absorb.

впи́сывать, *v. imp. (perf.* **вписа́ть**), inscribe; register, enter in writing.

впи́тывать, *v. imp. (perf.* **впита́ть**), absorb; imbibe.

вплотну́ю, *adv.* close, closely.

вплоть, *adv.* close to the end; (до + *gen.*) up to, close to.

вполза́ть, *v. imp. (perf.* **вползти́**), crawl in, creep in.

вполне́, *adv.* entirely, completely, fully; quite.

впопыха́х, *adv.* hastily, in a hurry.

впосле́дствии, *adv.* later, afterwards; consequently.

вправля́ть, *v. imp. (perf.* **впра́вить**), *tr.*, *(surg.)* set.

впра́во, *adv.* to the right of.

впредь, *adv.* henceforth; in the future.

впро́чем, *adv.* however; nevertheless.

впры́гивать, *v. imp. (perf.* **впры́гнуть**), в + *acc.* jump in; на + *acc.* jump on.

впры́скивание, *nt.* injection.

впры́скивать, *v. imp. (perf.* **впры́снуть**), inject.

впуска́ть, *v. imp. (perf.* **впусти́ть**), *tr.* admit.

впусту́ю, *adv.* in vain; to no purpose.

впу́тывать, *v. imp. (perf.* **впу́тать**), involve; entangle. **-ся**, meddle, interfere; become involved.

враг, *m.* enemy, foe.

вражда́, *f.* enmity, hostility.

вражде́бный, *adj.* hostile.

вра́жеский, *adj.* hostile.

вразуми́тельный, *adj.* intelligible, clear.

врасплóх, *adv.* by surprise, unawares.

врата́рь, *m.* goal keeper, goalie.

врать, *v. imp. (perf.* **совра́ть**), lie, tell lies.

врач, *m.* physician, doctor. **-е́бный**, *adj.* medical.

враща́ть, *v. imp. tr.*, revolve, rotate, turn. **-ся**, *intr.*, revolve, rotate; turn; mingle, associate with.

вред, *m.* harm; hurt; injury.

вреди́тель, *m.* pest; vermin; wrecker, saboteur. **-ство**, *nt.* sabotage.

вреди́ть, *v. imp. (perf.* **повреди́ть**), harm, injure, hurt; damage.

вре́дный, *adj.* harmful, injurious; unhealthful.

времена́ми, *adv.* at times, from time to time.

вре́менный, *adj.* temporary; provisional.

вре́мя, *nt. (pl.* **времена́)** time; *(gram.)* tense.

вре́мя гóда, season.

времяисчисле́ние, *nt.* calendar.

времяпрепровожде́ние, *nt.* pastime.

вро́де, *prep.* (+ *gen.*) like; not unlike.

врождённый, *adj.* innate, inborn.

врозь, *adv.* apart; separately.

врун *m.*, **-ья**, *f.*, liar, fibber.

вруча́ть, *v. imp. (perf.* **вручи́ть**), present, award; deliver

вруче́ние, *nt.* presentation; delivery.

врыва́ться, *v. imp. (perf.* **ворва́ться)**, в + *acc.*, burst in or into; — *(perf.* **врыться**), в + *acc.*, dig in; be dug in.

вса́дник, *m.* rider, horseman.

вса́сывать, *v. imp. (perf.* **всоса́ть)**, absorb.

все, *see* **весь.** — *pron.* everyone, all.

всё, *see* **весь.** — *pron.* all, everything. — *adv.* always; still, yet.

всевозмо́жный, *adj.* all possible.

всегда́, *adv.* always.

всего́, *pron., gen. of* **весь.** — *adv.* all; only.

вселе́нная, *f.* universe; world.

вселя́ть, *v. imp. (perf.* **всели́ть)**, install; establish; instill.

всеми́рный, *adj.* universal.

всео́бщий, *adj.* general, universal.

всерьёз, *adv.* seriously; in earnest.

всесою́зный, *adj.* All-Soviet.

всесторо́нний, *adj.* comprehensive, thorough.

всё-таки, *adv.* nevertheless; still, however.

всеце́ло, *adv.* entirely, completely, wholly.

всея́дный, *adj.* omnivorous.

вска́кивать, *v. imp.* (*perf.* **вскочи́ть**), на + *acc.*, в + *acc.*, jump on or into; jump or leap up.

вска́пывать, *v. imp.* (*perf.* **вскопа́ть**), dig.

вскипа́ть, *v. imp.* (*perf.* **вскипе́ть**), *intr.*, boil, begin to boil; become enraged.

вскипяти́ть, *v.*, *perf. of* **кипяти́ть**.

вско́льзь, *adv.* casually, in passing.

вско́ре, *adv.* shortly or soon after.

вска́кивать, *v.*, *perf. of* **вска́кивать**.

вскри́кивать, *v. imp.* (*perf.* **вскри́кнуть**), scream, shriek.

вскрыва́ть, *v. imp.* (*perf.* **вскры́ть**), open, unseal; disclose, reveal; dissect, lance.

вскры́тие, *nt.* opening, unsealing; revelation, disclosure; dissection; autopsy.

всле́дствие, *prep.* (+ *gen.*) owing to, on account of.

всоса́ть, *v.*, *perf. of* **вса́сывать**.

вспо́мнить, *v.*, *perf. of* **по́мнить**.

вспомога́тельный, *adj.* auxiliary.

вспоте́ть, *v.*, *perf. of* **поте́ть**.

вставно́й зуб, false tooth.

встрево́жить, *v.*, *perf. of* **трево́жить**.

встреча́ть, *v. imp.* (*perf.* **встре́тить**), meet, encounter; greet.

встре́чный, *adj.* contrary.

вступа́ть, *v. imp.* (*perf.* **вступи́ть**), в + *acc.*, enter; join; enter into or upon.

вступи́тельный, *adj.* introductory; entrance; opening.

вступле́ние, *nt.* entry; prelude, preamble, introduction.

всходи́ть, *v. imp.* (*perf.* **взо-** йти́), на + *acc.*, mount, ascend, rise.

всю́ду, *adv.* everywhere.

вся, *see* **весь**.

вся́кий, *adj.* any; every. — *pron.* anyone; everyone.

вся́чески, *adv.* in every possible way or manner.

вта́йне, *adv.* secretly, in secret.

втира́ть, *v. imp.* (*perf.* **вте-** ре́ть), rub in or into.

втихомо́лку, *adv.* secretly, stealthily.

вторга́ться, *v. imp.* (*perf.* **вто́ргнуться**), в + *acc.*, invade; trespass; intrude on or into.

вторже́ние, *nt.* invasion; intrusion.

втори́чно, *adv.* for the second time.

вто́рник, *m.* Tuesday.

вто́рничный, *adj.* Tuesday.

второ́й, *adj.* second; the latter.

второстепе́нный, *adj.* secondary, minor; grade B.

втро́е, *adv.* thrice; three times as much.

втыка́ть, *v. imp.* (*perf.* **вотк-** ну́ть), в + *acc.*, run, drive, stick, thrust in or into.

втя́гивать, *v. imp.* (*perf.* **втяну́ть**), draw, pull in or into.

вуа́ль, *f.* veil.

вуз, *abbr. of* **вы́сшее уче́бное заведе́ние**, institution of higher learning.

вулка́н, *m.* volcano. **-и́ческий**, *adj.* volcanic.

вулканизи́ровать, *v. imp. & perf.* vulcanize.

вход, *m.* entrance, entry; admittance. **-но́й**, *adj.* entrance.

входи́ть, *v. imp.* (*perf.* **войти́**), enter, go or come in.

вчера́, *adv.* yesterday. **-шний**, *adj.* yesterday's.

въезд, *m.* entry, entrance (*by conveyance*).

въезжа́ть, *v. imp.* (*perf.* **въе́хать**), в + *acc.*, enter; drive in or into.

вы, *pron. pl.* you.

выбега́ть, *v. imp.* (*perf.* **вы́бежать**), run out *or* out of.

выбира́ть, *v. imp.* (*perf.* **вы́брать**), choose; elect.

вы́бор, *m.* choice, selection. **-ный**, *adj.* elective, electoral. **-ы**, *pl.* elections.

выбра́сывать, *v. imp.* (*perf.* **вы́бросить**), throw out.

вы́брать, *v.*, *perf. of* выбира́ть.

вы́везти, *v.*, *perf. of* вывози́ть.

вы́вернуть, *v.*, *perf. of* вывора́чивать.

вы́веска, *f.* sign.

вы́вести, *v.*, *perf. of* выводи́ть.

выве́шивать, *v. imp'* (*perf.* **вы́весить**), hang out.

вы́вих, *m.* dislocation.

вы́вихнуть, *v. perf.*, dislocate, sprain.

вы́вод, *m.* conclusion, inference; withdrawal, removal.

вы́вод, *m.* conclusion, inference; withdrawal, removal.

выводи́ть, *v. imp.* (*perf.* **вы́вести**), withdraw, remove; exterminate; conclude, infer.

вы́воз, *m.* export.

вывози́ть, *v. imp.* (*perf.* **вы́везти**), remove; export.

вывора́чивать, *v. imp.* (*perf.* **вы́вернуть**), unscrew.

выгиба́ть, *v. imp.* (*perf.* **вы́гнуть**), bend; curve.

вы́гладить, *v.*, *perf. of* гла́дить.

выгля́дывать, *v. imp.* (*perf.* **вы́глянуть**), look out, peep out.

вы́гнать, *v.*, *perf. of* выгоня́ть.

вы́гнуть, *v.*, *perf. of* выгиба́ть.

вы́говор, *m.* reprimand; pronunciation.

вы́года, *f.* gain, profit; advantage.

вы́годный, *adj.* profitable; advantageous.

выгоня́ть, *v. imp.* (*perf.* **вы́гнать**), drive out; turn out.

выграви́ровать, *v.*, *perf. of* грави́ровать.

выгружа́ть, *v. imp.* (*perf.* **вы́грузить**), unload.

выдава́ть, *v. imp.* (*perf.* **вы́дать**), distribute, give out; betray.

вы́дача, *f.* distribution; extradition.

выдаю́щийся, *adj.* outstanding; eminent, distinguished.

выдвига́ть, *v. imp.* (*perf.* **вы́двинуть**), pull out.

вы́делка, *f.* manufacture.

выде́лывать, *v. imp.* (*perf.* **вы́делать**), manufacture, make.

выделя́ть, *v. imp.* (*perf.* **вы́делить**), single out; choose; detach; secrete.

вы́держанность, *f.* endurance, firmness, steadfastness.

выде́рживать, *v. imp.* (*perf.* **вы́держать**), bear, endure; sustain; control *or* contain oneself.

вы́драть, *v.*, *perf. of* **дра́ть**.

вы́думка, *f.* invention; fib.

выду́мывать, *v. imp.* (*perf.* **вы́думать**), invent, make up, conceive.

вы́езд, *m.* departure.

выезжа́ть, *v. imp.* (*perf.* **вы́ехать**), leave, depart.

выжива́ть, *v. imp.* (*perf.* **вы́жить**), survive.

выжима́ть, *v. imp.* (*perf.* **вы́жать**), wring out, squeeze out.

вы́звать, *v.*, *perf. of* вызыва́ть.

выздора́вливать, *v. imp.* (*perf.* **вы́здороветь**), recover, get well.

выздоровле́ние, *nt.* convalescence, recovery.

вы́зов, *m.* summons; challenge.

вызыва́ть, *v. imp.* (*perf.* **вы́звать**), call, summon; challenge; evoke; cause.

вызыва́ющий, *adj.* defiant; challenging.

выи́грывать, *v. imp.* (*perf.* **вы́играть**), win; gain.

вы́игрыш, *m.* winnings; prize. **-ный**, *adj.* winning.

вы́йти, *v.*, *perf. of* выходи́ть.

вы́кидыш, *f.* abortion; miscarriage.

выкла́дывать, *v. imp.* (*perf.*

вы́ложить), lay out, spread out; cover with.

выключа́тель, m. switch.

выключа́ть, v. imp. (perf. вы́ключить), turn off, shut off; switch off.

выкра́ивать, v. imp. (perf. вы́кроить), cut out.

вы́кройка, f. pattern.

вы́купать, v., perf. of купа́ть.

выкупа́ть, v. imp. (perf. вы́купить), redeem; ransom.

выку́ривать, v. imp. (perf. вы́курить), smoke; smoke out.

вылеза́ть, v. imp. (perf. вы́лезть), climb out; come out, get out; emerge.

вылепля́ть, v., perf. of лепи́ть.

вылета́ть, v. imp. (perf. вы́лететь), fly out; take off; dash out.

вылечивать, v. imp. (perf. вы́лечить), cure.

вылива́ть, v. imp. (perf. вы́лить), pour out.

вы́ложить, v., perf. of выкла́дывать.

вы́мести, v., perf. of мести́.

вымира́ть, v. imp. (perf. вы́мереть), die out; become extinct.

вымога́тельство, nt. extortion.

вымога́ть, v. imp. extort; wring.

вы́мысел, m. fabrication, fiction; lie.

вынима́ть, v. imp. (perf. вы́нуть), take out.

выноси́ть, v. imp. perf. вы́нести), carry out, take out; endure.

выно́сливость, f. endurance.

выно́сливый, adj. hardy; capable of extreme endurance.

вы́нуть, v., perf. of вынима́ть.

вы́пад, m. attack; thrust.

выпада́ть, v. imp. (perf. вы́пасть), fall out, drop out; come out; (snow) fall.

выпека́ть, v. imp. (perf. вы́печь), bake.

выпива́ть, v. imp. (perf. вы́пить), drink (up); drain.

выпи́сывать, v. imp. (perf.

вы́писать), write out; copy; order; discharge.

вы́писка, f. certificate.

вы́пить, v., perf. of выпива́ть.

вы́плата, f. payment.

выпла́чивать, v. imp. (perf. вы́платить), pay, pay out, pay off.

выполне́ние, nt. execution; fulfilment.

выполня́ть, v. imp. (perf. вы́полнить), execute, carry out; fulfil.

вы́пуклый, adj. bulging; prominent; convex.

вы́пуск, m. issue, edition; output.

выпуска́ть, v. imp. (perf. вы́пустить), release, let out; issue; publish; omit.

выраба́тывать, v. imp. (perf. вы́работать), manufacture, produce; work out; earn.

вы́работка, f. output, produce.

выража́ть, v. imp. (perf. вы́разить), express.

выраже́ние, nt. expression.

вырази́тельный, adj. expressive.

вы́разить, v., perf. of выража́ть.

выраста́ть, v. imp. (perf. вы́расти), grow; grow up; grow out of.

выра́щивать, v. imp. (perf. вы́растить), bring up, rear; grow.

выреза́ть, v. imp. (perf. вы́резать), cut out, carve out; engrave.

вырожда́ться, v. imp. (perf. вы́родиться), degenerate.

вырожде́ние, nt. degeneration.

выруга́ть, v., perf. of руга́ть.

вырыва́ть, v. imp. (perf. вы́рвать), pull out, tear out. — (perf. вы́рыть), dig up, dig out.

выселе́ние, nt. eviction.

выселя́ть, v. imp. (perf. вы́селить), evict.

выска́зывание, nt. opinion, saying; declaration.

выска́зывать, v. imp. (perf. вы́сказать), express; declare.

-ся, express oneself, speak out.

высла́ть, v., perf. of высыла́ть.

выслу́шивать, v. imp. (perf. вы́слушать), hear, hear out; listen; (med.) ausculate.

высморка́ться, v., perf. of сморка́ться.

высо́кий, adj. high; tall.

высо́ко, adv. high, high up.

высокоме́рный, adj. haughty.

высота́, f. height; altitude.

вы́сохнуть, v., perf. of высыха́ть.

вы́ставка, f. exhibition.

выставля́ть, v. imp. (perf. вы́ставить), exhibit; expose.

выступа́ть, v. imp. (perf. вы́ступить), appear, come out; come forward.

выступле́ние, nt. appearance.

вы́сушить, v., perf. of сушить.

вы́сший, adj. higher; superior.

высыла́ть, v. imp. (perf. вы́слать), send out, forward; dispatch.

высыпа́ться, v. imp. (perf. вы́спаться), intr., spill. — (perf. вы́спаться), have one's fill of sleep.

высыха́ть, v. imp. (perf. вы́сохнуть), dry out; wither.

высь, f. height.

выта́скивать, v. imp. (perf. вы́тащить), drag out; pull out.

вытека́ть, v. imp. (perf. вы́течь), flow out, leak out.

вытира́ть, v. imp. (perf. вы́тереть), dry; wipe.

выть, v. imp. howl.

вытя́гивать, v. imp. (perf. вы́тянуть), stretch out.

вы́ход, m. egress; exit, outlet; issue.

выходи́ть, v. imp. (perf. вы́йти), go out; look out on.

выходно́й день, day off.

вы́честь, v., perf. of вычита́ть.

вы́чет, m. deduction.

вычисля́ть, v. imp. (perf. вы́числить), calculate.

вычита́ние, nt. (math.) subtraction.

вычита́ть, v. imp. (perf. вы́честь), deduct; subtract.

вычища́ть, v. imp. (perf. вы́чистить), clean; brush; polish.

вы́ше, adj., adv. higher.

вышеука́занный, adj. above-named, above-mentioned.

вышеупомя́нутый, adj. above-mentioned.

вышива́ть, v. imp. (perf. вы́шить), embroider.

вышина́, f. height.

вы́шка, f. tower.

выявля́ть, v. imp. (perf. вы́явить), reveal.

выясня́ть, v. imp. (perf. вы́яснить), elucidate.

вьетна́мец m., вьетна́мка f., Vietnamese.

вью́га, f. snowstorm, blizzard.

вью́чное живо́тное, beast of burden.

вяз, m. elm, elm tree.

вяза́ние, nt. knitting; crocheting.

вяза́ть, v. imp. (perf. связа́ть), tie, bind; knit.

вя́зкий, adj. viscous; swampy, marshy.

вя́лый, adj. flabby; sluggish.

вя́нуть, v. imp. (perf. завя́нуть), wither, fade; droop.

Г

Гаа́га, f. The Hague.

Гава́йи, nt. ind. Hawaii.

га́вань, f. harbor; haven.

Гаврю́ша, dim. of name Гаврии́л.

гад, m. reptile.

гада́тельный, adj. conjectural; problematical; hypothetical.

гада́ть v. imp. (perf. погада́ть), tell fortunes; surmise, conjecture.

га́дкий, *adj.* repulsive, vile, horrid.

газ, *m.* gas; gauze, gossamer.

газе́та, *f.* newspaper.

га́зовый, *adj.* gas; gauze.

га́йка, *f.* (*mach.*) nut.

Га́йти, *nt. ind.* Haiti.

гала́нтный, *adj.* gallant.

галере́я, *f.* gallery.

гало́п, *m.* gallop; (*dance*) galop.

Га́лочка, *dim. of name* Гали́на.

гало́ши, *f. pl.* galoshes, rubbers.

га́лстук, *m.* tie, necktie.

га́лька, *f.* pebble.

Га́ля, *dim. of name* Гали́на.

га́мма, *f.* (*mus.*) scale; (*fig.*) gamut.

гара́ж, *m.* garage.

гаранти́ровать, *v. imp. & perf.* guarantee; vouch.

гардеро́б, *m.* wardrobe.

гармонизи́ровать, *v. imp. & perf.* harmonize.

гармо́ния, *f.* harmony; concord.

гарниту́р, *m.* set; (*furniture*) suite.

гаси́ть, *v. imp.* (*perf.* погаси́ть) extinguish.

га́снуть, *v. imp.* go out, stop burning; decline.

гастри́ческий, *adj.* gastric.

гастро́ль, *f.* tour.

гастроно́м, *m.* epicure.

гвозди́ка, *f.* carnation; clove.

гвоздь, *m.* nail.

где, *adv.* where. **где-либо**, **где-нибудь**, **где-то**, somewhere; anywhere.

генера́льный, *adj.* general.

гене́тика, *f.* genetics.

гениа́льность, *f.* genius.

гениа́льный, *adj.* exceptionally gifted, talented.

ге́ний, *m.* genius.

Генрие́тта, *f.* Henriette.

Ге́нрих, *m.* Henry.

гео́граф, *m.* geographer.

геогра́фия, *f.* geography.

гео́лог, *m.* geologist.

геоло́гия, *f.* geology.

геоме́трия, *f.* geometry.

гера́нь, *f.* geranium.

герб, *m.* coat of arms.

Геркуле́с, *m.* Hercules.

герма́нец *m.*, **герма́нка** *f.*, Teuton; (*colloq.*) German.

Герма́ния, *f.* Germany.

герма́нский, *adj.* German.

геро́иня, *f.* heroine.

герои́ческий, *adj.* heroic; epic.

геро́й, *m.* hero. **-ство**, *nt.* heroism.

ги́бель, *f.* death; annihilation; destruction. **-ный**, *adj.* destructive, ruinous.

ги́бкий, *adj.* flexible; supple; pliable, pliant.

ги́бнуть, *v. imp* (*perf.* поги́бнуть), perish, lose one's life.

гига́нт, *m.* giant. **-ский**, *adj.* gigantic.

гигие́на, *f.* hygiene.

гидра́влика, *f.* hydraulics.

Гимала́и (*also* **Гимала́йские го́ры**), The Himalayas, Himalaya Mountains.

гимн, *m.* anthem.

гимнази́ст *m.*, **-ка** *f.*, secondary school student.

гимна́зия, *f.* secondary school; Gymnasium.

гимна́стика, *f.* gymnastics.

гипно́з, *m.* hypnosis.

гипнотизи́ровать, *v. imp.* (*perf.* загипнотизи́ровать), hypnotize.

гипоте́за, *f.* hypothesis.

гиппопота́м, *m.* hippopotamus.

гипс, *m.* gypsum; plaster. **-овый**, *adj.* plaster.

ги́ря, *f.* dumbbell; weight (*of a clock*).

гита́ра, *f.* guitar.

глава́, *f.* chapter (*of a book*); head, chief.

главнокома́ндующий, *m.* commander in chief.

гла́вный, *adj.* main, chief, principal. **гла́вным о́бразом**, mainly.

глаго́л, *m.* (*gram.*) verb.

гла́дить, *v. imp.* (*perf.* вы́гладить, погла́дить), iron, press; stroke, pat.

гла́дкий, *adj.* smooth, even, sleek.

глаз, *m.* eye. в глаза́, to one's face. за глаза́, behind one's back.

глазни́ца, *f.* eye socket.

глазно́й, *adj.* optic(al), eye.

глазу́нья, *f.* fried eggs.

гла́сный, *adj.* vowel.

гли́на, *f.* clay.

гли́нистый, *adj.* clayey, loamy.

гли́няный, *adj.* clay; earthenware.

гло́бус, *m.* globe; sphere.

глота́ть, *v. imp.* swallow, gulp.

гло́тка, *f.* throat; gullet. во всю гло́тку, (*colloq.*) at the top of one's voice.

глото́к, *m.* swallow, sip, mouthful.

гло́хнуть, *v. imp.* (*perf.* огло́хнуть), grow deaf.

глубина́, *f.* depth, depths; heart, interior; substance.

глубо́кий, *adj.* deep; profound. глубо́кая о́сень, late fall.

глубокомы́сленный, *adj.* profound.

глумле́ние, *nt.* mockery.

глуми́ться, *v. imp.* (*perf.* поглуми́ться), mock, jeer.

глупе́ц, *m.* dolt, blockhead.

глупова́тый, *adj.* doltish, stupid.

глу́пость, *f.* stupidity; dullness.

глу́пый, *adj.* stupid; dull.

глухо́й, *adj.* deaf.

глухонемо́й, *adj.* deaf and dumb. — *n.* deaf-mute.

глухота́, *f.* deafness.

глуши́тель, *m.* silencer; muffler.

гляде́ть, *v. imp.* (*perf.* погляде́ть), на + *acc.*, look at, stare at.

гнать, *v. imp.* drive; pursue; persecute.

гнев, *m.* anger. -ный, *adj.* angry.

гневи́ть, *v. imp.* (*perf.* прогневи́ть), anger.

гнезди́ться, *v. imp.* nest; nestle.

гнездо́, *nt.* nest; (*tech.*) socket; family (*of languages*).

гнёт, *m.* oppression.

гние́ние, *nt.* decay, rotting; corruption.

гнило́й, *adj.* rotten, decayed.

гнить, *v. imp.* (*perf.* сгнить), rot, decay.

гной, *m.* pus. -ный, *adj.* purulent, festering.

гну́сный, *adj.* infamous; villainous.

гнуть, *v. imp.* (*perf.* согну́ть), *tr.*, bend.

говори́ть, *v. imp.* (*perf.* сказа́ть), say, tell; (*perf.* поговори́ть) speak.

говя́дина, *f.* beef.

год, *m.* year. -а́ми, *adv.* for years and years, for years on end. -и́чный (*also* -ово́й), *adj.* annual; yearly. -овщи́на, *f.* anniversary.

годи́ться, *v. imp.* be fit *or* suited for.

го́дный, *adj.* fit; suitable.

голла́ндец *m.*, голла́ндка *f.*, Hollander.

Голла́ндия, *f.* Holland.

голла́ндский, *adj.* Dutch.

голова́, *f.* (*anat.*) head.

головна́я боль, headache.

головокруже́ние, *nt.* dizziness.

головоло́мка, *f.* (*colloq.*) puzzle.

го́лод, *m.* hunger; starvation. -о́вка, *f.* hunger strike.

голода́ть, *v. imp.* (*perf.* проголода́ть), *intr.*, starve.

голо́дный, *adj.* hungry.

го́лос, *m.* voice; vote. в оди́н го́лос, unanimously.

голосло́вный, *adj.* unfounded; unsubstantiated.

голосова́ть, *v. imp.* vote.

голубе́ц, *m.* stuffed cabbage.

голубо́й, *adj.* blue.

го́лубь, *m.* pigeon, dove.

го́лый, *adj.* naked, bare.

Гонду́рас, *m.* Honduras.

гоне́ние, *nt.* persecution.

гоне́ц, *m.* messenger.

го́нка, *f.* haste, hurry.

го́нки, *pl.* races; regatta.

Гонко́нг, *m.* Hong Kong.

Гонолу́лу, *m. ind.* Honolulu.

гонора́р, *m.* fee.

гонча́рное иску́сство, ceramics.

го́нщик, *m.* racer.

гоня́ть, *v. imp.* drive; send.

гора́, *f.* mountain; heap, pile.

гора́здо, *adv.* much, far.

горб, *m.* hump, hunch. -а́тый, *adj.* hunchbacked. -у́н *m.*, -у́нья, *f.*, hunchback.

гордел́ивый, *adj.* proud.

горди́ться, *v. imp.* (+ *instr.*) be proud (of).

го́рдый, *adj.* proud.

го́ре, *nt.* grief; misfortune.

горева́ть, *v. imp.* grieve.

горе́лка, *f.* burner.

го́рестный, *adj.* sad.

горе́ть, *v. imp.* burn, blaze.

го́рец, *m.* mountaineer.

го́речь, *f.* bitterness; bitter taste.

горизо́нт, *m.* horizon. -а́льный, *adj.* horizontal.

гори́стый, *adj.* mountainous.

го́рло, *nt.* throat. дыха́тельное го́рло, windpipe.

горн, *m.* furnace, forge; bugle. -и́ст, *m.* bugler. -ый, *adj.* mountain; mine, mining. -я́к, *m.* miner.

горноста́й, *m.* ermine.

го́род, *m.* city; town. -ско́й, *adj.* city, municipal, urban, metropolitan.

горожа́нин *m.*, горожа́нка *f.*, metropolitan.

горо́х, *m.* (coll.) peas.

горсове́т, *abbr. of* городско́й сове́т, City Council.

горсть, *f.* handful.

горта́нный, *adj.* guttural.

горта́нь, *f.* larynx.

горчи́ца, *f.* mustard.

горшо́к, *m.* pot.

го́рький, *adj.* bitter.

горю́чее, *nt.* fuel.

горю́чий, *adj.* combustible.

горя́чий, *adj.* hot, warm; passionate, ardent, fervent.

горячи́ть, *v. imp.* (*perf.* разгорячи́ть), excite; anger.

горя́чка, *f.* fever.

горя́чность, *f.* ardor, fervor.

госпита́ль, *m.* military hospital. -ный, *adj.* hospital.

господи́н, *m.* gentleman; Mr.

госпо́дство, *nt.* supremacy, domination, reign.

госпо́дствовать, *v. imp.* reign; dominate.

госпожа́, *f.* Mrs.

гостеприи́мный, *adj.* hospitable.

гостеприи́мство, *nt.* hospitality.

гости́ная, *f.* living room.

гости́ница, *f.* hotel; inn.

гости́ть, *v. imp.* (у + *gen.*), be a guest in someone's home.

гость, *m.* guest; visitor.

госуда́рство, *nt.* State, nation, country.

готи́ческий, *adj.* Gothic.

гото́вить, *v. imp.* (*perf.* пригото́вить), *tr.*, prepare.

гото́вность, *f.* readiness; preparedness.

гото́вый, *adj.* ready; prepared.

грабёж, *m.* plunder; robbery.

граби́тель, *m.* burglar; plunderer.

гра́бить, *v. imp.* (*perf.* огра́бить), rob; sack, pillage, plunder.

гра́бли, *pl.* rake.

графи́ровать, *v. imp.* (*perf.* вы́гравировать), engrave.

грaвю́ра, *f.* engraving, print.

град, *m.* hail.

гра́дом, *adv.* profusely.

градуи́рованный, *adj.* graded.

гра́дус, *m.* degree. -ник, *m.* thermometer.

граждани́н *m.*, (*pl.* гра́ждане), гражда́нка *f.*, citizen.

гражда́нство, *nt.* citizenship.

грамм, *m.* gram.

грамма́тика, *f.* grammar.

граммати́ческий, *adj.* grammatical.

гра́мота, *f.* reading and writing; deed, charter; document.

гра́мотный, *adj.* literate.

грана́т, *m.* pomegranate; garnet.

грани́т, *m.* granite. -ный, *adj.* granite.

грани́ца, *f.* boundary; border,

frontier. **за грани́цей**, (*loc.*) abroad. **за грани́цу**, (*dir.*) abroad.

грани́чить, *v. imp.* (+ *instr.*) border (on *or* upon).

гра́фика, *f.* graphic arts.

графи́т, *m.* graphite.

графи́ческий, *adj.* graphic.

грацио́зный, *adj.* graceful.

гра́ция, *f.* grace.

грач, *m.* rook (*bird*).

гребёнка *f.*, **гребе́нь** *m.*, comb.

гребе́ц, *m.* oarsman.

гре́бля, *f.* rowing.

грёза, *f.* daydream.

гре́зить, *v. imp.* dream, daydream.

грек *m.*, **греча́нка** *f.*, Greek.

гре́лка, *f.* hot-water bottle.

греме́ть, *v. imp.* thunder.

грему́чий, *adj.* thundering; thunderous. **грему́чая змея́**, rattlesnake.

грести́, *v. imp.* row, pull; rake.

греть, *v. imp.* warm; give off warmth.

Гре́ция, *f.* Greece.

гре́цкий оре́х, walnut.

гре́ческий, *adj.* Greek.

гречи́ха, *f.* buckwheat.

гре́шник *m.*, **гре́шница** *f.*, sinner.

гре́шный, *adj.* sinful.

гриб, *m.* mushroom.

гри́ва, *f.* mane.

грим, *m.* stage make-up.

грима́са, *f.* grimace.

грима́сничать, *v. imp.* grimace.

грипп, *m.* flu, influenza; grippe.

Гри́ш(к)а, *dim. of name* Григо́рий.

гроб, *m.* coffin. **-ни́ца**, *f.* tomb.

гроза́, *f.* storm, thunderstorm.

грози́ть, *v. imp.* (*perf.* пригрози́ть), threaten.

гро́зный, *adj.* threatening; menacing; terrible.

гром, *m.* thunder.

грома́да, *f.* mass; heap.

грома́дный, *adj.* vast; huge.

громи́ть, *v. imp.* (*perf.* разгроми́ть), smash, destroy; rout.

гро́мкий, *adj.* loud; famous; celebrated.

громо́здкий, *adj.* unwieldy; cumbersome.

гро́хот, *m.* crash; rattle; rumble.

грохота́ть, *v. imp.* (*perf.* прогрохота́ть), rumble; crash; rattle.

грубе́ть, *v. imp.* (*perf.* огрубе́ть), become coarse, rude.

груби́ть, *v. imp.* (*perf.* нагруби́ть), +*dat.*, be rude (to).

гру́бый, *adj.* rude; coarse; rough.

гру́да, *f.* heap, pile.

грудь, *f.* breast; bosom; chest.

груз, *m.* load; cargo, freight; burden, weight.

Гру́зия, *f.* Georgia (*USSR*).

грузови́к, *m.* truck.

грузово́й, *adj.* freight; cargo.

гру́зчик, *m.* stevedore, longshoreman.

грунт, *m.* soil; ground, base.

гру́ппа, *f.* group.

группи́ровать, *v. imp.* (*perf.* сгруппи́ровать), *tr.*, group; gather.

грусти́ть, *v. imp.* be sad *or* melancholy.

гру́стный, *adj.* melancholy; sad, sorrowful.

грусть, *f.* melancholy; sadness.

гру́ша, *f.* pear; pear tree.

гры́жа, *f.* (*med.*) rupture, hernia.

грызть, *v. imp.* gnaw; nibble. **-ся**, *intr.*, (*of dogs*) fight; quarrel.

грызу́н, *m.* rodent.

гряда́ (*also* **гря́дка**), *f.* (*soil*) bed; (*clouds*) bank.

грязни́ть, *v. imp.* (*perf.* загрязни́ть), soil, sully; dirty.

гря́зный, *adj.* dirty; filthy.

грязь, *f.* dirt; filth.

губа́, *f.* lip; (*geog.*) inlet.

губи́тельный, *adj.* disastrous; destructive; fatal.

губи́ть, *v. imp.* (*perf.* погуби́ть), destroy; ruin.

гу́бка, *f.* sponge.

губна́я гармо́ника, harmonica, mouth organ.

губна́я пома́да, lipstick.

гудёть, v. imp. buzz; hoot, honk; drone.

гудо́к, m. whistle; horn.

гу́лкий, adj. hollow.

гуля́нье, nt. walking; promenade; public outdoor festivity.

гуля́ть, v. imp. walk, take a walk.

гумани́зм, m. humanism.

гуманита́рный, adj. humanitarian, humanistic.

гума́нность, f. humaneness, humanity.

гу́сеница, f. caterpillar; caterpillar tractor.

густе́ть, v. imp., intr., thicken.

густо́й, adj. thick; dense.

густота́, f. thickness; denseness.

гусь, f. goose.

гу́ща, f. grounds, lees; thickness; thicket.

гуще, adj. thicker, denser; adv. more thickly or densely.

Д

да, adv. yes. — conj. and; but.

дава́ть, v. imp. (perf. **дать**), give. **дава́ть (дать) знать**, let know.

дави́ться, v. imp. (perf. **пода-ви́ться**), be pressed; choke.

давле́ние, nt. pressure.

да́вний, adj. old, ancient; bygone. **с да́вних пор**, long, for a long time.

давно́, adv. long ago; for a long time. **-проше́дший**, adj. remote (of time).

да́вность, f. remoteness; antiquity.

давны́м-давно́, adv. long, long ago.

да́же, adv. even.

да́лее, adv. further.

далёкий, adj. distant, remote.

далеко́, adv. far. **далеко́ не**, far from.

даль, f. distance. **-нейший**, adj. further; subsequent. **-ний**, adj. distant, remote. **-ность**, f. distance; range. **-ше**, adv. farther.

дальнови́дный, adj. foresighted.

дальнозо́ркий, adj. far-sighted.

да́ма, f. lady; (cards) queen.

Дании́л, m. Daniel.

Да́ния, f. Denmark.

да́нные, pl. data, facts.

да́нный, adj. given; present.

дань, f. tribute; contribution.

дар, m. gift; donation. **-и́тель**, m. donor. **-моед**, m. (colloq.) sponger, parasite. **-ови́тый**, adj. talented, gifted. **-ово́й**, adj. (colloq.) free, gratuitous. **-ом**, adv. free, gratis; in vain.

дари́ть, v. imp. (perf. **подари́ть**), give, donate; favor.

да́та, f. date.

да́тельный, adj. (gram.) dative.

да́тский, adj. Danish.

датча́нин m., **датча́нка** f., Dane.

дать, v., perf. of **дава́ть**.

да́ча, f. summer cottage, country house; portion; act of testifying or giving. **на да́че**, in the country.

два, num. two.

двадца́тый, adj. twentieth.

два́дцать, num. twenty.

два́жды, adv. twice.

двена́дцатый, adj. twelfth.

двена́дцать, num. twelve.

дверь, f. door.

две́сти, num. two hundred.

дви́гатель, m. motor, engine. **-ный**, adj. motive, impellent.

движе́ние, nt. motion, movement; traffic.

дво́е, num. (coll.) two. **-бра́чие**, nt. bigamy. **-же́нец**, m. bigamist. **-то́чие**, nt. (gram.) colon.

двои́ть, v. imp. divide in two. **-ся**, to divide (or be divided) in two. — *impers.*: у меня двойтся в глазах, I see double.

двойка, *f.* two; (*cards*) deuce.

двойник, *m.* double; counterpart.

двойной, *adj.* double, twofold.

двойня, *f.* twins.

двор, *m.* court, yard. -éц, *m.* palace. -ник, *m.* janitor.

двоюродная сестра, first cousin, *f.*

двоюродный брат, first cousin *m.*

двойкий, *adj.* double.

двойко, *adv.* in two ways.

двукратный, *adj.* double, twofold.

двусмысленный, *adj.* ambiguous; equivocal; suggestive, indecent.

дебелый, *adj.* (*colloq.*) plump; buxom.

девица, *f.* girl; unmarried woman; spinster.

девичество, *nt.* girlhood.

девичий, *adj.* girlish, maidenly.

девочка, *f.* girl, little girl.

девственный, *adj.* virgin.

девушка, *f.* young girl.

девяносто, *num.* ninety.

девяностый, *adj.* ninetieth.

девятнадцатый, *adj.* nineteenth.

девятнадцать, *num.* nineteen.

девятый, *adj.* ninth.

девять, *num.* nine. -сот, *num.* nine hundred. -сотый, *adj.* nine hundredth.

дёготь, *m.* tar.

дед, *m.* grandfather; old man; (*pl.*) forefathers.

дед-мороз, *m.* Santa Claus.

дедушка, *m.* (*declined as f.*) grandpa, granddad.

деепричастие, *nt.* (*gram.*) gerund.

дежурить, *v. imp.* be on duty.

дезертир, *m.* deserter. -ство, *nt.* desertion.

дезертировать, *v. imp. & perf.* desert.

дезинфекция, *f.* disinfection.

дезинфицировать, *v. imp. & perf.* disinfect.

действенный, *adj.* effective, efficacious.

действие, *nt.* activity, action; operation; conduct.

действительный, *adj.* real, actual; valid; (*gram.*) active.

действовать, *v. imp.* (*perf.* подействовать), be active; operate, work; function; have an effect on *or* upon.

действующий, *adj.* active, operating, functioning, working; in force. действующие лица, cast of characters.

декабрь, *m.* December. -ский, *adj.* December.

декада, *f.* decade.

дисквалификация, *f.* disqualification.

дисквалифицироваться, *v. imp.* be disqualified; disqualify oneself.

декламация, *f.* recitation.

декламировать, *v. imp.* (*perf.* продекламировать), recite; declaim.

декларация, *f.* declaration.

декрет, *m.* decree, edict.

деланный, *adj.* artificial; feigned; affected.

делать, *v. imp.* (*perf.* сделать), make; do. -ся, become; get; grow; happen, occur.

делегат, *m.* delegate.

делегация, *f.* delegation.

делегировать, *v. imp. & perf.* delegate.

деление, *nt.* division; degree.

деликатный, *adj.* delicate; tactful.

делимое, *nt.* (*math.*) dividend.

делитель, *m.* (*math.*) divisor.

делить, *v. imp.* (*perf.* разделить), divide; dismember; share. — (*perf.* поделить), divide. -ся, (*perf.* разделиться), divide, be divided; (+ на) be divisible (by). — (*perf.* поделиться), share, give; transmit, communicate, impart.

дело, *nt.* affair, business, matter; cause; deed, act; (*pl.*) things, affairs. в самом деле, as a matter of fact.

делово́й, *adj.* business.

де́льный, *adj.* efficient, effective.

де́льта, *f.* delta.

демокра́тия, *f.* democracy.

демократизи́ровать, *v. imp. & perf.* democratize.

де́мон, *m.* demon. -и́ческий, *adj.* demoniac(al).

демонстра́ция, *f.* demonstration.

демонстри́ровать, *v. imp. & perf.* demonstrate.

дене́жный, *adj.* money, monetary, pecuniary; moneyed.

день, *m.* day. на днях, (*past*) the other day; (*future*) in a day or two, one of these days.

де́ньги, *pl.* money.

депе́ша, *f.* dispatch.

депони́ровать, *v. imp. & perf.* deposit.

депре́ссия, *f.* depression.

депута́т, *m.* deputy.

депута́ция, *f.* deputation.

дёргать, *v. imp.* (*perf.* дёрнуть,) pull, tug, jerk.

дереве́нский, *adj.* rural; rustic.

дере́вня, *f.* village; the country.

де́рево, *nt.* tree; wood.

деревя́нный, *adj.* wooden.

держа́ва, *f.* state; power.

держа́ть, *v. imp.* hold; keep. держа́ть пари́, to bet. держа́ть экза́мен, take an examination. -ся, hold (on); adhere; be held; restrain oneself; behave.

дерза́ть, *v. imp.* (*perf.* дерзну́ть,) dare.

де́рзкий, *adj.* impertinent, impudent; audacious.

де́рзость, *f.* impudence, insolence; audacity.

дёрн, *m.* turf, sod.

дёрнуть, *v.,* *perf.* of дёргать.

десе́рт, *m.* dessert.

десна́, *f.* (*anat.*) gum.

деспоти́ческий, *adj.* despotic.

десятибо́рье, *nt.* decathlon.

десяти́чный, *adj.* decimal.

деся́ток, *m.* ten; (*pl.*) tens; scores; dozens.

деся́тый, *adj.* tenth.

де́сять, *num.* ten.

дета́ль, *f.* detail. -ный, *adj.* detailed; minute.

детёныш, *m.* young one; calf, cub. *pl.* (*coll.*) the young.

де́ти, *pl.* children; (*colloq.*) kids.

деторо́дный, *adj.* genital.

де́тская, *f.* nursery.

де́тский, *adj.* childish; children's, child's.

де́тство, *nt.* childhood.

дефекти́вный, *adj.* defective.

дефи́с, *m.* hyphen.

дефици́т, *m.* deficit. -ный, *adj.* deficient.

дешеве́ть, *v. imp.* (*perf.* подешеве́ть,) become cheaper, cheapen.

дешеви́зна, *f.* cheapness.

дёшево, *adv.* cheap, cheaply.

дешёвый, *adj.* cheap.

де́ятель, *m.* worker; activist. -ность, *f.* activity; profession, occupation, vocation. -ный, *adj.* active; energetic.

джу́нгли, *pl.* jungle.

диа́гноз, *m.* diagnosis.

диагности́ровать, *v. imp. & perf.* diagnose.

диагона́ль, *f.* diagonal.

диале́кт, *m.* dialect. -ика, *f.* dialectics. -и́ческий, *adj.* dialectical.

диало́г, *m.* dialogue.

диа́метр, *m.* diameter.

дива́н, *m.* sofa.

диви́ться, *v. imp.* (*colloq.*) marvel, be astonished.

ди́вный, *adj.* wonderful, marvelous.

ди́во, *nt.* wonder, marvel.

дие́з, *n.* (*mus.*) sharp.

дие́та, *f.* diet.

ди́зель, *m.* Diesel engine.

дика́рь, *m.* savage.

ди́кий, *adj.* wild, savage; queer; preposterous, outrageous.

ди́кость, *f.* savagery, savageness.

диктату́ра, *f.* dictatorship

диктова́ть, *v. imp.* (*perf.* продиктова́ть,) dictate.

дикто́вка, *f.* dictation.

ди́ктор, *m.* (*radio*) announcer

ди́кция, *f.* diction, articulation, enunciation.

дина́мика, *f.* dynamics.

дипло́м, *m.* diploma.

диплома́тия, *f.* diplomacy.

директи́ва, *f.* directive; instructions, directions.

дире́ктор, *m.* director.

дирижа́бль, *m.* dirigible.

дирижёр, *m.* (*mus.*) conductor.

дирижи́ровать, *v. imp.* (*mus.*) conduct.

диск, *m.* discus. **-обо́л**, *m.* discus thrower.

дискредити́ровать, *v. imp. & perf.* discredit.

дискримина́ция, *f.* discrimination.

дискримини́ровать, *v. imp. & perf.* discriminate.

дискуссия, *f.* discussion.

дискути́ровать, *v. imp. & perf.* discuss.

диспансе́р, *m.* dispensary.

ди́спут, *m.* dispute, debate.

дисципли́на, *f.* discipline.

дисциплини́ровать, *v. imp. & perf.* discipline.

дитя́, *nt.* child.

дифференци́ровать, *v. imp. & perf.* differentiate.

дичь, *f.* game, wildfowl.

длина́, *f.* length. **в длину́**, lenthwise.

дли́нный, *adj.* long.

дли́тельный, *adj.* long, prolonged; protracted.

длить, *v. imp.* (*perf.* **продли́ть**) prolong; continue; protract.

для, *prep.* (+ *gen.*) for; to.

дневни́к, *m.* diary; journal.

дневно́й, *adj.* day; daily. **дневно́й свет**, fluorescent light. **дневно́й спекта́кль**, matinee performance.

днём, in the daytime; by day.

дно, *nt.* bottom. **вверх дном**, upside down. **до дна**, bottoms up.

до, *prep.* (+ *gen.*) to, till, until; under; about; before.

доба́вка, *f.* addition.

добавле́ние, *nt.* addition; appendix.

добавля́ть, *v. imp.* (*perf.* **доба́вить**), add.

добива́ть, *v. imp.* (*perf.* **доби́ть**), finish off. **-ся**, obtain; attain; achieve; secure; strive.

до́блесть, *f.* valor.

добро́, *nt.* good, benefit; property, possessions. **-во́лец**, *m.* volunteer. **-во́льный**, *adj.* voluntary. **-лу́ше**, *nt.* good nature. **-жела́тель**, *m.* wellwisher. **-ка́чественный**, *adj.* of high quality. **-со́вестность**, *f.* conscientiousness. **-со́вестный**, *adj.* conscientious.

доброта́, *f.* goodness, kindness.

до́брый, *adj.* good, kind.

добыва́ть, *v. imp.* (*perf.* **добы́ть**), get, obtain; procure; extract; mine.

добы́ча, *f.* obtainment; procurement; extraction; loot, plunder.

довезти́, *v.*, *perf. of* **довози́ть**.

дове́ренный, *adj.* possessing power of attorney; — *m.* proxy; agent.

дове́рие, *nt.* trust, confidence.

дове́рить, *v.*, *perf. of* **доверя́ть**.

дове́рчивый, *adj.* trustful, trusting; credulous.

доверша́ть, *v. imp.* (*perf.* **доверши́ть**), complete; conclude.

доверя́ть, *v. imp.* (*perf.* **дове́рить**), entrust; trust.

до́вод, *m.* reason; argument; **до́воды за и про́тив**, pros and cons.

доводи́ть, *v. imp.* (*perf.* **довести́**), bring to; drive into.

довое́нный, *adj.* pre-war.

дово́льно, *adv.* rather; fairly; sufficiently; quite.

дово́льный, *adj.* content, contented, satisfied.

дово́льствие, *nt.* allowance.

дово́льство, *nt.* contentment.

дога́дка, *f.* guess; conjecture.

дога́дливый, *adj.* shrewd, keen, quick-witted, penetrating.

догáдываться, v. imp. (perf. **догадáться**), guess, surmise, conjecture; suspect.

догнáть, v., perf. of **догонять**.

договóр, m. agreement; contract; pact, treaty. **-ённость**, f. understanding, arrangement.

догонять, v. imp. (perf. **догнáть**), overtake; catch up with or to.

доезжáть, v. imp. (perf. **доéхать**), reach; arrive (at).

доéние, nt. milking.

дождевóй, adj. pluvial; rain.

дождлúвый, adj. rainy.

дождь, m. rain. **дождь идёт**, it is raining. **на дождé**, in the rain.

дозволять, v. imp. (perf. **дозвóлить**), permit, allow.

дойть, v. imp. (perf. **подойть**), milk.

дойти, v., perf. of **доходить**.

доказáтельный, adj. conclusive, demonstrative.

доказáтельство, nt. proof, evidence.

докáзывать, v. imp. (perf. **доказáть**), prove.

доклáд, m. lecture. **-чик**, m. lecturer.

доклáдывать, v. imp. (perf. **доложить**), report, make a report; announce.

дóктор, m. doctor.

докумéнт, m. document.

докучáть, v. imp. (+ dat.) bother, pester.

докучлúвый, adj. bothersome, annoying.

долг, m. debt; duty.

дóлгий, adj. long.

дóлго, adv. long, for a long time. **-врéменный**, adj. lasting; of ong duration. **-срóчный**, adj. long-term.

долготá, f. length; (geog.) longitude.

должáть, v. imp. (perf. **задолжáть**), borrow (from); be in debt.

должнúк, m. debtor.

дóлжность, f. position, post.

дóлжный, adj due, proper.

долúна, f. valley.

доложить, v., perf. of **доклáдывать**.

долóй, adv. away with, down with.

дóльше, adv. longer.

дóля, f. portion, share; fate, lot.

дом, m. house, home. **-а**, adv. at home. **-óй**, adv. (dir.) home. **-áшний**, adj. domestic; home.

доминиóн, m. dominion.

доминúровать, v. imp. (над + instr). predominate (over).

дóмысел, m. conjecture; guess.

донáшивать, v. imp. (perf. **доносúть**), wear out.

донесéние, nt. report, dispatch, message.

дóнизу, adv. to the botom.

дóнор, m. blood donor.

доносúть, v. imp. (perf. **донестú**), denounce, inform (against); report. — v., perf. of **донáшивать**. **-ся**, v. imp. (perf. **донестúсь**), reach one's ears, be heard.

доплáта, f. additional payment.

доплáчивать, v. imp. (perf. **доплатúть**), make an additional payment.

дополнéние, nt. supplement; addition; (gram.) object.

дополнúтельный, adj. supplementary; additional.

дополнять, v. imp. (perf. **дополнить**), supplement; complete.

допрáшивать, v. imp. (perf. **допросúть**), examine, question; cross-examine.

допрóс, m. examination, inquest, cross-examination.

допускáть, v. imp. (perf. **допустúть**), admit; permit, allow; assume.

допустúмый, adj. permissible.

дореволюциóнный, adj. prerevolutionary.

дорóга, f. road; way; journey.

дóрого, adv. expensive, expensively; dear, dearly. **-вúзна**, f. dearness, expensiveness.

дорого́й, *adj.* dear, darling; dear, expensive.

доро́дный, *adj.* portly, corpulent.

дорожи́ть, *v. imp.* value; care for.

доро́жка, *f.* path, lane; runner; carpet.

Дорофе́я, *f.* Dorothy.

доса́да, *f.* nuisance, annoyance; disappointment.

досажда́ть, *v. imp.* (*perf.* досади́ть), annoy, vex.

доска́, *f.* board; plank. **от доски́ до доски́** from cover to cover.

досло́вный, *adj.* literal; word for word.

досмо́тр, *m.* examination.

досро́чный, *adj.* ahead of schedule.

достава́ть, *v. imp.* (*perf.* доста́ть), get, obtain, procure; (до + *gen.*) reach, touch.

доста́вка, *f.* delivery.

доставля́ть, *v. imp.* (*perf.* доста́вить), deliver; furnish, supply; convey.

доста́ток, *m.* sufficiency.

доста́точный, *adj.* sufficient.

доста́ть, *v., perf. of* доставать.

достига́ть, *v. imp.* (*perf.* дости́чь, дости́гнуть), + *gen.*, achieve, attain, reach.

достиже́ние, *nt.* achievement; attainment.

достове́рный, *adj.* trustworthy, reliable.

досто́инство, *nt.* dignity.

досто́йный, *adj.* worthy, deserving; fitting, suitable.

достопа́мятный, *adj.* memorable.

достопримеча́тельность, *f.* object or place of interest; sight.

достопримеча́тельный, *adj.* notable, remarkable; of especial interest.

достоя́ние, *nt.* property; holdings.

до́ступ, *m.* access; approach.

досту́пный, *adj.* accessible.

досу́г, *m.* leisure.

до́сыта, *adv.* to the point of satiation; to one's heart's content.

досю́да, *adv.* (*colloq.*) to here, up to here, as far as this.

досяга́емость, *f.* attainability.

до́хлый, *adj.* (*of animals*) dead.

дохля́тина, *f.* carrion.

до́хнуть, *v. imp.* (*of animals*) die.

дохну́ть, *v. perf.* breathe.

дохо́д, *m.* income; return. **-ный**, *adj.* income producing; profitable.

доходи́ть, *v. imp.* (*perf.* дойти́) до + *gen.*, reach.

доце́нт, *m.* docent; university lecturer.

дочь, *f.* daughter.

дошко́льный, *adj.* pre-school.

драгоце́нность, *f.* jewel, precious stone; treasure.

драгоце́нный, *adj.* precious.

дразни́ть, *v. imp.* tease.

дра́ка, *f.* fight.

дра́ма, *f.* drama. **-ти́ческий** (*also* **-ти́чный**) *adj.* dramatic. **-ту́рг**, *m.* playwright.

дра́ный, *adj.* torn; ragged.

драть, *v. imp.* (*perf.* вы́драть), tear; flay, flog. **-ся**, *v. imp.* (*perf.* подра́ться), fight. — (*perf.* разодра́ться), *intr.*, tear.

древе́сный, *adj.* wood.

дре́вний, *adj.* ancient.

дре́вность, *f.* antiquity.

дрейф, *m.* (*ocean*) drift.

дрейфова́ть, *v. imp. & perf.* drift.

дрема́ть, *v. imp.* doze; nap.

дремо́та, *f.* drowsiness.

дрему́чий, *adj.* thick.

дресси́ровать, *v. imp.* (*perf.* вы́дрессировать), train; school.

дрессиро́вщик, *m.* trainer.

дроби́ть, *v. imp.* (*perf.* раздроби́ть), divide *or* split up; crush; splinter.

дробь, *f.* (*math.*) fraction.

дрова́, *pl.* firewood.

дро́ги, *pl.* hearse.

дро́гнуть, *v. perf.* quiver; waver; flinch.

дрожа́ть, v. imp. shiver; tremble.

дро́жжи, pl. yeast.

дрожь, f. tremor, quaver; trembling, quivering.

друг, m. friend. друг дру́га, one another.

други́е, pl. others; the rest.

друго́й, adj. the other; another next.

дру́жба, f. amity, friendship.

дру́жеский, adj. friendly.

дру́жный, adj. amicable, friendly; unanimous.

дрянно́й, adj. worthless, bad, trashy.

дрянь, f. rubbish; trash.

дря́хлый, adj. decrepit; senile.

дуб, m. oak. **-о́вый,** adj. oak, oaken.

ду́ло, nt. muzzle.

ду́ма, f. meditation; thought; Duma.

ду́мать, v. imp. (perf. поду́мать), think. — inf. intend.

Дуна́й, m. Danube.

Ду́нька (also Ду́ня, Ду́няш(к)а), dim. of name Евдо́кия.

дупло́, nt. hollow.

ду́ра, f., дура́к m., fool.

дурма́нить, v. imp. (perf. одурма́нить), stupefy; intoxicate.

дурно́й, adj. foul; bad; evil; ugly.

дурь, f. (colloq.) folly; foolishness.

дуть, v. imp. blow.

дух, m. spirit, heart, courage; ghost. **-и́,** pl. perfume; scent. **-ове́нство,** nt. (coll.) clergy. **-о́вный,** adj. spiritual.

духово́й инструме́нт, wind instrument

духово́й орке́стр, (mus.) brass band.

духота́, f. stuffiness, closeness.

душ, m. shower, shower bath.

душа́, f. soul.

душева́я, f. shower; shower bath.

душевнобольно́й, adj. mentally ill. — n. insane person; mental case.

душе́вный, adj. sincere, cordial, heartfelt; mental.

ду́шенька, f. (colloq.) dear, darling, sweetheart; my dear.

души́стый, adj. fragrant, scented.

души́ть, v. imp. (perf. задуши́ть), strangle; stifle; smother; oppress, repress, suppress. —(perf. надуши́ть), perfume, scent.

ду́шный, adj. close, stuffy.

дуэ́ль, f. duel.

дуэ́т, m. duet.

ды́бом, adv. on end.

дым, m. smoke. **-ка,** f. mist; haze. **-ный,** adj. smoky.

дыми́ть, v. imp. (perf. надыми́ть), fill with smoke. **-ся,** intr., smoke; become filled with smoke or steam.

ды́ня, f. melon, muskmelon.

дыра́ (also ды́рка), f. hole.

дыря́вый, adj. full of holes.

дыха́ние, nt. respiration, breathing.

дыха́тельный, adj. respiratory.

дыша́ть, v. imp. breathe, respire.

дья́вол, m. devil. **-ьский,** adj. devilish; awful, horrible.

дю́жина, f. dozen.

дюйм, m. inch.

дю́на, f. dune.

дя́дя, m. (declined as f.) uncle.

дя́тел, m. woodpecker.

Е

Е́ва, f. Eva, Eve.

ева́нгелие, nt. gospel.

евангели́ст, m. evangelist.

Евге́ний, m. Eugene.

евге́ника, f. eugenics.

Евге́ния, f. Eugenia.

еврей *m.*, -ка *f.*, Jew, Hebrew.
-ский, *adj.* Jewish, Hebrew.
Европа, *f.* Europe.
европеец *m.*, европейка *f.*,
　European.
европеизировать, *v. imp. &*
　perf. Europeanize.
европейский, *adj.* European.
Египет, *m.* Egypt.
египтянин *m.*, египтянка *f.*,
　Egyptian.
его, *pron.*, *gen. & acc. case of*
　он, оно́.
еда, *f.* food; meal.
едва, *adv.* hardly. едва не,
　nearly, almost.
единение, *nt.* unity.
единица, *f.* unit; one.
единичный, *adj.* single; iso-
　lated.
единобожие, *nt.* monotheism.
единобрачие, *nt.* monogamy.
единовременно, *adv.* once.
единогласие, *nt.* unanimity,
　unanimousness.
единомыслие, *nt.* complete
　uniformity of ideas *or* opin-
　ions.
единообразие, *nt.* uniformity.
единственный, *adj.* sole, only.
единство, *nt.* unity.
единый, *adj.* united.
едкий, *adj.* caustic.
её, *pron.*, *gen. & acc. case of*
　она.
ёж, *m.* porcupine.
ежевика, *f.* (*coll.*) black-
　berries.
ежегодник, *m.* annual.
ежегодный, *adj.* annual.
ежедневный, *adj.* daily.
ежемесячник, *m.* monthly.
ежемесячный, *adj.* monthly.
ежеминутный, *adj.* occurring
　every minute; continual, in-
　cessant.
еженедельник, *m.* weekly.

еженедельный, *adj.* weekly.
ежечасный, *adj.* occurring
　every hour.
езда, *f.* ride, drive; driving,
　traveling.
ездить *v. imp. indet.* (*det.*
　ехать, *perf.* поехать), ride;
　drive, go; travel, journey.
ездок, *m.* rider, horseman;
　cyclist.
ей, *pron.*, *dat. & instr. case of*
　она.
Екатерина, *f.* Catherine.
еле, *adv.* scarcely.
Елена, *f.* Helen, Helena.
Елизавета, *f.* Elizabeth.
ёлка, *f.* fir tree.
ёмкий, *adj.* capacious.
ёмкость, *f.* capacity, capa-
　ciousness.
ему, *pron.*, *dat. case of* он, оно́.
епископ, *m.* bishop. -альный,
　adj. episcopalian. -ский, *adj.*
　episcopal. -ство, *nt.* episco-
　pate.
ересь, *f.* heresy.
еретик, *m.* heretic.
ерунда, *f.* nonsense; rubbish.
ерундить, *v. imp.* (*colloq.*)
　talk nonsense.
если, *conj.* if; but for.
естественный, *adj.* natural.
естество, *nt.* nature; substance.
-ведение (*also* -знание), *nt.*
　natural science.
есть [1], *v. imp.* (*perf.* съесть),
　eat; smart; corrode.
есть [2], *impers.* there is, there
　are. — *adv.* (*mil.*) aye-aye.
ехать, *v. imp. det. of* ездить.
ехидный, *adj.* (*colloq.*) mali-
　cious, spiteful, venomous.
ехидство, *nt.* malice, spite,
　venom.
ещё, *adv.* still, yet; more,
　some more; as far back as.
ею, *pron.*, *instr. case of* она.

Ж

ж, *see* же.
жаба, *f.* toad; quinsy, tonsil-
　litis.

жаворонок, *m.* lark.
жадничать, *v. imp.* (*colloq.*)
　be greedy.

жа́дный, *adj.* greedy; avid, covetous.

жа́жда, *f.* thirst.

жа́ждать, *v. imp.* thirst; crave.

жале́ть, *v. imp.* (*perf.* пожале́ть), be *or* feel sorry; regret.

жа́лить, *v. imp.* (*perf.* ужа́лить), sting, bite.

жа́лкий, *adj.* pitiful, pitiable.

жа́лко, *adv.* pitifully. как жа́лко! what a pity!

жа́ло, *nt.* (*zool.*) sting.

жа́лоба, *f.* complaint.

жа́лобный, *adj.* plaintive, sorrowful, mournful.

жа́ловать, *v. imp.* (*perf.* пожа́ловать), grant, bestow, confer; favor, be gracious; visit. -ся, complain.

жа́лостливый, *adj.* pitiful, compassionate.

жа́лость, *f.* pity.

жаль, *impers.*: it's a pity. мне его́ жаль, I feel sorry for him.

жанр, *m.* genre.

жар, *m.* heat; ardor; fever.

жара́, *f.* heat.

жарго́н, *m.* jargon, slang.

жа́реный, *adj.* fried; grilled; broiled.

жа́риться, *v. imp.* (*perf.* изжа́риться), *intr.*, fry; roast; broil; grill; (*colloq.*) sun, bask.

жа́ркий, *adj.* hot, torrid; tropical; ardent.

жа́рко, *adv.* hotly, hot.

жарко́е, *nt.* meat dish; roast.

жаро́вня, *f.* brazier.

жасми́н, *m.* jasmine.

жа́тва, *f.* harvest, reaping; harvest time.

жать, *v. imp.* (*perf.* сжать), press, squeeze; pinch; reap.

жва́чные, *pl.* (*zool.*) ruminants.

жгу́чий, *adj.* burning.

ждать, *v. imp.* wait, await, expect.

жева́ние, *nt.* mastication.

жева́тельный, *adj.* masticatory; (for) chewing.

жева́ть, *v. imp.* chew, masticaate, ruminate.

жезл, *m.* rod; baton; staff.

жела́ние, *nt.* wish, desire; longing, hunger.

жела́тельный, *adj.* desirable.

жела́ть, *v. imp.* (*perf.* пожела́ть), wish, desire; covet.

железа́, *f.* gland.

желе́зистый, *adj.* glandular; ferriferous.

желе́зная доро́га, railway, railroad.

железнодоро́жный, *adj.* railway, railroad.

желе́зный, *adj.* iron; ferrous железо, *nt.* iron.

желте́ть, *v. imp.* (*perf.* пожелте́ть), *intr.* yellow.

желтизна́, *f.* yellowness.

желтова́тый, *adj.* yellowish.

желто́к, *m.* yolk (*of an egg*).

желту́ха, *f.* (*med.*) jaundice.

жёлтый, *adj.* yellow.

желу́док, *m.* stomach.

желу́дочек, *m.* ventricle.

жёлудь, *m.* acorn.

жёлчность, *f.* biliousness; jaundice.

жёлчный, *adj.* bilious; bitter.

жёлчь, *f.* bile; gall.

же́мчуг, *m.* (*coll.*) pearls.

же́мчужина, *f.* pearl.

же́мчужница, *f.* pearl oyster.

жена́, *f.* wife. -тый, *adj.* (*of a man*) married.

жени́ть, *v. imp. & perf.* marry, wed. -ся, (*of a man*) to marry, get married.

жени́тьба, *f.* marriage.

жени́х, *m.* fiancé, betrothed.

женонави́стник, *m.* misogynist.

женоподо́бный, *adj.* effeminate.

же́нский, *adj.* female, feminine, womanly.

же́нственность, *f.* femininity.

же́нщина, *f.* woman.

Же́ня, *dim. of names* Евге́ний, Евге́ния.

жердь, *f.* rod, pole.

жеребёнок, *m.* foal.

жеребе́ц, *m.* stallion.

жереби́ться, *v. imp.* (*perf.* ожереби́ться), foal.

же́ртва, *f.* sacrifice; victim.

жёртвовать, v. imp. (perf. **пожёртвовать**), donate, offer, endow; sacrifice.

жест, m. gesture.

жестикули́ровать, v. imp. gesticulate.

жёсткий, adj. hard, strong, firm, rigid.

жесто́кий, adj. cruel.

жесть, f. tin.

жестяно́й, adj. tin.

жечь, v. imp. (perf. **сжечь**), tr., burn.

жжёный, adj. burned, burnt.

живи́тельный, adj. vivifying; bracing.

жи́во, adv. lively, animatedly; quickly; vividly, graphically.

живо́й, adj. living, live, alive.

живопи́сец, m. painter, artist.

живопи́сный, adj. picturesque.

жи́вопись, f. (art) painting.

жи́вость, f. liveliness, animation.

живо́т, m. stomach, belly.

живо́тное, nt. animal, beast.

живо́тный, adj. animal; organic; bestial, brute.

живу́честь, f. viability; tenaciousness.

живу́чий, adj. viable; vital; living.

жи́дкий, adj. liquid; thin.

жидкова́тый, adj. watery.

жи́зненность, f. vitality.

жи́зненный, adj. vital.

жизнеописа́ние, nt. biography.

жизнера́достный, adj. cheerful, joyous.

жизнеспосо́бный, adj. viable.

жизнь, f. life.

жи́ла, f. vein; sinew.

жил-был, once upon a time there was or lived.

жиле́т, m., -ка, f., vest, waistcoat.

жиле́ц m., **жили́ца** f., tenant, lodger.

жи́листый, adj. sinewy, stringy, wiry.

жили́ще, m. dwelling, abode, living quarters.

жи́лка, f.(bot.) fibre; vein; nerve.

жило́й, adj. dwelling; habitable.

жильё, nt. dwelling; domicile; habitation.

жир, m. fat.

жира́ф, m. giraffe.

жире́ть, v. imp. (perf. **разжире́ть**), become or grow fat.

жи́рный, adj. fat; plump; rich; greasy; boldface.

жирово́й, adj. fatty; adipose.

жи́тель m., **-ница** f., inhabitant, resident. **-ство**, nt. residence; domicile.

жи́тница, f. granary.

жи́то, nt. rye, barley, wheat; grain in general.

жить, v. imp. live. **-ся**, impers.: **как вам живётся?** (colloq.) how are things?

житьё, nt. life; existence.

жнец, m. reaper.

жни́во (also **жнивьё**), nt. stubble; harvest.

жоке́й, m. jockey.

жо́лудь, m., see **жёлудь**.

жонглёр, m. juggler.

жре́бий, m. lot; fate, destiny.

жужжа́ть, v. imp. hum, buzz, drone.

жук, m. beetle.

жура́вль, m. crane (bird).

жури́ть, v. imp. (colloq.) rebuke, scold.

журна́л, m. magazine, periodical, journal; register, diary. **-и́ст** m., **-и́стка** f., journalist. **-и́стика**, f. journalism.

журча́ть, v. imp. gurgle, babble, murmur.

жу́ткий, adj. dreadful, horrible, terrible.

жу́ткость, f. dread, horror, terror.

жюри́, nt. ind. judges; umpire.

З

за, prep. (+ acc.) across, over; | out of; for, by. — (+

instr.) behind, beyond; after.

зааплоди́ровать, *v. perf.* begin to applaud.

заба́ва, *f.* amusement.

забавля́ть, *v. imp.* amuse, entertain.

заба́вный, *adj.* amusing.

забастова́ть, *v. imp. & perf.* strike, go on strike.

забасто́вка, *f.* strike.

забве́ние, *nt.* oblivion.

забе́г, *m.* (*athl.*) heat, round.

забере́менеть, *v.,* *perf. of* **бере́менеть.**

забива́ть, *v. imp.* (*perf.* **заби́ть**) drive *or* hammer in; stop *or* block up.

забинтова́ть, *v. imp. & perf.* bandage.

забира́ть, *v. imp.* (*perf.* **забра́ть**), take.

заблаговре́менно, *adv.* in good time; in advance; early.

заблуди́ться, *v. perf.* lose one's way.

заблужда́ться, *v. imp.* be mistaken; err.

заблужде́ние, *nt.* error.

заболева́ть, *v. imp.* (*perf.* **заболе́ть**), become ill; get an ache *or* pain.

забо́р, *m.* fence.

забо́та, *f.* care; anxiety.

забо́титься, *v. imp.* (*perf.* **позабо́титься**), be concerned; take care of.

забо́тливый, *adj.* careful, thoughtful; concerned.

забра́ть, *v.,* *perf. of* **забира́ть.**

забро́шенный, *adj.* neglected; deserted, abandoned.

забыва́ть, *v. imp.* (*perf.* **забы́ть**), forget.

забы́вчивый, *adj.* forgetful; absent-minded.

забы́тый, *adj.* forgotten.

зава́ливать, *v. imp.* (*perf.* **завали́ть**), fill up, overload; bury under.

зава́ривать, *v. imp.* (*perf.* **завари́ть**), brew.

заведе́ние, *nt.* institution; establishment.

заве́дование, *nt.* management.

заве́довать, *v. imp.* (+ *instr.*) manage; head.

заве́дующий, *m.* manager, director.

завербова́ть, *v.,* *perf. of* **вербова́ть.**

заверша́ть, *v. imp.* (*perf.* **заверши́ть**), complete, conclude.

заверше́ние, *nt.* completion.

заверя́ть, *v. imp.* (*perf.* **заве́рить**), assure; certify.

заве́са, *f.* curtain; screen.

завести́, *v.,* *perf. of* **заводи́ть.**

заве́т, *m.* precept; legacy; behest.

завеща́ние, *nt.* will; testament.

завеща́ть, *v. imp. & perf.* bequeath.

завзя́тый, *adj.* inveterate; confirmed.

завива́ть, *v. imp.* (*perf.* **зави́ть**), wave, curl.

зави́вка, *f.* hairdo; wave.

зави́дный, *adj.* enviable.

зави́довать, *v. imp.* (*perf.* **позави́довать**), + *dat.,* envy.

завизжа́ть, *v.,* *perf. of* **визжа́ть.**

зави́сеть, *v. imp.* (от + *gen.*) depend on *or* upon.

зави́симость, *f.* dependence. **в зави́симости от** (+ *gen.*), depending on.

зави́симый, *adj.* dependent.

зави́стливый, *adj.* envious.

за́висть, *f.* envy.

зави́ть, *v.,* *perf. of* **завива́ть.**

завладева́ть, *v. imp.* (*perf.* **завладе́ть**), + *instr.,* take possession of; seize, conquer, capture.

завладе́ть, *v.,* *perf. of* **владе́ть,** **завладева́ть.**

завлека́ть, *v. imp.* (*perf.* **завле́чь**), entice; lure.

заво́д, *m.* plant, works, mill.

заводи́ть, *v. imp.* (*perf.* **завести́**), bring, take, *or* lead to; acquire; establish; introduce.

завоева́тель, *m.* conqueror.

завоёвывать, *v. imp.* (*perf.* **завоева́ть**), conquer.

завсегда́тай, *m.* habitué.

за́втра, *adv.* tomorrow. **-ний**, *adj.* tomorrow's.

за́втрак, *m.* breakfast.

за́втракать, *v. imp.* (*perf.* поза́втракать), breakfast, eat breakfast.

завя́зка, *f.* string; lace; (*lit.*) plot.

завя́зывать, *v. imp.* (*perf.* завяза́ть), bind; fasten; tie.

завя́зь, *f.* (*bot.*) ovary.

завя́нуть, *v., perf. of* вя́нуть.

зага́дка, *f.* riddle; enigma; mystery.

зага́дочный, *adj.* enigmatic; mysterious.

зага́дывать, *v. imp.* (*perf.* загада́ть), ask riddles; think of, conceive.

зага́р, *m.* sunburn.

загаси́ть, *v. perf.* put out, extinguish.

заги́б, *m.* bend; (*colloq.*) exaggeration.

загиба́ть, *v. imp.* (*perf.* загну́ть), bend; turn up or down; earmark.

загипнотизи́ровать, *v., perf. of* гипнотизи́ровать.

загла́вие, *nt.* title, heading.

загла́вная бу́ква, capital letter.

загла́живать, *v. imp.* (*perf.* загла́дить), press, iron; make amends (for).

загло́хнуть, *v., perf. of* гло́хнуть.

заглуша́ть, *v. imp.* (*perf.* заглуши́ть), muffle; drown out; deaden; alleviate; suppress, stifle.

загля́дывать, *v. imp.* (*perf.* загляну́ть), look or peep in.

загна́ть, *v., perf. of* загоня́ть.

загнива́ть, *v. imp.* (*perf.* загни́ть), rot, decay.

за́говор, *m.* conspiracy, plot. **-щик**, *m.* conspirator, plotter.

заголо́вок, *m.* title, heading; headline.

заго́н, *m.* enclosure.

загоня́ть, *v. imp.* (*perf.* загна́ть), drive in, into or out; exhaust.

загора́ть, *v. imp., intr.* (*perf.*

загоре́ть), sunburn, tan; bask in the sun. **-ся**, catch fire; light up; break out.

загоре́лый, *adj.* sunburned; tanned.

за́городный, *adj.* out-of-town; country; rural.

загота́вливать, *v. imp.* (*perf.* загото́вить), prepare; lay in store.

загото́вка, *f.* procurement, purchase; storage.

загражда́ть, *v. imp.* (*perf.* загради́ть), block.

заграни́чный, *adj.* foreign.

загреба́ть, *v. imp.* (*perf.* загрести́), rake up; gather in.

загри́вок, *m.* withers.

загроможда́ть, *v. imp.* (*perf.* загромозди́ть), encumber; jam, block.

загрязня́ть, *v. imp.* (*perf.* загрязни́ть), soil, dirty; pollute.

загуби́ть, *v. perf.* ruin.

зад, *m.* back, hind part; buttocks; posterior; hind quarters.

задава́ть, *v. imp.* (*perf.* зада́ть), set, pose.

зада́ние, *nt.* task.

зада́ток, *m.* deposit, advance.

зада́ча, *f.* problem, task.

задви́жка, *f.* bolt, door bolt.

задержа́ние, *nt.* detention; arrest.

заде́рживать, *v. imp.* (*perf.* задержа́ть), detain, delay; arrest; retard.

заде́ржка, *f.* delay.

задира́ть, *v. imp.* (*perf.* задра́ть), turn up; pull up; lift up.

за́дний, *adj.* back, hind, rear.

задо́лго, *adv.* long before.

задолжа́ть, *v., perf. of* должа́ть.

задо́лженность, *f.* indebtedness; liabilities.

за́дом, *adv.* backwards; with one's back.

задо́р, *m.* fervor, enthusiasm. **-ный**, *adj.* fervent, enthusiastic; defiant.

задра́ть, v., perf. of задира́ть.

заду́мчивость, f. pensiveness.

заду́мывать, v. imp. (perf. **заду́мать**), conceive; plan; + inf., intend. **-ся,** become pensive; become thoughtful; meditate.

задуши́ть, v., perf. of души́ть.

заём, m. loan.

зажа́ть, v., perf. of зажима́ть.

заже́чь, v., perf. of зажига́ть.

за́живо, adv. alive.

зажига́лка, f. cigarette lighter.

зажига́тельный, adj. incendiary.

зажига́ть, v. imp. (perf. **заже́чь**), set fire (to); light.

зажима́ть, v. imp. (perf. **зажа́ть**), squeeze; clutch, grip; suppress, keep down.

зажи́точный, adj. prosperous.

заи́грывать, v. imp. (perf. **заигра́ть**), strike up a tune; begin to play.

заика́ться, v. imp. (perf. **заикну́ться**), stutter; stammer; mention.

заи́мствовать, v. imp. (perf. **позаи́мствовать**), adopt; borrow.

заи́ндеветь, v., perf. of и́ндеветь.

заинтересова́ть, v. perf. interest. **-ся,** + instr. take interest in; become interested in.

заинтригова́ть, v., perf. of интригова́ть.

заи́скивать, v. imp. court; be ingratiating; make up to.

зайти́, v., perf. of заходи́ть.

зака́з, m. order. **-но́й,** adj. made to order or measure; registered. **-чик,** m. customer, client.

зака́зывать, v. imp. (perf. **заказа́ть**), order.

закалённый, adj. tempered; hardened.

зака́лывать, v. imp. (perf. **заколо́ть**), stab; kill, slaughter.

закаля́ть, v. imp. (perf. **закали́ть**), temper, strengthen.

зака́нчивать, v. imp. (perf. **зако́нчить**), finish, complete; conclude.

зака́пывать, v. imp. (perf. **закопа́ть**), bury.

зака́т, m. sunset; decline.

закла́д, m. pledge; pawn, pawning.

закла́дка, f. bookmark.

закла́дывать, v. imp. (perf. **заложи́ть**), place, put, lay; install; pawn.

закле́ивать, v. imp. (perf. **закле́ить**), glue, seal.

заклейми́ть, v., perf. of клейми́ть.

заклина́ть, v. imp. conjure; invoke.

заключа́ть, v. imp. (perf. **заключи́ть**), conclude, infer; close, wind up.

заключе́ние, nt. conclusion; inference; detention, imprisonment.

заключённый, adj. concluded; confined, detained. — n. prisoner, convict.

заключи́тельный, adj. closing, final; conclusive.

закля́тый, adj. sworn.

заколо́ть, v., perf. of зака́лывать.

зако́н, m. law. **-ность,** f. legality; legitimacy. **-ове́дение,** nt. jurisprudence. **-ода́тельный,** adj. legislative. **-оме́рный,** adj. in conformance with law; natural, regular.

зако́нчить, v., perf. of зака́нчивать.

закопа́ть, v., perf. of зака́пывать.

закорене́лый, adj. inveterate; deep-rooted.

закостене́лый, adj. numb, numbed; stiff.

закра́дываться, v. imp. (perf. **закра́сться**), steal in or into.

закрепля́ть, v. imp. (perf. **закрепи́ть**), fasten, secure, attach.

закрича́ть, v. perf. shout; begin to shout or cry.

закруже́ние, *nt.* curve; round, rounding.

закру́чивать, *v. imp.* (*perf.* **закрути́ть**), twist, twirl.

закрыва́ть, *v. imp.* (*perf.* **закры́ть**), shut, close; shut off; cover; shut down, suppress.

закры́тый, *adj.* closed, shut; secret.

закули́сный, *adj.* backstage, hidden, secret; occurring behind the scenes.

заку́пка, *f.* purchase.

закури́ть, *v. perf.* have a smoke; light a cigarette *or* pipe.

заку́ска, *f.* snack; hors d'oeuvres.

заку́сочная, *f.* snack bar.

заку́сывать, *v. imp.* (*perf.* **закуси́ть**), have a snack.

зал, *m.* hall; room.

залата́ть, *v. perf. of* **лата́ть**.

залежа́лый, *adj.* stale.

за́лежь, *f.* deposit).

зали́в, *m.* (*geog.*) bay.

залива́ть, *v. imp.* (*perf.* **зали́ть**), flood, inundate.

зало́г, *m.* pledge, security; (*gram.*) voice.

заложи́ть, *v.*, *perf. of* **закла́дывать**.

зало́жник, *m.* hostage.

залп, *m.* volley.

зама́зка, *f.* putty.

зама́лчивать, *v. imp.* (*perf.* **замолча́ть**), ignore; hush up; be *or* keep silent about.

зама́нивать, *v. imp.* (*perf.* **замани́ть**), tempt, lure.

зама́нчивый, *adj.* tempting.

замара́ть, *v.*, *perf. of* **мара́ть**.

замаскиро́вывать, *v. imp.* (*perf.* **замаскирова́ть**), mask, disguise; conceal, hide; camouflage.

замедля́ть, *v. imp.* (*perf.* **заме́длить**), *tr.*, slow down; delay.

заме́на, *f.* substitution, replacement; substitute.

заменя́ть, *v. imp.* (*perf.* **замени́ть**), substitute; replace.

замерза́ть, *v. imp.* (*perf.*

замёрзнуть), *intr.*, freeze.

замести́тель, *m.* assistant; deputy.

замести́ть, *v.*, *perf. of* **замеща́ть**.

заме́тка, *f.* note, notice; paragraph.

заме́тный, *adj.* noticeable; visible; noted.

замеча́ние, *nt.* remark, observation.

замеча́тельный, *adj.* remarkable.

замеча́ть, *v. imp.* (*perf.* **заме́тить**), note, observe, notice, remark.

замеша́тельство, *nt.* confusion, disorder.

замеща́ть, *v. imp.* (*perf.* **замести́ть**), replace; substitute for.

за́мкнутый, *adj.* closed, reserved; secluded.

замкну́ть, *v.*, *perf. of* **замыка́ть**.

за́мок, *m.* castle.

замо́к, *m.* lock; padlock. **под замко́м**, under lock and key.

замолка́ть, *v. imp.* (*perf.* **замо́лкнуть, замолча́ть**), *intr.*, become silent; cease.

замора́живать, *v. imp.* (*perf.* **заморо́зить**), *tr.*, freeze.

заморо́женный, *adj.* frozen.

за́муж, *adv.*: **вы́йти за́муж**, (*of a woman*) to marry. **-ем**, *adv.*: **быть за́мужем**, (*of a woman*) be married.

заму́жняя, *adj.* (*of a woman*) married.

замучить, *v. perf.* torture, torment; wear out.

за́мша, *f.* suede, chamois.

замыка́ние, *nt.*: **коро́ткое замыка́ние**, (*elec.*) short circuit.

замыка́ть, *v. imp.* (*perf.* **замкну́ть**), *tr.*, lock; close.

за́мысел, *m.* plant, conception; intention.

замышля́ть, *v. imp.* (*perf.* **замы́слить**), conceive; plan.

замя́ть, *v. perf.* stifle; hush up.

за́навес, *m.* (*theat.*) curtain.

занести́, v., perf. of заноси́ть.

занима́тельный, adj entertaining, diverting, engaging.

занима́ть, v. imp. (perf. заня́ть), occupy; borrow. -ся, be occupied (with); be engaged (in); study.

зано́во, adv. again, over again, new.

зано́за, f. splinter.

зано́с, m. snowdrift.

заноси́ть, v. imp. (perf. занести́), carry away; write down, enter.

зано́счивый, adj. arrogant.

заня́тие, nt. occupation.

заня́тный, adj. engaging, amusing, entertaining.

занято́й, adj. busy; occupied.

заня́ть(ся), v., perf. of занима́ть(ся).

заодно́, adv. in unison, in concert.

заостре́нный, adj. pointed, sharp, acute.

заостри́ть, v. imp. (perf. заостря́ть), sharpen; stress, emphasize.

зао́чно, adv. in absentia.

за́пад, m. west. -ный, adj. west, western.

западня́, f. trap, snare; pitfall.

запа́здывать, v. imp. (perf. запозда́ть), be late.

запа́л, m. heaves.

запа́льчивый, adj. quick-tempered; passionate.

запа́с, m. supply, stock; reserve

запаса́ть, v. imp. (perf. запасти́), store, stock. -ся, + instr., supply oneself with.

запасно́й (also запа́сный), adj. spare; reserve; emergency.

за́пах, adj. smell, odor; scent.

запира́тельство, nt. denial, disavowal.

запира́ть, v. imp. (perf. запере́ть), lock; bolt.

запи́ска, f. note, memorandum

запи́ски, pl. notes; papers; memoirs; transactions.

запи́сывать, v. imp. (perf. записа́ть), note, jot down, write down.

за́пись, f. entry, notation.

запла́та, f. patch.

заплати́ть, v. perf. of плати́ть.

заплече́е, nt. shoulder blade.

заплы́в, m. (swim.) heat, round.

запове́дник, m. reserve; preserve.

запове́дный, adj. forbidden.

за́поведь, f. commandment.

запозда́лый, adj. late, tardy; belated, delayed.

запозда́ть, v., perf. of запа́здывать.

заполня́ть, v. imp. (perf. запо́лнить), fill, fill up.

запомина́ть, v. imp. (perf. запо́мнить), remember; memorize.

за́понка, f. cuff link.

запо́р, m. bolt, lock; constipation.

запотева́ть, v. imp. (perf. запоте́ть), become misted.

запоте́ть, v., perf. of запотева́ть, поте́ть.

запре́т, m. prohibition. -и́тельный, adj. prohibitive.

запреща́ть, v. imp. (perf. запрети́ть), prohibit, forbid.

запреще́ние, nt. prohibition, ban.

запроекти́ровать, v., perf. of проекти́ровать.

запро́с, m. inquiry. це́ны без запро́са, fixed prices.

за́просто, adv. informally, without ceremony.

запру́да, f. dam.

запряга́ть, v. imp. (perf. запря́чь), harness.

запуска́ть, v. imp. (perf. запусти́ть), neglect. запуска́ть зме́й, fly a kite.

запусте́лый, adj. desolate; neglected.

запу́танный, adj. tangled; confused; intricate;

запу́тывать, v. imp. (perf. запу́тать), tangle; muddle; confuse.

запу́щенный, adj. neglected.

запята́я, f. comma.

зараба́тывать, v. imp. (perf. зарабо́тать), earn.

за́работок, m. earnings.

заража́ть, v. imp. (perf.

заразить), infect; contaminate.

заражёние, *nt.* infection.

зараз, *adv.* simultaneously, at the same time.

зараза, *f.* contagion; infection.

заразительный (*also* **заразный**), *adj.* infectious; contagious.

заразить(ся), *v.*, *perf. of* **заражать(ся)**.

зарáнее, *adv.* beforehand.

зарево, *nt.* glow.

зарегистрировать, *v. perf. of* **регистрировать**.

зарéзать, *v. perf., tr.*, slaughter, butcher; cut the throat.

зарекаться, *v. imp.* (*perf.* **заречься**), *colloq.*, renounce.

заржавёть, *v. perf.* become rusty.

зарница, *f.* summer lightning.

зародыш, *m.* embryo.

зарождать, *v. imp.* (*perf.* **зародить**), conceive; engender. -**ся**, be born; be conceived *or* engendered.

зарождёние, *nt.* conception.

зарóк, *m.* vow, pledge; solemn promise.

зáросль, *f.* growth, overgrowth.

зарплáта, *abbr. of* **заработная плáта**, wages.

зарубёжный, *adj.* foreign; beyond a country's border.

зарубка, *f.* notch, incision.

зарывать, *v. imp.* (*perf.* **зарыть**), bury; waste.

заря, *f.* light, glow. **ýтренняя заря**, dawn, daybreak. **вечéрняя заря**, dusk, twilight.

засáда, *f.* ambush.

зáсветло, *adv.* before nightfall.

засвидéтельствовать, *v. perf. of* **свидéтельствовать**.

засéв, *m.* sowing, seeding.

засевáть, *v. imp.* (*perf.* **засéять**), sow; seed.

заседáние, *nt.* meeting, conference.

заседáтель, *m.* assessor.

засилье, *nt.* dominance.

заслонять, *v. imp.* (*perf.* **заслонить**), screen, hide, shield.

заслуга, *f.* merit.

заслуживать, *v. imp.* (*perf.* **заслужить**), earn, merit, deserve.

засмеяться, *v. perf.* ridicule, scoff at. -**ся**, laugh, begin to laugh.

заснуть, *v.*, *perf. of* **засыпáть**.

засóхнуть, *v.*, *perf. of* **засыхáть**.

засóхший, *adj.* dry, withered.

застáва, *f.* gate, gates.

заставáть, *v. imp.* (*perf.* **застáть**), find in or at home.

заставлять, *v. imp.* (*perf.* **застáвить**), compel; force; fill, cram.

застёгивать, *v. imp.* (*perf.* **застегнуть**), button, button up; buckle, clasp.

застёжка, *f.* fastening; buckle, clasp.

застéнчивость, *f.* shyness, bashfulness.

застóй, *m.* stagnation, stagnancy.

застраховáть, *v. perf. of* **страховáть**.

застрелить, *v. perf.* shoot. -**ся**, shoot oneself.

застуживать, *v. imp.* (*perf.* **застудить**), chill, cool.

зáступ, *m.* spade.

заступáться, *v. imp.* (*perf.* **заступиться**), за + *acc.*, intercede (for), stand up (for).

застывáть, *v. imp.* (*perf.* **застыть**, **застынуть**), congeal, set; thicken, harden.

áсухая, *f.* drought.

засучивать, *v. imp.* (*perf.* **засучить**), roll, roll up.

засыпáть, *v. imp.* (*perf.* **заснуть**), fall asleep. — (*perf.* **засыпать**) fill, fill up; cover, bury; strew.

засыхáть, *v. imp.* (*perf.* **засóхнуть**), dry up, wither.

затаённый, *adj.* secret; moderated, restrained, repressed.

затаить, *v. perf.* hold, restrain.

затáпливать, *v. imp.* (*perf.* **затопить**), light *or* make a fire.

затвóр, *m.* lock; bolt; shutter; seclusion.

затворя́ть, *v. imp. (perf.* затвори́ть), close, shut.

зате́м, *adv.* then; thereupon; subsequently.

затемне́ние, *nt.* darkening; blackout.

затемня́ть, *v. imp. (perf.* затемни́ть), darken; obscure.

затеря́ть, *v. perf.* mislay; lose.

зате́я, *f.* venture, undertaking.

зати́шье, *nt.* calm, lull.

заткну́ть, *v., perf. of* затыка́ть

затме́ние, *nt.* eclipse.

зато́, *conj.* in return, for this.

затону́ть, *v. perf., intr.,* sink.

затопи́ть, *v., perf. of* зата́пливать, затопля́ть.

затопля́ть, *v. imp. (perf.* зато́пить), flood, inundate; submerge.

затра́гивать, *v. imp. (perf.* затро́нуть), affect.

затра́та, *f.* expenditure, expense.

затре́бовать, *v. perf.* request, order, ask for.

затрудне́ние, *nt.* difficulty.

затрудни́тельный, *adj.* difficult, embarrassing.

затрудня́ть, *v. imp. (perf.* затрудни́ть), render difficult, hamper, impede.

за́тхлый, *adj.* musty.

затыка́ть, *v. imp. (perf.* заткну́ть), stop up, cork up.

заты́лок, *m.* back of the head, occiput.

затя́гивать, *v. imp. (perf.* затяну́ть), tighten; cover; delay.

захва́т, *m.* seizure, capture.

захва́тывать, *v. imp. (perf.* захвати́ть), seize, capture; invade, occupy.

захлёбываться, *v. imp. (perf.* захлебну́ться), + *instr.,* choke (with).

захло́пывать, *v. imp. (perf.* захло́пнуть), *tr.,* slam.

захо́д со́лнца, sunset.

заходи́ть, *v. imp. (perf.* зайти́), set; call on, drop in; call at.

захоте́ть(ся), *v., perf. of* хоте́ть(ся).

зацепля́ть, *v. imp. (perf.* заце-

пи́ть), hook, catch; engage.

зачасту́ю, *adv.* often, frequently.

зача́тие, *nt.* conception.

зача́ток, *m.* embryo; sprout; source; rudiment.

зача́точный, *adj.* rudimentary.

заче́м, *adv.* why, for what reason.

заче́м-то, *adv.* for some reason (or purpose) or other.

зачёркивать, *v. imp. (perf.* зачеркну́ть), cross out; strike out.

зачёсывать, *v. imp. (perf.* зачеса́ть), comb.

зачёт, *m.* test, examination.

зачина́тель, *m.* pioneer, initiator.

зачи́нивать, *v. imp. (perf.* зачини́ть), mend; patch.

зачи́нщик, *m.* instigator.

зачисле́ние, *nt.* enrollment, enlistment.

зачисля́ть, *v. imp. (perf.* зачи́слить), *tr.,* include; enlist, enroll.

заши́вать. *v. imp. (perf.* заши́ть), sew up; mend.

защи́та, *f.* defence.

защити́тельный, *adj.* defending.

защища́ть, *v. imp. (perf.* защити́ть), defend; protect.

заявле́ние, *nt.* declaration, statement; application.

заявля́ть, *v. imp. (perf.* заяви́ть), declare, announce.

зая́длый, *adj.* inveterate.

за́яц, *m.* hare.

зва́ние, *nt.* rank, title.

зва́ный ве́чер, party.

звать, *v. imp. (perf.* позва́ть), call, call upon (+ *inf.);* invite. как вас зову́т? what is your name? -ся, *v. imp.,* be called.

звезда́, *f.* star.

звёздный, *adj.* starry.

звене́ть, *v. imp., intr.,* ring; jangle, clank.

звено́, *nt.* link.

звери́нец, *m.* menagerie.

зве́рский, *adj.* bestial, brutal.

зве́рствовать, *v. imp.* behave

зверь, *m.* beast; brute.

звон, *m.* ringing; peal.

звони́ть, *v. imp.* (*perf.* **по-звони́ть**), ring; clang. **звони́ть по телефо́ну**, to telephone.

зво́нкий, *adj.* ringing; clear; (*phonet.*) voiced.

звоно́к, *m.* bell. **звоно́к по телефо́ну**, telephone call.

звук, *m.* sound. **-оизоляцио́нный**, *adj.* soundproof. **-оподража́ние**, *nt.* onomatopoeia.

звуча́ть, *v. imp.* (*perf.* **прозвуча́ть**), sound; resound, be heard.

зву́чный, *adj.* resounding, sonorous.

зда́ние, *nt.* building, edifice.

здесь, *adv.* here.

зде́шний, *adj.* local, pertaining to this place.

здоро́ваться, *v. imp.* (*perf.* **поздоро́ваться**), с + *instr.*, greet, hail.

здорове́нный, *adj.* (*colloq.*) healthy, hale; robust, strapping.

здо́рово, *adv.* well, excellently. — *interj.* well done; excellent.

здоро́вый, *adj.* healthy.

здоро́вье, *nt.* health.

здра́вствовать, *v. imp.* be well; prosper, thrive.

здра́вствуй(те), (*greeting*) how do you do; good morning; good afternoon; good evening; hello.

здра́вый, *adj.* sensible.

зев, *m.* pharynx.

зева́ть, *v. imp.* (*perf.* **зевну́ть**), yawn.

Зевс, *m.* Zeus.

зелене́ть, *v. imp.* (*perf.* **позелене́ть**), turn *or* become green.

зеленова́тый, *adj.* greenish.

зелёный, *adj.* green.

зе́лень, *f.* verdure; greens, vegetables.

земе́льный, *adj.* earth, ground, land.

землевладе́лец, *m.* landowner.

земледе́лец, *m.* farmer, agriculturist.

земледе́лие, *nt.* agriculture.

землеме́р, *m.* surveyor; geodesist.

землетрясе́ние, *nt.* earthquake.

земли́стый, *adj.* earthy; sallow.

земля́, *f.* earth, soil.

земля́к, *m.* fellow countryman.

земляни́ка, *f.* (*coll.*) strawberries.

земно́й, *adj.* terrestrial; earthly.

зени́т, *m.* zenith.

зени́ца, *f.* pupil (*of the eye*).

зе́ркало, *nt.* mirror, looking-glass.

зерни́стый, *adj.* grainy; granular.

зерно́, *nt.* grain; seed, bean; kernel.

зима́, *f.* winter. **зимо́й**, in winter; in the winter.

зи́мний, *adj.* winter, wintry.

зимова́ть, *v. imp.* (*perf.* **прозимова́ть**), winter; pass *or* spend the winter.

зия́ние, *nt.* hiatus.

злак, *m.* cereal.

злить, *v. imp.* anger; irritate.

зло, *nt.* evil; anger, annoyance.

зло́ба, *f.* spite; malice.

зло́бный, *adj.* malicious; spiteful.

злободне́вный, *adj.* actual, topical.

злове́щий, *adj.* sinister, ominous.

злово́нный, *adj.* stinking, fetid.

зловре́дный, *adj.* harmful, noxious.

злоде́й, *m.* villain, scoundrel.

злодея́ние, *nt.* crime; evil act.

злой, *adj.* wicked, evil; malicious, vicious.

злока́чественный, *adj.* malignant.

злопа́мятный, *adj.* vindictive.

злосло́вие, *nt.* malicious gossip

злость, *f.* malice.

злоупотребле́ние, *nt.* abuse; misuse.

злоупотребля́ть, *v. imp.* (*perf.* **злоупотреби́ть**), abuse.

змей, *m.* serpent, dragon; kite.

змея́, *f.* snake; serpent.

знак, *m.* sign, token, symbol, mark; omen; signal.

знако́мить, *v. imp.* (*perf.* **познако́мить**), acquaint; introduce. **-ся**, **с** + *instr.* make one's acquaintance; meet; get to know.

знако́мство, *nt.* acquaintance.

знако́мый, *adj.* familiar; (**с** + *instr.*) acquainted with. — *m.* acquaintance, friend.

знамена́тель, *m.* denominator. **-ный**, *adj.* significant.

знаме́ние, *nt.* sign.

знамени́тость, *f.* celebrity.

знамени́тый, *adj.* celebrated.

зна́мя, *nt.* (*pl.* **знамёна**) banner colors; standard.

зна́ние, *nt.* knowledge; erudition.

зна́тный, *adj.* distinguished, notable.

знато́к, *m.* authority, expert, connoisseur.

знать, *v. imp.* know; be aware of; be acquainted with; have a knowledge of. **-ся**, (*colloq.*), **с** + *instr.*, know, be acquainted with, be associated with.

значе́ние, *nt.* meaning.

зна́чит, *interj.* so; well then.

значи́тельный, *adj.* considerable; sizable, substantial.

зна́чить, *v. imp.* mean, signify.

значо́к, *m.* mark; badge.

зна́ющий, *adj.* learned, scholarly.

зноби́ть, *v. imp., impers.*: **меня зноби́т**, I feel feverish.

зной, *m.* intense heat.

зоб, *m.* crop; (*med.*) goiter.

зов, *m.* call; summons.

зодиа́к, *m.* zodiac.

зо́дчество, *nt.* architecture.

зо́дчий, *m.* architect.

зола́, *f.* (*sg. only*) ashes.

золо́вка, *f.* sister-in-law (*husband's sister*).

золоти́ть, *v. imp.* (*perf.* **позолоти́ть**), gild.

зо́лото, *nt.* gold.

золото́й, *adj.* gold; golden.

зо́на, *f.* zone.

зонт (*also* **зо́нтик**), *m.* umbrella.

зоо́лог, *m.* zoologist. **-и́ческий**, *adj.* zoological. **зооло́гия**, *f.* zoology.

зо́ркий, *adj.* eagle-eyed; vigilant, alert.

зрачо́к, *m.* pupil (*of the eye*).

зре́лище, *nt.* spectacle, sight; performance; attraction.

зре́лость, *f.* ripeness; maturity.

зре́лый, *adj.* ripe; mature.

зре́ние, *nt.* sight, eyesight; vision. **то́чка зре́ния**, point of view.

зреть [1], *v. imp.* (*perf.* **созре́ть**), *intr.*, ripen.

зреть [2], *v. imp.* (*perf.* **узре́ть**), behold.

зри́тель *m.*, **-ница** *f.*, spectator. **-ный**, *adj.* visual, optical.

зуб, *m.* tooth. **-но́й**, *adj.* dental, tooth. **-очи́стка**, *f.* toothpick. **-ча́тый**, *adj.* toothed; cogged; jagged.

зуд, *m.* itch.

зуде́ть, *v. imp.*, itch.

зыби́ться, *v. imp.* surge; swell.

зы́бкий, *adj.* unstable, unsteady.

зы́чный, *adj.* stentorian.

зя́бнуть, *v. imp., intr.*, shiver; freeze; suffer from cold.

зять, *m.* son-in-law; brother-in-law (*sister's husband*).

И

и, *conj.* and. **и... и...**, both ... and ...

и́бо, *conj.* for.

и́ва, *f.* willow.

игла́, *f.* needle.

Игна́тий, *m.* Ignatius.

Игна́ш(к)а, *dim. of* **Игна́тий**.

игнори́ровать, *v. imp. & perf.* ignore, disregard.

и́го, *nt.* yoke.

иго́лка, *f.* needle.

игра́, *f.* game; play; acting.

игра́ть, *v. imp.* (*perf.* сыгра́ть), play; act.

игро́к, *m.* player; gambler.

игру́шечка, *f.* toy.

игри́вый, *adj.* playful.

идеа́л, *m.* ideal. **-исти́ческий**, *adj.* idealistic. **-ьный**, *adj.* ideal.

идеализи́ровать, *v. imp. & perf.* idealize.

иде́йный, *adj.* ideological; lofty.

идентифици́ровать, *v. imp. & perf.* identify.

иденти́чность, *f.* identity.

иденти́чный, *adj.* identical.

идео́лог, *m.* ideologist. **-и́ческий**, *adj.* ideological.

иде́я, *f.* idea, notion, concept.

идио́ма, *f.* idiom.

идио́т, *m.* idiot.

и́дол, *m.* idol.

и др., *abbr.* of и други́е.

идти́, *v. imp. det.* (*indet.* ходи́ть, *perf.* пойти́), go; start, leave.

Иерони́м, *m.* Hieronymus.

из (и́зо), *prep.* (+ gen.) from, out, out of; of.

изба́, *f.* cottage, hut, hovel.

избави́тель, *m.* redeemer, savior.

избавле́ние, *nt.* deliverance; rescue.

избавля́ть, *v. imp.* (*perf.* изба́вить), save, rescue; deliver. **-ся, от** + *gen.*, get rid of.

избало́вывать, *v. imp.* (*perf.* избалова́ть), spoil.

избега́ть, *v. imp.* (*perf.* избежа́ть, избе́гнуть), avoid; evade; shun.

избива́ть, *v. imp.* (*perf.* изби́ть) beat; slaughter, massacre; assault.

избие́ние, *nt.* slaughter, massacre; assault and battery.

избира́тель, *mt.* voter; elector. **-ный**, *adj.* electoral, elective, election.

избира́ть, *v. imp.* (*perf.* избра́ть), elect; choose.

изби́ть, *v.*, *perf.* of избива́ть.

избра́ние, *nt.* election.

избра́нник *m.*, **избра́нница** *f.*, one who is elected.

избра́ть, *v.*, *perf.* of избира́ть.

избы́ток, *m.* surplus.

избы́точный, *adj.* surplus.

изва́ять, *v.*, *perf.* of вая́ть.

изве́дывать, *v. imp.* (*perf.* изве́дать), experience.

изверга́ть, *v. imp.* (*perf.* изве́ргнуть), *tr.*, disgorge, eject; erupt.

изверже́ние, *nt.* eruption; discharge, ejection, excretion.

изве́риться, *v.*, *perf.*, lose faith in.

извести́, *v.*, *perf.* of изводи́ть.

изве́стие, *nt.* news, tidings; information.

извести́ть, *v.*, *perf.* of извеща́ть.

изве́стно, *impers.* it is known.

изве́стность, *f.* fame, reputation.

изве́стный, *adj.* famous, well-known.

и́звесть, *f.* lime.

извеща́ть, *v. imp.* (*perf.* извести́ть), inform, notify.

извеще́ние, *nt.* notification, notice.

извива́ться, *v. imp.* (*perf.* изви́ться), coil; wriggle, twist, wind; cringe.

изви́листый, *adj.* sinuous, tortuous; winding.

извине́ние, *nt.* apology; excuse.

извини́тельный, *adj.* pardonable, excusable; apologetic.

извиня́ть, *v. imp.* (*perf.* извини́ть), excuse, pardon.

изви́ться, *v.*, *perf.* of извива́ться.

извлека́ть, *v. imp.* (*perf.* извле́чь), extract; elicit; evoke.

извлече́ние, *nt.* extraction, extract.

извне́, *adv.* from without.

изво́д, *m.* recension.

изводи́ть, v. imp. (perf. извести́), expend, spend; exterminate; exhaust.

изво́зчик, m. carrier; cab driver.

изворо́тливый, adj. resourceful.

извраща́ть, v. imp. (perf. изврати́ть), pervert; misconstrue, misinterpret.

извраще́ние, nt. perversion; distortion, misconstruing.

изга́живать, v. imp. (perf. изга́дить), colloq., spoil, befoul.

изгна́ние, nt. banishment.

изгна́нник m., изгна́нница f., exile.

изголо́вье, nt. head of a bed.

изгоня́ть, v. imp. (perf. изгна́ть), banish.

изготовля́ть, v. imp. (perf. изгото́вить), make, manufacture.

издава́ть, v. imp. (perf. изда́ть), publish.

и́здавна, adv. long since.

издалека́ (also и́здали), adv. from afar or far away.

изда́ние, nt. publication; edition, issue.

изда́тель, m. publisher.

изда́ть, v., perf. of издава́ть.

издева́тельство, nt. mockery.

издева́ться, v. imp., над + instr., mock.

изде́лие, nt. product, manufactured article.

издыха́ть, v. imp. (perf. издо́хнуть), colloq., die.

из-за, prep. (+ gen.) from behind; because of.

излага́ть, v. imp. (perf. изложи́ть), state, set forth; expound.

излече́ние, nt. recovery; cure; medical treatment.

изле́чивать, v. imp. (perf. излечи́ть), (med.), cure.

излечи́мый, adj. curable.

изли́шек, m. surplus; excess.

изли́шний, adj. superfluous; unnecessary.

излия́ние, nt. outpouring.

изложе́ние, nt. account; statement.

изло́м, m. fracture; break -анный, adj. broken.

излуче́ние, nt. radiation; emanation.

изме́на, f. treason; treachery

измене́ние, nt. change, alteration.

изме́нник, m. traitor.

изме́нчивый, adj. changeable fickle.

изменя́ть, v. imp. (perf. измени́ть), tr., change, alter; b unfaithful.

измере́ние, nt. measurement measuring.

измеря́ть, v. imp. (perf измери́ть), measure, gauge

измучивать, v. imp. (perf нзму́чить), torture; tire, exhaust.

измя́ть, v. perf. rumple, crumple.

изнаси́лование, nt. rape; violation.

изнаси́ловать, v., perf. o наси́ловать.

изна́шивать, v. imp. (perf износи́ть), tr., wear out.

изно́шенный, adj. worn out shabby.

изнуре́ние, nt. physical exhaustion.

изнутри́, adv. from within.

изоби́лие, nt. abundance.

изоби́льный, adj. abundant

изобличе́ние, nt. exposure unmasking.

изобража́ть, v. imp. (perf. изобрази́ть), portray; represent

изобрази́тельный, adj. figurative; pictorial.

изобрета́тель, m. inventor -ный, adj. inventive.

изобрета́ть, v. imp. (perf изобрести́), invent; devise.

изобрете́ние, nt. invention.

изоли́ровать, v. imp. & perf isolate; insulate.

изоля́ция, f. isolation; quarantine; insulation.

из-под, prep. from under.

Изра́иль, m. Israel.

израильтя́нин m., израиль

тя́нка f., (pl. израильтя́не) Israeli; Israelite.

и́зредка, adv. rarely; now and then, from time to time.

изрека́ть, v. imp. (perf. изре́чь), say or speak solemnly; utter.

изрече́ние, nt. dictum; saying.

изорва́ть, v. perf. rend; tear.

изрыва́ть, v. imp. (perf. изры́ть), dig up.

и́зрядно, adv, fair, fairly; pretty well.

изуми́тельный, adj. amazing, wonderful.

изумле́ние, nt. amazement, wonder.

изумля́ть, v. imp. (perf. изуми́ть), amaze.

изуро́довать, v., perf. of уро́довать.

изуча́ть, v. imp. (perf. изучи́ть), study; learn; master.

изъя́тие, nt. withdrawal, removal; exception.

изыма́ть, v. imp. (perf. изъя́ть) withdraw, remove.

изы́сканность, f. refinement.

изю́м, m. (sg. only) raisins.

изя́щество, nt. refinement; elegance.

изя́щный,' adj. refined; elegant.

изя́щные иску́сства, fine arts.

ика́ть, v. imp. (perf. икну́ть), hiccup.

икра́, f. roe; caviar.

ил, m. silt.

и́ли, conj. or. и́ли ... и́ли ..., either ... or ...

иллюстра́ция, f. illustration.

иллюстри́ровать, v. imp. & perf. illustrate.

Ильи́ч, patronymic of name Илья́.

Илю́ш(к)а, dim. of name Илья́.

им, pron., instr. of он, оно́; dat. of они́.

име́ние, nt. estate.

имени́ны, pl. name-day.

имени́тельный, adj. (gram.) nominative.

и́менно, adv, namely; that is.

именно́й, adj. nominal.

именова́ть, v. imp. (perf. наименова́ть), name.

име́ть, v. imp. have. име́ть в виду́, mean; bear in mind. име́ть ме́сто, take place, occur. -ся, used impers. be had or possessed; be.

име́ющийся, adj. available.

и́ми, pron., instr. of они́.

империали́зм, m. imperialism.

импорти́ровать, v. imp. & perf. import.

импровиза́ция, f. improvisation.

импровизи́ровать, v. imp. & perf. improvise.

и́мпульс, m. impulse.

иму́щество, nt. property; belongings.

и́мя, nt. (pl. и́мени), name. и́мя прилага́тельное, adjective. и́мя существи́тельное, noun; substantive. и́мя чи́слительное, (gram.) numeral. от и́мени, in the name of.

ина́че, adv, otherwise; otherwise.

инвали́д, m. invalid.

и́ндеветь, v. imp. (perf. заи́ндеветь), be covered with frost.

инде́ец m., индиа́нка f., (American) Indian.

инде́йский, adj. (American) Indian.

индивидуа́льный, adj. individual.

инди́ец m., индиа́нка f., Indian.

инди́йский, adj. Indian.

Индоста́н, m. Hindustan.

инду́с m., -ка f., Hindu. -кий, adj. Hindu.

индустриализи́ровать, v. imp. industrialize.

индю́к m. turkey. индю́шка, f. turkey hen.

инжене́р, m. engineer.

инжи́р, m. fig; fig tree.

инициати́ва, f. initiative.

инко́гнито, nt. ind., adv. incognito.

иногда́, adv. sometimes.

иноземе́ц m., иноземка f., foreigner.

инозе́мный, adj. foreign.

ино́й, adj. another, other; different.

иностра́нец *m.*, **иностра́нка** *f.*, foreigner.

иностра́нный, *adj.* foreign.

инстинкти́вный, *adj.* instinctive.

институ́т, *m.* institute; institution.

инструкти́ровать, *v. imp. & perf.* instruct.

инстру́кция, *f.* instructions; directions.

инструме́нт, *m.* instrument; tool.

инструменти́ровать, *v. imp. & perf.* orchestrate.

инсцени́ровать, *v. imp. & perf.* stage; dramatize.

инсцениро́вка, *f.* staging; dramatization.

интегри́ровать, *v. imp. & perf.* (*math.*) integrate.

интеллектуа́льный, *adj.* intellectual.

интеллиге́нт *m.*, **-ка**, intellectual. **-ный**, *adj.* educated, cultured.

интеллиге́нция, *f.* intelligentsia.

интенси́вность, *f.* intensity.

интенси́вный, *adj.* intense.

интенсифици́ровать, *v. imp. & perf.* intensify.

интерве́нция, *f.* intervention.

интервью́, *nt. ind.* interview.

интервью́и́ровать, *v. imp. & perf.* interview.

интере́с, *m.* interest. **-ный**, *adj.* interesting; attractive.

интересова́ть, *v. imp.* interest. **-ся**, + *instr.*, be interested in.

Интернациона́л, *m.* Internationale.

интернациона́льный, *adj.* international.

интерни́ровать, *v. imp. & perf.* intern.

интерполи́ровать, *v. imp. & perf.* interpolate.

инти́мный, *adj.* intimate.

интона́ция, *f.* intonation.

интри́га, *f.* intrigue.

интригова́ть, *v. imp.* (*perf.* **заинтригова́ть**), plot, scheme; mystify.

инфе́кция, *f.* infection, contagion.

инфинити́в, *m.* infinitive.

инфля́ция, *f.* inflation.

информа́тор, *m.* informant.

информа́ция, *f.* information.

информбюро́, *abbr. of* **информацио́нное бюро́**, information bureau.

информи́ровать, *v. imp. & perf.* (*perf.* **проинформи́ровать**) inform.

инциде́нт, *m.* incident.

инъе́кция, *f.* injection.

ио́н, *m.* ion. **-ный**, *adj.* ionic.

иони́йский, *adj.* Ionic, Ionian.

Иони́ческое мо́ре, Ionian Sea.

Иорда́н, *m.* Jordan (*river*).

Иорда́ния, *f.* Jordan.

Ио́сиф, *m.* Joseph.

и пр., *abbr. of* **и про́чее**, and so forth.

Ира, *dim. of* **Ири́на**.

ира́нец *m.*, **ира́нка** *f.*, Iranian.

Ири́на, *f.* Irene.

ирла́ндец, *m.* Irishman. **ирла́ндка**, *f.* Irishwoman.

Ирла́ндия, *f.* Ireland.

ирони́ческий, *adj.* ironic(al).

иро́ния, *f.* irony.

иррациона́льный, *adj.* irrational.

иррига́ция, *f.* irrigation.

иск, *m.* legal action, suit.

искажа́ть, *v. imp.* (*perf.* **исказить**), distort; misrepresent.

искале́чить, *v.*, *perf. of* **кале́чить**..

иска́ть, *v. imp.* search (for); seek; look (for).

исключа́ть, *v. imp.* (*perf.* **исключи́ть**), exclude; except; rule out.

исключа́я, *prep.* except, excepting.

исключе́ние, *nt.* exception, exclusion; expulsion.

исключи́тельный, *adj.* exceptional; exclusive.

иско́нный, *adj.* primordial; indigenous.

ископа́емые, *pl.* minerals.

ископа́емый, *adj.* fossil, fossilized.

искорене́ние, *nt.* eradication.

искореня́ть, v. imp. (perf. искорени́ть), eradicate.

и́скоса, adv. askance.

и́скра, f. spark.

и́скренний, adj. sincere.

искривле́ние, nt. bend, crook; distortion.

искривля́ть, v. imp. (perf. искриви́ть), bend, crook; distort.

и́скус, m. trial, test; ordeal.

иску́сный, adj. skillful.

иску́сственный, adj. artificial; synthetic.

иску́сство, nt. art; skill, proficiency.

искуша́ть, v. imp. (perf. искуси́ть), tempt; seduce.

искуше́ние, nt. temptation; seduction.

исла́м, m. Islam.

исла́ндец m., исла́ндка f., Icelander.

испа́нец m., испа́нка f., Spaniard.

Испа́ния, f. Spain.

испа́нский, adj. Spanish.

испаре́ние, nt. evaporation.

испаря́ть, v. imp. (perf. испари́ть), tr., evaporate; exhale. -ся, intr., evaporate; disappear.

испа́чкать, v., perf. of па́чкать.

испе́чь, v., perf. of печь.

испове́довать, v. imp. & perf., tr., confess.

и́споведь, f. confession.

исподво́ль, adv. slowly, gradually.

исподтишка́, adv. stealthily; on the sly.

исполко́м, abbr. of исполни́тельный комите́т, executive committee.

исполне́ние, nt. execution, fulfillment.

исполни́тель, m. executor; performer. -ный, adj. executive.

исполня́ть, v. imp. (perf. испо́лнить), fulfill, carry out; execute.

испо́льзовать, v. imp. & perf. utilize; take advantage of; exploit.

испо́ртить, v., perf. of по́ртить.

испо́рченный, adj. depraved, perverted; spoiled; tainted.

исправля́ть, v. imp. (perf. испра́вить), tr., correct; repair, mend; reform.

испра́вный, adj. in good condition; in working order.

испражне́ние, nt. defecation, evacuation.

испражня́ться, v. imp. (perf. испражни́ться), defecate.

испу́г, m. fright, scare. -анный, adj. frightened; startled.

испуга́ть, v., perf. of пуга́ть.

испыта́ние, nt. trial, probation; test, examination.

испы́танный, adj. tested, tried; experienced.

испы́тывать, v. imp. (perf. испыта́ть), try, test; experience.

израсхо́довать, v., perf. of расхо́довать.

иссле́дование, nt. investigation; research; analysis; exploration.

иссле́довать, v. imp. & perf. investigate; explore; examine; analyse.

иссыха́ть, v. imp. (perf. иссо́хнуть), dry up; shrivel; wither.

истека́ть, v. imp. (perf. исте́чь), expire; elapse.

исте́рика (also исте́рия), f. hysterics.

истече́ние, nt. expiration; outflow.

исте́чь, v., perf. of истека́ть.

и́стина, f. truth.

и́стинный, adj. veritable, true.

исто́к, m. source. -и, pl. headwaters.

исто́рик, m. historian.

истори́ческий, adj. historical.

исто́рия, f. history; event; story.

исто́чник, m. source, spring.

истоща́ть, v. imp. (perf. истощи́ть), exhaust; drain; wear out.

истоще́ние, nt. exhaustion; emaciation.

истра́тить, v., perf. of тра́тить.

истреби́тельный, *adj.* destructive.

истребля́ть, *v. imp.* (*perf.* **истреби́ть**), destroy; annihilate, exterminate.

истяза́ть, *v. imp.* torture.

исхо́д, *m.* outcome, result; end. **-ный**, *adj.* initial.

исчеза́ть, *v. imp.* (*perf.* **исче́знуть**), disappear, vanish.

исче́рпывать, *v. imp.* (*perf.* **исче́рпать**), exhaust.

исче́рпывающий, *adj.* exhaustive; comprehensive.

исчисле́ние, *nt.* calculation; (*math.*) calculus.

исчисля́ть, *v. imp.* (*perf.* **исчи́слить**), calculate; estimate. **-ся**, в + *prep.*, amount to.

ита́к, *conj.* thus, so.

и так да́лее, and so forth.

италья́нец *m.*, **италья́нка** *f.*, Italian.

италья́нский, *adj.* Italian.

и т. д., (*abbr. of* **и так да́лее**).

ито́г, *m.* sum, total; result; score.

итого́, *adv.* in all.

ито́говый, *adj.* total; concluding.

и тому́ подо́бное, and the like.

и т.п., *abbr. of* **и тому́ подо́бное.**

иудаи́зм *m.*, **иуде́йство** *nt.*, Judaism.

иуде́й, *m.* Jew; Israelite. **-ский**, *adj.* Judaic.

их, *pron., gen., acc. of* **они́.** — *poss. pron.,* their, theirs.

ище́йка, *f.* bloodhound; police dog.

ию́ль, *m.* July. **-ский**, *adj.* July.

ию́нь, *m.* June. **-ский**, *adj.* June.

йог, *m.* yogi. **-а**, *f.* Yoga.

йод, *m.* iodine.

йон, *see* **ио́н.**

йо́та, *f.* iota.

йота́ция, *f.* iotation.

йоти́ровать, *v. imp. & perf.* iotate.

К

к (ко), *prep.* (+ *dat.*) to, towards; by; for, of, to.

ка́бель, *m.* cable.

каби́на, *f.* booth; cockpit; cabin.

кабине́т, *m.* study; conference room; (*polit.*) cabinet.

каблу́к, *m.* heel.

Кавка́з, *m.* Caucasus.

кавка́зец *m.*, **кавка́зка** *f.*, Caucasian.

кавы́чки, *pl.* quotation marks.

Ка́дикс, *m.* Cadiz.

кады́к, *m.* Adam's apple.

ка́ждый, *adj.* each, every. — *pron.* everyone, each one.

ка́жется, *impers. pred.* it seems.

каза́к *m.*, **каза́чка** *f.*, Cossack.

каза́рма, *f.* barracks.

каза́ть, *v. imp.* (*perf.* **показа́ться**), seem, appear; strike as.

каза́х, *m.* Kazakh.

казённый, *adj.* fiscal; formal; trite, banal.

казни́ть, *v. imp. & perf.* execute; put to death.

казнь, *f.* punishment, penalty; execution; death penalty.

Ка́ин, *m.* (*Bible*) Cain.

Каи́р, *m.* Cairo.

кака́о, *nt. ind.* cocoa.

как-либо (*also* **ка́к-нибудь**), *adv.* somehow, anyhow.

како́й, *pron.* what.

какой-либо (*also* **какой-нибудь**), *pron.* some, some kind of.

ка́к-то, *adv.* somehow.

ка́ктус, *m.* cactus.

каламбу́р, *m.* pun.

кале́ка, *f., m.* (*declined as f.*), cripple.

календа́рь, *m.* calendar.

кале́ние, *nt.* incandescence.

кале́чить, *v. imp.* (*perf.*

искалечить), mutilate; cripple, maim.

калибр, *m.* caliber.

калория, *f.* calorie.

калька, *f.* tracing paper.

калькировать, *v. imp.* trace.

камбольный, *adj.* worsted.

камелия, *f.* camelia.

каменеть, *v. imp. (perf.* окаменеть), turn to stone, petrify; harden.

каменистый, *adj.* stony, rocky.

каменный уголь, coal.

каменоломня, *f.* quarry.

камень, *m.* stone, rock; *(coll.)* stones.

камера, *f.* chamber; cell; inner tube.

камертон, *m.* tuning fork.

камин, *m.* fireplace.

кампания, *f.* campaign.

камфара, *f.* camphor.

канава, *f.* ditch.

канадец *m.*, канадка *f.*, Canadian.

канадский, *adj.* Canadian.

канал, *m.* canal; channel; duct. -изация, *f.* sewerage.

канарейка, *f.* canary.

канат, *m.* cable; rope.

канва, *f.* canvas.

кандалы, *pl.* irons; shackles.

кандидат *m.*, -ка *f.*, candidate; nominee. -ура, *f.* candidacy.

каникулы, *pl.* vacation.

каноист *m.*, -ка *f.*, canoeist.

канонизировать, *v. imp. & perf.* canonize.

каноэ, *nt. ind.* canoe.

канун, *m.* eve.

канцелярия, *f.* office.

каньон, *m.* canyon.

капать, *v. imp.* drip, dribble.

капелла, *f.* choir; chapel.

капелька, *f.* droplet.

капилляр, *m.* capillary.

капитал, *m.* capital (money). -изм, *m.* capitalism.

капитулировать, *v. imp. & perf.* capitulate.

капитуляция, *f.* capitulation, surrender.

капля, *f.* drop.

каприз, *m.* whim; caprice.

капризничать, *v. imp. & perf.* behave capriciously.

капуста, *f.* cabbage. цветная капуста, cauliflower.

кара, *f.* penalty, punishment.

караемый, *adj.* punishable.

Карайбское море, Caribbean Sea.

каракуль, *m.* astrakhan. -ча́, *f.* broadtail.

карандаш, *m.* pencil.

карантин, *m.* quarantine.

карат, *m.* carat.

карательный, *adj.* punitive.

карать, *v. imp. (perf.* покарать), punish; chastise; penalize.

караул, *m.* watch; guard.

караулить, *v. imp.* stand watch *or* guard.

карбонизировать, *v. imp. & perf.* carbonize.

карел *m.*, -ка *f.*, Karelian.

карета скорой помощи, ambulance.

карий, *adj.* brown.

карикатура, *f.* caricature.

карлик, *m.* dwarf; pygmy.

карман, *m.* pocket. -ник, *m.* (*colloq.*) pickpocket.

кармин, *m.* carmine. -ный, *adj.* carmine.

карнавал, *m.* carnival.

карп, *m.* carp.

Карпатские горы, Carpathian Mountains.

Карское море, Kara Sea.

карта, *f.* map; playing card.

картина, *f.* picture; painting, canvas; scene.

картограф, *m.* cartographer.

картон, *m.* cardboard. -ка, *f.* cardboard box.

картотека, *f.* card index.

картофель, *m.* (*sg. only*) potatoes.

карточка, *f.* photograph, snapshot.

картошка, *f.* (*colloq.*) potato, potatoes.

карусель, *f.* carousel, merry-go-round.

карьера, *f.* career.

касательная, *f.* (*math.*) tangent.

касáтельно, *prep.* (+ *gen.*) concerning.

касáться, *v. imp.* (*perf.* коснýться), touch, touch upon; concern. что касается (+ *gen.*) as for.

касáющийся, *adj.* pertinent to; concerning.

Каспийское мóре, Caspian Sea.

кáсса, *f.* box-office; safe; cashier's desk.

кассир *m.*, -ша *f.*, cashier.

кáста, *f.* caste.

кастóровое мáсло, castor oil.

каталéпсия, *f.* catalepsy.

каталóг, *m.* catalogue.

каталогизúровать, *v. imp. & perf.* catalogue.

катáние, *nt.* drive, driving; rolling.

катáр, *m.* catarrh.

катарáкта, *m.* cataract.

катастрóфа, *f.* catastrophe.

катáть, *v. imp.* drive, take for a drive; roll, wheel, trundle; mangle (*clothing*), -ся, *v. imp.* take a drive; roll.

категóрия, *f.* category.

Кáтенька, *dim. of* Екатерúна.

катóд, *m.* cathode.

катóлик, *m.* Catholic.

католúческий, *adj.* Catholic.

Кáтька (*also* Катюша, Кáтя), *dim. of* Екатерúна.

каучýк, *m.* rubber.

кафé, *nt. ind.* café.

кафéдра, *f.* chair, rostrum; department; faculty.

кáфель, *m.* tile.

качáлка, *f.* rocking chair, rocker.

качáть, *v. imp.* (*perf.* качнýть), *tr.*, rock, swing; shake.

кáчественный, *adj.* qualitative.

кáчество, *nt.* quality.

кáша, *f.* porridge; gruel.

кáшель, *m.* cough.

кáшлять, *v. imp.* cough.

каштáн, *m.* chestnut.

каюта, *f.* cabin, room, state-room, suite.

квадрáт, *m.* square.

квалификáция, *f.* qualifica-

квалифицúровать, *v. imp. & perf.* qualify.

квáрта, *f.* quart.

квартáл, *m.* quarter; city block.

квартéт, *m.* quartet.

квартúра, *f.* apartment; quarters.

квартирáнт *m.*, -ка *f.*, tenant.

квартиронанимáтель *m.*, -ница *f.*, tenant.

квас, *m.* quass.

квáсить, *v. imp., tr.*, sour.

квáшенный, *adj.* fermented.

квéрху, *adv.* upward(s), up.

квинтéт, *m.* quintet.

квитáнция, *f.* acknowledgment; receipt.

кегль, *m.* (*typog.*) point.

кéльнер, *m.* waiter.

кем, *pron., instr. of* кто.

кенгурý, *m. ind.* kangaroo.

керáмика, *f.* ceramics.

керосúн, *m.* kerosene.

кивáть, *v. imp.* (*perf.* кивнýть), nod; motion (to).

кидáть, *v. imp.* (*perf.* кúнуть), throw, cast, fling.

кий, *m.* billiard cue.

килó, *nt. ind.* (*abbr. of* килогрáмм) kilogram. -мéтр, *m.* kilometer.

кинó, *nt. ind.*, motion picture; movie house.

кино-хрóника, *f.* newsreel.

кúнуть, *v.*, *perf. of* кидáть.

киóск, *m.* booth, kiosk; news-stand.

кипéть, *v. imp.* boil; seethe.

кипýчий, *adj.* boiling; seething.

кипятúльник, *m.* boiler.

кипятúть, *v. imp.* (*perf.* вскипятúть), *tr.*, boil.

кипятóк, *m.* boiling water.

киргúз, *m.*, -ка *f.*, Kirghiz.

кирúллица, *f.* Cyrillic alphabet.

кирпúч, *m.* brick.

кисéт, *m.* pouch, tobacco pouch.

кисея, *f.* muslin.

кисловáтый, *adj.* sourish.

кислорóд, *m.* oxygen.

кислотá, *f.* sourness; acidity; (*chem.*) acid.

кислóтность, *f.* acidity.

кúслый, *adj.* sour.

киста́, f. cyst.

кисть, f. cluster; bunch.

кит, m. whale.

кита́ец m., китая́нка f., Chinese.

Кита́й, m. China.

кише́чник, m. intestine; bowels.

кишка́, f. intestine.

Кла́ва, dim. of Кла́вдия.

Кла́вдия, f. Claudia.

клавиату́ра, f. keyboard.

кла́виш m., -а f., (piano, etc.) key.

кла́дбище, nt. cemetery.

кладова́я, f. pantry; larder; storeroom.

кла́няться, v. imp. (perf. поклони́ться), bow, greet; extend one's regards.

кла́пан, m. valve; vent.

кларне́т, m. clarinet.

класс, m. class; classroom.

кла́ссик, m. classic. -а f., classics.

классифици́ровать, v. imp. & perf. classify.

класси́ческий, adj. classic(al).

кла́ссный, adj. class, classroom.

кла́ссовый, adj. class (social).

класть, v. imp. (perf. положи́ть), put, place, lay; put down, place down.

клева́ть, v. imp. (perf. клю́нуть), peck; bite.

клёвер, m. clover.

клевета́, f. slander.

клевета́ть, v. imp. (на + gen.) slander.

клеветни́к, m. slanderer.

кле́ить, v. imp. (perf. скле́ить), glue; paste.

клей, m. glue. -кий, adj. sticky. -мо́, nt. stamp, mark, brand; trademark.

клейми́ть, v. imp. (perf. заклейми́ть), stamp, mark, brand.

клён, m. maple. кленóвый, adj. maple.

кле́тка, f. cage, coop; check, square; cell. в кле́тку, checked (design).

клетча́тый, adj. checked (design).

кле́щи, pl. pincers, nippers, tongs.

клие́нт m., -ка f., client, customer.

кли́зма, f. enema.

кли́ка, f. clique, faction.

кли́кать, v. imp. (perf. кли́кнуть), call, cry.

кли́мат, m. climate. -и́ческий, adj. climatic.

клин, m. wedge.

кли́ника, f. clinic.

клини́ческий, adj. clinical.

клино́к, m. blade.

кличка, f. nickname.

клоп, m. bug, bedbug.

кло́ун, m. clown.

клочо́к, m. scrap.

клуб, m. club; cloud, puff.

клубни́ка, f. strawberry.

клубо́к, m. ball.

клу́мба, f. flowerbed.

клык, m. fang; tusk.

клю́ква, f. cranberry.

клю́нуть, v., perf. of клева́ть.

ключ, m. key; (mus.) clef.

ключи́ца, f. collarbone; clavicle.

клясть, v. imp., tr., curse. -ся, intr., swear.

кля́тва, f. oath.

кни́га, f. book.

кни́жный, adj. book.

книзу, adv. down, downwards.

кнут, m. whip.

ко, see к.

кобы́ла, f. mare.

кóваный, adj. forged.

кова́рный, adj. perfidious.

кова́ть, v. imp. forge; shoe.

ковёр, m. carpet; rug.

когда́, adv. when.

когда́-либо (also когда́-нибудь), adv. some time, some day.

когда́-то, adv. once, at one time.

кого́, pron., gen., acc. of кто.

кóготь, m. claw, talon.

кóдекс, m. code.

кóе-где́, adv. here and there.

кóе-кто́, pron. someone, somebody.

кóе-что́, pron. something.

ко́жа, f. skin; leather. -ный, adj. leather.

ко́жица, f. skin; peel.

кожура́, f. rind, peel.

коза́, f., козёл m., goat.

ко́зырь, m. trump.

ко́йка, f. cot, bunk; berth.

коклю́ш, m. whooping cough.

коко́с m. coconut.

кокс, m. coke.

кол, m. stake.

колбаса́, f. sausage.

колдовство́, nt. witchcraft.

колду́н, m. wizard.

колеба́ться, v. imp., oscillate; fluctuate; hesitate.

коле́но, nt. knee.

Ко́ленька, dim. of Никола́й.

колесо́, nt. wheel.

колея́, f. rut; track.

коли́чественный, adj. quantitative.

коли́чество, nt. quantity; amount.

колле́дж, m. college.

коллекти́в, m. collective body. -ный adj. collective.

колле́кция, f. collection.

коло́да, f. (wood) log; (cards) deck, pack.

коло́дец, m. well.

ко́локол, m. bell.

колоко́льня, f. belfry.

колониа́льный, adj. colonial.

колониза́ция, f. colonization.

коло́ния, f. colony.

коло́нна, f. column.

ко́лос, m. ear (of corn).

коло́ть, v. imp. prick, thrust, stab; chop.

колу́н, m. ax, axe.

колхо́з, abbr. of коллекти́вное хозя́йство, collective farm. -ник, m. collective farmer.

колыбе́ль, f. cradle.

колю́чий, adj. prickly, thorny.

Ко́ля, dim. of Никола́й.

кома́нда, f. command; (athl.) team.

командова́ние, nt. command; headquarters.

кома́ндовать, v. imp. order, command; be in command.

кома́р, m. mosquito; gnat.

коме́дия, f. comedy.

комисса́р, m. commissar.

коми́ссия, f. commission.

комите́т, m. committee.

коми́ческий (also коми́чный), adj. comic(al).

комме́рческий, adj. commercial.

коммуни́зм, m. communism.

коммуни́ст, m. communist. -и́ческий, adj. communist.

ко́мната, f. room.

комо́д, m. chest of drawers.

компа́ния, f. company.

компа́ртия, abbr. of коммунисти́ческая па́ртия, Communist Party.

ко́мпас, m. compass.

компенса́ция, f. compensation.

компенси́ровать, v. imp. & perf. compensate.

компози́тор, m. composer.

компози́ция, f. composition.

компо́т, m. stewed fruit; compote.

компромети́ровать, v. imp. (perf. скомпромети́ровать), compromise.

компроми́сс, m. compromise.

комсомо́л, m. (abbr. of Коммунисти́ческий Сою́з Молодёжи) Komsomol. -ец m., -ка f., a member of the Young Communist League.

кому́, pron., dat. of кто.

конве́йер, m. conveyor.

конве́рт, m. envelope.

конгре́сс, m. congress.

конди́терская, f. confectionery shop.

Кондра́тий m. Conrad.

конёк, m. skate.

коне́ц, m. end. в конце́ концо́в, in the end.

коне́чно, adv. of course.

коне́чности, f. pl. extremities.

коне́чный, adj. final, terminal.

конкре́тный, adj. concrete.

конкуре́нт, m. competitor.

конкури́ровать, v. imp. с + instr., compete.

ко́нкурс, m. competition, contest.

конопля́, f. hemp.

консервати́вный, *adj.* conservative.

консервато́рия, *f.* conservatory.

консерви́ровать, *v. imp.* preserve.

консе́рвы, *pl.* canned food.

конспе́кт, *m.* synopsis, summary, abstract.

Константи́н, *m.* Constantine.

Конста́нция, *f.* Constance.

констати́ровать, *v. imp. & perf.* ascertain; state.

конститу́ция, *f.* constitution.

констру́ировать, *v. imp. & perf.* construct; design; form.

констру́кция, *f.* construction, structure, design.

ко́нсул, *m.* consul. **-ство,** *nt.* consulate. **-ьта́нт,** *m.* consultant.

консульти́ровать, *v. imp.* (*perf.* проконсульти́ровать), advise; (*c* + *instr.*), consult (with).

контине́нт, *m.* continent, mainland.

конто́ра, *f.* office.

контра́кт, *m.* contract, agreement.

контрибу́ция, *f.* contribution.

контроли́ровать, *v. imp.* control.

конту́зия, *f.* contusion.

конура́, *f.* kennel.

конфере́нция, *f.* conference.

конфискова́ть, *v. imp. & perf.* confiscate.

конфу́зить, *v. imp.* (*perf.* сконфу́зить), disconcert, confuse.

концентри́ровать, *v. imp.* (*perf.* сконцентри́ровать), *tr.*, concentrate; mass.

конце́рт, *m.* concert, recital. **-ме́йстер,** *m.* first violinist.

концерти́ровать, *v. imp.* give concerts.

концла́герь, *m.*, *abbr. of* концентрацио́нный ла́герь, concentration camp.

конча́ть, *v. imp.* (*perf.* ко́нчить), *tr.*, finish, end, complete; (+ *inf.*) stop, cease.

ко́нчик, *m.* tip, end.

кончи́на, *f.* death, decease.

конь, *m.* horse, steed; (*chess*) knight.

коньки́, *pl.* skates.

коню́шня, *f.* stable.

кооперати́в, *m.* co-operative.

коопера́ция, *f.* co-öperation.

коопери́ровать, *v. imp. & perf.* organize into a co-öperative. **-ся,** co-öperate; be organized into a co-öperative.

копе́йка, *f.* kopeck.

ко́пи, *pl.* mines, pits.

копи́ровать, *v. imp.* (*perf.* скопи́ровать), copy; imitate, mimic.

копи́ть, *v. imp.*, *tr.*, accumulate, save; store up.

ко́пия, *f.* copy.

ко́поть, *f.* soot, lampblack.

копчёная ры́ба, smoked fish.

копы́то, *nt.* hoof.

копьё, *nt.* javelin.

кора́, *f.* bark; crust.

кораблекруше́ние, *nt.* shipwreck.

кора́бль, *m.* ship.

кора́лл, *m.* coral.

коре́ец *m.,* **коре́йка** *f.,* Korean.

коре́йский, *adj.* Korean.

коренно́й, *adj.* radical; native, indigenous.

ко́рень, *m.* root.

Коре́я, *f.* Korea.

корзи́на (*also* корзи́нка), *f.* basket.

коридо́р, *m.* corridor.

кори́чневый, *adj.* brown.

ко́рка, *f.* crust; rind.

корм, *m.* fodder.

корма́, *f.* (*naut.*) stern.

корми́ть, *v. imp.* (*perf.* накорми́ть), feed; suckle.

кормле́ние, *nt.* feeding; suckling.

коро́бка, *f.* box.

коро́ва, *f.* cow.

короле́ва, *f.* queen.

короле́вский, *adj.* royal.

короле́вство, *nt.* kingdom.

коро́ль, *m.* king.

коро́на, *f.* crown.

коро́нка, *f.* (*dental*) crown.

коро́ткий, *adj.* short.

ко́рпус, *m.* (*athl.*) length.

корректи́ровать, *v. imp.* (*perf.*

прокорректи́ровать), correct; proof.

корре́ктор, *m.* proofreader.

корректу́ра, *f.* proof, proof sheet.

корреспонде́нция, *f.* correspondence.

корсе́т, *m.* corset.

коры́стный, *adj.* mercenary.

коры́то, *nt.* trough.

корь, *f.* measles.

коса́, *f.* scythe; plait.

ко́свенный, *adj.* indirect.

коси́ть, *v. imp.* (*perf.* скоси́ть), mow.

косма́тый, *adj.* shaggy.

космополи́т, *m.* cosmopolite.

ко́сность, *f.* stagnation, stagnancy; inertness.

косноязы́чный, *adj.* tongue-tied.

косну́ться, *v., perf. of* каса́ться.

ко́сный, *adj.* stagnant; inert.

косо́й, *adj.* slanting, oblique; squinting.

костёр, *m.* bonfire.

косты́ль, *m.* crutch.

кость, *f.* bone. **игра́льные ко́сти**, dice. **слоно́вая кость**, ivory.

костю́м, *m.* costume; dress, suit.

Ко́стя, *dim. of* Константи́н.

костя́к, *m.* skeleton.

кот, *m.* tomcat.

котёл, *m.* boiler.

котело́к, *m.* kettle, pot.

котёнок, *m.* kitten.

котле́та, *f.* cutlet; chop.

кото́рый, *pron.* which.

ко́фе, *m.* coffee.

кофе́йник, *m.* coffeepot.

кофе́йный, *adj.* coffee.

кочева́ть, *v. imp.* wander; lead a nomadic life.

коче́вник, *m.* nomad.

коша́чий, *adj.* feline.

кошелёк, *m.* purse.

ко́шка, *f.* cat.

кошма́р, *m.* nightmare.

кра́деный, *adj.* stolen.

кра́жа, *f.* theft.

край, *m.* border, brim, edge;

land, country. **-ний**, *adj.* extreme. **по кра́йней ме́ре**, at least. **-ность**, *f.* extreme, extremity.

кран, *m.* faucet; hydrant.

краса́вец, *m.* handsome man.

краса́вица, *f.* beautiful woman, beauty.

краси́вый, *adj.* beautiful.

кра́сить, *v. imp.* (*perf.* покра́сить), color, dye, paint.

кра́ска, *f.* color, paint, dye.

кра́сная строка́, new paragraph.

красне́ть, *v. imp.* (*perf.* покрасне́ть), flush, redden; blush.

кра́сное де́рево, mahogany.

краснознамённый, *adj.* decorated with the Order of the Red Banner (USSR).

красноречи́вый, *adj.* eloquent.

кра́сный, *adj.* red.

красота́, *f.* beauty.

красть, *v. imp.* (*perf.* укра́сть), steal.

кра́ткий, *adj.* brief, short.

кра́тко, *adv.* briefly. **-вре́менный**, *adj.* of short duration; transitory; **-сро́чный**, *adj.* short-term. **-сть**, *f.* brevity.

кра́тное, *nt.* (*math.*) multiple.

кратча́йший, *adj.* shortest.

крах, *m.* crash, bankruptcy; failure.

крахма́л, *m.* starch.

крахма́лить, *v. imp.* (*perf.* накрахма́лить), starch.

кра́шенный, *adj.* painted, dyed colored.

креди́т, *m.* credit. **-оспосо́бный**, *adj.* solvent.

крем, *m.* cream.

кремато́рий, *m.* crematorium.

креме́нь, *m.* flint.

Кремль, *m.* Kremlin.

креп, *m.* crêpe.

крепи́ть, *v. imp.* strengthen; reinforce.

кре́пкий, *adj.* strong; firm, sturdy; robust.

кре́пость, *f.* fortress; strength.

кре́сло, *nt.* armchair.

крест, *m.* cross.

крести́ть, *v. imp.* (*perf.*

окрести́ть), baptize, christen.
кре́стник, m. godson.
кре́стница, f. goddaughter.
крестья́нин m. крестья́нка f., peasant.
крестья́нство, nt. peasantry.
кривизна́, f. crookedness; curvature.
криво́й, adj. crooked; curved.
кри́зис, m. crisis.
крик, m. shout, cry. -ли́вый, adj. loud.
кри́тик, m. critic.
кри́тика, f. criticism.
критикова́ть, v. imp. criticize.
крича́ть, v. imp. (perf. кри́кнуть), shout, cry.
кров, m. roof, shelter, house.
крова́вый, adj. bloody; murderous.
крова́ть, f. bed.
кро́вный, adj. blood.
кровоизлия́ние, nt. hemorrhage.
кровообраще́ние, nt. blood circulation.
кровопроли́тие, nt. bloodshed.
кровотече́ние, nt. bleeding.
кровоточи́ть, v. imp. bleed.
кровь, f. blood.
кровяно́й ша́рик, blood corpuscle.
кро́ить, v. imp. (perf. скрои́ть), cut, cut out.
кро́лик, m. rabbit.
кролл, m. (swim.) crawl.
кро́ме, prep. (+ gen.) except; besides, in addition to.
кро́мка, f. selvage.
кропотли́вый, adj. laborious; painstaking.
кросс, m. cross-country race.
кро́ссворд, m. crossword puzzle.
крот, m. mole; moleskin.
кро́ткий, adj. gentle; meek.
кро́тость, f. gentleness; meekness.
кроха́, f. crumb.
кроши́ть, v. imp., tr., crumble.
кро́шка, f. crumb.
круг, m. circle. -лый, adj. round. -овой, adj. circular. -ом, adv., prep. round, around
кру́жево, nt. lace.

кружи́ть, v. imp., tr., turn, spin, whirl. — intr., circle, wander.
кружо́к, m. disk; circle, club.
крупа́, f. groats.
кру́пный, adj. big, large; large-scale.
крути́ть, v. imp., tr., turn, roll.
круто́е яйцо́, hard-boiled egg.
круто́й, adj. steep; stern.
круше́ние, nt. accident, wreck; downfall, ruin.
крыла́тый, adj. winged.
крыло́, nt. wing.
крыльцо́, nt. porch.
Крым, m. Crimea.
кры́са, f. rat.
крыть, v. imp. (perf. покры́ть), cover. -ся, v. imp., intr., hide, conceal oneself; be covered.
кры́ша, f. roof.
кры́шка, f. cover, lid.
крюк (also крючо́к), m. hook.
кста́ти, adv. by the way.
кто, pron. who, whom; that. кто́-либо (also кто́-нибудь), pron. somebody, someone; anybody, anyone.
кто́-то, pron. somebody.
куб, m. (geom.) cube; boiler, still.
ку́бок, m. goblet.
кубоме́тр, m. cubic meter.
куда́, adv. where, whither.
куда́-нибудь, adv. somewhere, anywhere.
куда́-то, adv. somewhere, anywhere.
ку́дри, pl. curls.
кудря́вый, adj. curly, curly-headed.
кузне́ц, m. blacksmith.
кузне́чик, m. grasshopper.
ку́кла, f. doll, puppet.
кукуру́за, f. maize, corn.
куку́шка, f. cuckoo.
кула́к, m. fist; kulak.
кулина́рный, adj. culinary.
кули́сы, pl. (theat.) wings; scenes.
культ, m. cult. -у́ра, f. culture.
культиви́ровать, v. imp. cultivate.
купа́льня, f. bathhouse.

купа́ние, *nt.* bathing.

купа́ть, *v. imp.* (*perf.* вы́купать), *tr.*, bathe.

купе́, *nt. ind.* train compartment.

купе́ц, *m.* merchant.

Купидо́н, *m.* Cupid.

купи́ть, *v.*, *perf. of* покупа́ть.

куре́ние, *nt.* smoking.

кури́льщик, *m.* smoker.

кури́ть, *v. imp.* smoke.

ку́рица, *f.* hen, chicken.

куропа́тка, *f.* partridge.

куро́рт, *m.* health resort.

курс, *m.* course; rate of exchange.

курси́в, *m.* italics.

курье́р, *m.* messenger.

курье́рский по́езд, express train.

куса́ть, *v. imp., tr.* sting, bite.

кусо́к, *m.* piece; lump.

куст, *m.* bush, shrub. -а́рник, *m.* shrubbery.

куха́рка, *f.* cook.

ку́хня, *f.* kitchen; cuisine.

ку́хонный, *adj.* kitchen.

ку́ча, *f.* heap; hill.

ку́шанье, *nt.* food; dish; eating.

ку́шать, *v. imp.* (*perf.* поку́шать), eat.

куше́тка, *f.* couch

Л

лаборато́рия, *f.* laboratory.

ла́ва, *f.* lava.

лави́на, *f.* avalanche.

лави́ровать, *v. imp.* maneuver.

ла́вка, *f.* bench; shop.

ла́вочник, *m.* shopkeeper.

лавр, *m.* laurel.

ла́герь, *m.* camp.

ла́дан, *m.* incense.

ла́дно, *adv.* well; all right.

Ла́дожское о́зеро, Lake Ladoga.

ладо́нь, *f.* palm.

лазаре́т, *m.* hospital; infirmary

лазу́рь, *f.* azure.

ла́йка, *f.* Eskimo dog; kidskin.

лак, *m.* varnish.

лака́ть, *v. imp.* lap.

лакирова́ть, *v. imp. & perf.* varnish.

Ла-Ма́нш, проли́в (Англи́йский кана́л), English Channel.

ла́мпа, *f.* lamp.

ла́мпочка, *f.* bulb.

ландша́фт, *m.* landscape.

лань, *f.* doe.

ла́па, *f.* paw.

лапша́, *f.* noodles; noodle soup.

ларёк, *m.* stall.

ла́ска, *f.* caress, endearment; kindness, goodness.

ласка́ть, *v. imp.* caress, pet.

ла́сковый, *adj.* affectionate, tender.

ла́сточка, *m.* swallow (*bird*).

лата́ть, *v. imp.* (*perf.* зала́тать), patch.

латви́ец *m.*, латви́йка *f.*, Latvian.

латви́йский, *adj.* Latvian.

лати́нский, *adj.* Latin.

лату́нь, *f.* brass.

латы́нь, *f.* Latin.

латы́ш *m.*, -ка *f.*, Lett.

лауреа́т, *m.* laureate.

ла́ять, *v. imp.* bark.

лгать, *v. imp.* (*perf.* солга́ть), lie, tell a lie.

лгун, *m.* liar.

лебедь, *m.* swan.

лев, *m.* lion.

левша́, *m., f.* left-handed person; southpaw.

ле́вый, *adj.* left.

лега́льный, *adj.* legal.

лёгкие, *pl.* lungs.

лёгкий, *adj.* light; easy; slight.

легкове́рный, *adj.* credulous.

легкомы́сленный, *adj.* flippant, frivolous.

лёд, m. ice.

леденёть, v. imp. freeze; become numb.

ледни́к, m. glacier.

Ледови́тый океа́н, Arctic Ocean.

ледяно́й, adj. icy.

лежа́ть, v. imp., intr., lie, be situated; be.

ле́звие, nt. blade, edge.

лезть, v. imp. (perf. поле́зть), climb, clamber; в + acc., get in or into.

лека́рство, nt. medicine; drug.

ле́ктор, m. lecturer.

ле́кция, f. lecture.

лён, m. flax.

Ле́на, f. Lena.

лени́вый, adj. lazy.

ле́нинский, adj. Leninist.

лени́ться, v. imp. be lazy.

ле́нта, f. ribbon, tape; band.

Лён(уш)ка, dim. of Еле́на.

лень, f. laziness.

лепесто́к, m. petal.

лепи́ть, v. imp. (perf. вы́лепить), model, fashion, shape. — (perf. слепи́ть), build, make.

лес, m. forest, wood; timber. -и́стый, adj. wooded. -но́й, adj. wood, forest. -ово́дство, nt. forestry.

леса́, f. scaffold, scaffolding.

ле́стница, f. staircase, stairs; ladder.

ле́стный, adj. flattering.

лесть, f. flattery.

лёт, m. flight. на лету́, in flight.

лета́, pl. years, age.

лета́ть, v. imp. ind. (det. лете́ть, perf. полете́ть), fly, flutter.

ле́тний, adj. summer.

ле́то, nt. summer. ле́том, in summer.

ле́топись, f. chronicle, annal.

летоисчисле́ние, nt. chronology.

летучий, adj. flying.

лётчик, m. flyer, pilot.

лече́бный, adj. curative, medical.

лече́ние, nt. treatment, cure.

лечи́ть, v. imp. treat, cure.

лечь, v., perf. of ложи́ться.

лжец, m. liar.

лжи́вый, adj. false, lying.

ли, conj. whether, if.

ли́бо, conj. or. ли́бо... ли́бо..., either... or....

Лива́н, m. Lebanon.

ли́вень, m. downpour.

ли́га, f. league.

Ли́дия, f. Lydia.

Ли́за (also Ли́занька, Ли́з(оч)ка), dim. of Елизаве́та.

лиза́ть, v. imp. (perf. лизну́ть), lick.

ликвиди́ровать, v. imp. & perf. liquidate.

ли́лия, f. lily.

лило́вый, adj. violet.

лимо́н, m. lemon. -а́д, m. lemonade.

лингви́стика, f. linguistics.

лине́йка, f. ruler.

ли́нза, f. lens.

ли́ния, f. line.

ли́па, f. linden tree.

ли́пкий, adj. sticky.

ли́рика, f. lyrics.

лири́ческий, adj. lyric(al).

лиса́, лиси́ца, f. fox.

Лиссабо́н, m. Lisbon.

лист, m. (pl. ли́стья) leaf; (pl. листы́) sheet. -ва́, f. foliage.

Литва́, f. Lithuania.

литерату́ра, f. literature.

лито́вец m., лито́вка f., Lithuanian.

лито́вский, adj. Lithuanian.

литр, m. liter.

лить, v. imp., tr., pour; spill.

лифт, m. elevator.

лихо́й, adj. evil.

лихора́дка, f. fever.

лихора́дочный, adj. feverish.

лицева́я сторона́, right side; front, facade.

лицеме́р, m. hypocrite.

лицо́, nt. face; person, personage; right side; (gram.) person. лицо́м к лицу́, face to face.

ли́чность, f. personality.

ли́чный, adj. personal, individual, private.

ли́чный соста́в, personnel.

лиша́ть, v. imp. (perf. **лиши́ть**), + gen., deprive of. **лиши́ть себя́ жи́зни,** commit suicide.

лише́ние, nt. deprivation; privation, hardship.

ли́шний, adj. surplus; superfluous.

лишь, adv. only. **лишь бы,** if only. — conj. (also **лишь то́лько**) as soon as.

лоб, m. forehead.

лове́ц, m. hunter; fisherman.

лови́ть, v. imp. (perf. **пойма́ть**), catch; entrap, trap.

ло́вкий, adj. adroit, dexterous.

ло́вкость, f. adroitness, dexterity.

лову́шка, f. snare, trap.

ло́гика, f. logic.

логи́ческий (also **логи́чный**), adj. logical.

ло́говище, nt. lair, den.

ло́дка, f. boat.

ло́жа, f. (theat.) box.

ложи́ться, v. imp. (perf. **лечь**), lie down. **ложи́ться спать,** go to bed or sleep.

ло́жка, f. spoon.

ло́жный, adj. false.

ложь, f. lie, falsehood.

ло́зунг, m. slogan.

лойя́льный, adj. loyal.

локомоти́в, m. locomotive.

ло́коть, m. lock, curl.

лом, m. crowbar; (coll.) scrap.

лома́ть, v. imp. (perf. **слома́ть**), tr., break.

ломба́рд, m. pawnshop.

ломо́ть, f. hunk, chunk, piece.

ло́мтик, m. slice.

ло́но, nt. bosom; lap.

ло́пасть, f. fan; vane.

лопа́та, f. spade, shovel.

лоск, m. luster, gloss.

лососи́на, f. salmon.

лось, m. elk.

Лотари́нгия, f. Lorraine.

лотере́я, f. lottery.

лохма́тый, adj. shaggy.

лохмо́тья, pl. rags.

ло́шадь, f. horse.

Луа́ра, f. Loire.

луг, m. meadow.

лу́жа, f. puddle.

лук, m. onion; bow.

лука́вство, nt. slyness, cunning.

лука́вый, adj. sly, cunning.

луна́, f. moon.

лу́нный, adj. lunar, moon.

лу́па, f. magnifying glass.

лупи́ть, v. imp. (perf. **облупи́ть**), peel, pare. — (perf. **отлупи́ть**), thrash, flog.

луч, m. ray, beam. **-еза́рный,** adj. radiant. **-и́стый,** adj. radiant.

лу́чше, adv. better.

лу́чший, adj. better.

лущи́ть, v. imp. husk; shell.

лы́жа, f. ski; snowshoe.

лы́жник, m. skier.

лысе́ть, v. imp. grow bald.

лы́сина, f. baldness, bald spot.

лы́сый, adj. bald.

льви́ца, f. lioness.

льго́та, f. privilege.

льго́тный, adj. privileged; favorable.

льди́на, f. ice floe.

льняно́й, adj. flaxen; linen.

льстец, m. flatterer.

льсти́вый, adj. flattering.

льсти́ть, v. imp. (perf. **польсти́ть**), flatter.

Лю́ба, dim. of **Любо́вь.**

любе́зность, f. courtesy, kindness.

любе́зный, adj. courteous, kind, amiable; obliging, polite.

люби́мец, m. favorite, pet.

люби́мый, adj. beloved, favorite, pet.

люби́тель, m. lover; amateur. **-ский,** adj. amateur.

люби́ть, v. imp. love; like.

любова́ться, v. imp., + instr. admire.

любо́вник, m. lover.

любо́вница, f. mistress.

любо́вный, adj. love, loving.

любо́вь, f. love.

Любо́вь, f. pers. name.

любо́й, adj. any. — n. anyone; either (of two).

любопы́тный, adj. curious.

лю́бящий, adj. affectionate; loving.

лю́ди, *pl.* people.
людный, *adj.* crowded; populous.
Людо́вик, *m.* Ludwig.
людско́й, *adj.* human.
лю́лька, *f.* cradle.
лю́тик, *m.* buttercup.

лю́тый, *adj.* severe; fierce.
ляга́ть, *v. imp.* (*perf.* лягну́ть), *tr.* kick.
лягу́шка, *f.* frog.
ля́жка, *f.* thigh; haunch.
ля́мка, *f.* strap.

М

м., *abbr. of* метр.
мавзоле́й, *m.* mausoleum.
магази́н, *m.* store, shop.
магистра́ль, *f.* water main; highway.
магни́т, *m.* magnet. -ный, *adj.* magnetic. -офо́н, *m.* tape recorder.
магни́тить, *v. imp.* magnetize.
Магоме́т, *m.* Mohammed.
магомета́нин *m.*, магомета́нка *f.*, Mohammedan.
магомета́нский, *adj.* Mohammedan.
мажо́р, *m.* (*mus.*) major.
маза́ть, *v. imp.* oil, grease, lubricate; smear; daub.
мази́лка, *f.* brush.
мазь, *f.* ointment.
май, *n.* May. -ский, *adj.* May.
майоне́з, *m.* mayonnaise.
мак, *m.* poppy; poppy seed.
макаро́ны, *pl.* macaroni.
мака́ть, *v. imp.* dip in *or* into.
македо́нец *m.*, македо́нка *f.*, Macedonian.
макре́ль, *f.* mackerel.
максима́льный, *adj.* maximum.
ма́ксимум, *m.* maximum.
малайский, *adj.* Malayan.
Ма́лая А́зия, Asia Minor.
малейший, *adj.* smallest, least, slightest.
ма́ленький, *adj.* small, little; diminutive. — *n.* baby, child.
мале́ц, *m.* lad.
мали́на, *f.* raspberry; (*coll.*) raspberries.
мали́новка, *f.* robin; raspberry brandy.
ма́ло, *adv., pron.* little; a little.
-ду́шный, *adj.* faint-hearted.

-иму́щий, *adj.* poor. -кро́вие, *nt.* anemia. -ле́тний, *adj.* underage; juvenile.
ма́ло-пома́лу, *adv.* little by little; gradually.
ма́лый, *adj.* small, little.
ма́льчик, *m.* boy, lad.
маля́р, *m.* house painter.
маля́рия, *f.* malaria.
ма́ма, *f.* mother, mama.
мандари́н, *m.* tangerine.
мане́вр, *m.* maneuver.
маневри́ровать, *v. imp.* maneuver.
мане́ра, *f.* manner.
манже́та, *f.* cuff.
мани́ть, *v. imp.* beckon; wave to; lure, attract, entice.
манифе́ст, *m.* manifesto. -а́ция, *f.* demonstration.
манчжу́р *m.*, -ка *f.*, Manchurian. -ский, *adj.* Manchurian.
Ма́нька (*also* Ма́ня), *dim. of* Мари́я.
мара́ть, *v. imp.* (*perf.* зама́рать), soil, stain, sully. — (*perf.* нама́рать), daub, scribble.
марафо́н, *m.* marathon.
Маргари́та, *f.* Margaret.
маргари́тка, *f.* daisy.
мари́ец *m.*, мари́йка *f.*, Mari.
Мари́на, *f.* Marina.
маринова́ть, *v. imp.* (*perf.* замаринова́ть), marinate, pickle.
Мари́я (*also* Ма́рья), *f.* Maria.
ма́рка, *f.* postage stamp; brand, grade, sort; trademark.
маркси́зм, *m.* Marxism.
Марс, *m.* Mars.

март, *m.* March. -овский, *adj.* March.

Ма́рфа, *f.* Martha.

Ма́рфуш(к)а, *dim. of* Ма́рфа.

марш, *m.* march.

маршал, *m.* marshal.

маршировать, *v. imp.* march.

маршру́т, *m.* itinerary; route.

Ма́рья, *see* Мари́я.

ма́ска, *f.* mask. -ра́д, *m.* masquerade.

маскировать, *v. imp.* (*perf.* замаскирова́ть), mask, disguise; camouflage.

маслёнка, *f.* butter dish; oil can.

масли́на, *f.* olive; olive tree.

ма́сло, *nt.* butter; oil.

ма́сса, *f.* mass.

масса́ж, *m.* massage.

масси́вный, *adj.* massive.

масси́ровать, *v. imp. & perf.* massage, rub.

ма́ссы, *pl.* masses.

ма́стер, *m.* foreman; expert. -ска́я, *f.* workshop; studio. -ско́й, *adj.* masterly. -ство́, *nt.* skill, mastery; craftmanship.

масти́тый, *adj.* venerable.

масть, *f.* color, shade; (*cards*) suit.

масшта́б, *m.* scale.

мат, *m.* (*chess*) checkmate, mate.

Матве́й, *m.* Matthew.

матема́тик, *m.* mathematician. -а, *f.* mathematics.

материа́л, *m.* material. -и́зм, *m.* materialism. -ьный, *adj.* material.

матери́к, *m.* mainland; continent.

матери́нский, *adj.* maternal.

матери́нство, *nt.* motherhood.

мате́рия, *f.* matter; pus.

ма́тка, *f.* uterus; womb; (*of animals*) female, dam, queen.

ма́товый, *adj.* mat, dull.

матра́ц, *m.* mattress.

матро́с, *m.* sailor, seaman.

матч, *m.* (*athl.*) match.

мать, *f.* mother.

мах, *m.* stroke.

маха́ть, *v. imp.* (*perf.* мах-

ну́ть), wave one's hand.

маче́ха, *f.* stepmother.

ма́чта, *f.* mast.

Ма́ша (*also* Ма́шенька), *dim. of* Мари́я.

маши́на, *f.* engine; machine; car.

машина́льный, *adj.* mechanical, automatic.

машини́ст, *m.* machinist; engineer.

машини́стка, *f.* typist.

маши́нка, *f.* typewriter; sewing machine.

мая́к, *m.* lighthouse.

ма́ятник, *m.* pendulum.

мгла, *f.* mist, haze.

мгли́стый, *adj.* misty, hazy.

мгнове́ние, *ni.* instant, moment.

мгнове́нный, *adj.* instantaneous, momentary.

ме́бель, *f.* furniture.

меблирова́ть, *v. imp. & perf.* furnish.

меблиро́вка, *f.* furnishings, furniture; furnishing.

мёд, *m.* honey.

меда́ль, *f.* medal.

медве́дь, *m.* bear.

медици́на, *f.* medicine.

медици́нский, *adj.* medical.

ме́дленный, *adj.* slow.

ме́длить, *v. imp.* linger; delay.

ме́дный, *adj.* copper.

медо́вый, *adj.* honey.

медь, *f.* copper. жёлтая медь, brass.

межа́, *f.* boundary.

междоме́тие, *nt.* (*gram.*) interjection.

ме́жду, *prep.* (+ *instr.*) between; among, amongst. ме́жду тем, meanwhile. ме́жду тем как, while. ме́жду про́чим, by the way, incidentally.

междунаро́дный, *adj.* international.

Ме́ксика, *f.* Mexico.

мел, *m.* chalk.

ме́лкий, *adj.* small; fine; shallow; petty, minor.

мелоди́чный, *adj.* melodious.

мело́дия, *f.* melody.

мело́чный, *adj.* petty; mean.

ме́лочь, *f.* trifle; trivia; (*money*) change.

мель, *f.* shoal; bank. **сесть на ме́ле**, run aground.

ме́льком, *adv.* in passing; cursorily.

ме́льник, *m.* miller.

ме́льница, *f.* mill.

ме́на, *f.* exchange, barter.

ме́нее, *comp. adv.* less. **тем не ме́нее**, nonetheless.

ме́ньше, *adj.* smaller. — *adv.* less.

ме́ньший, *adj.* lesser, smaller, younger.

меньшинство́, *nt.* minority.

меню́, *nt., ind.,* menu.

меня́, *pron., gen., acc.* of я.

меня́ть, *v. imp.* (*perf.* поменя́ть), change; exchange (for).

ме́ра, *f.* measure.

мерза́вец, *m.* rascal, scoundrel.

ме́рзкий, *adj.* vile.

мёрзлый, *adj.* frozen.

мёрзнуть, *v. imp.* freeze.

меридиа́н, *m.* meridian.

ме́рило, *nt.* criterion, standard.

ме́рить, *v. imp.* measure; try on.

ме́рка, *f.* measure.

ме́ркнуть, *v. imp.* (*perf.* поме́ркнуть), grow dark or dim.

Мерку́рий, *n.* Mercury.

ме́рный, *adj.* measured; measuring.

мёртвенный, *adj.* deathly, ghastly.

мертве́ть, *v. imp.* grow numb or stiff.

мертве́ц, *m.* corpse. **-ка́я,** *f.* mortuary.

мертворождённый, *adj.* stillborn.

мёртвый, *adj.* dead.

мерца́ть, *v. imp.*, shimmer, glimmer.

меси́ть, *v. imp.* (*perf.* смеси́ть), knead.

мести́, *v, imp.* (*perf.* вы́мести) sweep.

местко́м, *abbr. of* ме́стный коми́тет.

ме́стность, *f.* locality.

ме́стный, *adj.* local.

ме́сто, *nt.* place; room; seat; job. **-жи́тельство,** *nt.* place of residence.

местоиме́ние, *nt.* pronoun.

месть, *f.* vengeance. revenge.

ме́сяц, *m.* month; moon.

ме́сячный, *adj.* monthly.

мета́лл, *m.* metal. **-и́ческий,** *adj.* metallic. **-у́ргия,** *f.* metallurgy.

мета́тель, *m.* thrower, hurler.

мета́ть, *v. imp.* (*perf.* метну́ть) throw, cast, fling. — (*perf.* смета́ть), baste.

метёлка, *f.* whiskbroom.

мете́ль, *f.* snowstorm.

метеороло́гия *f.* meteorology.

ме́тить, *v. imp.* mark, stamp; в + *acc.*, aim at; aspire to.

ме́тка, *f.* mark.

ме́ткий, *adj.* well-aimed, accurate.

ме́ткость, *f.* accuracy.

метла́, *f.* broom.

метну́ть, *v., perf. of* мета́ть.

ме́тод, *m.* method.

метр, *m.* meter.

ме́трика *f.*, birth certificate.

метро́ *nt. ind.* (*also* метрополи́тен *m*) subway.

Мефо́дий, *m.* Methodius.

мех, *m.* (*pl.* меха́) fur; (*pl.* мехи́) bellows.

механизи́ровать, *v. imp. & perf.* mechanize.

меха́ник, *m.* mechanic.

механи́ческий, *adj.* mechanical.

Ме́хико, *nt. ind.* Mexico City.

мехово́й, *adj.* fur.

меч, *m.* sword.

мече́ть, *f.* mosque.

мечта́, *f.* dream.

мечта́ть, *v. imp.* dream.

меша́ть, *v. imp.* (*perf.* помеша́ть); disturb; hinder, hamper; interfere.

мешо́к, *m.* bag, sack.

миг, *m.* instant. **-ом,** in a flash.

мига́ть, *v. imp.* (*perf.* мигну́ть), wink; twinkle.

мизи́нец, *m.* little finger.

миллиа́рд, *m.* billion.

миллиме́тр, *m.* millimeter.

миллио́н, *m.* million. -ный, *adj.* millionth.

милови́дный, *adj.* comely.

милосе́рдие, *nt.* charity, charitableness.

ми́лостивый, *adj.* gracious.

ми́лостыня, *f.* alms.

ми́лость, *f.* favor, kindness; mercy.

ми́лый, *adj.* pleasant, nice.

ми́ля, *f.* mile.

ми́мо, *adv., prep.* (+ *gen.*) past, by. -лётный, *adj.* fleeting, passing. -хо́дом, *adv.* in passing; by the way.

ми́на, *f.* countenance, facial expression; mine.

минда́ль, *m.* almond tree; (*coll.*) almonds.

минера́л, *m.* mineral.

минима́льный, *adj.* minimum.

министе́рство, *nt.* ministry, department.

мини́стр, *m.* minister, secretary.

минова́ть, *v. imp.* (*perf.* мину́ть), pass, pass by.

мино́р, *m.* (*mus.*) minor.

мину́вший, *adj.* past.

ми́нус, *m.* minus; defect.

мину́та, *f.* minute; moment, instant.

мину́тный, *adj.* momentary.

мину́ть, *v.,* *perf. of* минова́ть.

мир, *m.* peace; world. -ный, *adj.* peaceful. -ово́й, *adj.* world; universal.

мири́ть, *v. imp.* (*perf.* помири́ть), reconcile. -ся, с + *instr.,* be reconciled with.

ми́ска, *f.* basin; tureen.

ми́ссия, *f.* mission.

Ми́тенька, *dim. of name* Дми́трий.

миф, *m.* myth.

Михаи́л, *m.* Michael.

Ми́ша (*also* Мишу́тка), *dim. of* Михаи́л.

мише́нь, *f.* target. я́блоко мише́ни, bull's-eye.

младе́нец, *m.* infant.

младе́нчество, *nt.* infancy.

мла́дший, *adj.* younger; junior.

млекопита́ющее, *pl.* mammals.

Мле́чный путь, Milky Way.

мне, *pron., dat., prep. of* я.

мне́ние, *nt.* opinion.

мни́мый, *adj.* imaginary.

мно́гие, *adj., pron.* many.

мно́го, *adv., adj.* much. -зна́чительный, *adj.* very significant. -кра́тный, *adj.* repeated, frequent; (*gram.*) frequentative. -чи́сленный, *adj.* multiple, numerous. -язы́чный, *adj.* polyglot.

мно́жественный, *adj.* plural.

мно́жество, *nt.* multitude.

мно́жимое, *m.* multiplicand.

мно́житель, *m.* multiplier, factor.

мно́жить, *v. imp.* (*perf.* помно́жить), multiply. — (*perf.* умно́жить), increase.

мной (*also* мно́ю), *pron., instr. of* я.

мобилизова́ть, *v. imp. & perf.* mobilize.

моги́ла, *f.* grave.

могу́чий, *adj.* powerful, mighty.

могу́щество, *nt.* power, might.

мо́да, *f.* fashion.

моде́ль, *f.* model.

мо́дный, *adj.* fashionable.

мо́жет быть, perhaps, maybe.

мо́жно, *impers.* it is possible; one may, one can.

мозг, *m.* brain; marrow. -ово́й, *adj.* cerebral.

Моисе́й, *m.* Moses.

мой, *pron.,* my.

мо́кнуть, *v. imp.* become wet; soak.

мокро́та, *f.* phlegm.

мокрота́, *f.* humidity.

мо́крый, *adj.* wet.

мол, *m.* pier.

молва́, *f.* rumor.

молдава́нин, *m.,* молдава́нка *f.,* Moldavian.

молдава́нский (*also* молда́вский), *adj.* Moldavian.

моли́тва, *f.* prayer.

моли́ть, *v. imp.* entreat, implore, beseech. -ся, (о + *prep.*) pray (for); (на + *acc.*) adore, idolize.

мо́лния, *f.* lightning.

молодёжь, *f.* youth; the young.

молодо́й, *adj.* young.

мо́лодость, *f.* youth.

молоко́, *nt.* milk.

мо́лот, *m.* (large) hammer.

молоти́ть, *v. imp.* thresh; thrash.

молото́к, *m.* hammer.

моло́ть, *v. imp.* (*perf.* **смоло́ть**), grind; mill.

моло́чный, *adj.* dairy; creamery.

мо́лча, *adv.* silently, in silence. **-ли́вый**, *adj.* reticent; taciturn.

молча́ние, *nt.* silence.

молча́ть, *v. imp.* be *or* keep silent.

моль, *f.* clothes moth.

мольба́, *f.* entreaty, plea.

мольбе́рт, *m.* easel.

моме́нт, *m.* moment. **-а́льный**, *adj.* instantaneous.

монасты́рь, *m.* monastery; cloister, nunnery, convent.

мона́х, *m.* monk.

монго́л *m.*, **-ка** *f.*, Mongolian.

моне́та, *f.* coin.

моне́тный, *adj.* monetary.

моното́нный, *adj.* monotonous

монти́ровать, *v. imp.* (*perf.* **смонти́ровать**), assemble, mount.

мор, *m.* pestilence; plague.

мора́ль, *f.* moral.

мордви́н *m.*, **-ка** *f.*, Mordovian.

мордо́вский, *adj.* Mordovian.

морга́ть, *v. imp.* (*perf.* **моргну́ть**), wink; blink.

мо́рда, *f.* muzzle.

мо́ре, *nt.* sea. **-пла́вание**, *nt.* navigation.

морж, *m.* walrus.

мори́ть, *v. imp.* exterminate.

морко́вь, *f.* carrot.

моро́женое, *nt.* ice cream.

моро́з, *m.* frost.

моро́зить, *v. imp., tr.*, freeze.

моро́зный, *adj.* frosty.

мороси́ть, *v. imp.* drizzle.

морско́й, *adj.* sea; maritime, nautical; marine.

морщи́на, *f.* wrinkle.

мо́рщить, *v. imp.* (*perf.* **намо́рщить**, **смо́рщить**), wrinkle.

моря́к, *m.* seaman, sailor.

Москва́, *f.* Moscow.

москви́ч, *m.* Muscovite.

моско́вский, *adj.* Moscow, Muscovite.

мост, *m.* bridge.

мостова́я, *f.* pavement.

моти́в, *m.* motive, reason; (*mus.*) motif.

мото́р, *m.* motor, engine.

мотоци́кл (*also* **мотоцикле́т**) *m.*, **мотоцикле́тка** *f.*, motorcycle.

мотылёк, *m.* butterfly; moth.

мох, *m.* moss.

мохна́тый, *adj.* hairy; shaggy.

моча́, *f.* urine.

мочи́ть, *v. imp.* soak; wet. **-ся**, *v. imp.* (*perf.* **помочи́ться**), urinate; be soaked.

мо́чка у́ха, ear lobe.

мочь, *v. imp.* (*perf.* **смочь**), be able to. — *f.* power, might. **что есть мо́чи**, with all one's might.

моше́нник, *m.* swindler.

моше́нничать, *v. imp.* (*perf.* **смоше́нничать**), swindle.

мо́щный, *adj.* powerful.

мощь, *f.* power, might.

мрак, *m.* gloom; darkness, blackness.

мра́мор, *m.* marble.

Мра́морное мо́ре, Sea of Marmara.

мра́чный, *adj.* gloomy; dark, black.

мсти́ть, *v. imp.* (*perf.* **отомсти́ть**), revenge oneself; avenge.

му́дрость, *f.* wisdom.

му́дрый, *adj.* wise, sage.

муж, *m.* husband. **-ественный**, *adj.* courageous, manly. **-ество**, *nt.* courage. **-ско́й**, *adj.* masculine, male. **-чи́на**, *m.* (*declined as f.*) man; male.

музе́й, *m.* museum.

му́зыка, *f.* music.

музыка́нт, *m.* musician.

му́ка, *f.* suffering, torment.

мука́, *f.* flour; meal.

мул, *m.* mule.

му́мия, *f.* mummy.

мунди́р, *m.* uniform.

мундшту́к, *m.* cigarette *or*

cigar holder; mouthpiece.

муравей, *m.* ant.

мурлыкать, *v. imp.* purr.

мускул, *m.* muscle. **-истый**, *adj.* muscular.

мусор, *m.* rubbish, trash.

мутный, *adj.* turbid; cloudy; muddy.

муфта, *f.* muff.

муха, *f.* fly.

мучение, *nt.* torture.

мученик, *m.* martyr.

мученичество, *nt.* martyrdom.

мучитель, *m.* tormentor, torturer. **-ный**, *adj.* agonizing.

мучить, *v. imp.* torture; harass, torment, worry.

мщение, *nt.* vengeance.

мы, *pron.* we.

мылить, *v. imp.* (*perf.* **намылить**), soap, lather.

мылкий, *adj.* soapy.

мыло, *nt.* soap.

мыльный, *adj.* soapy.

мыс, *m.* cape.

мысленный, *adj.* mental.

мыслимый, *adj.* conceivable.

мыслить, *v. imp.* think.

мысль, *f.* thought, idea.

мыть, *v. imp.* (*perf.* **помыть**), *tr.*, wash.

мычать, *v. imp.* low.

мышеловка, *f.* mousetrap.

мышление, *nt.* thinking; mentality.

мышца, *f.* muscle.

мышь, *f.*, mouse. **летучая мышь**, bat.

мышьяк, *m.* arsenic.

Мюнхен, *m.* Munich.

мягкий, *adj.* soft; mild, gentle.

мягкость, *f.* softness; gentleness, mildness.

мясистый, *adj.* fleshy.

мясная, *f.* meat market.

мясник, *m.* butcher.

мясное, *nt.* meat dish.

мясо, *nt.* meat; flesh.

мята, *f.* mint.

мятеж, *m.* mutiny; rebellion, revolt.

мять, *v. imp.* (*perf.* **помять**), crumple, rumple; knead.

мяукать, *v. imp.* mew.

мяч, *m.* ball.

Н

на, *prep.* (+ *acc.*) on, onto; upon; to; till; for; (+ *prep.*) during; in, at; on.

набавлять, *v. imp.* (*perf.* **набавить**) add (to); increase.

набег, *m.* raid.

набережная, *f.* embankment.

набивать, *v. imp.* (*perf.* **набить**), stuff (with); fill (with).

набивка, *f.* stuffing, filling.

набирать, *v. imp.* (*perf.* **набрать**), gather, collect; recruit.

наблюдатель, *m.* observer. **-ный**, *adj.* observant.

наблюдать, *v. imp.* observe.

набожный, *adj.* pious, devout.

наборщик, *m.* compositor, typesetter.

набрать, *v.*, *perf. of* **набирать**.

набросок, *m.* sketch, outline.

навеки, *adv.* for ever.

наверно, *adv.* probably.

наверняка, *adv.* (*colloq.*) for sure, for certain.

навёртывать, *v. imp.* (*perf.* **наверстать**), make up (for).

наверх, *adv.* up, upwards; upstairs. **-ý**, *adv.* above; upstairs.

навещать, *v. imp.* (*perf.* **навестить**), visit, call on *or* upon.

навлекать, *v. imp.* (*perf.* **навлечь**), incur.

наводить, *v. imp.* (*perf.* **навести**), direct (at); cover, coat.

наводнение, *nt.* flood.

наводнять, *v. imp.* (*perf.* **наводнить**), flood, inundate.

навоз, *n.* manure.

навсегда, *adv.* for ever. **раз-**

навсегда́, once and for all.

навстре́чу, *adv.* from the opposite direction.

на́вык, *m.* habit.

навя́зчивый, *adj.* obtrusive.

навя́зывать, *v. imp.* (*perf.* **навяза́ть**), tie, fasten; force *or* thrust (on).

нагиба́ть, *v. imp.* (*perf.* **нагну́ть**), bend.

на́глухо, *adv.* tightly.

на́глый, *adj.* impudent, insolent.

нагля́дный, *adj.* visual; obvious, clear.

нагное́ние, *nt.* festering, suppuration.

нагова́ривать, *v. imp.* (*perf.* **наговори́ть**), на + *acc.,* calumniate, slander.

наго́й, *adj.* nude.

нагоня́ть, *v. imp.* (*perf.* **нагна́ть**), overtake.

нагото́ве, *adv.* in readiness.

награ́да, *f.* reward; decoration.

награжда́ть, *v. imp.* (*perf.* **награди́ть**), reward; decorate

нагрева́ть, *v. imp.* (*perf.* **нагре́ть**), warm, warm up; heat.

нагруби́ть, *v., perf. of* **груби́ть.**

нагру́дник, *m.* bib.

нагружа́ть, *v. imp.* (*perf.* **нагрузи́ть**), load.

нагру́зка, *f.* load.

над (надо), *prep.* (+ *instr.*) over, above.

надба́вка, *f.* increment, increase.

надвига́ющийся, *adj.* approaching; imminent.

надгро́бный па́мятник *or* **ка́мень,** tomb, tombstone.

надева́ть, *v. imp.* (*perf.* **наде́ть**), put on, don.

наде́жда, *f.* hope.

надёжный, *adj.* dependable, reliable, safe.

наде́л, *m.* allotment.

На́денька, *dim. of name* **Наде́жда.**

наде́ть, *v., perf. of* **надева́ть.**

наде́яться, *v. imp.* hope for; rely on.

надзе́мный, *adj.* above ground; overhead.

надзира́тель, *m.* supervisor; overseer.

надзо́р, *m.* surveillance.

надлежа́щий, *adj.* proper, suitable, fit.

надло́м, *m.* fracture, break.

надме́нный, *adj.* haughty, arrogant.

на́до, *prep., see* **над. — impers.** it is necessary.

надо́бность, *f.* need, necessity.

надоеда́ть, *v. imp.* (*perf.* **надое́сть**), plague, bother, annoy.

надое́дливый, *adj.* boring, tiresome.

надо́лго, *adv.* for a long time.

на́дпись, *f.* inscription.

надре́з, *m.* incision, cut.

надрыва́ть, *v. imp.* (*perf.* **надорва́ть**), overtax, strain.

надсмо́тр, *m.* inspection, surveillance.

надстро́чный знак, superscript; diacritical mark.

надува́ть, *v. imp.* (*perf.* **наду́ть**), inflate; cheat, dupe.

надуши́ть, *v., perf. of* **души́ть.**

надыми́ть, *v., perf. of* **дыми́ть.**

На́дька, Надю́ш(к)а, На́дя, *dim. of name* **Наде́жда.**

наеда́ться, *v. imp.* (*perf.* **нае́сться**), eat one's fill.

наедине́, *adv.* in private, privately.

нае́зд, *m.* raid, incursion. **-ник,** *m.* horseman, rider.

наезжа́ть, *v. imp.* (*perf.* **нае́хать**), на + *acc.,* run into, collide with; (*imp. only*) visit from time to time.

наём, *m.* hire; rent.

нажа́ть, *v., perf. of* **нажима́ть.**

нажива́ть, *v. imp.* (*perf.* **нажи́ть**), acquire; gain.

нажи́вка, *f.* profit, gain.

нажи́м, *m.* pressure.

нажима́ть, *v. imp.* (*perf.* **нажа́ть**), press, push.

наза́д, *adv.* back, backwards. **тому́ наза́д,** ago. **-й,** *adv.* (*colloq.*) behind.

назва́ние, *nt.* name, title.

назва́ть, *v.*, *perf. of* называ́ть.

назида́тельный, *adj.* edifying.

назнача́ть, *v. imp.* (*perf.* назна́чить), appoint, nominate; prescribe.

назначе́ние, *nt.* appointment, nomination; prescription; purpose.

назо́йливый, *adj.* importunate; intrusive.

называ́ть, *v. imp.* (*perf.* назва́ть), name, call.

наибо́лее, *adv.* most.

наи́вный, *adj.* naive.

наизу́сть, *adv.* by heart.

наилу́чший, *adj.* best.

наиме́нее, *adv.* least.

наименова́ние, *nt.* name, title.

наименова́ть, *v.*, *perf. of* именова́ть.

найско́сь, *adv.* aslant; obliquely.

найти́(сь), *v.*, *perf. of* находи́ть(ся).

нака́з, *m.* order, instruction.

наказа́ние, *nt.* punishment, penalty.

нака́зывать, *v. imp.* (*perf.* наказа́ть), punish, penalize.

накану́не, *adv.* the day *or* evening before. — *prep.*, + *gen.*, on the eve (of).

наки́дывать, *v. imp.* (*perf.* наки́нуть), throw on *or* over; slip on.

накла́дывать, *v. imp.* (*perf.* наложи́ть), impose; lay *or* place on.

накле́йка, *f.* label.

накло́н, *m.* inclination; slope. -е́ние, *nt.* inclination; (*gram.*) mood. -ость, *f.* bent, inclination.

наклоня́ть, *v. imp.* (*perf.* наклони́ть), *tr.*, bend.

наконе́ц, *adv.* finally, at last.

накопле́ние, *nt.* accumulation.

нако́пливать, *v. imp.* (*perf.* накопи́ть), *tr.*, accumulate.

накорми́ть, *v.*, *perf. of* корми́ть.

накрахма́лить, *v.*, *perf. of* крахма́лить.

на́крест, *adv.* crosswise.

накрыва́ть, *v. imp.* (*perf.* накры́ть), cover, cover with; set a table.

налага́ть, *v. imp.* (*perf.* наложи́ть), impose.

нале́во, *adv.* to the left.

налёт, *m.* air raid; thin coating.

налива́ть, *v. imp.* (*perf.* нали́ть), pour, pour out; fill.

нали́чие, *nt.* presence.

нали́чный, *adj.* present; available.

нало́г, *m.* tax.

наложи́ть, *v.*, *perf. of* накла́дывать, налага́ть.

нам, *pron.*, *dat. of* мы.

намара́ть, *v.*, *perf. of* мара́ть.

намёк, *m.* hint, allusion.

намека́ть, *v. imp.* (*perf.* намекну́ть), на + *acc.*, hint (at); allude (to).

намерева́ться, *v. imp.* intend; mean.

наме́рение, *nt.* intention.

намеча́ть, *v. imp.* (*perf.* наме́тить), plan, contemplate.

на́ми, *pron.*, *instr. of* мы.

намо́рщить, *v.*, *perf. of* мо́рщить.

намы́лить, *v.*, *perf. of* мы́лить.

нанима́ть, *v. imp.* (*perf.* наня́ть), rent, hire, engage.

наноси́ть, *v. imp.* (*perf.* нанести́), bring, deposit; inflict, cause.

наоборо́т, *adv.* on the contrary; vice versa.

наобу́м, *adv.* at random.

напада́ть, *v. imp.* (*perf.* напа́сть), на + *acc.*, attack.

нападе́ние, *nt.* attack, assault.

напе́в, *m.* tune, air.

напёрсток, *m.* thimble.

напи́лок, *m.* file.

написа́ть, *v.*, *perf. of* писа́ть.

напи́ток, *m.* beverage, drink.

напи́ться, *v. imp.* have something to drink; get drunk.

напои́ть, *v.*, *perf. of* пои́ть.

наполня́ть, *v. imp.* (*perf.* напо́лнить), *tr.*, fill.

наполови́ну, *adv.* in half; by halves.

напомина́ние, *nt.* reminder; reminding; notice.

напомина́ть, *v. imp.* (*perf.* **напо́мнить**), remind.

напо́р, *m.* pressure.

напосле́док, *adv.* at last; in the end.

направле́ние, *nt.* direction.

направля́ть, *v. imp.* (*perf.* **напра́вить**), direct; send, refer. -ся. к + *dat.,* в + *acc.,* head towards *or* for.

напра́во, *adv.* to the right.

напра́сно, *adv.* in vain; uselessly.

напра́шиваться, *v. imp.* (*perf.* **напроси́ться**), obtrude oneself on *or* upon; be suggested.

наприме́р, for example.

напрока́т, *adv.* for hire.

напро́тив, *adv.* opposite; on the contrary; across the street — *prep.* (+ *gen.*) opposite.

напряжённе, *nt.* strain, effort; tension.

напряжённый, *adj.* strained; tense.

напу́дрить, *v.,* *perf. of* **пу́дрить.**

напы́шенный, *adj.* pompous; inflated.

наравне́, *adv.* on the same level; equally.

нараста́ть, *v. imp.* (*perf.* **нарасти́**), grow, increase.

нарва́ть, *v.,* *perf. of* **нарыва́ть, рвать.**

наре́чие, *n.* adverb.

нарисова́ть, *v.,* *perf. of* **рисова́ть.**

нарица́тельное существи́тельное, (*gram.*) common noun.

нарица́тельный, *adj.* nominal.

наро́д, *m.* nation; people. -ность, *f.* nationality. -ный, *adj.* national; people's.

нарожда́ться, *v. imp.* arise; come into being.

наро́ст, *m.* growth.

наро́читый, *adj.* deliberate.

наро́чно, *adv.* on purpose, purposely.

нару́жность, *f.* exterior, appearance.

нару́жный, *adj.* external.

нару́жу, *adv.* out, outside.

наруша́ть, *v. imp.* (*perf.* **нару́шить**), violate.

наруше́ние, *nt.* violation, breach.

нары́в, *m.* abscess.

нарыва́ть, *v. imp.* (*perf.* **нарва́ть**), gather, pluck, pull.

наря́д, *m.* order, warrant; attire, apparel. -ный, *adj.* smart, well-dressed; elegant.

нас, *pron.,* gen., acc. of **мы.**

насажда́ть, *v. imp.* (*perf.* **насади́ть**), plant.

насеко́мое, *nt.* insect.

населе́ние, *nt.* population.

населя́ть, *v. imp.* (*perf.* **насели́ть**), settle, populate; inhabit.

наси́лие, *nt.* violence; force.

наси́ловать, *v. imp.* (*perf.* **изнаси́ловать**), violate; force.

наси́льно, *adv.* by force.

наси́льственный, *adj.* forced; violent.

наскво́зь, *adv.* through; through and through; throughout.

наско́лько, *adv.* as far as, so far as.

наслажда́ться, *v. imp.* (*perf.* **наслади́ться**), + *instr.,* enjoy, take pleasure in.

наслажде́ние, *nt.* delight, enjoyment, pleasure.

насле́дие, *nt.* legacy.

насле́дник, *m.* heir.

насле́дственный, *adj.* hereditary.

насле́дство, *nt.* inheritance.

насме́шка, *f.* mockery, mocking.

насме́шливый, *adj.* mocking.

на́сморк, *m.* catarrh.

насори́ть, *v.,* *perf. of* **сори́ть.**

насо́с, *m.* pump.

наставле́ние, *nt.* admonition, exhortation; instruction, directions.

наста́ивать, *v. imp.* (*perf.* **настоя́ть**), insist; persist (in).

Наста́сья, *var. of* **Анаста́сия.**

на́стежь, *adv.* wide open.

На́стенька, *dim. of* **Наста́сья.**

насто́йчивый, *adj.* persistent.

настолько, *adv.* so. настолько насколько, *as much as.*

настоя́тельный, *adj.* urgent, pressing.

настоя́ть, *v., perf. of* наста́ивать.

настоя́щий, *adj.* present; genuine, real.

на́строго, *adv.* strictly.

настрое́ние, *nt.* mood; humor.

настро́ить, *v. imp.* tune.

наступле́ние, *nt.* approach, coming.

насу́щный, *adj.* urgent; vital.

насчёт, *prep.*, + *gen.*, regarding.

насчи́тывать, *v. imp. (perf.* насчита́ть), count, number.

насыпа́ть, *v. imp. (perf.* насы́пать), pour, pour in or into.

на́сыпь, *f.* embankment.

насыща́ть, *v. imp. (perf.* насы́тить), satiate; saturate.

Ната́лия, *f.* Natalie.

ната́лкиваться, *v. imp. (perf.* натолкну́ться), на + *acc.*, come across; encounter.

Ната́ша, *dim. of* Ната́лия.

нату́ра, *f.* nature.

натура́льный, *adj.* natural.

натюрмо́рт, *m.* still life.

натя́гивать, *v. imp. (perf.* натяну́ть), stretch, strain; draw or pull on.

нау́ка, *f.* science.

научи́ть(ся), *v., perf. of* учи́ть(ся).

нау́чный, *adj.* scientific.

нау́шники, *pl.* earphones; earflaps.

наха́льный, *adj.* impudent.

нахму́риться, *v., perf. of* хму́риться.

находи́ть, *v. imp. (perf.* найти́), find, discover; на + *acc.*, come across or upon. -ся, turn up, be found; be, be situated or located.

нахо́дка, *f.* find.

национализи́ровать, *v. imp. & perf.* nationalize.

национа́льность, *f.* nationality.

национа́льный, *adj.* national.

нача́ло, *nt.* beginning.

нача́льный, *adj.* elementary; beginning, initial.

нача́тки, *pl.* rudiments.

начерта́ние, *nt.* tracing; inscription.

начина́ть, *v. imp. (perf.* нача́ть), *tr.,* begin, start, commence.

начина́ющий, *adj.* beginning. — *m.* beginner.

начи́танный, *adj.* well-read.

наш, *pron.,* our, ours.

наше́ствие, *nt.* invasion.

небе́сный, *adj.* celestial, heavenly.

неблагода́рный, *adj.* ungrateful.

неблагоразу́мный, *adj.* imprudent.

нёбный, *adj.* palatal.

не́бо, *nt.* sky, heaven.

нёбо, *nt.* palate.

небосво́д, *m.* firmament.

небоскрёб, *m.* skyscraper.

небре́жный, *adj.* careless, negligent.

небыва́лый, *adj.* unprecedented.

неведе́ние, *nt.* ignorance.

неве́домый, *adj.* unknown.

неве́жественный, *adj.* ignorant.

неве́жливый, *adj.* rude.

неве́рный, *adj.* incorrect; unfaithful, disloyal.

невероя́тный, *adj.* incredible.

неве́ста, *f.* bride; fiancée.

неве́стка, *f.* daughter-in-law; sister-in-law (*brother's wife*).

неви́данный, *adj.* unprecedented.

неви́димый, *adj.* invisible.

не́где, *adv.* nowhere.

неви́нный, *adj.* innocent.

невозвра́тный, *adj.* irrevocable.

невозмо́жный, *adj.* impossible.

нево́льный, *adj.* involuntary.

невреди́мый, *adj.* unharmed; safe.

невыноси́мый, *adj.* unbearable.

него́дный, *adj.* unfit.

негодова́ние, *nt.* indignation.

негодова́ть, *v. imp.* be indignant.

негр, *m.* Negro. **-итя́нка**, *f.* Negress.

негра́мотный, *adj.* illiterate.

неда́вний, *adj.* recent.

недалеко́, *adv.* not far.

неда́ром, *adv.* not in vain.

недви́жимый, *adj.* immovable.

недействи́тельный, *adj.* invalid; ineffective.

недели́мый, *adj.* indivisible.

неде́льный, *adj.* weekly.

неде́ля, *f.* week.

недобросо́вестный, *adj.* unscrupulous.

недове́рие, *nt.* distrust, mistrust.

недово́льный, *adj.* discontented.

недозво́ленный, *adj.* unlawful.

недо́лго, *adv.* not long.

недооце́нивать, *v. imp.* (*perf.* **недооцени́ть**), underestimate.

недопусти́мый, *adj.* inadmissible.

недоразуме́ние, *nt.* misunderstanding.

недоста́ток, *m.* lack, shortage.

недостижи́мый, *adj.* unattainable.

недоуме́ние, *nt.* perplexity.

недочёт, *m.* deficit; shortcoming.

неду́г, *m.* ailment.

неесте́ственный, *adj.* unnatural, affected.

нежда́нный, *adj.* unexpected.

нежена́тый, *adj.* (*of a man*) unmarried.

не́жный, *adj.* tender, affectionate, loving.

незави́симый, *adj.* independent.

незако́нный, *adj.* illegal, illegitimate, illicit.

незамени́мый, *adj.* irreplaceable.

незаме́тный, *adj.* imperceptible.

незащищённый, *adj.* unprotected.

незнако́мец, *m.* stranger.

незнако́мый, *adj.* unknown.

незна́ние, *nt.* ignorance.

незначи́тельный, *adj.* insignificant.

незре́лый, *adj.* immature; unripe.

неизбе́жный, *adj.* inevitable.

неизве́стный, *adj.* unknown.

неизмери́мый, *adj.* immeasurable.

неи́скренный, *adj.* insincere, false.

неисправи́мый, *adj.* incorrigible.

неиспра́вный, *adj.* out of order.

неистощи́мый, *adj.* inexhaustible.

нейтралите́т, *m.* neutrality.

нейтра́льный, *adj.* neutral.

не́кий, *pron.*, a certain.

не́когда, there is no time.

не́который, *pron.* some.

некроло́г, *m.* obituary.

некста́ти, *adv.* inopportunely; not to the point.

не́кто, *pron.* someone.

не́куда, *adv.* (+ *inf.*) nowhere.

неле́пый, *adj.* absurd; nonsensical.

нело́вкий, *adj.* awkward.

нельзя́, *impers.* one must not; it is prohibited.

нелюбо́вь, *f.* (к + *dat.*) dislike (for).

неме́дленно, *adv.* immediately.

не́мец *m.*, **не́мка** *f.*, German.

неме́цкий, *adj.* German.

неми́лость, *f.* disgrace.

немно́гие, *pron.* few; not many.

немно́го, *adv.* a little, not much.

немо́й, *adj.* dumb, mute.

ненави́деть, *v. imp.* hate, abhor.

не́нависть, *f.* hatred.

нена́стный, *adj.* foul.

нена́стье, *nt.* foul weather.

нену́жный, *adj.* unnecessary.

необду́манный, *adj.* hasty, rash.

необита́емый, *adj.* uninhabited.

необосно́ванный, *adj.* groundless, without foundation.

необразо́ванный, *adj.* uneducated.

необходи́мый, *adj.* necessary, urgent, essential.

необыкнове́нный, *adj.* unusual, uncommon.

неограни́ченный, *adj.* unlimited.

неоднокра́тно, *adv.* time and again, repeatedly.

неодобре́ние, *nt.* disapproval.

неожи́данный, *adj.* unexpected.

неопределённый, *adj.* indefinite, vague.

нео́пытный, *adj.* inexperienced.

неоснова́тельный, *adj.* unfounded.

неосторо́жный, *adj.* careless.

неотку́да, *adv.* from nowhere.

неохо́та, *f.* reluctance.

неоцени́мый, *adj.* invaluable.

непа́рный, *adj.* odd.

непереходный, *adj.* intransitive.

неплодоро́дный, *adj.* infertile.

непобеди́мый, *adj.* invincible.

непого́да, *f.* foul weather.

неподви́жный, *adj.* immovable.

неподчине́ние, *nt.* insubordination.

неподходя́щий, *adj.* unsuitable.

непоме́рный, *adj.* excessive.

непоня́тный, *adj.* incomprehensible.

непоря́док, *m.* disorder.

непоря́дочный, *adj.* dishonorable.

непосле́довательный, *adj.* inconsistent, inconsequential.

непосре́дственный, *adj.* direct.

непостоя́нный, *adj.* inconstant, changeable.

непохо́жий, *adj.* unlike.

непра́вда, *f.* untruth.

непра́вильный, *adj.* incorrect.

непра́вый, *adj.* irregular.

непредви́денный, *adj.* unforeseen.

непреме́нно, *adv.* without fail.

непреме́нный, *adj.* indispensible.

непреры́вный, *adj.* continuous.

неприе́млемый, *adj.* unacceptable.

неприкоснове́нный, *adj.* inviolable.

неприли́чный, *adj.* indecent.

непримири́мый, *adj.* irreconcilable

непринуждённый, *adj.* natural, free, easy.

непристу́пный, *adj.* inaccessible.

неприя́тель, *m.* enemy.

неприя́тность, *f.* unpleasantness; nuisance, annoyance, trouble.

непромока́емый, *adj.* waterproof; impermeable.

непроница́емый, *adj.* impenetrable.

неравноме́рный, *adj.* uneven, irregular.

неразвито́й, *adj.* undeveloped.

неразгово́рчивый, *adj.* uncommunicative.

неразрешённый, *adj.* unsolved, not solved; forbidden, prohibited.

неразры́вый, *adj.* indissoluble.

неразу́мный, *adj.* unwise, unreasonable.

нераствори́мый, *adj.* insoluble.

нерв, *m.* nerve. **-ный**, *adj.* nervous.

не́рвничать, *v. imp.* to be nervous.

неред́ко, *adv.* often.

нереши́тельный, *adj.* undecisive, irresolute.

несваре́ние желу́дка indigestion.

несве́жий, *adj.* stale.

несвя́зный, *adj.* incoherent.

несгора́емый, *adj.* incombustible; fireproof.

не́сколько, *num.* several, a few.

нескро́мный, *adj.* immodest.

несло́жный, *adj.* simple.

неслы́ханный, *adj.* unheard of; unprecedented.

несмотря́ на, in spite of.

несмыва́емые черни́ла, indelible ink.

несовершенноле́тний, *adj.* under age; — *n.* minor.

несоверше́нный, *adj.* imperfect; (*gram.*) imperfective.

несовмести́мый, *adj.* incompatible.

несогла́сие, *nt.* disagreement, discord.

несозна́тельный, *adj.* unconscious.

несомне́нно, *adv.* undoubtedly.

неспосо́бный, *adj.* incapable; unfit.

несправедли́вый, *adj.* unjust, unfair.

несравне́нный, *adj.* incomparable.

нести́, *v. imp. det.* (*indet.* носи́ть, *perf.* понести́), carry; bear. — (*perf.* снести́): нести́ яйцо́, lay an egg. -сь, be carried. — (*perf.* снести́сь), lay eggs.

несча́стный, *adj.* unhappy, unfortunate, unlucky. несча́стный слу́чай, accident.

несча́стье, *nt.* misfortune, disaster. к несча́стью, unfortunately.

несчётный, *adj.* innumerable.

нет, *neg.* no; not. ещё нет, not yet.

нетерпели́вый, *adj.* impatient.

нето́чный, *adj.* inexact; inaccurate.

нетре́звый, *adj.* intoxicated, drunk.

нетрудоспосо́бный, *adj.* disabled, invalid.

неуве́ренный, *adj.* uncertain.

неуда́ча, *f.* failure.

неудо́бство, *nt.* inconvenience.

неудовлетворённый, *adj.* dissatisfied.

неудовлетвори́тельный, *adj.* unsatisfactory.

неуже́ли, *adv.* indeed, really.

неумоли́мый, *adj.* implacable.

неурожа́й, *m.* poor harvest.

неутоли́мый, *adj.* unquenchable, unsatiable.

неутоми́мый, *adj.* indefatigable.

нефть, *f.* petroleum, oil.

нехорошо́, *adj.* bad, badly; unwell.

нехотя́, *adv.* unwillingly.

неча́янно, *adv.* unintentionally; unexpectedly.

не́чего, *pron.* (+ *inf.*): it is useless (to). не́чего де́лать, there is nothing one can do.

нечётный, *adj.* odd.

нечи́стый, *adj.* unclean; impure; shady.

не́что, *pron.* something.

неща́дный, *adj.* unmerciful, merciless.

нея́вка, *f.* absence; non-attendance.

нея́сный, *adj.* vague; unclear.

ни, *conj.* not. ни . . . ни . . ., neither . . . nor . . . ни оди́н, not one.

нигде́, *adv.* nowhere.

ни́же, *adv.* lower; below; beneath, under.

ни́жний, *adj.* lower.

низ, *m.* bottom.

низверга́ть, *v. imp.* (*perf.* низве́ргнуть), overthrow.

низверже́ние, *nt.* overthrow.

ни́зкий, *adj.* low; base, mean.

ни́зменность, *f.* lowland.

ни́зость, *f.* baseness.

ника́к, *adv.* in no way, by no means. -о́й, *pron.* no, none; none whatever.

никогда́, *adv.* never.

Никола́й, *m.* Nicholas.

никто́, *pron.* nobody, no one.

Нил, *m.* Nile.

никуда́, *adv.* (*dir.*) nowhere.

ниско́лько, *adv.* not in the least.

ни́тка, *f.* thread.

ничего́, *pron.* nothing.

ниче́й, *pron.* nobody's.

ничто́, *pron.* nothing. -жный, *adj.* insignificant.

ничу́ть, *adv.* not in the least.

ничья́, *f.* (*sports*) draw, drawn game.

нищета́, *f.* poverty.

ни́щий, *adj.* beggarly. — *n.* beggar.

но, *conj.* but.

нове́йший, *adj.* newest, latest.

новизна́, *f.* novelty.

новобра́чный, *pl.* newlyweds.

нововведе́ние, *nt.* innovation.

новолу́ние, *nt.* new moon.

новорождённый, *adj.* newborn.

новосе́лье, *nt.* house-warming.

Новосиби́рские острова́, New Siberian Islands.

но́вость, *f.* news; novelty.

но́вый, *adj.* new. с Но́вым го́дом, Happy New Year!

новь, *f.* virgin soil.

нога́, *f.* foot, leg.

ноготь, m. fingernail; toenail.
нож, m. knife. **-ик**, small knife.
ножка, f. (furniture) leg.
ножницы, pl. scissors.
ноздря, f. nostril.
Ной, m. Noah.
нокаут, m. knockout.
нокаутировать, v. imp. + perf. (boxing) knock out.
нокдаун, m. knockdown.
номер, m. number; room, apartment; size.
нора, f. hole; lair, den, burrow.
Норвегия, f. Norway.
норвежец m., **норвежка** f., Norwegian.
норвежский, adj. Norwegian.
норка, f. mink.
норма, f. norm, standard; rate.
нормальный, adj. normal.
нос, m. nose.
носилки, pl. stretcher.
носильщик, m. porter.
носитель, m. bearer.
носить v. imp. ind. (det. **нести**, perf. **понести**), carry, bear; wear. **-ся**, rush, rush about; be carried or worn.
носовой ~ платок, handkerchief.
носок, m. sock.
носорог, m. rhinoceros.
нота, f. (mus.) note.
ноты, pl. sheet music.
ночевать, v. imp. (perf. **переночевать**), spend the night.

ночлег, m. lodging for the night.
ночная бабочка, moth.
ночной, adj. night.
ночь, f. night. **ночью**, at night.
ноябрь, m. November. **-ский**, adj. November.
нрав, m. disposition, temper. **-ы**, pl. customs; manners.
нравится, v. imp. (perf **понравиться**), + dat., please.
нравственность, f. morals.
ну! interj. well.
нудный, adj. tedious, tiresome, boring.
нужда, f. need.
нуждаться, v. imp. (в + prep.) need.
нуждающийся, adj. indigent, needy.
нужно, impers. it is necessary; one must; one should.
нужный, adj. necessary.
нуль, m. nought; zero.
нумерация, f. numeration.
нумеровать, v. imp. number.
ныне, adv. now, at present. **-шний**, adj. present.
нырять, v. imp. (perf. **нырнуть**), dive.
н. э., abbr. of **нашей эры**: A.D.
нюх, m. scent; sense of smell.
нюхать, v. imp. (perf. **понюхать**), smell, sniff.
нянчить, v. imp. nurse.
няня, f. nurse, nursemaid.

О

о (**об**, **обо**), prep. (+ prep.) of, about; (+ acc.) against.
оба num., m., nt., **обе** f. both.
обвал, m. fall, collapse, landslide.
обваливаться, v. imp. (perf. **обвалиться**), fall, collapse.
обаятельный, adj. charming, fascinating.
обветшалый, adj. decayed.
обвинение, nt. accusation.
обвинить, v., perf. of **винить**, **обвинять**.

обвинять, v. imp. (perf. **обвинить**), accuse.
обвислый, adj. sagging.
обгорелый, adj. charred, burned.
обдумывать, v. imp. (perf. **обдумать**), consider.
обе, see **оба**.
обед, m. dinner.
обедать, v. imp. (perf. **пообедать**), dine.
обеднеть, v. perf. become or grow poor.

обезопáсить, v. perf. guarantee or secure against.

обезорýживать, v. imp. (perf. обезорýжить), disarm.

обезья́на, f. monkey. ape.

оберегáть, v. imp. (perf. оберéчь), guard against; defend.

обёрточная бумáга, wrapping paper.

обессилéть, v. perf. grow or become weak.

обесси́ливать, v. imp. (perf. обесси́лить), tr., weaken.

обéт, m. promise; vow.

обещáние, nt. promise.

обещáть, v. imp. & perf. promise.

обжóрство, nt. gluttony.

обзóр, m. survey.

обивáть, v. imp. (perf. оби́ть), cover; pad; upholster.

оби́вка, f. upholstering; upholstery.

оби́да, f. offense.

оби́дный, adj. offensive.

обижáть, v. imp. (perf. оби́деть), offend.

оби́лие, nt. abundance.

оби́льный, adj. abundant, plentiful.

обитáтель, m. inhabitant.

обитáть, v. imp. inhabit.

оби́ть, v., perf. of обивáть.

облáдать, v. imp. possess, own.

óблако, nt. cloud.

областнóй, adj. regional.

óбласть, f. region; district; province.

облáчный, adj. cloudy.

облегчáть, v. imp. (perf. облегчи́ть), lighten; relieve; facilitate.

облегчéние, nt. relief.

обложéние, nt. taxation.

обложи́ть, v. imp. face, cover.

облóжка, f. cover.

облóмок, m. fragment.

облупи́ть, v., perf. of лупи́ть.

обмáн, m. fraud, deception. -чивый, adj. deceptive.

обмáнывать, v. imp. (perf. обману́ть), deceive; cheat.

обмéн, m. exchange.

обнажáть, v. imp. (perf. обнажи́ть), bare, uncover; reveal.

обнарýживать, v. imp. (perf. обнарýжить), discover; reveal.

обнимáть, v. imp. (perf. обня́ть), embrace.

обнищáть, v. imp. become impoverished.

обновлéние, nt. renovation.

обновля́ть, v. imp. (perf. обнови́ть), renovate.

обня́ть, v., perf. of обнимáть.

обо, see о.

обобщáть, v. imp. (perf. обобщи́ть), generalize.

обобществлéние, nt. socialization; collectivization.

обобществля́ть, v. imp. (perf. обобществи́ть), socialize.

обобщи́ть, v., perf. of обобщáть.

обогащáть, v. imp. (perf. обогати́ть), enrich.

обогащéние, nt. enrichment.

обогревáть, v. imp. (perf. обогрéть), warm.

ободрéние, nt. encouragement.

ободря́ть, v. imp. (perf. ободри́ть), encourage.

обожáтель m., -ница f., admirer.

обожáть, v. imp. admire, worship.

обозначáть, v. imp. mean. — (perf. обознáчить), designate, mark.

обозначéние, nt. designation.

обозрéние, nt. review.

обóи, pl. wallpaper.

обойти́(сь), v., perf. of обходи́ть(ся).

обольсти́тельный, adj. seductive.

обольщáть, v. imp. (perf. обольсти́ть), seduce.

обоня́ние, nt. sense of smell.

обрывáть(ся), v., perf. of обрывáть(ся).

оборóна, f. defense.

оборонáть, v. imp. (perf. оборони́ть), defend.

оборóт, m. revolution.

оборýдование, nt. equipment.

оборýдовать, v. imp. equip.

обоснова́ние, *nt.* basis.

обосно́вывать, *v. imp.* (*perf.* **обоснова́ть**), base, ground. **-ся**, settle.

обостря́ть, *v. imp.* (*perf.* **обостри́ть**), sharpen; aggravate, strain.

обою́дный, *adj.* mutual.

обоюдоо́стрый, *adj.* double-edged.

обрабо́тка, *f.* treatment; processing; cultivation, tillage.

обра́довать, *v., perf. of* **ра́довать.**

о́браз, *m.* form, image; mode, manner, way.

образе́ц, *m.* example, model, standard.

образова́ние, *nt.* education.

образо́ванный, *adj.* educated.

образо́вывать, *v. imp.* (*perf.* **образова́ть**), form, make, shape; organize.

образцо́вый, *adj.* model.

обра́зчик, *m.* specimen, sample; pattern.

обра́тно, *adj.* back, backwards; conversely, inversely.

обра́тный, *adj.* reverse; opposite; return.

обраща́ть, *v. imp.* (*perf.* **обрати́ть**), turn; direct. **-ся**, address; turn into.

обраще́ние, *nt.* address; treatment; circulation.

обреза́ть, *v. imp.* (*perf.* **обре́зать**), cut, cut off, clip, pare.

обрека́ть, *v. imp.* (*perf.* **обре́чь**), doom.

обременя́ть, *v. imp.* (*perf.* **обремени́ть**), burden.

обруба́ть, *v. imp.* (*perf.* **обруби́ть**), cut off.

обру́бок, *m.* stump.

о́бруч, *m.* hoop.

обры́в, *m.* precipice.

обрыва́ть, *v. imp.* (*perf.* **обо́рва́ть**), *tr.*, break or tear off.

обря́д, *m.* rite, ritual, ceremony. **-ный** (*also* **-овый**), *adj.* ritual.

обсле́довать, *v. imp.* inspect; investigate.

обслу́живание, *nt.* service.

обслу́живать, *v. imp.* (*perf.* **обслужи́ть**), attend, serve; service.

обстано́вка, *f.* furniture; (*theat.*) set; situation.

обстоя́тельный, *adj.* detailed, thorough.

обстоя́тельственный, *adj.* circumstantial.

обстоя́тельство, *nt.* circumstance; (*gram.*) adverbial modifier.

обступа́ть, *v. imp.* (*perf.* **обступи́ть**), surround.

обсужда́ть, *v. imp.* (*perf.* **обсуди́ть**), discuss.

обсужде́ние, *nt.* discussion.

обтека́емый, *adj.* streamlined.

обува́ть, *v. imp.* (*perf.* **обу́ть**), shoe.

о́бувь, *f.* footwear.

обу́здывать, *v. imp.* (*perf.* **обузда́ть**), bridle.

обусло́вливать, *v. imp.* (*perf.* **обусло́вить**), stipulate; condition; cause, evoke.

обу́ть, *v., perf. of* **обува́ть.**

обуча́ть, *v. imp.* (*perf.* **обучи́ть**), instruct, teach. **-ся**, learn; be instructed or taught

обходи́ть, *v. imp.* (*perf.* **обойти́**), go or pass around; make the rounds; avoid. **-ся**, treat; manage, do.

обхо́дный, *adj.* roundabout

обши́рный, *adj.* vast, extensive spacious.

обща́ться, *v. imp.*, **с** + *instr.* associate (with).

общедосту́пный, *adj.* generally accessible or available.

общежи́тие, *nt.* hostel; society community.

обще́ние, *nt.* intercourse, personal contact.

общепри́нятый, *adj.* in genera use; conventional.

обще́ственный, *adj.* public social.

о́бщество, *nt.* society.

о́бщий, *adj.* common; genera

объедине́ние, *nt.* unification.

объединя́ть, *v. imp.* (*perf.* **объедини́ть**), unite.

объекти́вный, *adj.* objective

объём, *m.* extent; volume; size

объявле́ние, *nt.* declaration; announcement.

объявля́ть, *v. imp.* (*perf.* объяви́ть), declare; announce.

объясне́ние, *nt.* explanation.

объясни́тельный, *adj.* explanatory.

объясня́ть, *v. imp.* (*perf.* объясни́ть), explain.

объя́тие, *nt.* embrace.

обыкнове́нно, *adv.* usually, as a rule.

обыкнове́нный, *adj.* usual; ordinary, plain, simple.

обы́скивать, *v. imp.* (*perf.* обыска́ть), *tr.*, search.

обы́чай, *m.* custom.

обы́чный, *adj.* usual; ordinary, commonplace.

обя́занность, *f.* duty.

обя́занный, *adj.* obliged.

обяза́тельно, *adv.* without fail.

обяза́тельный, *adj.* obligatory.

обя́зывать, *v. imp.* (*perf.* обяза́ть), oblige; obligate; bind.

овёс, *m.* oats.

овладева́ть, *v. imp.* (*perf.* овладе́ть), + *instr.*, seize, take possession of.

о́вощи, *pl.* vegetables.

овся́нка, *f.* oatmeal.

овца́, *f.* sheep.

овча́рка, *f.* sheepdog.

оглавле́ние, *nt.* contents; table of contents.

огла́ска, *f.* publicity.

оглаша́ть, *v. imp.* (*perf.* огласи́ть), publish; announce.

огло́хнуть, *v., perf. of* гло́хнуть.

оглуша́ть, *v. imp.* (*perf.* оглуши́ть), deafen, stun.

о́гненный, *adj.* fiery.

огнеопа́сный, *adj.* flammable.

огнетуши́тель, *m.* fire extinguisher.

огово́рка, *f.* reservation; stipulation.

ого́нь, *m.* fire.

огоро́д, *m.* vegetable garden.

огорче́ние, *nt.* grief.

огра́бить, *v., perf. of* гра́бить.

огра́да, *f.* fence; wall.

огражда́ть, *v. imp.* (*perf.* огради́ть), guard against; protect against.

ограниче́ние, *nt.* limitation; restriction.

ограни́чивать, *v. imp.* (*perf.* ограни́чить), limit; restrict.

огро́мный, *adj.* enormous.

огрубе́ть, *v., perf. of* грубе́ть.

огуре́ц, *m.* cucumber.

одарённый, *adj.* gifted.

одева́ть, *v. imp.* (*perf.* оде́ть), *otr.*, dress, clothe; cover.

де́жда, *f.* clothes.

одея́ло, *nt.* blanket.

оди́н *m.*, одна́ *f.*, одно́ *nt.*, *num.*, one. — *adj.* a, a certain; alone.

одина́ковый, *adj.* identical.

оди́ннадцатый, *adj.* eleventh.

оди́ннадцать, *num.* eleven.

одино́кий, *adj.* lonely, solitary.

одино́чество, *nt.* solitude.

одна́, *see* оди́н.

одна́жды, *adv.* once.

одна́ко, *conj.* however; nevertheless; yet, still.

одно́, *see* оди́н.

одновреме́нный, *adj.* simultaneous.

однозву́чный, *adj.* monotonous.

одноро́дный, *adj.* homogeneous.

односло́жный, *adj.* monosyllabic.

односторо́нний, *adj.* one-sided.

одобре́ние, *nt.* approval.

одобря́ть, *v. imp.* (*perf.* одо́брить), approve, approve of.

одолжа́ть, *v. imp.* (*perf.* одолжи́ть), lend.

одолже́ние, *nt.* favor.

одуре́лый, *adj.* stupid.

одурма́нить, *v., perf. of* дурма́нить.

одушевле́ние, *nt.* animation.

одушевля́ть, *v. imp.* (*perf.* одушеви́ть), animate.

ожереби́ться, *v., perf. of* жереби́ться.

ожере́лье, *nt.* necklace.

ожесточа́ть, *v. imp.* (*perf.* ожесточи́ть), harden; embitter.

ожесточе́ние, *nt.* bitterness.

ожива́ть, *v. imp.* (*perf.* ожи́ть), come to life.

оживля́ть, *v. imp.* (*perf.* оживи́ть), become lively, animated.

ожида́ние, *nt.* expectation.

ожида́ть, *v. imp.* expect, await; wait for; look forward to.

ожи́ть, *v.,* *perf. of* ожива́ть.

озабо́ченный, *adj.* preoccupied.

озагла́вливать, *v. imp.* (*perf.* озагла́вить), entitle.

о́зеро, *nt.* lake.

озлобле́ние, *nt.* bitterness; animosity.

ознакомля́ться, *v. imp.* (*perf.* ознако́миться), **c** + *instr.,* become acquainted with.

ознаменова́ть, *v. perf.* mark; celebrate.

означа́ть, *v. imp.* mean, signify.

ока́зывать, *v. imp.* (*perf.* оказа́ть), render, show. **-ся** prove to be; turn out to be.

окамене́ть, *v.,* *perf. of* камене́ть.

ока́нчивать, *v. imp.* (*perf.* око́нчить), *tr.,* finish, end.

окая́нный, *adj.* damned, cursed.

океа́н, *m.* ocean. **-ский,** *adj.* oceanic.

окисле́ние, *nt.* oxidation.

о́кись, *f.* oxide.

оккупи́ровать, *v. imp. & perf.* occupy.

окно́, *nt.* window.

о́ко, *nt.* eye.

о́коло, *prep.* (+ *gen.*) by, near, around; about, nearly, approximately.

око́нное стекло́, windowpane.

оконча́ние, *nt.* termination, end, ending; graduation.

оконча́тельный, *adj.* final, definitive.

око́нчить, *v.,* *perf. of* ока́нчивать.

окостене́лый, *adj.* ossified; numb, stiff.

окра́ина, *f.* outskirts.

окра́ска, *f.* painting, dyeing; color.

окре́пнуть, *v. perf.* recover one's strength; become stronger.

окрести́ть, *v.,* *perf. of* крести́ть.

окре́стность, *f.* environs; environment.

окре́стный, *adj.* neighboring.

о́круг, *m.* district.

окружа́ть, *v. imp.* (*perf.* окружи́ть), surround.

окру́жность, *f.* circumference; circle.

октя́брь, *m.* October. **-ский,** *adj.* October.

оку́рок, *m.* cigarette butt.

оледене́лый, *adj.* frozen.

оле́нина, *f.* venison.

оле́нь, *m.* deer.

О́ленька, *dim. of* О́льга.

олимпи́йский, *adj.* Olympic.

олицетворе́ние, *nt.* personification.

олицетворя́ть, *v. imp.* (*perf.* олицетвори́ть), personify.

о́лово, *nt.* tin.

оловя́нный, *adj.* tin.

О́льга, *f.* Olga.

О́ля, *dim. of* О́льга.

омерзе́ние, *nt.* loathing.

омерзи́тельный, *adj.* loathsome.

омле́т, *m.* omelet.

он, *pron.* he.

она́, *pron.* she.

онеме́ть, *v. perf.* become dumb or numb.

они́, *pron.* they.

оно́, *pron.* it.

опа́здывать, *v. imp.* (*perf.* опозда́ть), be late.

опаса́ться, *v. imp.* fear.

опасе́ние, *nt.* fear, apprehension.

опасли́вый, *adj.* cautious.

опа́сность, *f.* danger.

опа́сный, *adj.* dangerous.

опеку́н, *m.* guardian.

о́пера, *f.* opera.

операти́вный, *adj.* operative; surgical.

опера́ция, *f.* operation.

опере́ние, *nt.* plumage.

опере́ться, *v.,* *perf. of* опира́ться.

оперировать, v. imp. & perf. operate.

оперный, adj. operatic, opera.

опечатка, f. misprint.

опилки, pl. sawdust.

опираться, v. imp. (perf. **опереться**), be based on or upon.

описание, nt. description.

описательный, adj. descriptive.

описывать, v. imp. (perf. **описать**), describe.

опись, f. list, inventory; schedule.

оплакивать, v. imp. (perf. **оплакать**), mourn.

оплата, f. payment.

оплачивать, v. imp. (perf. **оплатить**), remunerate, pay.

оплодотворение, nt. fecundation, fertilization.

оплодотворять, v. imp. (perf. **оплодотворить**), fecundate, impregnate, fertilize.

опоздать, v., perf. of. **опаздывать**.

опомниться, v. perf. come to one's senses.

опора, f. support.

оправа, f. setting, mounting.

оправдание, nt. justification.

оправдывать, v. imp. (perf. **оправдать**), justify.

определение, nt. definition; (gram.) attribute.

определённый, adj. definite; certain.

определимый, adj. definable.

определять, v. imp. (perf. **определить**), define; determine.

опровергать, v. imp. (perf. **опровергнуть**), refute.

опровержение, nt. refutation.

опрометчивый, adj. rash; imprudent.

опрос, m. inquest, interrogation.

опрятный, adj. neat, tidy.

оптика, f. optics.

оптический, adj. optic(al).

оптовый, adj. wholesale.

опубликование, nt. publication; promulgation.

опубликовать, v., perf. of **публиковать**.

опускать, v. imp. (perf. **опустить**), lower; pull down; omit.

опустеть, v., perf. of **пустеть**.

опустошать, v. imp. (perf. **опустошить**), devastate.

опустошение, nt. devastation.

опухать, v. imp. (perf. **опухнуть**), intr., swell.

опухоль, f. swelling; tumor.

опыт, m. experiment; experience. **-ный**, adj. experienced; experimental.

опьянеть, v., perf. of **пьянеть**.

опять, adv. again.

орган, m. organ.

орган, m. (mus.) organ.

организация, f. organization.

организовать, v. imp. & perf. organize.

органический, adj. organic.

орден, m. order, decoration.

орёл, m. eagle. **орёл или решка**, heads or tails.

орех, m. nut.

оригинальный, adj. original.

оркестр, m. orchestra.

орошение, nt. irrigation.

орудие, nt. instrument, tool, implement.

оружие, nt. weapon.

орфография, f. orthography.

оса, f. wasp.

осада, f. siege.

осадок, m. sediment.

осваивать, v. imp. (perf. **освоить**), master; assimilate. **-ся, с** + instr., make oneself familiar with.

осведомление, nt. information.

осведомлять, v. imp. (perf. **осведомить**), o + prep., inform of.

освещать, v. imp. (perf. **осветить**), illuminate, illumine; elucidate.

освещение, nt. light, lighting.

освидетельствовать, v., perf of **свидетельствовать**.

освободитель, m. liberator, emancipator.

освобождать, v. imp. (perf.

освободи́ть), free, liberate, emancipate; deliver.

освобождéние, nt. liberation, emancipation; deliverance.

освóбить(ся), v., perf. of освобождáть(ся).

оседáть, v. imp. (perf. осéсть), intr., settle; subside.

осёл, m. donkey; ass.

осéнний, adj. autumn, autumnal.

óсень, f. autumn, fall. -ю, in autumn.

осéсть, v., perf. of оседáть.

осётр, m. sturgeon.

осиротéть, v. perf. become an orphan; be deserted or abandoned.

оскверня́ть, v. imp. (perf. оскверни́ть), defile, profane.

оскóлок, m, splinter.

оскорби́тельный, adj. insulting; outrageous.

оскорблéние, nt. insult; offense.

оскорбля́ть, v. imp. (perf. оскорби́ть), insult, offend.

ослабевáть, v. imp. (perf. ослабéть), grow feeble or weak.

ослабéть, v., perf. of ослабевáть, слабéть.

ослаблéние, nt. weakening.

ослепи́тельный, adj. blinding; dazzling.

ослепля́ть, v. imp. (perf. ослепи́ть), blind.

ослепнýть, v. perf. of слéпнуть), become or go blind.

осложня́ть, v. imp. (perf. осложни́ть), complicate.

ослушáние, nt. disobedience.

ослы́шаться, v. perf. mishear.

осмáтривать, v. imp. (perf. осмотрéть), examine; survey; scan. -ся, look about or around; get one's bearings.

осмéивать, v. imp. (perf. осмея́ть), ridicule.

осмéливаться, v. imp. (perf. осмéлиться), dare.

осмóтр, m. examination, inspection. -и́тельный, adj. cautious; circumspect.

осмотрéть(ся), v., perf. of осмáтривать(ся).

основáние, nt. founding; foundation, basis.

основáтель, m. founder.

основáть, v., perf. of осно́вывать.

основнóй, adj. fundamental, basic; principal, cardinal.

основополóжник, m. founder.

осно́вывать, v. imp. (perf. основáть), found; base.

осóба, f. person.

осóбенно, adv. especially, particularly.

осóбенность, f. peculiarity, feature. в осóбенности, especially, in particular.

осóбенный, adj. especial, particular.

осознавáть, v. imp. (perf. осознáть), realize.

óспа, f. smallpox.

оставáться, v. imp. (perf. остáться), remain, stay; survive.

оставля́ть, v. imp. (perf. остáвить), leave, abandon; retain, keep; give up.

остальнóй, adj. rest, remaining.

останáвливать, v. imp. (perf. останови́ть), tr., stop, bring to a stop.

остáнки, pl. remains.

останóвка, f. stop, halt; interruption; station, stop.

остáток, m. rest; (math.) remainder; remnant.

остáтки, pl. remains.

остáться, v., perf. of оставáться.

остерегáть, v. imp. (perf. остерéчь), warn. -ся, beware.

осторóжный, adj. careful; cautious, wary.

остригáть, v. imp. (perf. остри́чь), cut; crop· shear.

остриё, nt. point; edge.

остри́чься, v. perf. of стри́чься.

óстров, m. island, isle. -итя́нин, m. islander. -нóй, adj. insular.

остротá, f. sharpness, acuteness, keenness.

остроýмный, adj. witty; clever.

óстрый, adj. sharp, cute, keen.

оступáться, v. imp. (perf. оступи́ться), stumble.

остыва́ть, v. imp. (perf. **осты́ть**), intr., cool.

осужда́ть, v. imp. (perf. **осуди́ть**), blame; condemn, convict.

осужде́ние, nt. blame; conviction.

осуше́ние, nt. drainage.

осуществля́ть, v. imp. (perf. **осуществи́ть**), realize; carry out; accomplish.

ось, f. axis; (tech.) axle.

осяза́емый, adj. tangible.

осяза́тельный, adj. tactile.

осяза́ть, v. imp. touch, feel.

от (**о́то**), prep. (+ gen.) from, away from.

отбира́ть, v. imp. (perf. **отобра́ть**), take away; confiscate.

о́тблеск, m. reflection.

отбо́р, m. selection, choice. **-ный**, adj. select, choice.

отбра́сывать, v. imp. (perf. **отбро́сить**), throw away or off; repulse; reject, discard.

отва́га, f. courage.

отва́жный, adj. brave, courageous.

отвезти́, v., perf. of **отвози́ть**

отверга́ть, v. imp. (perf. **отве́ргнуть**), reject.

отве́рстие, nt. opening; slot.

отве́ртка, f. screwdriver.

отвести́, v., perf. of **отводи́ть**

отве́т, m. reply, answer. **-ственный**, adj. responsible.

отве́тственный реда́ктор, editor-in-chief.

отвеча́ть, v. imp. (perf. **отве́тить**), **на** + acc., answer; **за** + acc., be responsible for.

отви́нчивать, v. imp. (perf. **отвинти́ть**), unscrew.

отвлека́ть, v. imp. (perf. **отвле́чь**), tr., distract, divert; abstract.

отвлече́ние, nt. abstraction; distraction.

отводи́ть, v. imp. (perf. **отвести́**), lead or draw aside; ward off.

отвози́ть, v. imp. (perf. **отвезти́**), take or drive away; take or drive back.

отворя́ть, v. imp. (perf. **отвори́ть**), tr., open.

отврати́тельный, adj. disgusting, repulsive.

отвраща́ть, v. imp. (perf. **отврати́ть**), avert, repulse.

отвыка́ть, v. imp. (perf. **отвы́кнуть**), grow out of a habit.

отвя́зывать, v. imp. (perf. **отвяза́ть**), tr., untie.

отга́дывать, v. imp. (perf. **отгада́ть**), guess.

отгова́ривать, v. imp. (perf. **отговори́ть**), dissuade.

отгово́рка, f. excuse, pretext.

отдава́ть, v. imp. (perf. **отда́ть**), return, give back; devote.

отдале́ние, nt. distance; removal.

отдалённый, adj. remote, distant.

отдаля́ть, v. imp. (perf. **отдали́ть**), remove. **-ся**, **от** + gen., move away from.

отда́ть, v., perf. of **отдава́ть**.

отда́ча, f. return; output.

отде́л, m. section; department. **-е́ние**, nt. separation; compartment, section; department, branch. **-и́мый**, adj. separable. **-ьный**, adj. separate.

отде́лывать, v. imp. (perf. **отде́лать**), dress, finish, trim.

отделя́ть, v. imp. (perf. **отдели́ть**), tr., separate, detach.

о́тдых, m. rest.

отдыха́ть, v. imp. (perf. **отдохну́ть**), rest; take a rest.

оте́ц, m. father.

оте́ческий, adj. paternal.

оте́чественный, adj. native; home; civil.

оте́чество, nt. fatherland.

о́тзыв, m. echo; repercussion.

о́тзыв, m. reference, opinion; response, comment.

отзыва́ться, v. imp. (perf. **отозва́ться**), answer, reply; recall.

отзы́вчивый, adj. sympathetic.

отка́з, m. refusal; rejection.

отка́зывать, v. imp. (perf. отказа́ть), refuse, deny. -ся, decline; renounce.

откла́дывать, v. imp. (perf. отложи́ть), lay or put aside; suspend.

отклоне́ние, nt. deflection; digression.

отклоня́ть, v. imp. (perf. отклони́ть), deflect; decline.

открове́нный, adj. frank, outspoken, candid.

открыва́ть, v. imp. (perf. откры́ть), open; reveal, disclose; unveil.

откры́тие, nt. discovery; unveiling.

откры́тка, f. postcard.

откры́тый, adj. open.

отку́да, adv. from where, whence.

отку́да-нибу́дь, adv. from anywhere or somewhere.

отку́сывать, v. imp. (perf. откуси́ть), bite off.

отлёт, m. takeoff.

отли́в, m. low tide.

отлича́ть, v. imp. (perf. отличи́ть), distinguish. -ся, от + gen., be different; distinguish oneself.

отли́чие, nt. difference.

отличи́тельный, adj. distinctive.

отли́чный, adj. different (from) excellent.

отложи́ть, v., perf. of откла́дывать.

отлупи́ть, v., perf. of лупи́ть.

отме́на, f. abolition.

отменя́ть, v. imp. (perf. отмени́ть), abolish; abrogate.

отме́тка, f. note; (school) mark.

отмеча́ть, v. imp. (perf. отме́тить), mark; note; mention.

отнести́(сь), v., perf. of относи́ть(ся).

отнима́ть, v. imp. (perf. отня́ть), take off or away; amputate.

относи́тельно, adv. relatively. — prep. (+ gen.) concerning.

относи́ть, v. imp. (perf. отнести́), carry away, remove.

-ся, к + dat., treat, regard, concern.

отноше́ние, nt. attitude; treatment.

отны́не, adv. from this moment on; from here on.

отню́дь, adv. by no means; not in the least.

отня́ть, v., perf. of отнима́ть. ото, see от.

отобра́ть, v., perf. of отбира́ть.

отовсю́ду, adv. from everywhere.

отож(д)ествля́ть, v. imp. (perf. отож(д)естви́ть), identify.

отозва́ть(ся), v., perf. of отзыва́ть(ся).

отойти́, v., perf. of отходи́ть.

отомсти́ть, v. perf. of мстить.

отопле́ние, nt. heating; heat.

оторва́ть, v., perf. of отрыва́ть.

отосла́ть, v., perf. of отсыла́ть.

отпеча́ток, m. imprint.

отплыва́ть, v. imp. (perf. отплы́ть), sail; depart; swim away.

отправля́ть, v. imp. (perf. отпра́вить), send, dispatch; forward. -ся, set off, depart, leave.

отпра́здновать, v., perf. of пра́здновать.

о́тпуск, m. leave; holiday.

отпуска́ть, v. imp. (perf. отпусти́ть), release, free; slacken.

отра́ва, f. poison.

отравля́ть, v. imp. (perf. отрави́ть), poison; spoil.

отража́ть, v. imp. (perf. отрази́ть), reflect.

отраже́ние, nt. reflection.

о́трасль, f. branch.

отреза́ть, v. imp. (perf. отре́зать), cut off.

отрека́ться, v. imp. (perf. отре́чься), от + gen., renounce, repudiate.

отрече́ние, nt. renunciation; abdication.

отрица́ние, nt. negation.

отрица́тельный, adj. negative.

отрица́ть, v. imp. deny; refute.

о́трочество, nt. adolescence.

отрыва́ть, v. imp. (perf. оторва́ть), tr., tear off or away.

отры́вок, m. fragment.

отря́д, m. detachment.

отсека́ть, v. imp. (perf. отсе́чь), cut off; chop off.

отсро́чивать, v. imp. (perf. отсро́чить), postpone.

отсро́чка, f. postponement.

отстава́ть, v. imp. (perf. отста́ть), fall behind; be backward or slow.

отста́вка, f. resignation, dismissal.

отставно́й, adj. retired.

отста́лый, adj. backward.

отста́ть, v., perf. of отстава́ть.

отступа́ть, v. imp. (perf. отступи́ть), retreat, fall back; deviate.

отступле́ние, nt. retreat; deviation.

отсу́тствие, nt. absence.

отсу́тствовать, v. imp. be absent.

отсыла́ть, v. imp. (perf. отосла́ть), send back; send.

отсю́да, adv. from here, hence.

отте́нок, m. shade; hue.

о́ттиск, m. impression.

отту́да, adv. from there.

отхо́д, m. departure; deviation.

отходи́ть, v. imp. (perf. отойти́), depart, leave.

отцо́вский, adj. paternal.

отча́сти, adv. partly, in part.

отча́яние, nt. despair.

отчего́, adv. why, for what reason.

о́тчество, nt. patronymic.

отчёт, m. acount; report. -ливый, adj. clear, distinct.

о́тчим, m. stepfather.

отъе́зд, m. departure.

отъезжа́ть, v. imp. (perf. отъе́хать), depart, drive off.

оты́скивать, v. imp. (perf. отыска́ть), find.

офице́р, m. officer.

официа́льный, adj. official.

охва́т, m. scope; inclusion.

охва́тывать, v. imp. (perf. охвати́ть), embrace, include; seize, overcome.

охлажде́ние, nt. cooling.

охо́та, f. hunt, hunting; wish, desire.

охо́титься, v. imp. hunt.

охо́тник, m. hunter; amateur, lover.

охо́тно, adv. willingly.

охра́на, f. guard, guarding.

охраня́ть, v. imp. (perf. охрани́ть), guard, protect.

охри́пнуть, v. perf. become hoarse.

оце́нивать, v. imp. (perf. оцени́ть), evaluate, estimate; value.

оце́нка, f. estimate, appraisal, appraisement.

очарова́тельный, adj. charming, fascinating.

очаро́вывать, v. imp. (perf. очарова́ть), charm, fascinate.

очеви́дец, m. eyewitness.

очеви́дный, adj. obvious.

о́чень, adv. very; very much.

очередно́й, adj. next, next in turn; usual.

о́чередь, f. turn.

о́черк, m. sketch; outline.

очерта́ние, nt. outline.

оче́рчивать, v. imp. (perf. очерти́ть), outline.

очини́ть, v., perf. of чини́ть.

очки́, pl. eyeglasses, spectacles.

очко́, nt. (games) point.

ошиба́ться, v. imp. (perf. ошиби́ться), make a mistake; err.

оши́бка, f. error, mistake.

оши́бочный, adj. erroneous, mistaken.

оштрафова́ть, v., perf. of штрафова́ть.

о́щупь, f. touch.

ощути́мый, adj. perceptible, tangible.

ощуща́ть, v. imp. (perf. ощути́ть), feel, sense.

ощуще́ние, nt. feeling, sensation.

П

Па́вел, m. Paul.

Павлу́ш(к)а, dim. of Па́вел.

па́даль, f. carrion.

па́дать, v. imp. (perf. пасть), fall.

паде́ж, m. (gram.) case.

паде́ние, nt. fall; downfall.

па́дчерица, f. stepdaughter.

паёк, m. ration.

пай, m. share.

пакова́ть, v. imp. pack.

па́кость, f. filth.

пакт, m. pact.

па́лец, m. finger.

пали́тра, f. palette.

пали́ть, v. imp. (perf. спали́ть), burn; scorch.

па́лка, f. stick; cane.

па́луба, f. (naut.) deck.

па́льма, f. palm.

пальто́, nt. coat, overcoat.

па́мятник, m. monument.

па́мятный, adj. memorable.

па́мять, f. memory.

панихи́да, f. requiem; burial ceremony.

па́па, m. papa, daddy; Pope.

папиро́са, f. cigarette.

па́пка, f. file; folder.

пар, m. steam; exhalation.

па́ра, f. pair, couple.

пара́д, m. parade; review.

парази́т, m. parasite.

парализова́ть, v. imp. & perf. paralyze.

парали́ч, m. paralysis.

паралле́льный, adj. parallel.

па́рень, m. lad, young lad.

пари́, nt. ind. bet, wager.

Пари́ж, m. Paris.

парижа́нин m., парижа́нка f., Parisian.

пари́к, m. wig. -ма́хер f. hairdresser, barber. -ма́херская, f. beauty shop, hairdresser's.

парк, m. park.

па́рный, adj. twin.

парово́з, m. locomotive, engine.

паро́м, m. ferry; raft.

парохо́д, m. steamship, steamer.

парте́р, m. (theat.) orchestra.

парти́ец, m. member of the Communist Party.

парти́йность, f. membership of the Communist Party; spirit or principle of the Communist Party.

парти́йный, adj. (Communist) Party.

партиту́ра, f. (mus.) score.

па́ртия, f. party; game, match.

парто́рг, abbr. of парти́йный организа́тор, Party organizer.

па́рус, m. sail. -и́на́ f., canvas, sailcloth. -ный, adj. sail; yacht.

па́смурный, adj. cloudy, gloomy, dull; sullen.

пассажи́р, m. passenger.

пасси́в, m. (financial) liabilities.

па́стбище, nt. pasture.

пасть, f. (animal) mouth, jaws. — v. (perf. of па́дать) fall; fall in action.

па́сха, f. Easter.

па́сынок, m. stepson.

патефо́нная (also грамофо́нная) пласти́нка, phonograph record.

па́уза, f. pause.

пау́к, m. spider.

паути́на, f. spiderweb.

пах, m. groin.

па́хнуть, v. imp., intr., smell.

па́хотный, adj. arable.

пацие́нт, m. patient.

па́чкать, v. imp. soil.

пая́ть, v. imp. solder.

пая́ц, m. clown.

певе́ц m., певи́ца f., singer.

педа́ль, f. pedal.

пейза́ж, m. landscape; view.

пека́рня, f. bakery.

пе́карь, m. baker.

пелёнка, f. diaper.

пе́мза, f. pumice.

пе́на, f. foam; lather.

пе́ние, nt. singing.

пе́нсия, f. pension.

пень, f. stump; stub.

пе́пел, m. ashes.

пе́пельница, f. ashtray.

пе́рвенство, *nt.* superiority; championship.

перви́чный, *adj.* primary; initial;

первобы́тный, *adj.* primitive.

первонача́льный, *adj.* primary; elementary.

первосо́ртный, *adj.* of the best quality; first-class.

пе́рвый, *ord.* first.

пергáмент, *m.* parchment.

перебегáть, *v. imp.* (*perf.* **перебежáть**), **чéрез** + *acc.*, run across, cross.

перевáл, *m.* mountain pass.

перевёртывать, *v. imp.* (*perf.* **переверну́ть**), turn over; overturn.

перевéс, *m.* preponderance, predominance.

перевóд, *m.* transfer, transference; translation. **-чик** *m.*, **-чица** *f.*, translator, interpreter.

переводи́ть, *v. imp.* (*perf.* **перевести́**), transfer; translate.

перевози́ть, *v. imp.* (*perf.* **перевезти́**), transport (across).

переворóт, *m.* revolution; upheaval.

перевя́зка, *f.* bandage, dressing.

перевя́зывать, *v. imp.* (*perf.* **перевязáть**), tie, tie up; bandage, dress.

пéревязь, *f.* sling.

перегорóдка, *f.* partition.

перегрызáть, *v. imp.* (*perf.* **перегры́зть**), bite through.

пéред (пéредо), *prep.* (+ *instr.*) before, in front of.

пéрёд, *m.* front.

передавáть, *v. imp.* (*perf.* **передáть**), pass, hand; give; broadcast; communicate, tell.

передáча, *f.* transmission; transfer; broadcast.

переде́лка, *f.* alteration.

передови́ца *f.* (*also* **передовáя статья́**) editorial, leading article.

передовóй, *adj.* advanced; front.

переду́мывать, *v. imp.* (*perf.*

переду́мать), change one's mind.

перее́зд, *m.* passage; crossing; move, moving.

переезжáть, *v. imp.* (*perf.* **перее́хать**), cross, cross over; move.

переживáние, *nt.* experience.

переживáть, *v. imp.* (*perf.* **пережи́ть**), experience, live through; endure.

пережи́ток, *m.* vestige, remnant; survival.

перейти́, *v.*, *perf. of* **переходи́ть**.

переклáдывать, *v. imp.* (*perf.* **переложи́ть**), lay *or* place in a different place; transfer; + *instr.* interlay; shift.

перекрёсток, *m.* crossing, crossroad.

перелёт, *m.* flight; migration.

перелетáть, *v. imp.* (*perf.* **перелете́ть**), fly over *or* across.

переложи́ть, *v.*, *perf. of* **переклáдывать**.

перелóм, *m.* fracture; crisis.

переме́на, *f.* change; recess, interval.

переме́нный, *adj.* variable; alternating.

переменя́ть, *v. imp.* (*perf.* **перемени́ть**), change.

перенимáть, *v. imp.* (*perf.* **переня́ть**), adopt; imitate.

переноси́ть, *v. imp.* (*perf.* **перенести́**), transfer; carry over; divide into syllables; endure.

переночевáть, *v.*, *perf. of* **ночевáть**.

перепи́ска, *f.* correspondence.

перепи́сываться, *v. imp.*, с + *instr.*, correspond with.

пéрепись, *f.* census.

перепóнка, *f.* membrane; web.

переса́дка, *f.* transplantation.

переса́живать, *v. imp.* (*perf.* **пересади́ть**), transplant; move to another seat.

пересмóтр, *m.* review; revision; reconsideration.

перестава́ть, *v. imp.* (*perf.* **перестáть**), stop, cease.

перестрáивать, *v. imp.* (*perf.*

перестро́ить), rebuild; reorganize.

перестро́йка, f. rebuilding; reorganization.

переу́лок, m. sidestreet; lane, alley.

переходи́ть, v. imp. (perf. перейти́), cross; turn into.

перехо́дный, adj. transitional; (gram.) transitive.

пе́рец, m. pepper.

пе́речень, m. list, listing.

пе́речница, f. pepper shaker, peppermill.

переше́ек, m. isthmus.

пери́од, m. period. -и́ческий, adj. periodic(al).

перо́, nt. feather, plume; pen.

перочи́нный но́жик, penknife.

пе́рсик, m. peach.

пе́рхоть, f. dandruff.

перча́тка, f. glove.

пёс, m. dog.

песнь (also пе́сня), f. song.

песо́к, m. sand.

петли́ца, f. buttonhole.

пе́тля, f. loop.

Пётр, m. Peter.

петру́шка, f. parsley.

Петру́шка, dim. of Пётр.

пету́х, m. rooster.

петь, v. imp. sing; crow.

Пе́тька (also Пе́тя), dim. of Пётр.

печа́лить, v. imp., tr., grieve.

печа́ль, f. sorrow, grief. -ный, adj. sad.

печа́тать, v. imp. (perf. напеча́тать), print; type.

печа́ть, f. seal; press, print, printing.

пе́чень, f. liver.

пече́нье, nt. pastry.

печь, f. stove; oven; heater. — v. imp. (perf. испе́чь) bake.

пешехо́д, m. pedestrian.

пе́шка, f. (chess) pawn.

пешко́м, adv. on foot.

пеще́ра, f. cave.

пиани́но, nt. upright piano.

пиани́ст m., -ка f., pianist.

пи́во, nt. beer.

пи́ки, pl. (cards) spades.

пила́, f. saw.

пили́ть, v. imp. saw.

пилю́ля, f. pill.

пионе́р, m. pioneer.

пир, m. banquet, feast.

пиро́г, m. pie.

пиро́жное, nt. pastry.

писа́тель m., -ница f., writer.

писа́ть, v. imp. (perf. написа́ть), write. писа́ть кра́сками, to paint.

пистоле́т, m. pistol.

письмо́, nt. letter.

пита́тельный, adj. nourishing.

пита́ть, v. imp. feed; nourish.

пить, v. imp. (perf. вы́пить), drink.

питьё, nt. drink; drinking.

пи́шущая маши́нка, typewriter.

пи́ща, f. food.

пищеваре́ние, nt. digestion.

пла́вание, nt. swimming; navigation; (swimming) stroke.

пла́вать, v. imp. indet. (det плыть, perf. поплы́ть) swim float; sail.

пла́вный, adj. fluent; smooth

плака́т, m. poster, placard.

пла́кать, v. imp. cry, weep.

пла́мя, nt. (pl. пла́мени) flame; blaze.

плане́та, f. planet.

плани́ровать, v. imp. plan, lay out; glide.

пла́новый, adj. planned.

пласт, m. layer, stratum.

пласти́нка, f. plate; record.

пла́та, f. payment, fee, fare.

платёж, m. payment.

плати́ть, v. imp. (perf. заплати́ть), pay.

плато́к, m. shawl. носово́й плато́к, handkerchief.

Плато́н, m. Plato.

пла́тье, nt. dress; (coll.) clothes, clothing.

плач, m. weeping.

плащ, m. cloak, coat.

плева́, f. membrane, film.

плева́ть, v. imp. (perf плю́нуть), spit.

пле́мя, nt. (pl. племён) tribe

племя́нник, m. nephew.

племя́нница, f. niece.

плен, m. captivity.

плёнка, f. film; tape.

пленя́ть, *v. imp.* fascinate, captivate.

пле́сень, *f.* mould.

плеск, *m.* splash.

плеска́ть, *v. imp.* (*perf.* плесну́ть), splash.

плечо́, *nt.* shoulder.

плита́, *f.* plate, slab.

пловец́, *m.* swimmer.

пловчи́ха, *f.* swimmer.

плодови́тый, *adj.* fruitful.

плодотво́рный, *adj.* fruitful.

пло́мба, *f.* (*dental*) filling.

пло́ский, *adj.* flat.

пло́скость, *f.* flatness; plane.

плот, *m.* raft.

пло́тность, *f.* density.

пло́тный, *adj.* dense.

плоть, *f.* flesh.

пло́хо, *adv.* badly.

плохо́й, *adj.* bad, inferior.

пло́щадь, *f.* area; square.

плуг, *m.* plow.

Плуто́н, *n.* Pluto.

плыть, *v. imp. det.* of пла́вать.

плю́нуть, *v.,* *perf.* of плева́ть.

плюс, *m.* (*math.*) plus; advantage.

пляж, *m.* beach.

пляса́ть, *v. imp.* dance.

по, *prep.* (+ *dat.*) on, along; according to; over; (+ *acc.*) to, up to; (+ *prep.*) after.

по-англи́йский, (in) English.

побе́да, *f.* victory.

побежа́ть, *v.,* *perf.* of бе́гать, бежа́ть.

побежда́ть, *v. imp.* (*perf.* победи́ть), conquer; be victorious.

побеле́ть, *v. perf.* of беле́ть.

побере́жье, *nt.* shore, coast.

побледне́ть, *v. perf.* turn pale.

побо́ище, *nt.* massacre; slaughter.

побо́чный, *adj.* accessory; collateral.

по-бра́тски, *adv.* fraternally; in a brotherly fashion.

побужда́ть, *v. imp.* (*perf.* побуди́ть), impel; induce; prompt.

побы́ть, *v. perf.* visit; stay, remain; spend some time.

повали́ть, *v.,* *perf.* of вали́ть.

пова́льный, *adj.* general; epidemic.

по́вар, *m.* cook.

пова́ренный, *adj.* culinary.

поведе́ние, *nt.* behavior, conduct.

повезти́, *v.,* *perf.* of вози́ть, везти́.

повели́тельный, *adj.* imperative, authoritative; (*gram.*) imperative.

повенча́ть, *v.,* *perf.* of венча́ть.

пове́рить, *v.* (*perf.* of ве́рить), believe; verify, check.

поверну́ть, *v.,* *perf.* of повора́чивать.

пове́рка, *f.* checkup; verification.

пове́рх, *prep.* (+ *gen.*) above, over. -ностный, *adj.* superficial. -ность, *f.* surface.

пове́сить(ся), *v.,* *perf.* of ве́шать(ся).

повести́, *v.,* *perf.* of води́ть, вести́.

пове́стка, *f.* notice; summons.

по́весть, *f.* narrative, story, tale.

по-ви́димому, *adv.* apparently.

пови́нность, *f.* duty.

повинова́ться, *v. imp. & perf.,* + *dat.* obey.

повинове́ние, *nt.* obedience.

пови́снуть, *v.,* *perf.* of висе́ть.

повлия́ть, *v.,* *perf.* of влия́ть.

по́вод, *m.* occasion, reason, cause; bridle, rein.

повора́чивать, *v. imp.* (*perf.* поверну́ть), *tr.,* turn; swing.

повреди́ть, *v.,* *perf.* of вреди́ть, поврежда́ть.

повреждать́, *v. imp.* (*perf.* повреди́ть), damage; harm, hurt.

повседне́вный, *adj.* daily, every day.

повторе́ние, *nt.* repetition.

повтори́тельный, *adj.* repetitive.

повторя́ть, *v. imp.* (*perf.* повтори́ть), repeat.

повыша́ть, *v. imp.* (*perf.* повы́сить), raise, increase.

повя́зка, *f.* bandage.

погада́ть, *v.,* *perf.* of гада́ть.

погаси́ть, v., perf. of гаси́ть.

погиба́ть, v. imp. (perf. поги́бнуть), perish.

поги́бший, adj. lost.

погла́дить, v., perf. of гла́дить.

поглоща́ть, v. imp. (perf. поглоти́ть), absorb; swallow up.

поглоще́ние, nt. absorption.

поглуми́ться, v., perf. of глуми́ться.

погляде́ть, v., perf. of гляде́ть.

погово́рка, f. proverb, saying.

пого́да, f. weather.

пограни́чный, adj. border, frontier.

по́греб, m. cellar.

погреба́льный, adj. funeral.

погребе́ние, nt. burial, internment.

погружа́ть, v. imp. (perf. погрузи́ть), immerse.

погуби́ть, v., perf. of губи́ть.

под, prep. (+ acc.) under; towards. (+ instr.) under; near, by.

подава́ть, v. imp. (perf. пода́ть), give; serve.

подави́ться, v., perf. of дави́ться.

пода́вленный, adj. depressed; dispirited.

подавля́ть, v. imp. (perf. подави́ть), suppress.

подари́ть, v., perf. of дари́ть.

пода́рок, m. gift.

пода́ть, v., perf. of подава́ть.

подбега́ть, v. imp. (perf. подбежа́ть), run up to.

подбо́р, m. selection.

подборо́док, m. chin.

подва́л, m. basement, cellar.

подверга́ть, v. imp. (perf. подве́ргнуть), subject; expose.

подвести́, v., perf. of подводи́ть.

по́двиг, m. feat; exploit.

подвижно́й (also подви́жный), adj. mobile.

подводи́ть, v. imp. (perf. подвести́), lead up to.

подво́дный, adj. submarine.

подвя́зка, f. garter; suspender.

подгото́вка, f. preparation.

подготовля́ть, v. imp. (perf. подгото́вить), tr., prepare.

поддава́ться, v. imp. (perf. подда́ться), intr., yield.

по́дданный, m. subject.

подде́лка, f. counterfeit; forgery.

подде́лывать, v. imp. (perf. подде́лать), counterfeit; forge.

подде́рживать, v. imp. (perf. поддержа́ть), support.

подде́ржка, f. support.

подде́йствовать, v., perf. of де́йствовать.

подели́ть(ся), v., perf. of дели́ть(ся).

поде́ржанный, adj. used, second-hand.

подешеве́ть, v., perf. of дешеве́ть.

поджига́ть, v. imp. (perf. подже́чь), set fire (to).

поджо́г, m. arson.

подзаголо́вок, m. subtitle.

подзе́мный, adj. underground.

подкла́дка, f. lining.

подкла́дывать, v. imp. (perf. подложи́ть), line (with); lay under.

подкра́дываться, v. imp. (perf. подкра́сться), steal up (to).

по́дкуп, m. bribery.

подкупа́ть, v. imp. (perf. подкупи́ть), bribe.

по́дле, prep. (+ gen.) near, by; beside, by the side of.

подлежа́щее, nt. (gram.) subject.

по́длинник, m. original.

по́длинный, adj. original.

подло́г, m. forgery.

подложи́ть, v., perf. of подкла́дывать.

по́длый, adj. mean, base.

подме́на, f. substitution.

подменя́ть, v. imp. (perf. подмени́ть), tr., substitute (for).

подмётка, f. sole (of a shoe).

поднима́ть, v. imp. (perf. подня́ть), lift, raise. -ся, rise; climb.

подно́жие, nt. pedestal.

подно́с, m. tray.

подноси́ть, v. imp. (perf.

поднести́, bring; present.

подня́ть(ся), v., perf. of поднима́ть(ся).

подо́бие, nt. likeness; similarity.

подо́бно, adv. similarly. -prep. (+ dat.) like, similar to.

подо́бный, adj. similar. и тому́ подо́бное, and the like. ничего́ подо́бного, nothing of the sort.

подогрева́ть, v. imp. (perf. подогре́ть), tr., warm up.

подожда́ть, v., perf. of ждать.

подозрева́ть, v. imp. suspect.

подозре́ние, nt. suspicion.

подозри́тельный, adj. suspicious.

подойти́, v., perf. of дойти́.

подойти́, v., perf. of подходи́ть.

подорва́ть v., perf. of подрыва́ть.

подорожа́ть, v. perf. become dearer or more expensive.

подохо́дный нало́г, income tax.

подпи́ска, f. subscription.

подпи́сывать, v. imp. (perf. подписа́ть), tr., sign. -ся, intr., sign; на + acc., subscribe (to).

по́дпись, f. signature.

подпо́рка, f. prop.

подража́ть, v. imp. imitate.

подразумева́ть, v. imp. imply.

подра́ться, v., perf. of дра́ться.

подро́бный, adj. detailed.

по-дру́жески, adv. friendly.

подрыва́ть, v. imp. (perf. подорва́ть), sap; undermine.

подря́д, adv. one after another.

подска́зывать, v. imp. (perf. подсказа́ть), prompt.

подслу́шивать, v. imp. eavesdrop. — (perf. подслу́шать) overhear.

подсо́лнечник, m. sunflower.

подста́вка, f. stand.

по́дступ, m. approach.

подсуди́мый, adj. accused; defendant.

подтвержда́ть, v. imp. (perf. подтверди́ть), confirm; acknowledge.

подтя́жки, pl. suspenders.

поду́мать, v. (perf. of ду́мать), think, think a little or for a while.

поду́шка, f. pillow; cushion.

подхо́д, m. approach; point of view.

подходи́ть, v. imp. (perf. подойти́), approach.

подходя́щий, adj. suitable.

подчёркивать, v. imp. (perf. подчеркну́ть), underline; emphasize.

подчине́ние, nt. submission; subordination.

подчиня́ть, v. imp. (perf. подчини́ть), subordinate. -ся, submit to.

подъезжа́ть, v. imp. (perf. подъе́хать) drive up to.

подъём, m. ascent; lifting; hoisting; slope, rise.

поеди́нок, m. duel.

по́езд, m. train.

пое́здка, f. trip, journey, excursion.

пое́хать, v., perf. of е́здить, е́хать.

пожале́ть, v., perf. of жале́ть.

пожа́ловать(ся), v., perf. of жа́ловать(ся).

пожа́луйста, please; don't mention it.

пожа́р, m. fire.

пожа́тие руки́, handshake.

пожела́ть, v., perf. of жела́ть.

пожелте́ть, v., perf. of желте́ть.

поже́ртвовать, v., perf. of же́ртвовать.

пожива́ть, v. imp. get along, get on. как вы пожива́ете?, how are you?

пожило́й, adj. elderly.

по́за, f. pose.

позабо́титься, v., perf. of забо́титься.

позави́довать, v., perf. of зави́довать.

поза́втракать, v., perf. of за́втракать.

позавчера́, adv. the day before yesterday.

позади́, adv., prep. (+ gen.) behind.

позаи́мствовать, *v.*, perf. of
заи́мствовать.

позва́ть, *v.*, perf. of зва́ть.

позволе́ние, *nt.* permission.

позволя́ть, *v. imp. (perf.*
позво́лить), allow, permit.

позвони́ть, *v.*, perf. of звони́ть.

позвоно́к, *m.* vertebra.

позвоно́чник, *m.* spine.

по́здний, *adj.* late.

поздоро́ваться, *v.*, perf. of
здоро́ваться.

поздравля́ть, *v. imp. (perf.*
поздра́вить), greet.

позелене́ть, *v.*, perf. of зелене́ть.

по́зже, *adv.* later, later on.

познава́ть, *v. imp. (perf.*
позна́ть), become acquainted
(with).

познако́мить(ся), *v.*, perf. of
знако́мить(ся).

позо́р, *m.* disgrace; shame.

пои́стине, *adv.* indeed; in truth.

пои́ть, *v. imp. (perf.* напои́ть),
(of animals) water.

пойма́ть, *v.*, perf. of пойма́ть,
catch.

пойти́, *v.*, perf. of ходи́ть,
идти́.

пока́, *conj.* while; until. —
adv. for the present.

пока́з, *m.* demonstration;
show. -а́ние, *nt.* testimony,
evidence; deposition. -а́тель,
m. index.

показа́ться, *v.*, perf. of ка-
за́ться.

пока́зывать, *v. imp. (perf.*
показа́ть), show.

покара́ть, *v.*, perf. of кара́ть.

покая́ние, *nt.* confession;
repentance.

пока́яться, *v.* perf. confess;
repent.

покида́ть, *v. imp. (perf.* по-
ки́нуть), leave; abandon.

поки́нутый, *adj.* abandoned.

покло́н, *m.* bow; compliments.
-е́ние, *nt.* worship. -ник, *m.*
admirer; worshipper.

поклони́ться, *v.* perf. of
кла́няться.

поко́й, *m.* rest; room, ward.
-ник, *m.* deceased.

поколе́ние, *nt.* generation.

поко́нчить, *v.* perf., с + *instr.*,
finish (with).

покоре́ние, *nt.* subjugation.

поко́рный, *adj.* submissive;
obedient.

покоря́ть, *v. imp. (perf.*
покори́ть), subdue, subjugate.
-ся, submit; give in, yield.

покра́сить, *v.*, perf. of кра́сить.

покрасне́ть, *v.*, perf. of крас-
не́ть.

покро́в, *m.* cover; shroud.
-и́тель, *m.* patron, protector.

покрыва́ть, *v. imp. (perf.*
покры́ть), cover.

покры́шка, *f.* cover, covering.

покупа́тель, *m.* buyer; customer.

покупа́ть, *v. imp. (perf.* ку-
пи́ть), buy.

поку́пка, *f.* purchase.

поку́шать, *v.*, perf. of ку́шать.

покуше́ние, *nt.* attempt.

пол, *m.* floor; sex.

пола́, *f.* skirt; flap.

полага́ть, *v. imp.* think, suppose; believe. -ся, rely.

полго́да, half a year.

по́лдень, *m.* noon.

по́ле, *nt.* field; margin, brim.

поле́зный, *adj.* useful.

поле́зть, *v. (perf.* of ле́зть),
start to climb.

полете́ть, *v.*, perf. of лета́ть,
лете́ть.

по́лзать, *v. imp. (perf.* ползти́),
creep, crawl.

полирова́ть, *v. imp.* polish.

поли́тика, *f.* politics.

полити́ческий, *adj.* political.

поли́ция, *f.* police.

по́лка, *f.* shelf.

полнокро́вный, *adj.* full-
blooded.

полнолу́ние, *nt.* full moon.

полномо́чный, *adj.* plenipo-
tentiary.

по́лностью, *adv.* completely,
in full.

по́лночь, *f.* midnight.

по́лный, *adj.* full.

по́ло, *nt. ind.* polo.

полови́на, *f.* half.

полово́й, *adj.* floor; sexual.

положе́ние, *nt.* position, location, situation; condition.

положи́тельный, *adj.* affirmative.

положи́ть, *v.*, *perf. of* класть.

полоса́, *f.* strip; region, zone.

полоска́ть, *v. perf. of* rinse; gargle.

по́лость, *f.* (anat.) cavity.

полоте́нце, *nt.* towel.

полотно́, *nt.* linen.

полотня́ный, *adj.* linen.

полтора́, *num.* one and a half.

-ста́, *num.* one hundred and fifty.

полуде́нный, *adj.* midday, noon.

полукру́г, *m.* semicircle.

полуме́сяц, *m.* half moon.

полуо́стров, *m.* peninsula.

получа́ть, *v. imp.* (*perf.* получи́ть), receive. -ся, result, turn out to be.

полуша́рие, *nt.* hemisphere.

полчаса́, *num.* half-hour.

по́льза, *f.* use, benefit.

по́льзоваться, *v. imp.*, + *instr.* make use of; profit by; enjoy.

по́льский, *adj.* Polish.

польсти́ть, *v. perf. of* льсти́ть.

По́льша, *f.* Poland.

полюби́ть, *v. perf.* become fond of; take a liking to.

полюбо́вный, *adj.* amicable.

по́люс, *m.* (geog.) pole.

поля́к *m.*, по́лька *f.*, Pole.

поля́рный, *adj.* polar.

поменя́ть, *v., perf. of* меня́ть.

поме́ркнуть, *v., perf. of* ме́ркнуть.

помёт, *m.* dung; litter, brood.

поме́тка, *f.* mark, note.

поме́шанный, *adj.* crazy, insane, mad.

помеша́ть, *v., perf. of* меша́ть. — *v. perf.* stir a little *or* for a while. -ся, go mad; become insane.

помеща́ть, *v. imp.* (*perf.* помести́ть), place; invest; accomodate, lodge.

помеще́ние, *nt.* location; investment; lodging.

помидо́р, *m.* tomato.

поми́мо, *prep.* besides.

помина́ть, *v. imp.* (*perf.* помяну́ть), mention; make mention (of).

помири́ть(ся), *v.*, *perf. of* мири́ть(ся).

по́мнить, *v. imp.* (*perf.* вспо́мнить), remember; recall.

помно́жить, *v.*, *perf. of* мно́жить.

помога́ть, *v. imp.* (*perf.* помо́чь), help.

по-мо́ему, *adv.* in my opinion; to my mind.

помо́щник, *m.* assistant, helper.

по́мощь, *f.* help, assistance.

по́мысел, *m.* thought; design.

помы́ть, *v., perf. of* мыть.

помяну́ть, *v., perf. of* помина́ть.

помя́ть, *v., perf. of* мять.

понеде́льник, *m.* Monday.

понеде́льный, *adj.* weekly.

понести́(сь), *v., perf. of* носи́ть(ся), нести́(сь).

понижа́ть, *v. imp.* (*perf.* пони́зить), lower; reduce.

понима́ние, *nt.* understanding.

понима́ть, *v. imp.* (*perf.* поня́ть), understand, comprehend.

поноси́ть, *v. perf.* carry *or* wear for a while.

понра́виться, *v.*, *perf. of* нра́виться.

понюха́ть, *v., perf. of* ню́хать.

поня́тие, *nt.* idea, notion, conception.

поня́тный, *adj.* clear, intelligible, understandable.

поня́ть, *v., perf. of* понима́ть.

пообе́дать, *v., perf. of* обе́дать.

попере́к, *adv.* crosswise. — *prep.* (+ *gen.*) across. вдоль и попере́к, far and wide; thoroughly.

поплы́ть, *v., perf. of* пла́вать, плыть.

попола́м, *adv.* in half.

пополу́дни, *adv.* in the afternoon.

пополу́ночи, *adv.* after midnight.

попра́вка, *f.* correction; recovery.

поправля́ть, v. imp. (perf. попра́вить), repair, mend; correct. -ся, get well, recover; improve.

по-пре́жнему, adv. as before, as usual.

попрёк, m. reproach.

по́прище, nt. field; walk of life.

попро́бовать, v., perf. of про́бовать.

попроси́ть, v., perf. of проси́ть.

по́просту, adv. simply; without ceremony.

попуга́й, m. parrot.

популя́рный, adj. popular.

попу́тно, adv. in passing; on one's way; incidentally.

попу́тчик, m. fellow traveler.

попыта́ться, v., perf. of пыта́ться.

попы́тка, f. attempt.

попяти́ться, v., perf. of пя́титься.

пора́, f. time. — impers. it is time. с тех пор, since then.

порабо́тать, v., perf. of рабо́тать.

порабоща́ть, v. imp. (perf. поработи́ть), enslave.

поража́ть, v. imp. (perf. порази́ть), defeat.

порази́тельный, adj. striking.

по́ристый, adj. porous.

порица́ть, v. imp. blame; reproach.

поро́г, m. threshold; rapids.

поро́да, f. breed; (geol.) rock.

поро́дистый, adj. pedigree.

по́рознь, adv. separately.

поро́к, m. vice; defect.

по́рох, m. powder.

поро́чный, adv. vicious; depraved.

порошо́к, m. powder.

порт, m. port; harbor.

по́ртить, v. imp. (perf. испо́ртить), tr., spoil, damage; corrupt.

портни́ха, f. dressmaker.

портно́й, m. tailor.

портре́т, m. portrait.

портфе́ль, m. briefcase.

по-ру́сски, adv. (in) Russian.

поруча́ть, v. imp. (perf.

поручи́ть), commission; charge (with).

поруче́ние, nt. commission; message.

поручи́ть, v., perf. of поруча́ть. -ся, v., perf. of руча́ться.

по́рция, f. portion.

поры́в, m. gust. -йстый, adj. gusty; impetuous.

поря́дковое числи́тельное, (gram.) ordinal numeral.

поря́док, m. order.

поря́дочный, adj. decent, honest.

посади́ть, v. perf. plant; imprison.

по-сво́ему, adv. on one's own way.

посвяща́ть, v. imp. (perf. посвяти́ть), devote; dedicate.

посети́тель, m. visitor, guest.

посеща́ть, v. imp. (perf. посети́ть), visit; attend.

посея́ть, v., perf. of се́ять.

поскака́ть, v., perf. of скака́ть.

поско́льку, adv. so far as.

посла́ние, nt. message.

посла́нник, m. minister.

посла́ть, v., perf. of посыла́ть.

по́сле, adv. later, afterwards. — prep. (+ gen.) after.

после́дний, adj. last; latter; the latest.

после́довательный, adj. successive, consecutive.

после́довать, v., perf. of сле́довать.

после́дствие, nt., consequence.

после́дующий, adj. following, next.

послеза́втра, adv. the day after tomorrow.

послесло́вие, nt. epilogue.

посло́вица, f. proverb.

послужи́ть, v., perf. of служи́ть.

послу́шать(ся), v., perf. of слу́шать(ся).

посме́ртный, adj. posthumous.

посмотре́ть, v., perf. of смотре́ть.

посо́бие, nt. text, textbook; grant, allowance; aid.

посоли́ть, v., perf. of соли́ть.

посо́льство, nt. embassy.

поспеши́ть, v., perf. of спеши́ть.

поспе́шный, adj. prompt, hurried, hasty; rash.

поспо́рить, v., perf. of спо́рить.

посреди́, adv. in the middle. — prep. (+ gen.) in the middle of.

посре́дник, m. mediator.

посре́дничество, nt. mediation.

посре́дственность, f. mediocrity.

посре́дством, prep. (+ instr.) by means of.

поста́вить, v., perf. of поставля́ть, ста́вить.

поставля́ть, v. imp. (perf. поста́вить), place, put; erect; produce, stage.

постано́вка, f. (theat.) production, staging.

постановле́ние, nt. decision; decree.

постановля́ть, v. imp. (perf. постанови́ть), decide; decree.

постара́ться, v., perf. of стара́ться..

посте́ль, f. bed.

постепе́нный, adj. gradual.

постига́ть, v. imp. (perf. пости́гнуть, пости́чь), comprehend, perceive; strike; overtake.

постиже́ние, nt. comprehension, understanding.

постижи́мый, adj. comprehensible, understandable.

посто́льку, conj. in so far as.

посторони́ться, v., perf. of сторони́ться.

посторо́нний, adj. strange, foreign.

постоя́нный, adj. constant, permanent.

пострада́ть, v., perf. of страда́ть.

постро́ение, nt. construction, erection.

постро́ить, v., perf. of стро́ить.

поступа́тельный, adj. progressive.

поступа́ть, v. imp. (perf. поступи́ть), act; treat, deal with; enter, join.

посту́пок, m. action, deed.

по́ступь, f. step.

посу́да, f. china, earthenware.

посыла́ть, v. imp. (perf. посла́ть), send.

посяга́ть, v. imp. (perf. посягну́ть), encroach on or upon.

пот, m. sweat, perspiration.

потемне́ть, v., perf. of темне́ть.

потепле́ть, v., perf. of тепле́ть.

поте́ря, f. loss; waste.

потеря́ть(ся), v., perf. of теря́ть(ся).

поте́ть, v. imp. (perf. вспоте́ть), sweat, perspire. — (perf. запоте́ть), intr., steam.

поте́шить, v., perf. of те́шить.

пото́к, m. stream, torrent; flow, flood.

потоло́к, m. ceiling.

потолсте́ть, v., perf. of толсте́ть.

пото́м, adv. afterwards; then. -ок, m. descendant; offspring. -ство, nt. posterity.

потому́, adv. for this reason. потому́, что, because; for.

пото́п, m. flood, deluge.

поторопи́ть(ся), v., perf. of торопи́ть(ся).

потребля́ть, v. imp. (perf. потреби́ть), consume, use.

потре́бный, adj. necessary; required.

потре́бовать, v., perf. of тре́бовать.

потряса́ть, v. imp. (perf. потрясти́), shake.

потрясе́ние, nt. shock.

потуши́ть, v., perf. of туши́ть.

потяну́ть(ся), v., perf. of тяну́ть(ся).

похвала́, f. praise.

похвали́ть(ся), v., perf. of похваля́ть(ся, хвали́ть(ся).

похваля́ть, v. imp. (perf. похвали́ть), praise. -ся, boast of, brag.

похища́ть, v. imp. (perf. похи́тить), kidnap; steal.

походи́ть, v. imp. resemble, look like.

похо́жий, adj. similar, resembling.

похорони́ть, *v.*, *perf. of* хорони́ть.

по́хороны, *pl.* burial, funeral.

по́хоть, *f.* lust.

похуде́ть, *v.*, *perf. of* худе́ть.

поцелова́ть, *v.*, *perf. of* целова́ть.

почелу́й, *m.* kiss.

по́чва, *f.* soil.

почём? *adv.* at what price?

почему́, *adv.* why.

почему́-либо, *adv.* for some reason or other.

по́черк, *m.* handwriting.

почёт, *m.* honor. -ный, *adj.* honorary, honorable.

почини́ть, *v.*, *perf. of* чини́ть.

по́чта, *f.* mail. -льо́н, *m.* postman. почта́мт, *m.* post office.

почте́ние, *nt.* respect.

почти́, *adv.* almost, nearly.

почти́тельный, *adj.* respectful.

почто́вый, *adj.* mail.

пошёл вон!, get out!

по́шлина, *f.* duty.

по́шлый, *adj.* vulgar.

поща́да, *f.* mercy.

пощади́ть, *v.*, *perf. of* щади́ть.

поэ́зия, *f.* poetry.

поэ́ма, *f.* poem.

поэ́т, *m.* poet. -и́ческий, *adj.* poetic(al).

поэ́тому, *adv.* therefore; for this reason.

появле́ние, *nt.* appearance.

появля́ться, *v.* *imp.* (*perf.* появи́ться), appear; emerge.

по́яс, *m.* belt; zone.

поясни́тельный, *adj.* explanatory.

пра́вда, *f.* truth.

правдоподо́бный, *adj.* likely, probable.

пра́вило, *nt.* rule.

пра́вильный, *adj.* right, correct.

прави́тельственный, *adj.* government(al).

пра́вить, *v.* *imp.* govern rule.

пра́во, *nt.* right.

правописа́ние, *nt.* spelling, orthography.

пра́вый, *adj* (*direction*) right; correct, just.

Пра́га, *f.* Prague.

пра́дед, *m.* great-grandfather.

пра́здник, *m.* holiday.

пра́здничный, *adj.* holiday.

пра́здновать, *v.* *imp.* (*perf.* отпра́здновать), celebrate.

пра́здный, *adj.* idle.

пра́ктика, *f.* practice.

практи́ческий (*also* практи́чный), *adj.* practical.

пра́чечная, *f.* laundry.

пра́чка, *f.* laundress.

пребыва́ть, *v.* *imp.* (*perf.* пребы́ть), stay, sojourn.

превосходи́ть, *v.* *imp.* (*perf.* превзойти́), surpass.

превосхо́дный, *adj.* excellent.

превраща́ть, *v.* *imp.* (*perf.* преврати́ть), transform.

превыша́ть, *v.* *imp.* (*perf.* превы́сить), exceed.

прегра́да, *f.* bar; obstacle.

прегражда́ть, *v.* *imp.* (*perf.* прегради́ть), bar; block.

предава́ть, *v.* *imp.* (*perf.* преда́ть), betray.

пре́данный, *adj.* devoted.

преда́тель, *m.* traitor. -ство, *nt.* treason; betrayal.

предвари́тельный, *adj.* preliminary.

преде́л, *m.* limit; boundary. -ьный, *adj.* limiting; extreme.

предисло́вие, *nt.* preface.

предлага́ть, *v.* *imp.* (*perf.* предложи́ть), present, offer; suggest; move, propose.

предло́г, *m.* (*gram.*) preposition; pretext.

предложе́ние, *nt.* offer, suggestion; motion, proposal; (*gram.*) sentence, clause.

предло́жный, *adj.* (*gram.*) prepositional.

предме́стье, *nt.* suburb.

предме́т, *m.* object, subject.

предназнача́ть, *v.* *imp.* (*perf.* предназна́чить), intend, destine, earmark.

предназначе́ние, *nt.* destination; predestination.

пре́док, *m.* ancestor.

предостереже́ние, *nt.* warning.

предпи́сывать, *v.* *imp.* (*perf.*

предписа́ть), order, direct; prescribe.

предполага́ть, v. imp. (perf. предположи́ть), assume; intend, propose.

предположе́ние, nt. supposition; assumption.

предпосле́дний, adj. next to last.

предпочита́ть, v. imp. (perf. предпоче́сть), prefer.

предпочте́ние, nt. preference.

предприи́мчивый, adj. enterprising.

предпринима́ть, v. imp. (perf. предприня́ть), undertake.

председа́тель, m. chairman.

предска́зывать, v. imp. (perf. предсказа́ть), foretell; predict; forecast.

представа́ть, v. imp. (perf. предста́ть), appear (before).

представи́тельный, adj. representative; imposing.

представле́ние, nt. performance; presentation; idea, notion.

представля́ть, v. imp. represent. — (perf.) предста́вить), present, introduce. -ся, occur present itself; introduce oneself.

предубежде́ние, nt. prejudice.

предупреди́тельный, adj. preventive; precautionary.

предупрежда́ть, v. imp. (perf. предупреди́ть), notify; warn, prevent; let know beforehand.

предусма́тривать, v. imp. (perf. предусмотре́ть), foresee.

предчу́вствие, nt. presentiment.

предчу́вствовать, v. imp. have a presentiment or foreboding.

предше́ственник, m. predecessor.

предше́ствовать, v. imp. precede.

предъявля́ть, v. imp. (perf. предъяви́ть), present; show; produce.

преды́дущий, adj. previous.

пре́жде, adv. formerly, before. — prep. (+ gen.) before.

преждевре́менный, adj. premature; untimely.

пре́жний, adj. previous, former.

презре́ние, nt. contempt, sorn.

презри́тельный, adj. contemptuous, scornful.

преиму́щественный, adj. principal.

преиму́щество, nt. advantage; preference.

прекло́нный, adj. extremely old.

прекра́сный, adj. beautiful; fine; excellent.

прекраща́ть, v. imp. (perf. прекрати́ть), break off; cut short; stop, cease, put an end (to).

прекраще́ние, nt. cessation.

пре́лесть, f. charm.

премье́ра, f. (theat.) first night, première.

пренебрега́ть, v. imp. (perf. пренебре́чь), neglect, disregard.

пренебреже́ние, nt. neglect, disregard.

преоблада́ть, v. imp. predominate, prevail.

препина́ние, nt.: знак препина́ния, punctuation mark.

преподава́ть, v. imp. teach. instruct.

препя́тствие, nt. obstacle.

препя́тствовать, v. imp. hinder; prevent (from).

прерыва́ть, v. imp. (perf. прерва́ть), interrupt; break off.

пресле́довать, v. imp. persecute; pursue, haunt.

пре́сная вода́, fresh water.

пре́сса, f. press.

прессконфере́нция, f. press conference.

преступа́ть, v. imp. (perf. преступи́ть), transgress; trespass.

преступле́ние, nt. crime, offense.

престу́пник, m. criminal.

преувели́чивать, v. imp. (perf. преувели́чить), exaggerate.

преуменьша́ть, v. imp. (perf.

преуме́ньшить), underestimate.

при, *prep.* (+ *prep.*) by, at near; in the presence of; in the time of, during; attached to.

прибавля́ть, *v. imp.* (*perf.* приба́вить), increase, add.

приближа́ться, *v. imp.* (*perf.* прибли́зиться), approach; draw near.

приблизи́тельный, *adj.* approximate.

прибо́р, *m.* apparatus; instrument, implement.

прибыва́ть, *v. imp.* (*perf.* прибы́ть), arrive; increase.

прибы́тие, *nt.* arrival.

приве́т, *m.* greeting(s).

приве́тствовать, *v. imp.* welcome; greet.

привлека́ть, *v. imp.* (*perf.* привле́чь), attract.

привози́ть, *v. imp.* (*perf.* привезти́), bring.

привыка́ть, *v. imp.* (*perf.* привы́кнуть), become accustomed or used to.

привы́чка, *f.* habit, custom.

привя́занный, *adj.* attached.

привя́зывать, *v. imp.* (*perf.* привяза́ть), tie, fasten.

приглаша́ть, *v. imp.* (*perf.* пригласи́ть), invite.

приглаше́ние, *nt.* invitation.

пригова́ривать, *v. imp.* (*perf.* приговори́ть), sentence; condemn.

пригово́р, *m.* sentence.

при́городный, *adj.* suburban.

приготови́тельный, *adj.* preparatory.

пригото́вить, *v., perf. of* гото́вить, приготовля́ть.

приготовля́ть, *v. imp.* (*perf.* пригото́вить), *tr.*, prepare.

пригрози́ть, *v., perf. of* грози́ть.

прида́ное, *nt.* dowry.

прида́точный, *adj.* additional, accessory; (*gram.*) subordinate.

приде́рживать, *v. imp.* (*perf.* придержа́ть) hold *or* stick to.

придоро́жный, *adj.* roadside.

приду́мывать, *v. imp.* (*perf.*

придума́ть), think up, invent.

прие́зд, *m.* arrival.

приезжа́ть, *v. imp.* (*perf.* прие́хать), arrive.

прие́м, *m.* reception; (*med.*) dose; method, way. -ная, *f.* reception room.

прижима́ть, *v. imp.* (*perf.* прижа́ть), press.

призва́ние, *nt.* vocation, calling.

признава́ть, *v. imp.* (*perf.* призна́ть), acknowledge, recognize. -ся, в + *prep.* confess, admit.

при́знак, *m.* sign.

призна́ние, *nt.* acknowledgement; recognition; confession.

призна́ть(ся), *v., perf. of* признава́ть(ся).

при́зрачный, *adj.* unreal; illusory.

призы́в, *m.* appeal, call; slogan.

призыва́ть, *v. imp.* (*perf.* призва́ть), call; call up.

прийти́(сь), *v., perf. of* приходи́ть(ся).

прика́з, *m.* order, command. -а́ние, *m.* order, instruction.

прика́зывать, *v. imp.* (*perf.* приказа́ть), order, command.

прикладно́й, *adj.* applied.

прикла́дывать, *v. imp.* (*perf.* приложи́ть), add; enclose; apply.

прикле́ивать, *v. imp.* (*perf.* прикле́ить), stock *or* paste to.

приключе́ние, *nt.* adventure.

приключи́ться, *v. perf.* (*colloq.*) happen, occur.

прикоснове́ние, *nt.* touch, contact.

прикрепля́ть, *v. imp.* (*perf.* прикрепи́ть), fasten; attach.

прикрыва́ть, *v. imp.* (*perf.* прикры́ть), cover; close.

прилага́тельное, *see* и́мя прилага́тельное.

прилага́ть, *v. imp.* (*perf.* приложи́ть), apply.

прилега́ющий, *adj.* adjoining, adjacent.

приле́жный, *adj.* diligent.

прилета́ть, *v. imp.* (*perf.*

прилете́ть), arrive by air.

прили́в, *m.* high tide.

прили́чный, *adj.* decent.

приложе́ние, *nt.* supplement; enclosure.

приложи́ть, *v.*, *perf.* of прикла́дывать, прилага́ть.

примене́ние, *nt.* application.

примени́тельно, *adv.* in conformity with.

применя́ть, *v. imp.* (*perf.* примени́ть), apply, adapt; employ, use.

приме́р, *m.* example. -ный, *adj.* exemplary.

приме́рить, *v. imp.* (*perf.* приме́рить), try on; fit.

при́месь, *f.* admixture; tinge; dash.

приме́та, *f.* sign, token, mark.

примеча́ние, *nt.* note, footnote; comment.

примеча́тельный, *adj.* notable, remarkable.

примире́ние, *nt.* reconciliation.

примири́тельный, *adj.* conciliatory.

примиря́ть, *v. imp.* (*perf.* примири́ть), reconcile; conciliate.

принадлежа́ть, *v. imp.* belong to.

принадле́жность, *f.* belonging to; affiliation; приналле́жности, *pl.* accessories.

принима́ть, *v. imp.* (*perf.* приня́ть), receive; accept.

приноси́ть, *v. imp.* (*perf.* принести́), bring; yield.

приноше́ние, *nt.* offering, gift.

принуди́тельный, *adj.* compulsory.

принужда́ть, *v. imp.* (*perf.* прину́дить), compel, force.

принужде́ние, *nt.* compulsion.

принципиа́льно, *adv.* in essence, in principle.

приня́тие, *nt.* adoption; reception; acceptance.

приня́ть, *v.*, *perf.* of принима́ть.

приобрета́ть, *v. imp.* (*perf.* приобрести́), acquire, gain.

припа́док, *m.* attack; fit.

припа́сы, *pl.* supplies, stores.

припе́в, *m.* (*mus.*) refrain.

припи́ска, *f.* postscript.

припи́сывать, *v. imp.* (*perf.* приписа́ть), add in writing; attribute.

припомина́ть, *v. imp.* (*perf.* припо́мнить), remember, recollect.

прираще́ние, *nt.* increase; increment.

приро́да, *f.* nature.

приро́дный, *adj.* natural; inborn, innate.

приро́ст, *m.* increase.

прируча́ть, *v. imp.* (*perf.* приручи́ть), domesticate; tame.

присва́ивать, *v. imp.* (*perf.* присво́ить), appropriate.

приседа́ть, *v. imp.* (*perf.* присе́сть), squat.

присла́ть, *v.*, *perf.* of присыла́ть.

присни́ться, *v.*, *perf.* of сни́ться.

присоединя́ть, *v. imp.* (*perf.* присоедини́ть), *tr.*, join, add; annex.

приспособле́ние, *nt.* adaptation; accommodation.

приспособля́ть, *v. imp.* (*perf.* приспосо́бить), adapt; accommodate.

пристава́ть, *v. imp.* (*perf.* приста́ть), stick *or* adhere (to); come alongside.

приста́вка, *f.* (*gram.*) prefix.

приставля́ть, *v. imp.* (*perf.* приста́вить), put *or* set against; lean against.

при́стальный, *adj.* fixed.

при́стань, *f.* pier, dock, wharf.

приста́ть, *v.*, *perf.* of пристава́ть.

пристра́стность, *f.* partiality.

при́ступ, *m.* assault; attack, fit.

приступа́ть, *v. imp.* (*perf.* приступи́ть), begin, start; proceed (to).

прису́тствие, *nt.* presence.

прису́тствовать, *v. imp.* be present, attend.

присыла́ть, *v. imp.* (*perf.* присла́ть), send.

прися́га, *f.* oath.

присяга́ть, v. imp. (perf. **присягну́ть**), swear; take an oath.

притво́рный, adj. affected, feigned; sham.

притворя́ться, v. imp. (perf. **притвори́ться**), intr., shut, close.

притесня́ть, v. imp. (perf. **притесни́ть**), oppress.

прито́к, m. tributary.

прито́м, conj. besides.

притяга́тельный, adj. attractive.

притя́гивать, v. imp. (perf. **притяну́ть**), attract.

притяжа́тельный, adj. possessive.

притяже́ние, nt. attraction.

притяза́тельный, adj. pretentious; exacting.

прихо́д, m. arrival; receipts.

приходи́ть, v. imp. (perf. **прийти́**), come, arrive. **-ся**, impers., have to; have occasion to.

прихотли́вый, adj. capricious, whimsical.

при́хоть, f. caprice, whim.

прицепля́ть, v. imp. (perf. **прицепи́ть**), hook; couple.

прича́стие, nt. participle.

прича́стный, adj. participating, involved in or with.

причёска, f. coiffure.

причёсывать, v. imp. (perf. **причеса́ть**), comb, dress (hair).

причи́на, f. cause; reason.

причиня́ть, v. imp. (perf. **причини́ть**), cause.

пришива́ть, v. imp. (perf. **приши́ть**), sew on.

прию́т, m. asylum, shelter, refuge. де́тский прию́т, orphanage.

прия́тель m., **-ица** f., friend. **-ский**, adj. friendly.

прия́тный, adj. pleasant.

про, prep. about; for.

проанализи́ровать, v., perf. of анализи́ровать.

про́ба, f. trial, test; sample.

пробе́г, m. run.

пробега́ть, v. imp. (perf.

пробежа́ть), run (by)

пробега́ть, v. perf. run around (for a certain length of time).

пробе́л, m. gap; flaw.

пробива́ть, v. imp. (perf. **проби́ть**), make or punch a hole in.

пробира́ться, v. imp. (perf. **пробра́ться**), make one's way through.

про́бка, f. cork, stopper.

пробле́ма, f. problem.

про́бовать, v. imp. (perf. **попро́бовать**), attempt, try; taste.

пробо́р, m. part, parting.

пробужда́ть, v. imp. (perf. **пробуди́ть**), wake up, awaken, arouse.

пробыва́ть, v. imp. (perf. **пробы́ть**), stay, remain.

прова́л, m. downfall; trap; failure, flop.

прова́ливаться, v. imp. (perf. **провали́ться**), fail; fall through.

провезти́, v., perf. of провози́ть

провентили́ровать, v., perf. of вентили́ровать.

прове́рка, f. check, examination; control.

проверя́ть, v. imp. (perf. **прове́рить**), check; verify.

провести́, v., perf. of проводи́ть.

прове́тривать, v. imp. (perf. **прове́трить**), air, ventilate.

прови́зия, f. provisions.

провини́ться, v. imp. be at fault.

провинциа́льный, adj. provincial.

про́вод, m. wire.

проводи́ть, v., perf. of провожа́ть. — v. imp. (perf. провести́) lead; build; conduct, carry out.

прово́дка, f. installation; wires.

проводни́к, m. guide; guard.

провожа́ть, v. imp. (perf. **проводи́ть**), accompany; see off.

провожа́тый, adj. guided.

прово́з, m. transport.

провозглаша́ть, v. imp. (perf.

провозгласи́ть), announce, proclaim.

провози́ть, v. imp. (perf. **провезти́**), transport, convey.

про́волока, f. wire.

проволо́чка, f. (colloq.) delay.

прово́рный, adj. quick, agile, adroit.

прога́лина, f. glade.

прогля́дывать, v. imp. (perf. **прогляну́ть**) appear, be visible or perceptible. — (perf. **прогляде́ть**) look through.

прогне́вить, v., perf. of **гне́вить**.

проголода́ться, v., perf. of **голода́ть**.

проголосова́ть, v. perf. vote.

прогоня́ть, v. imp. (perf. **прогна́ть**), drive away or off.

прого́рклый, adj. rank, rancid.

прогресси́ровать, v. imp. progress, advance.

прогрохота́ть, v., perf. of **грохота́ть**.

прогу́ливаться, v. imp. take a walk or stroll.

прогу́лка, f. walk, stroll.

продава́ть, v. imp. (perf. **прода́ть**), sell.

продаве́ц, m. salesman.

продавщи́ца, f. saleswoman.

прода́жа, f. sale; selling.

прода́жный, adj. for sale; corrupt, mercenary.

продвига́ться, v. imp. (perf. **продви́нуться**), advance.

продвиже́ние, nt. advancement, progress.

продеклами́ровать, v., perf. of **деклами́ровать**.

проде́лка, f. trick.

продиктова́ть, v., perf. of **диктова́ть**.

продлева́ть, v. imp. (perf. **продли́ть**), prolong.

продли́ть, v., perf. of **длить**.

продово́льствие, nt. food; foodstuffs.

продолгова́тый, adj. oblong.

продолжа́ть, v. imp. (perf. **продо́лжить**), tr., continue.

продолже́ние, nt. continuation.

продолжи́тельность, f. duration.

продолжи́тельный, adj. of long duration.

продо́льный, adj. longitudinal.

продукти́вность, f. productivity; efficiency.

проду́кция, f. production; output.

проду́мывать, v. imp. (perf. **проду́мать**), think over or through.

проеда́ть, v. imp. (perf. **прое́сть**), eat away, corrode.

прое́зд, m. passage; thoroughfare.

проезжа́ть, v. imp. (perf. **прое́хать**), pass; go by or past.

прое́зжий, m. traveller.

проекти́ровать, v. imp. (perf. **запроекти́ровать**), project; plan, design.

прое́сть, v., perf. of **проеда́ть**.

прое́хать, v., perf. of **проезжа́ть**.

прожéктор, m. searchlight.

прожива́ть, v. imp. (perf. **прожи́ть**), live, reside.

прожига́ть, v. imp. (perf. **проже́чь**), burn through.

прожо́рливый, adj. voracious.

про́за, f. prose.

про́звище, nt. nickname.

прозаи́ческий, adj. prosaic.

прозвуча́ть, v., perf. of **звуча́ть**.

прозимова́ть, v., perf. of **зимова́ть**.

прозо́рливый, adj. sagacious; perspicacious.

прозра́чный, adj. transparent.

прозыва́ть, v. imp. (perf. **прозва́ть**), nickname.

прои́грывать, v. imp. (perf. **проигра́ть**), lose.

про́игрыш, m. loss.

произведе́ние, nt. work; product.

производи́тель, m. producer. **-ный**, adj. productive.

производи́ть, v. imp. (perf. **произвести́**), produce.

произво́дный, adj. derivative.

произво́дственный, adj. industrial.

произво́дство, *nt.* production, manufacture.

произво́льный, *adj.* arbitrary.

произноси́ть, *v. imp.* (*perf.* **произнести́**), pronounce.

произноше́ние, *nt.* pronunciation.

про́иски, *pl.* intrigues; plotting.

происходи́ть, *v. imp.* (*perf.* **произойти́**), happen; descend (from), originate.

происхожде́ние, *nt.* origin.

происше́ствие, *nt.* incident, event.

пройти́, *v.,* *perf. of* **проходи́ть.**

прока́за, *f.* leprosy; mischief.

прока́лывать, *v. imp.* (*perf.* **проколо́ть**), pierce.

прока́т, *m.* hire.

прокла́дывать, *v. imp.* (*perf.* **проложи́ть**), build, construct; lay; interlay.

прокла́мация, *f.* leaflet.

проклами́ровать, *v. imp. & perf.* proclaim.

проклина́ть, *v. imp.* (*perf.* **прокля́сть**), damn; curse.

прокля́тие, *nt.* curse; damnation.

прокля́тый, *adj.* damned, cursed.

проколо́ть, *v.,* *perf. of* **прока́лывать.**

проконсульти́ровать, *v.,* *perf. of* **консульти́ровать.**

прокорректи́ровать, *v.,* *perf. of* **корректи́ровать.**

прокуро́р, *m.* prosecutor.

проле́жень, *m.* bedsore.

пролёт, *m.* flight; bridge span.

пролета́рий *m.,* **пролета́рка** *f.,* proletarian.

проли́в, *m.* (*geog.*) strait.

пролива́ть, *v. imd.* (*perf.* **проли́ть**), spill; shed.

проло́м, *m.* break; fracture.

прома́тывать, *v. imp.* (*perf.* **промота́ть**), squander; dissipate.

прома́чивать, *v. imp.* (*perf.* **промочи́ть**), drench.

прома́х, *m.* miss; blunder.

промедле́ние, *nt.* delay.

промежу́ток, *m.* interval; space.

промежу́точный, *adj.* intermediate.

проме́нивать, *v. imp.* (*perf.* **променя́ть**), exchange, barter.

промока́тельная бума́га, blotter.

промока́ть, *v. imp.* (*perf.* **промо́кнуть**), get wet; be drenched. — (*perf.* **промокну́ть**), blot.

промолча́ть, *v. perf.* keep silent.

промота́ть, *v.,* *perf. of* **прома́тывать.**

промча́ться, *v. perf.* rush past; fly by.

промыва́ть, *v. imp.* (*perf.* **промы́ть**), *tr.,* wash.

промы́шленник, *m.* industrialist; manufacturer.

промы́шленность, *f.* industry.

пронза́ть, *v. imp.* (*perf.* **пронзи́ть**), pierce; run through.

пронзи́тельный, *adj.* piercing.

пронизывать, *v. imp.* (*perf.* **пронизать**), penetrate.

проника́ть, *v. imp.* (*perf.* **прони́кнуть**), penetrate.

проникнове́ние, *nt.* penetration.

прони́кнутый, *adj.* imbued or inspired with.

проница́емый, *adj.* permeable.

проница́тельный, *adj.* perspicacious, acute.

пропаганди́ровать, *v. imp.* propagandize.

пропада́ть, *v. imp.* (*perf.* **пропа́сть**), disappear; be missing *or* lost.

пропа́жа, *f.* loss.

про́пасть, *f.* precipice, abyss.

пропа́сть, *v.,* *perf. of* **пропада́ть.**

пропи́сная бу́ква, capital letter.

пропи́сывать, *v. imp.* (*perf.* **прописа́ть**), *tr.,* prescribe; register.

пропита́ние, *nt.* subsistence.

пропи́тывать, *v. imp.* (*perf.* **пропита́ть**), saturate.

пропове́довать, *v. imp.* preach.

про́поведь, *f.* sermon.

пропо́рция, *f.* proportion.

про́пуск, *m.* absence; omission; pass, permit.

пропуска́ть, *v. imp.* (*perf.* пропусти́ть), pass, admit; omit, leave out; miss.

прорва́ть(ся), *v.*, *perf. of* прорыва́ть(ся).

прог зз, *m.* cut.

прореза́ть, *v. imp.* (*perf.* проре́зать), cut through.

прорица́ние, *nt.* soothsaying; prophecy.

прорица́ть, *v. imp.* prophesy.

проро́к, *m.* prophet.

проро́чество, *nt.* prophecy.

проры́в, *m.* break-through, breach, gap.

прорыва́ть, *v. imp.* (*perf.* прорва́ть), break through. — (*perf.* проры́ть), dig through or across. -ся, *v. imp.* (*perf.* прорва́ться), burst open, tear; break.

прорыча́ть, *v.*, *perf. of* рыча́ть.

проса́ливать, *v. imp.* (*perf.* проса́лить), grease. — (*perf.* просоли́ть), salt.

просвети́тельный, *adj.* instructive.

просветле́ние, *nt.* enlightenment.

просве́чивание, *nt.* x-ray, x-raying; radioscopy.

просве́чивать, *v. imp.* (*perf.* просвети́ть), x-ray.

просвеща́ть, *v. imp.* (*perf.* просвети́ть), enlighten.

просвеще́ние, *nt.* enlightenment; education.

просе́ивать, *v. imp.* (*perf.* просе́ять), sift.

проси́тель *m.*, -ница *f.*, applicant, petitioner.

проси́ть, *v. imp.* (*perf.* попроси́ть), ask; demand; beg; invite.

просия́ть, *v. perf.* clear up; brighten; light up (with).

проскрипе́ть, *v.*, *perf. of* скрипе́ть,.

просла́вить, *v.*, *perf. of* прославля́ть, сла́вить.

прославле́ние, *nt.* glorification.

прославля́ть, *v. imp.* (*perf.* просла́вить), glorify; make famous; bring fame to.

просле́живать, *v. imp.* (*perf.* проследи́ть), trace, track; observe.

просма́тривать, *v. imp.* (*perf.* просмотре́ть), look through; miss, overlook.

просмо́тр, *m.* examination; review.

просну́ться, *v.*, *perf. of* просыпа́ться.

просоли́ть, *v. perf. of* проса́ливать.

проспа́ть, *v.*, *perf. of* просыпа́ть.

просро́ченный, *adj.* overdue.

просро́чивать, *v. imp.* (*perf.* просро́чить), exceed a time limit.

проста́к, *m.* simpleton.

простира́ть, *v. imp.* (*perf.* простере́ть), reach out; extend. — *v. perf.* wash, wash out. -ся, *v. imp.* (*perf.* простере́ться), *intr.*, stretch; range.

прости́тельный, *adj.* pardonable, excusable.

прости́ть(ся), *v.*, *perf. of* проща́ть(ся).

про́сто, *adv.* simply. -ва́тый, *adj.* (*colloq.*) simple, simpleminded. -ду́шие, *nt.* artlessness. -ре́чие, *nt.* popular speech. -серде́чный, *adj.* simple-hearted.

просто́й, *adj.* simple; easy; plain, ordinary, common.

просто́р, *m.* spaciousness; scope.

простота́, *f.* simplicity.

простра́нный, *adj.* extensive, vast.

простра́нство, *nt.* space.

простра́ция, *f.* prostration.

просту́да, *f.* cold, chill.

простужа́ться, *v. imp.* (*perf.* простуди́ться), catch a cold.

просту́пок, *m.* fault; misdemeanor.

простыня́, *f.* bedsheet.

просчи́тываться, *v. imp.* (*perf.* просчита́ться), miscalculate.

просыпа́ть, *v. imp.* (*perf.*

проспа́ть), oversleep. —(perf. просыпа́ть), tr., spill. **-ся**, v. imp. (perf. просну́ться), wake up, awake. — (perf. просыпа́ться), intr., spill.

про́сьба, f. request.

протека́ть, v. imp. (perf. проте́чь), leak; elapse.

протере́ть, v., perf. of протира́ть.

протестова́ть, v. imp. protest.

про́тив, prep. (+ gen.) against; opposite.

проти́виться, v. imp. oppose; object to; resist.

проти́вник, m. opponent.

проти́вный, adj. opposite, contrary; disgusting.

противове́с, m. counterbalance.

противоде́йствовать, v. imp. oppose; counteract.

противозако́нный, adj. illegal.

противополо́жный, adj.. contrary; opposite.

противопоставля́ть, v. imp. (perf. противопоста́вить), oppose to; contrast with.

противоре́чить, v. imp. contradict.

противостоя́ть, v. imp. resist; withstand.

протира́ть, v. imp. (perf. протере́ть), wear out or through; dry, wipe dry.

протоко́л, m. minutes; record.

прото́чный, adj. flowing; running.

протя́гивать, v. imp. (perf. протяну́ть), stretch, stretch out; reach out.

протяже́ние, nt. extent; stretch.

протяжённый, adj. extensive, lengthy.

протя́жный, adj. drawn out; drawling.

протяну́ть, v., perf. of протя́гивать.

профани́ровать, v. imp. & perf. profane.

профессиона́л m., **-ка** f., professional. **-ьный**, adj. professional.

профе́ссия, f. profession.

профе́ссор, m. professor.

прохла́да, f. coolness.

прохла́дный, adj. cool, chilly, fresh.

прохлажда́ться, v. imp. (perf. прохлади́ться), colloq. refresh oneself.

прохо́д, m. passage.

проходи́ть, v. imp. (perf. пройти́), pass; elapse, come to an end; cover, study.

прохо́жий, m. passer-by.

процвета́ть, v. imp. prosper.

проце́нт, m. percentage, percent; interest.

проце́сс, m. process; lawsuit, case, trial.

проче́сть, v., perf. of чита́ть.

про́чий, adj. other. и про́чее, and others; etc. ме́жду про́чим, by the way.

прочита́ть, v. perf. read; spend time reading.

про́чный, adj. firm, solid; lasting.

прочу́вствовать, v. perf. feel deeply or acutely.

прочь, adv. away, off.

проше́дший, adj. past.

проше́ние, nt. petition.

про́шлое, nt. past.

про́шлый, adj. past; last.

проща́й(те), good-bye).

проща́льный, adj. farewell, parting.

проща́ние, nt. farewell, parting.

проща́ть, v. imp. (perf. прости́ть), forgive; excuse. **-ся**, take leave; say good-bye.

про́ще, adj., adv. simpler, easier.

проще́ние, nt. forgiveness; pardon.

проявитель, m. (phot.) developer).

проявле́ние, nt. display; manifestation.

проявля́ть, v. imp. (perf. прояви́ть), display, show; manifest.

пруд, m. pond.

пружи́на, f. spring.

пруса́к, m. (colloq.) cockroach.

пру́сский, adj. Prussian.

прут, m. twig; rod.

пры́гать, v. imp. (perf. пры́гнуть), jump, leap; hop.

прыжки́, pl. jumping, leaping; diving.

прыжо́к, m. jump, leap; dive.

пры́ткий, adj. (colloq.) quick.

прыщ (also прыщик), m. pimple.

пряди́льный, adj. spinning.

прядь, f. lock (of hair).

пря́жа, f. thread, yarn.

пря́жка, f. buckle, clasp.

пряма́я речь, (gram.) direct discourse.

пря́мо, adv. straight; frankly. -ду́шный, adj. frank; straightforward.

прямо́й, adj. straight; direct; frank. прямо́й у́гол, (math.) right angle.

прямо́й шрифт, (typog.) Roman type.

прямота́, f. uprightness.

прямоуго́льник, m. rectangle.

пря́тать, v. imp. (perf. спря́тать), hide; put away.

пря́тки, pl. hide-and-seek.

псевдони́м, m. pseudonym.

психиа́тр, m. psychiatrist.

пси́хика, f. psyche.

психи́ческий, adj. mental, psychic(al).

психоана́лиз, m. psychoanalysis.

психо́з, m. psychosis.

психо́лог, m. psychologist.

психоневро́з, m. psychoneurosis.

психопа́т m., -чка f., psychopath.

психотерапи́я, f. psychotherapy.

пти́ца, f. bird.

пу́блика, f. public; audience.

публикова́ть, v. imp. (perf. опубликова́ть), publish.

публи́чный, adj. public.

пу́гало, nt. scarecrow.

пуга́ть, v. imp. (perf. испуга́ть, пугну́ть), frighten, scare.

пугли́вый, adj. timid; fearful.

пу́говица, f. button.

пу́дра, f. powder.

пу́дрить, v. imp. (perf. напу́дрить), powder.

пузырёк, m. bubble.

пузы́рь, m. bubble; blister; bladder.

пульс, m. pulse.

пульси́ровать, v. imp. pulsate; throb.

пу́ля, f. bullet.

пункт, m. point; station; post.

пунктуа́льный, adj. punctual.

пунктуа́ция, f. (gram.) punctuation.

пунцо́вый, adj. crimson.

пу́рпур, m. purple. -овый, adj. purple.

пуска́ть, v. imp. (perf. пусти́ть), set free; let in, admit; permit.

пусте́ть, v. imp. (perf. опусте́ть), become empty or deserted.

пусто́й, adj. empty, hollow; uninhabited; vacant.

пустота́, f. emptiness; vacuum.

пусты́нник, m. hermit.

пусты́нный, adj. desert; uninhabited.

пусты́ня, f. desert.

пусть, particle (+ inf.) let: пусть он идёт, let him go.

пустя́к, m. trifle.

пу́таница, f. confusion.

пу́тать, v. imp. confuse.

путеводи́тель, m. guidebook.

путём, adv. by way of, by means of.

путеше́ственник, m. traveler.

путеше́ствие, nt. voyage, trip, journey.

путеше́ствовать, v. imp. & perf. travel.

путь, m. road, way; journey; means, way.

пух, m. down.

пу́хлый, adj. chubby, plump.

пу́хнуть, v. imp. (perf. распу́хнуть), intr., swell.

пухо́вка, f. powder puff.

пучи́на, f. gulf.

пучо́к, m. bunch; tuft, wisp.

пуши́нка, f. fluff; flake.

пуши́стый, adj. fluffy; downy.

пушно́й, adj. fur-bearing.

пу́ща, f. primeval forest.

пчела́, f. bee.

пчелово́дство, nt. bee-keeping.
пшени́ца, f. wheat.
пыл, m. ardor, passion.
пылесо́с, m. vacuum cleaner.
пы́лкий, adj. ardent; passionate.
пыль, f. dust.
пы́льный, adj. dusty.
пыта́ть, v. imp. torture. -ся, v. imp. (perf. попыта́ться), attempt, try, endeavor.
пытли́вый, adj. inquisitive.
пы́шность, f. splendor, magnificence.
пы́шный, adj. magnificent, luxuriant.
пье́са, f. (theat.) play; (mus.) piece.
пьяне́ть, v. imp. (perf. опьяне́ть), become drunk.
пья́ница, f. drunk, drunkard.

пья́ный, adj. drunk(en).
пядь, f. span.
пята́, f. (anat.) heel.
пя́теро, num. coll. five.
пятёрка, f. (num., cards) five; five-ruble note.
пятибо́рье, nt. pentathlon.
пятидеся́тый, adj. fiftieth.
пятиле́тка, f. five-year plan.
пяти́ться, v. imp. (perf. попя́титься), back; step back.
пя́тка, f. (anat.) heel.
пятна́дцатый, adj. fifteenth.
пятна́дцать, num. fifteen.
пяти́стый, adj. spotty, spotted.
пя́тница, f. Friday.
пятно́, nt. stain, spot.
пя́тый, adj. fifth.
пять, num. five.
пятьдеся́т, num. fifty.
пятьсо́т num. five hundred.

Р

раб, m. slave.
рабо́ле́пие, nt. servility.
рабо́ле́пный, adj. servile.
рабо́та, f. work.
рабо́тать, v. imp. (perf. порабо́тать), work.
рабо́тник m., рабо́тница f., worker.
рабо́чий, m. worker.
ра́бство, nt. slavery.
ра́венство, nt. equality.
равни́на, f. plain.
равно́, adv. equally.
равнове́сие, nt. equilibrium, balance. -де́йствие, nt. equinox. -ду́шный, adj. indifferent. -ме́рный, adj. even; uniform.
ра́вный, adj. equal.
равня́ть, v. imp. (perf. сравня́ть), equalize. -ся, compete; (math.) be equal to.
ра́ди, for the sake of.
радиа́ция, f. radiation.
ра́дио, nt. ind. radio. -веща́ние, nt. broadcasting. -переда́тчик, m. radio trans-

mitter. -прие́мник, m. radio receiver; tuner.
ра́диус, m. radius.
ра́довать, v. imp. (perf. обра́довать), gladden.
ра́дость, f. joy.
ра́дуга, f. rainbow.
раду́шный, adj. cordial.
раз, m. time; one. — conj. since.
разбавля́ть, v. imp. (perf. разба́вить), dilute.
разбе́г, m. running start.
разбега́ться, v. imp. (perf. разбежа́ться), intr., scatter, run away.
разбива́ть, v. imp. (perf. разби́ть), tr., break, fracture; defeat; divide, split.
разбира́ть, v. imp. (perf. разобра́ть), strip, dismantle, take apart; investigate; analyze.
разби́тый, adj. broken.
разбогате́ть, v. imp. get o become rich.
разбо́й, m. robbery.

разбóр, m. analysis. **-чивый,** adj. legible; fastidious.

разбрáсывать, v. imp. (perf. **разбросáть**), scatter.

разбрóсанный, adj. scattered; dispersed.

разбудить, v. perf. wake.

развáл, m. chaos, disorder.

развáливаться, v. imp. (perf. **развалиться**), collapse; fall into pieces.

развáлины, pl. ruins.

рáзве, particle really.

разведéние, nt. breeding; cultivation.

разведённый, adj. divorced.

развéдка, f. reconnaisance; intelligence.

развéдчик, m. scout; intelligence officer.

развёртывать, v. imp. (perf. **развернуть**), unfold, open; spread out.

развеселить(ся), v., perf. of веселить(ся).

развести(сь), v., perf. of разводить(ся).

развивáть, v. imp. (perf. **развить**), tr., develop.

развитие, nt. development.

развлекáть, v. imp. (perf. **развлечь**), amuse.

развлечéние, nt. amusement.

развóд, m. divorce.

разводить, v. imp. (perf. **развести**), tr., conduct; bring or pull apart; dilute; divorce; breed, rear. **-ся,** intr., divorce be divorced; breed, multiply.

развóлноваться, v. perf. become excited.

разврáт, m. depravity.

развращáть, v. imp. (perf. **развратить**), corrupt; deprave.

развязывать, v. imp. (perf. **развязáть**), untie; unleash.

разгáдывать, v. imp. (perf. **разгадáть**), solve; guess.

разгáр, m. climax.

разглашáть, v. imp. (perf. **разгласить**), divulge.

разговáривать, v. imp. speak, talk, converse.

разговóр, m. conversation. **-ный,** adj. colloquial. **-чивый,** adj. talkative.

разгонять, v. imp. (perf. **разогнáть**), tr., disperse.

разгорячить, v., perf. of горячить.

разграничивать, v. imp. (perf. **разграничить**), demarcate; delimit.

разгрóм, m. defeat, rout; devastation.

разгромить, v. perf. of громить.

разгружáть, v. imp. (perf. **разгрузить**), unload.

разгрузка, f. unloading.

раздавáть, v. imp. (perf. **раздáть**), distribute. **-ся,** resound; be heard; ring out.

раздавить, v. perf. crush; smash.

раздáча, f. distribution.

раздевáть, v. imp. (perf. **раздéть**), tr., undress.

раздéл, m. division; section. **-éние,** nt. division. **-ьный,** adj. separate.

разделить, v., perf. of делить, разделять. **-ся,** v., perf. of делиться.

разделять, v. imp. (perf. **разделить**), separate; divide.

раздóр, m. discord.

раздражáть, v. imp. (perf. **раздражить**), irritate.

раздражéние, nt. irritation.

раздражительный, adj. irritable.

раздроблять, v. imp. (perf. **раздробить**), break or smash to pieces.

раздувáть, v. imp. (perf. **раздуть**), fan, rouse; (colloq.) exaggerate.

раздумать, v. perf. change one's mind.

раздумье, nt. meditation; reflection.

разжигáть, v. imp. (perf. **разжечь**), kindle.

разжирéть, v., perf. of жирéть.

разительный, adj. striking.

разлагáть, v. imp. (perf. **разложить**), tr., lay out; decompose; demoralize. **-ся,** *intr.,* decompose, decay.

разла́д, *m.* discord.

разлени́ться, *v. perf.* become lazy.

разли́в, *m.* flood; overflow.

разлива́ть, *v. imp.* (*perf.* **разли́ть**), spill; pour out.

различа́ть, *v. imp.* (*perf.* **различи́ть**), distinguish. **-ся,** *v. imp.* differ.

разли́чие, *nt,* difference, distinction.

различи́тельный, *adj.* distinctive.

разли́чный, *adj.* different, diverse, various.

разложе́ние, *nt.* decomposition, decay; corruption, demoralization.

разложи́ть(ся), *v., perf. of* **разлага́ть(ся).**

разлу́ка, *f.* separation; parting.

разлуча́ть, *v. imp.* (*perf.* **разлучи́ть**), separate.

разма́тывать, *v. imp.* (*perf.* **размота́ть**), unwind.

разма́х, *m.* sweep, scope, range.

разма́хивать, *v. imp.* (*perf.* **размахну́ть**), brandish; swing; gesticulate.

разме́р, *m.* dimension, size; (*poetry*) meter; (*mus.*) measure.

разме́ривать, *v. imp.* (*perf.* **разме́рить**), measure off.

размеша́ть, ´*v. imp.* (*perf.* **размеша́ть**), stir.

размеща́ть, *v. imp.* (*perf.* **размести́ть**), place; accommodate, quarter.

размножа́ть, *v. imp.* (*perf.* **размно́жить**), multiply.

размноже́ние, *nt.* reproduction; propagation.

размота́ть, *v., perf. of* **разма́тывать.**

размышле́ние, *nt.* reflection.

размышля́ть, *v. imp.* (*perf.* **размы́слить**), reflect, ponder.

разнести́, *v., perf. of* **разноси́ть**

ра́зниться, *v. imp.* differ.

ра́зница, *f.* difference.

разнови́дность, *f.* variety.

разногла́сие, *nt.* variance, difference; disagreement; discord.

разнообра́зие, *nt.* variety, diversity.

разноро́дный, *adj.* heterogeneous.

разноси́ть, *v. imp.* (*perf.* **разнести́**), carry, convey; deliver; spread.

разносторо́нний, *adj.* manysided, versatile.

ра́зный, *adj.* different, diverse, various.

разоблача́ть, *v. imp.* (*perf.* **разоблачи́ть**), expose, unmask.

разобра́ть, *v., perf. of* **разбира́ть.**

разогна́ть, *v., perf. of* **разгоня́ть.**

разогрева́ть, *v. imp.* (*perf.* **разгре́ть**), warm up.

разодра́ться, *v., perf. of* **дра́ться.**

разозли́ть, *v. perf.* anger, enrage.

разойти́сь, *v., perf. of* **расходи́ться.**

разорва́ть(ся), *v., perf. of* **разрыва́ть(ся).**

разоре́ние, *nt.* ruin, destruction.

разоружа́ть, *v. imp.* (*perf.* **разоружи́ть**), *tr.,* disarm.

разоруже́ние, *nt.* disarmament.

разоря́ть, *v. imp.* (*perf.* **разори́ть**), ruin; destroy.

разочаро́вывать, *v. imp.* (*perf.* **разочарова́ть**), disillusion, disappoint.

разраба́тывать, *v. imp.* (*perf.* **разрабо́тать**), work out; elaborate; cultivate; exploit.

разре́з, *m.* cut; section.

разреза́ть, *v. imp.* (*perf.* **разре́зать**), cut, slit, snip; section; carve.

разреша́ть, *v. imp.* (*perf.* **разреши́ть**), permit, allow; solve.

разреше́ние, *nt.* permission; solution.

разро́зненный, *adj.* odd.

разру́ха, *f.* ruin, devastation.

разруша́ть, *v. imp.* (*perf.*

разру́шить), destroy, raze, demolish.

разруше́ние, *nt.* destruction.

разры́в, *m.* break, rupture; burst(ing).

разрыва́ть, *v. imp.* (*perf.* разры́ть), dig up. — разорва́ть), *tr.*, tear, rend. -ся, *v. imp.* (*perf.* разорва́ться), *intr.*, break; burst, explode.

разря́д, *m.* category; discharge. -ка, *f.* (*typog.*) spacing.

ра́зум, *m.* reason; mind, intellect.

разуме́ется, *impers.* of course; it goes without saying.

разу́мный, *adj.* reasonable.

разъеда́ть, *v. imp.* (*perf.* разъе́сть), eat away, corrode.

разъедини́ть, *v. imp.* (*perf.* разъедини́ть), disjoin, disconnect.

разъясни́ть, *v. imp.* (*perf.* разъясни́ть), explain, clarify.

разы́скивать, *v. imp.* (*perf.* разыска́ть), search for.

рай, *m.* paradise.

райо́н, *m.* region; district.

рак, *m.* crayfish; (*med.*) cancer.

раке́тка, *f.* (*athl.*) racket.

ра́ма, *f.* frame.

ра́мпа, *f.* footlights.

ра́на, *f.* wound.

ра́нить, *v. imp. & perf.* wound.

ра́нний, *adj.* early.

ра́но, *adv.* early. — *impers.* it is early.

ра́ньше, *adv.* earlier.

папи́ра, *f.* (*fencing*) foil.

ра́порт, *m.* report.

ра́са, *f.* race (*breed*).

раска́т, *m.* peal.

раска́яние, *nt.* remorse; repentance.

раско́л, *m.* split, break, crack.

раско́пки, *pl.* excavation(s).

раскрасне́ется, *v. perf.* flush, become flushed.

раскра́шивать, *v. imp.* (*perf.* раскра́сить), color, paint.

раскрепоща́ть, *v. imp.* (*perf.* раскрепости́ть), set free; liberate.

раскритикова́ть, *v. perf.* criticize severely.

раскрыва́ть, *v. imp.* (*perf.* раскры́ть), uncover, open; disclose.

раскупа́ть, *v. imp.* (*perf.* раскупи́ть), buy up.

раску́поривать, *v. imp.* (*perf.* раску́порить), uncork, open.

ра́совый, *adj.* racial.

распа́д, *m.* disintegration; collapse.

распада́ться, *v. imp.* (*perf.* распа́сться), disintegrate, break up; dissolve.

распако́вывать, *v. imp.* (*perf.* распакова́ть), unpack; undo.

распа́хивать, *v. imp.* (*perf.* распаха́ть), plow up. — (*perf.* распахну́ть), open wide; throw open.

распеча́тывать, *v. imp.* (*perf.* распеча́тать), unseal, open.

распина́ть, *v. imp.* (*perf.* распя́ть), crucify.

расписа́ние, *nt.* schedule, timetable.

распи́ска, *f.* receipt.

распи́сывать, *v. imp.* (*perf.* расписа́ть), paint; register.

распла́каться, *v. perf.* burst into tears.

распла́та, *f.* payment; atonement.

распла́чиваться, *v. imp.* (*perf.* расплати́ться), pay off; settle an account.

распознава́ть, *v. imp.* (*perf.* распозна́ть), distinguish; discern.

располага́ть, *v. imp.* (*perf.* расположи́ть), dispose (of); arrange, situate. -ся, settle; settle down.

расположе́ние, *nt.* disposition; arrangement; situation.

распоро́ть, *v. perf.* rip, rip up; undo.

распоряжа́ться, *v. imp.* (*perf.* распоряди́ться), order; be in command; decree.

распоряже́ние, *nt.* order, decree.

распра́ва, *f.* reprisal; violence.

распределе́ние, *nt.* distribution.

распределя́ть, *v. imp.* (*perf.* **распредели́ть**), distribute.

распрода́жа, *f.* clearance sale.

распространённый, *adj.* prevalent; widespread; widely disseminated.

распространя́ть, *v. imp.* (*perf.* **распространи́ть**), spread, disseminate.

ра́спря, *f.* discord; strife.

распуска́ние, *nt.* blossoming, blooming.

распуска́ть, *v. imp.* (*perf.* **распусти́ть**), dismiss, disband; let out, unfurl. -ся, *intr.*, dissolve.

распу́тный, *adj.* dissolute.

распу́тывать, *v. imp.* (*perf.* **распу́тать**), disentangle.

распу́тье, *pl.* crossroad(s).

распу́хнуть, *v.*, *perf. of* пу́хнуть.

распу́щенный, *adj.* dissolute.

распя́ть, *v.*, *perf. of* распина́ть.

рассве́т, *m.* dawn, daybreak.

рассе́ивать, *v. imp.* (*perf.* рассе́ять), *tr.*, disperse; scatter.

рассе́ливать, *v. imp.* (*perf.* рассели́ть), *intr.*, settle.

рассерди́ть, *v. perf.* anger.

рассе́янный, *adj.* scattered; absent-minded.

расска́з, *m.* story, tale, narrative.

расска́зывать, *v. imp.* (*perf.* рассказа́ть), narrate, tell.

рассле́довать, *v. imp. & perf.* investigate; inquire (into).

рассма́тривать, *v. imp.* (*perf.* рассмотре́ть), regard, consider; examine, scrutinize.

рассмея́ться, *v. perf.* begin to laugh; burst out laughing.

рассо́л, *m.* pickle.

расспра́шивать, *v. imp.* (*perf.* расспроси́ть), question; make inquiries (about).

рассро́чка, *f.* instalment.

расстава́ться, *v. imp.* (*perf.* расста́ться), *intr.*, part; separate.

расставля́ть, *v. imp.* (*perf.*

расста́вить), place, arrange; set; move apart.

расстёгивать, *v. imp.* (*perf.* расстегну́ть), undo, unbutton, unhook.

расстоя́ние, *nt.* distance.

расстра́ивать, *v. imp.* (*perf.* расстро́ить), disturb; put out of tune; cause indigestion.

расстро́енный, *adj.* upset; out of tune.

расстро́йство, *nt.* disorder.

рассуди́тельный, *adj.* reasonable; sensible.

рассу́док, *m.* reason; sense.

рассужда́ть, *v. imp.* (*perf.* рассуди́ть), discuss; reason.

рассчи́тывать, *v. imp.* (*perf.* рассчита́ть), calculate, reckon; intend.

рассыпа́ть, *v. imp.* (*perf.* рассы́пать), spill; scatter.

раста́ять, *v.*, *perf. of* та́ять.

раство́р, *m.* solution. -и́мый, *adj.* soluble.

растворя́ть, *v. imp.* (*perf.* раствори́ть), *tr.*, dissolve; open.

расте́ние, *nt.* plant.

растеря́нный, *adj.* confused; embarrassed.

растеря́ть, *v. perf.* lose.

расти́, *v. imp.*, *intr.*, grow; increase.

расти́тельность, *f.* vegetation.

расти́ть, *v. imp.* raise, grow, rear, bring up; cultivate.

растоло́чь, *v. perf.* grind; pound.

расторга́ть, *v. imp.* (*perf.* расто́ргнуть), dissolve; cancel, annul.

расторже́ние, *nt.* dissolution; cancellation.

расторо́пный, *adj.* quick; prompt.

расточа́ть, *v. imp.* waste; dissipate; lavish (on).

растра́та, *f.* embezzlement.

растра́тить, *v. perf.* embezzle.

растрёпанный, *adj.* tousled.

растро́гивать, *v. imp.* (*perf.* растро́гать), move, touch.

растя́гивать, *v. imp.* (*perf.* растяну́ть), stretch; prolong.

растяжение, *nt.* stretching; tension.

расхищать, *v. imp.* (*perf.* **расхитить**), plunder.

расход, *m.* expenditure.

расходиться, *v. imp.* (*perf.* **разойтись**), break up; separate; diverge.

расходовать, *v. imp.* (*perf.* **израсходовать**), spend.

расхождение, *nt.* divergence.

расхохотаться, *v. perf.* burst into laughter.

расцвет, *m.* prosperity; blossoming.

расцветать, *v. imp.* (*perf.* **расцвести**), blossom out; flourish.

расценивать, *v. imp.* (*perf.* **расценить**), estimate, value; consider.

расценка, *f.* evaluation; valuation.

расчёсывать, *v. imp.* (*perf.* **расчесать**), comb; comb out.

расчёт, *m.* calculation.

-ливый, *adj.* economical; prudent.

расчленять, *v. imp.* (*perf.* **расчленить**), dismember.

расшивать, *v. imp.* (*perf.* **расшить**), embroider.

расширение, *nt.* widening.

расширять, *v. imp.* (*perf.* **расширить**), widen; enlarge; extend.

расшифровывать, *v. imp.* (*perf.* **расшифровать**), decipher.

расщепление, *nt.* splitting; splintering.

ратификация, *f.* ratification.

рационализировать, *v. imp.* rationalize.

рациональный, *adj.* rational.

рвать, *v. imp.*, *tr.*, tear, rend; pick, pluck, pull.

рвение, *nt.* zeal; ardor.

рвота, *f.* vomiting.

рвотный, *adj.* emetic.

реабилитировать, *v. imp.* & *perf.* rehabilitate.

реагировать, *v. imp.* react; respond.

реакционный, *adj.* reactionary.

реальность, *f.* reality.

ребёнок, *m.* child; baby.

ребро, *nt.* rib; edge.

ребята, *pl.* children; boys.

ребячество, *nt.* childishness.

рёв, *m.* roar, bellow.

реветь, *v. imp.* roar, bellow; weep, howl.

ревизия, *f.* inspection; revision.

ревматизм, *m.* rheumatism.

ревнивый, *adj.* jealous.

ревновать, *v. imp.* be jealous.

ревностный, *adj.* zealous; ardent.

ревность, *adj.* jealousy.

революционер, *m.* revolutionary.

революция, *f.* revolution.

регистрировать, *v. imp.* (*perf.* **зарегистрировать**), *tr.*, register.

регулировать, *v. imp.* regulate.

регулярный, *adj.* regular.

регулятор, *m.* regulator.

редактировать, *v. imp.* edit.

редактор, *m.* editor.

редакция, *f.* editorial office(s).

редиска, *f.* radish.

редкий, *adj.* rare.

редко, *adv.* rarely, seldom.

редька, *f.* radish.

режим, *m.* regime.

режиссёр, *m.* director; producer.

резать, *v. imp.* cut; carve.

резвый, *adj.* playful.

резерв, *m.* reserve.

резина, *f.* rubber.

резинка, *f.* elastic; eraser; gum.

резиновый, *adj.* rubber.

резкий, *adj.* harsh; biting, sharp.

резня, *f.* slaughter.

резолюция, *f.* resolution.

результат, *m.* result.

резьба, *f.* carving.

рейс, *m.* trip, voyage.

река, *f.* river.

реквизировать, *v. imp.* requisition.

реклама, *f.* advertisement; publicity.

рекламировать, *v. imp.* advertise; publicize.

рекомендательный, *adj.* introduction, introductory.

рекомендовать, v. imp. recommend. -ся, recommend oneself; be advisable.

реконструкция, f. reconstruction.

рекорд, m. record.

религиозный, adj. religious.

религия, f. religion.

рельс, m. rail.

ремень, m. strap; belt.

ремесленник, m. artisan; handicraftsman.

ремесленный, adj. vocational; industrial.

ремесло, nt. trade; handicraft.

ремонт, m. repair; overhaul.

ремонтировать, v. imp. repair; overhaul.

реорганизовать, v. imp. reorganize.

репа, f. turnip.

репетиция, f. rehearsal.

репортёр, m. reporter.

репрессия, f. repression.

репродуктор, m. loudspeaker.

репутация, f. reputation.

ресница, f. eyelash.

республика, f. republic.

рессора, f. spring.

ресторан, m. restaurant.

ресурсы, pl. resources.

ретивый, adj. zealous.

ретуширование, nt. retouching.

реферат, m. essay, paper, lecture.

реформа, f. reform.

рецензия, f. review; criticism.

рецепт, m. prescription; recipe.

речка, f. river.

речной, adj. river.

речь, f. speech.

решать, v. imp. (perf. решить), decide; solve.

решающий, adj. decisive.

решение, nt. decision; solution.

решётка, f. grating; lattice.

решето, nt. sieve.

решимость, f. resolution.

решительный, adj. decisive; resolute.

решка, f. tails.

ржа (also ржавчина), f. rust. -вый, adj. rusty.

ржаветь, v. imp. rust.

ржаной, adj. rye.

ржать, v. imp. neigh.

Рим, m. Rome.

римский, adj. Roman.

рис, m. rice.

риск, m. risk.

рисковать, v. imp. (perf. рискнуть), risk.

рисование, nt. drawing.

рисовать, v. imp. (perf. нарисовать), draw; depict.

рисунок, m. drawing.

ритм, m. rhythm. -ический adj. rhythmical.

риторика, f. rhetoric.

риф, m. (geog.) reef.

рифма, f. rhyme.

рициновое масло, castor oil.

робкий, adj. timid, shy.

ров, m. ditch.

ровесник, m. contemporary.

ровно, adv. equally; evenly exactly.

ровный, adj. flat, even; equal

рог, m. horn, antler. -атый adj. horned.

род, m. kin, family stock sort, kind; (gram.) gender -ом, adv. by birth.

родина, f. native land, home land.

родители, pl. parents.

родительный, adj. (gram.) genitive.

родительский, adj. parental

родить(ся), v., perf. of рождать(ся).

родник, m. spring.

родной, adj. own; native.

родия, f. (coll.) relatives.

родовой, adj. ancestral.

родоначальник, m. ancestor forefather.

родословный, adj. genealogical.

родственник, m. relative, relation.

родственный, adj. kindred related.

родство, nt. relationship, kinship.

роды, pl. childbirth.

роение, nt. swarming.

рождаемость, f. birthrate.

рожда́ть, v. imp. (perf. роди́ть) give birth (to). -ся, be born.

рожде́ние, nt. birth.

рождество́, nt. Christmas.

рожь, f. rye.

ро́за, f. rose.

розмари́н, m. rosemary.

ро́зница, f. retail.

ро́зничный, adj. retail.

рознь, f. difference.

ро́зовый, adj. pink, rose-colored.

рой, m. swarm.

рок, m. fate. -ово́й, adj. fatal.

ро́кот, m. roar, rumble.

роль, f. role, part.

ром, m. rum.

рома́н, m. novel. -и́ческий, adj. romantic.

рома́нс, m. song; romance.

роня́ть, v. imp. (perf. урони́ть), drop; shed.

ро́пот, m. murmur; grumble.

ропта́ть, v. imp. murmur.

роса́, f. dew.

ро́скошь, f. luxury.

Росси́я, f. Russia.

рост, m. growth, increase, rise; height, stature.

рот, m. mouth.

ро́ща, f. grove.

роя́ль, m. (grand) piano.

РСФСР, abbr. of Росси́йская Сове́тская Федерати́вная Социалисти́ческая Респу́блика.

ртуть, f. mercury.

руба́ха, f. shirt.

руба́шка, f. shirt; chemise.

рубе́ж, m. boundary, border. за рубежо́м, abroad.

руби́н, m. ruby.

руби́ть, v. imp. fell, chop, hack.

рубль, m. ruble.

ру́бчатый, adj. ribbed.

ру́гань, f. abuse, swearing.

руга́тельство, nt. curse, swearing, oath.

руга́ть, v. imp. (perf. вы́ругать), scold, abuse, curse.

руда́, f. ore.

рудни́к, m. mine, pit.

ружьё, nt. gun; arms.

рука́, f. hand; handwriting. по́д руку, arm-in-arm.

рука́в, m. sleeve. -и́ца, f. mitten.

руководи́ть, v. imp. lead. -ся, follow; be guided (by).

руково́дство, nt. guidance, leadership.

руково́дствоваться, v. imp. follow; be guided (by).

ру́копись, f. manuscript.

рукоплеска́ть, v. imp. applaud, clap.

рукопожа́тие, nt. handshake.

рукоя́тка, f. handle; hilt.

рулево́е колесо́, f. steering wheel.

руле́тка, f. tape measure; roulette.

руль, m. rudder; helm.

румы́н, m., -ка f., Rumanian.

Румы́ния, f. Rumania.

румя́на, pl. rouge.

румя́нец, m. blush; flush.

румя́нить, v. imp. apply rouge.

румя́ный, adj. rosy, rubicund.

руса́к, m. hare.

руса́лка, f. mermaid.

ру́сло, nt. channel, riverbed.

ру́сский m., ру́сская f., Russian. — adj. Russian.

ру́сый, adj. light brown.

рути́на, f. routine.

ру́хнуть, v. perf. crash, tumble, collapse.

руча́тельство, nt. guaranty.

руча́ться, v. imp. (perf. поручи́ться), warrant; guarantee.

руче́й, m. brook, stream.

ру́чка, f. handle; knob.

ручно́й, adj. hand; manual; portable.

ры́ба, f. fish.

рыба́к, m. fisherman.

ры́бий, adj. fish.

рыга́ть, v. imp. (perf. рыгну́ть), belch.

рыда́ть, v. imp. sob.

ры́жий, adj. red; red-haired; ginger.

рыка́ть, v. imp. (perf. рыкну́ть), roar.

ры́ло, nt. snout.

ры́нок, m. marketplace.

рыса́к, m. trotter.

рысь, m. lynx; trot. -ю, adv. at a trot.

рыть, *v. imp.* dig, mine, burrow.

ры́царство, *tn.* knighthood; chivalry.

ры́царь, *m.* knight.

рыча́г, *m.* lever.

рыча́ть, *v. imp.* (*perf.* **про-рыча́ть**), growl; snarl.

рю́мка, *f.* wine *or* liqueur glass.

рябо́й, *adj.* pitted, pocked, pock-marked.

рябь, *f.* ripple(s).

ряд, *m.* row; line; series, number. **—овóй,** *adj.* ordinary, common. **—** *m.* (*mil.*) private. **-ом,** *adv.* side by side; next (to).

С

с (со), *prep.* (+ *gen.*) from; since; (+ *acc.*) about, approximately; (+ *instr.*) with.

са́бля, *f.* saber.

саботи́ровать, *v. imp. & perf.* sabotage.

сагити́ровать, *v., perf.* of **агити́ровать.**

сад, *m.* garden. де́тский сад, Kindergarten.

сади́ть, *v. imp.* (*perf.* посади́ть), plant. **-ся,** *v. imp.* (*perf.* сесть), sit down; board.

са́жа, *f.* soot.

сажа́ть, *v. imp.* (*perf.* посади́ть), seat.

сала́т, *m.* lettuce, salad.

са́ло, *nt.* fat; suet.

салфе́тка, *f.* napkin.

сам, *m.,* **сама́** *f.,* **само́** *nt.,* **са́ми** *pl.,* *pron.* oneself.

саме́ц, *m.* male.

са́мка, *f.* female.

само-, *prefix,* self-.

самова́р, *m.* samovar.

самоде́ятельный, *adj.* independent; amateur.

самолёт, *m.* aeroplane.

самолюби́вый, *adj.* proud; self-esteeming.

самомне́ние, *nt.* conceit, self-importance.

самоопределе́ние, *nt.* self-determination.

самоотве́рженный, *adj.* selfless.

самопоже́ртвование, *nt.* self-sacrifice.

самопроизво́льно, *adv.* spontaneously.

саморо́дный, *adj.* native; virgin.

самостоя́тельный, *adj.* independent.

самоуби́йство, *nt.* suicide.

са́мый, *pron.* the very. тот же са́мый, the very same.

санато́рий, *m.* sanitarium.

са́ни, *pl.* sleigh.

санита́р, *m.* hospital attendant *or* orderly. **-ный,** *adj.* sanitary.

санкциони́ровать, *v. imp. & perf.* sanction.

сантиме́тр, *m.* centimeter.

Са́ня, *dim.* of **Алекса́ндр, Алекса́ндра.**

сапо́г, *m.* boot.

сара́й, *m.* shed; barn.

саранча́, *f.* locust.

сарди́нка, *f.* sardine.

са́хар, *m.* sugar. **-ница,** *f.* sugarbowl. **-ный,** *adj.* sugar.

Са́ша (also Са́ш(ень)ка), *dim.* of **Алекса́ндр, Алекса́ндра.**

сберега́ть, *v. imp.* (*perf.* сбере́чь), save; preserve.

сближа́ть, *v. imp.* (*perf.* сбли́зить), *tr.,* draw *or* bring together. **-ся,** *intr.,* approach; draw near.

сближе́ние, *nt.* rapprochement.

сбо́ку, *adv.* from one side; on one side.

сбор, *m.* collection; harvest; vintage. **-ник,** *m.* collection.

сва́дьба, *f.* wedding.

сва́ривать, *v. imp.* (*perf.* свари́ть), weld.

свари́ть, *v., perf.* of **вари́ть, сва́ривать.**

сва́рка, *f.* welding.

сва́я, *f.* pile.

све́дение, *nt.* information; intelligence; knowledge.

све́дение, *nt.* reduction; (*med.*) cramp; contraction.

све́жесть, *f.* freshness.

све́жий, *adj.* fresh.

свёкла, *f.* beet.

свёкор, *m.* father-in-law (*husband's father*).

свекро́вь, *f.* mother-in-law (*husband's mother*).

сверже́ние, *nt.* overthrow; dethronement.

сверка́ть, *v. imp.* (*perf.* сверкну́ть), sparkle; twinkle.

сверло́, *nt.* drill, bore, perforator.

сверх, *prep.* (+ *gen.*) beyond; above; over. сверх того́, moreover.

све́рху, *adv.* from above, from the top.

сверхъесте́ственный, *adj.* supernatural.

свести́, *v.*, *perf. of* своди́ть.

свет, *m.* light; world; society. -и́ло, *nt.* luminary. -лый, *adj.* light. -ский, *adj.* secular, temporal.

света́ть, *v. imp.* begin to dawn.

свети́ть, *v. imp.* shine; give off light.

свеча́ (*also* све́чка), *f.* candle.

свиде́тель, *m.* witness. -ство, *nt.* evidence; certificate.

свиде́тельствовать, *v. imp.* (*perf.* засвиде́тельствовать), witness; testify. — (*perf.* освиде́тельствовать), examine, inspect.

свине́ц, *m.* (*metal*) lead.

свини́на, *f.* pork.

сви́нка, *f.* mumps.

свинцо́вый, *adj.* (*metal*) lead.

свинья́, *f.* pig.

свире́пый, *adj.* fierce, ferocious.

свист, *m.* (*sound*) whistle.

свиста́ть, свисте́ть, *v. imp.* whistle; sing.

свисто́к, *m.* whistle.

свить(ся), *v.*, *perf. of* вить(ся).

свобо́да, *f.* freedom, liberty.

свобо́дный, *adj.* free; vacant; loose; spare.

свод, *m.* arch, vault; code.

своди́ть, *v. imp.* (*perf.* свести́), bring together; remove.

сво́дный, *adj.* summary. сво́дный брат, step-brother.

своевре́менный, *adj.* timely, opportune.

своеобра́зный, *adj.* original; distinctive.

свой, *pron.* one's own.

сво́йство, *nt.* property, characteristic.

связа́ть, *v.*, *perf. of* вяза́ть, свя́зывать.

связа́нный, *adj.* connected, coherent.

свя́зывать, *v. imp.* (*perf.* связа́ть), tie, bind, connect.

связь, *f.* tie, bond, connection.

свя́тки, *pl.* yuletide.

свято́й, *adj.* holy, sacred.

свяще́нный, *adj.* sacred.

сгиб, *m.* bend.

сгиба́ть, *v. imp.* (*perf.* согну́ть), *tr.*, bend; curve.

сгни́ть, *v.*, *perf. of* гнить.

сгова́риваться, *v. imp.* (*perf.* сговори́ться), make arrangements; come to an agreement.

сгора́ние, *nt.* combustion.

сгора́ть, *v. imp.* (*perf.* сгоре́ть), burn down; burn, be consumed.

сгруппирова́ть, *v.*, *perf. of* группирова́ть.

сгущённый, *adj.* condensed; evaporated.

сдава́ть, *v. imp.* (*perf.* сдать), pass *or* hand in; surrender, yield; deal (*cards*); give change.

сда́ча, *f.* surrender; (*cards*) deal; (*money*) change.

сде́лать(ся), *v.*, *perf. of* де́лать(ся).

сде́ржанный, *adj.* reserved; discreet.

сде́рживать, *v. imp.* (*perf.* сдержа́ть), restrain, hold in, keep back; keep, fulfill.

сеа́нс, *m.* seance; performance; sitting.

себесто́имость, *f.* cost, price.

себя́, *refl. pron.* oneself.

сев, *m.* sowing.

се́вер, *m.* north. -ный, *adj.*

north, northern. -**я́нин** *m.*, -**я́нка** *f.*, northerner.
Се́верный Ледови́тый океа́н, Arctic Ocean.
сего́дня, *adv.* today. -**шний,** *adj.* today's.
седина́, *f.* grey hair.
седло́, *nt.* saddle.
седо́й, *adj.* grey.
седьмо́й, *adj.* seventh.
сезо́н, *m.* season, -**ный,** *adj.* seasonal.
сей *m.,* **сия́** *f.,* **сие́** *nt.,* **сии́** *pl.,* *pron.* this.
сейча́с, *adv.* now, at once.
секре́т, *m.* secret. -**ный,** *adj.* secret.
секретариа́т, *m.* secretariat.
секрета́рь *m.,* **секрета́рша** *f.,* secretary.
секу́нда, *f.* second.
се́кция, *f.* section.
селёдка, *f.* herring.
село́, *nt.* village.
сельдере́й, *m.* celery.
сельдь, *f.* herring.
се́льский, *adj.* rural; village. **се́льское хозя́йство,** agriculture.
сельскохозя́йственный, *adj.* agricultural.
сельсове́т, *abbr. of* **се́льский сове́т.**
сёмга, *f.* salmon.
семе́йный, *adj.* domestic family.
семе́йство, *nt.* family.
се́меро, *num. coll.* seven.
семидеся́тый, *adj.* seventieth.
семисо́тый, *adj.* seven hundredth.
семна́дцатый, *adj.* seventeenth.
семна́дцать, *num.* seventeen.
семь, *num.* seven.
се́мьдесят, *num.* seventy.
семьсо́т, *num.* seven hundred.
семья́, *f.* family.
се́мя, *nt.* seed; semen.
Се́на, *f.* Seine (*river*).
се́но, *nt.* hay.
сентя́брь, *m.* September. -**ский,** *adj.* September.
Сёнька (*also* **Се́ня**)*, dim. of* **Симео́н.**
се́ра, *f.* sulphur.

серде́чный, *adj.* heart; tender, cordial.
серди́тый, *adj.* angry.
серди́ть, *v. imp.* anger.
сердобо́льный, *adj.* tenderhearted.
се́рдце, *m.* heart. -**бие́ние,** *nt.* palpitation.
серебро́, *nt.* silver.
сере́бряный, *adj.* silver.
середи́на, *f.* middle.
Серёжа (*also* **Серёж(ень)ка**)*, dim. of name* **Серге́й.**
се́рия, *f.* series.
серова́тый, *adj.* greyish.
серп, *m.* sickle.
се́рый, *adj.* grey.
серьга́, *f.* earring.
серьёзный, *adj.* serious; earnest.
се́ссия, *f.* session.
сестра́, *f.* sister. **медици́нская сестра́,** nurse.
сесть, *v.,* *perf. of* **сади́ться.**
се́тка (*also* **сеть**)*, f.* net; system.
сечь, *v. imp.* flog, whip.
се́ять, *v. imp.* (*perf.* **посе́ять**), sow.
сжа́литься, *v. perf.* take pity on *or* upon.
сжа́тие, *nt.* pressure. pressing; compression.
сжать, *v.,* *perf. of* **сжима́ть,** **жать.**
сжечь, *v. perf. of* **жечь.**
сжима́ть, *v. imp.* (*perf.* **сжать**), press, squeeze; condense.
сза́ди, *adv.* from behind.
Сиби́рь, *f.* Siberia.
сига́ра, *f.* cigar.
сиде́ть, *v. imp.* sit, be seated, perch.
си́ла, *f.* strength, power.
си́лос, *m.* silo.
си́льный, *adj.* strong.
симпати́ческий, *adj.* sympathetic.
синева́тый, *adj.* bluish.
си́ний, *adj.* blue.
синя́к, *m.* bruise.
сире́на, *f.* siren.
сире́нь, *f.* lilac.
сирота́, *f.* orphan.

систе́ма, f. system. -ти́ческий, adj. systematic.

сия́ние, nt. radiance.

сия́ть, v. imp. shine, beam.

сказа́ние, nt. story; legend.

ска́зка, f. tale, story.

сказа́ть, v., perf. of говори́ть.

сказу́емое, nt. (gram.) predicate.

скака́ть, v. imp. (perf. поскака́ть), skip, jump; gallop.

скала́, f. rock.

скали́стый, adj. rocky.

ска́лывать, v. imp. (perf. сколо́ть), split or chop off; pin together.

скаме́йка, f. bench.

скамья́, f. bench.

сканда́л, m. scandal.

скат, m. slope, slant.

ска́терть, f. tablecloth.

ска́тывать, v. imp. (perf. скати́ть), roll or slide down.

скачо́к, m. jump, leap.

скве́рный, adj. nasty.

сквозь, prep. (+ acc.) through.

скеле́т, m. skeleton.

ски́дка, f. deduction, rebate.

склад, m. storehouse; constitution.

скла́дка, f. fold, crease, pleat. складно́й, adj. collapsible, folding.

скла́дывать, v. imp. (perf. сложи́ть), fold, fold up; compose; pack up.

склеи́ть, v., perf. of клеи́ть.

склон, m. slope. -е́ние, nt. declination; (gram.) declension. -ный, adj. inclined, disposed. -я́емый, adj. (gram.) declinable. -я́ть, v. imp. (perf. склони́ть), decline.

ско́бка, f. bracket, parenthesis.

ско́вывать, v. imp. (perf. скова́ть), forge.

сколо́ть, v., perf. of ска́лывать.

скользи́ть, v. imp. (perf. скользну́ть), slip, slide.

ско́льзкий, adj. slippery.

ско́лько, adv. how much or many.

ско́лько-нибудь, adv. any.

скомпромети́ровать, v., perf. of компромети́ровать.

сконфу́зить, v., perf. of конфу́зить.

сконча́ться, v. perf. pass away, die.

скопле́ние, nt. accumulation.

ско́рбный, adj. sorrowful, sad.

скорбь, f. sorrow, grief.

скорлупа́, f. shell.

ско́ро, adv. quickly; soon. -сть, f. speed.

ско́рый, adj. quick, fast.

коси́ть, v., perf. of коси́ть.

скот, m. (coll.) cattle.

скра́дывать, v. imp. (perf. скрасть), conceal.

скрепля́ть, v. imp. (perf. скрепи́ть), fasten together; strengthen.

скриви́ть, v. perf. bend; distort.

скрип, m. squeak.

скрипа́ч, m. violinist.

скрипе́ть, v. imp. (perf. проскрипе́ть), squeak.

скри́пка, f. violin.

скрои́ть, v., perf. of крои́ть.

скро́мный, adj. modest.

скрыва́ть, v. imp. (perf. скрыть), hide, conceal.

скры́тый, adj. reserved; secretive.

скрю́чиваться, v. imp. huddle.

ску́дный, adj. scanty, sparse.

ску́ка, f. boredom, tedium.

культу́ра, f. sculpture.

скупо́й, adj. stingy.

скуча́ть, v. imp. be bored.

ску́чный, adj. boring, tedious.

слабе́ть, v. imp. (perf. ослабе́ть), weaken, grow weak.

слаби́тельное, nt. laxative, purge.

сла́бый, adj. weak.

сла́ва, f. fame; glory.

сла́вить, v. imp. (perf. просла́вить), glorify.

сла́вный, adj. glorious, famous.

славяни́н m., славя́нка f., Slav.

сла́дкий, adj. sweet. сла́дкое блю́до, dessert.

сладостра́стный, adj. voluptuous.

сла́дость, *f.* sweetness.

сла́сти, *pl.* sweets.

сле́ва, *adv.* from the left.

слегка́, *adv.* somewhat.

след, *m.* trace; track; sign.

следи́ть, *v. imp.* watch; spy on *or* upon; follow, shadow.

сле́дователь, *m.* investigator.

сле́довательно, *adv.* consequently; therefore.

сле́довать, *v. imp.* (*perf.* после́довать), follow; come next; take after.

сле́дствие, *nt.* consequence.

сле́дующий, *adj.* next, following.

слеза́, *f.* tear.

слеза́ть, *v. imp.* (*perf.* слезть), get down *or* off.

слепе́ц, *m.* blind man.

слепи́ть, *v., perf. of* лепи́ть.

сле́пнуть, *v. imp.* (*perf.* осле́пнуть), become blind.

слепо́й, *adj.* blind.

слепота́, *f.* blindness.

сли́ва, *f.* plum.

слива́ть, *v. imp.* (*perf.* слить), pour out *or* off.

сли́вки, *pl.* cream.

слизь, *f.* mucus; slime.

сли́тный, *adj.* conjunct, conjunctional.

слить, *v., perf. of* слива́ть.

слича́ть, *v. imp.* (*perf.* сличи́ть), collate.

сли́шком, *adv.* too.

слия́ние, *nt.* confluence, junction; blending, merging.

слова́рь, *m.* dictionary; glossary, vocabulary.

слове́сный, *adj.* verbal, oral.

сло́во, *nt.* word. сло́во в сло́во, word for word.

сло́вом, *adv.* in short.

слог, *m.* syllable; style.

сложе́ние, *nt.* composition, constitution.

сложи́ть, *v., perf. of* скла́дывать.

сло́жный, *adj.* complex, complicated; compound.

слой, *m.* layer.

слома́ть, *v., perf. of* лома́ть.

слон, *m.* elephant.

слуга́, *f.* servant.

слу́жащий, *adj.* serving. — *m.* employee.

слу́жба, *f.* service; work.

служе́бный, *adj.* service; functional; auxiliary.

служи́ть, *v. imp.* (*perf.* послужи́ть), serve.

слух, *m.* hearing; rumor.

слу́чай, *m.* case; occasion, chance; event, incident. -но, *adv.* accidentally, by chance.

случи́ть, *v. imp.* (*perf.* случи́ть), couple, pair. -ся, happen, occur.

слу́шание, *nt.* audition, hearing.

слу́шать, *v. imp.* (*perf.* послу́шать), listen, hear; attend. -ся, obey; be heard; be listened to.

слыха́ть, *v. imp.* hear about *or* of.

слы́шать, *v. imp.* (*perf.* услы́шать), hear; hear of.

слы́шимый, *adj.* audible.

слюна́, *f.* saliva.

сме́шанный, *adj.* mixed; hybrid; compound.

сме́шивать, *v. imp.* (*perf.* сме́шать), *tr.*, mix, blend; confuse.

смеши́ть, *v. imp.* cause to laugh.

смешли́вый, *adj.* given to laughter.

смешно́й, *adj.* funny, ludicrous, ridiculous.

смеща́ть, *v. imp.* (*perf.* смести́ть), *v. imp.* displace; remove.

смея́ться, *v. imp.* chuckle, laugh; над + *instr.* laugh at.

смире́нный, *adj.* humble; meek; submissive.

сми́рно, *adv.* quietly; (*mil.*) attention!

сми́рный, *adj.* quiet; mild.

смиря́ть, *v. imp.* (*perf.* смири́ть), restrain; subdue.

смола́, *f.* resin; tar.

смоли́стый, *adj.* resinous.

смолка́ть, *v. imp.* (*perf.* смо́лкнуть), become *or* grow silent.

смоло́ть, *v., perf. of* моло́ть.

смонти́ровать, v., perf. of **монти́ровать**.

сморка́ться, v. imp. (perf. **вы́сморкаться**), blow one's nose.

сморо́дина, f. (coll.) currants.

смо́рщить, v., perf. of **мо́рщить**.

смотр, m. review.

смотре́ть, v. imp. (perf. **посмотре́ть**), look, look at; examine; look through.

смочи́ть, v., perf. of **сма́чивать**.

смочь, v., perf. of **мочь**.

смошённичать, v., perf. of **мошённичать**.

сму́глый, adj. dark-skinned.

сму́тный, adj. vague; dim.

смуща́ть, v. imp. (perf. **смути́ть**), confuse; embarrass; trouble.

смуще́ние, nt. confusion; embarrassment.

смысл, m. sense, meaning; purport.

смягча́ть, v. imp. (perf. **смягчи́ть**), tr., soften; mollify; relax; (phon.) palatalize.

смять, v. perf. rumple, crush, crumple.

снабжа́ть, v. imp. (perf. **снабди́ть**), supply, provide, furnish.

снабже́ние, nt. supply, provision.

снаружи́, adv. from the outside.

снача́ла, adv. at first; firstly; all over again.

снег, m. snow.

сне́жный, adj. snow, snowy.

снести́, v., perf. of **нести́**, **сноси́ть**. **-сь**, v., perf. of **нести́сь**.

снижа́ть, v. imp. (perf. **сни́зить**), lower, reduce, decrease.

снизойти́, v. perf. of **снисходи́ть**.

сни́зу, adv. from below, from the bottom.

снима́ть, v. imp. (perf. **снять**), take away or off; take down; photograph.

сни́мок, m. photograph.

снисходи́ть, v. imp. (perf. **снизойти́**), condescend.

снисхожде́ние, nt. condescension.

сни́ться, v. imp. (perf. **присни́ться**), impers. (with dat.) dream, have a dream: мне сни́лось, I had a dream.

сно́ва, adv. anew; again.

сноси́ть, v. imp. (perf. **снести́**), take down; demolish; discard; bring together.

сно́сный, adj. tolerable.

сноха́, f. daughter-in-law.

сноше́ния, nt. intercourse, dealings.

снять, v., perf. of **снима́ть**.

со, see **с**.

соба́ка, f. dog.

соба́чий, adj. canine, dog's.

собира́тельный, adj. (gram.) collective.

собира́ть, v. imp. (perf. **собра́ть**), gather; collect. **-ся**, intend.

соблазни́тельный, adj. seductive; tempting.

соблазня́ть, v. imp. (perf. **соблазни́ть**), entice, lure, tempt; seduce.

соблюда́ть, v. imp. (perf. **соблюсти́**), observe.

соблюде́ние, nt. observance; maintenance.

со́боль, m. sable.

собо́р, m. cathedral.

собра́ние, nt. meeting, gathering; collection.

собра́т, m. fellow.

собра́ть(ся), v., perf. of **собира́ть(ся)**.

со́бственность, f. property.

со́бственный, adj. own; personal.

собы́тие, nt. event.

сова́, f. owl.

соревнова́ние, nt. competition.

соверша́ть, v. imp. (perf. **соверши́ть**), accomplish; perform; commit.

соверше́ние, nt. accomplishment, fulfillment; perpetration.

соверше́нно, adv. completely,

absolutely. -ле́тний, *adj.* of, age, adult.

соверше́нный, *adj.* complete, absolute; perfect; (*gram.*) perfective.

соверше́нствовать, *v. imp.* (*perf.* усоверше́нствовать), perfect.

соверши́ть, *v.*, *perf. of* соверша́ть.

со́вестливый, *adj.* conscientious.

со́весть, *f.* conscience.

сове́т, *m.* Soviet; council; advice, counsel. -ник. *m.* counselor, adviser. -ский, *adj.* Soviet.

сове́товать, *v. imp.* advise. -ся, consult.

совеща́ние, *nt.* conference.

совеща́ться, *v. imp.* deliberate.

Совинформбюро́, *abbr. of* Сове́тское Информацио́нное Бюро́, Soviet Information Bureau.

совмести́мый, *adj.* compatible.

совме́стный, *adj.* common, joint, combined.

Совнарко́м, *abbr. of* Сове́т Наро́дных Комисса́ров, Council of People's Commissars.

совокупле́ние, *nt.* copulation.

совоку́пный, *adj.* aggregate, combined, total.

совпада́ть, *v. imp.* (*perf.* совпа́сть), coincide.

совпаде́ние, *nt.* coincidence.

совра́ть, *v.*, *perf. of* врать.

совраща́ть, *v. imp.* (*perf.* соврати́ть), seduce.

совреме́нник, *m.* contemporary.

совреме́нный, *adj.* contemporary; modern.

совсе́м, *adv.* completely, quite.

совхо́з, *m.* State farm.

согла́сие, *nt.* agreement, consent.

согла́сно, *adv.* in accord *or* agreement. — *prep.* (с + *instr.*) in accordance (with).

согла́сный, *adj.* agreeable. — *m.* consonant.

согласова́ние, *nt.* agreement, concordance.

согласо́вывать, *v. imp.* (*perf.* согласова́ть), coordinate.

соглаша́ться, *v. imp.* (*perf.* согласи́ться), agree.

соглаше́ние, *nt.* understanding; consent; agreement.

согну́ть, *v.*, *perf. of* гну́ть, сгиба́ть.

соде́йствовать, *v. imp.* assist.

содержа́тельность, *f.* pithiness

содержа́ть, *v. imp.* contain; maintain, keep, support.

содру́жество, *nt.* concord; collaboration.

соедине́ние, *nt.* combination, junction.

соединя́ть, *v. imp.* (*perf.* соедини́ть), *tr.*, join, unite; connect.

сожале́ние, *nt.* regret.

сожале́ть, *v. imp.* regret; be sorry.

сожже́ние, *nt.* cremation, burning.

созва́ть, *v. perf.* convoke; summon.

созве́здие, *nt.* constellation.

созву́чие, *nt.* accord.

создава́ть, *v. imp.* (*perf.* созда́ть), create.

созда́ние, *nt.* creation.

созерца́ть, *v. imp.* contemplate.

сознава́ть, *v. imp.* (*perf.* созна́ть), be conscious of; realize; recognize.

созна́ние, *nt.* consciousness; confession; acknowledgement.

созна́тельный, *adj.* conscious; deliberate.

созрева́ть, *v. imp.* (*perf.* созре́ть), ripen.

сойти́(сь), *v.*, *perf. of* сходи́ть(ся).

сок, *m.* juice, sap.

со́кол, *m.* falcon.

сокраща́ть, *v. imp.* (*perf.* сократи́ть), shorten; abbreviate.

сокраще́ние, *nt.* abbreviation; shortening.

сокрове́нный, *adj.* concealed; secret; innermost.

сокро́вище, *nt.* treasure.

сокруша́ть, *v.*, (*perf.* **сокруши́ть**), distress.

сокруше́ние, *nt.* destruction.

сокры́тый, *adj.* concealed; secret.

солга́ть, *v.*, *perf. of* **лга́ть**.

солда́т, *m.* soldier.

солёный, *adj.* salty, salt, saline.

соле́нье, *nt.* pickled food(s).

соли́дный, *adj.* solid; reliable.

соли́ст *m.*, **-ка** *f.*, soloist.

соли́ть, *v.* imp. (*perf.* **посоли́ть**), salt; pickle.

со́лнечный, *adj.* solar, sun; sunny.

со́лнце, *nt.* sun. **-стоя́ние**, *nt.* solstice.

солове́й, *m.* nightingale.

соло́ма, *f.* straw.

соло́нка, *f.* salt shaker.

соль, *f.* salt.

сомнева́ться, *v. imp.* doubt, have doubts.

сомне́ние, *nt.* doubt.

сомни́тельный, *adj.* doubtful, dubious.

сон, *m.* sleep; dream. **-ный**, *adj.* sleepy; sleeping.

Со́нька (*also* **Со́нюшка, Со́ня**) *dim. of* **Со́фья**.

соображать, *v. imp.* (*perf.* **сообрази́ть**), consider, ponder; grasp, understand.

сообра́зный, *adj.* consistent (with).

сообща́, *adv.* together.

сообща́ть, *v. imp.* (*perf.* **сообщи́ть**), announce, inform; communicate.

соотве́тсвенно, *adv.* accordingly.

соотве́тственный, *adj.* corresponding.

соотве́тствие, *nt.* accordance, conformity.

соотве́тствовать, *v. imp.* correspond (to).

соотéчественник, *m.* compatriot.

соотноси́тельный, *adj.* correlative.

соотноше́ние, *nt.* correlation.

сопе́рник, *m.* rival; competitor.

сопе́рничать, *v. imp.* compete (with).

сопоставля́ть, *v. imp.* (*perf.* **сопоста́вить**), compare.

соприкоснове́ние, *nt.* contact.

сопроводи́тельный, *adj.* accompanying.

сопровожда́ть, *v. imp.* (*perf.* **сопроводи́ть**), accompany.

сопротивля́ться, *v. imp.* resist.

сопу́тствовать, *v. imp.* accompany.

сор, *m.* litter.

сорва́ть(ся), *v.*, *perf. of* **срыва́ть(ся)**.

соревнова́ться, *v. imp.* compete.

сори́ть, *v. imp.* (*perf.* **насори́ть**), stop up; fill with dirt.

со́рок, *num.* forty. **-ово́й**, *adj.* fortieth.

сорт, *m.* sort, kind; quality.

сортирова́ть, *v. imp.* sort.

соса́ть, *v. imp.* suck.

сосе́д *m.*, **-ка** *f.*, neighbor. **-ний**, *adj.* neighboring. **-ский**, *adj.* neighborly. **-ство**, *nt* neighborhood.

соси́ска, *f.* sausage.

сослага́тельный, *adj.* (*gram.*) subjunctive.

сосла́ть, *v.*, *perf. of* **ссыла́ть**.

сосло́вие, *nt.* estate.

сосна́, *f.* pine; pine tree.

сосредото́чивать, *v. imp.* (*perf.* **сосредото́чить**), concentrate.

соста́в, *m.* composition; structure; staff. **-и́тель**, *m.* compiler; author. **-но́й**, *adj.* composite; component.

составля́ть, *v. imp.* (*perf.* **соста́вить**), compose; put together; draw up.

соста́риться, *v. perf. of* **ста́риться**.

состоя́ние, *nt.* condition; state.

состоя́ть, *v. imp.* be; consist (of). **-ся**, take place.

сострада́ние, *nt.* compassion.

сострада́тельный, *adj.* compassionate.

состяза́ние, *nt.* contest; competition.

состяза́тельный, *adj.* controversial.

сосу́д, *m.* vessel.

сосуществова́ть, *v. imp.* coexist.

сотворе́ние, *nt.* creation.

сотвори́ть, *v., perf. of* сотворя́ть, твори́ть. -ся, *perf. of* твори́ть(ся).

сотворя́ть, *v. imp.* (*perf.* сотвори́ть), create.

со́тня, *f.* (coll.) hundred.

сотру́дничать, *v. imp.* collaborate.

со́тый, *ord.* hundredth.

Со́фьюшка, *dim. of* Со́фья.

Со́фья, *f.* Sophie.

со́ус, *m.* sauce.

соуча́ствовать, *v. imp.* participate.

со́хнуть, *v. imp.* dry.

сохране́ние, *nt.* preservation; conservation.

сохраня́ть, *v. imp.* (*perf.* сохрани́ть), preserve; maintain, keep.

социализа́ция, *f.* socialization.

социа́льный, *adj.* social.

сочета́ть, *v. imp.* combine.

сочине́ние, *nt.* work; composition.

сочиня́ть, *v. imp.* (*perf.* сочини́ть), write; compose; invent.

со́чный, *adj.* juicy.

сочу́вствие, *nt.* sympathy.

сочу́вствовать, *v. imp.* sympathize.

сою́з, *m.* union; alliance. -ник, *m.* ally. -ный, *adj.* allied.

спада́ть, *v. imp.* (*perf.* спасть), fall down.

спали́ть, *v. perf. of* пали́ть.

спа́льня, *f.* bedroom.

спаса́ть, *v. imp.* (*perf.* спасти́), save; rescue.

спасе́ние, *nt.* rescue.

спаси́бо, thanks; thank you.

спаси́тель, *m.* rescuer.

спасти́, *v., perf. of* спаса́ть.

спасть, *v., perf. of* спада́ть.

спать, *v. imp.* sleep; be asleep.

спекта́кль, *m.* performance.

спе́лый, *adj.* ripe.

сперва́, *adv.* at first.

спе́реди, *adv.* at or from the front.

спесь, *f.* haughtiness; conceit.

специа́льный, *adj.* special.

спеши́ть, *v. imp.* (*perf.* поспеши́ть), hurry; (*of a watch*) be fast.

спе́шный, *adj.* urgent; hasty.

спина́, *f.* (anat.) back.

спира́льный, *adj.* spiral.

спирт, *m.* alcohol. -но́й, *adj.* alcoholic.

спи́сывать, *v. imp.* (*perf.* списа́ть), copy; (*colloq.*) crib; write off.

спи́чка, *f.* match.

спле́тничать, *v. imp.* gossip.

спле́тня, *f.* gossip.

сплочённый, *adj.* united.

сплошно́й, *adj.* continuous, unbroken.

сплошь, *adv.* entirely.

споко́йный, *adj.* quiet, calm. споко́йной но́чи, good night.

сполна́, *adv.* completely; in full.

спор, *m.* argument. -ный, *adj.* questionable.

спо́рить, *v. imp.* (*perf.* поспо́рить), argue.

спорт, *m.* sport.

спо́соб, *m.* way, method.

спосо́бность, *f.* ability, faculty.

спосо́бный, *adj.* able, clever; capable.

спосо́бствовать, *v. imp.* further; promote; be conducive (to).

спра́ва, *adv.* to the right of.

справедли́вость, *f.* justice.

справедли́вый, *adj.* just; fair.

справля́ть, *v. imp.* (*perf.* спра́вить), celebrate. -ся, ask (about); cope with, manage.

спра́вочник, *m.* reference book.

спра́шивать, *v. imp.* (*perf.* спроси́ть), ask.

спрос, *m.* demand.

спряже́ние, *nt.* (gram.) conjugation.

спря́тать, *v. perf. of* пря́тать.

спуск, *m.* descent; landing.

спуска́ть, *v. imp.* (*perf.* спусти́ть), let down; lower.

спустя́, *adv.* after.

спу́тник, *m.* companion; fellow traveler; (*astr.*) satellite.

спя́чка, *f.* hibernation.

сравне́ние, *nt.* comparison.

сра́внивать, *v. imp.* (*perf.* сравни́ть), compare. — (*perf.* сровня́ть), level.

сравни́тельный, *adj.* comparative.

сравни́ть(ся), *v., perf. of* равня́ть(ся).

сража́ть, *v. imp.* (*perf.* срази́ть), strike; overwhelm. -ся, fight, battle; engage in a fight.

сраже́ние, *nt.* battle.

сра́зу, *adv.* at once.

срамно́й, *adj.* (*colloq.*) shameful.

среда́, *f.* Wednesday; environment, surroundings.

среди́ (*also* средь), *prep.* (+ *gen.*) among; amidst.

Средизе́мное мо́ре, Mediterranean Sea.

средневеко́вый (*also* средневеко́вый), *adj.* medieval.

средневеко́вье, *nt.* Middle Ages.

сре́дний, *adj.* average; middle.

средото́чие, *nt.* focus.

сре́дство, *nt.* means; remedy.

средь, *see* среди́.

среза́ть, *v. imp.* (*perf.* сре́зать) cut off.

сровня́ть, *v., perf. of* сра́внивать.

сро́дство, *nt.* affinity.

срок, *m.* date; term; period.

сро́чный, *adj.* urgent, pressing.

сруба́ть, *v. imp.* (*perf.* сруби́ть), cut down, fell.

срыв, *m.* collapse; failure.

срыва́ть, *v. imp.* (*perf.* сорва́ть), tear off; pick. — (*perf.* срыть), level to the ground, raze. -ся, *v. imp.* (*perf.* сорва́ться), *intr.* break off; become loose.

ссо́ра, *f.* quarrel.

СССР, (*abbr. of* Сою́з Сове́тских Социалисти́ческих Респу́блик) USSR.

ссыла́ть, *v. imp.* (*perf.* сосла́ть), exile.

ссы́лка, *f.* exile; reference.

ста́вить, *v. imp.* (*perf.* поста́вить), put; stage.

ста́вка, *f.* rate; (*cards*) stake.

ста́вня, *f.* shutter.

стадио́н, *m.* stadium.

ста́дия, *f.* stage.

ста́до, *nt.* herd, flock.

стака́н, *m.* glass.

ста́лкивать, *v. imp.* (*perf.* столкну́ть), push off *or* down. -ся, collide.

сталь, *f.* steel. -но́й, *adj.* steel.

Стамбу́л, *m.* Istanbul.

стандартизи́ровать, *v. imp.* standardize.

станови́ться, *v. imp.* (*perf.* стать), become.

ста́нция, *f.* station.

стара́ние, *nt.* endeavor, effort.

стара́тельный, *adj.* diligent, assiduous.

стара́ться, *v. imp.* (*perf.* постара́ться), endeavor, try.

стари́к, *m.* old man.

стари́нный, *adj.* ancient; old.

ста́риться, *v. imp.* (*perf.* состари́ться), become *or* grow old.

старомо́дный, *adj.* old-fashioned.

ста́рость, *f.* old age.

стару́ха, *f.* old woman.

ста́рческий, *adj.* senile.

ста́рший, *adj.* oldest; eldest; senior.

старшинство́, *nt.* seniority.

ста́рый, *adj.* old.

стасова́ть, *v., perf. of* тасова́ть.

стати́стика, *f.* statistics.

ста́тный, *adj.* stately.

ста́туя, *f.* statue.

стать, *v., perf. of* станови́ться. — (+ *infinitive*) begin, commence.

статья́, *f.* article.

ста́я, *f.* flock.

сте́бель, *m.* stem, stalk.

стега́ть, *v. imp.* quilt. — (*perf.* стегну́ть), whip.

стека́ть, *v. imp.* (*perf.* стечь), flow down.

стекло́, *nt.* glass.

стекля́нный, *adj.* glass.

стена́, *f.* wall.

стенно́й, *adj.* wall.

Сте́нька, *dim. of name* Степа́н.

степе́нный, *adj.* sedate, staid.

сте́пень, *f.* degree; extent.

степь, *f.* steppe.

стере́ть, *v., perf. of* стира́ть.

стере́чь, *v. imp.* watch, guard.

стери́льный, *adj.* sterile.

стесне́ние, *nt.* constraint.

стесни́тельный, *adj.* shy, diffident; inconvenient.

стесня́ть, *v. imp. (perf.* стесни́ть*)*, hamper, constrain. -ся, be shy; feel constrained.

стече́ние, *nt.* confluence.

стечь, *v., perf. of* стека́ть.

стиль, *m.* style.

стира́ть, *v. imp. (perf.* стере́ть*)*, wash.

сти́рка, *f.* washing, laundry.

стихи́, *pl.* verses.

стихи́я, *f.* element.

сто, *num.* hundred.

стог, *m.* stack.

стогра́дусный, *adj.* centigrade.

сто́имость, *f.* cost; value.

сто́ить, *v. imp.* cost; be worth.

сто́йка, *f.* counter.

сто́йкий, *adj.* firm.

сток, *m.* gutter.

стокра́тный, *adj.* hundredfold.

стол, *m.* table; desk; board.

столб, *m.* pillar, post.

столбе́ц, *m.* newspaper column.

столе́тие, *nt.* century; centenary.

столи́ца, *f.* capital (*city*); metropolis.

столи́чный го́род, capital city.

столкнове́ние, *nt.* collision, clash.

столкну́ть(ся), *v., perf. of* ста́лкивать(ся).

столо́вая, *f.* dining room.

столо́чь, *v. perf.* grind, pound.

сто́лько, *adv.* so much, so many. сто́лько ско́лько, as many as, as much as.

стона́ть, *v. imp.* moan, groan.

стопа́, *f.* foot, step; ream.

сторожи́ть, *v. imp.* guard, watch.

сторона́, *f.* side; aspect.

сторони́ться, *v. imp.* (*perf.*

посторони́ться), avoid, shun.

сторо́нник, *m.* supporter, advocate.

стоя́нка, *f.* stand.

стоя́ть, *v. imp.* stand; be; be situated.

стоя́чий, *adj.* standing; stagnant.

страда́ние, *nt.* suffering.

страда́тельный, *adj.* (*gram.*) passive.

страда́ть, *v. imp. (perf.* пострада́ть*)*, suffer.

страна́, *f.* country.

страни́ца, *f.* page.

стра́нный, *adj.* strange.

стра́нствовать, *v. imp.* wander.

стра́стный, *adj.* passionate.

страсть, *f.* passion.

страх, *m.* fear.

страхова́ние, *nt.* insurance.

страхова́ть, *v. imp. (perf.* застрахова́ть*)*, insure.

страши́ть, *v. imp. (perf.* устраши́ть*)*, frighten.

стра́шный, *adj.* terrible; awful.

стрела́, *f.* arrow.

стре́лка, *f.* arrow, pointer, hand. по стре́лке, clockwise. про́тив стре́лки, counterclockwise.

стрельба́, *f.* shooting.

стреми́тельный, *adj.* impetuous.

стреми́ться, *v. imp.* aspire.

стремле́ние, *nt.* aspiration.

стре́мя, *nt.* stirrup.

стри́жка, *f.* haircut.

стри́чься, *v. imp. (perf.* остри́чься*)*, have one's hair cut; get a haircut.

стро́гий, *adj.* strict.

строе́ние, *nt.* structure; building.

строи́тель, *m.* builder.

стро́ить, *v. imp. (perf.* постро́ить*)*, build, construct.

строй, *m.* system, order. -ка, *f.* construction. -ный, *adj.* harmonious.

строка́, *f.* line; paragraph.

строчна́я бу́ква, lower case letter.

структу́рный, *adj.* structural.

струна́, *f.* string.

стручо́к, *m.* pod.

струя́, *f.* stream, jet; current.

стря́пать, *v. imp.* cook.

студе́нт *m.*, **-ка** *f.*, student.

студе́нчество, *nt.* (*coll.*) students; student body.

сту́день, *m.* jelly; galantine.

студи́ть, *v. imp.* cool.

сту́дия, *f.* studio.

стук, *m.* knock, tap; noise.

стул, *m.* chair.

ступа́ть, *v. imp.* (*perf.* **ступи́ть**), step.

ступе́нь, *f.* step; stage.

ступня́, *f.* foot.

стыд, *m.* shame.

стыди́ться, *v. imp.* be ashamed.

стыдли́вый, *adj.* modest, bashful, shy.

сты́нуть, *v. imp.*, *intr.* cool.

стя́гивать, *v. imp.* (*perf.* **стяну́ть**), tighten; tie up; gather.

суббо́та, *f.* Saturday.

субъекти́вный, *adj.* subjective.

сугро́б, *m.* snowdrift.

сугу́бый, *adj.* special, especial; particular.

суд, *m.* court. **-е́бный**, *adj.* court; legal. **-и́мость**, *f.* conviction.

суди́ть, *v. imp.* try, judge; umpire, referee.

су́дно, *nt.* ship, vessel.

су́дорога, *f.* cramp.

су́дорожный, *adj.* convulsive.

судьба́, *f.* fate, destiny.

судья́, *m.* judge.

суеве́рие, *nt.* superstition.

суета́, *f.* fuss.

сужде́ние, *nt.* judgment.

суже́ние, *nt.* narrowing; contraction.

сук, *m.* bough.

су́ка, *f.* bitch.

сукно́, *nt.* cloth.

сумасбро́дный, *adj.* wild, extravagant.

сумасше́ствие, *nt.* madness.

сумасше́дший, *adj.* mad. — *m.* madman, lunatic.

су́мерки, *pl.* twilight.

суме́ть, *v. perf.* succeed (in), be able (to).

су́мка, *f.* bag, handbag.

су́мма, *f.* sum.

су́мрак, *m.* dusk, twilight.

су́мрачный, *adj.* gloomy.

сунду́к, *m.* trunk, chest.

суп, *m.* soup.

супру́г, *m.* husband. **-а** *f.* wife.

супру́жество, *nt.* matrimony.

суро́вый, *adj.* severe, stern.

суста́в, *m.* joint.

су́тки, *pl.* twenty four hours; day.

су́точный, *adj.* daily.

суть, *f.* essence; main *or* principal point.

суфлёр, *m.* (*theat.*) prompter.

суфли́ровать, *v. imp.* prompt.

су́ффикс, *m.* suffix.

сухо́й, *adj.* dry.

су́хость, *f.* dryness.

сучи́ть, *v. imp.* twist; spin.

сучо́к, *m.* twig.

су́ша, *f.* land, dry land.

суше́ние, *nt.* drying.

суши́ть, *v. imp.* (*perf.* **вы́сушить**), dry; air.

суще́ственный, *adj.* essential.

существи́тельное, *see* **и́мя существи́тельное.**

существо́, *nt.* being; essence.

существова́ть, *v. imp.* exist.

су́щий, *adj.* real.

су́щность, *f.* essence; nature.

сфе́ра, *f.* sphere.

сформули́ровать, *v. perf. of* **формули́ровать.**

сфотографи́ровать, *v,. perf. of* **фотографи́ровать.**

схвати́ть, *v., perf. of* **схва́тывать**, **хвата́ть. -ся**, *perf. of* **хвата́ться.**

схва́тывать, *v. imp.* (*perf.* **схвати́ть**), grip, seize.

схе́ма, *f.* scheme. **-ти́ческий**, *adj.* schematic.

сходи́ть, *v. imp.* (*perf.* **сойти́**), go down; get off; leave. **-ся**, become intimate; agree; meet.

схо́дка, *f.* meeting.

схо́дни, *pl.* gangway, gangplank.

схо́дный, *adj.* similar.

схо́дство, *nt.* resemblance, similarity.

схорони́ть, *v., perf. of* **хорони́ть.**

сцена, *f.* (theat.) stage; scene.

сцепление, *nt.* coupling; cohesion.

счастливый, *adj.* happy; fortunate.

счастье, *nt.* happiness; luck.

счесть, *v., perf. of* считать.

счёт, *m.* calculation; account; bill, check; (athl.) score.

счетовод, *m.* bookkeeper.

счёты, *pl.* abacus.

считать, *v. imp.* (perf. счесть), consider; count.

США, (abbr. of Соединённые Штаты Америки) USA.

сшивать, *v. imp.* (perf. сшить), sew together; sew.

сшить, *v., perf. of* сшивать, шить.

съедать, *v. imp.* (perf. съесть), eat.

съезд, *m.* congress, convention; arrival.

съезжаться, *v. imp.* (perf. съехаться), assemble.

съёмка, *f.* survey; filming, photographing.

съестное, *nt.* edible.

съестной, *adj.* edible, eatable.

съесть, *v., perf. of* съедать.

съехаться, *v., perf. of* съезжаться.

сыграть, *v., perf. of* играть.

сын, *m.* son.

сыпать, *v. imp.* strew, pour.

сыпь, *f.* eruption; rash.

сыр, *m.* cheese.

сырой, *adj.* damp; raw; uncooked.

сырьё, *nt.* raw material.

сытный, *adj.* nourishing; substantial; satiating.

сытый, *adj.* satiated.

сюда, *adv.* (dir.) here, to this place.

сюрприз, *m.* surprise.

сяк, *adv.:* и так и сяк, this way and that (way).

сям, *adv.:* там и сям, here and there.

Т

та, *see* тот.

табак, *m.* tabacco.

табачный, *adj.* tabacco.

таблетка, *f.* tablet.

таблица, *f.* table; list.

табуретка, *f.* stool.

таз, *m.* washbasin; pelvis.

таинственный, *adj.* mysterious.

таить, *tr., v. imp.* conceal, hide.

тайком, *adv.* secretly.

тайна, *f.* mystery; secret.

тайник, *m.* hiding place.

тайный, *adj.* secret.

так, *adv.* so, thus; like this, like that. — *conj.* then. так как, *conj.* since.

также, *adv.* also, too.

такой, *pron.* such. что это такое? what is this?

такса, *f.* dachshund; tariff, price.

такт, *m.* tact; (mus.) time. **-ика**, *f.* tactics. **-ический**, *adj.* tactical. **-ичный**, *adj.* tactful.

талант, *m.* talent; gift. **-ливый**, *adj.* talented; gifted.

талия, *f.* waist.

талон, *m.* coupon.

тальк, *m.* talc.

там, *adv.* there.

таможня, *f.* custom house.

танец, *m.* dance.

танцевать, *v. imp.* dance.

танцовщик *m.,* **танцовщица** *f.,* dancer.

Таня, *dim. of name* Татьяна.

таракан, *m.* cockroach.

тарелка, *f.* plate.

таскать, *v. imp.* (perf. тащить), drag, pull.

тасовать, *v. imp.* (perf. стасовать), shuffle (cards).

ТАСС, *abbr. of* Телеграфное Агентство Советского Союза.

тачка, *f.* wheelbarrow.

таять, *v. imp.* (perf. растаять), intr., thaw; melt.

тварь, *f.* creature.

твердеть, *v. imp., intr.* harden.

тверди́ть, v. imp. reiterate; say over and over again.

твёрдый, adj. hard, solid; firm.

твой m., твоя́ f., твоё nt., твои́ pl., pron. your, yours.

творе́ние, nt. creation.

твори́тельный, adj. (gram.) instrumental.

твори́ть, v. imp. (perf. [со]твори́ть), create. -ся take place; be created.

тво́рчество, nt. creation, creative work; (pl.) works.

твои́, see твой.

те, see тот.

т.е. (abbr. of то есть), i.e.

теа́тр, m. theater.

тебе́, dat. of ты.

тебя́, gen., acc. of ты.

тёзка, m. & f. (declined as f.) namesake.

тексти́льный, adj. textile.

теку́чий, adj. fluid; fluctuating.

теку́щий, adj. flowing; current, present.

телеви́дение, nt. television.

телеви́зор, m. television set.

теле́га, f. cart.

телеграфи́ровать, v. imp. wire, telegraph.

телёнок, m. (pl. теля́та) calf.

теле́сный, adj. corporeal.

телефони́ровать, v. imp. telephone.

те́ло, nt. body; corpse.

телосложе́ние, nt. build; frame.

теля́та, see телёнок.

теля́тина, f. veal.

тем, instr. of тот. тем не ме́нее, nevertheless.

те́ма, f. subject, topic; theme.

Те́мза, f. Thames.

темне́ть, v. imp. (perf. потемне́ть), become or grow dark.

темнота́, f. darkness, dark; ignorance; obscurity.

тёмный, adj. dark; obscure; ignorant.

темп, m. rate; pace; tempo.

температу́ра, f. temperature.

тенде́нция, f. tendency.

те́ннис, m. tennis.

тень, f. shade; shadow.

Теодо́р, m. Theodore.

тео́рия, f. theory.

тепе́решний, adj. present-day.

тепе́рь, adv. now.

тепле́ть, v. imp. (perf. потепле́ть), grow warm.

тепли́ца, f. hothouse.

тепло́, nt. warmth; heat. — adv. warmly. —во́й, adj. thermal. -та́, f. warmth; heat.

тёплый, adj. warm.

терапевти́ческий, adj. therapeutic.

тере́ть, v. imp. rub; grate.

терза́ть, v. imp. torment.

те́рмин, m. term.

терни́стый, adj. thorny.

терпели́вый, adj. patient.

терпе́ние, nt. patience.

терпе́ть, v. imp. endure, suffer; have patience; tolerate. -ся, impers. (with dat.) be patient: мне не те́рпится пойти́ туда́, I can't wait to go there.

терпи́мый, adj. tolerant; tolerable.

те́рпкий, adj. tart.

терра́са, f. terrace.

террито́рия, f. territory.

терро́р, m. terror.

теря́ть, v. imp. (perf. потеря́ть), lose; waste. -ся, be or become lost; be at a loss.

теснота́, f. narrowness.

те́сный, adj. narrow.

те́сто, nt. dough.

тесть, m. father-in-law (wife's father).

тётка, f. aunt.

тетра́дь, f. notebook.

тётя, f. aunt.

те́хник, m. technician. -a, f. technique.

тече́ние, nt. flow; course. в тече́ние, during.

течь, v. imp. flow; leak.

те́шить, v. imp. (perf. поте́шить), amuse.

тёща, f. mother-in-law (wife's mother).

тигр, m. tiger.

Тимофе́й, m. Timothy.

Тимо́ш(ка), dim. of Тимофе́й.

ти́на, f. slime.

ти́нистый, adj. slimy.

тип, m. type. -и́чный, adj.

typical. -овой, *adj.* standard, model.

типогра́фия, *f.* printing plant, printer.

тира́ж, *m.* edition; circulation.

тира́н, *m.* tyrant.

тира́нить, *v. imp.* tyrannize.

тире́, *nt. ind.* (*typog.*) dash.

ти́скать, *v. imp.* (*perf.* ти́снуть), squeeze.

тиски́, *pl.* (*mech.*) vice.

ти́тул, *m.* title.

тиф, *m.* (*phys.*); typhoid.

ти́хий, *adj.* quiet, still; gentle, soft.

Ти́хий океа́н (also Вели́кий океа́н), Pacific Ocean.

ти́ше, *adv.* quietly.

тишина́, *f.* quiet; stillness.

ткань, *f.* cloth; fabric.

ткать, *v. imp.* weave.

ткнуть, *v.*, *perf. of* ты́кать.

тле́ние, *nt.* smoldering; decay, decaying.

тлеть, *v. imp.* smolder; rot, decay.

то, *pron.*, *see* тот. — *conj.* then. то есть, that is. а не то, or else; otherwise.

тобо́й (also тобо́ю), *instr. of* ты.

това́р, *m.* goods; commodity.

това́рищ, *m.* comrade; mate. -ество, *nt.* association.

тогда́, *adv.* then. тогда́ как, while.

тогда́шний, *adj.* pertaining to that time.

тожде́ственный, *adj.* identical.

тожде́ство, *nt.* identity.

то́же, *adv.* also, too, as well.

ток, *m.* (*electric*) current.

толк, *m.* sense.

толка́ть, *v. imp.* (*perf.* толкну́ть), push.

толкова́ть, *v. imp.* interpret.

толко́вый, *adj.* explanatory; intelligible.

толо́чь, *v. imp.* pound, crush.

толпа́, *f.* crowd.

толпи́ться, *v. imp.* crowd.

толсте́ть, *v. imp.* (*perf.* потолсте́ть), grow fat or stout.

то́лстый, *adj.* fat, stout.

толчо́к, *m.* push, jerk.

толщина́, *f.* fatness, stoutness.

то́лько, *adv.* only.

То́ля, *dim. of* Анато́лий.

том, *m.* (*book*) volume.

томи́ть, *v. imp.* weary, tire; wear out. -ся, pine *or* languish (for).

томле́ние, *nt.* languor.

то́мный, *adj.* languid.

тон, *m.* tone.

тони́ческий, *adj.* tonic.

то́нкий, *adj.* thin, slim, slender.

то́нкость, *f.* thinness, slimness; delicacy.

то́нна, *f.* ton.

тонна́ж, *m.* tonnage.

тонне́ль, *see* тунне́ль.

тону́ть, *v. imp.* drown; sink.

то́пать, *v. imp.* (*perf.* то́пнуть), stamp.

топи́ть, *v. imp.* (*perf.* утопи́ть), heat; melt; drown, sink.

то́пкий, *adj.* swampy.

то́пливо, *nt.* fuel.

то́пнуть, *v.*, *perf. of* то́пать.

то́поль, *m.* poplar.

топо́р, *m.* ax.

топта́ть, *v. imp.* trample.

торги́, *pl.* auction.

торгова́ть, *v. imp.* trade, deal. -ся, bargain.

торго́вец, *m.* merchant, dealer, tradesman.

торго́вля, *f.* trade, commerce.

торже́ственный, *adj.* solemn.

торжество́, *nt.* celebration.

торжеству́ющий, *adj.* triumphant.

то́рмоз, *m.* brake.

тормози́ть, *v. imp.* apply brakes; hinder, hamper.

торопи́ть, *v. imp.* (*perf.* поторопи́ть), *tr.*, hurry, hasten.

торопли́вость, *f.* haste, hurry.

торпе́да, *f.* torpedo.

торт, *m.* cake.

торф, *m.* peat.

торча́ть, *v. imp.* protrude.

тоска́, *f.* melancholy, longing.

тоскли́вый, *adj.* dull, dreary.

тоскова́ть, *v. imp.* be melancholy, long for.

тот *m.*, та *f.*, то *nt.*, те *pl.*, *pron.* that; the other.

то́тчас, *adv.* immediately.

точи́ть, v. imp. sharpen; grind.

то́чка, f. point; dot; period.

то́чно, adv. exactly. — conj. as if, as though.

то́чный, adj. exact, precise, accurate.

точь-в-то́чь, adv. (colloq.) exactly.

тошнота́, f. nausea, sickness.

то́щий, adj. meager; lean.

трава́, f. grass.

трави́ть, v. imp. hunt; persecute; etch.

тра́гик, m. tragedian.

траги́ческий, adj. tragic.

тради́ция, f. tradition.

тракта́т, m. treatise.

тракти́р, m. inn; tavern.

трамплин, m. springboard.

транскри́пция, f. transcription.

трансли́ровать, v. imp. broadcast.

трансля́ция, f. broadcast.

трансми́ссия, f. transmission.

транспорти́ровать, v. imp. transport.

трансформи́ровать, v. imp. transform.

тра́сса, f. route.

тра́та, f. expense, expenditure; waste.

тра́тить, v. imp. (perf. истра́тить), spend; waste.

тра́ур, m. mourning.

трафаре́т, m. stencil; stereotype.

тре́бовательный, adj. demanding, exacting.

тре́бовать, v. imp. (perf. потре́бовать), demand; require.

трево́га, f. alarm.

трево́жить, v. imp. (perf. встрево́жить), disturb; worry. trouble.

трево́жный, adj. anxious.

тре́звый, adj. sober.

трек, m. track, racecourse.

тре́нер, m. (sports) coach.

тре́ние, nt. friction.

трениро́вать, v. imp., tr., train.

тре́пет, m. quiver, quivering.

трепета́ть, v. imp. quiver, tremble.

треск, m. crash, crack.

треска́, f. cod.

трескотня́, f. rattle.

треску́чий моро́з, bitter cold.

тре́снуть, v. imp. crack; burst.

тре́тий, adj. third.

треть, f. third.

треуго́льник, m. triangle.

тре́фы, pl. (cards) clubs.

трёхсо́тый, adj. three hundredth.

треща́ть, v. imp. crack, crackle; chirp, chatter.

три, num. three.

трибу́на, f. tribune, rostrum.

тридца́тый, adj. thirtieth.

три́дцать, num. thirty.

три́жды, adv. thrice.

трина́дцатый, adj. thirteenth.

трина́дцать, num. thirteen.

три́ста, num. three hundred.

тро́гательный, adj. touching.

тро́гать, v. imp. (perf. тро́нуть), touch; move.

тро́е, num. coll. three.

тройно́й, adj. triple.

трон, m. throne.

тро́нуть, v., perf. of тро́гать.

тро́пики, pl. tropics.

тропи́нка, f. path; track.

тропи́ческий, adj. tropical.

тростни́к, m. reed.

трость, f. cane.

тротуа́р, m. pavement; sidewalk.

трофе́й, m. trophy.

труба́, f. pipe, chimney, smokestack; (mus.) trumpet.

тру́бка, f. tube; (telephone) receiver; pipe (smoking).

труд, m. labor, work; trouble, difficulty.

труди́ться, v. imp. work, toil.

тру́дность, f. difficulty.

тру́дный, adj. difficult.

трудолюби́вый, adj. industrious, diligent.

трудоспосо́бный, adj. capable, able-bodied.

трудя́щийся, m. worker.

труп, m. corpse.

тру́ппа, f. troupe, company.

трус, m. coward.

тру́сики, pl. shorts.

трусли́вый, adj. cowardly.

трусость, f. cowardice.

тряпка, f. rag; dusting rag.

трястись, v. imp., intr., shake, shiver.

туберкулёз, m. tuberculosis.

туго, adv. tightly, fast; with difficulty.

тугой, adj. tight.

туда, adv. (to) there, to that place.

туз, m. (cards) ace.

туземный, adj. native.

туловище, nt. trunk, body.

туман, m. fog, mist. -ный, adj. foggy, misty.

туннель, m. tunnel.

тупик, m. blind alley; deadlock.

тупой, adj. blunt.

турецкий, adj. Turkish.

турнир, m. tournament, contest.

турок, m. Turk.

Турция, f. Turkey.

тусклый, adj. dim; dull.

тут, adv. here.

тутовая ягода, mulberry.

туфля, f. slipper, shoe.

тухлый, adj. rotten.

туча, f. cloud; swarm.

тучный, adj. obese, fat; fertile.

тушить, v. imp. (perf. потушить), extinguish.

тушь, f. India ink.

тщательный, adj. careful.

тщеславие, nt. vanity.

тщеславный, adj. vain.

тщетный, adj. vain, futile.

ты, pron. sg. you.

тыкать, v. imp. (perf. ткнуть), poke.

тыква, f. pumpkin.

тыл, m. rear.

тысяча, num. thousand.

тысячный, adj. thousandth.

тьма, f. dark, darkness.

тюлень, m. seal.

тюльпан, m. tulip.

тюремный, adj. prison.

тюрьма, f. prison.

тюфяк, m. mattress.

тяга, f. draught; traction.

тягость, f. burden.

тяготение, nt. gravitation; attraction.

тяготеть, v. imp. gravitate.

тяготить, v. imp. be a burden.

тяжеловесный, adj. ponderous.

тяжёлый, adj. heavy; severe; hard, difficult.

тяжесть, f. weight; gravity; difficulty.

тяжкий, adj. heavy; grave, serious.

тянуть, v. imp. (perf. потянуть), pull, draw, tow. -ся, last; drag on; stretch.

У

у, prep. (+ gen.) at, by; with, at; from, of; in; (possession) (+ gen.): у меня, I have, у тебя, you have, etc.

убавлять, v. imp. (perf. убавить), diminish.

убаюкивать, v. imp. (perf. убаюкать) lull.

убегать, v. imp. (perf. убежать), run away, flee.

убедительный, adj. convincing; persuasive.

убеждать, v. imp. (perf. убедить), convince; persuade.

убеждение, nt. conviction; persuasion.

убежище, nt. refuge, shelter; sanctuary.

убивать, v. imp. (perf. убить), kill, murder.

убийственный, adj. deadly, murderous.

убийство, nt. murder.

убийца, m. murderer.

убирать, v. imp. (perf. убрать), remove; put away; harvest; clean or tidy up; decorate.

убить, v., perf. of убивать.

убогий, adj. poor, miserable.

убожество, nt. poverty.

убой, m. slaughter.

убор, m. attire.

убо́рка, *f.* harvest, harvesting; cleaning.

убо́рная, *f.* lavatory, toilet.

убра́ть, *v.*, *perf. of* убира́ть.

убыва́ть, *v. imp.* (*perf.* убы́ть), *intr.*, decrease.

у́быль, *f.* decrease, diminution.

убы́ток, *m.* loss.

убы́точный, *adj.* losing, unprofitable.

убы́ть, *v.*, *perf. of* убыва́ть.

уважа́емый, *adj.* respected, esteemed.

уважа́ть, *v. imp.* respect, esteem.

уведомле́ние, *nt.* information.

уведомля́ть, *v. imp.* (*perf.* уве́домить), inform.

увезти́, *v.*, *perf. of* увози́ть.

увекове́чивать, *v. imp.* (*perf.* увекове́чить), immortalize; perpetuate.

увели́чивать, *v. imp.* (*perf.* увели́чить), *tr.*, increase, enlarge.

увере́ние, *nt.* assurance.

уве́ренный, *adj.* assured, certain; confident.

уверну́ться, *v. perf.* dodge; evade.

уверти́ра, *f.* overture.

уверя́ть, *v. imp.* (*perf.* уве́рить), assure; convince.

увеселя́ть, *v. imp.* (*perf.* увесели́ть), amuse.

увести́, *v.*, *perf. of* уводи́ть.

уве́чить, *v. imp.* cripple.

уве́чье, *nt.* mutilation.

увеща́ние, *nt.* admonishment, admonition.

увещева́ть, *v. imp.* (*perf.* увеща́ть), admonish.

увида́ть, *v. imp.* (*perf.* уви́деть), see. **-ся**, *intr.*, meet.

увлажня́ть, *v. imp.* (*perf.* увлажни́ть), moisten.

увлека́тельный, *adj.* fascinating, captivating.

увлека́ть, *v. imp.* (*perf.* у влечь), fascinate. captivate; carry away *or* off.

увлече́ние, *nt.* animation; passion.

уводи́ть, *v. imp.* (*perf.* увести́), take away; withdraw.

увози́ть, *v. imp.* (*perf.* увезти́), take *or* carry away; steal; kidnap.

увольня́ть, *v. imp.* (*perf.* уво́лить), dismiss, discharge.

увы́! *interj.* alas.

увяда́ть, *v. imp.* (*perf.* увя́нуть), *intr.*, fade; wither; droop.

увя́зывать, *v. imp.* (*perf.* увяза́ть), tie *or* pack up; coordinate.

уга́дывать, *v. imp.* (*perf.* угада́ть), guess.

угаса́ть, *v. imp.* (*perf.* уга́снуть), fade, die away.

углеко́п, *m.* miner.

углепромы́шленность, *f.* coal industry.

углеро́д, *m.* carbon.

углова́тый, *adj.* angular; awkward.

углово́й, *adj.* corner; angular.

углубле́ние, *nt.* deepening.

углубля́ть, *v. imp.* (*perf.* углуби́ть), *tr.*, deepen. **-ся**, become deeper; be absorbed (in); delve (in).

угнета́тель, *m.* oppressor.

угнета́ть, *v. imp.* (*perf.* угнести́), oppress; depress.

угова́ривать, *v. imp.* (*perf.* уговори́ть), persuade.

угово́р, *m.* persuasion; agreement.

угода́, *f.*: **в уго́ду**, (*with dat.*) to please.

угоди́ть, *v.*, *perf. of* угожда́ть.

уго́дливый, *adj.* obsequious; officious.

уго́дно, *impers.*: **как вам уго́дно**, as you please.

угожда́ть, *v. imp.* (*perf.* угоди́ть), please.

у́гол, *m.* corner; angle.

уголо́вный, *adj.* criminal; penal.

уголо́к, *m.* corner, nook.

у́голь, *m.* coal.

у́гольный, *adj.* coal.

уго́льный, *adj.* (*colloq.*) corner.

у́горь, *m.* blackhead; eel.

угоща́ть, *v. imp.* (*perf.* угости́ть), entertain, treat.

угрожа́ть, *v. imp.* threaten.

угро́за, *f.* threat; menace.

угрю́мый, *adj.* sullen; morose.

удава́ться, *v. imp.* (*perf.* уда́ться), work *or* turn out successfully.

удавля́ть, *v. imp.* (*perf.* удави́ть), strangle.

удаля́ть, *v. imp.* (*perf.* удали́ть), remove; extract; send away.

уда́р, *m.* blow; (*med*) stroke. **-е́ние,** *nt.* accent; stress; emphasis. **-ный,** *adj.* shock; accelerated; percussive, percussion; accented.

ударя́ть, *v. imp.* (*perf.* уда́рить), strike; hit.

уда́ться, *v., perf. of* удава́ться.

уда́ча, *f.* success.

уда́чный, *adj.* successful.

удва́ивать, *v. imp.* (*perf.* удво́ить), *tr.,* double; redouble.

уде́л, *m.* lot, destiny.

уде́льный, *adj.* specific.

уделя́ть, *v. imp.* (*perf.* удели́ть), spare, give.

удержа́ние, *nt.* deduction; retention, keeping.

уде́рживать, *v. imp.* (*perf.* удержа́ть), retain; hold, **-ся,** refrain (from); hold one's ground.

удешевля́ть, *v. imp.* (*perf.* удешеви́ть), cheapen; reduce the price of.

удивля́ть, *v. imp.* (*perf.* удиви́ть), astonish, amaze, surprise.

удира́ть, *v. imp.* (*perf.* удра́ть), *colloq.,* run away.

удлиня́ть, *v. imp.* (*perf.* удлини́ть), lengthen.

удо́бный, *adj.* comfortable, convenient.

удобре́ние, *nt.* fertilization.

удо́бство, *nt.* comfort.

удовлетворя́ть, *v. imp.* (*perf.* удовлетвори́ть), satisfy.

удово́льствие, *nt.* pleasure.

удостовере́ние, *nt.* certificate.

удостоверя́ть, *v. imp.* (*perf.* удостове́рить), certify; testify.

у́дочка, *f.* fishing rod.

удра́ть, *v., perf. of* удира́ть.

удруча́ть, *v. imp.* (*perf.* удручи́ть), depress.

удушли́вый, *adj.* suffocating.

уду́шье, *nt.* asthma.

уедине́ние, *nt.* solitude.

уединённый, *adj.* solitary.

уезжа́ть, *v. imp.* (*perf.* уе́хать), leave; depart.

уж, *adv., see* уже́. — *particle* really.

ужа́лить, *v., perf. of* жа́лить.

у́жас, *m.* horror, terror.

ужаса́ть, *v. imp.* (*perf.* ужасну́ть), terrify, horrify, awe.

ужа́сный, *adj.* horrible, terrible.

уже́, *adv.* already.

у́жин, *m.* supper.

у́жинать, *v. imp.* (*perf.* поу́жинать), have supper.

узаконя́ть, *v. imp.* (*perf.* узако́нить), legalize.

узда́, *f.* bridle.

у́зел, *m.* knot; bundle.

у́зкий, *adj.* narrow.

узнава́ть, *v. imp.* (*perf.* узна́ть), learn; find out; recognize.

узо́р, *m.* pattern, design.

узре́ть, *v., perf. of* зреть.

уйти́, *v., perf. of* уходи́ть.

ука́з, *m.* edict. **-а́ние,** *nt.* indication. **-а́тель,** *m.* indicator.

ука́зывать, *v. imp.* (*perf.* указа́ть), indicate; show; point out.

ука́тывать, *v. imp.* (*perf.* укати́ть), roll.

ука́чивать, *v. imp.* (*perf.* укача́ть), rock to sleep.

укла́дывать, *v. imp.* (*perf.* уложи́ть), lay; pack; put to bed. **-ся,** pack up.

укло́н, *m.* slope; deviation. **-е́ние,** *nt.* deviation; evasion. **-чивый,** *adj.* evasive.

уклоня́ться, *v. imp.* (*perf.* уклони́ться), deviate; evade.

уко́л, *m.* prick, pricking.

уко́р, *m.* reproach.

укора́чивать, *v. imp.* (*perf.* укороти́ть), shorten.

укорени́вшийся, *adj.* ingrained, enrooted.

укореня́ться, *v. imp.* (*perf.* укорени́ться), take root; become enrooted.

укори́зненный, *adj.* reproachful.

укороти́ть, *v., perf. of* укора́чивать.

укоря́ть, *v. imp.* (*perf.* укори́ть), reproach.

укра́дкой, *adv.* stealthily.

украи́нец *m.*, **украи́нка** *f.*, Ukrainian.

укра́сть, *v., perf. of* красть.

украша́ть, *v. imp.* (*perf.* укра́сить), adorn, decorate.

укрепля́ть, *v. imp.* (*perf.* укрепи́ть), strengthen, fortify.

укро́мный, *adj.* secluded.

укро́п, *m.* dill; fennel.

укроти́тель *m.* tamer.

укроща́ть, *v. imp.* (*perf.* укроти́ть), tame; subdue.

укрыва́ть, *v. imp.* (*perf.* укры́ть), cover; conceal; harbor

укры́тие, *nt.* shelter, cover.

у́ксус, *m.* vinegar.

уку́с, *m.* bite.

укуси́ть(ся), *v., perf. of* куса́ть(ся).

ула́вливать, *v. imp.* (*perf.* улови́ть), catch.

ула́живать, *v. imp.* (*perf.* ула́дить), arrange; settle.

у́лей, *m.* beehive.

улета́ть, *v. imp.* (*perf.* улете́ть), fly away *or* off.

ули́ка, *f.* evidence.

у́лица, *f.* street.

улича́ть, *v. imp.* (*perf.* уличи́ть), convict; expose.

у́личный, *adj.* street.

улови́мый, *adj.* perceptible; audible.

улови́ть, *v., perf. of* ула́вливать.

уложе́ние, *nt.* (*law*) code.

уложи́ть(ся), *v., perf. of* укла́дывать(ся).

улучша́ть, *v. imp.* (*perf.* улучши́ть), improve; better; ameliorate.

улыба́ться, *v. imp.* (*perf.* улыбну́ться), smile.

улы́бка, *f.* smile.

ум, *m.* mind.

ума́лчивать, *v. imp.* (*perf.* умолча́ть), pass over in silence.

умаля́ть, *v. imp.* (*perf.* ума-ли́ть), belittle; derogate.

уме́лый, *adj.* skillful.

уме́ние, *nt.* skill.

уменьша́ть, *v. imp.* (*perf.* уме́ньшить), *tr.*, decrease, diminish.

уменьши́тельный, *adj.* (*gram.*) diminutive.

уме́ренный, *adj.* temperate.

умере́ть, *v., perf. of* умира́ть.

уме́рший, *adj., m.* deceased.

умерщвля́ть, *v. imp.* (*perf.* умертви́ть), kill.

умеря́ть, *v. imp.* (*perf.* уме́рить), moderate.

уме́стный, *adj.* proper; to the point.

уме́ть, *v. imp.* know, know how to.

умира́ть, *v. imp.* (*perf.* умере́ть), die.

умне́ть, *v. imp.* grow wiser.

умножа́ть, *v. imp.* (*perf.* умно́жить), *tr.*, increase; (*math.*) multiply.

умноже́ние, *nt.* multiplication.

у́мный, *adj.* clever; intelligent.

умолка́ть, *v. imp.* (*perf.* умо́лкнуть), become silent, lapse into silence.

умолча́ть, *v., perf. of* ума́лчивать.

умоля́ть, *v. imp.* entreat, implore.

умори́ть, *v. perf.* kill; starve to death.

у́мственный, *adj.* mental, intellectual.

у́мствовать, *v. imp.*, *colloq.*, philosophize; reason.

умыва́льник, *m.* washstand.

умыва́ть, *v. imp.* (*perf.* умы́ть) *tr.*, wash.

у́мысел, *m.* design, intent, intention,

умы́шленный, *adj.* designed; intentional, deliberate.

умышля́ть, *v. imp.* (*perf.* умы́слить), design; intend.

умягча́ть, *v. imp.* (*perf.* умягчи́ть), soften.

унести́, v., perf. of **уноси́ть**.

универма́г, **универса́льный магази́н**, department store.

универса́льный, adj. universal; many-sided; general-purpose.

университе́т, m. university.

унижа́ть, v. imp. (perf. **уни́зить**), humble, humiliate; abase; belittle.

униже́ние, nt. humiliation; abasement.

унима́ть, v. imp. (perf. **уня́ть**), quiet, calm; repress, soothe.

уничтожа́ть, v. imp. (perf. **уничто́жить**), destroy; abolish.

уничтоже́ние, nt. destruction, annihilation; abolition.

уничтожи́тельный, adj. destructive.

уноси́ть, v. imp. (perf. **унести́**), take or carry away; carry off.

у́нция, f. ounce.

уныва́ть, v. imp. lose heart; be dejected.

уны́лый, adj. dejected, dismal, sad, cheerless.

уны́ние, nt. despondency, dejection.

уня́ть, v., perf. of **унима́ть**.

упа́дочный, adj. decadent; depressive.

упако́вывать, v. imp. (perf. **упакова́ть**), pack, pack up.

упа́сть, v. perf. fall.

упира́ться, v. imp. rest or lean against; rest on.

упла́та, f. payment.

упла́чивать, v. imp. (perf. **уплати́ть**), pay.

уплотня́ть, v. imp. (perf. **у-плотни́ть**), condense.

уплотне́ние, nt. condensation.

уподобле́ние, nt. likening; (phon.) assimilation.

упое́ние, nt. ecstasy, rapture.

упои́тельный, adj. entrancing, ravishing.

уполномо́ченный, m. representative, authorized agent.

уполномо́чивать, v. imp. (perf. **уполномо́чить**), authorize, empower.

упомина́ть, v. imp. (perf. **упомяну́ть**), mention, refer to.

упо́мнить, v. perf., colloq., remember.

упо́рный, adj. stubborn; persistent.

упо́рствовать, v. imp. persist; be stubborn or obstinate.

употреби́тельный, adj. in common use.

употребля́ть, v. imp. (perf. **употреби́ть**), use; apply.

управле́ние, nt. management, government.

управля́ть, v. imp. (perf. **упра́вить**), manage, govern; operate.

управля́ющий, adj. managing, governing. — m. manager.

упражне́ние, nt. exercise.

упражня́ться, v. imp. exercise.

упраздня́ть, v. imp. (perf. **упраздни́ть**), abolish.

упра́шивать, v. imp. (perf. **упроси́ть**), beg, entreat.

упрёк, m. reproach; rebuke.

упрека́ть, v. imp. (perf. **упрекну́ть**), reproach.

упроси́ть, v., perf. of **упра́шивать**.

упро́чивать, v. imp. (perf. **упро́чить**), tr., strengthen; consolidate.

упроща́ть, v. imp. (perf. **упрости́ть**), simplify.

упру́гий, adj. elastic; resilient.

упря́мый, adj. stubborn, obstinate.

упуска́ть, v. imp. (perf. **упусти́ть**), miss; let go or escape.

упуще́ние, nt. omission.

упы́рь, m. vampire.

ура́! interj. hurrah!

уравне́ние, nt. equalization; (math.) equation.

ура́внивать, v. imp. (perf. **уравня́ть**), equalize; level. — (perf. **уровня́ть**); even; smooth.

уравнове́шенный, adj. balanced; steady; even-tempered.

урага́н, m. hurricane; tornado.

Ура́н, m. Uranus.

уре́зывать, v. imp. (perf. **уре́зать**), cut off.

ури́на, f. urine.

у́рна, *f.* urn.

у́ровень, *m.* level; standard.

уровня́ть, *v.*, *perf. of* ура́внивать.

уро́д, *m.* freak; monster, monstrosity. -ливость, *f.* deformity. -ливый, *adj.* deformed; ugly.

уро́довать, *v. imp.* (*perf.* изуро́довать*), disfigure, deform; mutilate.

урожа́й, *m.* harvest, yield. -ный, *adj.* fruitful, productive.

урождённая, *adj.* born, née.

уроже́нец, *m.* native.

уро́к, *m.* lesson.

уро́н, *m.* losses.

урони́ть, *v.*, *perf. of* роня́ть.

ус, *m.* mustache.

уса́живать, *v. imp.* (*perf.* усади́ть*), *tr.* seat. -ся, take a seat.

уса́тый, *adj.* mustached.

усва́ивать, *v. imp.* (*perf.* усво́ить*), master, learn; assimilate.

усвое́ние, *nt.* mastering, learning; adaptation.

усе́рдный, *adj.* zealous, diligent.

уси́дчивый, *adj.* assiduous; perseverant.

усиле́ние, *nt.* reinforcement; intensification; amplification.

уси́ливать, *v. imp.* (*perf.* уси́лить*), strengthen; intensify; amplify.

уси́лие, *nt.* effort.

ускольза́ть, *v. imp.* (*perf.* ускользну́ть*), slip away *or* off; steal away.

ускоре́ние, *nt.* acceleration.

ускори́тель, *m.* accelerator.

ускоря́ть, *v. imp.* (*perf.* уско́рить*), hasten, quicken; accelerate.

усла́да, *f.* pleasure, delight.

услажда́ть, *v. ·imp.* (*perf.* услади́ть*), delight.

усло́вие, *nt.* condition.

усло́вливаться, *v. imp.* (*perf.* усло́виться*), arrange, make arrangements; agree (on).

усло́вный, *adj.* conditional.

усложня́ть, *v. imp.* (*perf.* усложни́ть*), complicate.

услу́га, *f.* service.

услу́живать, *v. imp.* (*perf.* услужи́ть*), render a service; serve.

услу́жливый, *adj.* helpful; obliging.

услы́шать, *v.*, *perf. of* слы́шать.

усмеха́ться, *v. imp.* (*perf.* усмехну́ться*), smile ironically; grin.

усме́шка, *f.* ironical smile.

усмиря́ть, *v. imp.* (*perf.* усмири́ть*), pacify; suppress.

усну́ть, *v. perf.* fall asleep.

усовершенствование, *nt.* improvement.

усовершенствовать, *v.*, *perf. of* совершенствовать.

успева́ть, *v. imp.* (*perf.* успе́ть*) manage (to); have time (to); succeed (in).

успе́х, *m.* success.

успе́шный, *adj.* successful.

успока́ивать, *v. imp.* (*perf.* успоко́ить*), calm, quiet, soothe; assuage.

уста́в, *m.* regulations; statute.

устава́ть, *v. imp.* (*perf.* уста́ть*), become tired.

уста́лый, *adj.* fatigued, weary, tired.

устана́вливать, *v. imp.* (*perf.* установи́ть*), place; mount; establish.

устано́вка, *f.* installation; establishment; mounting; setting.

уста́ть, *v.*, *perf. of* устава́ть.

устаре́лый, *adj.* outdated, obsolete.

у́стный, *adj.* oral, verbal.

усто́йчивый, *adj.* steady, firm, stable.

устоя́ть, *v. perf.* keep one's balance.

устра́ивать, *v. imp.* (*perf.* устро́ить*), arrange, organize, establish; make, create.

устраня́ть, *v. imp.* (*perf.* устрани́ть*), remove; eliminate.

устраша́ть, *v. imp.* (*perf.* устраши́ть*), frighten, scare.

устраши́ть, v., perf. of страши́ть, устраша́ть.

устремле́ние, nt. aspiration.

у́стрица, f. oyster.

устро́ить, v., perf. of устра́ивать.

устро́йство, nt. arrangement; organization; structure.

усту́п, m. ledge; projection.

уступа́ть, v. imp. (perf. уступи́ть), yield; cede.

усту́пка, f. concession.

усту́пчивый, adj. yielding; pliant, tractable.

у́стье, nt. estuary, mouth; orifice.

усыновле́ние, nt. adoption.

усыновля́ть, v. imp. (perf. усынови́ть), adopt.

усыпля́ть, v. imp. (perf. усыпи́ть), lull to sleep; hypnotize, mesmerize.

утверди́тельный, adj. affirmative.

утвержда́ть, v. imp. (perf. утверди́ть), affirm; maintain, assert, contend; approve.

утёнок, m. duckling.

утека́ть, v. imp., (perf. уте́чь), flow off or away.

утере́ть, v., perf. of утира́ть.

утёс, m. rock; cliff.

уте́ха, f. joy, delight, pleasure; comfort, consolation.

утеша́ть, v. imp. (perf. уте́шить), comfort, console.

утира́ть, v. imp. (perf. утере́ть), wipe; dry.

утиха́ть, v. imp. (perf. ути́хнуть), cease; fade; become calm.

у́тка, f. duck.

утолще́ние, nt. thickening; bulge.

утоля́ть, v. imp. (perf. утоли́ть), quench; satisfy.

утоми́тельный, adj. tiresome, tiring, exhausting.

утомля́ть, v. imp. (perf. утоми́ть), tr., tire, weary, fatigue, exhaust.

тонча́ть, v. imp. (perf. утонча́ть), thin, thin out; refine.

утопи́ть, v., perf. of топи́ть.

уточня́ть, v. imp. (perf.

уточни́ть), specify; render more precise or accurate.

утра́та, f. loss.

у́тренний, adj. morning.

у́тро, nt. morning. по утра́м, in the morning(s). у́тром, in the morning.

утро́ба, f. womb.

утро́ение, nt. trebling, tripling.

утружда́ть, v. imp. (perf. утруди́ть), trouble.

утю́г, m. iron (appliance).

утю́жить, v. imp. iron, press.

уха́бистый, adj. bumpy.

уха́живать, v. imp. nurse, tend; court.

ухва́тывать, v. imp. (perf. ухвати́ть), catch, grasp.

ухитря́ться, v. imp. (perf. ухитри́ться), contrive.

ухищре́ние, nt. contrivance; device.

у́хо, nt. (pl. у́ши) ear.

ухо́д, m. departure.

уходи́ть, v., perf. of уйти́.

ухудша́ть, v. imp. (perf. уху́дшить), worsen, make worse.

уцеле́ть, v. perf. survive.

уча́ствовать, v. imp. participate.

уча́стие, nt. participation; share.

уча́стливый, adj. sympathetic, compassionate.

уча́стник, m. participant.

уча́сток, m. lot, plot, strip; parcel.

у́часть, f. lot, fate.

уча́щийся, m. student.

уче́бник, m. textbook, manual.

уче́бный, adj. educational, school.

уче́ние, nt. learning, studies.

учени́к, m., учени́ца f., pupil.

учёный, adj. learned, erudite. — m. scholar, scientist.

уче́сть, v., perf. of учи́тывать.

учёт, m. calculation; registration.

учи́лище, nt. school, college.

учи́тель m., -ница f., teacher.

учи́тывать, v. imp. (perf.

учесть), take into account; allow for.

учи́ть, v. imp. (perf. научи́ть), teach. -ся, learn; study.

учреди́тель, m. founder.

учрежда́ть, v. imp. (perf. учреди́ть), found, establish.

уши́б, m. injury.

ушиба́ться, v. imp. (perf. ушиби́ться), hurt oneself.

ушно́й, adj. aural, ear.

уще́лье, nt. ravine, gorge.

уще́рб, m. damage, loss; detriment.

ую́тный, adj. cosy; comfortable.

язви́мый, adj. vulnerable.

уясня́ть, v. imp. (perf. уясни́ть), understand; size up.

Ф

фа́брика,, f. factory.

фабрика́нт, m. manufacturer.

фабрика́т, m. product.

фабрикова́ть, v. imp. (perf. сфабрикова́ть), produce, manufacture.

фабри́чный, adj. factory.

фа́була, f. fable.

фа́за, f. phase.

фаза́н, m. pheasant.

фа́кел, m. torch.

факт, m. fact. -и́ческий, adj. factual, actual.

факультати́вный, adj. optional.

факульте́т, m. faculty, department.

фа́кция, f. faction.

фальсифици́ровать, v. imp. & perf. falsify.

фальши́вый, adj. false.

фальшь, f. falsity, falseness.

фами́лия, f. surname.

фамилья́рный, adj. unceremonious, familiar.

фанати́зм, m. fanaticism.

фане́ра, f. veneer; plywood.

фанта́зия, f. fantasy; fancy; imagination.

фанфа́ра, f. fanfare.

фа́ра, f. headlight.

фармаце́вт, m. pharmacist.

фарма́ция, f. pharmacy.

фа́ртук, m. apron.

фарфо́р, m. porcelain, china.

фарш, m. stuffing; minced meat.

фарширова́ть, v. imp. stuff.

фасо́н, m. fashion, mode, style.

февра́ль, m. February. -ский, adj. February.

федерати́вный, adj. federative.

федера́ция, f. federation.

Фе́дя (also Фе́дька), dim. of name Фёдор.

фейерве́рк, m. fireworks.

феноме́н, m. phenomenon.

феодали́зм, m. feudalism.

феода́льный, adj. feudal.

Фео́дор, m. Theodore.

Феодо́сий, m. Theodosius.

ферзь, f. (chess) queen.

фе́рма, f. farm; girder; truss.

фе́рмер, m. farmer. -ство, nt. farming.

фестива́ль, m. festival.

фетр, m. felt. -овый, adj. felt.

фехтова́льщик m., фехтова́льщица f., fencer.

фехтова́ть, v. imp. fence.

фиа́лка, f. violet.

фиа́ско, nt. ind. fiasco; failure.

фи́га, f. fig.

фигу́ра, f. figure; (cards) face-card; (chess) piece.

фигури́ровать, v. imp. figure or appear as.

фи́зик, m. physicist.

фи́зика, f. physics.

физиоло́гия, f. physiology.

физи́ческий, adj. physical.

физкульту́ра, f. abbr. of физи́ческая культу́ра.

физкульту́рник, m. athlete, gymnast.

фикти́вный, adj. fictitious.

фи́кция, f. fiction.

филиа́л, *m.* branch, department.

филоло́гия, *f.* philology.

фило́соф, *m.* philosopher.

филосо́фия, *f.* philosophy.

философ́ствовать. *v. imp.* philosophize.

фильм, *m.* film; movie.

фильтр, *m.* filter.

фина́л, *m.* finale.

фина́нсовый, *adj.* financial.

фина́нсы, *pl.* finances.

фи́ник, *m.* date (*fruit*).

финля́ндец (*also* финн) *m.*, финля́ндка (*also* фи́нка) *f.*, Finn.

фиоле́товый, *adj.* violet.

фи́рма, *f.* firm, company.

фиста́шка, *f.* pistachio.

фити́ль, *m.* wick.

флаг, *m.* flag, banner.

флако́н, *m.* bottle.

флане́ль, *f.* flannel.

флéгма, *f.* phlegm, apathy.

фле́йта, *f.* flute.

фли́гель, *m.* wing.

флот, *m.* fleet. -ский, *adj.* naval.

фля́га (*also* фля́жка), *f.* flask.

фойе́, *nt. ind.* foyer.

фо́кус, *m.* focus; trick, whim, freak.

фома́, *m.* Thomas.

фон, *m.* background.

фона́рь, *m.* lantern, lamp; street lamp; flashlight.

фонд, *m.* fund.

фоне́тика, *f.* phonetics.

фонта́н, *m.* fountain.

форе́ль, *f.* trout.

фо́рма, *f.* form, shape; mould; uniform.

форма́льный, *adj.* formal.

форма́т, *m.* size.

форма́ция, *f.* formation; structure.

формирова́ть, *v. imp.* (*perf.* фсформирова́ть), form, mold.

формули́ровать, *v. imp.* formulate.

форси́ровать, *v. imp.* force.

фортепиа́но, *nt. ind.* piano.

фортифика́ция, *f.* fortification.

фо́сфор, *m.* phosphorus.

фо́то, *nt. ind.* photo.

фотоаппара́т, *m.* camera.

фото́граф, *m.* photographer.

фотографи́ровать, *v. imp.* (*perf.* сфотографи́ровать), photograph.

фотогра́фия, *f.* photograph.

фотока́рточка, *f.* photograph.

фрагме́нт, *m.* fragment. -а́рный, *adj.* fragmentary.

фра́за, *f.* phrase.

франт, *m.* dandy.

Фра́нция, *f.* France.

францу́женка, *f.* Frenchwoman.

францу́з, *m.* Frenchman. -ский *adj.* French.

фрахт, *m.* freight.

фре́ска, *f.* fresco.

фронт, *m.* front.

фрукт, *m.* fruit. -о́вый, *adj.* fruit.

фунда́мент, *m.* foundation; groundwork. -а́льный, *adj.* fundamental.

функциони́ровать, *v. imp. & perf.* function.

фу́нкция, *f.* function.

фура́ж, *m.* forage, fodder.

фут, *m.* foot.

футбо́л, *m.* football; soccer. -и́ст, *m.* football *or* soccer player.

футля́р, *m.* case.

фуфа́йка, *f.* jersey.

X

хала́т, *m.* bathrobe; overalls.

хала́тный, *adj.* negligent.

хам, *m.* boor; crude person. -ский, *adj.* crude, vulgar.

хамелео́н, *m.* chameleon.

ха́нжеский, *adj.* bigoted; hypocritical.

ха́ос, *m.* chaos.

хаоти́ческий (also хаоти́чный), adj. chaotic.

хара́ктер, m. character; nature. -и́стика, f. characteristic. -ный, adj. characteristic; typical.

характеризова́ть, v. imp. characterize.

ха́ркать, v. imp. (perf. ха́ркнуть), spit, expectorate.

ха́та, f. hut.

хвала́, f. praise.

хвале́бный, adj. laudatory.

хвали́ть, v. imp. (perf. похвали́ть), praise. -ся, boast.

хвастовство́, nt. boasting, bragging.

хвасту́н, m. braggart.

хвата́ть, v. imp. (perf. схвати́ть), grab, grasp. — (perf. хвати́ть), suffice. -ся, v. imp. (perf. схвати́ться), grip; snatch (at).

хво́йный, adj. coniferous.

хвора́ть, v. imp. (colloq.) be ill.

хвост, m. tail.

хижина, f. hut, cabin.

хи́лый, adj. feeble; sickly.

химе́ра, f. chimera.

хи́мик, m. chemist. -а́лии, pl. chemicals.

хими́ческий, adj. chemical.

хи́мия, f. chemistry.

хини́н, m. quinine.

хиру́рг, m. surgeon. -и́ческий, adj. surgical. -и́я, f. surgery.

хи́трый, adj. cunning.

хище́ние, nt. plunder, plundering.

хищник, m. beast (or bird) of prey.

хищный, adj. predatory; rapacious.

хладнокро́вный, adj. composed; cool.

хлеб, m. bread; corn, grain.

хлев, m. pigsty.

хлеста́ть, v. imp. lash.

хло́пать, v. imp. (perf. хло́пнуть), bang, slam.

хлопко́вый, adj. cotton.

хло́пок, m. cotton.

хло́пья, pl. flakes; flocks.

хлор, m. chlorine.

хмель, m. hop(s); drunken-

ness, intoxication. -но́е, nt. intoxicating beverage. -но́й, adj. intoxicating.

хму́риться, v. imp. (perf. нахму́риться), frown.

хму́рый, adj. gloomy.

хны́кать, v. imp. (colloq.) whimper.

хо́бот, m. trunk, proboscis.

ход, m. motion, speed; turn, move, lead.

ходи́ть, v. imp. indet. (det. идти́, perf. пойти́), go; walk.

хо́дкий, adj. current; marketable.

ходу́ли, pl. stilts.

ходьба́, f. walking.

хозя́ин, m. master; owner, proprietor; host.

хозя́йка, f. mistress, hostess.

хозя́йничать, v. imp. keep house; be a host.

хозя́йство, nt. economy; household.

хокке́й, m. hockey.

холе́ра, f. cholera.

холм, m. hill. -и́стый adj. hilly.

хо́лод, m. cold.

холоди́льник, m. icebox; refrigerator.

холо́дный, adj. cold.

холосто́й, adj. unmarried; idle; blank.

холостя́к, m. bachelor.

холст, m. canvas; linen.

хор, m. chorus, choir.

Хорва́тия, f. Croatia.

хорони́ть, v. imp. (perf. схорони́ть, похорони́ть) bury, inter; hide, conceal.

хоро́шенький, adj. pretty.

хоро́ший, adj. good.

хорошо́, adv. well. — impers. all right; good.

хоте́ть, v. imp. (perf. захоте́ть), want, wish, have a desire. -ся, impers., + dat., want, wish, have a yen. мне хо́чется есть (спать), I want to eat (sleep), I'm hungry (sleepy).

хоть, conj. at least. хоть бы, if only.

хотя́, conj. although. хотя́ бы, even though.

хо́хот, *m.* loud laughter.

хохота́ть, *v. imp.* roar with laughter.

хра́брый, *adj.* brave, courageous.

храм, *m.* temple; church.

хране́ние, *nt.* keeping, storing, storage.

храни́лище, *nt.* storage; warehouse.

храни́тель, *m.* custodian, keeper.

храни́ть, *v. imp.* keep, store.

храпе́ть, *v. imp.* snore.

хребе́т, *m.* (anat.) spine; mountain range.

хрен, *m.* horseradish.

хрип, *m.* wheeze. **-лый**, *adj.* hoarse. **-ота́**, *f.* hoarseness.

христиани́н *m.*, **христиа́нка** *f.*, Christian.

христиа́нский, *adj.* Christian.

христиа́нство, *nt.* Christianity.

Христо́с, *m.* Christ.

Христофо́р, *m.* Christopher.

хрома́ть, *v. imp.* limp.

хромо́й, *adj.* lame. — *m.* lame person.

хромота́, *f.* lameness.

хро́ника, *f.* chronicle.

хрони́ческий, *adj.* chronic.

хронологи́ческий, *adj.* chronological.

хру́пкий, *adj.* frail, delicate.

хруст, *m.* crackle, crunch.

хруста́ль, *f.* crystal.

хрусте́ть, *v. imp.* (*perf.* **хру́стнуть**), crackle, crunch.

хрю́кать, *v. imp.* (*perf.* **хрю́кнуть**), grunt.

хрящ, *m.* (anat.) cartilage; gravel.

худе́ть, *v. imp.* (*perf.* **похуде́ть**), become *or* grow thin; lose weight.

ху́до, *adv.* bad, badly. — *n.* harm, evil. — *impers.* (with *dat.*) feel unwell.

худо́жество, *nt.* art.

худо́жник *m.*, **худо́жница** *f.*, artist.

худо́й, *adj.* lean; meagre; evil, bad; ill.

ху́дший, *adj.* worst.

ху́же, *adv.* worse.

хулига́н, *m.* ruffian.

ху́тор, *m.* farmstead.

Ц

ца́пля, *f.* heron.

цара́пать, *v. imp.*, *tr.*, scratch.

цара́пина, *f.* scratch.

цари́ть, *v. imp.* reign.

ца́рство, *nt.* kingdom.

ца́рствовать, *v. imp.* reign.

царь, *m.* tsar.

цвести́, *v. imp.* bloom, flower, blossom.

цвет, *m.* color; flower; blossom. **-ни́к**, *m.* flower garden. **-но́й**, *adj.* colored. **-о́к**, *m.* flower; blossom. **-у́щий**, *adj.* flowering; flourishing.

цветна́я капу́ста, cauliflower.

цеди́ть, *v. imp.* strain; filter.

Це́зарь, *m.* Caesar.

целе́бный, *adj.* medicinal, curative.

целесообра́зный, *adj.* expedient.

целеустремлённый, *adj.* purposeful.

целико́м, *adv.* entirely, completely.

целина́, *f.* virgin soil.

це́лить, *v. imp.* aim.

целова́ть, *v. imp.* (*perf.* **поцелова́ть**), *tr.*, kiss.

це́лое, *nt.* whole.

целому́дрие, *nt.* chastity.

це́лостный, *adj.* integral.

це́лость, *f.* safety; integrity. **в це́лости**, intact.

це́лый, *adj.* whole.

цель, *f.* aim, purpose, intention.

цеме́нт, *m.* cement.

цена́, *f.* price; cost.

цензу́ра, *f.* censorship.
цени́ть, *v. imp.* value; estimate.
це́нность, *f.* value.
це́нный, *adj.* valuable.
центр, *m.* center.
централизова́ть, *v. imp.* centralize.
центра́льный, *adj.* central.
центробе́жный, *adj.* centrifugal.
цепля́ться, *v. imp.* cling (to).
цепь, *f.* chain.
церемо́ниться, *v. imp.* stand on ceremony.
церемо́нный, *adj.* ceremonious.
Цере́ра, *f.* (*myth.*) Ceres.
це́рковь, *f.* church.
цивилиза́ция, *f.* civilization.
цивилизова́ть, *v. imp.* civilize.
цикл, *m.* cycle.
цикло́н, *m.* cyclone.
цико́рий, *m.* chicory.

цили́ндр, *m.* cylinder. **-и́ческий**, *adj.* cylindrical.
цини́зм, *m.* cynicism.
цини́ческий, *adj.* cynical.
цинк, *m.* zinc. **-овый**, *adj.* zinc.
цирк, *m.* circus.
циркуля́р, *m.* circular. **-ный**, *adj.* circular.
циркуля́ция, *f.* circulation.
цита́та, *f.* quotation.
цити́ровать, *v. imp.* quote.
ци́тра, *f.* zither.
цифербла́т, *m.* dial, face.
ци́фра, *f.* figure.
Цицеро́н, *m.* Cicero.
цыга́н *m.*, **-ка** *f.*, gypsy.
цы́кать, *v. imp.* (*perf.* цы́кнуть), silence; hush.
цы́нга, *f.* scurvy.
цыплёнок, *m.* chick.
цы́почки, *pl.*: на цы́почках, on tiptoe.

Ч

чад, *m.* fumes.
чай, *m.* tea. **-ный**, *adj.* tea.
ча́йка, *f.* seagull.
ча́йник, *m.* teapot.
ча́лый, *adj.* roan.
чан, *m.* tub, vat.
чарова́ть, *v. imp.* charm; bewitch.
чароде́й, *m.* magician, sorcerer.
час, *m.* hour; o'clock. кото́рый час, what time is it?
часово́й, *adj.* hour; time. — *m.* sentry.
части́ца, *f.* (*gram.*) particle.
части́чный, *adj.* partial.
ча́стность, *f.* particular; detail.
ча́стный, *adj.* private.
ча́сто, *adv.* frequently.
ча́стый, *adj.* frequent.
часть, *f.* part.
часы́, *m.* clock, watch.
чахо́тка, *f.* (*med.*) consumption.
ча́шка, *f.* cup.
ча́ща, *f.* thicket.
ча́ще, *adv.* more frequently *or* often.

ча́яние, *nt.* expectation; hope.
чва́нство, *nt.* blast, boasting.
чего́, *gen. of* что.
чей, *pron.* whose.
чек, *m.* check.
чека́нить, *v. imp.* coin, mint.
челове́к, *m.* man.
челове́ческий, *adj.* human.
челове́чество, *nt.* humanity.
челове́чность, *f.* humaneness.
че́люсть, *f.* jaw.
чем, *instr. of* что. — *conj.* than.
чемода́н, *m.* trunk; suitcase; valise.
чемпиона́т, *m.* championship.
чему́, *dat. of* что.
чепуха́, *f.* nonsense.
червь, (*also* червя́к) *m.* worm.
черда́к, *m.* garret.
чередова́ться, *v. imp., intr.* alternate.
че́рез (чрез), *prep.* (+ *acc.*) across, over; through; (*time*) in. че́рез день, every other day.
че́реп, *m.* skull.
черепа́ха, *f.* tortoise, turtle.
черепи́ца, *f.* tile.
чересчу́р, *adv.* too; exceedingly.

черёшня, f. cherry; cherry tree.

чернéть, v. imp. become or turn black.

чернúла, pl. ink.

чернúльница, f. inkstand.

чернúть, v. imp. blacken; slander.

черновúк, m. draft; rough copy.

чернорабóчий, m. unskilled worker.

чернослúв, m. (coll.) prunes.

чёрный, adj. black.

черпáть, v. imp. draw, draw up.

черствéть, v. imp. become or grow stale.

чёрствый, adj. stale.

чертá, f. trait, characteristic; line.

чертёж, m. sketch; draft.

чертúть, v. imp. draw.

черчéние, nt. drawing.

чесáть, v, imp. comb; card. **-ся,** scratch oneself.

чеснóк, m. garlic.

чествовáть, v. imp. celebrate; honor.

чéстный, adj. honest; fair.

честолюбúвый, adj. ambitious.

честь, f. honor.

четвéрг, m. Thursday.

четвéреньки, pl.: **на четвéреньках,** on all fours.

четвёрка, f. four; foursome.

четверо, num. coll. four. **-нóгое,** nt. quadruped.

четвёртый, adj. fourth.

четвéрть, f. quarter; fourth.

чёткий, adj. clear; legible.

чётный, adj. even.

четыре, num. four. **-ста,** num. four hundred.

четырёхсóтый, adj. four hundredth.

четырнáдцатый, adj. fourteenth.

четырнáдцать, num. fourteen.

чех m., **чéшка** f., Czech.

чéшский, adj. Czech.

чин, m. grade, rank.

чинúть, v. imp. cause. — (perf. починúть), repair. — (perf. очинúть), sharpen.

чинóвник, m. official; bureaucrat.

чúсленность, f. number, quantity.

чúсленный, adj. numeral.

числúтель, m. (math.) numerator.

числúтельное, see úмя числúтельное and порядковое числúтельное.

числó, nt. number, quantity; date; (gram.) number.

чистúльщик, m. bootblack.

чúстить, v. imp. clean; brush; peel.

чúстка, f. cleaning; purge, purging.

чистокрóвный, adj. thoroughbred.

чистосердéчный, adj. frank, sincere.

чистотá, f. cleanliness; purity, innocence.

чúстый, adj. clean.

читáльня, f. reading room.

читáть, v. imp. read. **читáть лéкцию,** deliver a lecture.

чихáть, v. imp. (perf. чихнýть), sneeze.

член, m. member; (gram.) article. **-ство,** nt. membership.

чорт, m. devil.

чрезвычáйный, adj. extraordinary.

чрезмéрный, adj. excessive; exceeding.

чтéние, nt. reading.

чтить, v. imp. honor; respect.

что, pron. what. — conj. that.

чтóбы, conj. in order to or that.

чтó-либо (also **чтó-нибудь**), pron. something; anything.

чтó-то, pron. something.

чýвственный, adj. sensual.

чувствúтельный, adj. sensitive; sentimental.

чýвство, nt. sense; feeling.

чýвствовать, v. imp. sense; feel.

чудáк, m. (person) crank, eccentric.

чудéсный, adj. wonderful, miraculous.

чýдиться, v. imp. seem.

чуднóй, adj. odd, strange.

чýдный, adj. wonderful; beautiful.

чу́до, *nt.* wonder.

чудо́вище, *nt.* monster.

чудо́вищный, *adj.* monstrous.

чужда́ться, *v. imp.* keep away from; keep aloof; avoid.

чу́ждый, *adj.* alien.

чужо́й, *adj.* strange; someone else's.

чуло́к, *m.* stocking; hose.

чума́, *f.* plague.

чу́ткий, *adj.* sensitive; delicate; considerate.

чуть, *adv.* slightly; hardly; almost.

чутьё, *nt.* scent; intuition.

чу́ять, *v. imp.* feel.

чьё, чьи, чья, *see* чей.

Ш

шабло́н, *m.* stencil; pattern; mould.

шаг, *m.* step. **-ом,** *adv.* at a walking pace.

шага́ть, *v. imp.* step, pace, stride.

ша́йка, *f.* gang, band.

шака́л, *m.* jackal.

шала́ш, *m.* hut.

шали́ть, *v. imp.* misbehave; be naughty.

шалу́н, *m.* mischievous child.

шаль, *f.* shawl.

шампа́нское, *nt.* champagne.

шанта́ж, *m.* blackmail.

ша́пка, *f.* cap.

шар, *m.* ball; sphere. **возду́шный шар,** balloon.

шара́да, *f.* charade.

шарж, *m.* cartoon; caricature.

ша́рик, *m.* bead; small ball; globule.

ша́рить, *v. imp.* fumble around rummage (in).

ша́ркать, *v. imp.* shuffle one's feet.

шарлата́н, *m.* charlatan. **-ство,** *nt.* quackery.

шарови́дный, *adj.* spherical.

шарф, *m.* scarf.

шата́ть, *v. imp.* sway; rock; shake. **-ся,** become loose; stagger, reel.

ша́ткий, *adj.* unsteady; precarious.

ша́фер, *m.* best man.

шах, *m.* (*chess*) check. **шах и мат,** (*chess*) checkmate.

шахмати́ст *m.,* **-ка** *f.,* chess player.

ша́хматы, *pl.* chess.

ша́хта, *f.* mine; pit.

шахтёр, *m.* miner.

ша́шечница, *f.* checkerboard.

ша́шки, *pl.* (*game*) checkers.

шве́дский, *adj.* Swedish.

шве́йный, *adj.* sewing.

швейца́р, *m.* porter; doorman.

швейца́рец *m.,* **швейца́рка** *f.,* Swiss.

Швейца́рия, *f.* Switzerland.

Шве́ция, *f.* Sweden.

швея́, *f.* seamstress.

шевели́ть, *v. imp.,* move, stir.

шеде́вр, *m.* masterpiece.

ше́лест, *m.* rustle, rustling.

шелесте́ть, *v. imp.* rustle.

шёлк, *m.* silk.

шелкови́стый, *adj.* silky.

шёлковый, *adj.* silk.

шелуши́ть, *v. imp.* shell, husk.

шепеля́вить, *v. imp.* lisp.

шепеля́вый, *adj.* lisping.

шепта́ть, *v. imp.* whisper.

шере́нга, *f.* rank.

шерохова́тый, rough; rugged.

шерсти́стый, *adj.* woolly.

шерсть, *f.* hair; wool; worsted.

шерстяно́й, *adj.* woolen.

ше́ршень, *m.* hornet.

шест, *m.* pole.

ше́ствие, *nt.* procession; train.

шестна́дцатый, *adj.* sixteenth.

шестна́дцать, *num.* sixteen.

шесто́й, *adj.* sixth.

шесть, *num.* six. **-деся́т,** *num.* sixty. **-со́т,** *num.* six hundred.

шеф, *m.* chief; chef. **-ство,** *nt.* patronage.

ше́я, *f.* neck.

шика́рный, adj. chic, smart.
ши́ло, nt. awl.
ши́на, f. tire; (med.) splint.
шине́ль, f. overcoat.
шип, m. thorn.
шипе́ние, nt. hissing; spitting; sizzling.
шипе́ть, v. imp. hiss.
шипу́чий, adj. sparkling.
ширина́, f. width, breadth.
широ́кий, adj. wide.
широковеща́ние, nt. broadcasting.
широта́, f. width; breadth; (geog.) latitude.
шить, v. imp. (perf. сшить), sew.
шитьё, nt. sewing; embroidering; embroidery.
шифр, m. cipher.
ши́шка, f. (bot.) cone; bump, lump; kernel.
шкала́, f. scale.
шкату́лка, f. box, case; casket.
шкаф, m. cupboard; dresser; wardrobe.
шко́ла, f. school; schoolhouse.
шко́льник, m. schoolboy.
шко́льный, adj. school, scholastic.
шку́ра, f. skin; hide.
шланг, m. hose.
шлем, m. helmet.
шлифова́ть, v. imp. grind; polish.
шля́па, f. hat.
шмель, m. bumblebee.
шнур, m. string; cord.
шнурова́ть, v. imp. string; lace, lace up.
шов, m. seam.
шовини́зм, m. chauvinism.
шокола́д, m. chocolate.
шо́пот, m. whisper.
шо́рох, m. rustle.
шоссе́, nt. ind. highway.
Шотла́ндия, f. Scotland.
шотла́ндский, adj. Scotch, Scottish.
шофёр, m. chauffeur, driver.

шпа́га, f. sword, épée.
шпи́лька, f. hairpin; tack; brad, stud.
шпина́т, m. spinach.
шпио́н, m. spy. -а́ж, m. espionage.
шпио́нить, v. imp. spy.
шпо́ра, f. spur.
шприц, m. syringe.
шпу́лька, f. spool, bobbin.
шрам, m. scar.
шрифт, m. print; type.
штаб, m. staff; headquarters.
штамп, m. stamp; cliché.
шта́нга, f. (athl.) weight.
штанги́ст m.,-ка f.,weightlifter
штаны́, pl. trousers.
штат, m. (USA) state. -ский adj. civil, civilian.
штиль, m. (naut.) calm.
што́пать, v. imp. darn.
што́пка, f. darning; darning cotton or wool.
што́пор, m. corkscrew.
шторм, m. storm.
штраф, m. fine; penalty.
штрафова́ть, v. imp. (perf оштрафова́ть), fine.
шту́ка, f. piece; thing.
штукату́рить, v. imp. plaster
шту́рман, m. navigator.
штурмова́ть, v. imp. storm assault.
штык, m. bayonet.
шу́ба, f. fur coat.
шум, m. noise. -ный, adf noisy, loud; tumultuous.
шуме́ть, v. imp. make a noise be noisy.
Шу́ра, dim. of Алекса́ндр Алекса́ндра.
шу́рин, m. brother-in-law (wife's brother).
шурша́ть, v. imp. rustle.
шут, m. fool. -ка, f. joke, jes -ли́вый, adj. playful. -очны adj. comical; facetious.
шути́ть, v. imp. joke, jest.
шушу́каться, v. imp. whisper

Щ

щади́ть, v. imp. spare; have mercy.

щебета́ть, v. imp. chirrup.
ще́дрый, adj. generous.

щека́, *f.* cheek.

щекота́ть, *v. imp.* tickle.

щекотли́вый, *adj.* ticklish; delicate.

щёлкать, *v. imp.* click; smack; crack.

щелочно́й, *adj.* alkaline.

щель, *f.* crack, chink; (*anat*) glottis.

щено́к, *m.* pup, puppy.

щепети́льный, *adj.* scrupulous.

ще́пка, *f.* chip.

щети́на, *f.* bristle.

щётка, *f.* brush.

щи, *pl.* Russian cabbage soup.

щи́колотка (*also* щи́колка), *f.* ankle.

щипа́ть, *v. imp.* (*perf.* щипну́ть), pinch; nibble.

щипцы́, *pl.* tongs, pincers.

щит, *m.* shield.

щу́ка, *f.* (*fish*) pike.

щу́пальце, *nt.* tentacle; feeler.

щу́пать, *v. imp.* feel.

щу́плый, *adj.* puny.

Э

эбе́новый, *adj.* ebony.

эвакуа́ция, *f.* evacuation.

эвакуи́ровать, *v. imp. & perf.* evacuate.

эволюцио́нный, *adj.* evolutional; evolutionary.

Эге́йское мо́ре, Aegean Sea.

эго́изм, *m.* egoism.

эква́тор, *m.* equator. **-на́льный**, *adj.* equatorial.

экза́мен, *m.* examination.

экзаменова́ть, *v. imp.* examine. **-ся**, take an examination; be examined.

экземпля́р, *m.* copy; specimen.

эконо́мика, *f.* economics.

эконо́мить, *v. imp.* economize.

экономи́ческий, *adj.* economic.

эконо́мия, *f.* economy.

эконо́мный, *adj.* economical.

экра́н, *m.* screen.

экску́рсия, *f.* excursion.

экспа́нсия, *f.* expansion.

экспеди́ция, *f.* expedition.

экспериме́нт, *m.* experiment. **-а́льный**, *adj.* experimental.

экспе́рт, *m.* expert.

эксплуати́ровать, *v. imp.* exploit.

экспона́т, *m.* exhibit.

экспорти́ровать, *v. imp. & perf.* export.

экспре́сс, *m.* express. **-и́вный**, *adj.* expressive.

экстренный, *adj.* special; unforeseen.

эласти́чный, *adj.* elastic.

элега́нтный, *adj.* elegant.

эле́гия, *f.* elegy.

электри́ческий, *adj.* electric.

электри́чество, *nt.* electricity.

элеме́нт, *m.* element. **-а́рный**, *adj.* elementary.

эма́левый, *adj.* enamel.

эма́ль, *f.* enamel.

эмбле́ма, *f.* emblem.

эмигри́ровать, *v. imp. & perf.* emigrate.

Эне́й, *m.* Aeneas.

энерги́чный, *adj.* energetic.

эне́ргия, *f.* energy.

энтузиасти́ческий, *adj.* enthusiastic.

энциклопеди́ческий, *adj.* encyclopedic.

энциклопе́дия, *f.* encyclopedia.

эпиде́мия, *f.* epidemic.

эпизо́д, *m.* episode.

эпи́ческий, *adj.* epic.

эпо́ха, *f.* epoch.

э́ра, *f.* era.

эруди́ция, *f.* erudition.

эски́з, *m.* sketch.

эскимо́с, *m.* Eskimo. **-ский**, *adj.* Eskimo.

эстафе́та, *f.* relay race; relays.

эсте́тика, *f.* esthetics.

эсто́нец *m.*, **эсто́нка** *f.*, Estonian.

эсто́нский, *adj.* Estonian.

эстра́да, *f.* platform.

эстуа́рий, *m.* estuary.

эта, see э́тот.

этаж, *m.* floor, story.

эта́п, *m.* stage, phase.

э́ти, see э́тот.

э́тика, *f.* ethics.

этике́тка, *f.* label.

эти́чный, *adj.* ethic(al).

э́то, this, that, it; see э́тот.

э́тот *m.*, э́та *f.*, э́то *nt.*, э́ти *pl.*, *pron.* this; that.

этю́д, *m.* (*mus.*) etude; study, exercise; sketch.

эфи́р, *m.* ether.

эффе́кт, *m.* effect.

эффе́кт, *m.* effect. -и́вный, *adj.* effective; efficient. -ный, *adj.* effective, spectacular.

э́хо, *nt.* echo.

Ю

юбиле́й, *m.* jubilee; anniversary.

ю́бка, *f.* skirt; slip.

ювели́р, *m.* jeweler.

юг, *m.* south.

югосла́вский, *adj.* Yugoslav.

юдофо́б, *m.* anti-Semite. -ство *nt.* anti-Semitism.

ю́жанин *m.*, ю́жанка *f.*, southerner.

ю́жный, *adj.* south, southern.

ю́мор, *m.* humor. -исти́ческий *adj.* humoristic; comic(al).

ю́ность, *f.* youth.

ю́ноша, *m.* youth; young man.

ю́ношеский, *adj.* youthful.

ю́ношество, *nt.* youth; (*coll.*) young people.

ю́ный, *adj.* young; youthful.

юриди́ческий, *adj.* juridical, legal.

юрисди́кция, *f.* jurisdiction.

юри́ст, *m.* lawyer.

ю́ркий, *adj.* brisk; nimble.

юсти́ция, *f.* justice.

юти́ться, *v. imp.* huddle; huddle together; take shelter.

Я

я, *pron.* I.

я́блоко, *nt.* apple. глазно́е я́блоко, eyeball.

я́блоня, *f.* appletree.

я́блочный, *adj.* apple.

яви́ться, *v.*, *perf. of* явля́ться.

я́вка, *f.* appearance; presence.

явле́ние, *nt.* appearance; occurrence; (*theat.*) scene.

явля́ться, *v. imp.* (*perf.* яви́ться), appear, seem; come.

я́вный, *adj.* evident, obvious.

я́вственный, *adj.* clear; distinct.

ягнёнок, *m.* lamb.

я́года, *f.* berry.

я́годица, *f.* buttock.

яд, *m.* poison.

ядови́тый, *adj.* poisonous, venomous.

ядро́, *nt.* nucleus. толка́ние ядра́, (*athl.*) shot put.

я́зва, *f.* ulcer.

язви́тельный, *adj.* biting.

язы́к, *m.* tongue; language. -ове́дение, *nt.* linguistics.

язы́ческий, *adj.* pagan.

язы́чник, *m.* pagan, heathen.

яичко́, *nt.* small egg; (*anat.*) testicle.

яи́чник, *m.* ovary.

яи́чница, *f.* scrambled eggs; omelet.

яйцо́, *nt.* egg.

я́кобы, *conj.* as if; as though.

Я́ков, *m.* Jacob.

я́корь, *m.* anchor.

я́ловый, *adj.* barren; dry.

я́ма, *f.* pit.

янва́рский, *adj.* January.

янва́рь, *m.* January.

янта́рь, *m.* amber.

япо́нец *m.*, япо́нка *f.*, Japanese.

Япо́ния, *f.* Japan.

япо́нский, *adj.* Japanese.

яр, *m.* steep bank.

я́ркий, *adj.* bright; clear.

ярлы́к, *m.* label.

я́рмарка, *f.* fair.

ярмо́, *nt.* yoke.

я́ростный, *adj.* fierce, furious, violent.

я́рость, *f.* fury, rage; violence.

я́рус, *m.* (*theat.*) tier, circle.

я́рый, *adj.* ardent; violent.

я́сли, *pl.* feeding crib; creche.

я́сный, *adj.* clear.

я́стреб, *m.* hawk.

я́хта, *f.* yacht.

яхтсме́н, *m.* yachtsman.

яче́йка, *f.* cell.

ячме́нь, *m.* barley; (*med.*) sty.

я́щерица, *f.* lizard.

я́щик, *m.* box; drawer.

A

a, *indef. art., no equivalent in Russian.*

abandon, *n.* непринуждённость *f.* — *v.* покидáть *imp.,* покúнуть *perf.;* оставлять *imp.,* остáвить *perf.* **-ed,** *adj.* покúнутый, забрóшенный. **-ment,** *n.* оставлéние *nt.,* заброшённость *f.*

abate, *v.* уменьшáть (ся) *imp.,* умéньшить (ся) *perf.;* ослаблять *imp.,* ослáбить *perf.*

abbreviate, *v.* сокращáть *imp.,* сократúть *perf.*

abbreviation, *n.* аббревиатýра *f.,* сокращéние *nt.*

abdomen, *n.* брюшнáя пóлость; живóт *m.*

abdominal, *adj.* брюшнóй.

abduct, *v.* похищáть *imp.,* похúтить *perf.;* уводúть (увестú) сúлой.

abduction, *n.* похищéние *nt.,* увóд *m.*

abet, *v.* подстрекáть *imp.,* подстрекнýть *perf.;* содéйствовать *imp.* & *perf.*

abeyance, *n.* состояние неопределённости.

abhor, *v.* ненавúдеть *imp.;* питáть отвращéние.

abhorrence, *n.* отвращéние *nt.*

abhorrent, *adj.* отвратúтельный.

abiding, *adj.* постоянный.

ability, *n.* спосóбность *f.*

ablaze, *adj.* в огнé, в плáмени.

able, *adj.* спосóбный; умéлый **to be able,** мочь; быть в состоянии.

ably, *adv.* умéло.

abnormal, *adj.* ненормáльный, анормáльный. **-ity,** *n.* ненормáльность *f.,* непрáвильность *f.* **-ly,** *adv.* ненормáльно, анормáльно.

aboard, *adv.* (*location*) на корáблé, на бортý, в вагóне; (*motion*) на корáбль, на борт, в вагóн; **all aboard!** посáдка зáкончена!

abode, *n.* жилúще *nt.,* местопребывáние *nt.*

abolish, *v.* стменять *imp.,* отменúть *perf.*

abominable, *adj.* отвратúтельный.

abominate, *v.* питáть отвращéние, ненавúдеть.

abomination, *n.* отвращéние *nt.*

aboriginal, *adj.* искóнный, тузéмный.

abortion, *n.* абóрт *m.,* выкúдыш *f.*

abortive, *adj.* неудáвшийся, безплóдный.

abound, *v.* изобúловать *imp*

about, *adv.* кругóм; óколо; в обрáтном направлéнии; **a face!** кругóм! **be a. to,** собирáться *imp.* — *prep* вокрýг; по; о, об; óколо.

above, *adv* (*direction*) выше, наверх; (*location*) выше, наверхý. **from a.,** сверхý — *prep.* нáд; выше, бóльше свыше; **a. all,** бóльше всегó — *adj.* вышеупомянутый — *n.* **the above,** вышеупомянутое *nt.*

abrasion, *n.* абрáзия *f.;* шлифóвка *f.;* (*med.*) ссáдина *f.*

abrasive, *adj.* обдирáющий шлифýющий. — *n.* абразúвный (*or* шлифовáльный материáл.

abreast, *adv.* рядом; бок с бок; на однóй лúнии; на ýровне.

abridge, *v.* сокращáть *imp.* сократúть *perf.* **-ment,** *n* сокращéние *nt.;* сокращённый текст; крáткое изложéние.

abroad, *adv.* за границей; зá границу. **from a.,** из-зá границы.

abrupt, *adj.* обрывúстый; внезáпный; рéзкий. **-ly,** *adv* обрывисто; внезáпно; рéзко **-ness,** *n.* обрывистость *f* внезáпность *f.*

abscess, *n.* абсцесс *m.*, нарыв *m.*, гнойник *m.*

abscond, *v.* скрываться *imp.*, скрыться *perf.*; бежать *imp.*

absence, *n.* отсутствие *nt.*

absent, *adj.* отсутствующий. be a., отсутствовать *imp.*

absentee, *n.* отсутствующий; отлынивающий (от).

absent-minded, *adj.* рассеянный. -ness, *n.* рассеянность *f.*

absolute, *adj.* полный; безусловный; абсолютный. -ly, *adv.* абсолютно; совершенно; безусловно. -ness, *n.* абсолютность *f.*; совершенность *f.*; безусловность *f.*

absolution, *n.* прощение *nt.*; отпущение грехов.

absolutism, *n.* абсолютизм *m.*

absolve, *v.* прощать *imp.*, простить *perf.*; **a. of sins,** отпускать (отпустить) грехи.

absorb, *v.* абсорбировать *imp.* & *perf.*; поглощать *imp.*, поглотить *perf.*; всасывать *imp.*, всосать *perf.* -ent, *adj.* поглощающий; всасывающий. — *n.* поглотитель *m.*; всасывающее средство. -ing, *adj.* поглощающий; всасывающий.

absorption, *n.* абсорбция *f.*; поглощение *nt.*; (mind) погружённость *f.*

abstain, *v.* воздерживаться *imp.*, воздержаться *perf.*

abstract, *adj.* абстрактный; отвлечённый. — *n.* резюме *nt.*; извлечение *nt.*; конспект *m.* — *v.* отвлекать *imp.*, отвлечь *perf.*; абстрагировать *imp.* & *perf.*

absurd, *adj.* абсурдный, нелепый. -ity, *n.* нелепость *f.*, глупость *f.* -ly, *adv.* нелепо.

abundance, *n.* изобилие *nt.*

abundant, *adj.* обильный, изобильный. -ly, *adv.* обильно.

abuse, *n.* злоупотребление *nt.*, оскорбление *nt.*; неправильное употребление. —

v. злоупотреблять *imp.*, злоупотребить *perf.*; оскорблять *imp.*, оскорбить *perf.*

abusive, *adj.* оскорбительный, ругательный.

abyss, *n.* бездна *f.*, пропасть *f.*, пучина *f.*

academic, *adj.* академический.

academy, *n.* академия *f.*

accelerate, *v.* ускорять *imp.*, ускорить *perf.*

acceleration, *n.* ускорение *nt.*

accelerator, *n.* (auto) ускоритель *m.*, акселератор *m.*

accent, *n.* ударение *nt.*, акцент *m.* — *v.* ставить ударение; акцентировать *imp.* & *perf.*; подчёркивать *imp.*, подчеркнуть *perf.*

accentuate, *v.* подчёркивать *imp.*, подчеркнуть *perf.*; делать ударение.

accept, *v.* принимать *imp.*, принять *perf.*; допускать *imp.*, допустить *perf.*; признавать *imp.*, признать *perf.* -ance, *n.* принятие *nt.*, приём *m.*

access, *n.* доступ *m.* -ible, *adj.* доступный.

accessory, *adj.* добавочный, соучаствующий. — *n.* соучастник *m.*

accident, *n.* несчастный случай; случайность *f.* -al, *adj.* случайный. -ally, *adv.* случайно.

acclaim, *v.* провозглашать *imp.*, провозгласить *perf.*; шумно приветствовать. — *n.* шумное одобрение.

acclimate, *v.* акклиматизировать *imp.* & *perf.*

accommodate, *v.* приспособлять *imp.*, приспособить *perf.*; (lodge) давать пристанище; помещать *imp.*, поместить *perf.*

accomodating, *adj.* услужливый, приспособляющийся.

accomodation, *n.* приспособление *nt.*; удобство *nt.*

accompaniment, *n.* аккомпанемент *m.*

accompany, v. аккомпани́ровать imp. & perf.

accomplice, n. соуча́стник m., сообщник m.

accomplish, v. соверша́ть imp., соверши́ть perf.; заверша́ть imp., заверши́ть perf. -ment, n. заверше́ние nt., выполне́ние nt., достиже́ние nt.

accord, n. согла́сие, соглаше́ние — v. (agree) согласова́ть imp.; (grant) предоставля́ть imp. -ance, n. соотве́тствие nt.

according to, adv. согла́сно с, в соотве́тствии с (& instr.).

accordingly, adv. соотве́тственно.

accordion, n. аккордео́н m., гармо́ника f.

account, n. счёт m., расчёт m., отчёт m. on a. of, и́з-за, всле́дствие (& gen.). on no a., ни в ко́ем слу́чае. -able, adj. отве́тственный; объясни́мый.

accountant, n. бухга́лтер m.

accounting, n. бухгалте́рия f.

accumulate, v. аккумули́ровать imp. & perf.; нака́пливать (ся) imp., накопля́ть (ся) perf.

accumulation, n. накопле́ние nt., аккумуля́ция f.

accuracy, n. то́чность f., пра́вильность f.; ме́ткость f.

accurate, adj. ме́ткий; то́чный; пра́вильный. -ly, adv. то́чно.

accusation, n. обвине́ние nt.

accuse, v. обвиня́ть imp., обвини́ть perf.

accused, adj., n. обвиня́емый.

accuser, n. обвини́тель m.

accustom, v. привыка́ть imp., привы́кнуть perf.; приуча́ть imp., приучи́ть perf. -ed, adj. привы́кший, приуче́нный; привы́чный. become a., приуча́ться imp., приучи́ться perf.

ace, n. (cards) туз m.

ache, n. боль f. — v. боле́ть imp.

achieve, v. достига́ть imp.,

дости́гнуть perf. -ment, n. достиже́ние nt.

Achilles, n. Ахилле́с m.

acid, n. кислота́ f. — adj. ки́слый; кисло́тный. -ity, n. кисло́тность f., е́дкость f.

acknowledge, v. признава́ть imp., (admit) призна́ть perf.; сознава́ть imp., созна́ть perf.; a. (receipt) подтвержда́ть получе́ние.

acme, n. вы́сшая то́чка; верх m.

acoustics, n. аку́стика f.

acquaint, v. знако́мить imp., познако́мить perf. a. oneself with, знако́миться с imp., познако́миться perf. -ance, n. знако́мство nt.; (person) знако́мый. -ed, adj. знако́мый (с & instr.).

acquiesce, v. молчали́во согла́шаться imp., согласи́ться perf.

acquiescence, n. мопчали́вое согла́сие nt.

acquire, v. приобрета́ть imp., приобрести́ perf.

acquisition, n. приобрете́ние.

acquisitive, adj. стяжа́тельный.

acquit, v. опра́вдывать imp., оправда́ть perf.; освобожда́ть imp., освободи́ть perf.

acquittal, n. опра́вдание nt.

acre, n. акр m.

acrid, adj. о́стрый, е́дкий; ре́зкий.

acrobat, n. акроба́т m.

across, prep. сквозь, че́рез, по. — adv. поперёк; по ту сто́рону.

act, n. де́йствие nt.; (theat.) акт m.; (law) зако́н m. — v. поступа́ть imp., поступи́ть perf.; (behave) вести́ себя́. де́йствовать imp., поде́йствовать perf.

acting, n. игра́ f. — adj. де́йствующий.

action, n. де́йствие nt.; де́ятельность f.; посту́пок m.

active, adj. акти́вный, де́ятельный.

activity, n. де́ятельность f., акти́вность f.

actor, n. актёр m.

actress, n. актриса f.

actual, adj. действительный, настоящий. -ity, n. действительность f. -ly, adv, фактически; в действительности; на самом деле.

acute, adj. острый; проницательный. -ly adv. проницательно. -ness, n. острота f., пронзительность f.

Adam's apple, кадык m., адамово яблоко.

adapt, v. приспособлять imp., приспособить perf. -ation, n. приспособление nt., применение nt.

add, v. добавлять imp., добавить perf.; прибавлять imp., прибавить perf.

addition, n. добавление nt., сложение nt. in a., вдобавок; кроме того. in a. to, в дополнение к (& dat.). -al, adj. добавочный; дополнительный.

address, n. адрес m.; (speech) обращение nt. — v. t. (a letter) адресовать imp., направлять imp., направлять imp.; (speak to) обращаться imp., обратиться perf.

adequate, adj. отвечающий требованиям; достаточный.

adherence, n. приверженность f.

adhesive, adj. липкий. a. tape, липкий пластырь.

adieu, interj. прощай, прощайте. — n. прощание nt.

adjacent, adj. соседний.

adjective, n. имя прилагательное.

adjoining, adj. соседний, смежный.

adjourn, v. t. отсрочивать imp. отсрочить perf. — v. i. объявлять перерыв. объявить перерыв. -ment, n. отсрочка f., перерыв m.

adjust, v. улаживать imp., уладить perf.; прилаживать imp.; регулировать imp. & perf.; приводить в порядок.

administer, v. управлять imp.

administration, n. администрация f., управление nt.

administrative, adj. административный, исполнительный

administrator, n. администратор m., управляющий m.

admirable, adj. восхитительный.

admiration, n. восхищение nt., восторг m.

admire, v. t. восхищаться imp., восхититься perf.

admirer, n. поклонник m., поклонница f.; обожатель m.

admissible, adj. допустимый, приемлемый.

admission, n. допущение nt., вход m.; (confession) признание nt.

admit, v. допускать imp., допустить perf.; впускать imp., впустить perf.; (confess) признавать imp., признать perf.

admittance, n. доступ m., вход m.

admonish, v. увещать, увещевать imp.

amonitiond, n. увещание m., упрёк m.

adolescence, n. отрочество nt.

adopt, v. t. принимать imp., принять perf.; усыновлять imp., усыновить perf.; заимствовать imp.

adoption, n. усыновление nt., принятие nt.

adore, v. обожать imp.; поклоняться imp.

adorn, v. украшать imp., украсить perf. -ment, n. украшение nt.

adrenalin, n. адреналин m.

adroit, adj. ловкий, находчивый.

adult, adj., n. взрослый, совершеннолетний.

adulterate, v. примешивать imp., примешать perf

adultery, n. супружеская измена.

advance, n. продвижение nt.

in a., вперёд, заранее. — *v.* продвигаться вперёд; повышаться *imp.*, повыситься *perf.*

advanced, *adj.* передовой; выдвинутый.

advancement, *n.* продвижение *nt.*; выдвижение *nt.*

advantage, *n.* преимущество *nt.* **take a.** of, воспользоваться *imp.* **-ous,** *adj.* выгодный, благоприятный.

adventure, *n.* приключение *nt.*

adventurer, *n.* авантюрист *m.*

adventurous, *adj.* смелый; предприимчивый.

adverb, *n.* наречие *nt.*

adversary, *n.* противник *m.*

advertise, *v.* извещать *imp.*, объявлять *imp.*, **-ment,** *n.* объявление *nt.*

advertising, *n.* рекламное дело.

advice, *n.* совет *m.*

advisable, *adj.* рекомендуемый, целесообразный.

advise, *v.* советовать *imp.*

adviser, *n.* советник *m.*, консультант *m.*

advocate, *n.* сторонник *m.*, защитник *m.* — *v.* отстаивать *imp.*

Aegean Sea, Эгейскре море.

aerial, *adj.* воздушный. — *n.* антенна *f.*

afar, *adv.* вдалеке. **from afar,** издалека.

affair, *n.* дело *nt.*

affect, *v.* воздействовать *imp. & perf.*; (*emotionally*) трогать, волновать *imp.* **-ation,** *n.* аффектация *f.* **-ed,** *adj.* тронутый; (*unnatural*) аффектированный.

affection, *n.* привязанность *f.* **-ate,** *adj.* любящий, нежный. **-ately,** *adv.* нежно.

affiliation, *n.* присоединение, соединение *f.*

affinity, *n.* родственность *f.*; сходство *nt.*

affirmative, *n.* утвердительный ответ. — *adj.* утвердительный.

afflict, *v.* причинять страда-

ние. **-ion,** *n.* бедствие, несчастье *nt.*

affluence, *n.* изобилие *nt.*; приток *m.*

afford, *v.* быть в состоянии.

affront, *n.* оскорбление. *nt.* — *v.* оскорблять *imp.*, оскорбить *perf.*

aforementioned, *adj.* вышепомянутый.

afraid, *adj.* испуганный. **be a.,** бояться *imp.*; пугаться *imp.*

Africa, *n.* Африка *f.*

African, *adj.* африканский. — *n.* африканец *m.*, африканка *f.*

after, *prep.* после. — *conj.* после того как. — *adv.* после.

afternoon, *n.* время после полудня.

afterward(s), *adv.* впоследствии.

again, *adv.* опять, снова.

against, *prep.* (*opposed*) против (& *gen.*).

age, *n.* возраст *m.*; (*era*) век *m.*, эпоха *f.* **old age,** старость *f.* — *v. i.* стареть *imp.*, постареть *perf.*

aged, *adj.* пожилой.

agency, *n.* агенство.

aggravate, *v.* ухудшать *imp.*, ухудшить *perf.*

aggravation, *n.* ухудшение *nt.*

aggregate, *adj.* совркупный. — *n.* совокупность *f.*

aggregation, *n.* агрегат *m.*, скопление *nt.*

aggression, *n.* агрессия *f.*, нападение *nt.*

aggressive, *adj.* агрессивный. **-ly,** *adv.* агрессивно. **-ness,** *n.* агрессивность *f.*

agile, *adj.* подвижной, проворный.

agility, *n.* подвижность *f.*

agitate, *v.* агитировать *imp. & perf.*

agitation, *n.* агитация *f.*

agitator, *n.* агитатор *m.*

ago, *adv.* (тому) назад. **long ago,** давно, давно тому назад.

agony, *n.* агония *f.*; сильнейшая боль.

agree, *v.* соглаша́ться *imp.*, согласи́ться *perf.* **-able**, *adj.* прия́тный; согла́сный.
-ment, *n.* соглаше́ние, согла́сие *nt.*
agriculture, *n.* се́льское хозя́йство; земледе́лие *nt.*
agricultural, *adj.* сельскохозя́йственный, земледе́льческий.
ahead, *adv.* (*dir.*) вперёд; (*loc.*) впереди́.
aid, *n.* по́мощь *f.* — *v.* помога́ть *imp.*, помо́чь *perf.*
ailment, *n.* неду́г *m.*, боле́знь *f.*
aim, *n.* цель *f.* — *v.* прице́ливаться *imp.*, прице́литься *perf.*; стреми́ться *imp.* **-less**, *adj.* бесце́льный.
air, *n.* во́здух *m.* — *v.* прове́тривать *imp.*, прове́трить *perf.*
air mail, авиапо́чта *f.* (*abbr.* of авиацио́нная по́чта), возду́шная по́чта.
air-conditioned, *adj.* с кондициони́рованным во́здухом.
air conditioning, кондициони́рование во́здуха.
airplane, *n.* самолёт *m.*
airport, *n.* аэропо́рт *m.*
aisle, *n.* прохо́д *m.*
alarm, *n.* трево́га *f.* — *v.* встрево́жить *perf.*
alarm-clock, *n.* буди́льник *m.*
alas! *interj.* увы́!
Alaska, *n.* Аля́ска *f.*
album, *n.* альбо́м *m.*
alcohol, *n.* алкого́ль *m.* **-ic**, *adj.* алкого́льный, алкоголи́ческий. — *n.* алкого́лик *m.*
ale, *n.* пи́во *nt.*, эль *m.*
alert, *adj.* насторо́женный, бди́тельный. — *n.* трево́га *f.*
Alexander, *n.* Алекса́ндр *m.*
algebra, *n.* а́лгебра *f.*
Algeria, *n.* Алжи́р *m.*
alias, *n.* вы́мышленное и́мя.
alibi, *n.* а́либи *nt. ind.*
Alice, *n.* Элис *f. ind.*, Али́са *f.*
alien, *adj.* чу́ждый. — *n.* иностра́нец *m.* **-ate**, *v.* отчужда́ть *imp.*, отчужди́ть *perf.*
alike, *adj.* похо́жий, подоб-

ный. — *adv.* подо́бно, одина́ково; то́чно так же.
alive, *adj.* живо́й.
alkaline, *adj.* щелочно́й.
all, *adj.* весь, вся, всё. — *pron.* всё. **all the more**, тем бо́лее, что. **not at all**, совсе́м не (нет); ниско́лько.
allay, *v.* успока́ивать *imp.*, успоко́ить *perf.*
allegation, *n.* утвержде́ние *nt.*
allege, *v.* утвержда́ть *imp.*, утверди́ть *perf.*
Allegheny Mountains, Аллега́нские го́ры.
allegiance, *n.* ве́рность *f.*
allegory, *n.* аллего́рия *f.*
allergy, *n.* аллерги́я *f.*
alley, *n.* алле́я *f.* у́зкий переу́лок.
alliance, *n.* сою́з *m.*
allied, *adj.* сою́зный.
alligator, *n.* аллига́тор *m.*
allotment, *n.* распределе́ние *nt.*; до́ля *f.*
allow, *v.* позволя́ть *imp.*, позво́лить *perf.*
allowance, *n.* позволе́ние, разреше́ние *nt.*; (*money*) паёк *m.* **make a. for**, принима́ть в расчёт.
alloy, *n.* сплав *m.*
all right, хорошо́, ла́дно.
allude, *v.* намека́ть *imp.*, намекну́ть *perf.*
alluring, *adj.* соблазни́тельный.
allusion, *n.* намёк *m.*
ally, *v.* соединя́ться *imp.*, соедини́ться *perf.* — *n.* сою́зник *m.*
almanac, *n.* альмана́х *m.*
almighty, *adj.* всемогу́щий.
almond, *n.* минда́ль *m.*
almost, *adv.* почти́.
alone, *adj.* оди́н; одино́кий.
along, *prep.* вдоль (+ *gen.*); по (+ *dat.*); у (+ *gen.*). **-side**, *adv.* ря́дом; бок о́ бок.
aloud, *adv.* вслух; гро́мко.
alphabet, *n.* алфави́т *m.*, а́збука *f.* **-ical**, *adj.* по алфави́ту. **-ically**, *adv.* по алфави́ту. **-ize**, *v.* располага́ть в алфави́тном поря́дке.

Alps, *pl.* А́льпы *pl.*

already, *adv.* уже́.

also, *adv.* та́кже, то́же.

altar, *n.* алта́рь *m.*

alteration, *n.* чередова́ние *nt.*

alter, *v.* изменя́ть *imp.,* измени́ть *perf.;* переде́лывать *imp.,* переде́лать *perf.*

alternate, *adj.* череду́ющийся, переме́нный. — *v. t.* чередова́ть *imp.* — *v. i.* череду́ться *imp.*

alternating current, (*elec.*) переме́нный ток.

alternative, *adj.* альтернати́вный. — *n.* альтернати́ва *f.*

although, *conj.* хотя́.

altitude, *n.* высота́ *f.*

alto, *n.* альт *m.*

altogether, *adv.* всего́, вполне́.

aluminum, *n.* алюми́ний *m.*

always, *adv.* всегда́.

amateur, *n.* люби́тель *m.* — *adj.* люби́тельский.

amaze, *v.* изумля́ть *imp.* -ment, *n.* удивле́ние *nt.*

amazing, *adj.* удиви́тельный.

Amazon, *n.* (*river*) Амазо́нка *f.*

ambassador, *n.* посо́л *m.*

ambiguity, *n.* двусмы́сленность *f.*

ambiguous, *adj.* двусмы́сленный.

ambitious, *adj.* честолюби́вый.

ambulance, *n.* каре́та ско́рой по́мощи.

ambush, *n.* заса́да *f.* — *v.* напада́ть из заса́ды.

amen, *n.* ами́нь *m.*

amend, *v.* исправля́ть *imp.,* испра́вить *perf.* -ment, *n.* попра́вка *f.,* исправле́ние *nt.*

America, *n.* Аме́рика *f.*

American, *adj.* америка́нский. — *n.* америка́нец *m.,* америка́нка *f.*

amiable, *adj.* любе́зный.

ammonia, *n.* аммиа́к *m.*

amnesia, *n.* амнези́я *f.*

amnesty, *n.* амни́стия *f.*

among, *prep.* ме́жду (+ *instr.*); среди́ (+ *gen.*).

amorous, *adj.* любо́вный.

amount, *n.* коли́чество *nt.,* су́мма *f.*

ampere, *n.* ампе́р *m.*

amphibian, *adj.* земново́дный. — *n.* амфи́бия *f.*

amphibious, *adj.* земново́дный.

ample, *adj.* оби́льный; доста́точный.

amplify, *v.* уси́ливать *imp.,* уси́лить *perf.*

amputate, *v.* ампути́ровать *imp. & perf.*

amuse, *v.* забавля́ть *imp.* **a. oneself,** забавля́ться *imp.* -ment, *n.* развлече́ние *nt.*

anachronism, *n.* анахрони́зм *m.*

analogous, *adj.* аналоги́чный.

analogy, *n.* анало́гия *f.,* схо́дство *nt.*

analysis, *n.* ана́лиз *m.*

analyst, *n.* анали́тик *m.*

analyze, *v.* анализи́ровать *imp.,* проанализи́ровать *perf.*

anarchy, *n.* ана́рхия *f.*

anatomy, *n.* анато́мия *f.*

ancestor, *n.* пре́док *m.*

ancestral, *adj.* насле́дственный.

ancestry, *n.* происхожде́ние *nt.*

anchor, *n.* я́корь *m.* — *v.* стать на я́корь.

anchovy, *n.* анчо́ус *m.*

ancient, *adj.* стари́нный; дре́вний.

and, *conj.* и; а.

Andrew, *n.* Андре́й *m.,* Эндрю *m. ind.*

anecdote, *n.* анекдо́т *m.*

anemia, *n.* анеми́я *f.,* малокро́вие *nt.*

anesthetic, *n.* анестези́рующее сре́дство.

anew, *adv.* сы́знова, за́ново.

angel, *n.* а́нгел *m.*

anger, *n.* гнев *m.* — *v. t.* серди́ть *imp.*

angle, *n.* у́гол *m.*

angrily, *adv.* гне́вно, серди́то.

angry, *adj.* серди́тый.

animal, *n.* живо́тное *nt.* — *adj.* живо́тный.

animate, *adj.* одушевлённый. — *v.* одушевля́ть *imp.,* одушеви́ть *perf.*

animation, *n.* оживле́ние *nt.,* жи́вость *f.*

animosity, *n.* враждебность *f.*

ankle, *n.* лодыжка *f.*

Anna, *n.* Анна *f.*, Энна *f.*

annals, *n. pl.* летопись *f.*, хроника *f.*

annexation, *n.* присоединение *nt.*, аннексия *f.*

annihilate, *v.* уничтожать *imp.*, уничтожить *perf.*

anniversary, *n.* годовщина *f.*

annotate, *v.* аннотировать *imp. & perf.*

annotation, *n.* аннотация *f.*, примечание *nt.*

announce, *v.* объявлять *imp.*, объявить *perf.*

announcer, *n.* диктор *m.*

annoy, *v.* досаждать *imp.*, досадить *pref.* надоедать *imp.*, надоесть *perf.* **-ance,** *n.* раздражение *nt.*

annual, *adj.* ежегодный, годовой. — *n.* ежегодник *m.*

annul, *v.* аннулировать *imp. & perf.*

anode, *n.* анод *m.*

anomalous, *adj.* неправильный, ненормальный.

anonymous, *adj.* анонимный.

another, *pron.* другой.

answer, *n.* ответ *m.* — *v.* отвечать *imp.*, ответить *perf.*

ant, *n.* муравей *m.*

antagonism, *n.* антагонизм *m.*, вражда *f.*

antagonistic, *adj.* враждебный, антагонистический.

antagonize, *v.* вызывать антагонизм.

antarctic, *adj.* антарктический.

Antarctic, the, *n.* Антарктика *f.*

Antarctica, *n.* Антарктида *f.*

antelope, *n.* антилопа *f.*

antenna, *n.* антенна *f.*; (*insects*) щупальце *pl.*

anterior, *adj.* предшествующий.

anthem, *n.* гимн *m.*

anthology, *n.* антология *f.*

Anthony, *n.* Антоний *m.*, Энтони *m. ind.*

anthropologist, *n.* антрополог *m.*

anthropology, *n.* антропология *f.*

anticipate, *v.* ожидать *imp.*, предчувствовать *imp.*

anticipation, *n.* предвкушение *nt.*

antidote, *n.* противоядие *nt.*

antipathy, *n.* антипатия *f.*

antiquated, *adj.* устарелый, старомодный.

antique, *adj.* старинный, античный. — *n.* античное произведение искусства.

antiquity, *n.* древность *f.*

antiseptic, *adj.* антисептический. — *n.* антисептическое средство.

antisocial, *adj.* антиобщественный, необщительный.

antitoxin, *n.* противоядие *nt.*, антитоксин *m.*

Antoinette, *n.* Антуанетта *f.*

anxiety, *n.* беспокойство *nt.*

anxious, *adj.* озабоченный, беспокоящийся. **be a.,** беспокоиться *imp.*

any, *pron.* кто-нибудь. — *adj.* какой-нибудь. **-body,** *pron.* всякий; кто-нибудь. **-how,** *adv.* как-нибудь, кое-как. **-where,** *adv.* где-нибудь. **any угодно.**

apart, *adv.* в сторону; в стороне; порознь.

apartment, *n.* квартира *f.*, комната *f.*

apathetic, *adj.* равнодушный, апатичный.

apathy, *n.* апатия *f.*

ape, *n.* обезьяна *f.* — *v.* подражать *imp.*

aperture, *n.* отверстие *nt.*

aphorism, *n.* афоризм *m.*

apiece, *adv.* за штуку, с головы.

apologetic, *adj.* извиняющийся.

apologize, *v.* извиняться *imp.*, извиниться *perf.*

apology, *n.* извинение *nt.*

apoplexy, *n.* апоплексия *f.*

apostle, *n.* апостол *m.*

apparatus, *n.* аппарат *m.*, прибор *m.*

apparel, *n.* платье *nt.*, одежда *f.*

apparent, *adj.* явный, очевидный. **-ly,** *adv.* очевидно.

apparition, *n.* проявле́ние *nt.*, привиде́ние *nt.*

appeal, *n.* апелля́ция *f.*; призы́в *m.*, воззва́ние *nt.* — *v.* апелли́ровать *imp. & perf.*

appear, *v.* явля́ться *imp.*, яви́ться *perf.* появля́ться *imp.*, появи́ться *perf.*; (*seem*) каза́ться *imp.* -ance, *n.* появле́ние *nt.*; вне́шний вид.

appease, *v.* умиротворя́ть *imp.*, умиротвори́ть *perf.*; успока́ивать *imp.*, успоко́ить *perf.* -ment, *n.* умиротворе́ние *nt.*, успокое́ние *nt.*

appendage, *n.* приве́сок *m.*; прида́ток *m.*

appendicitis, *n.* аппендици́т *m.*

appendix, *n.* аппе́ндикс *m.*

appetite, *n.* аппети́т *m.*

appetizer, *n.* заку́ска *f.*

appetizing, *adj.* аппети́тный.

applaud, *v.* аплоди́ровать *imp. & perf.*

applause, *n.* аплодисме́нты *pl.*

apple, *n.* я́блоко *nt.* **a. tree**, я́блоня *f.*

appliance, *n.* примене́ние *nt.*, прибо́р *m.*

applicant, *n.* проси́тель *m.*

application, *n.* примене́ние *nt.*, приложе́ние *nt.*; про́сьба *f.*, стара́ние *nt.*

applied, *adj.* прикладно́й.

apply, *v.* прикла́дывать *imp.*, приложи́ть *perf.* применя́ть *imp.*, примени́ть *perf.*

appoint, *v.* назнача́ть *imp.*, назна́чить *perf.* -ment, (*rendezvous*) свида́ние *nt.* (*nomination*) *n.* назначе́ние *nt.*

apportion, *v.* распределя́ть *imp.*, распредели́ть *perf.*; дели́ть пропорциона́льно.

appraise, *v.* оце́нивать *imp.*, оцени́ть *perf.*

appreciate, *v.* оце́нивать *imp.*, оцени́ть *perf.*

appreciation, *n.* уваже́ние *nt.*, высо́кая оце́нка.

apprehend, *v.* схва́тывать *imp.*, схвати́ть *perf.*

apprehension, *n.* задержа́ние *nt.*, аре́ст *m.*

apprehensive, *adj.* озабо́ченный; опаса́ющийся.

apprentice, *n.* учени́к *m.*, подмасте́рье *m.*

approach, *n.* приближе́ние *nt.*, подхо́д *m.* — *v.* приближа́ться *imp.*, прибли́зиться *perf.*; подходи́ть *imp.*, подойти́ *perf.*

appropriate, *adj.* подходя́щий. — *v.* присва́ивать *imp.*, присво́ить *perf.*; предназнача́ть *imp.*, предназна́чить *perf.*

appropriation, *n.* присвое́ние *nt.*; ассигнова́ние *nt.*

approval, *n.* одобре́ние *nt.*

approve, *v.* одобря́ть *imp.*, одо́брить *perf.*

approximate, *adj.* приблизи́тельный. — *v.* приблизи́тельно равня́ться *imp.* -ly, *adv.* приблизи́тельно.

apricot, *n.* абрико́с *m.*

April, *n.* апре́ль *m.* — *adj.* апре́льский.

apron, *n.* пере́дник *m.*, фа́ртук *m.*

apt, *adj.* подходя́щий; скло́нный.

aptitude, *n.* спосо́бность *f.*; скло́нность *f.*

aquarium, *n.* аква́риум *m.*

aquatic, *adj.* во́дный.

Arab, Arabian, *n.* ара́б *m.*, ара́бка *f.* — *adj.* (*also* **Arabic**) ара́бский.

arable, *adj.* па́хотный.

Aral Sea, Ара́льское мо́ре.

arbitrary, *adj.* произво́льный.

arbitration, *n.* трете́йский суд; арбитра́ж *m.*

arbitrator, *n.* трете́йский судья́; арби́тр *m.*

arc, *n.* дуга́ *f.*

arch, *n.* а́рка *f.*, свод *m.*; дуга́ *f.*

archaeology, *n.* археоло́гия *f.*

archaic, *adj.* архаи́ческий.

archbishop, *n.* архиепи́скоп *m.*

archery, *n.* стрельба́ из лу́ка.

architect, *n.* архите́ктор *m.*, зо́дчий *m.*

architectural, *adj.* архитекту́рный.

architecture, *n.* архитекту́ра *f.*, зо́дчество *nt.*

archive, *n.* архи́в *m.*

arctic, *adj.* аркти́ческий.

ardent, *adj.* ре́вностный; горя́чий.

ardor, *n.* рве́ние *nt.*, пыл *m.*

area, *n.* пло́щадь *f.*, террито́рия *f.*

arena, *n.* аре́на *f.*

Argentine, Argentinean, *adj.* аргенти́нский. — *n.* аргенти́нец *m.*, аргенти́нка *f.*

argue, *v.* спо́рить *imp.*

argument, *n.* спор *m.*, диску́ссия *f.*; (reason) до́вод *m.*

aria, *n.* а́рия *f.* "

arid, *adj.* сухо́й; беспло́дный.

arise, *v.* встава́ть *imp.*, встать *perf.*; возника́ть *imp.*, возни́кнуть *perf.*; появля́ться *imp.*, появи́ться *perf.*

aristocracy, *n.* аристокра́тия *f.*

aristocratic, *adj.* аристократи́ческий.

arithmetic, *n.* арифме́тика. -al, *adj.* арифмети́ческий.

arm, *n.* рука́ *f.*; (weapon) ору́жие *nt.* — *v. t.* вооружа́ть *imp.* вооружи́ть *perf.* — *v. i.* вооружа́ться *imp.*, вооружи́ться *perf.*

armchair, *n.* кре́сло *nt.*

Armenia, *n.* Арме́ния *f.*

Armenian, *adj.* армя́нский. — *n.* армя́нин *m.*, армя́нка *f.*

army, *n.* а́рмия *f.*, во́йско *nt.*

aroma, *n.* арома́т *m.* -tic, *adj.* арома́тный, благово́нный.

around, *prep.* вокру́г (+ gen.) — *adv.* круго́м, в окре́стностях.

arouse, *v.* вызыва́ть *imp.*, вы́звать *perf.*

arrange, *v.* устра́ивать *imp.*, устро́ить *perf.* организо́вывать *imp.*, организова́ть *perf.* -ment, *n.* устро́йство *nt.*, расположе́ние *nt.*

arrest, *n.* заде́ржание *nt.*, аре́ст *m.* — *v.* арестова́ть *perf.*; заде́рживать *imp.*

arrival, *n.* прибы́тие *nt.*, появле́ние *nt.*

arrive, *v.* приезжа́ть *imp.*, прие́хать *perf.*; прибыва́ть *imp.*, прибы́ть *perf.*

arrogance, *n.* высокоме́рие *nt.*, надме́нность *f.*

arrogant, *adj.* высокоме́рный, надме́нный.

arson, *n.* поджо́г *m.*

art, *n.* иску́сство *nt.*

artery, *n.* арте́рия *f.*

arthritis, *n.* артри́т *m.*

Arthur, *n.* Арту́р *m.*

artichoke, *n.* артишо́к *m.*

article, *n.* статья́ *f.*; (gram.) арти́кль, член *m.*

articulation, *n.* артикуля́ция *f.*

artificial, *adj.* иску́сственный.

artisan, *n.* реме́сленник *m.*

artist, *n.* худо́жник *m.* -ic, *adj.* худо́жественный, артисти́ческий.

as, *adv.* как; когда́, в то вре́мя как. **as for,** что каса́ется.

asbestos, *n.* асбе́ст *m.*

ascend, *v.* восходи́ть *imp.*, взойти́ *perf.* поднима́ться *imp.*, подня́ться *perf.*

ascent, *n.* восхожде́ние *nt.*, подъём *m.*

ascertain, *v.* установи́ть *perf.*; удостове́риться *perf.*

ascetic, *adj.* аскети́ческий. — *n.* аске́т *m.*

ashamed, *adj.* пристыжённый.

ashes, *n.* зола́ *f.* пе́пел *m.*

ashore, *adv.* к бе́регу, на бе́рег **go a.,** сходи́ть на бе́рег.

ashtray, *n.* пе́пельница *f.*

Asia, *n.* А́зия *f.*

Asian, Asiatic, *adj.* азиа́тский. — *n.* азиа́т *m.*, азиа́тка *f.*

aside, *adv.* в сто́рону; прочь.

ask, *v.* спра́шивать *imp.*, спроси́ть *perf.*; (request) проси́ть *imp.*, попроси́ть *perf.*; (invite) приглаша́ть *imp.*, пригласи́ть *perf.* **ask a question,** зада́ть вопро́с.

asleep, *adj.* спя́щий.

asparagus, *n.* спа́ржа *f.*

aspect, *n.* аспе́кт *m.*, взгляд *m.*; (gram.) вид *m.*

aspersion, *n.* клевета́ *f.*; обры́згивание *nt.*

asphalt, n. асфа́льт m.

asphyxiate, v. души́ть imp., задуши́ть perf.

aspiration, n. стремле́ние nt., жела́ние nt.; (phon.) придыха́ние nt.

aspire, v. стреми́ться imp.; домога́ться imp.

aspirin, n. аспири́н m.

ass, n. осёл m.

assail, v. напада́ть imp., напа́сть perf. **-ant,** n. напада́ющий m.; зачи́нщик m.

assassin, n. уби́йца m. **-ate,** v. уби́ть perf. **-ation,** n. уби́йство nt.

assault, n. нападе́ние nt. — v. напада́ть imp., напа́сть perf.

assemble, v. i. собира́ть imp., собра́ть perf. — v. i. собира́ться imp. собра́ться perf.

assembly, n. собра́ние nt.; ассамбле́я f.

assert, v. утвержда́ть imp.; отста́ивать imp. **-ion,** n. утвержде́ние nt.

assess, v. расце́нивать imp., расцени́ть perf.

asset, n. иму́щество nt.; це́нное ка́чество nt. **assets and liabilities,** акти́в и пасси́в.

assign, v. назнача́ть imp., назна́чить perf.; предпи́сывать imp., предписа́ть perf. **-ment,** n. зада́ние nt.

assimilation, n. усвое́ние nt.

assist, v. помога́ть imp., помо́чь perf. **-ance,** n. по́мощь f. **-ant,** n. помо́щник, ассисте́нт m.

associate, n. това́рищ, соуча́стник m. — v. ассоции́роваться imp. обща́ться imp.

association, n. о́бщество nt.; ассоциа́ция f.

assort, v. подбира́ть imp., подобра́ть perf. **-ment,** n. подбо́р m.; ассортиме́нт m.

assume, v. предполага́ть imp., предположи́ть perf.; присва́ивать imp., присво́ить perf.

assumption, n. присвое́ние nt.; предположе́ние nt.

assurance, n. уве́ренность f.; завере́ние nt.

assure, v. уверя́ть imp., уве́рить perf.

assured, adj. уве́ренный; гаранти́рованный; самоуве́ренный.

asterisk, n. звёздочка f.

asthma, n. а́стма, одышка f.

astigmatism, n. астигмати́зм m.

astonish, v. удивля́ть imp., удиви́ть perf.; изумля́ть imp., изуми́ть perf. **-ment,** n. удивле́ние, изумле́ние nt.

astound, v. изумля́ть imp., изуми́ть perf.; поража́ть imp., порази́ть perf.

astray, adj., adv.: **go a.,** заблуди́ться perf. **lead a.,** сби́ть с пути́.

astringent, adj. вя́жущий. — n. вя́жущее сре́дство.

astrology, n. астроло́гия f.

astronomer, n. астроно́м m.

astronomy, n. астроно́мия f.

astute, adj. проница́тельный, хи́трый.

asylum, n. (refuge) прию́т m., убе́жище nt.; (institution) психиатри́ческая больни́ца.

at, prep. у; во́зле; о́коло; при; (time) в, на.

atheism, n. атеи́зм m.

atheist, n. атеи́ст m. **-ic,** adj. атеисти́ческий.

Athens, n. Афи́ны pl.

athlete, n. атле́т m., атле́тка f.

athletic, adj. атлети́ческий.

athletics, n. атле́тика f. физкульту́ра f.

Atlantic Ocean, Атланти́ческий океа́н.

atlas, n. а́тлас m.

atmosphere, n. атмосфе́ра f.

atmospheric, adj. атмосфе́рный, атмосфери́ческий.

atom, n. а́том m. **-ic,** adj. а́томный.

atone, v. искупа́ть imp., искупи́ть perf.; возмеща́ть imp., возмести́ть perf. **-ment,** n. искупле́ние, возмеще́ние nt.

atrocious, adj. жесто́кий; ужа́сный.

atrocity, n. зве́рство nt., жесто́кость f.

atrophy, *n.* атрофи́я *f.* — *v.* атрофи́роваться *imp.* & *perf.*

attach, *v.* прикрепля́ть *imp.*, прикрепи́ть *perf.*; придава́ть *imp.*, прида́ть *perf.* -**ment.** *n.* прикрепле́ние *nt.*; (*emotional*) привя́занность *f.*

attaché, *n.* атташе́ *m. ind.*

attack, *n.* наступле́ние *nt.*; нападе́ние *nt.* — *v.* наступа́ть *imp.*, наступи́ть *perf.*, атакова́ть *imp.* & *perf.*

attain, *v.* дости́гнуть *perf.* доби́ться *perf.* -**able,** *adj.* достижи́мый. -**ment,** *n.* дости-же́ние *nt.*

attempt, *n.* попы́тка *f.* — *v.* пыта́ться *imp.*, про́бовать *imp.*, попро́бовать *perf.*

attend, *v.* посеща́ть *imp.*, посети́ть *perf.* -**ance,** *n.* прису́тствие *nt.*; посеща́е-мость *f.* -**ant,** *n.* провожа́-тый *m.*, слуга́ *m.* — *adj.* сопровожда́ющий, сопу́т-ствующий.

attention, *n.* внима́ние *nt.* pay a. to, обраща́ть внима́ние.

attentive, *adj.* внима́тельный.

attest, *v.*; свиде́тельствовать *imp.*; удостоверя́ть *imp.*, удостове́рить *perf.*

attic, *n.* мансáрда *f.*, чердáк *m.*

attire, *n.* пла́тье *nt.*, наря́д *m.* — *v.* наряжа́ть *imp.*, наря-ди́ть *perf.*

attitude, *n.* отноше́ние *nt.*; по́за *f.*, вид *m.*

attract, *v.* привлека́ть *imp.*, привле́чь *perf.* -**ion,** *n.* притяже́ние, тяготе́ние *nt.* аттра́кция *m.* -**ive,** *adj.* привлека́тельный; притя-га́тельный.

attribute, *n.* сво́йство *nt.*, при́знак *m.*; (*gram.*) опреде-ле́ние *nt.* — *v.* припи́сы-вать *imp.*, приписа́ть *perf.*

attune, *v.* настра́ивать *imp.*, настро́ить *perf.*

auction, *n.* аукцио́н *m.* — *v.* продава́ть с молотка́ (*or* с аукцио́на). -**eer,** *n.* аук-циони́ст *m.*

audacious, *adj.* сме́лый; де́рз-кий.

audacity, *n.* сме́лость *f.*; де́рзость *f.*

audible, *adj.* слы́шимый.

audience, *n.* аудито́рия *f.*, слу́шатели *pl.*, пу́блика *f.*; (*interview*) аудие́нция *f.*

audition, *n.* слу́шание, выслу́-шивание *nt.*

auditorium, *n.* зри́тельный зал; аудито́рия *f.*

aunt, *n.* тётя, тётка *f.*

auspicious, *adj.* благоприя́т-ный.

austere, *adj.* суро́вый; тёрп-кий.

Australia, *n.* Австра́лия *f.*

Australian, *adj.* австрали́й-ский. — *n.* австрали́ец *m.*, австрали́йка *f.*

Austria, *n.* А́встрия *f.*

Austrian, *adj.* австри́йский. — *n.* австри́ец *m.*, австри́йка *f.*

authentic, *adj.* по́длинный, достове́рный. -**ity,** *n.* по́д-линность *f.*; достове́рность *f.*

author, *n.* а́втор *m.*

authoritative, *adj.* авторите́т-ный; повели́тельный.

authority, *n.* авторите́т *m.*; (*power*) власть *f.*, полно-мо́чие *nt.*

authorization, *n.* уполномо́-чивание *nt.*; разреше́ние *nt.*

authorize, *v.* уполномо́чивать *imp.*, уполномо́чить *perf.*

autobiography, *n.* автобио-гра́фия *f.*

autocracy, *n.* самодержа́вие *nt.*

autograph, *n.* авто́граф *m.*; оригина́л ру́кописи.

automatic, *adj.* автомати́че-ский. -**ally,** *adv.* автомати́-чески.

automobile, *n.* автомоби́ль *m.*

autonomous, *adj.* автоно́мный.

autonomy, *n.* автоно́мия *f.*

autopsy, *n.* вскры́тие (тру́па).

autumn, *n.* о́сень *f.* in the a., о́сенью. — *adj.* осе́нний.

auxiliary, *adj.* вспомога́тель-ный.

available, *adj.* достижи́мый; име́ющийся в распоряже́нии.

avarice, *n.* ску́пость *f.*

avaricious, *adj.* скупо́й.

avenge, *v.* мстить *imp.*, отомсти́ть *perf.*

avenue, *n.* прохо́д *m.*, алле́я *f.*; проспе́кт *m.*

average, *adj.* сре́дний. — *n.* сре́днее число́. on the a., в сре́днем. — *v.* выводи́ть сре́днее число́.

averse, *adj.* неохо́тный; пита́ющий отвраще́ние.

aversion, *n.* отвраще́ние *nt.*, антипа́тия *f.*

avert, *v.* отводи́ть *imp.*, отвести́ *perf.*

aviation, *n.* авиа́ция *f.*

avid, *adj.* жа́дный.

avocation, *n.* заня́тие, призва́ние *nt.*

avoid, *v.* избега́ть *imp.*, избе́гнуть *perf.* **-able,** *adj.* то, чего́ мо́жно избежа́ть. **-ance,** *n.* избега́ние *nt.*

await *v.* ожида́ть *imp.*, ждать *imp.*

awake, *v. i.* просыпа́ться *imp.*, просну́ться *perf.* — *adj.* бо́дрствующий.

award, *n.* присужде́ние *nt.* — *v.* присужда́ть *imp.*, присуди́ть *perf.* награжда́ть *imp.*, награди́ть *perf.*

aware, *adj.* осведомлённый.

away, *adv.* прочь.

awe, *n.* благогове́ние *nt.*, страх, тре́пет *m.*

awful, *adj.* ужа́сный.

awhile, *adv.* ненадо́лго, на не́которое вре́мя.

awkward, *adj.* неуклю́жий, нело́вкий. **-ness,** *n.* нело́вкость, неуклю́жесть *f.*

awning, *n.* наве́с, тент *m.*

ax, *n.* топо́р *m.*

axiom, *n.* аксио́ма *f.*

axis, *n.* ось *f.*

axle, *n.* ось *f.*

Azov, Sea of, Азо́вское мо́ре.

azure, *adj.* голубо́й; лазу́рный. — *n.* лазу́рь *f.*

B

baby, *n.* ма́ленький ребёнок.

bachelor, *n.* холостя́к *m.*

back, *adv.* наза́д, обра́тно. — *n.* оборо́тная (*or* за́дняя) сторона́, (spine) спина́ *f.*

background, *n.* фон *m.*, за́дний план.

backward, *adj.* обра́тный; отста́лый. — *adv.* наза́д, за́дом; наоборо́т. **-ness,** *n.* отста́лость *f.*

bacon, *n.* беко́н *m.*

bacteria, *n.* бакте́рия *f.*

bacteriologist, *n.* бактерио́лог *m.*

bacteriology, *n.* бактериоло́гия *f.*

bad, *adj.* плохо́й, дурно́й, вре́дный. **-ly,** *adv.* пло́хо, вре́дно, (*very much*) о́чень, си́льно. **-ness,** *n.* вре́дность *f.*, него́дность *f.*

badge, *n.* значо́к *m.*

baffle, *v.* расстра́ивать *imp.*, расстро́ить *perf.* сбива́ть с то́лку.

bag, *n.* су́мка *f.*, мешо́к *m.* — *v.* схвати́ть *perf.*

baggage, *n.* бага́ж *m.*

bagpipe, *n.* волы́нка *f.*

bait, *n.* прима́нка *f.*, искуше́ние *nt.* — *v.* ста́вить прима́нку.

bake, *v.* печь *imp.*, спечь *perf.*

baker, *n.* пе́карь *m.*

bakery, *n.* пека́рня *f.*

balance, *n.* равнове́сие *nt.*; бала́нс *m.* — *v.* взве́шивать *imp.*; приводи́ть в равнове́сие.

balcony, *n.* балко́н *m.*

bald, *adj.* лы́сый.

ball, *n.* мяч *m.*; (dance) бал *m.*, танцева́льный ве́чер.

ballad, n. балла́да f.

ball bearing, шарикоподши́пник.

ballerina, n. балери́на f.

ballet, n. бале́т m.

balloon, n. возду́шный шар.

ballot, n. баллотиро́вка f.; избира́тельный бюллете́нь. — v. голосова́ть imp., баллоти́ровать imp.

ballroom, n. танцева́льный зал.

balm, n. бальза́м m.

Baltic Sea, Балти́йское мо́ре.

bamboo, n. бамбу́к m.

ban, n. запре́т m., запреще́ние nt. — v. запреща́ть imp. запрети́ть perf.

banal, adj. бана́льный.

banana, n. бана́н m. **banana tree,** бана́новое де́рево.

band, n. отря́д m., гру́ппа люде́й f. (music) орке́стр m.; (ribbon) ле́нта f. — v. свя́зывать imp. связа́ть perf.

bandage, n. бинт m., повя́зка f., банда́ж m. — v. перевяза́ть perf.; бинтова́ть imp., забинтова́ть perf.

bandit, n. банди́т m.

bang, n. хло́панье nt., уда́р m. — v. хло́пать imp., хло́пнуть perf.; ударя́ть imp., уда́рить perf.

banish, v. изгоня́ть imp. изгна́ть perf. **-ment,** n. изгна́ние nt.

banister, n. пери́ла pl.

banjo, n. ба́нджо nt. ind.

bank, n. (money) банк m.; (river) бе́рег m.; (slope) на́сыпь f. — v. (embank делать на́сыпь; (money) класть де́ньги в банк.

bankbook, n. ба́нковая кни́жка.

banker, n. банки́р m.

banking, n. ба́нковое де́ло.

bank note, n. банкно́та f.

bankrupt, n. несостоя́тельный. **-су,** n. банкро́тство nt.

banner, n. зна́мя nt.

banquet, n. банке́т m.

banter, n. шу́тка f., подшучи-

вание nt. — v. доброду́шно подшу́чивать.

baptism, n. креще́ние nt.

Baptist, n. бапти́ст m.

baptize, v. крести́ть imp.

bar, n. полоса́ f., брусо́к m.; (tavern) бар m.; (law) адвокату́ра f. — v. прегражда́ть imp.; прегради́ть perf.; запреща́ть imp. запрети́ть perf.

Barbara, n. Варва́ра f., Барба́ра f.

barbarian, adj. ва́рварский. — n. ва́рвар m.

barbarism, n. ва́рварство nt.; (ling.) варвари́зм m.

barbarous, adj. ва́рварский.

barbed wire, колю́чая про́волока.

barber, n. парикма́хер m.

bare, adj. го́лый. — v. обнажа́ть imp. обнажи́ть perf. **-ly,** adv. едва́. **-ness,** n. нагота́ f.

barefoot(ed), adj. босоно́гий.

Barents Sea, Ба́ренцево мо́ре.

bargain, n. торго́вая сде́лка, уда́чная поку́пка. — v. торгова́ться imp.

barge, n. ба́ржа f.

baritone, n. барито́н m.

barium, n. ба́рий m.

bark, n. кора́ f.; (of a dog) лай m. — v. ла́ять imp.

barley, n. ячме́нь m.

barn, n. амба́р m., сара́й m.; гумно́ nt.

barometer, n. баро́метр m.

barometric, adj. барометри́ческий.

baroque, n. баро́кко nt. and adj.

barracks, n. бара́к m., каза́рма f.

barrel, n. бо́чка f., бочо́нок m.; (of gun) ствол m., ду́ло nt.

barren, adj. беспло́дный; неплодоро́дный.

barricade, n. баррика́да f.

barrier, n. барье́р m., прегра́да f.

bartender, n. буфе́тчик m.

barter, n. менова́я торго́вля. — v. меня́ть imp., поменя́ть *perf.*; обме́нивать *imp.* обменя́ть *perf.*

base, *adj.* ни́зкий, по́длый. — *n.* ба́зис *m.*, осно́ва *f.*, ба́за *f.* — *v.* осно́вывать *imp.* основа́ть *perf.*

baseball, *n.* бейсбо́л *m.*

basement, *n.* подва́льное помеще́ние *or* эта́ж.

bashful, *adj.* засте́нчивый, ро́бкий. **-ness**, *n.* засте́нчивость, ро́бкость *f.*

basic, *adj.* основно́й.

basin, *n.* таз *m.*, ми́ска *f.*

basis, *n.* осно́ва *f.*, основа́ние *nt.*, ба́зис *m.*

bask, *v.* гре́ться *imp.*

basket, *n.* корзи́на, корзи́нка *f.*

basketball, *n.* баскетбо́л *m.*

bass, *n. (fish)* о́кунь *m.*; *(mus.)* бас *m.* — *adj.* басо́вый.

bassoon, *n.* фаго́т *m.*

bastard, *n.* внебра́чный ребёнок. — *adj.* внебра́чный, подде́льный.

bat, *n.* летучая мышь; *(baseball)* бита́ *f.*

batch, *n.* ку́чка, па́чка *f.*

bath, *n.* ба́ня; купа́льня *f.*; *(wash)* ва́нна *f.*, купа́ние *nt.*

bathroom, *n.* ва́нная *f.*

bathe, *v.* купа́ться *imp.*

baton, *n.* па́лочка *f.*; *(mus.)* дирижёрская па́лочка; *(athl)* эстафе́тная па́лочка.

batter, *n.* взби́тое те́сто. — *v.* колоти́ть *imp.*

battery, *n.* батаре́я *f.*

battle, *n.* би́тва *f.*, сраже́ние *nt.* — *v.* сража́ться *imp.* **-field**, *n.* по́ле сраже́ния. **-ship**, *n.* лине́йный кора́бль; линко́рь *m.*

bawl, *v.* крича́ть *imp.*, ора́ть *imp.*

bay, *adj.* гнедо́й. — *n.* *(geog.)* бу́хта *f.*, зали́в *m.*; *(dog)* лай *m.* — *v.* ла́ять *imp.*

bayonet, *n.* штык *m.*

bazaar, *n.* ры́нок *m.*, база́р *m.*

beach, *n.* пляж *m.*

beacon, *n.* ба́кен *m.*; ма́як *m.*

be, *v.* быть *imp.*; *(loc.)* находи́ться *imp.*, найти́сь *perf.*

bead, *n.* бу́синка, ка́пля *f.*

beak, *n.* клюв *m.*

beam, *n.* *(light)* луч *m.*; *(wood)* ба́лка *f.*

bean, *n.* боб *m.*

bear, *n.* медве́дь. — *v.* *(give birth to)* рожда́ть *imp.*; роди́ть, *perf.*; *(endure)* выноси́ть *imp.*, вы́нести *perf.*; *(carry)* носи́ть *imp.* **-able**, *adj.* терпи́мый, сно́сный.

beard, *n.* борода́ *f.* **-ed**, *adj.* борода́тый.

bearer, *n.* носи́тель *m.*; предъяви́тель *m.*

bearing, *n.* поведе́ние *nt.*, отноше́ние *nt.*; *(tech.)* подши́пник *m.*

beast, *n.* зверь *m.*

beat, *v.* бить *imp.*, поби́ть *perf.*; *(defeat)* побежда́ть *imp.* победи́ть *perf.* **-en**, *adj.* би́тый, разби́тый. *(defeated)* побеждённый. **-ing**, *n.* би́тьё *nt.*, бие́ние *nt.*; *(defeat)* пораже́ние *nt.*

beautiful, *adj.* краси́вый, прекра́сный. **-ly**, *adv.* краси́во, прекра́сно.

beautify, *v.* украша́ть *imp.*, укра́сить *perf.*

beauty, *n.* красота́ *f.*

because, *conj.* потому́ что; так как. **because of**, из-за.

become, *v.* станови́ться *imp.*, стать *perf.*; быть к лицу́.

becoming, *adj.* подходя́щий; к лицу́.

bed, *n.* крова́ть *f.*, посте́ль *f.*; *(river)* дно *nt.*

bedclothes *n.* посте́льное-бельё.

bedroom, *n.* спа́льня *f.*

bedspread, *n.* посте́льное покрыва́ло.

bee, *n.* пчела́ *f.*

beef, *n.* говя́дина *f.*

beefsteak, *n.* бифште́кс *m.*

beehive, *n.* у́лей *m.*

beer, *n.* пи́во *nt.*

beet, *n.* свёкла *f.*

beetle, *n.* жук *m.*

before, *prep.* пе́ред; до. — *adv.* вы́ше, ра́ньше. **-hand**, *adv.* зара́нее.

befriend, *v.* отнести́сь дру́-
жески.

beg, *v.* проси́ть *imp.*, по-
проси́ть *perf.*; (entreat) умо-
ля́ть *imp.*

beggar, *n.* ни́щий *m.*, **-ly,** *adj.*
ни́щенский, жа́лкий.

begin, *v.* начина́ть *imp.*, на-
ча́ть *perf.* — *v. i.* начина́ться
imp., нача́ться *perf.*

beginner, *n.* начина́ющий *m.*

beginning, *n.* нача́ло *nt.* **at the
beginning,** в нача́ле. **from
the beginning,** с нача́ла.

begrudge, *v.* зави́довать *imp.*

behalf, *n.:* **in behalf of,** для,
ра́ди, в по́льзу. **on behalf of,**
от и́мени; в интере́сах.

behave, *v.* вести́ себя́; посту-
па́ть *imp.*

behavior, *n.* поведе́ние *nt.*

behead, *v.* обезгла́вить *perf.*

behind, *adv.* позади́. — *prep.*
за (+ *instr.*), позади́ (+*gen.*).

being, *n.* (existence) бытие́ *nt.*,
существова́ние *nt.*; (creature)
существо́ *nt.*

belated, *adj.* запозда́лый.

belch, *v.* отрыга́ть *imp.* — *v.*
рыга́ть *imp.*, рыгну́ть *perf.*

Belgian, *adj.* бельги́йский. —
n. бельги́ец *m.*, бельги́йка *f.*

Belgium, *n.* Бе́льгия *f.*

belief, *n.* ве́ра *f.*; (opinion)
убежде́ние *nt.*, мне́ние *nt.*
beyond belief, вне вероя́т-
ности.

believable, *adj.* вероя́тный;
правдоподо́бный.

believe, *v.* ве́рить *imp.*; (suppose) полага́ть *imp.*, ду́мать
imp.

believer, *n.* ве́рующий.

belittle, *v.* умаля́ть *imp.*;
принижа́ть *imp.*

bell, *n.* ко́локол *m.*; (doorbell)
звоно́к *m.*

bellboy, *n.* посы́льный.

belligerent, *adj.* вою́ющий.

bellow, *v.* мыча́ть *imp.*

bellows, *n.* мехи́ *pl.*

belly, *n.* живо́т *m.*

belong, *v.* принадлежа́ть *imp.*

beloved, *adj.* люби́мый.

below, *adv.* ни́же, внизу́, вниз.
— *prep.* под, ни́же.

belt, *n.* по́яс *m.*, реме́нь *m.*

bench, *n.* скаме́йка *f.*

bend, *v.* изги́б *m.* — *v.* сгиба́ть
imp., согну́ть *perf.* — *v. i.*
сгиба́ться *imp.* согну́ться
perf.

beneath, *adv.* внизу́. — *prep.*
под, ни́же.

benefactor, *n.* благоде́тель
m.

beneficial, *adj.* поле́зный;
вы́годный.

benefit, *n.* вы́года *f.*; по́льза *f.*
— *v. t.* приноси́ть по́льзу.
— *v. i.* извлека́ть по́льзу.

benevolent, *adj.* благотвори́-
тельный; благоскло́нный.

benign, *adj.* ми́лостивый, ве-
ликоду́шный.

Benjamin, *n.* Вениами́н, Вень-
ями́н *m.*, Бе́нджамен *m.*

bent, *adj.* изо́гнутый. — *n.*
скло́нность, наклю́ность *f.*

benzene, *n.* бензи́н *m.*

bequeath, *v.* завеща́ть *imp.* &
perf.

bequest, *n.* насле́дство *nt.*;
оставле́ние насле́дства.

bereavement, *n.* тяжёлая
утра́та.

Bering Sea, Бе́рингово мо́ре.

berry, *n.* я́года *f.*

berth, *n.* спа́льное ме́сто; (on
a ship) ко́йка *f.*

beside, *prep.* ря́дом с (+*instr.*),
во́зле (+ *gen.*).

besides, *prep.* кро́ме, помимо
(+ *gen.*). — *adv.* кро́ме того́;
к тому́ же.

besiege, *v.* осажда́ть *imp.*,
осади́ть *perf.*

best, *adj.* лу́чший, са́мый
лу́чший. — *adv.* лу́чше всего́
at best, в лу́чшем слу́чае.

bestial, *adj.* ско́тский.

bet, *n.* пари́ *nt. ind.* — *v.*
держа́ть пари́.

betray, *v.* предава́ть *imp.*,
преда́ть *perf.*; изменя́ть *imp.*
измени́ть *perf.* **-al,** *n.* пре-
да́тельство *nt.*, изме́на *f.*

betroth, *v.* обруча́ть *imp.*

обручи́ть *perf.* -al, *n.* обруче́ние *nt.*, помо́лвка *f.*

better, *adj.* лу́чший. — *adv.* лу́чше. — *v.* улучша́ть *imp.*, улучши́ть *perf.* **better oneself,** улучша́ться *imp.*, улучши́ться *perf.*

between, *prep.* ме́жду (& *instr.*)

beverage, *n.* напи́ток *m.*

beware, *v.* остерега́ться *imp.*

bewilder, *v.* сбива́ть с то́лку. **-ment,** *n.* смуще́ние *nt.*; замеша́тельство *nt.*

bewitch, *v.* заколдова́ть *perf.*; очарова́ть *perf.*

beyond, *prep.* за; по ту сто́рону; вы́ше, свы́ше. — *adv.* вдали́, на расстоя́нии.

bias, *n.* (*slant*) укло́н, накло́н, склон *m.*; (*prejudice*) преду-бежде́ние *nt.*

bib, *n.* нагру́дник *m.*

Bible, *n.* би́блия *f.*

Biblical, *adj.* библе́йский.

bibliography, *n.* библиогра́-фия *f.*

biceps, *n.* би́цепс *m.*

bicycle, *n.* велосипе́д *m.*

bid, *n.* предложе́ние цены́. — *v.* предлага́ть це́ну.

bidder, *n.* покупщи́к *m.*

bide, *v.*: **bide one's time,** жда́ть благоприя́тного слу́чая.

bier, *n.* похоро́нные дро́ги.

bifocal, *adj.* двухфо́кусный.

big, *adj.* большо́й, кру́пный, обши́рный.

bigamist, *n.* двоеже́нец *m.*, двумужни́ца *f.*

bigamy, *n.* бига́мия *f.*

bile, *n.* жёлчь *f.*

bilingual, *adj.* двуязы́чный.

bilious, *adj.* жёлчный.

bill, *n.* (*account*) счёт *m.*; (*money*) банкно́та *f.*; (*bird*) клюв *m.*

billet, *n.* кварти́ры *pl.*; помеще́ние для посто́я. — *v.* (*mil.*) расквarти́ровать *perf.*

billiards, *n.* билли́ард *m.*

billion, *n.* миллиа́рд *m.*

bimonthly, *adj.* двухме́сячный. — *adv.* раз в два ме́сяца.

bin, *n.* я́щик *m.*; закром *m.*

bind, *n.* свя́зывать *imp.*,

свя́зать *perf.*; перевя́зывать *imp.*, перевяза́ть *perf.*; (*book*) переплета́ть *imp.*, переплести́ *perf.*

bindery, *n.* переплётная мас-те́рская.

binding, *n.* переплёт *m.*

binoculars, *pl.* бино́кль *m.*

biographer, *n.* био́граф *m.*

biographical, *adj.* биографи́-ческий.

biography, *n.* биогра́фия *f.*

biological, *adj.* биологи́ческий

biology, *n.* биоло́гия *f.*

bipartisan, *adj.* двупарти́йный.

bird, *n.* пти́ца *f.* **bird of prey** хи́щная пти́ца.

birth, *n.* рожде́ние *nt.* **give birth to,** рожда́ть *imp.*, роди́ть *perf.*

birth certificate, ме́трика *f.*

birthday, *n.* день рожде́ния.

birthmark, *n.* роди́мое пятно́; ро́динка *f.*

birth rate, *n.* рожда́емость *f.*

Biscay, Bay of, Биска́йский зали́в.

biscuit, *n.* суха́рь *m.*, сухо́е пече́нье.

bisect, *v.* разреза́ть попола́м.

bisexual, *adj.* двупо́лый.

bishop, *n.* епи́скоп *m.*; (*chess*) слон *m.*

bison, *n.* бизо́н *m.*

bit, *n.* кусо́к, кусо́чек *m.*; (*mach.*) сверло́ *nt.*; (*horse*) удила́ *pl.*

bitch, *n.* су́ка *f.*

bite, *n.* уку́с *m.*; (*morsel*) кусо́чек *m.* — *v.* куса́ть *imp.*, укуси́ть *perf.*

biting, *adj.* о́стрый, е́дкий.

bitter, *adj.* го́рький. **-ness,** *n.* го́речь *f.*

black, *adj.* чёрный.

blackberry, *n.* ежеви́ка *f.*

blackboard, *n.* кла́ссная доска́ *f.*

blacken, *v.* черни́ть *imp.*, начерни́ть *perf.* — *v. i.* черне́ть очерне́ть.

blackmail, *n.* шанта́ж *m.*, вымога́тельство *nt.* — *v.* шантажи́ровать *imp.*; вымога́ть де́ньги.

black market, *n.* чёрный ры́нок.

Black Sea, Чёрное мо́ре.

bladder, *n.* пузы́рь *m.*; мочево́й пузы́рь *m.*

blade, *n.* ле́звие *nt.*; (*of grass*) трави́нка *f.*

blame, *v.* порица́ть *imp.*, вини́ть *imp.* — *n.* порица́ние, обвине́ние *nt.*; вина́ *f.* -less- *adj.* неви́нный; безупре́чный.

blank, *adj.* пусто́й, неиспи́санный. — *n.* бланк *m.*; пусто́е ме́сто.

blanket, *n.* одея́ло *nt.*

blare, *n.* рёв *m.*; зву́ки труб. — *v.* гро́мко труби́ть.

blaspheme, *v.* богоху́льствовать *imp.*

blasphemous, *adj.* богоху́льный.

blasphemy, *n.* богоху́льство *nt.*

blast, *n.* поры́в ве́тра; взрыв *m.* — *v.* взрыва́ть *imp.*, взорва́ть *perf.*

blatant, *adj.* шу́мный, крикли́вый.

blaze, *n.* пла́мя *nt.*; блеск *m.* — *v.* горе́ть *imp.*; пыла́ть *imp.*

bleach, *v. t.* бели́ть *imp.*; отбе́ливать *imp.*, отбели́ть *perf.* — *v. i.* отбе́ливаться *imp.*, отбели́ться *perf.* — *n.* хло́рная и́звесть.

bleak, *adj.* лишённый расти́тельности; уны́лый.

bleed, *v.* истека́ть кро́вью.

blemish, *n.* пятно́ *nt.*, позо́р *m.* — *v.* пятна́ть *imp.*, позо́рить *imp.*

blend, *n.* смесь *f.* — *v.* сме́шивать *imp.*, смеша́ть *perf.*

bless, *v.* благословля́ть *imp.*, благослови́ть *perf.*

blight, *n.* скру́чивание *nt.* — *v.* приноси́ть вред.

blind, *adj.* слепо́й. — *v.* ослепля́ть *imp.*, ослепи́ть *perf.* -ly, *adv.* сле́по. -ness, *n.* слепота́ *f.*; ослепле́ние *nt.*

blindfold, *v.* завя́зывать глаза́.

blink, *v.* мига́ть *imp.* мигну́ть *perf.*; мерца́ть *imp.*

bliss, *n.* блаже́нство *nt.* -ful, *adj.* блаже́нный.

blister, *n.* волды́рь *m.*

blithe, *adj.* весёлый, жизнера́достный.

blizzard, *n.* бура́н *m.*, мете́ль *f.*

bloat,— *v.* раздува́ться *imp.*, разду́ться *perf.*

block, *n.* чурба́н *m.*, коло́да *f.*; (*street*) кварта́л *m.* — *v.* загороди́ть *perf.*

blonde, *adj.* белоку́рый. — *n.* блонди́н *m.*, блонди́нка *f.*

blood, *n.* кровь *f.*

bloodhound, *n.* ище́йка *f.*

bloodless, *a.* бескро́вный.

bloodshed, *n.* кровопроли́тие *nt.*

bloodshot, *adj.* нали́тый кро́вью.

bloodthirsty, *adj.* кровожа́дный.

blood vessel, кровено́сный сосу́д.

bloody, *adj.* крова́вый.

bloom, *n.* цвете́ние *nt.* — *v.* цвести́ *imp.*

blooming, *adj.* цвету́щий.

blossom, *n.* цвето́к *m.* — *v.* цвести́ *imp.*

blotter, *n.* промока́тельная бума́га.

blouse, *n.* блу́за *f.*

blow, *n.* уда́р *m.* **at one blow**, одни́м уда́ром; сра́зу. — *v.* дуть *imp.* **b. out**, туши́ть *imp.*, потуши́ть *perf.* **b. up**, *v. t.* взрыва́ть *imp.*, взорва́ть *perf.* — *v.i.* взрыва́ться *imp.*, взорва́ться *perf.*

blowout, *n.* разры́в (ши́ны) *m.*

blue, *adj.* си́ний, голубо́й.

bluff, *n.* (*deception*) блеф *m.*, обма́н *m.*; (*cliff*) отве́сный бе́рег. — *v.* запу́гивать *imp.*, запуга́ть *perf.*

blunder, *n.* гру́бая оши́бка. — *v.* сде́лать гру́бую оши́бку.

blunt, *adj.* тупо́й. -ness, *n.* ту́пость. *f.*

blush, *n.* кра́ска стыда́; кра́ска смуще́ния. — *v.* красне́ть *imp.*, покрасне́ть *perf.*

board, n. доска́ f.; борт m.
— v. сесть perf.

boast, n. хвастовство́ nt. — v.
хва́статься imp., похва́-
ста́ться perf. **-ful**, adj. хваст-
ли́вый.

boat, n. ло́дка f.; (ship) су́дно
nt., кора́бль m.

bobbin, n. шпу́лька f.; кату́ш-
ка f.

bodily, adj. теле́сный, физи́-
ческий.

body, n. те́ло nt.

boil, n. нары́в m. — v. кипя-
ти́ть imp.; вари́ть imp. — v.i.
кипе́ться imp.; вари́ться
imp.

boiler, n. парово́й котёл.

bold, adj. сме́лый. **-ly**, adv.
сме́ло. **-ness**, n. сме́лость f.

bold type, жи́рный шрифт.

bolt, n. (door) засо́в m.,
задви́жка f.; (lightning) мо́л-
ния f., уда́р гро́ма. — v.
запира́ть на засо́в.

bomb, n. бо́мба f. — v.
бомби́ть imp. & perf.

bond, n. связь f.; облига́ция f.

bondage, n. ра́бство n.

bone, n. кость f. **-less**, adj.
бескостный.

bonus, n. пре́мия f.; тантье́ма
f.

bony, adj. кости́стый.

book, n. кни́га f.

bookcase, n. кни́жный шкаф.

bookkeeper, n. бухга́лтер m.

bookkeeping, n. бухгалте́рия f.

booklet, n. брошю́ра f.

boor, n. гру́бый, невоспи́-
танный челове́к.

boot, n. сапо́г m.

bootblack, n. чи́стильщик
сапо́г.

booth, n. бу́дка f., кио́ск m.

border, n. грани́ца f. — v.
грани́чить (с) imp.

boredom, n. ску́ка f.

boric acid, n. бо́рная кислота́ f.

boring, adj. ску́чный.

born, adj. прирождённый.

borrow, v. займствовать imp.;
занима́ть imp., заня́ть perf.

bosom, n. грудь f., па́зуха f.

Bosporus, n. Босфо́р m.

boss, n. хозя́ин m., предпри-
нима́тель m. — v. хозя́йни-
чать imp. управля́ть imp.

botany, n. бота́ника f.

both, pron. & adj. о́ба m. & nt.,
о́бе f. both . . . and, и . . . и;
как . . . так и.

bother, v. беспоко́ить imp.

bottle, n. буты́лка f. — v.
разлива́ть в буты́лки.

bottom, n. дно nt., низ m.,
ни́жняя часть.

bough, n. сук m.

boulder, n. валу́н m.

boulevard, n. бульва́р m.

bounce, n. отска́кивать imp.,
отскочи́ть perf.

bound, n. грани́ца f., преде́л
m. — v. пры́гать imp.,
бы́стро бежа́ть; ограни́чи-
вать imp., ограни́чить perf.

boundary, n. грани́ца f.

bouquet, n. буке́т m.; (of wine)
арома́т m.

bout, n. схва́тка f.

bow, n. покло́н m.; (ship) нос
m.; (archery) лук m.; (ribbon)
бант m. — v. кла́няться imp.,
поклони́ться perf.

bowels, n. кишка́ f., вну́трен-
ности pl., не́дра pl.

bowl, n. ча́ша f., ку́бок m. —
v. игра́ть в шары́ (or в
ке́гли). **-ing**, n. игра́ в шары́
(or в ке́гли).

bowlegged, adj. кривоно́гий.

box, n. коро́бка f., я́щик m.;
(theat.) ло́жа f. — v. бокси́-
ровать imp.

boxing, n. бокс m.

boy, n. ма́льчик m. **-hood**, n.
о́трочество nt. **-ish**, adj.
о́троческий, мальчи́шеский.

boycott, n. бойко́т m. —
v. бойкоти́ровать imp. &
perf.

brace, n. скре́па f. — v.
скрепля́ть imp., скрепи́ть
perf.

bracelet, n. брасле́т m.

bracket, n. (print.) ско́бка f.;
(support) подпо́рка f., подс-
та́вка f.

brag, v. хва́статься imp.

braggart, n. хвасту́н m.

braid, *n.* коса́ *f.* — *v.* плести́ *imp.*, заплета́ть *imp.*

brain, *n.* мозг *m.*; рассу́док *m.*

brainy, *adj.* у́мный.

brake, *n.* то́рмоз *m.* — *v.* тормози́ть *imp.*

bran, *n.* о́труби *pl.*

branch, *n.* (*offshoot*) о́трасль *f.*, (*district*) о́бласть *f.*, (*department*) отделе́ние *nt.* (*tree*) ветвь, ве́тка *f.*; — *v.* разветвля́ться *imp.*, разветви́ться *perf.*

brand, *n.* головня́ *f.*; (*trade-mark*) фабри́чная ма́рка *f.*

brandy, *n.* конья́к *m.*

brass, *n.* лату́нь *f.*, жёлтая медь.

brass band, духово́й орке́стр.

brassière, *n.* бюстга́льтер *m.*

brave, *adj.* хра́брый.

bravery, *n.* хра́брость *f.*

Brazil, *n.* Брази́лия *f* **-ian,** *adj.* брази́льский.

breach, *n.* (*break*) проло́м *m.*, (*of law, etiquette, etc.*) наруше́ние *nt.*

bread, *n.* хлеб *m.*

breadth, *n.* ширина́ *f.*

break, *n.* проры́в *m.*; переры́в *m.*, (*pause*) па́уза *f.* — *v.* лома́ть *imp.*, слома́ть *perf.* — *v. i.* лома́ться *imp.*, сло-ма́ться *perf.* **b. into,** вла́мываться *imp.*, вломи́ться *perf.* **b. through,** прорыва́ться *imp.* прорва́ться *perf.*

breakable, *adj.* ло́мкий.

breakage, *n.* поло́мка *f.*

breakfast, *n.* за́втрак *m.* — *v.* за́втракать *imp.*, поза́втракать *perf.*

breakwater, *n.* волноре́з *m.*

breast, *n.* грудь *f.*

breast stroke, *n.* брасс *m* ; пла́вание бра́ссом *nt.*

breath, *n.* дыха́ние *nt.*

breathe, *v.* дыша́ть *imp.*

breathing, *n.* дыха́ние *nt.*

breathless, *adj.* запыха́вшийся.

breeches, *n. pl.* штаны́ *pl.*

breed, *n.* поро́да *f.* — *v.* выводи́ть, разводи́ть *imp.*

breeding, *n.* воспита́ние *nt.*; разведе́ние *nt.*

breeze, *n.* бриз *m.*, лёгкий ветеро́к.

breezy, *adj.* прохла́дный. **it is breezy,** прохла́дно.

brevity, *n.* кра́ткость *f.*

brew, *v.* (*beer*) вари́ть *imp.* (*пиво*)

brewery, *n.* пивова́ренный заво́д.

bribe, *n.* взя́тка *f.*, по́дкуп *m.* — *v.* подкупа́ть *imp.*, подкупи́ть *perf.*

bribery, *n.* взя́точничество *nt.*

brick, *n.* кирпи́ч *m.*

bricklayer, *n.* ка́менщик *m.*

bridal, *adj.* сва́дебный.

bride, *n.* неве́ста *f.*

bridegroom, *n.* жени́х *m.*

bridge, *n.* мост *m.*; (*cards*) бридж *m.*

bridle, *n.* узда́ *f.*

brief, *adj.* кра́ткий. **-ly,** *adv.* кра́тко. **-ness,** *n.* кра́ткость *f.*

briefcase, *n.* портфе́ль *m.*

brigade, *n.* брига́да *f.*

bright, *adj.* я́ркий, блестя́щий. **-ten,** *v.* проясня́ться *imp.*, проясни́ться *perf.* **-ness,** *n* я́ркость *f.*

brilliance, *n* блеск *m*

brilliant, *adj* блестя́щий

brim, *n* край *m*; (*hat*) поля́ *pl*

brine, *n.* соляно́й раство́р; морска́я вода́; солёная вода́

bring, *v* приноси́ть *imp* , принести́ *perf* доставля́ть *imp* , доста́вить *perf.*

brink, *n.* край *m.*

brisk, *adj.* живо́й, прово́рный. **-ly,** *adv.* жи́во.

bristle, *n.* щети́на *f.* — *v.* ощети́ниться *perf.*

Britain, see Great Britain.

British, *adj.* брита́нский. **-er,** *n.* брита́нец *m.*, брита́нка *f.*

brittle, *adj.* хру́пкий, ло́мкий.

broad, *adj.* широ́кий.

broadcast, *n.* радиовеща́ние *nt.*, радиопереда́ча *f.* — *v.* передава́ть по ра́дио. **-er,** *n.* ди́ктор *m.* **-ing,** *n.* радиопереда́ча *f.*, трансля́ция *f.*

broaden, *v.* расширя́ть *imp.*, расши́рить *perf.* — *v. i.* расширя́ться *imp.*, расши́риться *perf*

broil, v. жа́рить imp.

broken, adj. разби́тый, ло́маный.

broker, n. ма́клер m.

bronchial, adj. бронхиа́льный.

bronchitis, n. бронхи́т m.

bronze, n. бро́нза f. — adj. бронзо́вый.

brooch, n. брошь f.

brook, n. руче́й m.

broom, n. метла́ f.

broth, n. бульо́н m., жи́дкий суп.

brothel, n. публи́чный дом.

brother, n. брат m.

brotherhood, n. бра́тство nt.

brother-in-law, n. (sister's husband) зять m.; (wife's brother) шури́н m.

brow, n. бровь f.; лоб m.

brown, adj. кори́чневый.

bruise, n. синя́к m. — v. ушиби́ть perf.

brunette, n. брюне́т m., брюне́тка f.

brush, n. щётка f.; (paintbrush) кисть f. — v. чи́стить щёткой.

brusque, adj. ре́зкий; гру́бый.

brutal, adj. жесто́кий. **-ity,** n. жесто́кость, f. **-ly,** adv. жесто́ко.

bubble, n. пузы́рь m.

bucket, n. ведро́ nt.

buckle, n. пря́жка f. — v. застёгивать пря́жку.

buckram, n. клеёнка f.

bud, n. по́чка f. — v. пуска́ть ростки́; дава́ть по́чки.

budge, v. пошевельну́ть perf. — v. i. пошевельну́ться perf.

budget, n. бюдже́т m.

buffalo, n. бу́йвол m.

buffer, n. бу́фер m.

buffet, n. буфе́т m.

bug, n. клоп m., насеко́мое n.

build, v. стро́ить imp., устро́ить perf. **-er,** n. строи́тель m. **-ing,** n. зда́ние nt.; (construction) постро́йка f., строе́ние nt.

bulb, n. лу́ковица f.; (lamp) электри́ческая ла́мпочка.

Bulgarian, adj. болга́рский.

bulge, n. вы́пуклость f. — v.

выпя́чиваться imp., вы́пятиться perf.

bulk, n. объём m.; ма́сса f.; больша́я часть.

bulky, adj. объёмистый.

bull, n. бык m.

bullet, n. пу́ля f.

bulletin, n. бюллете́нь m.; сво́дка f.

bulldozer, n. бульдо́зер m.

bull's-eye, n. я́блоко мише́ни.

bulwark, n. бастио́н m.; опло́т m.

bum, n. ло́дырь m.; безде́льник m.

bump, n. (collision столкнове́ние m.; (swelling) ши́шка f. — v. сту́кнуть perf. — v. i. сту́кнуться perf.

bumper, n. бока́л m.

bun, n. бу́лочка f.

bunch, n. связка f., пучо́к m.

bundle, n. свя́зка f., у́зел m. — v. свя́зывать в у́зел.

bungalow, n. бу́нгало nt. ind.

bunk, n. ко́йка f.

buoy, n. ба́кен, буй m.

buoyant, adj. спосо́бный держа́ться на пове́рхности.

burden, n. бре́мя nt. — v. обременя́ть imp. **-some,** adj. обремени́тельный.

bureau, n. бюро́ nt., конто́ра f.; (furn.) бюро́ nt., шкаф m.

burglar, n. вор, взло́мщик m. **-y,** n. кра́жа со взло́мом.

burial, n. по́хороны pl.

burlap, n. холст m., холсти́на f.

Burma, n. Би́рма f.

burn, v. сжига́ть imp., сжечь perf.; горе́ть imp., сгоре́ть perf.

burner, n. горе́лка f.

burst, v. взорва́ться perf.

bury, v. хорони́ть imp., похорони́ть perf.

bus, n. авто́бус m.

bush, n. куста́рник m.

bushy, adj. пуши́стый.

business, n. де́ло nt., заня́тие nt.; дела́ pl. **-like,** adj. делово́й. **-man,** n. деле́ц, бизнесме́н m.

bust, n. бюст m.

bustle, *n.* суматóха *f.*

busy, *adj.* занятóй, зáнятый.

but, *conj.* но, однáко. — *adv.* тóлько, лишь.

butcher, *n.* мяснúк *m.*

butchery, *n.* бóйня *f.*

butt, *n.* (*target*) мишéнь *f.*; (*of a cigarette*) окýрок *m.* — *v.* бодáться *imp.*

butter, *n.* мáсло *nt.*

butterfly, *n.* бáбочка *f.*; (*swimming*) баттерфлáй.

button, *n.* пýговица *f.*; (*elect.*) кнóпка.

buttonhole, *n.* пéтля *f.*

buy, *v.* покупáть *imp.*, купúть *perf.* -**er**, *n.* покупáтель *m.*

buzz, *n.* жужжáние *nt.* — *v.* жужжáть *imp.*

buzzer, *n.* гудóк *m.*

by, *prep.* пóдле, к; за; (*place*) вóзле, óколо, мúмо. — *adv.* мúмо. **by the way**, кстáти, междý прóчим.

bygone, *adj.* прóшлый.

by-pass, *n.* обходúть *imp.*, обойтú *perf.*

by-product, *n.* побóчный продýкт.

Byzantine, *adj.* византúйский.

C

cab, *n.* извóзчик *m.*, таксú *nt. ind.*

cabbage, *n.* капýста *f.*

cabin, *n.* хúжина *f.*; (*ship*) кабúна *f.*, каюта *f.*

cabinet, *n.* кабинéт *m.*, шкатýлка *f.*

cable, *n.* кáбель *m.*, канáт *m.*; телегрáмма *f.*

cablegram, *n.* каблогрáмма *f.*

cactus, *n.* кáктус *m.*

cadaver, *n.* труп *m.*

café, *n.* кафé *nt. ind.*

cafeteria, *n.* кафетéрий *m.*

caffeine, *n.* кофеúн *m.*

cage, *n.* клéтка *f.* — *v.* сажáть в клéтку.

cajole, *v.* льстить *imp.*

cake, *n.* торт *m.*, кекс *m.*, пирóжное *nt.*

calamitous, *adj.* пáгубный.

calamity, *n.* бéдствие *nt.*

calcium, *n.* кáльций *m.*

calculate, *v.* вычислять *imp.*, вычислить *perf.*

calculating, *adj.* расчитывающий.

calculation, *n.* вычислéние *nt.*, расчёт *m.*

caldron, *n.* котёл *m.*

calendar, *n.* календáрь *m.*

calf, *n.* телёнок *m.*

calfskin, *n.* телячья кóжа.

caliber, *n.* калúбр *m.*

call, *n.* призýв *m.* — *v.* звать *imp.*; (*name*) называть *imp.*, назвáть *perf.*; (*telephone*) звонúть по телефóну.

callous, *adj.* мозóлистый.

calm, *adj.* спокóйный. — *n.* тишинá *f.*, спокóйствие *nt.* — *v.* успокáивать *imp.*, успокóить *perf.* **c. down**, успокáиваться *imp.*, успокóиться *perf.* -**ly**, *adv.* спокóйно. -**ness**, *n.* спокóйствие *nt.*

calorie, *n.* калóрия *f.*

camel, *n.* верблюд *m.*

camelia, *n.* камéлия *f.*

camera, *n.* фотографúческий аппарáт.

camouflage, *n.* маскирóвка *f.* — *v.* маскировáть *imp.*, замаскировáть *perf.*

camp, *n.* лáгерь *m.* — *v.* располагáться лáгерем.

campaign, *n.* кампáния *f.*

camphor, *n.* камфорá *f.*

campus, *n.* университéтский двор.

can, *n.* бидóн *m.*; (*tin*) жестянáя бáнка; жестянка *f.* — *v.* консервúровать *imp. &. perf. see* **able**.

Canadian, *adj.* канáдский. — *n.* канáдец *m.*, канáдка *f.*

canal, *n.* кана́л *m.*

canary, *n.* канаре́йка *f.*

cancel, *v.* вычёркивать *imp.*, вы́черкнуть *perf.*; аннули́ровать *imp. & perf.*

cancellation, *n.* аннули́рование, вычёркивание *nt.*

cancer, *n.* рак *m.*

candid, *adj.* и́скренний.

candidacy, *n.* кандидату́ра *f.*

candidate, *n.* кандида́т *m.*

candle, *n.* свеча́ *f.*

candlestick, *n.* подсве́чник *m.*

candor, *n.* прямота́, и́скренность *f.*

candy, *n.* ледене́ц *m.*

cane, *n.* па́лка *f.*; *(walking)* трость *f.*

canine, *adj.* соба́чий.

canned, *adj.* консерви́рованный.

cannibal, *n.* людое́д *m.* **-ism**, *n.* людое́дство *nt.*

cannon, *n.* пу́шка *f.*

canoe, *n.* кано́э *nt. ind.*, байда́рка *f.*

canonize, *v.* канонизи́ровать *imp. & perf.*

canopy, *n.* балдахи́н *m.*

cantaloupe, *n.* канталу́па *f.*

canvas, *n.* паруси́на *f.*

canyon, *n.* каньо́н *m.*

cap, *n.* ша́пка, фура́жка *f.*

capability, *n.* спосо́бность *f.*

capable, *adj.* спосо́бный.

capacious, *adj.* просто́рный, объёмистый.

capacity, *n.* объём *m.*, вмести́мость *f.*; спосо́бность *f.*

cape, *n.* (*geog.*) мыс *m.*; плащ *m.*

capital, *n.* (*money*) капита́л *m.*; (*city*) столи́ца *f.*, столи́чный го́род. **c. letter**, загла́вная (*or* прописна́я) бу́ква. **c. punishment**, сме́ртная казнь.

capitalism, *n.* капитали́зм *m.*

capitalist, *n.* капитали́ст *m.* **-ic**, *adj.* капиталисти́ческий.

capitalization, *n.* капитализа́ция *f.*

capitalize, *v.* капитализи́ровать *imp. & perf.*

capitulate, *v.* сдава́ться *imp.*, сда́ться *perf.*

caprice, *n.* капри́з *m.*

capricious, *adj.* капри́зный.

capsize, *v. t.* опроки́дывать *imp.*, опроки́нуть *perf.* — *v. i.* опроки́дываться *imp.*, опроки́нуться *perf.*

capsule, *n.* ка́псюль *f.*

captain, *n.* капита́н *m.*

caption, *n.* заголо́вок *m.*

captivate, *v.* очаро́вывать *imp.* очарова́ть *perf.*

captivating, *adj.* очарова́тельный.

captivity, *n.* плен *m.*

capture, *n.* захва́т *m.*, взя́тие в плен. — *v.* захвати́ть *perf.*, взять в плен.

car, *n.* автомоби́ль *m.*; ваго́н *m.*

caramel, *n.* караме́ль *f.*

carat, *n.* кара́т *m.*

caravan, *n.* карава́н *m.*

caraway, *n.* тмин *m.*

carbon, *n.* углеро́д *m.*

carbon paper, копирова́льная бума́га.

carburetor, *n.* карбюра́тор *m.*

card, *n.* ка́рта, ка́рточка *f.*

cardboard, *n.* карто́н *m.*

cardiac, *adj.* серде́чный.

cardinal, *adj.* основно́й, гла́вный. — *n.* кардина́л *m.*

care, *n.* забо́та *f.* — *v.* забо́титься *imp.*, позабо́титься *perf.*

career, *n.* карье́ра *f.*

careful, *adj.* осторо́жный, тща́тельный.

careless, *adj.* небре́жный, невнима́тельный.

caress, *n.* ла́ска *f.* — *v.* ласка́ть *imp.*

cargo, *n.* груз *m.*

Caribbean Sea, Кари́бское мо́ре.

caricature, *n.* карикату́ра *f.* — *v.* изобража́ть в карикату́рном ви́де.

carnal, *adj.* пло́тский, теле́сный.

carnation, *n.* гвозди́ка *f.*

carnival, *n.* карнава́л *m.*

carnivorous, *adj.* плотоя́дный.

carouse, v. пирова́ть imp.

carpenter, n. плóтник m.

carpet, n. ковёр m.

carrier, n. носи́тель m.

carrot, n. морко́вь f.

carry, v. носи́ть imp. indet., нести́ imp. det., понести́ perf.; (convey) вози́ть imp. indet., везти́ imp. det., повезти́ perf. **c. in,** вноси́ть imp., внести́ perf. **c. out,** выноси́ть imp., вы́нести perf.; выполня́ть imp., вы́полнить perf.

cartilage, n. хрящ m.

carton, n. карто́н m.

cartoon, n. карикату́ра f. **-ist,** n карикатури́ст m.

carve, v. выреза́ть imp., вы́резать perf.

case, n. слу́чай m.; дело nt.; (box) я́щик m.; (gram.) падеж m. **in case,** в слу́чае е́сли. **in any case,** во вся́ком слу́чае.

cashier, n. касси́р m.

casket, n. шкату́лка f.

Caspian Sea, Каспи́йское мо́ре.

cast, n. (mold) фóрма для литья́; (theat.) состáв исполни́телей. — v. броса́ть imp., бро́сить perf. отлива́ть imp., отли́ть perf.

caste, n. ка́ста f.

castigate, v. нака́зывать imp., наказа́ть perf.; бичева́ть imp.

castle, n. за́мок m.; (chess) ладья́ f.

casual, adj. случа́йный, непреднаме́ренный.

cat, n. кóшка f.

catalogue, n. катало́г m.

cataract, n. водопа́д m.; (eye) катара́кта f.

catastrophe, n. катастро́фа f.

catch, v. лови́ть imp., пойма́ть perf. **c. up,** догна́ть perf.

categorical, adj. категори́ческий.

category, n. катего́рия f.

cater, v. снабжа́ть прови́зией. **c. to,** угожда́ть imp.

caterpillar, n. гу́сеница f.

cathartic n. слаби́тельное сре́дство.

cathedral, n. собо́р m.

Catherine, n. Екатери́на f., Ке́трин f. ind.

cathode, n. като́д m.

Catholic, adj. католи́ческий. — n. като́лик m. **-ism,** n. католи́чество nt., католици́зм m.

cattle, n. скот m.

Caucasus, n. Кавка́з m.

cauliflower, n. цветна́я капу́ста f.

cause, n. причи́на f.; дело nt. — v. причиня́ть imp., причи́ть perf.

caustic, adj. каусти́ческий; язви́тельный.

cauterize, v. прижига́ть imp., приже́чь perf.

caution, n. осторо́жность f.

cautious, adj. осторо́жный;.

cave, n. пеще́ра f.

caviar, n. икра́ f.

cavity, n. пóлость f.; впа́дина f.

cease, v. перестава́ть imp., переста́ть perf.

cedar, n. кедр m.

cede, v. сдава́ть imp., сдать perf.

ceiling, n. потоло́к m.

celebrate, v. пра́здновать imp.

celebration, n. пра́зднование nt.

celebrity, n. знамени́тость f.

celery, n. сельдере́й m.

celestial, adj. небе́сный.

celibacy, n. безбра́чие nt.

celibate, adj. холосто́й.

cell, n. яче́йка f.; (biol.) кле́тка f.

cellar, n. пóгреб m.; подва́л m.

cellist, n. виолончели́ст m.

cello, n. виолонче́ль f.

cellophane, n. целлофа́н m.

cement, n. цемéнт m. — v. цементи́ровать imp. & perf.

cemetery, n. кла́дбище nt.

censor, n. цéнзор m. — v. подверга́ть цензу́ре. **-ship,** n. цензу́ра f.

censure, n. осужде́ние nt. — v. порица́ть imp.; осужда́ть imp., осуди́ть perf.

census, n. пе́репись f.

cent, n. цент m.

centenary, adj. столе́тний. — n. столе́тняя годовщи́на.

center, n. центр m.

centigrade, adj. стогра́дусный; Це́льсия. 10 degrees centigrade, 10 гра́дусов Це́льсия

central, adj. центра́льный.

centralize, v. централизова́ть imp. & perf.

century, n. век m., столе́тие nt.

ceramic, adj. керами́ческий.

ceramics, n. кера́мика f.

cereal, n. овся́нка f.

cerebral, adj. мозгово́й.

ceremonial, adj. церемониа́льный.

ceremonious, adj. церемониа́льный; церемо́нный.

ceremony, n. церемо́ния f.

certain, adj. (fixed) определённый; (indefinite) не́кий, не́который. to be c., быть уве́ренным. -ly, adv. коне́чно. -ty, n. уве́ренность f.

certificate, n. удостовере́ние nt.; свиде́тельство nt.

certify, v. свиде́тельствовать imp., засвиде́тельствовать perf.

cessation, n. прекраще́ние nt.

chagrin, n. доса́да f., огорче́ние nt.

chain, n. цепь f.; цепо́чка f. — v. ско́вывать imp., скова́ть perf.

chair, n. стул m.; (univ) ка́федра f. -man, n. председа́тель m.

chalk, n. мел m.

challenge, n. вы́зов m. — v. вызыва́ть imp., вы́звать perf.

chamber, n. ко́мната f.; пала́та f.

chambermaid, n. го́рничная f.

chamber music, ка́мерная му́зыка.

chameleon, n. хамелео́н m.

chamois, n. за́мша f.

champagne, n. шампа́нское nt.

champion, n. чемпио́н m., чемпио́нка f. — v. защища́ть imp., защити́ть perf.;

поде́рживать imp., поддержа́ть perf. -ship, n. чемпиона́т m., пе́рвенство nt.

chance, n. возмо́жность f. by c., случа́йно. take a c., рискова́ть imp., рискну́ть perf.

chandelier, n. лю́стра f.

change, n. измене́ние nt., переме́на f. — v. t. меня́ть imp. — v. i. меня́ться imp. -able, adj. изме́нчивый.

channel, n. проли́в m., кана́л m.; путь f.

chant, n. песнь f.; (eccles.) песнопе́ние nt. — v. петь imp.

chaos, n. ха́ос m.

chaotic, adj. хаоти́ческий.

chapel, n. часо́вня f.; капе́лла f.

chaplain, n. капелла́н m.

chapter, n. глава́ f.

char, v. обжига́ть imp., обже́чь perf.

character, n. хара́ктер m.

characteristic, adj. хара́ктерный — n. характери́стика f., хара́ктерная осо́бенность.

characterization, n. характери́стика f.

characterize, v. характеризова́ть imp. & perf.

charcoal, n. древе́сный у́голь.

charge n. (order) предписа́ние nt., поруче́ние nt.; (responsibility) отве́тственность f. — v. (entrust) поруча́ть imp., поручи́ть perf.; (accuse) обвиня́ть imp., обвини́ть perf.; (set a price) назнача́ть це́ну.

charitable, adj. милосе́рдный.

charity, n. благотвори́тельность f.

charlatan, n. шарлата́н m.

Charles, n. Карл m., Чарл(ь)з m.

charm, n. ча́ры pl.; обая́ние nt. — v. очаро́вывать imp., очарова́ть perf.

charming, adj. очарова́тельный.

chart, n. морска́я ка́рта. — v. наноси́ть на ка́рту.

chase, n. пого́ня f. — v. гна́ться imp.

chasm, n. расселина f.

chassis, n. шасси nt. ind.

chaste, adj. целомудренный.

chastise, v. наказывать imp., наказать perf.

chastity, n. целомудрие nt.

chat, n. болтовня f. — v. болтать imp.

chauffeur, n. шофёр m.

cheap, a. дешёвый.

cheap, a. дешёвый. **-en**, v. дешеветь imp., подешеветь perf. **-ly**, adv. дёшево.

cheat, v. обманывать imp., обмануть perf. **-er**, n. обманщик m.

check, n. контроль m., проверка f.; (bank) чек m.; (chess) шах m. — v. проверять imp., проверить perf. (chess) шаховать imp.

checkmate, n. шах и мат.

cheek, n. щека f.

cheer, n. весёлье nt. — v. ободрять imp.; аппплодировать imp.

cheerful, adj. весёлый. **-ly**, adv. весело. **-ness**, n. весёлость f.

cheese, n. сыр m.

chef, n. главный повар.

chemical, adj. химический. — n. химическое средство; pl. химикалий pl. **-ly**, adv. химически.

chemist, n. химик m.

chemistry, n. химия f.

cherish, v. лелеять imp., хранить imp.

cherry, n. вишня f.

chess, n. шахматы pl.

chest, n. (trunk) сундук m., ящик m.; (anat.) грудная клетка f.

chestnut, n. каштан m. — adj. каштановый.

chew, v. жевать imp.

chic, adj. шикарный, модный.

chicanery, n. придирка f.

chick, n. цыплёнок m.

chicken, n. курица f., цыплёнок m.

chicken pox, n. ветряная оспа.

chicory, n. цикорий m.

chief, adj. главный. — n.

глава f., начальник m. **ly** adv. главным образом.

child, n. ребёнок m., дитя nt. (pl. дети). **-hood**, n. детство nt. **-ish**, adj. детский **-less**, adj. бездетный.

chill, n. простуда f. — v. охлаждать imp., охладить perf.

chilly, adj. прохладный.

chimney, n. труба f.

chimpanzee, n. шимпанзе nt. ind.

chin, n. подбородок m.

china, n. фарфор f., фарфоровая посуда.

China, n. Китай m.

Chinese, adj. китайский. — n. китаец m., китайка f.

chisel, n. резец m., долото nt. — v. ваять imp.; высекать imp., высечь perf.

chivalrous, adj. рыцарский.

chivalry, n. рыцарство nt.

chloride, n. хлорид m.

chlorine, n. хлор m.

chloroform, n. хлороформ m.

chlorophyll, n. хлорофилл m.

chocolate, n. шоколад m. — adj. шоколадный.

choice, n. отборный. — n. выбор m.

choir, n. хор m.

choke, v. — v. t. душить imp. — v. i. задыхаться imp.

cholera, n. холера f.

choose, v. выбирать imp., выбрать perf.

choral, a. adj. хоровой.

chop, n. (meat) отбивная котлета. — v. рубить imp.; высекать imp., высечь perf.

chord, n. (musical instrument) струна f.; (harmony) аккорд m.

choreography, n. хореография f.

chorus, n. хор m.

Christ, n. Христос m.

christen, v. крестить imp., окрестить perf.

Christian, adj. христианский. —n. христианин m., христианка f.

Christianity, n. христиа́нство nt.

Christmas, n. рождество́ nt.

Christopher, n. Христофо́р m., Кри́стофер m.

chromium, n. хром m.

chronic, adj. хрони́ческий.

chronicle, n. хро́ника f., ле́топись f.

chronological, adj. хронологи́ческий.

chrysanthemum, n. хризанте́ма f.

church, n. це́рковь f.

churn, n. маслобо́йка f. — v. сбива́ть.

chute, n. стремни́на f.

cider, n. я́блочный сок; сидр m.

cigar, n. сига́ра f.

cigarette, n. папиро́са. сигаре́та f.

cinder, n. шлак m.

cinema, n. кино́ nt., кинотеа́тр m.

cinnamon, n. кори́ца f.

cipher, n. (code) шифр m.; (number) ара́бская ци́фра.

circle, n. круг m., кружо́к m.

circuit, n. кругооборо́т m.

circuitous, adj. кру́жный, око́льный.

circular, adj. кру́глый.

circulate, v. циркули́ровать imp. & perf.

circulation, n. циркуля́ция f.; (newspaper, etc.) тира́ж m.

circumcision, n. обреза́ние nt.

circumference, n. окру́жность f.

circumlocution, n. укло́нчивость f.

circumscribe, v. ограни́чивать imp., ограни́чить perf.

circumspect, adj. осмотри́тельный.

circumstance, n. обстоя́тельство nt. **in (or under) the circumstances,** при да́нных обстоя́тельствах.

circumstantial, adj. обстоя́тельный.

circumvention, n. обма́н m., хи́трость f.

circus, n. цирк m.

cirrhosis, n. цирро́з печени.

cistern, n. цисте́рна f.

citation, n. цита́та f., ссы́лка f., цити́рование nt.

cite, v. цити́ровать imp. & perf., ссыла́ться imp., сосла́ться perf.

citizen, n. граждани́н m., гражда́нка f. **-ship,** n. гражда́нство nt.

citric, adj. лимо́нный.

city, n. го́род m.

civic, adj. гражда́нский.

civil, adj. гражда́нский; (polite) вежли́вый.

civilization, n. цивилиза́ция f.

civilize, v. цивилизова́ть imp., & perf.

civilized, adj. цивилизо́ванный.

claim, n. прете́нзия f., тре́бование nt. — v. тре́бовать imp., потре́бовать perf.

clairvoyant, adj. яснови́дящий.

clamp, n. зажи́м m. — v. скрепля́ть imp., скрепи́ть perf.; зажима́ть imp., зажа́ть perf.

clan, n. род, клан m.

clandestine, adj. та́йный, скры́тый.

clap, v. хло́пать imp., похло́пать perf.

claret, n. кларе́т m.

clarification, n. проясне́ние nt.

clarify, v. проясни́ть perf.

clarinet, n. кларне́т m.

clarity, n. я́сность f., прозра́чность f.

clash, n. столкнове́ние nt. — v. ста́лкиваться imp., столкну́ться perf.

clasp, n. застёжка f., (hand) рукопожа́тие nt. — v. застёгивать imp., застегну́ть perf.; (hand) сжима́ть imp.

class, n. класс m. — adj. кла́ссный, кла́ссовый.

classic, classical, adj. класси́ческий.

classicism, n. классици́зм m.

classification, n. классифика́ция f.

classify, v. классифици́ровать imp. & perf.

classmate, n. однокла́ссник m.

classroom, *n.* кла́ссная ко́мната.

clause, *n.* (*legal*) статья́ *f.*; (*gram.*) предложе́ние *nt.*

claw, *n.* ко́готь *f.*, ла́па *f.*; *pl.* (*of a hammer*) клещи́ *pl.*

clay, *n.* гли́на *f.*

clean, *adj.* чи́стый. — *v.* чи́стить *imp.*, почи́стить *perf.*

cleanliness, *n.* чистота́ *f.*

cleanse, *v.* чи́стить *imp.*, почи́стить *perf.*; очища́ть *imp.*, очи́стить *perf.*

clear, *adj.* я́сный. — *v.* очища́ть *imp.*, очи́стить *perf.*; опра́вдывать *imp.*, оправ-да́ть *perf.*

clearance, *n.* зазо́р *m.*

clearness, *n.* я́сность *f.*

cleavage, *n.* расщепле́ние, *nt.*; расхожде́ние *nt.*

cleaver, *n.* дроково́л *m.*

clef, *n.* ключ *m.*

clemency, *n.* милосе́рдие *nt.*

clench, *v.* сжима́ть *imp.*, сжать *perf.*

clergy, *n.* духове́нство *nt.*

clergyman, *n.* свяще́нник *m.*

clerical, *adj.* клерика́льный, канцеля́рский.

clerk, *n.* клерк *m.*, слу́жащий *m.*, чино́вник *m.*

clever, *adj.* у́мный.

cliché, *n.* клише́ *nt. ind.*

client, *n.* клие́нт *m.*

clientele, *n.* клиенту́ра *f.*

cliff, *n.* утёс *m.*

climate, *n.* кли́мат *m.*

climatic, *adj.* климати́ческий.

climax, *n.* кульминацио́нный пункт.

climb, *v.* взбира́ться *imp.*, взобра́ться *perf.*; (*colloq.*) кара́бкаться.

cling, *v.* цепля́ться *imp.*

clinic, *n.* кли́ника *f.* -al, *adj.* клини́ческий.

clip, *n.* ско́ба *f.*; скре́пка *f.* — *v.* скрепля́ть *imp.*, скре-пи́ть *perf.*; зажима́ть *imp.*, зажа́ть *perf.*

clippers, *pl.* но́жницы *pl.*

clique, *n.* кли́ка *f.*

cloak, *n.* плащ *m.*

cloakroom, *n.* гардеро́б *m.* (*colloq.*) раздева́льня *f.*

clock, *n.* часы́ *pl.* -wise, по стре́лке.

clod, *n.* ком *m.*

cloister, *n.* монасты́рь *m.*

close, *adj.* бли́зкий. — *adv.* бли́зко. — *v.* закрыва́ть *imp.* закры́ть *perf.* -ly, *adv.* бли́з-ко; (*attentively*) внима́тель-но.

closet, *n.* чула́н *m.*; кабине́т *m.*

clot, *n.* комо́к *m.*; тромб *m.* — *v.* сгуща́ться *imp.*, сгус-ти́ть *perf.*; свёртываться *imp.*, сверну́ться *perf.*

cloth, *n.* сукно́ *nt.*, ткань *f.*, мате́рия *f.*

clothe, *v.* покрыва́ть *imp.*, покры́ть *perf.* c. oneself, одева́ться *imp.*, оде́ться *perf.*

clothes, clothing, *n.* оде́жда *f.*

cloud, *n.* о́блако *n.*, ту́ча *f.*

cloudiness, *n.* о́блачность *f.*

cloudy, *adj.* о́блачный.

clove, *n.* гвозди́ка *f.*

clover, *n.* кле́вер *m.*

clown, *n.* кло́ун *m.*

cloy, *v.* пресыща́ть *imp.*, преси́тить *perf.*

club, *n.* клуб *m.*

clue, *n.* клубо́к *m.*, ключ к разга́дке.

clump, *n.* глы́ба *f.*

clumsiness, *n.* неуклю́жесть *f.*

clumsy, *adj.* неуклю́жий.

cluster, *n.* гроздь *f.*

clutter, *n.* сумато́ха *f.* — *v.* суети́ться *imp.*

coach, *n.* каре́та *f.*; (*sports*) тре́нер *m.* — *v.* тренирова́ть *imp.*

coagulate, *v.* ство́ра́живаться *imp.*, створо́живаться *imp.*

coagulation, *n.* коагуля́ция *f.*

coal, *n.* у́голь *m.*

coalition, *n.* коали́ция *f.*

coarse, *adj.* гру́бый; (*material*) необрабо́танный.

coast, *n.* (морско́й) бе́рег *m.*

coastal, *adj.* берегово́й.

coast guard, *n.* берегова́я охра́на; пограни́чная слу́жба.

coastline, n. побере́жье nt.

coat, n. пальто́ nt., пиджа́к m.; (paint) слой m. — v. покрыва́ть imp., покры́ть perf.

coax, v. упра́шивать imp., упроси́ть perf.

cobblestone, n. булы́жник m.

cobweb, n. паути́на f.

cocaine, n. кока́ин m.

cock, n. (rooster) пету́х m.; (faucet) кран m.; (of a gun) куро́к m.

cockroach, n. тарака́н m.

cocktail, n. кокте́йль m.

cocoa, n. кака́о nt. ind.

coconut, n. коко́с m., коко́совый оре́х.

cocoon, n. ко́кон m.

cod, n. треска́ f.

code, n. (rules) ко́декс m.; (communication) шифр m.

codify, v. кодифици́ровать imp. & perf.

coeducation, n. совме́стное обуче́ние nt.

coerce, v. принужда́ть imp., прину́дить perf.

coercion, n. принужде́ние nt.

coercive, adj. принуди́тельный.

coexist, v. сосуществова́ть imp.

coffee, n. ко́фе m. ind.

coffin, n. гроб m.

cog, n. зубе́ц m.

cogent, adj. убеди́тельный.

cogitate, v. обду́мывать imp., обду́мать perf.

cognizance, n. зна́ние nt.; подсу́дность f.

cognizant, adj. зна́ющий, осведомлённый.

coherent, adj. свя́зный.

cohesion, n. сцепле́ние nt.

cohesive, adj. спосо́бный к сцепле́нию.

coiffure, n. причёска f.

coil, n. кату́шка f.; кольцо́ nt. — v. свёртывать спира́лью.

coin, n. моне́та f.

coincide, v. совпада́ть imp., совпа́сть perf.

coincidence, n. совпаде́ние nt.

coincident, adj. совпада́ющий.

colander, n. дуршла́г m.

cold, adj. холо́дный. — n. хо́лод m.; (med.) просту́да f., на́сморк m.

cold-blooded, adj. хладнокро́вный.

coldness, n. хо́лод m.

collaborate, v. сотру́дничать imp.

collaboration, n. сотру́дничество nt.

collaborator, n. сотру́дник m.

collapse, n. разруше́ние, круше́ние nt. — v. ру́шиться perf.

collar, n. воротни́к m.

collarbone, n. ключи́ца f.

colleague, n. колле́га m.

collect, v. собира́ть imp., собра́ть perf. — v. i. собира́ться imp., собра́ться perf.

collection, n. колле́кция f., собра́ние nt., скопле́ние nt.

collective, adj. коллекти́вный.

collective farm, колхо́з m.

collective farmer, колхо́зник m.

collector, n. сбо́рщик m., коллекционе́р m.

college, n. колле́дж m.

collegiate, n. коллегиа́льный; университе́тский, академи́ческий.

collide, v. ста́лкиваться imp. столкну́ться perf.

collision, n. столкнове́ние nt.

colloquial, adj. разгово́рный.

colon, n. (punctuation) двоето́чие nt.; (anat.) ободо́чная кишка́.

colonel, n. полко́вник m.

colonial, adj. колониа́льный.

colonist, n. колони́ст. пере́селенец m.

colonization, n. колониза́ция f.

colonize, v. колонизи́ровать imp. & perf.

colony, n. коло́ния f.

color, n. цвет m.; (paint) кра́ска f. — v. t. кра́сить imp., покра́сить perf. — v. i. красне́ть imp. покрасне́ть perf. **-ed,** adj. цветно́й цветноко́жий. **-ful,** adj. кра́-

сочный, я́ркий. **-less,** adj. бесцве́тный.

colossal, adj. колосса́льный.

colt, n. жеребёнок m.

column, n. коло́нна f.; столбе́ц m.

coma, n. ко́ма f.

comb, n. гре́бень m. — v. чеса́ть imp., почеса́ть perf.

combat, n. бой m., сраже́ние nt. — v. боро́ться про́тив.

combination, n. сочета́ние, соедине́ние nt.

combine, v. сочета́ть imp. & perf.

combustible, adj. горю́чий.

combustion, n. сгора́ние nt.

come, v. (on foot) приходи́ть imp., прийти́ perf.; (by vehicle) приезжа́ть imp., прие́хать perf. c. **from,** быть ро́дом c (+ gen.).

comedian, n. ко́мик m.

comedy, n. коме́дия f.

comet, n. коме́та f.

comfort, n. комфо́рт m.; (consolation) утеше́ние nt. — v. утеша́ть imp., уте́шить perf. **-able,** adj. удо́бный.

comic, comical, adj. коми́ческий.

coming, n. прие́зд, прихо́д m. — adj. бу́дущий, наступа́ющий.

comma, n. запята́я f.

command, n. прика́з m., распоряже́ние nt. — v. прика́зывать imp., приказа́ть perf.

commander in chief, n. главноко́мандующий m.

commandment, n. за́поведь f.

commemorate, v. пра́здновать imp., отпра́здновать perf.

commemoration, n. пра́зднование nt.

commence, v. начина́ть imp., нача́ть perf.

commencement, n. (beginning) нача́ло nt.

commend, v. поруча́ть imp., поручи́ть perf. **-able,** adj. похва́льный. **-ation,** n. похвала́ f.

commensurate, adj. соотве́тственный.

comment, n. коммента́рий m., примеча́ние nt. — v. комменти́ровать imp. & perf.

commentary, n. коммента́рий m.

commentator, n. коммента́тор m.

commerce, n. торго́вля f.

commercial, adj. торго́вый, комме́рческий.

commission, n. поруче́ние nt.; полномо́чие nt. — v. дава́ть поруче́ние.

commit, v. соверша́ть imp., соверши́ть perf.

committee, n. комите́т m.

commodity, n. това́р m.

common, adj. о́бщий, обыкнове́нный.

commonplace, adj. бана́льный.

commotion, n. волне́ние nt.; суматоха f.

communal, adj. о́бщинный, коммуна́льный.

communicable, adj. поддаю́щийся переда́че; (med.) зара́зный.

communicate, v. сообща́ть imp., сообщи́ть perf. — v. i. сообща́ться imp., сообщи́ться perf.

communication, n. коммуника́ция, связь f., сообще́ние nt.

communiqué, n. коммюнике́ nt. ind.

Communism, n. коммуни́зм m.

Communist, n. коммуни́ст m., коммуни́стка f. **-ic,** adj. коммунисти́ческий.

community, n. о́бщина f.

compact, n. прессо́ванная пу́дра. — adj. компа́ктный, сжа́тый.

companion, n. това́рищ m.; спу́тник m. **-ship,** n. това́рищество n.

company, n. компа́ния f., о́бщество nt.

comparable, adj. сравни́мый.

comparative, adj. сравни́тельный. **-ly,** adv. сравни́тельно.

compare, v. сра́внивать imp., сравни́ть perf.

comparison, *n.* сравне́ние *nt.*

compartment, *n.* купе́ *nt.*

compass, *n.* объём, обхва́т *m.*; (*naut.*) ко́мпас *m.*

compassion, *n.* сострада́ние *nt.*

compassionate, *adj.* сострада́тельный.

compatible, *adj.* совмести́мый.

compatriot, *n.* соо́течественник *m.*

compel, *v.* вынужда́ть *imp.*, вы́нудить *perf.*

compensate, *v.* компенси́ровать *imp. & perf.*

compensation, *n.* возмеще́ние *nt.*; жа́лованье *nt.*

compete, *v.* состяза́ться *imp.*, соревнова́ться *imp.*

competent, *adj.* компете́нтный; доста́точный.

competition, *n.* конкуре́нция *f.*; состяза́ние, соревнова́ние *nt.*

competitive, *adj.* сопернича́ющий; ко́нкурсный.

competitor, *n.* конкуре́нт *m.*

compile, *v.* собира́ть *imp.*, собра́ть *perf.*; составля́ть *imp.*, соста́вить *perf.*

complacent, *adj.* самодово́льный.

complain, *v.* жа́ловаться *imp.*

complaint, *n.* жа́лоба *f.*; недово́льство *nt.*

complement, *n.* дополне́ние *nt.*; компле́кт *m.*

complete, *adj.* по́лный, зако́нченный. — *v.* зака́нчивать *imp.*, зако́нчить *perf.* **-ly,** *adv.* соверше́нно. **-ness,** *n.* зако́нченность *f.*; полнота́ *f.*

completion, *n.* оконча́ние *nt.*; заверше́ние *nt.*

complex, *adj.* сло́жный; составно́й.

complexion, *n.* цвет лица́.

complexity, *n.* сло́жность *f.*

compliance, *n.* согла́сие *n.* **in compliance with,** в соотве́тствии с.

complicate, *v.* усложня́ть *imp.*, усложни́ть *perf.*

complicated, *adj.* сло́жный; запу́танный.

complication, *n.* сло́жность *f.*; запу́танность *f.*

compliment, *n.* комплиме́нт *m.*; *pl.* приве́т *m.*, покло́н *m.*

complimentary, *adj.* ле́стный (*free*) беспла́тный.

comply, *v.* подчиня́ться пра́вилам.

component, *n.* составно́й — *n.* составна́я часть.

compose, *v.* сочиня́ть *imp.* сочини́ть *perf.*; составля́ть *imp.*, соста́вить *perf.*

composer, *n.* компози́тор *m.*

composite, *adj.* комбини́ро́ванный, составно́й. — *n.* смесь *f.*

composition, *n.* сочине́ние *nt.*

composure, *n.* споко́йствие *nt.*

compote, *n.* компо́т *m.*

compound, *adj.* составно́й сло́жный. — *n.* соста́в *m.*

comprehend, *v.* понима́ть *imp.* поня́ть *perf.*

comprehensible, *adj.* поня́тный

comprehension, *n.* понима́ние *nt.*

comprehensive, *adj.* исче́рпывающий, всесторо́нний.

compress, *n.* компре́сс *m.* — *v.* сжима́ть *imp.* сжать *perf.* **-ion,** *n.* сжа́тие *nt.*

comprise, *v.* заключа́ть в себе́ содержа́ть *imp.*

compromise, *n.* компроми́с *m.* — *v.* компромети́ровать *imp.*

compulsion, *n.* принужде́ни *nt.*

compulsive, *adj.* принуди́тельный.

compulsory, *adj.* обяза́тельный.

compunction, *n.* угрызе́ние со́вести; сожале́ние *nt.*

compute, *v.* подсчи́тывать *imp.*, подсчита́ть *perf.*

comrade, *n.* това́рищ *m.* **-ship,** *n.* това́рищество *nt.*; това́рищеские отноше́ния.

concave, *adj.* во́гнутый, впа́лый.

conceal, *v.* скрыва́ть *imp* скрыть *perf.* **-ment,** *n.* ута́ивание *nt.*

concede, *v.* уступа́ть *imp.,* уступи́ть *perf.;* признава́ть *imp.,* призна́ть *perf.*

conceit, *n.* тщесла́вие *nt.;* самомне́ние *nt.* **-ed.** *adj.* тщесла́вный.

conceivable, *adj.* мы́слимый.

conceive, *v.* заду́мывать *imp.,* заду́мать *perf.*

concentrate, *v.* сосредото́чивать *imp.,* сосредото́чить *perf.*

concentration, *n.* концентра́ция *f.*

concept, *n.* поня́тие *nt.*

conception, *n.* поня́тие, пони́мание *nt.*

concern, *n.* забо́та, *f.,* интере́с *m.* — *v.* каса́ться *imp.*

concerning, *prep.* относи́тельно.

concert, *n.* конце́рт *m.*

concession, *n.* усту́пка *f.*

conciliate, *v.* примиря́ть *imp.,* примири́ть *perf.*

conciliation, *n.* примире́ние *nt.*

concise, *adj.* сжа́тый, кра́ткий.

conclude, *v.* заключа́ть *imp.,* заключи́ть *perf.*

conclusion, *n.* заключе́ние *nt.*

conclusive, *adj.* заключи́тельный.

concoct, *v.* состря́пать *imp* ; приду́мать *perf.*

concoction, *n.* стряпня́ *f.,* ва́рево *nt.*

concord, *n.* согла́сие *nt.*

concrete, *adj.* конкре́тный. **-ly,** *adv.* конкре́тно.

concur, *n.* соглаша́ться *imp.,* согласи́ться *perf.*

concurrence, *n.* совпаде́ние *nt.;* согла́сие *nt.*

concurrent, *adj.* совпада́ющий

concussion, *n.* потрясе́ние *nt.*

condemn, *v.* осужда́ть *imp.,* осуди́ть *perf.* **-ation,** *n.* осужде́ние *nt.*

condensation, *n.* сгуще́ние *nt.,* конденса́ция *f.*

condense, *v.* сгуща́ть *imp.,* сгусти́ть *perf.*

condescend, *v.* снизойти́ *perf.*

condiment, *n.* припра́ва *f.*

condition, *n.* положе́ние *nt.,*

состоя́ние *nt.;* (*stipulation*) усло́вие *nt.* — *v.* обусло́вливать *imp.,* обусло́вить *perf.*

conditional, *adj.* усло́вный. **-ly,** *adv.* усло́вно.

condolence, *n.* соболезнова́ние *nt.;* сочу́вствие *nt.*

condone, *v.* проща́ть *imp.*

conducive, *adj.* способству́ющий.

conduct, *n.* поведе́ние *nt.* — *v.* вести́ *imp.*

conductor, *n.* руководи́тель *m.;* (*mus.*) дирижёр *m.*

cone, *n.* ко́нус *m.;* (*bot.*) ши́шка *f.*

confection, *n.* сла́сти *pl.*

confectionery, *n.* конди́терская *f.*

confederate, *n.* соуча́стник *m.* — *adj.* сою́зный.

confederation, *n.* конфедера́ция *f.*

confer, *v.* присужда́ть *imp.,* присуди́ть *perf.* — *v. i.* совеща́ться *imp.*

conference, *n.* совеща́ние *nt.*

confess, *v.* признава́ться *imp.,* призна́ться *perf.* **-ion,** *n.* призна́ние *nt.*

confide, *v.* доверя́ть *imp.,* дове́рить *perf.*

confidence, *n.* дове́рие *nt.*

confident, *adj.* уве́ренный.

confidentially, *adv.* по секре́ту; секре́тно.

confine, *v.* ограни́чивать *imp.,* ограни́чить *perf.* **confine oneself,** ограни́чиваться *imp.,* ограни́читься *perf.*

confirm, *v.* подтвержда́ть *imp.,* подтверди́ть *perf.* **-ation,** *n.* подтвержде́ние *nt.*

confiscate, *v.* конфискова́ть *imp. &. perf.*

confiscation, *n.* конфиска́ция *f.*

conflict, *n.* конфли́кт *m.* — *v.* противоре́чить *imp.*

conformation, *n.* устро́йство *nt.*

conformist, *n.* конформи́ст *m.*

conformity, *n.* соотве́тствие *nt.* **in conformity with,** в соотве́тствии с.

confound, *v.* спу́тывать *imp.,*

спута́ть *perf.* разруша́ть *imp.*, разру́шить *perf.*

confront, *v.* стоя́ть лицо́м к лицу́; смотре́ть в лицо́.

confuse, *v.* смуща́ть *imp.*, сбива́ть с то́лку.

confusion, *n.* беспоря́док *m.*, смуще́ние *nt.*

congeal, *v.* замора́живать *imp.*, заморо́зить *perf.*

congenial, *adj* благоприя́тный, конгениа́льный.

congenital, *adj.* прирождённый; врождённый.

congested, *adj.* перенаселённый, те́сный.

congestion, *n.* теснота́ *f.*; перенаселённость *f.*

conglomerate, *v.* ска́пливаться *imp.*, скопи́ться *perf.* — *n.* конгломера́т *m.*

conglomeration, *n.* конгломера́ция *f.*, скопле́ние *nt.*

congratulate, *v.* поздравля́ть *imp.*, поздра́вить *perf.*

congratulation, *n.* поздравле́ние *nt.*

congratulatory, *adj.* поздрави́тельный.

congregate, *v.* собира́ть *imp.*, собра́ть *perf.* — *v. i.* собира́ться *imp.*, собра́ться *perf.*

congregation, *n.* скопле́ние, собра́ние *nt.*

congress, *n.* конгре́сс *m.*

conjecture, *n.* предположе́ние *nt.* — *v.* предполага́ть *imp.*, предположи́ть *perf.*

conjugate, *v.* спряга́ть *imp.*

conjugation, *n.* спряже́ние *nt.*

conjunction, *n.* соедине́ние *nt.*; (*gram.*) сою́з *m.*

conjure, *v.* умоля́ть *imp.*, умоли́ть *perf.*

connect, *v.* свя́зывать *imp.*, связа́ть *perf.*; соединя́ть *imp.*, соедини́ть *perf.*

connection, *n.* связь *f.*

connive, *v.* потво́рствовать *imp.*

connoisseur, *n.* знато́к *m.*

connotation, *n.* дополни́тельное значе́ние.

connote, *v.* име́ть дополни́-

тельное значе́ние; означа́ть *imp.*

conquer, *v.* завоёвывать *imp.*, завоева́ть *perf.* -*or,* *n.* завоева́тель *m.*, покори́тель *m.*

conquest, *n.* завоева́ние *nt.*

Conrad, *n.* Кондра́тий *m.*, Ко́нрад *m.*

conscience, *n.* со́весть *f.*

conscientious, *adj.* со́вестливый; добросо́вестный.

conscious, *adj.* созна́тельный -*ness,* *n.* созна́ние *nt.*

conscription, *n.* набо́р *m.*

consecrate, *v.* посвяща́ть *imp.*, посвяти́ть *perf.*

consecration, *n.* посвяще́ние *nt.*

consecutive, *adj.* после́довательный.

consent, *n.* согла́сие, разреше́ние *nt.* — *v.* соглаша́ться *imp.*, согласи́ться *perf.*

consequence, *n.* сле́дствие, после́дствие *nt.* in c. of, всле́дствие.

consequent, *adj.* после́довательный. -*ly,* *adv.* сле́довательно.

conservation, *n.* сохране́ние *nt.*

conservative, *adj.* консервати́вный.

conservatory, *n.* консервато́рия *f.*

conserve, *v.* консерви́ровать *imp. & perf.*

consider, *v.* (*regard as*) счита́ть *imp.*, счесть *perf.*; (*contemplate*) рассма́тривать *imp.*, рассмотре́ть *perf.*; (*take into account*) принима́ть во внима́ние.

considerable, *adj.* значи́тельный.

considerate, *adj.* внима́тельный к други́м.

consideration, *n.* размышле́ние *nt.*; внима́ние *nt.* be under c., рассма́триваться.

considering, *prep.,* принима́я во внима́ние.

consist, *v.* состоя́ть из.

consistency, *n.* постоя́нность, после́довательность *f.*

consistent, *adj.* после́довательный.

consolation, *n.* утеше́ние *nt.*

console, *v.* утеша́ть *imp.*, уте́шить *perf.*

consolidate, *v.* укрепля́ть *imp.*, укрепи́ть *perf.*

consonant, *n.* согла́сный.

conspicuous, *adj.* ви́димый, заме́тный.

conspiracy, *n.* за́говор *m.*

conspire, *v.* устра́ивать за́говор *m.*

Constance, *n.* Ко́нстанс *f. ind.*; Конста́нция *f.*

constancy, *n.* постоя́нство *nt.*

constant, *adj.* постоя́нный.

constellation, *n.* созве́здие *nt.*

consternation, *n.* оцепене́ние *nt.*, у́жас *m.*

constipation, *n.* запо́р *m.*

constitute, *v.* составля́ть *imp.*

constitution, *n.* конститу́ция *f.* **-al,** *adj.* конституцио́нный.

constraint, *n.* принужде́ние *nt.*, принужде́нность *f.*

constrict, *v.* стя́гивать *imp.*, стяну́ть *perf.*

construct, *v.* стро́ить *imp.*, постро́ить *perf.* **-ion,** *n.* стро́ительство *nt.* **-ive,** *adj.* конструкти́вный, стро́ительный.

construe, *v.* толкова́ть *imp.*

consul, *n.* ко́нсул *m.* **-ate,** *n.* ко́нсульство *nt.*

consult, *v.* сове́товаться *imp.*, посове́товаться *perf.* **-ant,** *n.* консульта́нт *m.* **-ation,** *n.* консульта́ция *f.*

consume, *v.* потребля́ть *imp.*, потреби́ть *perf.*

consumer, *n.* потреби́тель *m.*

consummation, *n.* заверше́ние *nt.*

consumption, *n.* потребле́ние *nt.*, расхо́д *m.*; (*med.*) чахо́тка *f.*, туберкулёз лёгких.

consumptive, *adj.* больно́й туберкулёзом. — *adj.* туберкулёзный.

contact, *n.* конта́кт *m.*, соприкоснове́ние *nt.* — *v.* приводи́ть в соприкоснове́ние.

contagious, *adj.* зара́зный; (*fig.*) зарази́тельный.

contain, *v.* содержа́ть *imp.*

container, *n.* конте́йнер *m.*

contaminate, *v.* по́ртить *imp.*, испо́ртить *perf.*

contamination, *n.* загрязне́ние *nt.*

contemplate, *v.* созерца́ть *imp.*

contemplation, *n.* созерца́ние *nt.*

contemplative, *adj.* созерца́тельный.

contemporary, *adj.* совреме́нный. — *n.* совреме́нник *m.*

contempt, *n.* презре́ние *nt.* **-ible,** *adj.* презре́нный. **-uous,** *adj.* презри́тельный.

contend, *v.* утвержда́ть *imp.*, утверди́ть *perf.*

content, *adj.* дово́льный. — *n. pl.* содержа́ние *nt.* — *v.* удовлетворя́ть *imp.*, удовлетвори́ть *perf.*

contention, *n.* утвержде́ние *nt.*

contentment, *n.* удовлетворённость *f.*, дово́льствие *nt.*

contest, *n.* ко́нкурс *m.*; состяза́ние *nt.* — *v.* спо́рить *imp.*

context, *n.* конте́кст *m.*

continent, *n.* матери́к *m.*, контине́нт *m.*

continental, *adj.* материко́вый, континента́льный.

continual, *adj.* непреры́вный.

continuation, *n.* продолже́ние *nt.*

continue, *v.* продолжа́ть *imp.*, продо́лжить *perf.*

continuity, *n.* непреры́вность *f.*

continuous, *adj.* непреры́вный.

contour, *n.* ко́нтур *m.*

contraband, *n.* контраба́нда *f.*

contract, *n.* догово́р, контра́кт *m.* — *v.* заключа́ть догово́р; сжима́ться *imp.*, сжа́ться *perf.*

contraction, *n.* сжа́тие *nt.*; сокраще́ние *nt.*

contradict, *v.* противоре́чить *imp.* **-ion,** *n.* противоре́чие *nt.* **-ory,** *adj.* противоречи́вый.

contrary, *adj.* противополо́жный. — *n.* противополо́жность *f.* **c. to,** вопреки́. **on the c.,** наоборо́т.

contrast, *n.* контра́ст *m.* — *v.* противопоставля́ть *imp.*, противопоста́вить *perf.*

contribute, *v.* сде́лать вклад.

contribution, *n.* вклад *m.*, контрибу́ция *f.*

contributor, *n.* соде́йствующий, соуча́стник *m.*

contrite, *adj.* сокруша́ющийся

contrive, *v.* приду́мывать *imp.*, приду́мать *perf.*

control, *n.* прове́рка *f.*, контро́ль *m.* — *v.* контроли́ровать *imp.* & *perf.*

controversial, *adj.* спо́рный.

controversy, *n.* спор *m.*, поле́мика *f.*

convalesce, *v.* выздора́вливать *imp.*

convalescence, *n.* выздора́вливание *nt.*

convene, *v.* собира́ться *imp.*, собра́ться *perf.*

convenience, *n.* удо́бство *nt.*

convenient, *adj.* удо́бный.

convent, *n.* же́нский монасты́рь.

convention, *n.* (*assembly*) съезд *m.*

conventional, *adj.* усло́вный.

converge, *v.* сходи́ться *imp.*, сойти́сь *perf.*

convergence, *n.* схожде́ние *nt.*

conversant, *adj.* све́дущий.

conversation, *n.* разгово́р *m.* **-al,** *adj.* разгово́рный.

converse, *v.* бесе́довать *imp.*

conversion, *n.* превраще́ние *nt.*

convert, *v.* превраща́ть *imp.*, преврати́ть *perf.* **-ible,** *adj.* обрати́мый, измени́мый.

convex, *adj.* вы́пуклый.

convey, *v.* перевози́ть *imp.*, перевезти́ *perf.*; передава́ть *imp.*, переда́ть *perf.* **-ance,** *n.* перево́зка *f.*

conviction, *n.* осужде́ние *nt.*; (*belief*) убежде́ние *nt.*, уве́ренность *f.*

convince, *v.* убежда́ть *imp.*, убеди́ть *perf.* **become ~,** *v.* убежда́ться *imp.*, убеди́ться *perf.*

convincing, *adj.* убеди́тельный

convulsion, *n.* конву́льсия *f.*

convulsive, *adj.* судоро́жный.

cook, *n.* по́вар *m.*, куха́рка *f.* — *v.* гото́вить *imp.*, пригото́вить *perf.*; стря́пать *imp.*

cool, *adj.* прохла́дный. — *v.* охлажда́ть *imp.*, охлади́ть *perf.*

coop, *n.* куря́тник *m.*

coöperate, *v.* сотру́дничать *imp.*

coöperation, *n.* сотру́дничество *nt.*

coöperative, *adj.* совме́стный, коoperatíвный.

coördinate, *v.* координи́ровать *imp.* & *perf.*

coördination, *n.* координа́ция *f.*

copious, *adj.* оби́льный.

copper, *n.* медь *f.*

copy, *n.* экземпля́р *m.*, ко́пия *f.* — *v.* копи́ровать *imp.*

copyright, *n.* а́вторское пра́во.

coral, *n.* кора́лл *m.*

cord, *n.* верёвка *f.*

cordial, *adj.* серде́чный. **-ity,** *n.* серде́чность *f.*

core, *n.* сердцеви́на *f.*

cork, *n.* про́бка *f.*

corkscrew, *n.* што́пор *m.*

corn, *n.* кукуру́за *f.*, зерно́ *nt.*

corner, *n.* у́гол *m.* **around the c.,** (*dir.*) за у́гол. (*loc.*) за угло́м.

coronation, *n.* корона́ция *f.*

corporal, *n.* капра́л *m.* — *adj.* теле́сный.

corporation, *n.* корпора́ция *f.*; акционе́рное о́бщество.

corps, *n.* ко́рпус *m.*

corpse, *n.* труп *m.*

corpulent, *adj.* доро́дный.

corpuscle, *n.* кровяно́й ша́рик.

correct, *adj.* пра́вильный. — *v.* поправля́ть *imp.*, поправля́ть *imp.*, попра́вить *perf.*, исправля́ть *imp.*, испра́вить *perf.* **-ion,** *n.* попра́вка *f.* **-ive,** *adj.* исправи́тельный. **-ness,** *n.* пра́вильность *f.*

correlate, *v.* устана́вливать соотноше́ние.

correlation, *n.* соотноше́ние *nt.*, корреля́ция *f.*

correspond, *v.* перепи́сываться

imp.; соответствовать *imp.*

correspondence, *n.* корреспонде́нция *f.*, перепи́ска *f.*; *(conformity)* соотве́тствие *nt.* **by c.,** зао́чна.

correspondent, *n.* корреспонде́нт *m.*

corresponding, *adj.* соотве́тствующий.

corridor, *n.* коридо́р *m.*

corroborate, *v.* подтвержда́ть *imp.*, подтверди́ть *perf.*

corroboration, *n.* подтвержде́ние *nt.*

corrode, *v.* разъеда́ть *imp.*, разъе́сть *perf.*

corrosion, *n.* корро́зия *f.*

corrupt, *adj.* развращённый. — *v.* развраща́ть *imp.*, разврати́ть *perf.* **-ion,** *n.* развраще́ние *nt.*

cosmetic, *adj.* космети́ческий. — *n.* космети́ческое сре́дство.

cosmic, *adj.* косми́ческий.

cosmopolitan, *adj.* космополити́ческий.

cost, *n.* сто́имость *f.* **at all costs,** любо́й цено́й. — *v.* сто́ить *imp.*

costly, *adv.* дорого́й, це́нный.

costume, *n.* костю́м *m.*

cosy, *adj.* ую́тный.

cot, *n.* крова́тка *f.*; ко́йка *f.*

cottage, *n.* да́ча *f.*

cotton, *n.* хло́пок *m.*

cough, *n.* ка́шель *m.* — *v.* ка́шлять *imp.*

council, *n.* сове́т *m.*

counsel, *n.* совеща́ние *nt.*; сове́т *m.*; *(legal)* адвока́т *m.* — *v.* сове́товать *imp.*, посове́товать *perf.* **-or,** *n.* сове́тник, консульта́нт *m.*

count, *n.* счёт *m.* — *v.* счита́ть *imp.*, сосчита́ть *perf.*

counteract, *v.* противоде́йствовать *imp.*

counterclockwise, *adv.* про́тив стре́лки.

counterfeit, *adj.* подде́льный. — *v.* подде́лывать *imp.*, подде́лать *perf.*

countless, *adj.* бесчи́сленный.

country, *n.* страна́ *f.*; *(native)* ро́дина *f.*, оте́чество *nt.*; *(rural districts)* дере́вня *f.*

countryman, *n.* соотве́ственник *m.*

county, *n.* о́круг *m.*

couple, *n.* па́ра *f.* — *v.* спа́ривать *imp.*, спа́рить *perf.*

coupon, *n.* купо́н *m.*; тало́н *m.*

courage, *n.* му́жество *nt.*, сме́лость *f.*

courageous, *adj.* му́жественный, сме́лый.

course, *n.* курс *m.*; направле́ние *nt.* **of c.,** коне́чно. **in the c. of,** в тече́ние.

court, *n.* суд *m.*

courteous, *adj.* ве́жливый.

courtesy, *n.* ве́жливость *f.*

courtship, *n.* уха́живание *nt.*

cousin, *n.* двою́родный брат *m.* двою́родная сестра́ *f.*

cover, *n.* *(lid)* кры́шка *f.*; *(protection)* прикры́тие *nt.* — *v.* покрыва́ть *imp.*, покры́ть *perf.*; *(embrace)* охва́тывать *imp.*, охвати́ть *perf.*

cow, *n.* коро́ва *f.*

coward, *n.* трус *m.* **-ice,** *n.* тру́сость *f.* **-ly,** *adj.* трусли́вый.

cowboy, *n.* ковбо́й *m.*

coy, *adj.* засте́нчивый.

cozy, *adj.* ую́тный.

crab, *n.* краб *m.*

crack, *n.* *(noise)* треск *m.* трещи́на *f.* — *v. t.* раска́лывать *imp.*, расколо́ть *perf.* — *v. i.* раска́лываться *imp.*, расколо́ться *perf.*; тре́скаться *imp.*

cracker, *n.* сухо́е пече́нье.

cradle, *n.* колыбе́ль *f.*

craft, *n.* ремесло́ *f.*; *(coll.)* суда́ *pl.*

craftsman, *n.* реме́сленник *m.* **-ship,** *n.* мастерство́ *nt.*

crafty, *adj.* хи́трый.

cram, *v.* набива́ть *imp.*, наби́ть *perf.*; ната́скивать *imp.*, ната́скать *perf.*

cramp, *n.* су́дорога, спа́зма *f.*

cranberry, *n.* клю́ква *f.*

crane, *n.* *(bird)* жура́вль *m.*; *(mach.)* подъёмный кран.

crank, *n.* кривоши́п *m.,* руко́ятка *f.* — *v.* заводи́ть руко́яткой.

crash, *n.* гро́хот *m.,* треск *m.* — *v.* разби́ться. *perf.*

crate, *n.* клеть *f.;* корзи́на *f.*

crater, *n.* кра́тер *m.*

crave, *v.* жа́ждать *imp.*

craving, *n.* стра́стное жела́ние *nt.*

crawl, *v.* по́лзать *imp.,* ползти́ *imp.*

crazy, *adj.* сумасше́дший.

creak, *v.* скрипе́ть *imp.*

cream, *n.* (*milk product*) сли́вки *pl.;* (*cosmetic*) крем *m.*

creamery, *n.* масло́би́йня *f.*

create, *v.* твори́ть *imp.,* сотвори́ть *perf.;* создава́ть *imp.,* созда́ть *perf.*

creation, *n.* созда́ние, творе́ние *nt.*

creative, *adj* тво́рческий.

creator, *n.* творе́ц, созда́тель *m.;* а́втор *m.*

creature, *n.* существо́ *nt.*

credentials, *n. pl.* манда́т *m.;* вери́тельные гра́моты.

credible, *adj.* вероя́тный.

credit, *n.* креди́т *m.* — *v.* кредитова́ть *imp. & perf.;* припи́сывать *imp.,* приписа́ть *perf.*

credulity, *n.* дове́рчивость *f.*

credulous, *adj.* легкове́рный.

creed, *n.* вероуче́ние *nt.;* кре́до *nt. ind.*

creek, *v.* руче́й *m.*

crescent, *n.* полукру́г *m.;* (*moon*) полуме́сяц *m.*

crest, *n.* гре́бень *m.,* верши́на *f.*

crew, *n.* экипа́ж *m.,* кома́нда *f.*

crime, *n.* преступле́ние *nt.*

Crimea, *n.* Крым *m.*

criminal, *adj.* престу́пный. — *n.* престу́пник *m.*

crimson, *adj.* тёмнокра́сный, мали́новый. — *n.* мали́новый цвет.

cringe, *v.* раболе́пствовать *imp.*

cripple, *n.* кале́ка *m. & f.* (*declined as f.*) — *v.* кале́чить *imp.,* искале́чить *perf.*

crisis, *n.* кри́зис *m.;* перело́м *m.*

crisp, *adj.* хрустя́щий, ло́мкий.

criterion, *n.* крите́рий *m.*

critic, *n.* кри́тик *m.* **-al,** *adj.* крити́ческий.

criticism, *n.* кри́тика *f.*

criticize, *v.* критикова́ть *imp.*

croak, *n.* ква́канье *nt.;* ка́рканье *nt.* — *v.* ква́кать *imp.;* ка́ркать *imp.*

Croatia, *n.* Хорва́тия *f.*

crocodile, *n.* крокоди́л *m.*

crooked, *adj.* криво́й; (*dishonest*) нече́стный.

crop, *n.* урожа́й *nt.*

cross, *adj.* попере́чный, перекрёстный; (*angry*) злой, серди́тый. — *n.* крест *m.* — *v. t.* скре́щивать *imp.,* скрести́ть *perf.;* переходи́ть *imp.,* перейти́ *perf.* — *v. i.* скре́щиваться *imp.,* скрести́ться *perf.*

cross-eyed, *adj.* косогла́зый.

crossing, *n.* перепра́ва *f.,* пересече́ние *nt.;* (*crossroads*) перекрёсток *m.*

crossword puzzle, кро́ссворд *m.*

crotch, *n.* разви́лина *f.;* крюк *m.*

crow, *n.* воро́на *f.*

crowd, *n.* толпа́ *f.* — *v.* толпи́ться *imp.* **-ed,** *adj.* перепо́лненный.

crown, *n.* коро́на *f.* — *v.* коронова́ть *imp. & perf.*

crucial, *adj.* реша́ющий, крити́ческий.

crucify, *v.* распина́ть *imp.,* распя́ть *perf.*

crude, *adj.* сыро́й; (*rude*) гру́бый; (*unfinished*) необрабо́танный.

cruel, *adj.* жесто́кий. **-ty,** *n.* жесто́кость *f.*

cruise, *n.* рейс *m.,* пла́вание *nt.* — *v.* соверша́ть рейс.

crumb, *n.* кро́шка *f.*

crumble, *v.* кроши́ться *imp.*

crumple, *v.* мять *imp.,* помя́ть *perf.* — *v. i.* мя́ться *imp.,* помя́ться *perf.*

crusade, *n.* похо́д *m.,* кампа́ния *f.;* (*hist.*) кресто́вый похо́д.

crush, v. давить *imp.*; подавлять *imp.*, подавить *perf.*

crust, n. корка f.

crutch, n. костыль f.

сгу, n, крик m., клич m., плач m. — v. плакать *imp.*, кричать *imp.*

cryptic, adj. сокровенный.

crystal, n. хрусталь f.; — adj. хрустальный.

crystallize, v. кристализовать *imp. & perf.* — v. i. кристализоваться *imp. & perf.*

cube, n. куб m.

cubic, adj. кубический.

cucumber, n. огурец m.

cue, n. намёк m.; (billiards) кий m.

cuff, n. манжета f.

cuisine, n. кухня f.

culinary, adj. кулинарный.

culmination, n. кульминация f., кульминационный пункт.

cult, n. культ m.

cultivate, v. обрабатывать *imp.*, обработать *perf.*; культивировать *imp. & perf.*

cultivated, adj. обработанный; (cultured) культурный.

cultivation, n. возделывание nt., обработка f.

cultural, adj. культурный.

culture, n. культура f.

cultured, adj. культурный.

cumbersome, adj. затруднительный.

cumulative, adj. совокупный, кумулятивный.

cunning, n. ловкость, хитрость m. — adj. ловкий-хитрый.

cup, n. чашка f.

curable, adj. излечимый.

curb, n. обочина f.

curdle, v. свёртываться *imp.*, свернуться *perf.*

cure, n. лечение nt. — v. лечить *imp.*, вылечить *perf.*

curiosity, n. любопытство m.

curious, adj. любопытный.

curl, n. завивка f.; спираль f. — v. t. завивать *imp.*, завить *perf.* — v. i. виться *imp.* свиться *perf.*

curly, adj. вьющийся.

currency, n. (money) валюта f.; (prevalence) распространённость f.

current, adj. текущий. — n. (flow) течение nt.; (elec.) ток m.

curriculum, n. учебный план; программа f.

curse, n. проклятие nt. — v. ругаться *imp.*; проклинать *imp.*

cursory, adj. беглый, поверхностный.

curt, adj. краткий; отрывистый.

curtail, v. укорачивать *imp.*, укоротить *perf.*

curtain, n. занавеска f.; (theat) занавес m.

curve, n. закругление nt.; (math.) кривая f. — v. t. изгибать *imp.*, изогнуть *perf.* — v. i. изгибаться *imp.*, изогнуться *perf.*

cushion, n. подушка f.

custodian, n. хранитель, опекун m.

custody, n. охрана, опека f.

custom, n. обычай m.; привычка f.

customary, adj. обычный.

customer, n. покупатель, клиент m.

customhouse, customs, n. таможня f.

cut, n. порез m., вырезка f. — v. резать *imp.*, зарезать, срезать *perf.* — v. oneself. c. резаться *imp.*, прорезаться *perf.*

cute, adj. милый, красивый.

cutlet, n. котлета f.

cycle, n. цикл m. — v. ездить на велосипеде.

cyclone, n. циклон m.

cylinder, n. цилиндр m.

cylindrical, adj. цилиндрический.

cynic, n. циник m. -al, adj. циничный. -ism, n. цинизм m.

Cyprus, n. Кипр m.

cyst, n. киста f.

Czechoslovakia, n. Чехословакия f.

D

dad, *n.* па́па, оте́ц *m.*

dagger, *n.* кинжа́л *m.*

daily, *adj.* ежедне́вный. — *adv.* ежедне́вно.

dairy, *n.* масло́де́льня *f.*; моло́чная *f.*

daisy, *n.* маргари́тка *f.*

dam, *n.* да́мба, плоти́на *f.*

damage, *n.* уще́рб *m.* — *v.* наноси́ть уще́рб.

damn, *v.* проклина́ть *imp.*, прокля́сть *perf.* **-ation,** *n.* прокля́тие *nt.* **-ed,** *adj.* прокля́тый.

damp, *adj.* сыро́й, вла́жный. **-ness,** *n.* сы́рость *f.*

dance, *n* та́нец *m* — *v.* танцева́ть *imp.*

dancer, *n.* танцо́вщик *m.*

dancing, *n.* та́нцы *pl.*, пля́ска *f.*

dandelion, *n.* одува́нчик *m.*

dandruff, *n.* пе́рхоть *f.*

Dane, *n.* датча́нин *m.*, датча́нка *f.*

danger, *n.* опа́сность *f.* **-ous,** *adj.* опа́сный.

Daniel, *n.* Дании́л *m.*

Danish, *adj.* да́тский.

dapper, *adj.* опря́тный.

dare, *v.* осме́ливаться *imp.*, осме́литься *perf.*

daring, *n.* отва́га, сме́лость *f.* — *adj.* отва́жный, сме́лый.

dark, *adj.* тёмный. — *n.* тьма *f.* **-en,** *v.* затемня́ть *imp.*, затемни́ть *perf.* **-ness,** *n.* темнота́ *f.*

darn, *v.* што́пать *imp.*, зашто́пать *perf.*

dart, *n.* стрела́ *f.*

dash, *n.* рыво́к *m.*; (*punctuation*) чёрточка *f,* тире́ *nt. ind.* — *v.* ри́нуться *perf.*

data, *n.* да́нные *pl.*

date, *n.* да́та *f.*, число́ *nt.*; (*engagement*) свида́ние *nt.*; (*fruit*) фи́ник *m.*

daughter, *n.* дочь *f.*

daughter-in-law, *n.* сноха́ *f.*

David, *n.* Дави́д *m.*

day, *n.* день *m.* **a day or two ago,** на дня́х. **day by day,** изо дня в день; с ка́ждым днём. **by day,** днём. **by the day,** поде́нно. **every other day,** че́рез день. **in a day or two,** на дня́х. **the day after tomorrow,** послеза́втра. **the day before,** накану́не. **the day before yesterday,** позавчера́, тре́тьего дня.

daybreak, *n.* рассве́т *m.*

daylight, *n.* дневно́й свет.

dawn, *n.* заря́ *f.* — *v.* рассвета́ть *imp.*

daze, *v.* изумля́ть *imp.*, изуми́ть *perf.*

dead, *adj.* мёртвый. **-ly,** *adj.* смерте́льный.

Dead Sea, Мёртвое мо́ре.

deaf, глухо́й. **-en,** *v.* оглуша́ть *imp.*, оглуши́ть *perf.* **-ness,** *n.* глухота́ *f.*

deaf-mute, *n.* глухонемо́й.

deal, *n.* до́ля *f.*; (*agreement*) сде́лка *f.*; (*cards*) сда́ча *f.* — *v.* обходи́ться *imp.*, трактова́ть *imp.*; (*cards*) тасова́ть ка́рты. **-er,** *n.* торго́вец *m.*

dean, *n.* дека́н *m.*

dear, *adj.* дорого́й.

death, *n.* смерть *f.*

debase, *v.* понижа́ть *imp.*, пони́зить *perf.*; унижа́ть *imp.*, уни́зить *perf.*

debate, *n.* деба́ты *pl.*, спор *m.* — *v.* спо́рить *imp.*

debit, *n.* де́бет *m.*

debris, *n.* оско́лки *pl.*, разва́лины *pl.*

debt, *n.* долг *m.* **-or,** *n.* должни́к *m.*

debut, *n.* дебю́т *m.*

decade, *n.* десятиле́тие *nt.*, дека́да *f.*

decadence, *n.* упа́док *m.*; декаде́нтство *nt.*

decadent, *adj.* декаде́нтский, упа́дочный.

decapitate, *v.* обезгла́вливать *imp.*, обезгла́вить *perf.*

decay, *n.* гние́ние *nt.* — *v.* гнить *imp.*, сгнить *perf.*

deceased, *adj.* поко́йный, уме́рший.

deceit, *n.* обма́н *m.* **-ful,** *adj.* обма́нчивый.

deceive, *v.* обма́нывать *imp.*, обману́ть *perf.*

December, *n.* дека́брь *m.* — *adj.* дека́брьский.

decency, *n.* прили́чие *nt.*

decent, *adj.* прили́чный.

deception, *n.* обма́н *m.*

deceptive, *adj.* обма́нчивый; вводя́щий в заблужде́ние.

decide, *v. v. t.* реша́ть *imp.*, реши́ть *perf.;* — *v. i.* реша́ться *imp.* реши́ться *perf.*

decimal, *n.* десяти́чная дробь *f.*

decipher, *v.* расшифро́вывать *imp.*, расшифрова́ть *perf.*

decision, *n.* реше́ние *nt.*

decisive, *adj.* реши́тельный.

deck, *n.* па́луба *f.((cards)* коло́да карт.

declaration, *n.* деклара́ция *f.;* объявле́ние *nt.*; заявле́ние *nt.*

declare, *v.* объявля́ть *imp.*, объяви́ть *perf.* заявля́ть *imp.* заяви́ть *perf.*

declension, *n.* склоне́ние *nt.*

decline, *n. (decrease)* уменьше́ние *nt.; (slope)* склон *m.*, зака́т *m.* — *v. t.* отка́зываться *imp.*, отказа́ться *perf. (gram.)* склоня́ть *imp.*, склони́ть *perf.* — *v. i.* уменьша́ться *imp.*, уменьши́ться *perf.*; наклоня́ться *imp.*, наклони́ться *perf.*

decompose, *v. t.* разлага́ть *imp.*, разложи́ть *perf.* — *v. i.* разлага́ться *imp.*, разложи́ться *perf.*

decorate, *v.* украша́ть *imp.*, укра́сить *perf. (reward)* награжда́ть *imp.*, награди́ть *perf.*

decoration, *n.* награ́да *f.*

decorative, *adj.* декорати́вный.

decorator, *n.* декора́тор *m.*

decorum, *n.* прили́чие *nt.*

decrease, *v. t.* уменьша́ть *imp.*, уменьши́ть *perf.* — *v. i.* уменьша́ться *imp.*, уменьши́ться *imp.*, уменьше́ние *nt.*, убыль *f.*

decree, *n.* декре́т *m.*, ука́з *m.*

dedicate, *v.* посвяща́ть *imp.*, посвяти́ть *perf.*

dedication, *n.* посвяще́ние *nt.*

deduct, *v.* вычита́ть *imp.*, вы́честь *perf.*

deduction, *n.* вычита́ние *nt.*; вы́вод *m.*, заключе́ние *nt.*

deed, *n.* посту́пок *m.*; де́йствие *nt.*

deep, *adj.* глубо́кий. **-en, v.** углубля́ть *imp.*, углуби́ть *perf.*

deer, *n.* оле́нь *m.*

deface, *v.* обезобра́живать *imp.*, обезобра́зить *perf.*

defamation, *n.* клевета́ *f.*

defame, *v.* клевета́ть *imp.*, наклевета́ть *perf.*

defeat, *n.* разгро́м *m.* — *v.* побежда́ть *imp.*, победи́ть *perf.*

defect, *n.* недоста́ток *m.*; дефе́кт *m.* **-ive,** *adj.* повреждённый, дефе́ктный.

defend, *v.* защища́ть *imp.*, защити́ть *perf.*; обороня́ть *imp.*, оборони́ть *perf.* **-ant,** *n.* подсуди́мый, обвиня́емый. **-er,** *n.* защи́тник *m.*

defense, *n.* оборо́на, защи́та *f.*

defensive, *adj.* оборони́тельный.

defer, *v.* откла́дывать *imp.*, отложи́ть *perf.*

defiant, *adj.* вызыва́ющий.

deficiency, *n.* недоста́ток *m.*

deficient, *adj.* недоста́точный.

deficit, *n.* дефици́т *m.*, недочёт *m.*

define, *v.* определя́ть *imp.*, определи́ть *perf.*

definite, *adj.* определённый.

definition, *n.* определе́ние *nt.*

definitive, *adj.* оконча́тельный.

deflation, *n.* выка́чивание *nt.*; *(econ.)* дефля́ция *f.*

deflect, *v.* отклоня́ть *imp.*, отклони́ть *perf.*

deform, *v.* деформи́ровать *imp. & perf.* **-ity,** *n.* безобра́зие *nt.*

defraud, *v.* выма́нивать *imp.*, вы́манить *perf.*

defy, *v.* вызыва́ть *imp.*, вы́звать *perf.*

degenerate, *adj.* вырожда́ющийся. - *v.* вырожда́ться *imp.*, вы́родиться *perf.*

degeneration, *n.* вырожде́ние *nt.*

degradation, *n.* деграда́ция *f.*

degrade, *v.* дегради́ровать *imp. & perf.*

degree, *n.* (*unit*) гра́дус *m.*; (*extent*) сте́пень *f.*; (*educ.*) зва́ние *nt.*, учёная сте́пень.

deity, *n.* божество́ *nt.*

dejected, *adj.* удручённый.

dejection, *n.* удручённость *f.*

delay, *n.* промедле́ние *nt.* - *v.* откла́дывать *imp.*, отложи́ть *perf.*

delegate, *n.* делега́т *m.* - *v.* делеги́ровать *imp. & perf.*

delegation, *n.* делега́ция *f.*

delete, *v.* вычёркивать *imp.*, вы́черкнуть *perf.*

deliberate, *adj.* наме́ренный, умы́шленный. - *v.* совеща́ться *imp.*

deliberation, *n.* обсужде́ние, обду́мывание *nt.*

delicate, *adj.* делика́тный.

delicious, *adj.* восхити́тельный.

delight, *n.* восто́рг *m.*, восхище́ние *nt.* - *v.* восхища́ть *imp.*, восхити́ть *perf.* **-ful,** *adj.* восхити́тельный.

delinquent, *adj.* правонаруши́тель, престу́пник *m.*

delirious, *adj.* находя́щийся в бреду́.

delirium, *n.* бред *m.*

deliver, *v.* доставля́ть *imp.*, доста́вить *perf.*; освобожда́ть *imp.*, освободи́ть *perf.*; (*speech*) чита́ть *imp.*, прочита́ть *perf.*

deliverance, *n.* освобожде́ние, избавле́ние *nt.*

delivery, *n.* доста́вка, переда́ча *f.*; (*birth*) ро́ды *pl.*

delta, *n.* де́льта *f.*

delude, *v.* обма́нывать *imp.*, обману́ть *perf.*

delusion, *n.* заблужде́ние *nt.*

demand, *n.* тре́бование *nt.*; запро́с *m.* **in d.,** в спро́се.

on d., по тре́бованию. — *v.* тре́бовать *imp.*, потре́бовать *perf.*

demobilize, *v.* демобилизова́ть *imp. & perf.*

democracy, *n.* демокра́тия *f.*

democrat, *n.* демокра́т *m.* **-ic,** *adj.* демократи́ческий.

demolish, *v.* разруша́ть *imp.*, разру́шить *perf.*

demonstrate, *v.* демонстри́ровать *imp.*, уча́ствовать в демонстра́ции.

demonstration, *n.* демонстри́рование *nt.*; демонстра́ция *f.*

demonstrative, *adj.* демонстрати́вный; (*gram.*) указа́тельный.

demoralization, *n.* деморализа́ция *f.*

demoralize, *v.* деморализова́ть *imp. & perf.*

den, *n.* ло́говище *nt.*

denial, *n.* отрица́ние *nt.*

Denmark, *n.* Да́ния *f.*

denomination, *n.* наименова́ние, назва́ние *nt.*

denominator, *n.* знамена́тель, дели́тель *m.*

denote, *v.* обознача́ть *imp.*, обозна́чить *perf.*; означа́ть *imp.*, озна́чить *perf.*

denounce, *v.* денонси́ровать *imp. & perf.*

dense, *adj.* густо́й.

density, *n.* пло́тность *f.*

dent, *n.* вы́емка *f.* — *v.* вда́вливать *imp.*, вда́вить *perf.*

dental, *adj.* зубно́й.

dentist, *n.* зубно́й врач.

dentistry, *n.* зуболече́ние *nt.*

dentures, *pl.* вставны́е зу́бы.

denunciation, *n.* денонси́рование *nt.*

deny, *v.* отрица́ть *imp.*

deodorant, *n.* дезодора́тор *m.*

depart, *v.* уходи́ть *imp.*, уйти́ *perf.*; уезжа́ть *imp.*, уе́хать *perf.*

department, *n.* отде́л *m.*, отделе́ние *nt.*

department store, универма́г *m.* (*abbr. of* универса́льный магази́н).

departure, *n.* отъе́зд, ухо́д *m.*

depend, *v.* зави́сеть (от) *imp.*

-able, *adj.* надёжный. **-ence**, *n.* зави́симость *f.* **-ent**, *adj.* зави́симый. — *n.* иждиве́нец *m.*

depict, *v.* изобража́ть *imp.*, изобрази́ть *perf.*

deplorable, *adj.* плаче́вный.

deport, *v.* ссыла́ть *imp.*, сосла́ть *perf.* **-ation**, *n.* ссы́лка *f.*

depose, *v.* сверга́ть *imp.*, све́ргнуть *perf.*

deposit, *n.* (*payment*) взнос, зада́ток *m.*; (*sediment*) оса́док *m.* — *v.* положи́ть *perf.* **-or**, *n.* вкла́дчик *m.*

depraved, *adj.* развращённый.

deprecate, *v.* возража́ть *imp.*, возрази́ть *perf.*

depreciate, *v.* обесце́нивать *imp.*, обесце́нить *perf.*

depreciation, *n.* обесце́нивание *nt.*

depress, *v.* подавля́ть *imp.*, подави́ть *perf.* **-ion**, *n.* депре́ссия *f.*; впа́дина *f.*

deprive, *v.* лиша́ть *imp.*, лиши́ть *perf.*

depth, *n.* глубина́, глубо́кость *f.*

deputy, *n.* депута́т *m.*

derision, *n.* высме́ивание *nt.*

derivation, *n.* происхожде́ние *nt.*

derivative, *adj.* происхо́дный.

derive, *v.* происходи́ть *imp.*

derogatory, *adj.* унизи́тельный.

descend, *v.* сходи́ть *imp.*, сойти́ *perf.*; происходи́ть *imp.* произойти́ *perf.* **-ant**, *n.* пото́мок *m.*

descent, *n.* спуск *m.*; происхожде́ние *nt.*

describe, *v.* опи́сывать *imp.*, описа́ть *perf.*

description, *n.* описа́ние *nt.*

descriptive, *adj.* описа́тельный.

desert, *n.* пусты́ня *f.* — *v. t.* покида́ть *imp.*, поки́нуть *perf.* — *v. i.* дезерти́ровать. **-er**, *n.* дезерти́р *m.* **-ion**, *n.* дезерти́рство *nt.*

deserve, *v.* заслу́живать *imp.*, заслужи́ть *perf.*

design, *n.* прое́кт *m.*, план *m.*; (*pattern*) рису́нок *m.*, (*drawing*) узо́р *m.* — *v.* проекти́ровать *imp.*, запроекти́ровать *perf.*

designate, *v.* назнача́ть *imp.*, назна́чить *perf.*

designation, *n.* указа́ние, назначе́ние *nt.*

designer, *n.* проекти́ровщик *m.*

desirability, *n.* жела́тельность *f.*

desirable, *adj.* жела́тельный.

desire, *n.* жела́ние *nt.* — *v.* жела́ть *imp.*

desirous, *adj.* жела́ющий.

desk, *n.* канцеля́рский стол, пи́сьменный стол.

desolation, *n.* опустоше́ние *nt.*

despair, *n.* отча́яние *nt.*

desperate, *adj.* отча́янный.

despicable, *adj.* по́длый.

despise, *v.* презира́ть *imp.*

despite, *prep.* вопреки́ (+ *dat.*) несмотря́ на (+ *acc.*).

despondent, *adj.* пода́вленный.

despot, *n.* де́спот, тира́н *m.*

dessert, *n.* десе́рт *m.*

destination, *n.* назначе́ние, предназначе́ние *nt.*

destiny, *n.* судьба́ *f.*

destitute, *adj.* нужда́ющийся.

destitution, *n.* лише́ние *nt.*, нищета́ *f.*

destroy, *v.* уничтожа́ть *imp.*, уничто́жить *perf.*; истребля́ть *imp.*, истреби́ть *perf.*; разруша́ть *imp.*, разру́шить *perf.* **-er**, *n.* эсми́нец *m.*

destruction, *n.* разруше́ние, уничтоже́ние *nt.*

destructive, *afdj.* разруши́тельный.

desultory, *adj.* несвя́зный.

detach, *v.* отделя́ть *imp.*, отдели́ть *perf.* **-ment**, *n.* отря́д *m.*

detail, *n.* подро́бность, дета́ль. **-ed**, *adj.* подро́бный.

detain, *v.* заде́рживать *imp.*, задержа́ть *perf.*

detect, *v.* открыва́ть *imp.*,

открыть *perf.* **-ion**, *n.* открытие, обнаружение *nt.*

detective, *n.* сыщик *m.*

detention, *n.* задержание *nt.*

deter, *v.* удерживать *imp.*, удержать *perf.*

deteriorate, *v. t.* ухудшать *imp.*, ухудшить *perf.* — *v. i.* ухудшаться *imp.*, ухудшиться *perf.*

deterioration, *n.* ухудшение *nt.*

determination, *n.* решимость *f.*

determine, *v.* определять *imp.*, определить *perf.*

detour, *n.* окольный путь, обход, объезд *m.*

devaluation, *n.* девальвация *f.*

devastation, *n.* опустошение*nt.*

develop, *v. t.* развивать *imp.*, развить *perf.* — *v. i.* развиваться *imp.*, развиться *perf.* **-ment**, *n.* развитие *nt.*

deviation, *n.* отклонение *nt.*

device, *n.* изобретение *nt.*

devil, *n.* дьявол, чёрт *m.*

devious, *adj.* извилистый.

devise, *v.* придумывать *imp.*, придумать *perf.*

devote, *v.* посвящать *imp.*, посвятить *perf.* **d. oneself**, посвящать себя.

devoted, *adj.* преданный.

devotion, *n.* преданность *f.*

devour, *v.* пожирать *imp.*, пожрать *perf.*

devout, *adj.* набожный.

dew, *n.* роса *f.*

dexterity, *n.* проворство *nt.*, ловкость *f.*

dexterous, *adj.* проворный, ловкий.

diabetes, *n.* диабет *m.*, сахарная болезнь.

diabolic(al), *adj.* дьявольский.

diagnose, *v.* ставить диагноз.

diagnosis, *n.* диагноз *m.*

diagonal, *adj.* диагональный. — *n.* диагональ *f.*

diagram, *n.* диаграмма *f.*

dial, *n.* циферблат *m.*, шкала *f.*

dialect, *n.* диалект *m.*, наречие *nt.*, говор *m.*

dialogue, *n.* диалог *m.*

diameter, *n.* диаметр *m.*

diamond, *n.* алмаз *m.*; (*polished*) бриллиант *m.*

diarrhea, *n.* понос *f.*

diary, *n.* дневник *m.*

dice, pl. игральные кости.

dictate, *v.* диктовать *imp.*, продиктовать *perf.*

dictation, *n.* диктант *m.*, диктовка *f.*

dictator, *n.* диктатор *m.* **-ship**, *n.* диктатура *f.*

diction, *n.* дикция *f.*

dictionary, *n.* словарь *m.*

die, *v.* умирать *imp.*, умереть *perf.* **die out**, вымирать *imp.*, вымереть *perf.*

diet, *n.* диета *f.* **-ary**, *adj.* диетический.

differ, *v.* различаться *imp.*

difference, *n.* разница *f.*, различие *nt.*

different, *adj.* различный, разный, отличный.

differentiate, *v.* различать *imp.*, различить *perf.*; отличать *imp.*, отличить *perf.*

difficult, *adj.* трудный.

difficulty, *n.* трудность *f.*

diffusion, *n.* распространение *nt.*

dig, *v.* копать *imp.*; рыть *imp.*

digest, *n.* краткое изложение, — *v.* переваривать *imp.*, переварить *perf.* **-ible**, *adj.* удобоваримый. **-ion**, *n.* пищеварение *nt.* **-ive**, *adj.* пищеварительный.

dignity, *n.* достоинство *nt.*

digress, *v.* отступать *imp.*, отступить *perf.* **-ion**, *n.* отступление *nt.*

dike, *n.* дамба, плотина *f.*

dilation, *n.* расширение *nt.*

dilemma, *n.* дилемма *f.*

dilettante, *n.* дилетант, любитель *m.*

diligent, *adj.* прилежный.

dilute, *v.* разводить *imp.*, развести *perf.*

dim, *adj.* тусклый. — *v.* делать тусклым.

dimension, *n.* измерение *nt.*

diminish, *v. t.* уменьшать *imp.*, уменьшить *perf.* — *v. i.*

уменьша́ться *imp.*, уме́ньшиться *perf.*

diminutive, *adj.* (*gram.*) уменьши́тельный.

dimple, *n.* я́мочка *f.*

din, *n.* грохо́т, шум *m.*

dine, *v.* обе́дать *imp.*, пообе́дать *perf.*

diner, *n.* ваго́н-рестора́н *m.*

dining-room, *n.* столо́вая *f.*

dinner, *n.* обе́д *m.*

diphtheria, *n.* дифтери́я *f.*, дифтери́т *m.*

diploma, *n.* дипло́м *m.*

diplomacy, *n.* диплома́тия *f.*

diplomat, *n.* диплома́т *m.*

-ic, *adj.* дипломати́ческий.

dire, *adj.* ужа́сный, стра́шный.

direct, *adj.* прямо́й; непосре́дственный. — *v.* направля́ть *imp.*, напра́вить *perf.*; руководи́ть *imp.* **direct current,** постоя́нный ток.

direction, *n.* направле́ние *nt.*; (*management*) управле́ние *nt.* руково́дство *nt.*

directly, *adv.* пря́мо, непосре́дственно.

director, *n.* дире́ктор *m.*, руководи́тель *m.*; (*theat.*) режиссёр *m.*

dirt, *n.* грязь *f.*; (*soil*) по́чва *f.*

dirty, *adj.* гря́зный.

disability, *n.* неспосо́бность *f.*

disable, *v.* де́лать неспосо́бным.

disadvantage, *n.* невы́года *f.*, невы́годное положе́ние *nt.*

disagree, *v.* не соглаша́ться *imp.*, согласи́ться *perf.*; расходи́ться во мне́ниях. **-able,** *adj.* неприя́тный. **-ment,** *n.* расхожде́ние по мне́ниям; разногла́сие *nt.*

disappear, *v.* исчеза́ть *imp.*, исче́знуть *perf.* **-ance,** *n.* исчезнове́ние *nt.*

disappoint, *v.* разочаро́вывать *imp.*, разочарова́ть *perf.* **-ment,** *n.* разочарова́ние *nt.*

disapproval, *n.* неодобре́ние *nt.*

disapprove, *v.* не одобря́ть *imp.*

disarm, *v. t.* разоружа́ть *imp.*,

разоружи́ть *perf.* — *v. i.* разоружа́ться *imp.* разоружа́ться *imp.*, разоружи́ться *perf.*

disarmament, *n.* разоруже́ние *nt.*

disaster, *n.* бе́дствие *nt.*

disastrous, *adj.* бе́дственный, ги́бельный.

disbelief, *n.* неве́рие *nt.*

discard, *v.* сбра́сывать *imp.*, сбро́сить *perf.*

discern, *v.* различа́ть *imp.*, различи́ть *perf.* **-ing,** *adj.* проница́тельный. **-ment,** *n.* проница́тельность *f.*

discharge, *v.* выпуска́ть *imp.*, вы́пустить *perf.*; выполня́ть *imp.*, вы́полнить *perf.*

discipline, *n.* дисципли́на *f.*

disclaim, *v.* отрека́ться *imp.*, отре́чься *perf.*

disclose, *v.* обнару́живать *imp.*, обнару́жить *perf.*

disclosure, *n.* откры́тие, обнаруже́ние *nt.*

discomfort, *n.* неудо́бство *nt.*

disconnect, *v.* разъединя́ть *imp.*, разъедини́ть *perf.*

discontent, *n.* недово́льство *nt.* **-ed,** *adj.* недово́льный.

discontinue, *v.* прерыва́ть *imp.*, прерва́ть *perf.*

discord, *n.* разногла́сие *nt.*

discount, *n.* диско́нт *m.*, ски́дка *f.*

discourage, *v.* обескура́живать *imp.*, обескура́жить *perf.* **-ment,** *n.* обескура́живание *nt.*

discover, *v.* открыва́ть *imp.*, откры́ть *perf.*

discovery, *n.* откры́тие *nt.*

discreet, *adj.* осмотри́тельный.

discrepancy, *n.* расхожде́ние *nt.*; несхо́дство *nt.*

discretion, *n.* осмотри́тельность *f.*

discriminate, *v.* дискримини́ровать *imp. & perf.*

discrimination, *n.* дискримина́ция *f.*

discuss, *v.* обсужда́ть *imp.*, обсуди́ть *perf.* **-ion,** *n.* диску́ссия *f.*, обсужде́ние *nt.*

disdainful, *adj.* пренебрежи́тельный.

disease, *n.* боле́знь *f.*

disembark, *v.* выса́живаться на бе́рег.

disfigure, *v.* обезобра́живать *imp.*, обезобра́зить *perf.*

disgrace, *n.* бесче́стие *nt.*, позо́р *m.* — *v.* позо́рить *perf.* -ful, *adj.* бесче́стный, позо́рный.

disguise, *n.* маскиро́вка *f.* — *v.* маскирова́ть *imp.*, замаскирова́ть *perf.*

disgust, *n.* отвраще́ние *nt.* — *v.* внуша́ть отвраще́ние.

dish, *n.* посу́да *f.*; ˟ (food) блю́до *nt.*

dishearten, *v.* приводи́ть в уны́ние.

dishonest, *adj.* нече́стный.

dishonesty, *n.* нече́стность *f.*

dishonor, *v.* бесче́стить *imp.*, обесче́стить *perf.* -able, *adj.* бесче́стный.

dishtowel, *n.* посу́дное полоте́нце.

disillusion, *v.* разочаро́вывать *imp.*, разочарова́ть *perf.*

disinfect, *v.* дезинфици́ровать *imp. & perf.* -ant, *n.* дезинфици́рующее сре́дство.

disinherit, *v.* лиша́ть насле́дства.

disinterested, *adj.* бескоры́стный.

disk, *n.* диск *m.*

dislike, *v.* нелюбо́вь *f.* — *v.* не люби́ть.

dislocate, *v.* вы́вихнуть *perf.*

disloyal, *adj.* неве́рный, вероло́мный. -ty, *n.* неве́рность *f.*, вероло́мство *nt.*

dismal, *adj.* мра́чный.

dismiss, *v.* отпуска́ть *imp.*, отпусти́ть *perf.* -al, *n.* увольне́ние *nt.*

disobedience, *n.* непослуша́ние *nt.*

disobedient, *adj.* непослу́шный.

disobey, *v.* не слу́шаться.

disorder, *n.* беспоря́док *f.* -ly, *adj.* беспоря́дочный.

disown, *v.* не признава́ть за своё.

dispassionate, *adj.* бесстра́стный.

dispatch, *n.* отпра́вка *f.*; депе́ша *f.* — *v.* посыла́ть *imp.*, посла́ть *perf.*

dispel, *v.* разгоня́ть *imp.*, разогна́ть *perf.*

dispensary, *n.* амбулато́рия *f.*

displace, *v.* смеща́ть *imp.*, смести́ть *perf.*

display, *v.* выставля́ть *imp.*, вы́ставить *perf.* — *n.* пока́з *m.*, вы́ставка *f.*

displeasure, *n.* неудово́льствие *nt.*

disposal, *n.* расположе́ние *nt.*; распоряже́ние *nt.*

disposition, *n.* диспози́ция *f.*

dispossess, *v.* лиша́ть владе́ния.

disproportion, *n.* непропорциона́льность. -ate, *adj.* непропорциона́льный.

dispute, *n.* ди́спут, спор *m.* — *v.* спо́рить *imp.*

disqualification, *n.* дисквалифика́ция *f.*

disqualify, *v.* дисквалифици́ровать *imp. & perf.*

disregard, *n.* невнима́ние *nt.* — *v.* игнори́ровать *imp.*

disreputable, *adj.* по́льзующийся дурно́й репута́цией.

disrespect, *n.* неуваже́ние *nt.* — *adj.* непочти́тельный.

disrupt, *v.* разрыва́ть *imp.*, разорва́ть *perf.*

dissatisfaction, *n.* неудовлетворённость *f.*

dissatisfy, *v.* не удовлетворя́ть.

dissect, *v.* расчленя́ть *imp.*, расчлени́ть *perf.*

disseminate, *v.* распространя́ть *imp.*, распространи́ть *perf.*

dissent, *n.* разногла́сие *nt.* *v.* расходи́ться в мне́ниях.

dissertation, *n.* диссерта́ция *f.*

dissimilar, *adj.* несхо́дный.

dissipate, *v.* расточа́ть *imp.*, расточи́ть *perf.*

dissipation, *n.* расточе́ние *nt.*

dissolute, *adj.* распу́щенный.

dissolution, *n.* растворе́ние *nt.*; разложе́ние *nt.*

dissolve, *v. t.* растворя́ть *imp.*, раствори́ть *perf.* — *v. i.* раствори́ться *imp.*, раствори́ться *perf.*

dissuade, *v.* отгова́ривать *imp.*, отговори́ть *perf.*

distance, *n.* расстоя́ние *nt.*

distance, *n.* расстоя́ние *nt.* at a d., издалека́. in the d., вдали́.

distant, *adj.* отдалённый.

distasteful, *adj.* не вку́сный.

distill, *v.* дистилли́ровать *imp.* & *perf.* -ery, *n.* винокуре́нный заво́д.

distinct, *adj.* отчётливый. -ion *n.* отли́чие, разли́чие *nt.* -ive, *adj.* отличи́тельный.

distinguish, *v.* отлича́ть *imp.*, отличи́ть *perf.*; различа́ть *imp.*, различи́ть *perf.* -ed, *adj.* выдаю́щийся.

distort, *v.* искривля́ть *imp.*, искриви́ть *perf.*

distract, *v.* отвлека́ть *imp.*, отвле́чь *perf.* -ion, *n.* развлече́ние *nt.*

distribute, *v.* раздава́ть *imp.*, разда́ть *perf.*

distribution, *n.* разда́ча *f.*

district, *n.* райо́н *m.*

distrust, *n.* недове́рие *nt.* — *v.* не доверя́ть *imp.* -ful, *adj.* недове́рчивый.

disturb, *v.* волнова́ть *imp.*, взволнова́ть *perf.*; беспоко́ить *imp.* -ance, *n.* беспоко́йство *nt.*; волне́ние *nt.*

ditch, *n.* кана́ва *f.*, ров *m.*

dive, *n.* ныря́ние *nt.*; (*swim.*) прыжо́к *m.* — *v.* ныря́ть *imp.*, нырну́ть *perf.*: (*swim.*) пры́гнуть *imp.*, пры́гнуть *perf.*

diver, *n.* (*swim.*) прыгу́н в во́ду.

diverse, *adj.* ра́зный.

diversion, *n.* отклоне́ние *nt.*; отвлече́ние *nt.*

divert, *v.* отклоня́ть *imp.*, отклони́ть *perf.*; отвлека́ть *imp.*, отвле́чь *perf.*

divide, *v.* дели́ть *imp.*, раздели́ть *perf.*

dividend, *n.* дивиде́нд *m.*; (*math.*) дели́мое *nt.*

divine, *adj.* боже́ственный.

division, *n.* разделе́ние *nt.*, (*math.*) деле́ние *nt.*; (*department*) отде́л *m.*

divorce, *n.* разво́д *m.* — *v.* разводи́ться *imp.*, развести́сь *perf.*

divulge, *v.* разглаша́ть *imp.*, разгласи́ть *perf.*

do, *v.* де́лать *imp.*, сде́лать *perf.* do without, обходи́ться без.

dock, *n.* док *m.*, верфь *f.* — *v.* ста́вить су́дно в док.

doctor, *n.* врач, до́ктор *m.*

doctorate, *n.* до́кторская сте́пень.

doctrine, *n.* доктри́на *f.*

document, *n.* докуме́нт *m.*, свиде́тельство *nt.* — *v.* документи́ровать *imp.* & *perf.*

documentary, *adj.* документа́льный.

dog, *n.* соба́ка *f.*

dogma, *n.* до́гма *f.*, до́гмат *m.* -tic, *adj.* догмати́ческий.

doll, *n.* ку́колка *f.*

dollar, *n.* до́ллар *m.*

domain, *n.* владе́ние *nt.*; о́бласть, сфе́ра *f.*

dome, *n.* ку́пол *m.*

domestic, *adj.* дома́шний.

domesticate, *v.* выра́щивать *imp.*, вы́растить *perf.*; культиви́ровать *imp.* & *perf.*

dominant, *adj.* госпо́дствующий, преоблада́ющий.

dominate, *v.* преоблада́ть *imp.*; госпо́дствовать *imp.*

domination, *n.* преоблада́ние *nt.*; госпо́дство *nt.*

dominion, *n.* доминио́н *m.*

donation, *n.* дар *m.*, де́нежное поже́ртвование.

donkey, *n.* осёл *m.*

doom, *n.* рок *m.* — *v.* обрека́ть *imp.*, обре́чь *perf.*

door, *n.* дверь *f.* out of doors, на откры́том во́здухе.

doorway, *n.* вход *m.*, дверно́й проём.

dope, *n.* нарко́тик *m.*

dormant, adj. дре́млющий, безде́йствующий.

dormitory, n. студе́нческое общежи́тие.

Dorothy, n. Дорофе́я f., До́роти f. ind.

dose, n. до́за f.

dot, n. то́чка f.

double, adj. двойно́й, дво́йственный. — n. двойни́к m. — v. удва́ивать imp., удво́ить perf.

double-breasted, adj. двубо́ртный.

doubly, adv. вдвойне́, вдво́е.

doubt, n. сомне́ние nt. — v. сомнева́ться imp. **-ful**, adj. сомни́тельный. **-less**, adj. несомне́нный.

Douglas, n. Ду́глас m.

dove, n. го́лубь m.

Dover, Strait of, Па-де-Кале́ nt. ind.

down, adv. (dir.) вниз, (loc.) внизу́.

downfall, n. паде́ние nt.

downpour, n. ли́вень m.

downstairs, adv. (dir.) вниз; (loc.) внизу́, в ни́жшем этаже́.

downward, adv. вниз.

doze, v. дрема́ть imp.

dozen, n. дю́жина f.

draft, n. (sketch) чертёж, рису́нок, эски́з m.; (mil.) призы́в в а́рмию. — v. де́лать чертёж; составля́ть план; (mil.) призыва́ть в а́рмию.

drag, v. t. тяну́ть imp.; тащи́ть imp. — v. i. тяну́ться imp.; тащи́ться imp.

drain, n. кана́ва f., дрена́жная труба́. — v. дрени́ровать imp. & perf. **-age**, n. дрена́ж m., осуше́ние nt.

drama, n. дра́ма f.

dramatic, adj. драмати́ческий.

dramatize, v. инсцени́ровать imp. & perf., драматизи́ровать imp. & perf.

drastic, adj. реши́тельный.

draw, v. t. че́рпать imp.; (sketch) рисова́ть imp., на-

рисова́ть perf. — n. (games): **in a draw**, вничью́ adv.

drawback, n. препя́тствие nt., отрица́тельная сторона́.

drawer, n. я́щик m.

drawing, n. рису́нок m.

dread, n. страх m. — v. боя́ться imp. **-ful**, adj. ужа́сный, стра́шный.

dream, n. мечта́ f. — v. мечта́ть imp. **-er**, n. мечта́тель m.

dreary, adj. мра́чный; ску́чный.

dredge, n. дра́га, землечерпа́лка f. — v. драги́ровать imp. & perf.

dregs, n. отбро́сы pl.; оса́док m.

drench, v. прома́чивать наскво́зь..

dress, n. пла́тье nt., (attire) оде́жда f. — v. t. одева́ть imp.; оде́ть perf. — v. i. одева́ться imp.; оде́ться perf.

dressing, n. (med.) перевя́зочное сре́дство; (cooking) припра́ва f.

dressmaker, n. портни́ха f.

drift, n. тече́ние nt.; (ocean) дрейф m.; — v. сноси́ться ве́тром (or водо́й); плыть по тече́нию.

drill, n. (exercise) упражне́ние nt., трениро́вка f.; (tool) сверло́ nt. — v. (train) тренирова́ть imp.; (mech.) сверли́ть imp.

drink, n. питьё nt., напи́ток m. — v. пить imp., вы́пить perf.

drip, v. ка́пать imp., па́дать ка́плями.

drive, n. ката́нье nt., прогу́лка f.; (motivation) побужде́ние nt. — v. е́здить imp. ind., е́хать imp. det., пое́хать perf.; вести́ автомоби́ль. **d. out**, выгоня́ть imp., вы́гнать perf. **d. up to**, подъе́хать perf.

driver, n. води́тель m.

driveway, n. прое́зд m.

drizzle, n. ме́лкий дождь, моро́сящий дождь.

droop, v. поникать imp.

drop, n. (liquid) капля f.; (reduction) опускание, понижение nt. — v. t. опускать imp., опустить perf. — v. i. опускаться imp., опуститься perf.

drought, n. засуха f.

drown, v. t. топить imp., утопить perf. — v. i. тонуть imp., утонуть perf.

drowsy, adj. сонный.

drug, n. лекарство nt.; наркотик m.

druggist, n. аптекарь m.

drugstore, n. аптека f.

drum, n. барабан m.

drunk, adj. пьяный. — n. пьяница m.

drunkard, n. пьяница m.

drunken, adj. пьяный.

dry, adj. сухой. — v. сушить imp., высушить perf.

dual, adj. двойственный.

dubious, adj. мнительный.

duct, n. проток m.

due, adj. должный. **due to,** из-за, благодаря.

duel, n. поединок m.

dues, pl. сборы, налоги pl.

duet, n. дуэт m.

dull, adj. тупой; (boring) скучный.

duly, adv. должным образом.

dumb, adj. (mute) немой; (stupid) глупый.

dumfound, v. ошарашить perf.

dummy, n. манекен m.; (cards) болван m.

dune, n. дюна f.

dung, n. навоз m.

dupe, v. обманывать imp., обмануть perf.

duplicate, adj. двойной, удвоенный. — n. копия f., дубликат m. — v. удваивать imp., удвоить perf.

duplication, n. удваивание nt.

duplicity, n. двойственность f.; двуличность f.

durable, adj. прочный.

duration, n. продолжительность f.

duress, n. принуждение nt.

during, prep. в течение.

dusk, n. сумерки pl.

dust, n. пыль f. — v. вытирать пыль.

dusty, adj. пыльный.

Dutch, adj. голландский.

-man, n. голландец m., голландка f.

dutiful, adj. послушный.

duty, n. обязанность f.; (customs) пошлина f. **be on d.,** быть дежурным.

dwarf, n. карлик m.

dwell, v. жить imp., обитать imp.

dwelling, n. жилой дом.

dwindle, v. уменьшаться imp., уменьшиться perf.

dye, n. краска f. — v. красить imp., покрасить perf.

dynamic, adj. динамический.

dynamite, n. динамит m.

dynasty, n. династия f.

dysentery, n. дизентерия f.

E

each, adj. & pron. каждый.

eager, adj. нетерпеливый.

eagle, n. орёл m.

ear, n. ухо nt.; (corn) колос m.

early, adj. ранний. — adv. рано.

earn, v. зарабатывать imp., заработать perf.; (deserve) заслуживать imp., заслужить perf.

earnest, adj. серьёзный.

earnings, n. заработок m.

earring, n. серьга f.

earth, n. земля f.

earthquake, n. землетрясение nt.

ease, n. лёгкость f. — v. облегчать imp., облегчить perf.

easily, adv. легко.

east, *n.* восто́к *m.* **-ern,** *adj.* восто́чный. **-ward,** *adv.* к восто́ку, на восто́к.

Easter, *n.* па́сха *f.*

easy, *adj.* лёгкий.

eat, *v.* есть *imp.,* съесть *perf.*

ebb, *n.* отли́в *m.,* упа́док *m.* — *v.* отлива́ть *imp.,* отли́ть *perf.*

ebony, *n.* чёрное де́рево.

eccentric, *adj.* эксцентри́чный, стра́нный.

ecclesiastical *adj.* церко́вный.

echo, *n.* э́хо *nt.* — *v.* отда́ваться *imp.,* отда́ться *perf.*

eclipse, *n.* затме́ние *nt.* — *v.* затмева́ть *imp.,* затми́ть *perf.*

economic, *adj.* экономи́ческий.

economical, *adj.* эконо́мный.

economics, *n.* эконо́мика *f.*

economist, *n.* экономи́ст *m.*

economize, *v.* эконо́мить *imp. & perf.*

economy, *n.* эконо́мика *f.,* хозя́йство *nt.*

ecstasy, *n.* экста́з *m.*

Ecuador, *n.* Эквадо́р *m.*

eczema, *n.* экзе́ма *f.*

edge, *n.* край *m.,* ле́звие *nt.*

edible, *adj.* съедо́бный.

edict, *n.* эди́кт, указ *m.*

edit, *v.* редакти́ровать *imp.,* отредакти́ровать *perf.*

edition, *n.* изда́ние *nt.*

editor, *n.* реда́ктор *m.*

editorial, *adj.* редакцио́нный, реда́кторский. — *n.* передова́я статья́.

educate, *v.* дава́ть образова́ние; воспи́тывать *imp.,* воспита́ть *perf.*

educated, *adj.* образо́ванный.

education, *n.* образова́ние *nt.,* воспита́ние *nt.* **-al,** *adj.* образова́тельный, воспита́тельный, уче́бный.

eel, *n.* у́горь *f.*

effect, *n.* сле́дствие *nt.,* результа́т *m.;* эффе́кт *m.* — *v.* соверша́ть *imp.,* соверши́ть *perf.* **-ive,** эффекти́вный.

effeminate, *adj.* женоподо́бный, изне́женный.

efficient, *adj.* де́йственный,

эффекти́вный, производи́тельный.

effigy, *n.* изображе́ние *nt.*

effort, *n.* уси́лие *nt.*

egg, *n.* яйцо́ *nt.*

egoism, egotism, *n.* эгои́зм *m.*

egoist, egotist, *n.* эгои́ст *m.*

Egypt, *n.* Еги́пет *m.* **-ian,** *adj.* еги́петский.

eight, *adj., n.* во́семь *num.; n. (cards)* восьмёрка *f.*

eighteen, *adj., n.* восемна́дцать, *num.*

eighth, *adj.* восьмо́й.

eightieth, *adj.* восьмидеся́тый.

eighty, *adj., n.* во́семьдесят *num.*

either, *adj., pron.* тот и́ли друго́й; любо́й. — *conj.* **either . . . or,** и́ли . . . и́ли.

ejaculate, *v.* восклица́ть *imp.,* воскли́кнуть *perf.; (liquid)* изверга́ть *imp.,* изве́ргнуть *perf.*

eject, *v.* изверга́ть *imp.,* изве́ргнуть *perf.*

elaborate, *adj.* вы́работанный, сло́жный. — *v.* тща́тельно разраба́тывать в дета́лях.

elapse, *v.* проходи́ть *imp.,* пройти́ *perf.*

elastic, *adj.* эласти́чный. — *n.* рези́нка. **-ity,** *n.* эласти́чность *f.*

elation, *n.* припо́днятое настрое́ние.

elbow, *n.* ло́коть *m.*

elder, *adj.* ста́рший. — *n.* ста́рец *m.* **-ly,** *adj.* пожило́й.

elect, *v.* избира́ть *imp.,* избра́ть *perf.* **-ion,** *n.* вы́боры *pl.*

electric, electrical, *adj.* электри́ческий.

electrician, *n.* эле́ктрик *m.*

electricity, *n.* электри́чество *nt.*

electron, *n.* электро́н *m.*

electronics, *n.* электро́ника *f.*

elegance, *n.* элега́нтность *f.*

elegant, *adj.* элега́нтный.

elegy, *n.* эле́гия *f.*

element, *n.* элеме́нт *m.,* составна́я часть.

elementary, *adj.* элемента́рный, первонача́льный. e. school, *n.* нача́льная шко́ла.

elephant, *n.* слон *m.* — *adj.* слоно́вый.

elevate, *v.* возвыша́ть *imp.*, возвы́сить *perf.*

elevation, *n.* возвыше́ние *nt.*; подъём *m.*

elevator, *n.* лифт, элева́тор *m.*

eleven, *adj.*, *n.* оди́ннадцать *num.* -th, *adj.* оди́ннадцатый.

eligible, *adj.* могу́щий быть и́збранным.

eliminate, *v.* исключа́ть *imp.*, исключи́ть *perf.*; элими́нировать *imp. & perf.*

elimination, *n.* исключе́ние *nt.*, элимина́ция *f.*

Elizabeth, *n.* Елизаве́та *f.*; Эли́забет *f. ind.*

elk, *n.* лось *m.*

elm, *n.* вяз, ильм *m.*

elongate, *v.* удлиня́ть *imp.*, удлини́ть *perf.*

elope, *v.* сбега́ть *imp.*, сбежа́ть *perf.*

eloquence, *n.* красноре́чие *nt.*

eloquent, *adj.* красноречи́вый.

else, *adv.* ина́че.

elsewhere, *adv.* где-нибудь в друго́м ме́сте.

elude, *v.* избега́ть *imp.*, избе́гнуть *perf.*

elusive, *adj.* укло́нчивый.

emanate, *v.* исходи́ть *imp.*

emancipate, *v.* освобожда́ть *imp.*, освободи́ть *perf.*

emancipation, *n.* освобожде́ние *nt.*

embalm, *v.* бальзами́ровать *imp. & perf.*

embankment, *n.* на́сыпь, плоти́на *f.*

embargo, *n.* эмба́рго *nt. ind.*

embark, *v.* сади́ться на кора́бль.

embarrass, *v.* стесня́ть *imp.*, стесни́ть *perf.* -ing, *adj.* вызыва́ющий замеша́тельство. -ment, *n.* замеша́тельство, затрудне́ние *nt.*

embassy, *n.* посо́льство *nt.*

embezzle, *v.* присва́ивать (*or* затра́чивать) чужи́е де́ньги.

emblem, *n.* эмбле́ма *f.*, си́мвол *m.*

embody, *v.* воплоща́ть *imp.*, воплоти́ть *perf.*

embrace, *n.* объя́тия *pl.* — *v.* обнима́ть *imp.*, обня́ть *perf.*

embroider, *v.* вышива́ть *imp.*, вы́шить *perf.*

embroidery, *n.* вы́шивка *f.*

embryo, *n.* заро́дыш *f.*

emerald, *n.* изумру́д *m.*

emerge, *v.* всплыва́ть *imp.*, всплыть *perf.*

emergency, *n.* крити́ческое обстоя́тельство (*or* положе́ние).

emery, *n.* нажда́к *m.*

emetic, *adj.* рво́тный. — *n.* рво́тное *nt.*, рво́тное сре́дство.

emigrant, *adj.* эмигри́рующий — *n.* эмигра́нт *m.*

emigrate, *v.* эмигри́ровать *imp. & perf.*

emigration, *n.* эмигра́ция *f.*

eminence, *n.* возвы́шенность, знамени́тость *f.*

eminent, *adj.* выдаю́щийся, замеча́тельный.

emit, *v.* испуска́ть *imp.*, испусти́ть *perf.*; выпуска́ть *imp.*, вы́пустить *perf.*

emotion, *n.* волне́ние *nt.*; эмо́ция *f.* -al, *adj.* эмоциона́льный.

emperor, *n.* импера́тор *m.*

emphasis, *n.* эмфа́за *f.*, ударе́ние *nt.*

emphasize, *v.* де́лать ударе́ние; подчёркивать *imp.*, подчеркну́ть *perf.*

emphatic, *adj.* вырази́тельный, эмфати́ческий.

empire, *n.* импе́рия *f.*

empirical, *adj.* эмпири́ческий.

employ, *v.* (use) употребля́ть *imp.*, употреби́ть *perf.*; (hire) нанима́ть *imp.*, наня́ть *perf.* -ee, *n.* служа́щий. -er, *n.* нанима́тель *m.*, работода́тель *m.* -ment, *n.* наём *m.*; слу́жба *f.*, заня́тие *nt.*

empty, *adj.* пусто́й. — *v.* опорожни́ть *perf.*

emulate, *v.* подража́ть *imp.*

emulsion, *n.* эму́льсия *f.*

enable, *v.* дава́ть возмо́жность

enact, *v.* постанови́ть *perf.*; вводи́ть зако́н. **-ment**, *n.* введе́ние зако́на в си́лу.

enamel, *n.* эма́ль *f.*

enchant, *v.* очаро́вывать *imp.*, очарова́ть *perf.* **-ment**, *n.* очарова́ние *nt.*

enclose, *v.* вкла́дывать *imp.*, вложи́ть *perf.*; включа́ть *imp.*, включи́ть *perf.*

enclosure, *n.* огоро́женное ме́сто; вложе́ние, приложе́ние *nt.*

encompass, *v.* окружа́ть *imp.*, окружи́ть *perf.*; заключа́ть *imp.*, заключи́ть *perf.*

encounter, *n.* столкнове́ние *nt.*, встре́ча *f.* — *v.* встре́тить *perf.*; ната́лкивать *imp.*, натолкну́ть *perf.*

encourage, *v.* ободря́ть *imp.*, ободри́ть *perf.* **-ment**, *n.* ободре́ние *nt.*

encyclopedia, *n.* энциклопе́дия *f.*

end, *n.* коне́ц *m.* — *v. t.* конча́ть *imp.*, ко́нчить *perf.* — *v. i.* конча́ться *imp.*, ко́нчиться *perf.*

endanger, *v.* подверга́ть опа́сности.

endeavor, *n.* попы́тка *f.* — *v.* пыта́ться *imp.*, стара́ться *imp.*

ending, *n.* оконча́ние *nt.*

endless, *adj.* бесконе́чный.

endorse, *v.* индосси́ровать *imp. & perf.* **-ment**, *n.* индоссаме́нт *f.*

endurance, *n.* выно́сливость *f.*

endure, *v.* вы́носить *perf.*

enema, *n.* кли́зма *f.*

enemy, *n.* враг *m.*, неприя́тель *m.*

energetic, *adj.* энерги́чный.

energy, *n.* эне́ргия *f.*

enforce, *v.* проводи́ть в жизнь. **-ment**, *n.* принужде́ние *nt.*

engage, *v.* занима́ть *imp.*, заня́ть *perf.*

engine, *n.* маши́на *f.*, мото́р *m.*

engineer, *n.* инжене́р *m.* **-ing**,

n. инжене́рное иску́сство; те́хника *f.*

England, *n.* А́нглия *f.*

English, *adj.* англи́йский. **in E.**, по-англи́йски. **-man**, *n.* англича́нин *m.* **-woman**, *n.* англича́нка *f.*

English Channel, проли́в Ла-Ма́нш (Англи́йский кана́л).

engrave, *v.* гравирова́ть *imp.*, вы́гравировать *perf.*

engraver, *n.* гравёр *m.*

engraving, *n.* гравирова́ние *nt.*; (*an etching*) гравю́ра *f.*

enhance, *v.* повыша́ть *imp.*, повы́сить *perf.*

enigma, *n.* зага́дка *f.* **-tic**, *adj.* зага́дочный.

enjoy, *v.* наслажда́ться *imp.* **-able**, *adj.* прия́тный. **-ment**, *n.* наслажде́ние *nt.*

enlarge, *v.* увели́чивать *imp.*, увели́чить *perf.* **-ment**, *n.* увеличе́ние *nt.*

enlighten, *v.* просвеща́ть *imp.*, просвети́ть *perf.* **-ment**, *n.* просвеще́ние *nt.*

enlist, *v. t.* вербова́ть *imp.*, заверобва́ть *perf.* — *v. i.* поступа́ть на вое́нную слу́жбу.

enmity, *n.* вражда́ *f.*

enormous, *adj.* огро́мный.

enough, *adj.*, *adv.* дово́льно, доста́точно.

enrage, *v.* беси́ть *imp.*, взбеси́ть *perf.*

enrich, *v.* обогаща́ть *imp.*, обогати́ть *perf.*

enrollment, *n.* регистра́ция *f.* внесе́ние в спи́ски.

enslave, *v.* порабоща́ть *imp.*, поработи́ть *perf.*

entangle, *v.* запу́тать *perf.*

enter, *v.* (*on foot*) входи́ть *imp.*, войти́ *perf.*; (*by vehicle*) въезжа́ть *imp.*, въе́хать *perf.*; (*join*) вступа́ть *imp.*, вступи́ть *perf.*

enterprise, *n.* (*undertaking*) предприя́тие *nt.*; (*spirit*) предприи́мчивость *f.*

enterprising, *adj.* предприи́мчивый.

entertain, *v.* развлека́ть *imp.*,

развлечь *perf.*; принимать гостей. -ing, *adj.* забавный, развлекательный. -ment, *n.* развлечение *nt.*

enthusiasm, *n.* энтузиазм *m.*

enthusiast, *n.* энтузиаст *m.* -ic, *adj.* восторженный, полный энтузиазма.

entice, *v.* переманивать *imp.*, переманить *perf.*

entire, *adj.* целый. -ly, *adv.* полностью. -ty, *n.* полнота, цельность *f.*

entitle, *v.* давать право; (*book*) озаглавливать *imp.*, озаглавить *perf.*

entrails, *n.* внутренности *f. pl.* кишки *f. pl.*

entrance, *n.* вход *m.*

entreat, *v.* умолять *imp.*

entrust, *v.* вверять *imp.*, вверить *perf.*; поручать *imp.*, поручить *perf.*

entry, *n.* вход *m.*, вступление *nt.*

enumerate, *v.* перечислять *imp.*, перечислить *perf.*

enumeration, *n.* перечисление *nt.*

enunciate, *v.* произносить *imp.*, произнести *perf.*

enunciation, *n.* хорошее произношение.

envelop, *v.* обёртывать *imp.*, обернуть *perf.*

envelope, *n.* конверт *m.*

enviable, *adj.* завидный.

envious, *adj.* завистливый.

environment, *n.* окружение *nt.*

envoy, *n.* посланник *m.*

envy, *n.* зависть *f.* — *v.* завидовать *imp.*

eon, *n.* зон *m.*, эра *f.*

ephemeral, *adj.* эфемерный.

epic, *adj.* эпический. — *n.* эпическая поэма.

epicure, *n.* эпикуреец *m.*

epidemic, *adj.* эпидемический. — *n.* эпидемия *f.*

epigram, *n.* эпиграмма *f.*

epilepsy, *n.* эпилепсия *f.*

epileptic, *adj.* эпилептический. — *n.* эпилептик *m.*

episode, *n.* эпизод *m.*

epitaph, *n.* эпитафия *f.*

epitome, *n.* конспект *m.*

epoch, *n.* эпоха *f.*

equal, *adj.* равный. — *v.* равняться *imp.* -ity, *n.* равенство *nt.* -ize, *v.* уравнивать *imp.*, уравнять *perf.*

equanimity, *n.* уравновешенность *f.*

equation, *n.* уравнение *nt.*

equator, *n.* экватор *m.* -ial, *adj.* экваториальный.

equestrian, *adj.* конный. — *n.* всадник *m.*

equilibrium, *n.* равновесие *nt.*

equinox, *n.* равноденствие *nt.*

equip, *v.* оборудовать *imp. & perf.*; снабжать *imp.*, снабдить *perf.* -ment, *n.* оборудование *nt.*

equivalent, *adj.* эквивалентный. — *n.* эквивалент *m.*

era, *n.* эра *f.*

eradicate, *v.* искоренять *imp.*, искоренить *perf.*

erase, *v.* стирать *imp.*, стереть *perf.*

eraser, *n.* резинка *f.*

erect, *adj.* прямой, вертикальный. — *v.* воздвигать *imp.*, воздвигнуть *perf.*

erection, *n.* выпрямление *nt.*

erode, *v.* разъедать *imp.*, разъесть *perf.*

erosion, *n.* разъедание *nt.*

erotic, *adj.* эротический.

err, *v.* ошибаться *imp.*, ошибиться *perf.*

errand, *n.* поручение *nt.*

erratic, *adj.* неустойчивый.

erroneous, *adj.* ошибочный.

error, *n.* ошибка *f.*

erudition, *n.* эрудиция *f.*

eruption, *n.* извержение *nt.*

escalator, *n.* эскалатор *m.*

escapade, *n.* выходка, проделка *f.*

escape, *n.* бегство *nt.* — *v.* убегать *imp.*, убежать *perf.*

escort, *n.* охрана *f.*, эскорт *m.* — *v.* эскортировать *imp. & perf.*

Eskimo, *n.* эскимос *m.*

esophagus, *n.* пищевод *m.*

especially, *adv.* особенно.

espionage, *n.* шпиона́ж *m.*

essay, *n.* о́черк, этю́д *m.*

essence, *n.* су́щность *f.*

essential, *adj.* суще́ственный.
-ly, *adv.* по существу́.

establish, *v.* устана́вливать
imp., установи́ть *perf.* **-ment,**
n. учрежде́ние *nt.,* заведе́ние
nt.

estate, *n.* поме́стье *nt.*

esteem, *n.* уваже́ние *nt.* — *v.*
уважа́ть *imp.*

estimate, *v.* оце́нивать *imp.,*
оцени́ть *perf.* — *n.* оце́нка *f.*

estimation, *n.* сужде́ние, мне́-
ние *nt.*

Estonian, *adj.* эсто́нский. — *n.*
эсто́нец *m.,* эсто́нка *f.*

estrange, *v.* отчужда́ть *imp.,*
отчуди́ть *perf.*

et cetera, и так да́лее.

etching, *n.* гравю́ра *f.*

eternal, *adj.* ве́чный.

eternity, *n.* ве́чность *f.*

ether, *n.* эфи́р *m.* **-eal,** *adj.*
эфи́рный.

ethical, эти́чный, эти́ческий.

ethics, *n.* э́тика *f.*

Ethiopia, *n.* Эфио́пия *f.*

etiquette, *n.* профессиона́ль-
ная э́тика *f.*

etymology, *n.* этимоло́гия *f.*

Eugene, *n.* Евге́ний *m.,*
Юджи́н *m. ind.*

eulogy, *n.* панеги́рик *m.,*
похвала́ *f.*

euphonious, *adj.* благозву́ч-
ный.

Europe, *n.* Евро́па *f.*

European, *adj.* европе́йский. —
n. европе́ец *m.,* европе́йка
f.

Eva, Eve, *n.* Е́ва *f.*

evacuate, *v.* эвакуи́ровать
imp. & perf.

evade, *v.* извега́ть *imp.,* избе́-
гнуть *perf.*

evaluate, *v.* оце́нивать *imp.,*
оцени́ть *perf.*

evaluation, *n.* оце́нка *f.*

evangelist, *n.* евангели́ст *m.*

evaporate, *v.* выпа́ривать *imp.,*
вы́парить *perf.*

evaporation, *n.* испаре́ние
nt.

evasion, *n.* уклоне́ние *nt.*

evasive, *adj.* укло́нчивый.

eve, *n.* кану́н *m.* **on the eve of,**
накану́не.

even, *adj.* ра́вный, ро́вный;
(*number*) чётный. — *adv.*
да́же.

evening, *n.* ве́чер *m.* **in the e.,**
ве́чером.

event, *n.* собы́тие *nt.* **-ful,** *adj.*
по́лный собы́тиями.

eventual, *adj.* коне́чный. **-ly,**
adv. в коне́чном счёте.

ever, *adv.* когда́-либо, когда́-
нибудь. **e. since,** с того́
вре́мени как.

everlasting, *adj.* ве́чный.

every, *adj.* ка́ждый, вся́кий.
-body, *pron.* ка́ждый, вся́кий;
все *pl.* **-day,** *adj.* повседне́в-
ный. **-one,** *pron.* ка́ждый,
вся́кий; все *pl.* **-thing,** *pron.*
всё *nt.* **-where,** *adv.* (*dir.*)
всю́ду; (*loc.*) везде́.

evict, *v.* выселя́ть *imp.,* вы́се-
лить *perf.* **-ion,** *n.* выселе́ние
nt.

evidence, *n.* свиде́тельство *nt.,*
свиде́тельское показа́ние.

evident, *adj.* очеви́дный. **-ly,**
adv. очеви́дно.

evil, *adj.* дурно́й, злой. — *n.*
зло *nt.,* вред *m.*

evoke, *v.* вызыва́ть *imp.,*
вы́звать *perf.*

evolution, *n.* разви́тие *nt.,*
эволю́ция *f.*

evolve, *v. t.* развёртывать
imp., разверну́ть *perf.* — *v. i.*
развёртываться *imp.,* раз-
верну́ться *perf.*

exact, *adj.* то́чный, аккура́т-
ный. — *v.* взы́скивать *imp.,*
взыска́ть *perf.*

exacting, *adj.* тре́бователь-
ный.

exactly, *adv.* то́чно.

exaggerate, *v.* преувели́чивать
imp., преувели́чить *perf.*

exaggeration, *n.* преувеличе́-
ние *nt.*

examination, *n.* экза́мен *m.;*
осмо́тр *m.* **take an e.,**
держа́ть экза́мен.

examine, *v.* рассма́тривать

example 203 ENGLISH-RUSSIAN

imp., рассмотре́ть *perf.*; экзаменова́ть *imp.*, проэкза-менова́ть *perf.*; осма́три-вать *imp.*, осмотре́ть *perf.*

example, *n.* приме́р *m.* **for e.**, наприме́р.

exasperate, *v.* раздража́ть *imp.*, раздражи́ть *perf.*

exasperation, *n.* раздраже́ние *nt.*

excavate, *v.* выка́пывать *imp.*, вы́копать *perf.*

exceed, *v.* превыша́ть *imp.*, превы́сить *perf.*

exceedingly, *adv.* чрезвыча́йно.

excel, *v.* превосходи́ть *imp.*, превзойти́ *perf.*

excellence, *n.* превосхо́дство *nt.*

excellent, *adj.* отли́чный, превосхо́дный.

except, *prep.* кро́ме, за исключе́нием. **-ion**, *n.* исключе́ние *nt.* **-ional**, *adj.* исключи́тельный.

excerpt, *n.* отры́вок *m.*, цита́та *f.*

excess, *n.* изли́шек *m.* **-ive**, *adj.* чрезме́рный, изли́шний.

exchange, *n.* обме́н, заме́н *f.* **in e.**, взаме́н. — *v. t.* обме́нивать *imp.*, обменя́ть *perf.* — *v. i.* обме́ниваться *imp.*, обменя́ться, обменя́ться *perf.*

excite, *v.* волнова́ть *imp.*, взволнова́ть *perf.*; возбужда́ть *imp.*, возбуди́ть *perf.* **-ment**, *n.* возбужде́ние, волне́ние *nt.*

exciting, *adj.* волну́ющий.

exclaim, *v.* восклица́ть *imp.*, воскли́кнуть *perf.*

exclamation, *n.* восклица́ние *nt.* **exclamation point**, восклица́тельный знак.

exclude, *v.* исключа́ть *imp.*, исключи́ть *perf.*

exclusion, *n.* исключе́ние *nt.*

exclusive, *adj.* исключи́тельный.

excommunicate, *v.* отлуча́ть от це́ркви.

excommunication, *n.* отлуче́ние от це́ркви.

excrement, *n.* экскреме́нты *pl.*

excursion, *n.* экску́рсия *f.*

excuse, *n.* извине́ние, оправда́ние *nt.* — *v.* извиня́ть *imp.*, извини́ть *perf.*

execute, *v.* (*perform*) исполня́ть *imp.*, испо́лнить *perf.*, выполня́ть *imp.*, вы́полнить *perf.*; (*kill legally*) казни́ть *imp. & perf.*

execution, *n.* исполне́ние, выполне́ние *nt.*; (*legal killing*) казнь, экзеку́ция *f.* **-er**, *n.* пала́ч *m.*

executive, *adj.* исполни́тельный. — *n.* должностно́е лицо́.

exemplary, *adj.* образцо́вый.

exemplify, *v.* служи́ть приме́ром.

exempt, *adj.* освобождённый. — *v.* освобожда́ть *imp.*, освободи́ть *perf.*

exercise, *n.* упражне́ние *nt.* — *v.* упражня́ть *imp.*

exert, *v.* напряга́ть *imp.*, напря́чь *perf.* **-ion**, *n.* напряже́ние *nt.*

exhale, *v.* выдыха́ть *imp.*, вы́дохнуть *perf.*

exhaust, *n.* (*auto*) выхлопна́я труба́. — *v.* истоща́ть *imp.*, истощи́ть *perf.*; исче́рпывать *imp.*, исче́рпать *perf.* **-ion**, *n.* изнеможе́ние, истоще́ние *nt.*

exhibit, *n.* вы́ставка *f.*, экспона́т *m.* — *v.* выставля́ть *imp.*, вы́ставить *perf.*; экспони́ровать *imp. & perf.*

exhort, *v.* увещева́ть *imp.*

exhume, *v.* выка́пывать *imp.*, вы́копать *perf.*

exile, *n.* ссы́лка *f.*, изгна́ние *nt.*; (*person*) изгна́нник *m.* — *v.* ссыла́ть *imp.*, сосла́ть *perf.*; изгоня́ть *imp.*, изгна́ть *perf.*

exist, *v.* существова́ть *imp.* **-ence**, *n.* существова́ние *nt.*

exit, *n.* вы́ход *m.*

exodus, *n.* ма́ссовый исхо́д.

exonerate, *v.* опра́вдывать *imp.*, оправда́ть *perf.*

exorbitant, *adj.* непоме́рный.

exotic, *adj.* экзоти́ческий.

expand, *v. t.* расширя́ть *imp.*, расши́рить *perf.* — *v. i.* расширя́ться *imp.*, расши́риться *perf.*

expanse, *n.* протяже́ние, простра́нство *nt.*

expansion, *n.* экспа́нсия *f.*

expansive, *adj.* экспанси́вный.

expect, *v.* ожида́ть *imp.* **-ation**, *n.* ожида́ние *nt.*

expedite, *v.* бы́стро заверши́ть *perf.*

expedition, *n.* экспеди́ция *f.*

expel, *v.* выгоня́ть *imp.*, вы́гнать *perf.*

expend, *v.* тра́тить *imp.*, истра́тить *perf.*

expenditure, *n.* тра́та *f.*, расхо́д *m.*

expense, *n.* расхо́д *m.* **at the e. of.**, за счёт.

expensive, *adj.* дорого́й.

experience, *n.* о́пыт *m.*, испыта́ние *nt.* — *v.* испы́тывать *imp.*, испыта́ть *perf.*

experienced, *adj.* о́пытный.

experiment, *n.* экспериме́нт *m.*, о́пыт *m.* — *v.* экхпериме́нти́ровать *imp. & perf.* **-al**, *adj.* эксперимента́льный.

expert, *adj.* о́пытный. — *n.* экспе́рт *m.*

expiration, *n.* выдыха́ние *nt.*; (*time*) истече́ние *nt.*

expire, *v.* истека́ть *imp.*, исте́чь *perf.*; (*exhale*) выдыха́ть *imp.*, вы́дохнуть *perf.*

explain, *v.* объясня́ть *imp.*, объясни́ть *perf.*

explanation, *n.* объясне́ние *nt.*

explanatory, *adj.* объясни́тельный.

expletive, *n.* вставно́е сло́во.

explicit, *adj.* то́чный, определённый.

explode, *v. i.* взрыва́ться *imp.*, взорва́ться *perf.* — *v. t.* взрыва́ть *imp.*, взорва́ть *perf.*

exploit, *n.* по́двиг *m.* — *v.* эксплуати́ровать *imp. & perf.* **-ation**, *n.* эксплуата́ция *f.*

exploration, *n.* иссле́дование *nt.*

exploratory, *adj.* иссле́дующий.

explore, *v.* иссле́довать *imp.*

explorer, *n.* иссле́дователь *m.*

explosion, *n.* взрыв *m.*

explosive, *adj.* взрывча́тый. — *n.* взрывча́тое вещество́.

export, *n.* э́кспорт *m.* — *v.* экспорти́ровать *imp. & perf.* **-ation**, *n.* экспорти́рование *nt.*

expose, *v.* разоблача́ть *imp.*, разоблачи́ть *perf.*

exposition, *n.* (*description*) описа́ние *nt.*; (*exhibit*) вы́ставка *f.*

exposure, *n.* выставле́ние *nt.*; разоблаче́ние *nt.*

express, *adj.* курье́рский. — *n.* э́кспресс *m.*; (*messenger*) курье́р *m.* — *v.* выража́ть *imp.*, вы́разить *perf.* **-ion**, *n.* выраже́ние *nt.* **-ive**, *adj.* вырази́тельный.

expulsion, *n.* изгна́ние *nt.*

exquisite, *adj.* изы́сканный, преле́стный.

extemporaneous, *adj.* импровизи́рованный.

extend, *v.* вытя́гивать *imp.*, вы́тянуть *perf.* — *v. i.* тяну́ться *imp.*

extension, *n.* вытя́гивание, расшире́ние, добавле́ние *nt.* продле́ние *nt.*

extensive, *adj.* обши́рный; экстенси́вный.

extent, *n.* сте́пень *f.*, разме́р *m.*

exterior, *adj.* вне́шний, нару́жный. — *n.* вне́шность, нару́жность *f.*

exterminate, *v.* истребля́ть *imp.*, истреби́ть *perf.*

extermination, *n.* истребле́ние *nt.*

external, *adj.* вне́шний, нару́жный.

extinct, *adj.* поту́хший; вы́мерший. **-ion**, *n.* потуха́ние *nt.*; вымира́ние *nt.*

extinguish, *v.* гаси́ть *imp.*, погаси́ть *perf.*

extortion, *n.* вымога́тельство *nt.*

extra, *adj.* дополни́тельный; ли́шний.

extract, *n.* экстра́кт *m.* — *v.* извлека́ть *imp.*, извле́чь *perf.* -**ion,** *n.* извлече́ние *nt.*, экстра́кция *f.*

extraneous, *adj.* чу́ждый, вне́шний.

extraordinary, *adj.* чрезвы́чайный.

extravagant, *adj.* непоме́рный; расточи́тельный.

extreme, *adj.* кра́йний. — *n.* кра́йность *f.*

extremity, *n.* коне́чность *f.*

exuberant, *adj.* оби́льный, роско́шный.

exude, *v.* выделя́ть *imp.*, вы́делить *perf.*

eye, *n.* глаз *m.* — *v.* смотре́ть *imp.*; наблюда́ть *imp.* -**ball,** *n.* глазно́е я́блоко. -**brow,** *n.* бровь *f.* -**glasses,** *n.* очки́ *pl.* -**lash,** *n.* ресни́ца *f.* -**lid,** *n.* ве́ко *nt.* -**sight,** *n.* зре́ние *nt.*

F

fable, *n.* ска́зка, ба́сня *f.*

fabric, *n.* ткань, мате́рия *f.*

fabricate, *v.* выду́мывать *imp.*, вы́думать *perf.*; подде́лывать *imp.*, подде́лать *perf.*

fabulous, *adj.* ска́зочный; легенда́рный.

face, *n.* лицо́ *nt.* — *v.* стоя́ть лицо́м к лицу́.

facetious, *adj.* шутли́вый.

facial, *adj.* лицево́й.

facilitate, *v.* облегча́ть *imp.*, облегчи́ть *perf.*

facility, *n.* (*ease*) лёгкость *f.*; *pl.* удо́бства, сре́дства *nt. pl.*

facsimile, *n.* факси́миле *nt. ind.*

fact, *n.* факт *m.* **in f.,** факти́чески; на са́мом де́ле; в действи́тельности.

faction, *n.* фра́кция, кли́ка *f.*

factory, *n.* фа́брика *f.*, (*plant*) заво́д *m.*

factual, *adj.* факти́ческий.

faculty, *n.* спосо́бность *f.*, дарова́ние *nt.*; (*dept*) факульте́т *m.*, (*staff*) педагоги́ческий персона́л.

fad, *n.* причу́да *f.*

fade, *v.* вя́нуть *imp.*, завя́нуть *perf.*; (*color*) выцвета́ть *imp.*, вы́цвести *perf.*

fail, *v.* оказа́ться не в состоя́нии сде́лать; (*exam*) прова́ливаться *perf.*; обанкро́титься *perf.* — *n.*: **without f.,** непреме́нно, обяза́тельно.

-**ure,** *n.* неуда́ча *f.*; банкро́тство *nt.*

faint, *adj.* сла́бый; (*dim*) нея́сный, ту́склый. — *n.* о́бморок *m.* — *v.* па́дать в о́бморок; теря́ть созна́ние.

fair, *adj.* поря́дочный, справедли́вый; (*hair*) белоку́рый; (*weather*) благоприя́тный. — *n.* я́рмарка, вы́ставка *f.*

faith, *n.* ве́ра *f.* -**ful,** *adj.* ве́рный, пре́данный.

fake, *n.* фальши́вка, подде́лка *f.* — *v.* фальсифици́ровать *imp. & perf.*; подде́лывать *imp.*, подде́лать *perf.*

falcon, *n.* со́кол *m.*

fall, *n.* паде́ние *nt.*; (*season*) о́сень *f.* — *v.* па́дать *imp.*, пасть *perf.*; обва́ливаться *imp.*, обвали́ться *perf.*

false, *adj.* ло́жный; -**hood,** *n.* ложь *f.* -**ness,** *n.* фальши́вость, лжи́вость *f.*

falsification, *n.* фальсифика́ция *f.*

falsify, *v.* фальсифици́ровать *imp. & perf.*

fame, *n.* сла́ва *f.*

familiar, *adj.* знако́мый, бли́зкий. -**ize,** *v.* знако́мить *imp.*, познако́мить *perf.*

family, *n.* семья́ *f.*

famine, *n.* го́лод *m.*

famous, *adj.* знамени́тый.

fan, *n.* ве́ер, вентиля́тор *m.*; (*sports*) боле́льщик *m.*

fanatic, *n.* фана́тик *m.* **-al**, *adj.* фанати́ческий. **-ism**, *n.* фанати́зм *m.*

fancy, *adj.* причу́дливый; орнамента́льный. — *n.* фанта́зия *f.*; (*whim*) при́хоть, причу́да *f.*

fang, *n.* клык *m.*, ядови́тый зуб.

fantastic, *adj.* фантасти́ческий.

fantasy, *n.* фанта́зия *f.*

far, *adv.* далеко́. **as far as**, наско́лько.

farce, *n.* фарс *m.*

fare, *n.* сто́имость прое́зда.

farewell, *n.* проща́ние *nt.* **to say f.**, проща́ться *imp.* — *interj.* проща́йте! до свида́ния!

far-fetched, *adj.* натя́нутый.

farm, *n.* фе́рма *f.*, сельское хозя́йство *nt.* **-er**, *n.* фе́рмер *m.* **-house**, *n.* жило́й дом на фе́рме. **-ing**, *n.* сельское хозя́йство.

farther, *adv.* да́льше.

fascinate, *v.* очаро́вывать *imp.*, очарова́ть *perf.*

fascination, *n.* очарова́ние *nt.*

fascism, *n.* фаши́зм *m.*

fashion, *n.* мо́да *f.*, фасо́н *m.* **-able**, *adj.* мо́дный.

fast, *adj.* бы́стрый, ско́рый. — *adv.* бы́стро, ско́ро. — *n.* пост *m.* — *v.* пости́ться *imp.*

fasten, *v.* привя́зывать *imp.*, привяза́ть *perf.*; запира́ть *imp.*, запере́ть *perf.* **-er**, *n.* запо́р, зажи́м *m.*; застёжка *f.*

fastidious, *adj.* приверед́ли́вый.

fat, *adj.* жи́рный. — *n.* жир *m.*, са́ло *nt.*

fatal, *adj.* смерте́льный, па́губный. **-ity**, *n.* фата́льность *f.*; (*death*) смерть *f.*

fate, *n.* судьба́ *f.*, рок *m.* **-ful**, *adj.* роково́й.

father, *n.* оте́ц *m.* **-ly**, *adj.* оте́ческий.

father-in-law, *n.* (*husband's father*) свёкор *m.*; (*wife's father*) тесть *m.*

fatherland, *n.* оте́чество *nt.*, отчи́зна *f.*

fathom, *n.* морска́я са́жень. — *v.* измеря́ть глубину́ мо́ря; (*understand*) понима́ть *imp.*, поня́ть *perf.*

fatigue, *n.* уста́лость *f.* — *v.* утомля́ть *imp.*, утоми́ть *perf.*

faucet, *n.* водопрово́дный кран.

fault, *n.* вина́ *f.*; оши́бка *f.* **-less**, *adj.* безоши́бочный. **-y**, *adj.* оши́бочный, неиспра́вный.

favor, *n.* благоскло́нность *f.*; по́льза *f.* **in f.**, в по́льзу. — *v.* благоприя́тствовать *imp.* **-able** *adj.* благоприя́тный.

favorite, *adj.* люби́мый. — *n.* люби́мец *m.*

fear, *n.* боя́знь *f.*, страх *m.* — *v.* боя́ться *imp.* **-ful**, *adj.* ужа́сный, стра́шный. **-less**, *adj.* бесстра́шный.

feasible, *adj.* возмо́жный.

feast, *n.* пра́здник *m.*, пир *m.*

feat, *n.* по́двиг *m.*

feather, *n.* перо́ *nt.*

feature, *n.* осо́бенность *f.*

February, *n.* февра́ль *m.* — *adj.* февра́льский.

federal, *adj.* федера́льный.

federation, *n.* федера́ция *f.*

fee, *n.* пла́та *f.*, гонора́р *m.*; взнос *m.*

feeble, *adj.* сла́бый.

feed, *n.* пита́ние *f.*, еда́ *f.*, корм *m.* — *v.* пита́ть *imp.*, корми́ть *imp.*

feel, *v.* чу́вствовать *imp.*, почу́вствовать *perf.* — *v. i.* чу́вствовать себя́. **f. like**, (*dat.* +) хоте́ться *imp.* **I f. like**, мне хо́чется

feeling, *n.* чу́вство *nt.*; ощуще́ние *nt.*; эмо́ция *f.*

feign, *v.* симули́ровать *imp.* & *perf.*

fellow, *n.* това́рищ, прия́тель *m.*; (*colleague*) собра́т *m.* **-ship**, *n.* това́рищество, о́бщество *nt.*; (*study*) стипе́ндия *f.*

felony, *n.* уголо́вное преступле́ние.

felt, *n.* фетр, войлок *m.*

female, *adj.* женский. — *n.* женщина *f.*

feminine, *adj.* женский; (*gram.*) женского рода.

fence, *n.* забор *m.*, изгородь *f.* — *v.* (*enclose*) огораживать *imp.*, огородить *perf.*

fencing, *n.* фехтование *nt.*

fender, *n.* крыло *f.*

ferment, *n.* фермент *m.*, закваска *f.* — *v.* бродить *imp.* **-ation,** *n.* ферментация *f.*

ferocious, *adj.* свирепый.

ferocity, *n.* свирепость *f.*

ferry, *n.* паром *m.*

fertile, *adj.* плодородный.

fertility, *n.* плодородие *nt.*

fertilize, *v.* удобрять *imp.*, удобрить *perf.*

fertilizer, *n.* удобрительный тук.

fervent, *adj.* горячий, пылкий.

fervor, *n.* пыл *m.*

fester, *v.* гноиться *imp.*

festival, *n.* фестиваль *m.*

festive, *adj.* праздничный.

fetish, *n.* фетиш *m.*

feud, *n.* вражда *f.*

feudal, *adj.* феодальный. **-ism** *n.* феодализм *m.*

fever, *n.* жар *m.*, лихорадка *f.* **-ish,** *adj.* лихорадочный.

few, *adj.* немногие; немного, мало.

fiancé, *n.* жених *m.*

fiancée, *n.* невеста *f.*

fiasco, *n.* фиаско *nt. ind.*; провал *m.*, неудача *f.*

fiber, *n.* фибра *f.*, волокно *nt.*

fibrous, *adj.* фиброзный, волокнистый.

fickle, *adj.* изменчивый. **-ness,** *n.* изменчивость *f.*

fiction, *n.* фикция *f.*, вымысел *m.*; (*lit.*) беллетристика.

fictitious, *adj.* фиктивный, вымышленный.

fidelity, *n.* верность *f.*

field, *n.* поле *nt.*; (*area*), область *f.*

fiend, *n.* дьявол, бес *m.*

fierce, *adj.* жестокий, свирепый.

fiery, *adj.* огненный; вспыльчивый.

fifteen, *adj.*, *n.* пятнадцать *num.*

fifth, *adj.* пятый.

fiftieth, *adj.* пятидесятый.

fifty, *adj.*, *n.* пятьдесят *num.*

fig, *n.* фига *f.*

fight, *n.* борьба *f.*, битва *f.*, сражение *nt.*, драка *f.* — *v.* бороться *imp.*, сражаться *imp.*, драться *imp.* **-er,** *n.* боец *m.*

figurative, *adj.* переносный.

figure, *n.* фигура, статуя *f.*; (*number*) цифра *f.*; (*form*) образ *m.* — *v.* вычислять *imp.*, вычислить *perf.*

file, *n.* (*for papers*) картотека *f.*; (*tool*) напильник *m.*; (*row*) очередь *f.*, ряд *m.* — *v.* (*tool*) подпиливать *imp.*, подпилить *perf.*; (*papers*) регистрировать *imp.* & *perf.*

fill, *v.* наполнять *imp.*, наполнить *perf.* **-ing,** *n.* насыпь *f.*; (*dental*) пломба *f.*

film, *n.* фильм *m.* — *v.* производить киносъёмку *f.*

filter, *n.* фильтр *m.* — *v.* фильтровать *imp.*; процеживать *imp.*, процедить *perf.*

filth, *n.* грязь *f.*

filthy, *adj.* грязный.

fin, *n.* плавник *m.*

final, *adj.* финальный. — *n.* (*sports*) финал *m.* **-ly,** *adv.* окончательно; наконец.

finance, *n.* финансы *pl.*

financial, *adj.* финансовый.

find, *v.* находить *imp.*, найти *perf.* **f. out,** узнавать *imp.*, узнать *perf.*

fine, *adj.* хороший, прекрасный; (*thin*) тонкий. — *adv.* хорошо. — *n.* штраф *m.* — *v.* налагать штраф

finger, *n.* палец *m.* **-nail,** *n.* ноготь *m.* **-print,** *n.* отпечаток пальца. — *v.* снимать отпечатки пальцев.

finish, *n.* конец *m.* — *v.* кончать *imp.*, кончить *perf.* **-ed,** *adj.* законченный.

Finland, *n.* Финляндия *f.*

Finn, *n.* финля́ндец, финн *m* финля́ндка, фи́ннка *f.* **-ish,** *adj.* финля́ндский, фи́нский.

fir, *n.* ель *f.*

fire, *n.* ого́нь *m.,* пожа́р *m.*

to catch f., загоре́ться *perf.*

set on f., поджига́ть *imp.,* подже́чь *perf.* — *v.* (*shoot,* стреля́ть *imp.,* вы́стрелить *perf.*

fire escape, пожа́рная ле́стница.

fire extinguisher, *n.* огнетуши́тель *m.*

fireman, *n.* пожа́рный *m.*

fireplace, *n.* ками́н *m.*

fireplug, *n.* пожа́рный кран.

fireproof, *adj.* огнеупо́рный.

fireworks, *n. pl.* фейерве́рк *m.*

firm, *adj.* кре́пкий; сто́йкий. — *n.* фи́рма *f.*

first, *adj.* пе́рвый. — *adv.* сперва́, снача́ла; впервы́е. **at f.,** сперва́ adv., снача́ла adv. **f. of all,** пре́жде всего́.

first aid, пе́рвая по́мощь.

first-class, *adj.* первокла́ссный.

first-hand, *adj., adv.* из пе́рвых рук.

fish, *n.* ры́ба *f.*

fisherman, *n.* рыба́к *m.*

fishing, *n.* ры́бная ло́вля.

fist, *n.* кула́к *m.*

fit, *adj.* го́дный, подходя́щий. — *n.* (*impulse*) поры́в *m.* — *v.* *t.* прила́живать *imp.,* прила́дить *perf.* — *v.* *i.* годи́ться *imp.* **-ness,** *n.* го́дность, приго́дность *f.*

five, *adj.,* *n.* пять *num.*

fix, *n.* диле́мма *f.,* затрудни́тельное положе́ние. — *v.* исправля́ть *imp.,* испра́вить *perf.;* приводи́ть в поря́док.

fixation, *n.* фикса́ция *f.*

fixed, *adj.* неподви́жный; назна́ченный.

fixture, *n.* приспособле́ние *nt.;* прибо́р *m.*

flabby, *adj.* отви́слый.

flag, *n.* флаг *m.,* зна́мя *nt.*

flagrant, *adj.* вопию́щий.

flake, *n.* хло́пья *pl.* — *v.* па́дать хло́пьями.

flame, *n.* пла́мя *nt.*

flannel, *n.* флане́ль *f.* — *adj.* флане́левый.

flap, *n.* кла́пан *m.,* засло́нка *f.* — *v.* хло́пать *imp.;* шлёпать *imp.*

flare, *n.* фа́кел *m.,* вспы́шка *f.* — *v.* вспы́хивать *imp.*

flash, *n.* вспы́шка *f.* — *v.* вспыхну́ть *perf.;* сверкну́ть *perf.*

flashlight, *n.* электри́ческий фона́рь.

flask, *n.* фля́га, фля́жка *f.*

flat, *adj.* пло́ский, ро́вный. — *n.* (*apartment*) кварти́ра *f.;* (*mus.*) бемо́ль *m.* **-ness,** *n.* пло́скость *f.*

flatten, *v.* выра́внивать *imp.,* вы́ровнять *perf.*

flatter, *v.* льсти́ть *imp.*

flattery, *n.* лесть *f.*

flaunt, *v.* разма́хивать *imp.*

flavor, *n.* арома́т *m.,* прия́тный вкус. — *v.* приправля́ть *imp.,* припра́вить *perf.*

flaw, *n.* недоста́ток, поро́к *m.*

flax, *n.* лён *m.*

flea, *n.* блоха́ *f.*

flee, *v.* бежа́ть *imp.*

fleece, *n.* шерсть *f.* — *v.* стричь ове́ц *f.* — (*fig.*) обдира́ть *imp.,* ободра́ть *perf.*

fleet, *n.* флот *m.*

fleeting, *adj.* мимолётный.

flesh, *n.* плоть *f.*

flex, *v.* *t.* сгиба́ть *imp.,* согну́ть *perf.;* — *v.* *i.* сгиба́ться *imp.,* согну́ться *perf.* **-ible,** *adj.* ги́бкий.

flier, *n.* лётчик *m.*

flight, *n.* полёт *m.*

flint, *n.* креме́нь *m.*

flippant, *adj.* непочти́тельный, де́рзкий.

flirt, *n.* коке́тка *f.* — *v.* флиртова́ть *imp.* **-ation,** *n.* флирт *m.*

float, *v.* пла́вать *imp.* — *n.* поплаво́к *m.;* плот *m.*

flock, *n.* ста́до *m.,* ста́я *f.;* (*people*) толпа́ *f.* — *v.* толпи́ться *imp.*

flood, *n.* прили́в, пото́к *m.* — *v.* залива́ть *imp.,* зали́ть *perf.*

floor, *n.* пол *m.;* (*story*) эта́ж *m.*

floral, *adj.* цвето́чный.

florist, *n.* торго́вец цвета́ми.

flounder, *n.* ка́мбала *f.* — *v.* бара́хтаться *imp.*

flour, *n.* мука́ *f.*

flourish, *n.* ро́счерк *m.*, цвети́стое выраже́ние. — *v.* процвета́ть *imp.*

flow, *n.* тече́ние *nt.*, струя́ *f.* — *v.* течь *imp.*; ли́ться *imp.*

flower, *n.* цвето́к *m.* — *v.* цвести́ *imp.*

fluctuate, *v.* колеба́ться *imp.*

fluctuation, *n.* колеба́ние *nt.*

fluency, *n.* пла́вность, бе́глость *f.*

fluent, *adj.* пла́вный, бе́глый.

fluid, *adj.* жи́дкий; теку́чий. — *n.* жи́дкость *f.*

fluorescent light, дневно́й свет.

flush, *adj.* на одно́м у́ровне; в край. *n.* изоби́лие *nt.*; кра́ска *f.*, румя́нец *m.*; — *v.* (with water) промыва́ть *imp.*, промы́ть *perf.*; (blush) красне́ть *imp.*

flute, *n.* фле́йта *f.*

flutter, *n.* порха́ние *nt.* — *v.* развева́ться *imp.*

fly, *n.* му́ха *f.* — *v.* лета́ть *imp.*

foam, *n.* пе́на *f.* — *v.* пе́ниться *imp.*

focal, *adj.* фо́кусный.

focus, *n.* фо́кус *m.*, средото́чие *nt.* — *v.* сосредото́чивать *imp.*, сосредото́чить *perf.*

fodder, *n.* фура́ж, корм *m.*

foe, *n.* враг *m.*

fog, *n.* тума́н *m.*, мгла *f.*

foggy, *adj.* тума́нный, мгли́стый.

foil, *n.* фо́льга *f.*; (fencing) рапи́ра *m.* — *v.* расстра́ивать *imp.*, расстро́ить *perf.*; срыва́ть *imp.*, сорва́ть *perf.*

foist, *n.* всучи́ть *perf.*, всуну́ть *perf.*

fold, *n.* скла́дка *f.*, сгиб *m.* — *v.* скла́дывать *imp.*, сложи́ть *perf.*

folder, *n.* па́пка *f.*

foliage, *n.* листва́ *f.*

folklore, *n.* фолькло́р *m.*

follow, *v.* сле́довать *imp.*, после́довать *perf.* **-er**, *n.*

после́дователь, покло́нник *m.*

folly, *n.* глу́пость *f.*

foment, *v.* подстрека́ть *imp.*; разжига́ть *imp.*, разже́чь *perf.*

fond, *adj.* лю́бящий. **-ness**, *n.* не́жность *f.*

fondle, *v.* ласка́ть *imp.*

food, *n.* пи́ща *f.*, пита́ние *nt.*

fool, *n.* глупе́ц *m.* — *v.* дура́чить *imp.*, одура́чить *perf.*; (joke) шути́ть *imp.*, пошути́ть *perf.*

foolish, *adj.* глу́пый. **-ness**, *n.* глу́пость *f.*

foot, *n.* нога́ *f.*, ступня́ *f.* on f., пешко́м.

football, *n.* футбо́л *m.*; футбо́льный мяч *m.*

footlights, *n. pl.* ра́мпа *f.*

footnote, *n.* примеча́ние *nt.*

footstep, *n.* шаг *m.*

for, *prep.* для, ра́ди; (time) на, в тече́ние; (distance) на протяже́нии; (direction) в, к. **for a few minutes**, на не́сколько мину́т. — *conj.* и́бо, так как, потому́ что.

forbid, *v.* запреща́ть *imp.*, запрети́ть *perf.*

forbidding *adj.* отта́лкивающий.

force, *n.* си́ла *f.*, кре́пость *f.* — *v.* заставля́ть *imp.*, заста́вить *perf.*; форси́ровать *imp.* & *perf.* **-ful**, *adj.* си́льный.

forcible, наси́льственное.

forearm, *n.* предпле́чье *nt.*

forecast, *n.* предсказа́ние, *nt.*, прогно́з *m.* — *v.* предска́зывать *imp.*, предсказа́ть *perf.*

forefinger, *n.* указа́тельный па́лец.

forego, *v.* отка́зываться *imp.*, отказа́ться *perf.*

foreground, *n.* пере́дний план.

forehead, *n.* лоб *m.*

foreign, *adj.* иностра́нный. **-er**, *n.* иностра́нец *m.*, иностра́нка *f.*

foremost, *adj.* передово́й, пере́дний; са́мый выдаю́щийся.

forerunner, n. предше́ственник m.

foresee, v. предви́деть perf.

foresight, n. предусмотри́тельность f.

forest, n. лес m.

forestall, v. предупреди́ть perf.

foretell, v. предска́зывать imp., предсказа́ть perf.

forever, adv. навсегда́.

foreword, n. предисло́вие nt.

forfeit, n. штраф m.; фант m. — v. лиши́ться perf.

forge, n. ку́зница f. — v. кова́ть imp.; подде́лывать imp., подде́лать perf.

forgery, n. подде́лка f.

forget, v. забыва́ть imp., забы́ть perf. **-ful,** adj. забы́вчивый. **-fulness,** n. забы́вчивость f.

forgive, v. проща́ть imp., прости́ть perf. **-ness,** n. проще́ние nt.

fork, n. ви́лка f.; (road) развили́на f. — v. разветвля́ться imp., разветви́ться perf.

forlorn, adj. поки́нутый.

form, n. фо́рма f.; очерта́ние nt.; (document) бланк m. — v. t. формирова́ть imp., сформирова́ть perf.; образо́вывать imp., образова́ть perf. — v. i. формирова́ться imp. сформирова́ться perf. образо́вываться imp., образова́ться perf.

formal, adj. форма́льный; официа́льный. **-ity,** n. форма́льность f.

format, n. форма́т m.

formation, n. форма́ция f., образова́ние nt.

former, adj. пре́жний, бы́вший. **-ly,** adv. пре́жде.

formidable, adj. гро́зный, стра́шный; тру́дный.

formless, adj. бесфо́рменный.

formula, n. фо́рмула f.

formulation, n. формулиро́вка f.

forsake, v. покида́ть imp., поки́нуть perf.

fort, n. форт m.

forth, adv. вперёд, впредь. **back and f.,** взад и вперёд.

forthcoming, adj. предстоя́щий.

fortieth, adj. сороково́й.

fortification, n. фортифика́ция f.

fortify, v. укрепля́ть imp., укрепи́ть perf.

fortitude, n. сто́йкость f., му́жество nt.

fortress, n. кре́пость f.

fortunate, adj. счастли́вый.

fortune, n. форту́на f.; (fate) судьба́ f. **-teller,** n. гада́льщик m., гада́лка f.

forty, adj., n. со́рок num.

forum, n. фо́рум m.

forward, adj. пере́дний, передово́й. — adv. вперёд.

foster child, приёмыш m.

foster father, приёмный оте́ц.

foster mother, приёмная мать.

foul, adj., гря́зный, воню́чий.

found, v. закла́дывать imp., заложи́ть perf.; учрежда́ть imp., учреди́ть perf.

foundation, n. основа́ние nt., осно́ва f.; (building) фунда́мент m.

foundry, n. лите́йный заво́д.

fountain, n. фонта́н m.

fountain pen, авторучка f. (abbr. of автомати́ческая ру́чка).

four, adj., n. четы́ре num. **-teen,** adj., n. четы́рнадцать num. **-th,** adj. четвёртый.

fowl, n. дома́шняя пти́ца.

fox, n. лиси́ца f.

foyer, n. фойе́ nt. ind.

fraction, n. дробь f.

fracture, n. перело́м ко́сти. — v. лома́ть imp., слома́ть perf.

fragile, adj. хру́пкий.

fragment, n. обло́мок, отры́вок m. **-ary,** adj. отры́вочный.

fragrance, n. арома́т m.

fragrant, adj. арома́тный, души́стый.

frail, adj. хру́пкий, хи́лый.

frame, n. ра́ма f. — v. обрамля́ть imp., обра́мить perf.

France, n. Фра́нция f.

Frances, *n.* Франче́ска, Фра́нциска *f.*, Фра́нсис *f. ind.*

franchise, *n.* пра́во го́лоса; привиле́гия *f.*

frank, *adj.* и́скренний. **-ness,** *n.* и́скренность *f.*

frantic, *adj.* неи́стовый.

fraternal, *adj.* бра́тский.

fraternity, *n.* бра́тство *nt.*

fraternization, *n.* брата́ние *nt.*

fraternize, *v.* брата́ться *imp.*

fraud, *n.* моше́нничество *nt.*, обма́н *m.* **-ulent,** *adj.* моше́ннический, обма́нный.

freak, *n.* чуда́к *m.*; причу́да *f.*

freckle, *n.* весну́шка *f.*

freckled, *adj.* весну́шчатый.

Frederick, *n.* Фри́дрих *m.*, Фредери́к *m.*

free, *adj.* свобо́дный; (*gratis*) беспла́тный. — *v.* освобожда́ть *imp.*, освободи́ть *perf.* **-dom,** *n.* свобо́да *f.*

freeze, *v.* замерза́ть *imp.*, замёрзнуть *perf.*

freezer, *n.* моро́женица *f.*

freight, *n.* фрахт, груз *m.* **f. train,** това́рный по́езд. **-er,** *n.* грузово́е су́дно *nt.*

French, *adj.* францу́зский. **-man,** *n.* францу́з *m.* **-woman,** *n.* францу́женка *f.*

frenzy, *n.* бе́шенство *nt.*

frequency, *n.* частота́.

frequent, ча́стый. **-ly,** *adv.* ча́сто.

fresh, *adj.* све́жий; (*of water*) пре́сный. **-en,** *v.* освежа́ть *imp.*, освежи́ть *perf.* **-ness,** *n.* све́жесть *f.*

fretful, *adj.* раздражи́тельный **-ness,** *n.* раздражи́тельность *f.*

friction, *n.* тре́ние *nt.*

Friday, *n.* пя́тница *f.*

fried, *adj.* жа́реный.

friend, *n.* друг *m.*; прия́тель *m.* **-ly,** *adj.* дру́жеский. **-ship,** *n.* дру́жба *f.*

fright, *n.* испу́г *m.* **-en,** *v.* пуга́ть *imp.*, испуга́ть *perf.* **-ful,** *adj.* стра́шный.

frigid, *adj.* холо́дный.

fringe, *n.* бахрома́ *f.*

frisky, *adj.* ре́звый.

frivolous, *adj.* легкомы́сленный, пусто́й.

frog, *n.* лягу́шка *f.*

from, *prep.* из, от, с; из-за.

front, *n.* пере́дняя сторона́ *f.*, фаса́д *m.* (*mil.*) фронт *m.* **in f. of,** впереди́, пе́ред.

frontier, *n.* грани́ца *f.*

frost, *n.* моро́з *m.*

froth, *n.* пе́на, на́кипь *f.* — *v.* пе́ниться *imp.*

frothy, *adj.* пе́нистый.

frown, *n.* хму́рый взгляд. — *v.* хму́рить бро́ви.

frozen, *adj.* замёрзший, замо́роженный.

frugal, *adj.* бережли́вый, эконо́мный. **-ity,** *n.* бережли́вость *f.*

fruit, *n.* фрукт *m.*; (*benefits*) плод *m.* **-ful,** *adj.* плодотво́рный. **-less,** *adj.* беспло́дный.

frustrate, *v.* расстра́ивать *imp.*, расстро́ить *perf.*; срыва́ть *imp.*, сорва́ть *perf.*

frustration, *n.* расстро́йство *nt.*

fry, *v.* жа́рить *imp.*, изжа́рить *perf.*

fuel, *n.* то́пливо *nt.*

fugitive, *n.* бегле́ц, бе́женец, дезерти́р *m.*

fugue, *n.* фу́га *f.*

fulfill, *v.* выполня́ть *imp.*, вы́полнить *perf.* **-ment,** *n.* выполне́ние *nt.*, осуществле́ние *nt.*

full, *adj.* по́лный. **in f.,** по́лностью *adv.* **-ness,** *n,* полнота́ *f.*

fumes, *pl.* дым *m.*

fumigate, *v.* оку́ривать *imp.*, окури́ть *perf.*

fun, *n.* заба́ва *f.* **to make fun of,** высме́ивать *imp.*

function, *n.* фу́нкция *f.* — *v.* функциони́ровать *imp.* **-al,** *adj.* функциона́льный.

fund, *n.* фонд *m.*; (*supply*) запа́с *m.*

fundamental, *adj.* основно́й, коренно́й.

funeral, *n.* по́хороны *pl.*

funereal, *adj.* похоро́нный; (*fig.*) мра́чный, тра́урный.

fungus, *n.* пле́сень *f.*; (*med.*) наро́ст *m.*

funnel, *n.* воро́нка *f.*, дымова́я труба́.

funny, *adj.* заба́вный, смешно́.

fur, *n.* мех *m.*

furious, *adj.* ожесточённый, бе́шеный.

furlough, *n.* о́тпуск *m.*

furnace, *n.* пе́чка *f.*; горн *m.*

furnish, *v.* снабжа́ть *imp.*, снабди́ть *perf.*; (house) меблирова́ть *imp. & perf.*

furniture, *n.* ме́бель *f.*

further, *adj.* дальне́йший. — *adv.* да́льше, да́лее. — *v.* продвига́ть *imp.*, продви́нуть *perf.*

furthermore, *adv.* кро́ме того́, к тому́ же.

fury, *n.* я́рость *f.*, бе́шенство *nt.*

fuse, *n.* предохрани́тель *m.*, про́бка *f.* — *v.* пла́вить *imp.*

futile, *adj.* тще́тный.

futility, *n.* тще́тность *f.*

future, *adj.* бу́дущий. — *n.* бу́дущее *nt.*

fuzz, *n.* пуши́нка *f.*

G

gadget, *n.* приспособле́ние *nt.*

gaiety, *n.* весёлость *f.*

gain, *n.* при́быль, вы́игрыш *f.* — *v.* достига́ть *imp.*, дости́гнуть *perf.*

gait, *n.* похо́дка *f.*

gale, *n.* си́льный ве́тер.

gall, *n.* (bile) жёлчь *f.*; (impudence) наха́льство *nt.*

gallant, *adj.* хра́брый, до́блестный.

gallery, *n.* галере́я *f.*; (theat.) галёрка *f.*

gallon, *n.* галло́н *m.*

gallop, *n.* гало́п *m.* — *v.* галопи́ровать *imp. & perf.*

gallows, *n. pl.* ви́селица *f.*

gamble, *n.* риско́ванное предприя́тие. — *v.* игра́ть в аза́ртную игру́; рискова́ть *imp.*

game, *n.* игра́ *f.*; (hunting) дичь *f.*

gang, *n.* ба́нда *f.*

gangster, *n.* га́нгстер *m.*

gangrene, *n.* гангре́на *f.*

gap, *n.* уще́лье *m.*, брешь *f.*

garage, *n.* гара́ж *m.*

garbage, *n.* му́сор *m.*, отбро́сы *pl.*

garden, *n.* сад *m.*; (vegetable) огоро́д. **-er,** *n.* садо́вник *m.*

gargle, *v.* полоска́ть го́рло.

garland, *n.* гирля́нда *f.*

garlic, *n.* чесно́к *m.*

garment, *n.* оде́жда *f.*

garter, *n.* подвя́зка *f.*

gas, *n.* газ *m.*

gasoline, *n.* бензи́н *m.*

gate, *n.* воро́та *pl.*

gather, *v.* — *v. t.* собира́ть *imp.*, собра́ть *perf.* — *v. i.* собира́ться *imp.*, собра́ться *perf.*

gaudy, *adj.* крича́щий.

gauge, *n.* масшта́б, измери́тельный прибо́р. — *v.* измеря́ть *imp.*, изме́рить *perf.*

gaunt, *adj.* исхуда́лый, худо́й.

gauze, *n.* газ *m.*

gay, *adj.* весёлый.

gaze, *n.* пристальный взгляд. — *v.* пристально смотре́ть.

gear, *n.* переда́ча *f.*, приво́д *m.*

gem, *n.* драгоце́нный ка́мень *m.*

gender, *n.* род *m.*

general, *adj.* о́бщий. — *n.* генера́л *m.* in g., вообще́. **-ity,** *n.* всео́бщность *f.* **-ize,** *v.* обобща́ть *imp.*

generation, *n.* поколе́ние *m.*

generosity, *n.* великоду́шие *nt.*, ще́дрость *f.*

generous, *adj.* великоду́шный, ще́дрый.

genial, *adj.* дружелю́бный, серде́чный.

genius, *n.* ге́ний *m.*

gentle, *adj.* кро́ткий; благоро́дный. **-man,** *n.* джентльме́н *m.* **-ness,** *n.* благоро́дство *nt.*

genuine, *adj.* по́длинный, и́стинный.

geographical, *adj.* географи́ческий.

geography, *n.* геогра́фия *f.*

geology, *n.* геоло́гия *f.*

geometric, *adj.* геометри́ческий.

geometry, *n.* геоме́трия *f.*

Georgia, *n.* (*USSR*) Гру́зия *f.*; (*State*) Джо́рджия *f.*

Georgian, *adj.* (*USSR*) грузи́нский. — *n.* грузи́н *m.*, грузи́нка *f.*

geranium, *n.* гера́нь *f.*

germ, *n.* микро́б *m.*; заро́дыш *m.*

German, *adj.* герма́нский, неме́цкий. — *n.* не́мец *m.*, не́мка *f.*

Germany, *n.* Герма́ния *f.*

gesticulate, *v.* жестикули́ровать *imp.*

gesture, *n.* жест *m.*

get, *v.* достава́ть *imp.*, доста́ть *perf.*; получа́ть *imp.*, получи́ть *perf.*; (*become*) станови́ться *imp.*, стать *perf.*

get off, сойти́, *perf.* **get up,** встава́ть *imp.*, встать *perf.* **get well,** поправля́ться *imp.*, попра́виться *perf.*

ghastly, *adj.* стра́шный, ужа́сный.

ghost, *n.* дух *m.*

giant, *n.* велика́н *m.*

gift, *n.* пода́рок, дар *m.*; (*talent*) тала́нт *m.*

gild, *v.* золоти́ть *imp.*, позолоти́ть *perf.*

gin, *n.* джин *m.*

ginger, *n.* имби́рь *f.*

girdle, *n.* пояс, куша́к *m.*

girl, *n.* (*little*) де́вочка *f.*; (*grown-up*) де́вушка *f.*

give, *v.* дава́ть *imp.*, дать *perf.* **g. back,** отдава́ть *imp.*, отда́ть *perf.* **g. in,** уступа́ть *imp.*, уступи́ть *perf.* **g. up,** сдава́ться.

glacier, *n.* ледни́к *m.*

glad, *adj.* ра́достный. **be g.,** ра́доваться *imp.*; быть дово́льным. **-ly,** *adv.* с удово́льствием. **-ness,** *n.* ра́дость *f.*

glamor, *n.* обая́ние *nt.* **-ous,** *adj.* обая́тельный.

glance, *n.* бе́глый взгляд. — *v.* взгляну́ть *perf.*

gland, *n.* железа́ *f.*

glare, *n.* блеск *m.* — *v.* сверка́ть *imp.*

glass, *n.* стекло́ *nt.*; (*container*) стака́н *m.* **-es,** *n.* очки́ *pl.*

gleam, *n.* о́тблеск *m.* — *v.* свети́ться *imp.*

glee, *n.* весе́лье *nt.*

glide, *v.* скользи́ть *imp.*

glisten, *v.* блесте́ть *imp.*

glitter, *n.* блеск *m.* — *v.* блесте́ть *imp.*

globe, *n.* земно́й шар; гло́бус *m.*

gloom, *n.* уны́ние *nt.*

gloomy, *adj.* мра́чный, угрю́мый.

glorify, *v.* прославля́ть *imp.*, просла́вить *perf.*

glorious, *adj.* сла́вный.

glory, *n.* сла́ва *f.*

glossary, *n.* глосса́рий *m.*, слова́рь *m.*

glove, *n.* перча́тка *f.*

glow, *n.* жар *m.*; румя́нец *m.* — *v.* пыла́ть *imp.*

glue, *n.* клей *m.* — *v.* кле́ить *imp.*

glutton, *n.* обжо́ра *f.*

gnaw, *v.* грызть *imp.*

go, *v.* идти́ *imp.*, пойти́ *perf.* **go away,** уходи́ть *imp.*, уйти́ *perf.* **go back,** верну́ться *perf.* **go in,** входи́ть *imp.*, войти́ *perf.* **go on,** продолжа́ться *imp.* **go out,** выходи́ть *imp.*, вы́йти *perf.*

goal, *n.* цель *f.*; (*athl.*) гол *m.*

goat, *n.* коза́ *f.*

God, *n.* бог *m.*, божество́ *nt.*

godfather, *n.* крёстный оте́ц.

godmother, *n.* крёстная мать.

gold, *adj.* золото́й. — *n.*

зо́лото *nt.* -en, *adj.* золото́й; золоти́стый. — *n.* бла́го *nt.*

good, *adj.* хоро́ший, до́брый. — *n.* бла́го *nt.*

good-bye, *interj.* до свида́ния; проща́йте. — *n.* проща́ние *nt.* to say g., проща́ться *imp.,* попроща́ться *perf.*

good luck, *interj.* всего́ хоро́шего.

good-natured, *adj.* доброду́шный.

goodness, *n.* доброта́ *f.*

goods, *pl.* това́ры *pl.*

goose, *n.* гусь *m.*

gorge, *n.* уще́лье *nt.* — *v.* глота́ть *imp.*

gorgeous, *adj.* великоле́пный; пы́шный.

gorilla, *n.* гори́лла *f.*

gory, *adj.* окрова́вленный.

gospel, *n.* ева́нгелие *nt.*

gossip, *n.* спле́тня *f.* — *v.* спле́тничать *imp.*

Gothic, *adj.* готи́ческий.

gouge, *v.* выда́лбливать *imp.,* вы́долбить *perf.*

gourd, *n.* ты́ква *f.*

gourmand, *n.* гурма́н *m.;* обжо́ра *m.*

gourmet, *n.* гурма́н *m.*

govern, *v.* управля́ть *imp.*

government, *n.* прави́тельство *nt.* -al, *adj.* прави́тельственный.

governor, *n.* губерна́тор *m.;* (*mach.*) регуля́тор *m.;* тамбу́р *m.*

gown, *n.* пла́тье *nt.,* ма́нтия *f.*

grab, *v.* хвата́ть *imp.,* схвати́ть *perf.*

grace, *n.* гра́ция *f.;* ми́лость *f.* -ful, *adj.* грацио́зный.

gracious, *adj.* ми́лостивый.

grade, *n.* сте́пень *f.;* (*type*) сорт *m.;* (*school*) класс *m.* — *v.* сортирова́ть *imp.;* нивели́ровать *imp.*

gradual, *adj.* постепе́нный.

graduate, *n.* око́нчивший уче́бное заведе́ние. — *v.* конча́ть уче́бное заведе́ние.

graft, *n.* черено́к *m.,* приви́вка *f.;* (*colloq.*) взя́тка *f.,* взя́точничество *nt.* — *v.* прививать *imp.,* приви́ть *perf.*

grain, *n.* зерно́ *nt.;* хлеб *m.*

gram, *n.* грамм *m.*

grammar, *n.* грамма́тика *f.*

grammatical, *adj.* граммати́ческий.

granary, *n.* амба́р *m.*

grand, *adj.* вели́чественный, грандио́зный.

granddaughter, *n.* вну́чка *f.*

grandfather, *n.* де́душка *m.* (*declined as f.*), дед *m.*

grandiose, *adj.* грандио́зный.

grandmother, *n.* ба́бушка *f.*

grandson, *n.* внук *m.*

granite, *adj.* грани́тный. — *n.* грани́т *m.*

grant, *n.* дар *m.,* субси́дия *f.* — *v.* дарова́ть *imp. & perf.*

granular, *adj.* зерни́стый.

granulated sugar, *n.* са́харный песо́к.

grape, *n.* виногра́д *m.*

grapefruit, *n.* грейпфру́т *m.*

graph, *n.* диагра́мма *f.,* гра́фик *m.* -ic, *adj.* графи́ческий.

graphite, *n.* графи́т *m.*

grasp, *n.* сжа́тие *nt.,* хва́тка *f.;* (*sense*) овладе́ние *nt.* — *v.* схва́тывать *imp.,* схвати́ть *perf.;* ула́вливать *imp.,* улови́ть *perf.*

grass, *n.* трава́ *f.* — *adj.* травно́й.

grasshopper, *n.* кузне́чик *m.*

grate, *n.* решётка *f.*

grateful, *adj.* благода́рный.

gratify, *v.* удовлетворя́ть *imp.,* удовлетвори́ть *perf.*

gratitude, *n.* благода́рность *f.*

gratuitous, *adj.* дарово́й.

gratuity, *n.* пода́рок *m.;* (*tip*) чаевы́е *pl.*

grave, *adj.* серьёзный. — *n.* моги́ла *f.*

gravel, *n.* гра́вий *m.*

gravestone, *n.* надгро́бный па́мятник *or* ка́мень.

graveyard, *n.* кла́дбище *nt.*

gravitation, *n.* тяготе́ние *nt.*

gravity, *n.* тя́жесть *f.,* си́ла тя́жести.

gravy, *n.* подли́вка *f.,* со́ус *m.*

gray, *adj.* се́рый, (*hair*) седо́й. — *n.* се́рый цвет. become gray, седе́ть *imp.*

graze, *v.* пасти́сь *imp.*

grease, *n.* са́ло *nt.*, сма́зка *f.* — *v.* сма́зывать *imp.*, сма́зать *perf.*

greasy, *adj.* са́льный.

great, *adj.* вели́кий, большо́й, огро́мный.

Great Britain, Великобрита́ния *f.*

great-grandchild, *n.* пра́внук *m.*

great-grandfather, *n.* пра́дед *m.*

Greece, *n.* Гре́ция *f.*

greed, *n.* а́лчность *f.*, жа́дность *f.*

greedy, *adj.* а́лчный, жа́дный.

Greek, *adj.* гре́ческий. — *n.* грек *m.*, греча́нка *f.*

green, *adj.* зелёный. — *n.* зелёный цвет.

Greenland, *n.* Гренла́ндия *f.*

greet, *v.* приве́тствовать *imp.* -ing, приве́тствие *nt.*

gregarious, *adj.* общи́тельный.

greyhound, *n.* борза́я *f.*

grid, *n.* решётка *f.*

grief, *n.* го́ре *nt.*

grievance, *n.* жа́лоба *f.*; оби́да *f.*

grieve, *v.* горева́ть *imp.*

grievous, *adj.* го́рестный, печа́льный.

grill, *v.* жа́рить *imp.*, изжа́рить *perf.*; (*colloq.*) допра́шивать *imp.*

grim, *adj.* мра́чный, злове́щий.

grimace, *n.* грима́са *f.* — *v.* грима́сничать *imp.*

grime, *n.* грязь *f.*; (*soot*) са́жа *f.*

grimy, *adj.* гря́зный.

grin, *n.* усме́шка *f.* — *v.* усмеха́ться *imp.*, усмехну́ться *perf.*

grind, *v.* моло́ть *imp.*, смоло́ть *perf.*; точи́ть *imp.*, наточи́ть *perf.*

grip, *n.* сжима́ние *nt.*, схва́тывание *nt.* — *v.* схва́тывать *imp.*, схвати́ть *perf.*

gripe, *n.* зажи́м *m.*, зажа́тие *nt.* — *v.* притесня́ть *imp.*, притесни́ть *perf.*

grippe, *n.* грипп *m.*

grit, *n.* гра́вий *m.*; песо́к *m.*

groan, *n.* стон *m.* — *v.* стона́ть *imp.*

grocery, *n.* бакале́йная ла́вка.

groceries, *pl.* бакале́я *f.*

groin, *n.* пах *m.*

groom, *n.* грум *m.*; (*wedding*) жени́х *m.* — *v.* ходи́ть за лошадьми́.

groove, *n.* желобо́к *m.*; наре́зка *f.*, вы́емка *f.*

grope, *v.* идти́ ощупью.

gross, *adj.* грубый, большо́й, объёмистый, брутто. — *n.* гросс *m.*

grotesque, *adj.* гроте́скный.

grouch, *n.* дурно́е настрое́ние *nt.*

ground, *n.* земля́ *f.*, по́чва *f.*; (*base*) основа́ние *nt.*; (*pl.*) основа́ние *nt.* **-less**, *adj.* неоснова́тельный.

group, *n.* гру́ппа *f.* — *v.t.* группирова́ть *imp.*, сгруппирова́ть *perf.* — *v. i.* группирова́ться *imp.*, сгруппирова́ться *perf.*

grove, *n.* ро́ща *f.*

grow, *v.* расти́ *imp.*; (*become*) станови́ться *imp.*, стать *perf.* де́латься *imp.*, сде́латься *perf.*

growl, *n.* рыча́ние *f.* — *v.t.* рыча́ть *imp.*, прорыча́ть *perf.*

growth, *n.* рост *m.*, увеличе́ние *nt.*, разви́тие *nt.*

grudge, *n.* недово́льство *nt.* **to bear a g.,** име́ть зуб про́тив.

gruesome, *adj.* ужа́сный, отврати́тельный.

gruff, *adj.* грубова́тый, ре́зкий.

grumble, *v.* жа́ловаться *imp.*

grumpy, *adj.* сварли́вый, раздражи́тельный.

grunt, *v.* хрю́кать *imp.*, хрю́кнуть *perf.* — *n.* хрю́канье *nt.*

guarantee, *n.* гара́нтия *f.*, поручи́тельство *nt.*, зало́г *m.* — *v.* гаранти́ровать *imp.* & *perf.*

guard, *n.* стра́жа, охра́на *f.* — *v.* охраня́ть *imp.*; сторожи́ть *imp.*

guardian, *n.* опеку́н *m.*

guerilla, *n.* партиза́н *m.* — *adj.* партиза́нский.

guess, *n.* дога́дка *f.* — *v.* угáдывать *imp.*, угадáть *perf.*

guest, *n.* гость *m.*

Guiana, *n.* Гвиáна *f.*

guidance, *n.* руково́дство *nt.*

guide, *n.* проводни́к *m.*; руководи́тель *m.* — *v.* руководи́ть *imp.*; быть проводнико́м.

guilt, *n.* вино́вность *f.*; винá *f.*

guilty, *adj.* вино́вный.

guinea pig, *n.* морскáя сви́нка.

guise, *n.* о́блик *m.*

guitar, *n.* гитáра *f.*

gulch, *n.* ущéлье *nt.*

gulf, *n.* (*geog.*) зали́в *m.*; пучи́на *f.*

Gulf Stream, Го́льфстрим *m.*

gull, *n.* чáйка *f.*

gullet, *n.* пищево́д *m.*, гло́тка *f.*

gullible, *adj.* легкове́рный.

gulp, *n.* глото́к *m.* — *v.* глотáть *imp.*

gum, *n.* камéдь *f.*; (*anat.*) деснá *f.*; (*chewing*) рези́на *f.*

gun, *n.* ружьё *nt.*, револьвéр *m.* **-powder,** *n.* по́рох *m.*

gurgle, *n.* бу́льканье *nt.* — *v.* бу́лькать *imp.*

gush, *n.* си́льный пото́к. — *v.* хлы́нуть *perf.*

gust, *n.* поры́в *m.*

gusty, *adj.* бу́рный.

gut, *n.* кишкá *f.*; (*mus.*) струнá *f.*; *pl.* (*courage*) му́жество *nt.*

gutter, *n.* сто́чная канáвка.

guttural, *adj.* гортáнный. — *n.* гортáнный звук.

guy, *n.* пáрень *m.*

guzzle, *v.* жáдно глотáть.

gymnasium, *n.* гимнасти́ческий зал.

gymnast, *n.* гимнáст *m.*, гимнáстка *f.* **-ic,** *adj.* гимнасти́ческий. **-ics,** *n.* гимнáстика *f.*

gynecology, *n.* гинеколо́гия *f.*

gypsum, *n.* гипс *m.*

gypsy, *adj.* цыгáнский. — *n.*, цыгáн *m.*, цыгáнка *f.*

gyration, *n.* вращéние *nt.*, коловрáтное движéние.

gyroscope, *n.* гироско́п *m.*

H

haberdashery, *n.* галантерéя *f.*

habit, *n.* привы́чка *nt.*

habitation, *n.* жили́ще, жильё *nt.*

habitual, *adj.* привы́чный.

hackneyed, *adj.* банáльный.

haddock, *n.* пи́кша *f.*

hag, *n.* кáрга, ведьмá *f.*

haggard, *adj.* изможде́нный.

haggle, *v.* торговáться *imp.*

Hague, The, *n.* Гаáга *f.*

hail, *n.* град *m.*; — *interj.* привéт! — *v.* (*greet*) приветствовать *imp.*; сы́паться грáдом, **it is hailing,** идёт град.

hair, *n.* во́лос *m.* **-cut,** *n.* стри́жка *f.* **-do,** *n.* причéска *f.* **-dresser,** *n.* парикмáхер *m.* **-pin,** *n.* шпи́лька *f.*

hairy, *adj.* волосáтый.

Haiti, *n.* Гáйти *m. ind.*

hale, *adj.* крéпкий.

half, *adj.* полови́нный. — *n.* полови́на *f.*

half-breed, *n.* мети́с *m.*; ги́брид *m.*

half-hearted, *adj.* нереши́тельный.

halfway, *adv.* на полпути́.

half-wit, *n.* слабоу́мный *m.*

halibut, *n.* пáлтус *m.*

hall, *n.* зал *m.* **-way,** *n.* передняя *f.*, коридо́р *m.*

hallucination, *n.* галлюцинáция *f.*

halo, *n.* орео́л *m.*

halt, *n.* остано́вка *f.* — *v. i.* останáвливаться *imp.*, останови́ться *perf.* — *v. t,* останáвливать *imp.*, останови́ть *perf.* — *interj.* стой!

halter, *n.* по́вод, недоу́здок *m.*

halve, *v.* дели́ть попопáм.

ham, *n.* ветчина́ *f.*

hamburger, *n.* ру́бленый шни́цель.

hammer, *n.* молото́к *m.* — *v.* вбива́ть молотко́м.

hammock, *n.* гама́к *m.*

hamper, *n.* корзи́на *f.* — *v.* меша́ть *imp.*

hand, *n.* рука́ *f.*; — *v.* подава́ть *imp.*; пода́ть *perf.*

handbag, *n.* су́мка *f.*

handbook, *n.* руково́дство, посо́бие *nt.*, справочник, указа́тель *m.*

handcuff, *n.* нару́чник *m.* — *v.* надева́ть нару́чники.

handful, *n.* горсть *f.*

handicap, *n.* поме́ха *f.*

handkerchief, *n.* носово́й плато́к.

handle, *n.* ру́чка, рукоя́ть *f.* — *v.* управля́ть *imp.*; тракто́вать *imp.*

handmade, *adj.* ручно́й рабо́ты.

handshake, *n.* рукопожа́тие *nt.*

handsome, *adj.* краси́вый.

handwriting, *n.* по́черк *m.*

handy, *adj.* удо́бный.

hang, *v. t.* ве́шать *imp.*, пове́сить *perf. v. i.* висе́ть *imp.*

hangar, *n.* анга́р *m.*

hanger, *n.* ве́шалка *f.*

hanging, *n.* пове́шение *nt.* — *adj.* вися́чий.

hangman, *n.* пала́ч *m.*

hangnail, *n.* заусе́ница *f.*

haphazard, *adj.* случа́йный.

happen, *v.* случа́ться *imp.*, случи́ться *perf.*

happiness, *n.* сча́стье *nt.*

happy, *adj.* счастли́вый, уда́чный.

harass, *v.* беспоко́ить *imp.*

harbinger, *n.* предве́стник *m.*

harbor, *n.* га́вань *f.* — *v.* укрыва́ть *imp.*, укры́ть *perf.*; дава́ть убе́жище.

hard, *adj.* твёрдый; (difficult) тру́дный; — *adv.* си́льно, упо́рно.

hard-boiled egg, яйцо́ вкруту́ю.

harden, *v.* тверде́ть *imp.*; де́латься твёрдым.

hardly, *adv.* едва́.

hardness, *n.* твёрдость *f.*

hardship, *n.* тяжёлое испыта́ние.

hardware, *n.* скобяно́й това́р *m.*

hardy, *adj.* выно́сливый, сто́йкий.

hare, *n.* за́яц *m.*

harm, *n.* вред *m.* — *v.* вреди́ть *imp.*, повреди́ть *perf.* -**ful,** *adj.* вре́дный. -**less,** *adj.* безвре́дный.

harmonica, *n.* губна́я гармо́ника.

harmonious, *adj.* гармони́чный.

harmonize, *v.* гармони́ровать *imp.*

harmony, *n.* гармо́ния *f.*

Harold, *n.* Га́рольд *m.*

harp, *n.* а́рфа *f.*

harpoon, *n.* гарпу́н *m.*

harsh, *adj.* гру́бый, ре́зкий. -**ness,** *n.* ре́зкость *f.*

harvest, *n.* жа́тва *f.*, урожа́й *m.* — *v.* собира́ть урожа́й.

haste, *n.* спе́шка *f.*

hasten, *v. t.* торопи́ть *imp.* — *v. i.* торопи́ться *imp.*; спеши́ть *imp.*, поспеши́ть *perf.*

hasty, *adj.* поспе́шный.

hat, *n.* шля́па *f.*

hatchet, *n.* топо́рик *m.*

hate, *n.* не́нависть *f.* — *v.* ненави́деть *imp.* -**ful,** *adj.* ненави́стный.

hatred, *n.* не́нависть *f.*

haughty, *adj.* надме́нный.

haul, *v.* тяну́ть *imp.*, потяну́ть *perf.* — *n.* перево́зка *f.*; добы́ча *f.*

haunch, *n.* ля́жка *f.*

haunt, *v.* пресле́довать *imp.*

have, *v.* име́ть *imp.*; y + (gen.): I have, y меня́.

Hawaii, *n.* Гава́йи *m. ind.*

hawk, *n.* я́стреб *m.*

hay, *n.* се́но *nt.*

hay fever, сенна́я лихора́дка.

hayloft, *n.* сенова́л *m.*

hazard, *n.* риск *m.*, аза́ртная игра́. — *v.* рискова́ть *imp.*, рискну́ть *perf.* -**ous,** *adj.* риско́ванный; опа́сный.

haze, *n.* тума́н *m.*

hazel, *adj.* све́тло-кори́чневый.

hazelnut, *n.* обыкнове́нный оре́х.

hazy, *adj.* тума́нный, сму́тный.

he, *pron.* он.

head, *n.* голова́ *f.*; (*leader*) глава́ *f.*, вождь *m.*, руководи́тель *m.* — *v.* возглавля́ть *imp.*, возгла́вить *perf.*

headache, *n.* головна́я боль.

headlight, *n.* фа́ра *f.*

headline, *n.* заголо́вок *m.*

headquarters, *pl.* гла́вное управле́ние.

headstrong, *adj.* своево́льный.

heal, *v. i.* хажива́ть *imp.*, зажи́ть *perf.* — *v. t.* излечивать *imp.*, излечи́ть *perf.*

health, *n.* здоро́вье *nt.* -**ful**, *adj.* целе́бный. **-y**, *adj.* здоро́вый.

health resort, куро́рт *m.*

heap, *n.* гру́да, ку́ча *f.*

hear, *v.* слы́шать *imp.* -**ing**, *n.* слух *m.* -**say**, *n.* слух *m.*

hearse, *n.* похоро́нные дро́ги; катафа́лк *m.*

heart, *n.* се́рдце *nt.* by h., наизу́сть. h. **attack**, серде́чный припа́док.

heartbroken, *adj.* уби́тый го́рем.

heartburn, *n.* изжо́га *f.*

hearth, *n.* оча́г *m.*

heartless, *adj.* бессерде́чный.

hearty, *adj.* кре́пкий, здоро́вый; (*meal*) оби́льный.

heat, *n.* жара́ *f.*; (*track*) забе́г *m.*; (*swimming*) заплы́в *m.* — *v.* нагрева́ть *imp.*, нагре́ть *perf.* -**ed**, *adj.* горя́чий; разгоряче́нный. -**er**, *n.* нагрева́тельный прибо́р.

heathen, *n.* язы́чник *m.* — *adj.* язы́ческий.

heather, *n.* ве́реск *m.*

heave, *v.* бросо́к *m.* — *v.* броса́ть *imp.*, бро́сить *perf.*

heaven, *n.* не́бо *nt.* -**ly**, *adj.* небе́сный.

heavy, *adj.* тяже́лый; тру́дный.

Hebrew, *adj.* древнееврейский. — *n.* евре́й, иуде́й *m.*, евре́йка, иуде́йка *f.*

heed, *n.* внима́ние *nt.*, осторо́жность *f.* — *v.* обраща́ть внима́ние. -**less**, *adj.* невнима́тельный, неосторо́жный.

heel, *n.* пя́тка *f.*; (*shoe*) каблу́к *m.*

height, *n.* высота́ *f.*, рост *m.* -**en**, *n.* повы́сить *imp.*, повы́сить *perf.*; усили́вать *imp.*, усили́ть *perf.*

heinous, *adj.* отврати́тельный.

heir, *n.* насле́дник *m.* -**ess**, *n.* насле́дница *f.*

Helen, Helena, *n.* Еле́на *f.*, Эле́н *f.*

helicopter, *n.* геликопте́р, верто́лёт *m.*

helium, *n.* ге́лий *m.*

hell, *n.* ад *m.*

hello, *interj.* алло́!; (*good day*) здра́вствуйте.

help, *n.* по́мощь *f.* — *interj.* на по́мощь! — *v.* помога́ть *imp.*, помо́чь *perf.* -**er**, *n.* помо́щник *m.* -**ful**, *adj.* поле́зный. -**less**, *adj.* беспо́мощный.

hem, *n.* рубе́ц *m.*, кайма́ *f.*

hemisphere, *n.* полуша́рие *nt.*

hemorrhage, *n.* истече́ние кро́ви.

hemorrhoid, *n.* геморро́й *m.*

hemp, *n.* конопля́ *f.*

hen, *n.* ку́рица *f.*

hence, *adv.* сле́довательно; с э́тих пор. -**forth**, *adv.* отны́не.

Henry, *n.* Ге́нрих *m.*, Ге́нри *m. ind.*

her, *pron.* её, ей, — *adj.* её.

herb, *n.* расте́ние *nt.*

Herbert, *n.* Ге́рберт *m.*

herd, *n.* ста́до *nt.* — *v.* ходи́ть ста́дом.

here, *adv.* (*dir.*) сюда́; (*loc.*) здесь, тут. h. **and there**, там и сям. -**after**, *adv.* в бу́дущем. -**by**, *adv.* э́тим. -**in**, *adv.* в э́том; при сём. -**tofore**, *adv.* до э́того. -**with**, *adv.* при э́том.

hereditary, *adj.* насле́дственный.

heredity, *n.* насле́дственность *f.*

heresy, *n.* е́ресь *f.*

heretic, *n.* ерети́к *m.* **-al**, *adj.* ерети́ческий.

herring, *n.* сельдь *f.*

heritage, *n.* насле́дство, насле́дие *nt.*

hermit, *n.* отше́льник *m.*

hernia, *n.* гры́жа *f.*

hero, *n.* геро́й *m.* **-ic**, *adj.* геройческий. **-ine**, *n.* геройня *f.* **-ism**, *n.* герои́зм *m.*

hers, *pron.* её.

herself, *pron.* сама́. **she h.**, она́ сама́.

hesitate, *v.* колеба́ться *imp.*, поколеба́ться *perf.*

hesitation, *n.* колеба́ние *nt.*, нереши́тельность *f.*

heterogeneous, *adj.* разноро́дный; (*chem.*) гетероге́нный.

hexagon, *n.* шестиуго́льник *m.*

hibernate, *v.* зимова́ть *imp.*, прозимова́ть *perf.*

hibernation, *n.* зимо́вка *f.*

hiccup, *n.* ико́та *f.* — *v.* ика́ть *imp.*

hickory, *n.* ги́кори *nt. ind.*

hidden, *adj.* скры́тый.

hide, *n.* шку́ра *f.* — *v. t.* пря́тать *imp.*, скрыва́ть *imp.*, скрыть *perf.* — *v. i.* скрыва́ться *imp.*, скрыть *perf.* — *v. i.* скрыва́ться *imp.*, скры́ться *perf.*

hideous, *adj.* отврати́тельный.

hierarchy, *n.* иера́рхия *f.*

high, *adj.* высо́кий.

high school, *n.* сре́дняя шко́ла.

highway, *n.* шоссе́ *nt. ind.*

hilarious, *adj.* шу́мно весёлый.

hill, *n.* гора́ *f.*, холм *m.*

him, *pron.* его́, ему́.

Himalayas, The, Гимала́и; Гимала́йские го́ры.

himself, *pron.* сам. **he h.**, он сам.

hinder, *v.* меша́ть *imp.*

hindmost, *adj.* са́мый за́дний.

hindrance, *n.* поме́ха *f.*

Hindu, *adj.* инду́ский. — *n.* инду́с *m.*, инду́ска *f.*

hinge, *n.* пе́тля *f.* — *v. t.* прикрепля́ть *imp.*, прикрепи́ть *perf.* — *v. i.* враща́ться *imp.*

hint, *n.* намёк *m.* — *v.* намека́ть *imp.*, намекну́ть *perf.*

hip, *n.* бедро́ *m.*

hippopotamus, *n.* гиппопота́м *m.*

hire, *v.* нанима́ть *imp.*, наня́ть *perf.*

his, *pron.* его́.

hiss, *v.* шипе́ть *imp.* - *n.* свист *m.*

historian, *n.* исто́рик *m.*

historic(al), *adj.* истори́ческий.

history, *n.* исто́рия *f.*

hit, *n.* уда́р *m.*; (*success*) успе́х *m.*, уда́ча *f.* — *v.* ударя́ть *imp.*, уда́рить *perf.* **hit oneself**, ударя́ться *imp.*, уда́риться *perf.*

hitherto, *adv.* до сих пор.

hive, *n.* у́лей *m.*

hives, *n.* крапи́вница *f.*

hoard, *n.* запа́с *m.* — *v.* запаса́ть *imp.*

hoarse, *adj.* хри́плый.

hoax, *n.* обма́н *m.*

hobby, *n.* конёк *m.*, люби́мое заня́тие.

hobo, *n.* бродя́га *m.*

hockey, *n.* хокке́й *m.*

hodgepodge, *n.* вся́кая вся́чина *f.*

hoe, *n.* моты́га *f.* — *v.* моты́жить *imp.*

hog, *n.* свинья́ *f.*

hoist, *n.* подъёмник *m.* — *v.* поднима́ть *imp.*, подня́ть *perf.*

hold, *n.* захва́т *m.* — *v.* держа́ть *imp.* **-er**, *n.* ру́чка *f.*; опра́ва *f.* **-up**, *n.* налёт *m.*, ограбле́ние *nt.*

hole, *n.* дыра́ *f.*

holiday, *n.* пра́здник *m.*; (*vacation*) день о́тдыха, кани́кулы *pl.*

Holland, *n.* Голла́ндия *f.* **-er**, *n.* голла́ндец *m.*, голла́ндка *f.*

hollow, *adj.* пусто́й, по́лый. — *n.* впа́дина *f.*, углубле́ние *nt.*, по́лость *f.*

holly, *n.* остроли́ст, падуб *m.*

holy, *adj.* свято́й.

homage, *n.* почте́ние. уваже́ние *n.*

home, *n.* дом *m.* **at h.**, до́ма

adv. go h., идти́ домо́й.
-land, *n.* ро́дина *f.* -ly, *adj.*
некраси́вый. -sick, *adj.* тоску́ющий по до́му.
homicide, *n.* (*act*) уби́йство *nt.*,
(*person*) уби́йца *m.*
homogeneous, *adj.* одноро́дный.
homogenize, *v.* гомогенизи́ровать *imp. & perf.*
homosexual, *n.* гомосексуали́ст *m.* — *adj.* гомосексуа́льный.
Honduras, *n.* Гондура́с *m.*
honest, *adj.* че́стный.
honesty, *n.* че́стность *f.*
honey, *n.* мёд *m.* -moon, *n.*
медо́вый ме́сяц.
Hong Kong, Гонко́нг *m.*
honor, *n.* честь *f.* — *v.* ока́зывать *imp.* (*perf.* оказа́ть)
честь; чтить *imp.* -able,
adj. почётный. -ary, *adj.*
почётный.
hood, *n.* капюшо́н *m.*; (*auto.*)
колпа́к *m.*
hoodlum, *n.* хулига́н, гангстёр
m.
hoof, *n.* копы́то *nt.*
hook, *n.* крючо́к *m.* — *v.*
цепля́ть крючко́м.
hoop, *n.* о́бруч *m.*
hop, *n.* прыжо́к *m.* — *v.*
прыга́ть *imp.*, пры́гнуть *perf.*
hope, *n.* наде́жда *f.* — *v.*
наде́яться *imp.* -ful, *adj.*
наде́ющийся. -less, *adj.* безнадёжный.
horde, *n.* орда́ *f.*
horizon, *n.* горизо́нт *m.*
horizontal, *adj.* горизонта́льный.
hormone, *n.* гормо́н *m.*
horn, *n.* (*animals*) рог *m.*;
(*mus.*) рожо́к *m.*; горн *m.*;
(*auto*) гудо́к *m.*
hornet, *n.* ше́ршень *m.*
horny, *adj.* рогово́й; мозо́листый.
horoscope, *n.* гороско́п *m.*
horrible, *adj.* ужа́сный.
horrid, *adj.* стра́шный.
horrify, *v.* страши́ть *imp.*
horror, *n.* у́жас *m.*
horse, *n.* ло́шадь *f.*

horseback, *n.*: on h., верхо́м.
horseman, *n.* вса́дник *m.*
horsepower, *n.* лошади́ная
си́ла.
horseradish, *n.* хрен *m.*
horseshoe, *n.* подко́ва *f.*
horticulture, *n.* садово́дство *nt.*
hose, *n.* чулки́ *pl.*; (*garden*)
шланг *m.*
hosiery, *n.* чулки́ *pl.*, чуло́чные
изде́лия.
hospitable, *adj.* гостеприи́мный.
hospital, *n.* больни́ца *f.*, госпита́ль *m.*
hospitality, *n.* гостеприи́мство
nt.
hospitalize, *v.* госпитализи́ровать *imp. & perf.*
host, *n.* хозя́ин *m.*
hostage, *n.* зало́жник *m.*
hostel, *n.* общежи́тие *nt.*
hostess, *n.* хозя́йка *f.*
hostile, *adj.* вражде́бный,
вра́жеский.
hostility, *n.* вражде́бность *f.*
hot, *adj.* жа́ркий.
hotel, *n.* гости́ница *f.*
hothouse, *n.* тепли́ца *f.*
hound, *n.* го́нчая соба́ка. — *v.*
докуча́ть *imp.*
hour, *n.* час *m.* h. hand,
часова́я стре́лка. -ly, *adj.*
ежеча́сный. — *adv.* ежеча́сно.
house, *n.* дом *m.* — *v.* помеща́ть *imp.*, помести́ть *perf.*
-hold, *n.* дома́шнее хозя́йство. -wife, *n.* дома́шняя
хозя́йка.
hovel, *n.* шала́ш *m.*
hover, *v.* пари́ть *imp.*
how, *adv.* как; каки́м о́бразом
how many, how much, ско́лько.
Howard, *n.* Го́вард *m.*
however, *adv.* как бы ни. —
conj. одна́ко; тем не ме́нее.
howl, *n.* завыва́ние *nt.*, вой
m. — *v.* выть *imp.*, завы́ть
perf.
hub, *n.* сту́пица *f.*
hue, *n.* отте́нок *m.*
hug, *n.* объя́тие *nt.* — *v.*
обнима́ть *imp.*, обня́ть *perf.*

huge, *adj.* огро́мный.

hull, *n.* ко́рпус *m.*

hum, *n.* жужжа́ние *nt.* — *v.* жужжа́ть *imp.*

human, *n.* челове́к *m.* — *adj.* челове́ческий.

humane, *adj.* челове́чный, гума́нный.

humanitarian, *adj.* гуманита́рный.

humanities, *pl.* гуманита́рные нау́ки.

humanity, *n.* челове́чество *nt.*

humanly, *adv.* по-челове́чески.

humble, *adj.* поко́рный, сми-ре́нный.

humbug, *n.* надува́тельство *nt.*

humdrum, *adj.* ску́чный.

humid, *adj.* вла́жный. -ity, *n.* вла́жность *f.*

humiliate, *v.* унижа́ть *imp.*, унижи́ть *perf.*

humiliation, *n.* униже́ние *nt.*

humility, *n.* поко́рность *f.*, смире́ние *nt.*

humor, *n.* ю́мор *m.*; (*mood*) настрое́ние *nt.* — *v.* потака́ть *imp.* -ous, *adj.* юмори́стический.

hump, *n.* горб *m.*

humus, *n.* черно́зём *m.*

hunchback, *n.* горба́тый.

hundred, *adj.* & *n.* сто *num.* -th, *adj.* со́тый. — *n.* со́тая часть *f.*

Hungarian, *adj.* венге́рский. — *n.* венге́рец *m.*, венге́рка *f.*

Hungary, *n.* Ве́нгрия *f.*

hunger, *n.* го́лод *m.*

hungry, *adj.* голо́дный.

hunt, *n.* охо́та *f.* — *v.* охо́ти-ться *imp.* -er, *n.* охо́тник *m.* -ing, *n.* охо́та *f.* — *adj.* охо́тничий.

hurdle, *n.* препя́тствие *nt.*, барье́р *m.*

hurdler, *n.* барьери́ст *m.*, барьери́стка *f.*

hurl, *v.* броса́ть *imp.*, бро́сить *perf.*

hurricane, *n.* урага́н *m.*

hurry, *n.* спе́шка, торопли́-вость *f.* — *v.* спеши́ть *imp.*, поспеши́ть *perf.*

hurt, *n.* уще́рб, вред *m.* — *v. t.* вреди́ть *imp.*, повреди́ть *perf.* — *v. i.* боле́ть *imp.*, заболе́ть *perf.* -ful, *adj.* вре́дный.

husband, *n.* муж *m.*

husk, *n.* шелуха́ *f.* — *v.* снима́ть шелуху́.

hut, *n.* хижина́ *f.*

hyacinth, *n.* гиаци́нт *m.*

hybrid, *n.* гибри́д *m.* — *adj.* гибри́дный.

hydrangea, *n.* горте́нзия *f.*

hydraulic, *adj.* гивдравли́-ческий.

hydraulics, *n.* гивдра́влика *f.*

hydrochloric acid, хлористо-водоро́дная кислота́.

hydroelectric, *adj.* гидроэле́к-три́ческий.

hydrogen, *n.* водоро́д *m.*

hydrophobia, *n.* водобоя́знь *f.*

hyena, *n.* гие́на *f.*

hygiene, *n.* гигие́на *f.*

hygienic, *adj.* гигиени́ческий.

hymn, *n.* гимн *m.*

hyphen, *n.* дефи́с *m.* -ate, *v.* писа́ть че́рез дефи́с.

hypnosis, *n.* гипно́з *m.*

hypnotic, *adj.* гипноти́ческий.

hypnotism, *n.* гипнoти́зм *m.*

hypnotize, *v.* гипнотизи́ровать *imp.*, загипнотизи́ровать *perf.*

hypochondria, *n.* ипохо́ндрия *f.*

hypochondriac, *adj.* страда́-ющий ипохо́ндрией. — *n.* ипохо́ндрик *m.*

hypocrisy, *n.* лицеме́рие *nt.*

hypocrite, *n.* лицеме́р *m.*

hypocritical, *adj.* лицеме́рный.

hypodermic, *adj.* подко́жный.

hypothesis, *n.* гипоте́за *f.*

hypothetical, *adj.* гипотети́-ческий.

hysteria, *n.* истери́я *f.*

hysterical, *adj.* истери́ческий.

hysterics, *n.* исте́рика *f.*

I

I, *pron.* я.

ice, *n.* лёд *m.*

iceberg, *n.* а́йсберг *m.*

ice cream, сли́вочное моро́женое.

Iceland, *n.* Исла́ндия *f.* **-er,** *n.* исла́ндец *m.*, исла́ндка *f.* **-ic,** *adj.* исла́ндский.

ice skates, коньки́ *pl.*

icon, *n.* ико́на *f.*

icy, *adj.* ледяно́й.

idea, *n.* иде́я *f.*, поня́тие *nt.*

ideal, *adj.* идеа́льный. **-ist,** *n.* идеали́ст *m.* **-ize,** *v.* идеализи́ровать *imp.*

identical, *adj.* тожде́ственный.

identification, *n.* отождествле́ние *nt.*

identify, *v.* отождествля́ть *imp.*, отождестви́ть *perf.*

identity, *n.* тожде́ственность *f.*, тождество́ *nt.*

ideology, *n.* идеоло́гия *f.*

idiom, *n.* идиомати́ческое выраже́ние.

idiot, *n.* идио́т *m.* **-ic,** *adj.* идио́тский.

idle, *adj.* пра́здный. **-ness,** *n.* пра́здность *f.*

idol, *n.* идо́л *m.*

idolatry, *n.* идолопокло́нство *nt.*

idolize, *v.* поклоня́ться и́долам; боготвори́ть *imp.*

if, *conj.* е́сли.

ignite, *v.* зажига́ть *imp.*, заже́чь *perf.*

ignition, *n.* зажига́ние *nt.*

ignorance, *n.* неве́жество *nt.*

ignorant, *adj.* неве́жественный.

ignore, *v.* игнори́ровать *imp. & perf.*

ill, *adj.* больно́й. **be ill,** боле́ть *imp.* **become ill,** заболе́ть *perf.*

illegal, *adj.* нелега́льный.

illegible, *adj.* неразбо́рчивый, нечёткий.

illegitimate, *adj.* незаконорождённый; незако́нный.

illicit, *adj.* незако́нный.

illiteracy, *n.* негра́мотность *f.*

illiterate, *adj. & n.* негра́мотный.

illness, *n.* боле́знь *f.*

illogical, *adj.* нелоги́чный.

illuminate, *v.* освеща́ть *imp.*, освети́ть *perf.*

illumination, *n.* освеще́ние *nt.*, иллюмина́ция *f.*

illusion, *n.* иллю́зия *f.*

illustrate, *v.* иллюстри́ровать *imp. & perf.*

illustration, *n.* иллюстра́ция *f.*

illustrative, *adj.* иллюстрати́вный.

illustrious, *adj.* просла́вленный.

image, *n.* о́браз *m.*, изображе́ние *nt.*

imaginable, *adj.* вообрази́мый.

imaginary, *adj.* вообража́емый.

imagination, *n.* воображе́ние *nt.*

imaginative, *adj.* вообрази́тельный.

imagine, *v.* вообража́ть *imp.*, вообрази́ть *perf.*; представля́ть *imp.* (*perf.* предста́вить) себе́.

imbecile, *n.* слабоу́мный.

imitate, *v.* подде́лывать *imp.*, имити́ровать *imp. & perf.*

imitation, *n.* имита́ция *f.*, подража́ние *nt.*

immaculate, *adj.* безупре́чный.

immaterial, *adj.* невеще́ственный.

immature, *adj.* незре́лый.

immediate, *adj.* неме́дленный; непосре́дственный.

immense, *adj.* огро́мный. **—ly,** *adv.* чрезвыча́йно.

immersion, *n.* погруже́ние *nt.*

immigrant, *n.* иммигра́нт *m.*, иммигра́нтка *f.* **—** *adj.* иммигри́рующий.

immigrate, *v.* иммигри́ровать *imp. & perf.*

imminent, *adj.* грозя́щий; немину́емый.

immoderate, *adj.* неуме́ренный.

immoral, *adj.* безнра́вственный. **-ity**, *n.* безнра́вственность *f.*

immortal, *adj.* бессме́ртный. **-ity**, *n.* бессме́ртие *nt.*

immune, *adj.* невосприи́мчивый.

immunity, *n.* иммуните́т *m.*

impact, *n.* уда́р *m.*, столкнове́ние *nt.*

impair, *v.* поврежда́ть *imp.*, повреди́ть *perf.*

impart, *v.* наделя́ть *imp.*, надели́ть *perf.*

impartial, *adj.* беспристра́стный.

impatience, *n.* нетерпели́вость *f.*

impatient, *adj.* нетерпели́вый.

impede, *v.* препя́тствовать *imp.*

impediment, *n.* препя́тствие *nt.*

impel, *v.* приводи́ть в движе́ние.

impenetrable, *adj.* непроница́емый.

imperative, *adj.* повели́тельный, императи́вный.

imperceptible, *adj.* незаме́тный.

imperfect, *adj.* несоверше́нный. **-ion**, *n.* несоверше́нство *nt.* (*gram.*) несоверше́нный вид *m.*; имперфе́кт *m.*

impersonal, *adj.* безли́чный.

impersonate, *v.* олицетворя́ть *imp.*, олицетвори́ть *perf.*

impersonation, *n.* олицетворе́ние *nt.*

impertinence, *n.* де́рзость *f.*

impervious, *adj.* непроница́емый.

impetuous, *adj.* стреми́тельный.

impetus, *n.* и́мпульс *m.*

implacable, *adj.* неумоли́мый.

implicate, *v.* впу́тывать *imp.*, впу́тать *perf.*

implication, *n.* вовлече́ние *nt.*

implicit, *adj.* безогово́рочный.

implore, *v.* умоля́ть *imp.*

imply, *v.* подразумева́ть *imp.*

impolite, *adj.* неве́жливый, гру́бый.

import, *n.* и́мпорт, ввоз *m.* — *v.* ввози́ть *imp.*, ввезти́ *perf.* импорти́ровать *imp.* & *perf.*

importance, *n.* ва́жность *f.*

important, *adj.* ва́жный.

impose, *v.* облага́ть *imp.*, обложи́ть *perf.*

imposition, *n.* возложе́ние *nt.*

impossibility, *n.* невозмо́жность *f.*

impossible, *adj.* невозмо́жный.

impotence, *бессилие *nt.*; импоте́нция *f.*

impotent, *adj.* бесси́льный; импоте́нтный.

impregnate, *v.* оплодотворя́ть *imp.*, оплодотвори́ть *perf.*

impress, *v.* производи́ть *imp.* (*perf.* произвести́) впечатле́ние. **-ion**, *n.* впечатле́ние *nt.* **-ive**, *adj.* производя́щий впечатле́ние.

imprison, *v.* заключа́ть *imp.*, заключи́ть *perf.* **-ment**, *n.* заключе́ние *nt.*

improbable, *adj.* неправдоподо́бный.

impromptu, *adj.* импровизи́рованный. — *adv.* экспро́мтом.

improper, *adj.* неприли́чный, непристо́йный.

improve, *v.* улучша́ть *imp.*, улу́чшить *perf.* **-ment**, *n.* улучше́ние *nt.*

improvise, *v.* импровизи́ровать *imp.* & *perf.*

impudent, *adj.* бессты́дный, де́рзкий.

impulse, *n.* и́мпульс *m.*, побужде́ние *nt.*

impulsive, *adj.* побужда́ющий, импульси́вный.

impure, *adj.* нечи́стый; сме́шанный.

impurity, *n.* нечистота́ *f.*; при́месь *f.*

in, *prep.* в (во), на. — *adv.* внутри́, внутрь.

inadvertent, *adj.* неумы́шленный.

inalienable, *adj.* неотъе́млемый.

inane, *adj.* бессмы́сленный.

inaugural, *adj.* вступи́тельный.

inaugurate, *v.* открыва́ть *imp.*, откры́ть *perf.*

inauguration, *n.* торже́ственное откры́тие.

incarnation, *n.* воплоще́ние *nt.*

incense, *n.* ла́дан *m.* — *v.* серди́ть *imp.*

incentive, *n.* побужде́ние *nt.*, сти́мул *m.*

incessant, *adj.* непреры́вный.

incest, *n.* кровосмеше́ние *nt.*

inch, *n.* дюйм *m.*

incident, *n.* происше́ствие *nt.*, инциде́нт *m.*, слу́чай *m.* **-al**, *adj.* случа́йный. **-ally**, *adv.* ме́жду про́чим.

incinerator, *n.* мусоросжига́тельная ста́нция (печь).

incision, *n.* надре́з *m.*

incite, *v.* побужда́ть *imp.*, побуди́ть *perf.*

inclination, *n.* наклоне́ние *nt.*, накло́н *m,*

incline, *n.* накло́н *m.* — *v. t.* наклоня́ть *imp.*, наклони́ть *perf.* — *v. i.* наклоня́ться *imp.*, наклони́ться *perf.*

include, *v.* включа́ть *imp.*, включи́ть *perf.*

including, *prep.* включа́я.

inclusive, *adj.* включа́ющий.

incognito, *n.* инко́гнито *nt.* **ind.** —*adj.*, *adv.* инко́гнито.

income, *n.* дохо́д *m.* **i. tax**, подохо́дный нало́г.

incomparable, *adj.* несравне́нный.

incomplete, *adj.* непо́лный, незако́нченый.

incomprehensible, *adj.* непоня́тный.

inconceivable, *adj.* невообрази́мый.

inconsistent, *adj.* непосле́довательный.

inconvenience, *n.* неудо́бство *nt.* — *v.* причиня́ть неудо́бство.

inconvenient, *adj.* неудо́бный.

incorrect, *adj.* непра́вильный.

incorrigible, *adj.* неисправи́мый.

increase, *n.* увеличе́ние *nt.* — *v. t.* увели́чивать *imp.*, увели́чить *perf.* — *v.i.* увели́чиваться *imp.*, увели́читься *perf.*

incredible, *adj.* невероя́тный.

incredulous, *adj.* недове́рчивый.

increment, *n.* приро́ст *m.*, при́быль *f.*

incriminate, *v.* инкримини́ровать *imp. & perf.*

incrimination, *n.* инкримина́ция *f.*

incubator, *n.* инкуба́тор *m.*

incumbent, *adj.* возло́женный.

incur, *v.* навлека́ть на себя́.

incurable, *adj.* неизлечи́мый.

indebted, *adj.* обя́занный; в долгу́. **-ness**, *n.* задо́лженность *f.*

indeclinable, *adj.* (*gram.*) несклоня́емый.

indeed, *adv.* действи́тельно; неужéли.

indefinite, *adj.* неопределённый.

indelible, *adj.* несмыва́емый.

indemnity, *n.* компенса́ция *f.*

indent, *v.* де́лать абза́ц (*or* о́тступ). **-ation**, *n.* о́тступ, абза́ц *m.*

independence, *n.* незави́симость *f.*

independent, *adj.* самостоя́тельный, незави́симый.

index, *n.* указа́тель, и́ндекс *m.*

India, *n.* И́ндия *f.*

Indian, *adj.* (*USA*) инде́йский; (*Asia*) инди́йский. — *n.* (*USA*) инде́ец *m.*, инде́йка *f.*; (*Asia*) инди́ец *m.*, инди́йка *f.*

indicate, *v.* ука́зывать *imp.*, указа́ть *perf.*

indication, *n.* указа́ние *nt.*

indicative, *adj.* указа́тельный, ука́зывающий; (*gram.*) изъяви́тельный.

indict, *v.* предъявля́ть обвине́ние. **-ment**, *n.* обвини́тельный акт.

indifference, *n.* равноду́шие *nt.*

indifferent, *adj.* равноду́шный.

indigestion, *n.* расстройство желу́дка.

indignant, *adj.* негоду́ющий.

indignation, *n.* негодова́ние *nt.*

indirect, *adj.* ко́свенный.

indiscreet, *adj.* нескро́мный; неосторо́жный.

indiscretion, *n.* нескро́мность *f.*; неосмотри́тельность *f.*

indiscriminate, *adj.* неразбо́рчивый.

indispensable, *adj.* необходи́мый.

indisposed, *adj.* нездоро́вый.

individual, *adj.* индивидуа́льный. — *n.* индиви́дуум *m.* **-ity**, *n.* индивидуа́льность *f.*

indivisible, *adj.* недели́мый.

Indochina, *n.* Индокита́й *m.*

indoctrination, *n.* обуче́ние *nt.*

Indonesia, *n.* Индоне́зия *f.*

indoor, *adj.* находя́щийся внутри́ до́ма.

indoors, *adv.* внутри́ до́ма.

induce, *v.* склоня́ть *imp.*, склони́ть *perf.*

induction, *n.* инду́кция *f.*

inductive, *adj.* индукти́вный.

indulge, *v.* предава́ться *imp.*, преда́ться *perf.*

industrial, *adj.* индустриа́льный, промы́шленный.

industrious, *adj.* трудолюби́вый, приле́жный.

industry, *n.* инду́стрия *f.*, промы́шленность *f.*

inedible, *adj.* несъедо́бный.

ineligible, *adj.* неподходя́щий.

inert, *adj.* ине́ртный.

inertia, *n.* ине́рция *f.*

inevitable, *adj.* неизбе́жный.

inexperienced, *adj.* нео́пытный

infallible, *adj.* безоши́бочный.

infamous, *adj.* име́ющий позо́рную изве́стность.

infamy, *n.* позо́р *m.*

infant, *n.* ребёнок *m.*

infantry, *n.* пехо́та *f.*

infatuation, *n.* ослепле́ние *nt.*

infect, *v.* заража́ть *imp.*, зарази́ть *perf.* **-ion**, *n.* инфе́кция *f.* **-ious**, *adj.* зарази́тельный, зара́зный.

infer, *v.* выводи́ть заключе́ние. **-ence**, *n.* вы́вод *m.*

inferior, *adj.* ни́зший; подчинённый.

infernal, *adj.* а́дский.

infidelity, *n.* неве́рность *f.*

infiltrate, *v.* проника́ть *imp.*, прони́кнуть *perf.*

infinite, *adj.* безграни́чный.

infinitesimal, *adj.* мельча́йший

infinitive, *n.* (*gram.*) инфинити́в *m.*, неопределённая фо́рма глаго́ла.

infinity, *n.* бесконе́чность *f.*

infirmary, *n.* больни́ца *f.*

inflame, *v.* воспламеня́ть *imp.*, воспламени́ть *perf.*

inflammable, *adj.* огнеопа́сный.

inflammation, *n.* воспламене́ние *nt.*; (*med.*) воспале́ние *nt.*

inflate, *v.* надува́ть *imp.*, наду́ть *perf.*

inflation, *n.* инфля́ция *f.*

inflection, *n.* измене́ние *nt.*

inflict, *v.* наноси́ть *imp.*, нанести́ *perf.*

influence, *n.* влия́ние *nt.* — *v.* влия́ть *imp.* повлия́ть *perf.*

influential, *adj.* влия́тельный.

influenza, *n.* инфлюэ́нца *f.*, грипп *m.*

inform, *v.* уведомля́ть *imp.*, уве́домить *perf.*

informal, *adj.* неофициа́льный, неформа́льный.

information, *n.* информа́ция *f.*

infuriate, *v.* приводи́ть в я́рость.

ingenious, *adj.* изобрета́тельный.

ingenuity, *n.* изобрета́тельность *f.*

ingredient, *n.* составна́я часть *f.*

inhabit, *v.* жить; обита́ть *imp.*

inhabitant, *n.* жи́тель *m.*

inhale, *v.* вдыха́ть *imp.*, вдохну́ть *perf.*

inherent, *adj.* прису́щий.

inherit, *v.* насле́довать *imp.*, унасле́довать *perf.* **-ance**, *n.* насле́дство *f.*

inhibit, *v.* сде́рживать *imp.*, сдержа́ть *perf.* **-ion**, *n.* заде́рживание *nt.*

inhuman, *adj.* бесчелове́чный.

inimitable, *adj.* неподража́емый.

initial, *adj.* нача́льный. — *n.* инициа́л *m.*

initiate, *v.* положи́ть нача́ло.

initiation, *n.* посвяще́ние *nt.*; приня́тие *nt.*

initiative, *n.* инициати́ва *f.*

inject, *v.* впры́скивать *imp.*, впры́снуть *perf.* **-ion**, *n.* впры́скивание *nt.*

injunction, *n.* предписа́ние *nt.*

injure, *v.* уши́би́ть, ра́нить *perf.*

injurious, *adj.* вре́дный.

injury, *n.* поврежде́ние *nt.*

injustice, *n.* несправедли́вость *f.*

ink, *n.* черни́ла *pl.*

inland, *adv.* (*dir.*) внутрь страны́; (*loc.*) внутри́ страны́.

inlet, *n.* зали́в *m.*, бу́хточка *f.*

inmate, *n.* жиле́ц, обита́тель *m.*

inn, *n.* гости́ница *f.*

inner, *adj.* вну́тренний.

innocence, *n.* неви́нность *f.*

innocent, *adj.* неви́нный.

innovation, *n.* нововведе́ние *nt.*

innumerable, *adj.* бесчи́сленный.

inoculate, *v.* привива́ть *imp.*, приви́ть *perf.*

inoculation, *n.* приви́вка *f.*

inquest, *n.* дозна́ние, сле́дствие *nt.*

inquire, *v.* спра́шивать *imp.*, спроси́ть *perf.*

inquiry, *n.* спра́вка *f.*

insane, *adj.* безу́мный. **become i.**, сойти́ с ума́.

insanity, *n.* умопомеша́тельство *nt.*

inscribe, *v.* впи́сывать *imp.*, вписа́ть *perf.*

inscription, *n.* на́дпись *f.*

insect, *n.* насеко́мое *nt.*

inseparable, *adj.* неотдели́мый.

insert, *v.* вставля́ть *imp.*, вста́вить *perf.* — *n.* вста́вка *f.*

inside, *prep.* внутрь, внутри́.

— *adv.* внутри́. — *adj.* вну́тренний. — *n.* вну́тренность *f.*

insidious, *adj.* кова́рный.

insight, *n.* проница́тельность *f.*

insignificant, *adj.* незначи́тельный.

insinuate, *v.* намека́ть *imp.*, намекну́ть *perf.*

insinuation, *n.* инсинуа́ция *f.*

insipid, *adj.* безвку́сный.

insist, *v.* наста́ивать *imp.* **-ence**, *n.* насто́йчивость *f.* **-ent**, *adj.* насто́йчивый.

insolence, *n.* на́глость *f.*

insolent, *adj.* на́глый.

insomnia, *n.* бессо́нница *f.*

inspect, *v.* осма́тривать *imp.*, осмотре́ть *perf.* **-ion**, *n.* осмо́тр *m.* **-or**, *n.* инспе́ктор *m.*

inspiration, *n.* вдохнове́ние *nt.*

inspire, *v.* вдохновля́ть *imp.*, вдохнови́ть *perf.*

install, *v.* устра́ивать *imp.*, устро́ить *perf.* **-ation**, *n.* устано́вка *f.*, устро́йство *nt.* **-ment**, *n.* очередно́й взнос.

instance, *n.* приме́р *m.*; слу́чай *m.* **for i.**, наприме́р.

instant, *n.* мгнове́ние *nt.* **-ly**, *adv.* то́тчас.

instead, *adv.* взаме́н, вме́сто.

instigate, *v.* подстрека́ть *imp.*, подстрекну́ть *perf.*

instill, *v.* внуша́ть *imp.*, внуши́ть *perf.*

instinct, *n.* инсти́нкт *m.* **-ive**, *adj.* инстинкти́вный.

institute, *n.* институ́т *m.* — *v.* учрежда́ть *imp.*, учреди́ть *perf.*

institution, *n.* учрежде́ние *nt.*

instruct, *v.* обуча́ть *imp.*, обучи́ть *perf.*; инструкти́ровать *imp. & perf.* **-ion**, *n.* обуче́ние *nt.*, инстру́кция *f.* **-ive**, *adj.* поучи́тельный. **-or**, *n.* инстру́ктор *m.*

instrument, *n.* инструме́нт *m.* **-al**, *adj.* инструмента́льный; (*gram.*) твори́тельный.

insufficient, *adj.* недоста́точный.

insulate, v. изоли́ровать imp. & perf.

insulation, n. изоля́ция f.

insulin, n. инсули́н m.

insult, n. оскорбле́ние nt. — v. оскорбля́ть imp., оскорби́ть perf.

insurance, n. страхова́ние nt.

insure, v. страхова́ть imp., застрахова́ть perf.

insurgent, adj. восста́вший. — n. повста́нец m.

intact, adj. неповреждённый.

intangible, adj. неося́заемый.

integral, adj. неотдели́мый, (math.) интегра́льный.

integrate, v. интегри́ровать imp. & perf.

integrity, n. че́стность f.

intellect, n. интелле́кт m. **-ual,** adj. интеллектуа́льный.

intelligence, n. интеллиге́нция f.

intelligent, adj. интеллиге́нтный.

intelligible, adj. поня́тный.

intend, v. намерева́ться imp.

intense, adj. напряжённый.

intensity, n. напряжённость f.

intensive, adj. интенси́вный.

intention, n. наме́рение nt., цель f. **-al,** adj. умы́шленный.

intercept, v. перехвати́ть perf.

intercourse, n. обще́ние nt.

interest, n. интере́с m. — v. интересова́ть imp., заинтересова́ть perf. **-ed,** adj. заинтересо́ванный. be interested, интересова́ться. **-ing,** adj. интере́сный.

interfere, v. вме́шиваться imp., вмеша́ться perf.

interference, n. вмеша́тельство nt.

interior, adj. вну́тренний. — n. вну́тренность f.

interjection, n. междоме́тие nt.

intermediate, adj. промежу́точный.

intermission, n. переры́в m.; (theat.) антра́кт m.

intermittent, adj. перемежа́ющийся.

internal, adj. вну́тренний.

international, adj. междунаро́дный.

interpret, v. переводи́ть imp., перевести́ perf. **-ation,** n. перево́д m. **-er,** n. перево́дчик m.

interrogate, v. спра́шивать imp.

interrogation, n. вопро́с m.; допро́с m.

interrogative, adj. вопроси́тельный.

interrupt, v. прерыва́ть imp., прерва́ть perf. **-ion,** n. прерыва́ть imp., прерва́ть perf.

intersect, v. пересека́ть imp., пересе́чь perf. **-ion,** n. пересече́ние nt.

intersperse, v. пересыпа́ть perf.

interval, n. переры́в m., интерва́л m.

intervene, v. вме́шиваться imp., вмеша́ться perf.

intervention, n. интерве́нция f.

interview, n. интервью́ nt. ind. — v. интервью́и́ровать imp. & perf.

intestinal, adj. кише́чный.

intestines, n. кишки́ pl.

intimacy, n. бли́зость, инти́мность f.

intimate, adj. инти́мный; бли́зкий. — v. намека́ть imp., намекну́ть perf.

intimidate, v. запу́гивать imp., запуга́ть perf.

intimidation, n. запу́гивание nt.

into, prep. в (во) + (acc.).

intonation, n. интона́ция f.

intoxicate, v. опьяня́ть imp., опьяни́ть perf.

intoxication, n. опьяне́ние nt.

intricate, adj. сло́жный, затрудни́тельный.

intrigue, n. интри́га f. — v. интригова́ть imp.

introduce, v. вводи́ть imp., ввести́ perf.; (present) предста́вить perf.

introduction, n. введе́ние nt.; представле́ние nt.

introductory, adj. вступи́тельный.

intrude, v. вторга́ться imp., вто́ргнуться perf.

intrusion, *n.* вторже́ние *nt.*

intuition, *n.* интуи́ция *f.*

intuitive, *adj.* интуити́вный.

invade, *v.* вторга́ться *imp.*, вто́ргнуться *perf.*

invader, *n.* оккупа́нт *m.*

invalid, *adj.* недействи́тельный; (*sick*) больно́й. — *n.* больно́й.

invariable, *adj.* неизме́нный.

invasion, *n.* вторже́ние *nt.*

invent, *v.* изобрета́ть *imp.*, изобрести́ *perf.* -ion, *n.* изобрете́ние *nt.* -ive, *adj.* изобрета́тельный. -or, *n.* изобрета́тель *m.*

inventory, *n.* инвента́рь *m.*

invertebrate, *adj.* беспозвоно́чный. — *n.* беспозвоно́чное живо́тное.

invest, *v.* вкла́дывать *imp.*, вложи́ть *perf.*

investigate, *v.* иссле́довать *imp. & perf.*

investigation, *n.* иссле́дование *nt.*

investment, *n.* вклад *m.*

invigorate, *v.* подбодря́ть *imp.*, подбодри́ть *perf.*

invincible, *adj.* непобеди́мый.

invisible, *adj.* неви́димый.

invitation, *n.* приглаше́ние *nt.*

invite, *v.* приглаша́ть *imp.*, пригласи́ть *perf.*

invocation, *n.* призы́в *m.*

invoice, *n.* накладна́я *f.*

involuntary, *adj.* непроизво́льный.

involve, *v.* вовлека́ть *imp.*, вовле́чь *perf.*

involved, *adj.* запу́танный.

invulnerable, *adj.* неуязви́мый.

inward, *adv.* внутрь.

iodine, *n.* йод *m.*

Iran, *n.* Ира́н *m.* -ian, *adj.* ира́нский. — *n.* ира́нец *m.*, ира́нка *f.*

Iraq, *n.* Ира́к *m.*

Iraqi, *adj.* ассири́йский, ира́кский. — *n.* ассири́ец *m.*, ассири́йка *f.*

irate, *adj.* гне́вный.

Ireland, *n.* Ирла́ндия *f.*

Irene, *n.* Ири́на *f.*, Ирэ́н *f. ind.*

iris, *n.* (*eye*) ра́дужная обо-

ло́чка; (*flower*) и́рис *m.*

Irish, *adj.* ирла́ндский. -man, *n.* ирла́ндец *m.* -woman, *n.* ирла́ндка *f.*

irk, *v.* раздража́ть *imp.*, раздражи́ть *perf.*

iron, *adj.* желе́зный. — *n.* желе́зо *nt.*; (*appliance*) утю́г *m.* — *v.* гла́дить *imp.*, погла́дить *perf.*

ironical, *adj.* ирони́ческий.

irony, *n.* иро́ния *f.*

irrational, *adj.* иррациона́льный.

irregular, *adj.* непра́вильный, ненорма́льный. -ity, *n.* нерегуля́рность *f.*

irrelevant, *adj.* не относя́щийся к де́лу.

irresistible, *adj.* неотрази́мый.

irresponsible, *adj.* безотве́тственный.

irresponsibility, *n.* безотве́тственность *f.*

irreverent, *adj.* непочти́тельный.

irrevocable, *adj.* безвозвра́тный.

irrigate, *v.* ороша́ть *imp.*, ороси́ть *perf.*

irrigation, *n.* ороше́ние *nt.*

irritable, *adj.* раздражи́тельный.

irritate, *v.* раздража́ть *imp.*, раздражи́ть *perf.*

irritation, *n.* раздраже́ние *nt.*

island, *n.* о́стров *m.*

isolate, *v.* изоли́ровать *imp. & perf.*

isolation, *n.* изоля́ция *f.*

issue, *n.* изда́ние *nt.* — *v.* издава́ть *imp.*, изда́ть *perf.*; выпуска́ть *imp.*, вы́пустить *perf.*

isthmus, *n.* переше́ек *m.*

Israel, *n.* Изра́иль *m.*; госуда́рство Изра́иль.

Israeli, *adj.* изра́ильский. — *n.* израильтя́нин *m.*, израильтя́нка *f.*

it, *pron.* он *m.*, она́ *f.*, оно́ *nt.*; э́то *nt.*

Italian, *adj.* италья́нский. — *n.* италья́нец *m.*, италья́нка *f.*

italic, *adj.* курси́вный. — *n. pl.* курси́в *m.*, курси́вный, шрифт. -ize, *v.* вы́делить курси́вом.

Italy, *n.* Ита́лия *f.*

itch, *n.* зуд *m.*; чесо́тка *f.* — *v.* зуде́ть *imp.*

item, *n.* предме́т *m.*; пункт *m.* -ize, *v.* перечисля́ть по пу́нктам.

itinerary, *n.* маршру́т *m.*

its, *pron. poss.* его́ *m.*; её *f.*; свой.

itself, *pron.* сам *m.*, сама́ *f.*, само́ *nt.*; сам себя́, сама́ само́ себя́.

ivory, *n.* слоно́вая кость.

ivy, *n.* плющ *m.*

J

jab, *n.* толчо́к *m.* — *v.* толка́ть *imp.*, толкну́ть *perf.*

jack, *n.* (*mech.*) домкра́т *m.*; (*cards*) вале́т *m.*

jackass, *n.* осёл *m.*

jacket, *n.* жаке́т *m.*, ку́ртка *f.*

jaded, *adj.* изну́ренный.

jagged, *adj.* зубча́тый.

jaguar, *n.* ягуа́р *m.*

jail, *n.* тюрьма́ *f.* -er, *n.* тюре́мщик *m.*

jam, *n.* варе́нье *f.*, джем *m.* — *v.* загроможда́ть *imp.*, загромозди́ть *perf.*

janitor, *n.* дво́рник *m.*

January, *n.* янва́рь *m.* — *adj.* янва́рский.

Japan, *n.* Япо́ния *f.* -ese, *adj.* япо́нский — *n.* япо́нец *m.*, япо́нка *f.*

jar, *n.* (*container*) ба́нка *f.*; (*jolt*) потрясе́ние *nt.*, шок *m.* — *v.* дребезжа́ть *imp.*

jargon, *n.* жарго́н *m.*

jasmine, *n.* жасми́н *m.* — *adj.* жасми́нный.

jaundice, *n.* желту́ха *f.*

jaunt, *n.* прогу́лка *f.*

Java, *n.* Я́ва *f.*

javelin, *n.* копьё *nt.*

jaw, *n.* че́люсть *f.*

jazz, *n.* джаз *m.*

jealous, *adj.* ревни́вый, зави́стливый.

jealousy, *n.* ре́вность, за́висть *f.*

jelly, *n.* студе́нь *m.*

jeopardize, *v.* подверга́ть опа́сности.

jeopardy, *n.* опа́сность *f.*

Jerusalem, *n.* Иерусали́м *m.*

jest, *n.* шу́тка *f.* — *v.* шути́ть *imp.*, пошути́ть *perf.*

Jesus Christ, Иису́с Христо́с.

jet, *n.* струя́ *f.*

Jew, *n.* евре́й *m.*, евре́йка *f.* -ish, *adj.* евре́йский.

jewel, *n.* драгоце́нный ка́мень. -er, *n.* ювели́р *m.* -ry, *n.* ювели́рные изде́лия.

jilt, *v.* покида́ть *imp.*, покину́ть *perf.*

jingle, *n.* звя́кание *nt.* — *v.* звя́кать *imp.*

job, *n.* рабо́та, слу́жба *f.*

jockey, *n.* жоке́й *m.*

jocular, *adj.* шутли́вый.

John, *n.* Джон *m.*; (*Bibl.*) Иоа́нн *m.*

join, *v.* присоединя́ться *imp.*, присоедини́ться *perf.*

joint, *n.* суста́в *m.* -ly, *adv.* совме́стно.

joke, *n.* шу́тка *f.* -v. шути́ть *imp.*, пошути́ть *perf.*

joker, *n.* шутни́к *m.*; (*cards*) джо́кер *m.*

jolly, *adj.* весёлый.

jolt, *n.* тря́ска *f.* — *v.* трясти́ *imp.*, тряхну́ть *perf.*

Jordan, *n.* (*kingdom*) Иорда́ния *f.*; (*river*) Иорда́н *m.*

Joseph, *n.* Джо́зеф *m.*; (*Bibl.*) Ио́сиф *m.*

journal, *n.* журна́л *m.* -ism, *n.* журнали́стика *f.* -ist, *n.* журнали́ст *m.*

journey, *n.* путеше́ствие *nt* — *v.* путеше́ствовать *imp*

jowl, *n.* щека́ *f.*

joy, *n.* ра́дость *f.* **-ful,** *adj.* ра́достный.

jubilee, *n.* юбиле́й *m.*

Judaism, *n.* иудаи́зм *m.*

judge, *n.* судья́ *m.* — *v.* суди́ть *imp.*

judgment, *n.* сужде́ние *nt.*; реше́ние суда́; пригово́р *m.*

judicial, *adj.* суде́бный.

judicious, *adj.* рассуди́тельный.

jug, *n.* кувши́н *m.*

juggle, *v.* жонгли́ровать *imp.* & *perf.*

juice, *n.* сок *m.*

juicy, *adj.* со́чный.

July, *n.* ию́ль *m.* — *adj.* ию́льский.

jumble, *n.* толчея́, сумато́ха *f.* — *v.* сме́шивать *imp.*, смеша́ть *perf.*

jump, *n.* прыжо́к *m.* — *v.* пры́гать *imp.*, пры́гнуть *perf.*

junction, *n.* соедине́ние *nt.*, у́зел *m.*

June, *n.* ию́нь *m.* — *adj.* ию́ньский.

jungle, *n.* джу́нгли *pl.*

junior, *adj.* мла́дший.

jurisdiction, *n.* юрисди́кция *f.*

jurist, *n.* юри́ст *m.*

juror, *n.* прися́жный заседа́тель; член жюри́.

jury, *n.* жюри́ *nt. ind.*, прися́жные *pl.*

just, *adj.* справедли́вый. — *adv.* то́чно, и́менно, как раз; (*only*) то́лько.

justice, *n.* справедли́вость *f.*

justifiable, *adj.* прости́тельный.

justification, *n.* оправда́ние *nt.*

justify, *v.* опра́вдывать *imp.*, оправда́ть *perf.*

jut, *v.* выступа́ть *imp.*

juvenile, *adj.* ю́ный, ю́ношеский. — *n.* ю́ноша *m.*; подро́сток *m.*

K

kangóroo, *n.* кенгуру́ *nt. ind.*

kayak, *n.* кая́к *m.*

keel, *n.* киль *m.*

keen, *adj.* о́стрый; пронзи́тельный.

keep, *v.* держа́ть *imp.*, сохраня́ть *imp.*, сохрани́ть *perf.* **-er,** *n.* храни́тель *m.*

keg, *n.* бочо́нок *m.*

kennel, *n.* соба́чья конура́.

Kenya, *n.* Ке́ния *f.*

kernel, *n.* зерно́ *nt.*

kerosene, *n.* кероси́н *m.*

kettle, *n.* ча́йник для кипяче́ния воды́.

key, *n.* ключ *m.*; (*piano*) кла́виша *f.*

kick, *n.* уда́р ного́й. — *v.* ударя́ть ного́й.

kid, *n.* козлёнок *m.*; (*child*) ребёнок *m.* — *v.* (*jest*) высме́ивать *imp.*

kidnap, *v.* похища́ть *imp.*, похи́тить *perf.*

kidnapper, *n.* похити́тель *m.*

kidney, *n.* по́чка *f.*

kill, *v.* убива́ть *imp.*, уби́ть *perf.* **-er,** *n.* уби́йца *f.*

kilogram, *n.* килогра́мм *m.*

kilometer, *n.* киломе́тр *m.*

kilowatt, *n.* килова́тт *m.*

kin, *n.* ро́дственники *pl.*

kind, *adj.* до́брый, любе́зный, хоро́ший. — *n.* сорт, разря́д *m.*

kindergarten, *n.* де́тский сад.

kindle, *v. i.* загора́ться *imp.*, загоре́ться *perf.* — *v. t.* зажига́ть *imp.*, заже́чь *perf.*

kindly, *adj.* до́брый, любе́зный, доброжела́тельный. — *adv.* доброжела́тельно.

kindness, *n.* доброта́ *f.*

kindred, *adj.* ро́дственный, схо́дный.

kinetic, *adj.* кинети́ческий.

king, *n.* коро́ль *m.* **-dom,** *n.* короле́вство *nt.*

kinship, *n.* ро́дство *nt.*

kink, *n.* перекру́чивание *nt.*; (*body*) су́дорога *f.*

kiss, *n.* поцелу́й *m.* — *v. t.* целова́ть *imp.*, поцелова́ть *perf.* — *v. i.* целова́ться *imp.*, поцелова́ться *perf.*

kitchen, *n.* ку́хня *f.* — *adj.* ку́хонный.

kite, *n.* возду́шный змей. **to fly a k.,** запуска́ть змея́.

kitten, *n.* котёнок *m.*

kleptomaniac, *n.* клептома́н *m.*

knapsack, *n.* рюкза́к *m.*

knead, *v.* меси́ть *imp.*

knee, *n.* коле́но *nt.* **-cap,** *n.* коле́нная ча́шка.

kneel, *v.* станови́ться на коле́ни.

knife, *n.* нож *m.*

knight, *n.* ры́царь *m.*; (*chess*) конь *m.*

knit, *v.* вяза́ть *imp.*, связа́ть *perf.*

knob, *n.* ру́чка *f.*

knock, *n.* стук *m.* — *v.* стуча́ть *imp.*, постуча́ть *perf.* **-out,** *n.* нока́ут *m.* **k. out,** *v. t.* нокаути́ровать *imp.* & *perf.*

knot, *n.* у́зел *m.* — *v.* завя́зывать у́зел.

know, *v.* знать *imp.*; (*a person*) быть знако́мым.

knowledge, *n.* зна́ние *nt.*

knuckle, *n.* суста́в па́льца.

Korea, *n.* Коре́я *f.*

Kremlin, *n.* Кремль *m.*

L

label, *n.* ярлы́к *m.*; этике́тка *f.* — *v.* накле́ить ярлы́к.

labor, *n.* труд *m.* — *v.* труди́ться *imp.*

laboratory, *n.* лаборато́рия *f.*

laborer, *n.* рабо́чий *m.*

laborious, *adj.* утоми́тельный, тяжёлый.

labor union, *n.* профсою́з *m.* (*abbr. of* профессиона́льный сою́з).

labyrinth, *n.* лабири́нт *m.*

lace, *n.* кру́жево *nt.*; (*shoe*) шнуро́к *m.* — *v.* шнурова́ть *imp.*

laceration, *n.* разрыва́ние *nt.*

lack, *n.* недоста́ток *m.* — *v.* недостава́ть *imp.*

lackadaisical, *adj.* то́мный, мечта́тельный.

lacquer, *n.* лак *m.* — *v.* покрыва́ть ла́ком.

ladder, *n.* ле́стница *f.*

lady, *n.* да́ма *f.*; ле́ди *f. ind.*

ladybug, *n.* бо́жья коро́вка.

lag, *n.* запа́здывание *nt.* — *v.* запа́здывать *imp.*

lagoon, *n.* лагу́на *f.*

lake, *n.* о́зеро *nt.*

lamb, *n.* ягнёнок *m.*

lame, *adj.* хромо́й.

lament, *n.* жа́лоба *f.* — *v.* опла́кивать *imp.* **-ation,** *n.* ламента́ция *f.*

lamp, *n.* ла́мпа *f.*

land, *n.* земля́ *f.*; (*country*) страна́ *f.* **by l.,** сухи́м путём; сухопу́тным путём. **on l.,** на су́ше. — *v.* сходи́ть *imp.*, сойти́ *perf.*; выса́живаться *imp.*, вы́садиться *perf.*

landing, *n.* (*stairs*) площа́дка ле́стницы; (*ship*) ме́сто вы́садки; (*airplane*) ме́сто поса́дки.

landlady, *n.* хозя́йка кварти́ры.

landlord, *n.* хозя́ин кварти́ры; владе́лец *m.*

landscape, *n.* пейза́ж *m.*

landslide, *n.* обва́л *m.*

lane, *n.* тропи́нка *f.*; прохо́д *m.*; (*athl.*) бегова́я доро́жка.

language, *n.* язы́к *m.*

languid, *adj.* вя́лый, то́мный.

lanolin, *n.* ланоли́н *m.*

lantern, *n.* фона́рь *m.*

lap, *n.* коле́ни *pl.*, ло́но *nt.*; (*track*) эта́п, круг *m.*

lapel, *n.* ла́пкан *m.*

lapse, *n.* недосмо́тр, ля́псус *m.* — *v.* проходи́ть *imp.*, пройти́ *perf.*, истека́ть *imp.*, исте́чь *perf.*

larceny, *n.* воровство́ *nt.*

lard, *n.* са́ло *nt.*

large, *adj.* вели́кий, большо́й. **-ly,** *adv.* преиму́щественно; в большо́й сте́пени.

lariat, *n.* арка́н *m.*, лассо́ *nt. ind.*

lark, *n.* жа́воронок *m.*; (*fig.*) шу́тка *f.*

larva, *n.* личи́нка *f.*

laryngitis, *n.* ларинги́т *m.*

larynx, *n.* горта́нь *f.*

lascivious, *adj.* похотли́вый.

lash, *n.* бич *m.*; плеть *f.* — *v.* хлеста́ть *imp.*

last, *adj.* после́дний. **at l.,** наконе́ц. — *v.* продолжа́ться *imp.*, продолжи́ться *perf.* **-ing,** *adj.* дли́тельный.

latch, *n.* задви́жка *f.*, запо́р *m.*

late, *adj.* по́здний; (*deceased*) поко́йный. — *adv.* по́здно. **be l.,** опа́здывать *imp.*, опозда́ть *perf.* **-ly,** *adv.* за после́днее вре́мя.

latent, *adj.* скры́тый.

later, *adv.* по́зже.

lateral, *adj.* боково́й.

latest, *adj.* са́мый по́здний. **at the l.,** са́мое по́зднее.

lather, *n.* мы́льная пе́на. — *v.* намы́ливать *imp.*, намы́лить *perf.*

Latin, *n.* латы́нь *f.*, лати́нский язы́к. — *adj.* лати́нский, рома́нский.

latitude, *n.* широта́ *f.*

latter, *adj.* после́дний (из двух).

Latvian, *adj.* латви́йский. — *n.* латви́ец *m.*, латви́йка *f.*

laud, *v.* хвали́ть *imp.*, похвали́ть *perf.* **-able,** *adj.* похва́льный.

laugh, *n.* смех *m.* — *v.* смея́ться *imp.* **-ter,** *n.* смех *m.*

launder, *v.* стира́ть *imp.*, вы́стирать *perf.*

laundry, *n.* пра́чечная *f.*

laurel, *n.* лавр *m.*

lava, *n.* ла́ва *f.*

lavatory, *n.* убо́рная *f.*

lavender, *n.* лава́нда *f.*; (*color*) бледнолицо́вый свет.

lavish, *adj.* ще́дрый. — *v.* расточа́ть *imp.*, расточи́ть *perf.*

law, *n.* зако́н *m.* **-ful,** *adj.* зако́нный. **-less,** *adj.* беззако́нный.

lawn, *n.* лужа́йка *f.*, газо́н *m.*

lawyer, *n.* адвока́т *m.*, юри́ст *m.*

lax, *adj.* сла́бый, вя́лый.

laxative, *n.* слаби́тельное сре́дство.

lay, *n.* песнь, балла́да *f.* — *adj.* све́тский. — *v.* класть *imp.*, положи́ть *perf.*

layer, *n.* слой *m.*

lazy, *adj.* лени́вый.

lead 1, *n.* (*metal*) свине́ц *m.* — *adj.* свинцо́вый.

lead 2, *n.* приме́р *m.*; руково́дство *nt.*; пе́рвое ме́сто. (*theat.*) гла́вная роль. — *v.* води́ть *imp. ind.*, вести́ *imp. det.*, повести́ *perf.* **-er,** *n.* вождь *m.* **-ership,** *n.* руково́дство *nt.*

leaf, *n.* лист *m.*

leaflet, *n.* листо́вка *f.*

league, *n.* ли́га *f.*

leak, *n.* уте́чка *f.* — *v.* течь *imp.*

lean, *adj.* худо́й; ску́дный. — *v.* наклоня́ться *imp.*, наклони́ться *perf.*

leap, *n.* прыжо́к, скачо́к *m.* — *v.* прыга́ть *imp.*, пры́гнуть *perf.*

leap year, високо́сный год.

learn, *v.* учи́ться *imp.* **-ed,** *adj.* учёный. **-ing,** *n.* учёность *f.*; уче́ние *nt.*

lease, *n.* аре́нда *f.*, сда́ча в аре́нду. — *v.* (*to*) сдава́ть в аре́нду; (*from*) брать в аре́нду.

least, *adj.* наиме́ньший. **at l.,** по кра́йней ме́ре. **not in the l.,** ничу́ть. — *adv.* ме́ньше всего́.

leather, *n.* ко́жа *f.*

leave, *n.* (*of absence, etc.*)

óтпуск *m.*; (*permission*) разрешéние *nt.* — *v. i.* уходить *imp.*; уезжáть *imp.* — *v. t.* оставлять *imp.*, остáвить *perf.*

Lebanon, *n.* Ливáн *m.*

lechery, *n.* разврáт *m.*

lecture, *n.* лéкция *f.* — *v.* читáть лéкцию.

lecturer, *n.* лéктор *m.*

ledge, *n.* выступ *m.*

leech, *n.* пиявка *f.*

leek, *n.* лук-порéй *m.*

leer, *n.* косóй взгляд. — *v.* смотрéть искоса; смотрéть злóбно.

left, *adj.* лéвый. on the l., слéва. to the l., влéво. to the l. of, налéво от.

leg, *n.* ногá *f.*

legal, *adj.* закóнный. -ize, *v.* узакóнивать *imp.*, узакóнить *perf.*

legend, *n.* легéнда *f.* -ary, *adj.* легендáрный.

legible, *adj.* разбóрчивый, чёткий.

legion, *n.* легиóн *m.*

legislation, *n.* законодáтельство *nt.*

legislature, *n.* законодáтельная власть.

legitimate, *adj.* закóнный.

lemon, *n.* лимóн *m.* -ade, *n.* лимонáд *m.*

leisure, *n.* досýг *m.*; свобóдное врéмя.

lend, *v.* давáть взаймы.

length, *n.* длинá *f.*; (*athl.*) кóрпус *m.* -en, *v. t.* удлинять *imp.*, удлинить *perf.* — *v. i.* удлиняться *imp.*, удлиниться *perf.* -wise, *adv.* в длину.

lengthy, *adj.* растянутый.

lenient, *adj.* терпимый, снисходительный.

lens, *n.* линза *f.*, оптическое стекло.

lentil, *n.* чечевица *f.*

leopard, *n.* леопáрд *m.*

leper, *n.* прокажённый.

leprosy, *n.* прокáза *f.*

less, *adj.* мéньший. — *adv.* мéньше. — *prep.* без (бéзо).

none the l., тем не мéнее.

lesson, *n.* урóк *m.*

lest, *conj.* чтóбы не.

let, *v.* позволять *imp.*, позвóлить *perf.*, let be, оставлять в покóе. let know, давáть знать.

lethargic, *adj.* летаргический.

lethargy, *n.* летаргия *f.*

Lett, *n.* латыш *m.*, латышка *f.* -ish, *adj.* латышский.

letter, *n.* письмó *nt.*; (*alphabet*) бýква *f.*

lettuce, *n.* салáт, латýк *m.*

level, *adj.* рóвный; горизонтáльный. — *n.* ýровень *m.* — *v.* урáвнивать *imp.*, уравнять *perf.*

lever, *n.* рычáг *m.*

levy, *n.* обложéние налóгом. — *v.* облагáть налóг.

lewd, *adj.* похотливый.

liability, *n.* отвéтственность *f.*; обязáтельство *nt.* assets and liabilities, активи пассив

liable, *adj.* отвéтственный, обязáтельный.

liaison, *n.* связь *f.*

liar, *n.* лгун *m.*

libel, *n.* клеветá *f.* — *v.* клеветáть *imp.*, наклеветáть *perf.* -ous, *adj.* клеветнический.

liberal, *adj.* щéдрый, обильный; (*politics*) либерáльный. -ism, *n.* либерализм *m.*

liberate, *v.* освобождáть *imp.*, освободить *perf.*

liberty, *n.* свобóда, вóльность *f.*

librarian, *n.* библиотéкарь *m.*, библиотéкарша *f.*

library, *n.* библиотéка *f.*

Libya, *n.* Ливия *f.*

license, *n.* лицéнзия *f.*, свидéтельство *nt.*

licentious, *adj.* распýщенный.

lick, *v.* лизáть *imp.*, лизнýть *perf.*

licorice, *n.* лакрица *f.*

lid, *n.* крышка *f.*; (*eye*) вéко *nt.*

lie, *n.* ложь *f.* — *v.* (*tell untruths*) лгать *imp.*, солгáть *perf.*; (*recline*) лежáть *imp.* lie down, ложиться *imp.*

lieutenant, *n.* лейтена́нт *m.*

life, *n.* жизнь *f.* **-boat,** *n.* спаса́тельная ло́дка. **-guard,** *n.* член спаса́тельной кома́нды. **-less,** *adj.* безжи́зненный. **-time,** *n.* продолжи́тельность жи́зни.

lift, *v.* поднима́ть *imp.,* подня́ть *perf.*

ligament, *n.* свя́зка *f.*

light, *adj.* лёгкий; *(color)* све́тлый. — *n.* свет *m.,* освеще́ние *nt.* — *v. (illuminate)* освеща́ть *imp.,* освети́ть *perf.; (kindle)* зажига́ть *imp.,* заже́чь *perf.* **-en,** *v.,* облегча́ть *imp.,* облегчи́ть *perf.* **-ness,** *n.* лёгкость *f.*

lighthouse, *n.* мая́к *m.*

lightning, *n.* мо́лния *f.*

like, *adj.* похо́жий, подо́бный. — *adv.* подо́бно; так. — *n.* ро́вня *f.,* ра́вный *m.* — *v.* люби́ть *imp.* **-able,** *adj.* привлека́тельный, ми́лый. **-lihood,** *n.* вероя́тность *f.* **-ly,** *adj.* вероя́тный. — *adv.* вероя́тно. **-ness,** *n.* схо́дство *nt.* **-wise,** *adv.* та́кже.

lilac, *n.* сире́нь *f.* — *adj.* сире́невый.

lily, *n.* ли́лия *f.* — *adj.* лиле́йный.

limb, *n.* член *m.; (plant)* сук *m.,* ветвь *f.*

lime, *n.* и́звесть *f.; (fruit)* род лимо́на.

limestone, *n.* известня́к *m.*

limit, *n.* грани́ца; *f.* ограниче́ние *nt.* — *v.* ограни́чивать *imp.,* ограни́чить *perf.* **-ation,** *n.* ограниче́ние *nt.* **-less,** *adj.* безграни́чный.

limp, *adj.* безво́льный. — *n.* прихра́мывание *nt.* — *v.* прихра́мывать *imp.*

limpid, *adj.* прозра́чный.

line, *n.* ли́ния *f.; (print)* строка́ *f.,* *(row)* шере́нга *f.* — *v.* проводи́ть ли́нию.

lineage, *n.* родосло́вная *f.*

linear, *adj.* лине́йный.

linen, *n.* полотно́ *nt.* — *adj.* льняно́й.

liner, *n.* пассажи́рскии парохо́д.

linger, *v.* заде́рживаться *imp.,* затя́гиваться *imp.*

lingerie, *n.* да́мское бельё.

linguist, *n.* языкове́д, лингви́ст *m.* **-ic,** *adj.* языкове́дческий, лингвисти́ческий

liniment, *n.* жи́дкая мазь.

lining, *n.* подкла́дка *f.*

link, *n.* звено́ *nt.* — *v.* соединя́ть *imp.,* соедини́ть *perf.*

linoleum, *n.* лино́леум *m.*

lion, *n.* лев *m.*

lip, *n.* губа́ *f.* **-stick,** *n.* губна́я пома́да *f.*

liquer, *n.* ликёр *m.*

liquid, *n.* жи́дкость *f.* — *adj.* жи́дкий.

liquidate, *v.* ликвиди́ровать *imp. & perf.*

liquidation, *n.* ликвида́ция *f.*

liquor, *n.* спи́ртный напи́ток.

lisp, *n.* шепеля́вое произноше́ние. — *v.* шепеля́вить *imp.*

list, *n.* спи́сок *m.; (ship)* крен *m.* — *v.* составля́ть спи́сок; крени́ться *imp.*

listen, *v.* слу́шать *imp.*

listless, *adj.* апати́чный.

liter, *n.* литр *m.* — *adj.* литро́вый.

literal, *adj.* буква́льный.

literary, *adj.* литерату́рный.

literate, *adj.* гра́мотный.

literature, *n.* литерату́ра *f.*

Lithuania, *n.* Литва́ *f.*

Lithuanian, *adj.* лито́вский.

litter, *n.* носи́лки *pl.; (disorder)* помёт *n.* — *v.* разбра́сывать *imp.,* разбро́сить *perf.*

little, *adj. (size)* ма́ленький; *(quantity)* немно́го *adv.*

live, *v.* жить *imp.,* существова́ть *imp.; (inhabit)* обита́ть *imp.* **-lihood,** *n.* сре́дства к жи́зни; пропита́ние *nt.* **-ly,** *adj.* оживлённый.

liver, *n.* пе́чень *f.*

livestock, *n.* скот *m.,* живо́й инвента́рь.

livid, *adj.* мёртвенно бле́дный.

living, *adj.* живо́й, совреме́нный. — *n.* сре́дства к жи́зни (*or* существова́нию).

lizard, *n.* я́щерица *f.*

llama, *n.* ла́ма *f.*

load, *n.* груз *m.* — *v.* нагружа́ть *imp.*, нагрузи́ть *perf.*

loaf, *n.* буха́нка *f.*, карава́й *m.* — *v.* безде́льничать *imp.* -er, *n.* безде́льник *m.*

loan, *n.* заём *m.* — *v.* дава́ть взаймы́.

loathe, *v.* ненави́деть *imp.*, чу́вствовать отвраще́ние.

lobby, *n.* вестибю́ль *m.*, прихо́жая *f.*

lobe, *n.* до́ля, ло́пасть *f.*; (*ear*) мо́чка (у́ха).

lobster, *n.* ома́р *m.*

local, *adj.* ме́стный. **-ity,** *n.* ме́стность *f.* **-ize,** *n.* локализова́ть *imp. & perf.*

locate, *v.* определя́ть местонахожде́ние; поселя́ть *imp.*, посели́ть *perf.*

location, *n.* определе́ние ме́ста; ме́стность *f.*

lock, *n.* замо́к *m.* — *v.* запира́ть *imp.*, запере́ть *perf.*

locker, *n.* шкаф, шка́фчик *m.*

locket, *n.* медальо́н *m.*

lockjaw, *n.* спазм жева́тельных мышц.

locksmith, *n.* сле́сарь *m.*

locomotive, *n.* парово́з *m. adj.* дви́жущийся.

locust, *n.* саранча́ *f.*

lode, *n.* ру́дная жи́ла.

lodge, *n.* сто́рожка *f.* — *v.* приюти́ть *perf.*; квартирова́ть *imp. & perf.*

lodging, *n.* кварти́ра *f.*

loft, *n.* черда́к *m.*

lofty, *adj.* возвы́шенный.

log, *n.* чурба́н *m.*; (*naut.*) лаг *m.*, ва́хтенный журна́л.

loge, *n.* ло́жа *f.*

logic, *n.* ло́гика *f.* **-al,** *adj.* логи́ческий.

loin, *n.* филе́йная часть *f.*; *pl.* поясни́ца *f.*

lone, *adj.* одино́кий. **-ly,** *adj.* одино́кий.

long, *adj.* до́лгий; дли́нный *adv.* до́лго. — *v.* тоскова́ть давно́ *imp.*

longevity, *n.* долгове́чность *f.*

longing, *n.* тоска́ *f.*; стра́стное жела́ние.

longitude, *n.* долгота́ *f.*

look, *n.* (*glance*) взгляд; (*appearance*) вид *m.* — *v.* смотре́ть *imp.*; вы́глядеть *imp.*

loop, *n.* пе́тля *f.* — *v.* де́лать пе́тлю. **-hole,** *n.* бойни́ца *f.*; (*fig.*) лазе́йка *f.*

loose, *adj.* свобо́дный; не натя́нутый.

loosen, *v.* развя́зывать *imp.*, завя́зать *perf.*

loot, *n.* добы́ча *f.* — *v.* гра́бить *imp.*, огра́бить *perf.*

lose, *v.* теря́ть *imp.*, потеря́ть *perf.*; (*a game. bet, etc.*) прои́грывать *imp.*, проигра́ть *perf.*

loss, *n.* убы́ток *m.*, поте́ря *f.*

lost, *adj.* потеря́вший, поги́бший.

lot, *n.* (*fate*) жре́бий *m.*, у́часть, судьба́ *f.*; (*land*) уча́сток земли́. **a lot of,** мно́го.

lotion, *n.* примо́чка *f.*; жи́дкое косме́тическое сре́дство.

lottery, *n.* лотере́я *f.*

loud, *adj.* гро́мкий. — *adv.* гро́мко. **-speaker,** *n.* громкоговори́тель *m.*

louse, *n.* вошь *f.*

love, *n.* любо́вь *f.* **in l.,** влюблённый. **to fall in l.,** влюби́ться *perf.* — *v.* люби́ть *imp.* **-ly,** *adj.* преле́стный.

lover, *n.* любо́вник *m.*; (*amateur*) люби́тель *m.*

low, *adj.* ни́зкий. **-er,** *v.* понижа́ть *imp.*, пони́зить *perf.*; снижа́ть *imp.*, сни́зить *perf.*

lower case letter, строчна́я бу́ква.

loyal, *adj.* ве́рный, лойя́льный. **-ty,** *n.* ве́рность, лойя́льность *f.*

lubricant, *n.* сма́зочное вещество́.

lubricate, *v.* сма́зывать *imp.*, сма́зать *perf.*

lucid, *adj.* я́сный, прозра́чный.

luck, *n.* сча́стье *nt.*

lucky, *adj.* счастли́вый, уда́чливый.

lucrative, *adj.* прибы́льный.

ludicrous, *adj.* смешно́й.

luggage, *n.* бага́ж *m.*

lukewarm, *adj.* теплова́тый.

lull, *n.* зати́шье *nt.* — *v.* убаю́кивать *imp.*, убаю́кать *perf.*

lullaby, *n.* колыбе́льная пе́сня.

lumber, *n.* строево́й лес; хлам *m.*

luminous, *adj.* све́тлый, светя́щийся.

lump, *n.* кусо́к *m.*; глы́ба *f.*

lunar, *adj.* лу́нный.

lunatic, *n.* сумасше́дший.

lunch, *n.* второ́й за́втрак *m.* — *v.* за́втракать *imp.*, поза́втракать *perf.*

lung, *n.* лёгкое *nt.*

lunge, *n.* вы́пад *m.* — *v.* де́лать вы́пад.

lure, *n.* прима́нка *f.*, ва́би[m.] — *v.* прима́нивать *imp.* примани́ть *perf.*

lurid, *adj.* мра́чный, злове́щий.

luscious, *adj.* со́чный.

lust, *n.* страсть *f.*

luster, *n.* гля́нец, блеск *m.*

lusty, *adj.* здоро́вый, си́льный, живо́й.

lute, *n.* лю́тня *f.*

Lutheran, *adj.* лютера́нский. — *n.* лютера́нин *m.*

luxuriant, *adj.* бу́йный, пы́шный.

luxurious, *adj.* роско́шный.

luxury, *n.* ро́скошь *f.*

lymph, *n.* ли́мфа *f.*

lynch, *v.* линчева́ть *imp. & perf.*

lyric, lyrical, *adj.* лири́ческий

lyricism, *n.* лири́зм *m.*

M

macabre, *adj.* ужа́сный.

macaroni, *n.* макаро́ны *pl.*

machine, *n.* маши́на *f.*, механи́зм *m.*

machinery, *n.* маши́ны, механи́змы *pl.*

mackerel, *n.* макре́ль *f.*

mad, *adj.* сумасше́дший, бе́шеный. **-ness,** *n.* сумасше́ствие *nt.*

madam, *n.* мада́м *f. ind.*, госпожа́ *f.*

magazine, *n.* журна́л *m.*

magic, *n.* волшебство́ *nt.* — *adj.* волше́бный.

magician, *n.* волше́бник *m.*

magnanimous, *adj.* великоду́шный.

magnesium, *n.* ма́гний *m.*

magnet, *n.* магни́т *m.* **-ic,** *adj.* магни́тный.

magnificent, *adj.* великоле́пный.

magnify, *v.* увели́чивать *imp.*, увели́чить *perf.*

magnitude, *n.* величина́ *f.*

mahogany, *n.* кра́сное де́рево

maiden, *n.* деви́ца, де́ва *f.* — *adj.* де́вственная.

mail, *n.* по́чта *f.* — *v.* посыла́ть по́чтой. **-box,** *n.* почто́вый я́щик, **-man,** *n.* почтальо́н *m.*

main, *adj.* гла́вный. **-land,** *n.* матери́к *m.* **-ly,** *adv.* гла́вным о́бразом *adv.*

maintain, *n.* подде́рживать *imp.*, утвержда́ть *imp.*

maintenance, *n.* подде́ржка *f.*

maize, *n.* майс *m.*, кукуру́за *f.*

majestic, *adj.* вели́чественный

majesty, *n.* вели́чество *f.*

major, *adj.* бо́лее ва́жный гла́вный; (*mus.*) мажо́рный — *n.* майо́р *m.*: (*mus.*) мажо́р *m.*

majority, *n.* большинство́ *nt.*

make, *v.* де́лать *imp.*, сде́ла[ть]

perf.; (*earn*) зараба́тывать
imp., зарабо́тать *perf.*

maker, *n.* созда́тель, творе́ц
m.

make-up, *n.* грим *m.*

malady, *n.* боле́знь *f.*

malaria, *n.* маля́рия *f.*

male, *adj.* мужско́й. — *n.*
мужчи́на *m.* (declined as *f.*),
(*animal*) саме́ц *m.*

malevolent, *adj.* злора́дный.

malice, *n.* зло́ба *f.*

malicious, *adj.* зло́бный.

malignant, *adj.* зло́бный,
злока́чественный.

malnutrition, *n.* недоеда́ние *nt.*

malt, *n.* со́лод *m.*

mammal, *n.* млекопита́ющее
nt.

man, *n.* челове́к *m.*; (*male*)
мужчи́на *m.* (declined as *f.*).

manage, *v.* управля́ть *imp.*,
заве́довать *imp.* -ment, *n.*
управле́ние, заве́дование *nt.*

manager, *n.* заве́дующий,
руководи́тель *m.*

Manchurian, *adj.* манчжу́р-
ский.

mandate, *n.* манда́т *m.*

mandatory, *adj.* манда́тный.

mandolin, *n.* мандоли́на *f.*

mane, *n.* гри́ва *f.*

maneuver, *n.* манёвр *m.* — *v.*
маневри́ровать *imp. & perf.*

mangle, *n.* като́к *m.* — *v.*
ката́ть *imp.*, покати́ть *perf.*

manhood, *n.* му́жество *nt.*,
возмужа́лость *f.*

mania, *n.* ма́ния *f.*

maniac, *n.* манья́к *m.*

manicure, *n.* маникю́р *m.*

manifest, *adj.* очеви́дный,
я́сный. — *n.* манифе́ст *m.*
— *v.* проявля́ть *imp.*, прояви́ть *perf.*

manifesto, *n.* манифе́ст *m.*

manipulate, *v.* манипули́ровать *imp.*

mankind, *n.* челове́чество *nt.*

manliness, *n.* му́жественность
f.

manly, *adj.* му́жественный.

manner, *n.* о́браз, спо́соб *m.*,
мане́ра *f.*; *pl.* мане́ры. -ism,
n. манье́ризм *m.*

manual, *adj.* ручно́й.

manufacture, *v.* производи́ть
imp., произвести́ *perf.*;
выде́лывать *imp.*, вы́делать
perf.

manufacturer, *n.* фабрика́нт
m.

manufacturing, *n.* произво́д-
ство *nt.*, выде́лка *f.*

manure, *n.* наво́з *m.*

manuscript, *n.* ру́копись *f.*

many, *adj.* мно́гие *pl.* — *n.*
мно́жество *nt.* **how m.**,
ско́лько? **so m.**, сто́лько.
too m., сли́шком мно́го. **as
m. as**, сто́лько . . . ско́лько.

map, *n.* ка́рта *f.*

maple, *n.* клён *m.*

mar, *v.* испо́ртить *perf.*

marathon, *n.* марафо́н; мара-
фо́нский бег *m.*

marble, *n.* мра́мор *m.*

march, *n.* марш *m.* — *v.*
маршир́ова́ть *imp. & perf.*

March, *n.* март. — *adj.*
ма́ртовский.

mare, *n.* кобы́ла *f.*

Margaret, *n.* Маргари́та *f.*

margarine, *n.* маргари́н *m.*

margin, *n.* край *m.*, грани́ца *f.*

marine, *adj.* морско́й. — *n.*
солда́т морско́й пехо́ты *m.*

mariner, *n.* моря́к *m.*

marital, *adj.* супру́жеский.

maritime, *adj.* морско́й; при-
мо́рский.

mark, *n.* знак *m.*, отме́тка *f.*
— *v.* отмеча́ть *imp.*, отме́-
тить *perf.*

market, *n.* продово́льствен-
ный магази́н; ры́нок *m.*

marmalade, *n.* варе́нье *nt.*

maroon, *n.* (*color*) кашта́но-
вый. — *n.* (*color*) кашта́но-
вый цвет. — *v.* выса́жи-
вать на необита́емый ост-
ров.

marriage, *n.* брак *m.*, сва́дьба *f.*

married, *adj.* (*man*) жена́тый;
(*woman*) заму́жняя. **to get
m.**, (*man*) жени́ться; (*woman*)
выходи́ть за́муж.

marrow, *n.* спинно́й мозг *m.*

marry, *v.* (*man*) жени́ться;
(*woman*) выходи́ть за́муж.

marsh, *n.* боло́то *nt.*

Martha, *n.* Ма́рфа *f.*

martial, *adj.* вое́нный.

martyr, *n.* му́ченик *m.* **-dom,** *n.* му́ченичество *nt*

marvel, *n* чу́до, ди́во *nt.* — *v.* удивля́ться *imp.* **-ous,** *adj.* чуде́сный.

masculine, *adj.* мужско́й; (*gram.*) мужско́го ро́да.

mash, *v.* размина́ть *imp.,* размя́ть *perf.* **mashed potatoes,** карто́фельное пюре́.

mask, *n.* ма́ска *f.* — *v.* маскирова́ть *imp.,* замаскирова́ть *perf.*

mason, *n.* ка́менщик *m.;* (*lodge*) масо́н *m.*

masquerade, *n.* маскара́д *m.*

mass, *n.* ма́сса *f.* — *adj.* ма́ссовый. — *v.* собира́ться *imp.,* собра́ться *perf.*

Mass, *n.* обе́дня *f.*

massacre, *n.* резня́ *f.* — *v.* производи́ть резню́.

massage, *n.* масса́ж *m.* — *v.* де́лать масса́ж.

masseur, *n.* массажи́ст *m.*

massive, *adj.* масси́вный.

mast, *n.* ма́чта *f.*

master, *n.* хозя́ин *m.;* ма́стер *m.* — *v.* овладе́ть *perf.* **-piece** *n.* шеде́вр *m.* **-y,** *n.* мастерство́, госпо́дство *nt.*

mat, *n.* мат *m.,* цыно́вка *f.* — *adj.* (*dull*) ма́товый.

match, *n.* спи́чка *f.;* (*athl.*) состяза́ние *nt.,* матч *m.* — *v.* подбира́ть под па́ру.

mate, *n.* това́рищ *m.;* (*spouse*) супру́г *m.,* супру́га *f.;* (*chess*) мат *m.* — *v.* спа́ривать *imp.;* (*chess*) сде́лать мат.

material, *n.* материа́л *m.,* мате́рия *f.* — *adj.* материа́льный. **-ism** *n.* материали́зм *m.* **-ize** *v. t.* материализова́ться *imp. & perf.*

maternal, *adj.* матери́нский.

maternity, *n.* матери́нство *nt.*

mathematical, *adj.* математи́ческий.

mathematics, *n.* матема́тика *f.*

matinée, *n* дневно́й спекта́кль

matrimony, *n.* супру́жество *nt.,* брак *m.*

matter, *n.* вещество́ *nt.;* де́ло *nt.,* вопро́с *m.* **what's the m.?** в чём де́ло ? — *v.* име́ть значе́ние.

Matthew, *n.* Мэ́тью *m. ind.;* (*Bible*) Матфе́й *m.*

mattress, *n.* матра́ц *m.*

mature, *adj.* зре́лый; спе́лый. — *v.* созрева́ть *imp.,* созре́ть *perf.*

maturity, *n.* зре́лость *f.*

maxim, *n.* ма́ксима *f.*

maximum, *adj.* максима́льный. — *n.* ма́ксимум *m.*

may, *v.* (*possibility*) мочь *imp.*

May, *n.* май *m.* — *adj.* ма́йский.

maybe, *adv.* мо́жет быть.

mayonnaise, *n.* майоне́з *m.*

mayor, *n.* мэр *m.*

me, *pron.* меня́, мне, мно́ю.

meadow, *n.* луг *m.*

meager, *n.* ухло́й, то́щий.

meal, *n.* еда́ *f.;* (*flour*) мука́ *f.*

mean, *adj.* (*base*) по́длый, плохо́й; (*average*) сре́дний. — *n.* середи́на *f.* — *v.* зна́чить *imp.* **-ing,** *n.* значе́ние *nt.*

means, *pl.* сре́дство *nt.,* сре́дства *pl.* **by no m.,** нико́им о́бразом. **m. of,** посре́дством *adv.* **m. of communication,** пути́ сообще́ния.

meanwhile, *adv.* тем вре́менем

measles, *n.* корь *f.*

measure, *n.* ме́ра *f.;* (*mus.*) такт *m.* **beyond m.,** чрезме́рно. — *v.* измеря́ть *imp.,* изме́рить *perf.* **-ment,** *n.* разме́ры *pl.,* измере́ние *nt.*

meat, *n.* мя́со *nt.* **-y,** *adj.* мяси́стый; содержа́тельный.

mechanic, *n.* меха́ник *m.* **-al,** *adj.* механи́ческий; (*fig.*) маши́нальный.

mechanism, *n.* механи́зм *m.*

mechanize, *v.* механизи́ровать *imp. & perf.*

nedal, *n.* меда́ль *f.;* о́рден *m.*

meddle, *v.* вме́шиваться *imp.,* вмеша́ться *perf.*

medical *adj.* медици́нский.

medicine, *n.* медицина *f.*, лекарство *nt.*

medieval, *adj.* средневековый.

mediocre, *adj.* посредственный.

meditate, *v.* размышлять *imp.*

meditation, *n.* размышление *nt.*

Mediterranean Sea, Средиземное море.

medium, *adj.* средний. — *n.* (*mean*) середина *f.*; (*means*) средство *nt.*

meek, *adj.* покорный. -ness, *n.* покорность *f.*

meet, *v. t.* встречать *imp.*, встретить *perf.* — *v. i.* встречаться *imp.*, встретиться *perf.* -ing, *n.* митинг *m.*, собрание *nt.*; (*encounter*) встреча *f.*

melancholy, *adj.* грустный. — *n.* уныние *nt.*, грусть *f.*

mellow, *adj.* мягкий, спелый.

melodious, *adj.* мелодический, мелодичный.

melodrama, *n.* мелодрама *f.*

melody, *n.* мелодия *f.*

melon, *n.* дыня *f.*

melt, *v. t.* распускать *imp.*, распустить *perf.* — *v. i.* распускаться *imp.*, распуститься *perf.*

member, *n.* член *m.* -ship, *n.* членство *nt.*, количество членов.

membrane, *n.* перепонка, плёнка, оболочка *f.*

memento, *n.* напоминание *nt.*

memoir, *n.* воспоминание *nt.*, воспоминания *pl.*

memorable, *adj.* памятный.

memorandum, *n.* меморандум *m.*, заметка *f.*

memorial, *adj.* мемориальный. — *n.* памятник *m.*

memorize, *v.* заучивать наизусть.

memory, *n.* память *f.*

menace, *n.* угроза *f.* — *v.* угрожать *imp.*, угрозить *perf.*

mend, *v.* чинить *imp.*, починить *perf.*

menopause, *n.* климактерический период.

menstruation, *n.* менструация *f.*

mental, *adj.* умственный; психический. -ity, *n.* интеллект *m.*, склад ума.

menthol, *n.* ментол *m.*

mention, *n.* упоминание *nt.* — *v.* упоминать *imp.*, упомянуть *perf.*

menu, *n.* меню *nt. ind.*

mercenary, *adj.* продажный. — *n.* наёмник *m.*

merchandise, *n.* товары *pl.* — *v.* торговать *imp.*

merchant, *adj.* торговый. — *n.* купец *m.*

merciful, *adj.* милосердный.

merciless, *adj.* безжалостный.

mercury, *n.* ртуть *f.*

mercy, *n.* милосердие *nt.*

mere, *adj.* простой. -ly, *adv.* только, просто.

merge, *v.* сливаться *imp.*, слиться *perf.*

merit, *n.* заслуга *f.* — *v.* заслуживать *imp.*, заслужить *perf.*

merry, *adj.* весёлый.

merry-go-round, *n.* карусель *f.*

mesh, *n.* сеть *f.*

mess, *n.* беспорядок *m.*; (*mil.*) общее питание, общий стол

message, *n.* донесение *nt.*; сообщение *nt.*

messenger, *n.* вестник, посыльный.

metabolism, *n.* метаболизм *m.*

metal, *n.* металл *m.*

metallic, *adj.* металлический.

metallurgy, *n.* металлургия *f.*

meteor, *n.* метеор *m.*

meteorology, *n.* метеорология *f.*

meter, *n.* счётчик *m.*; (*measure*) метр *m.*

method, *n.* метод *m.*, система *f.* -ical, *adj.* методический.

meticulous, *adj.* мелочный, дотошный.

metric, *adj.* метрический.

metropolis, *n.* метрополия *f.*; столица *f.*

metropolitan, *adj.* столичный.

Mexican, *adj.* мексика́нский.

Mexico, *n.* Ме́ксика *f.*

mezzanine, *n.* полуэта́ж *m.*

Michael, (*n.* Майкл *m.*; (*Bible*) Михаи́л *m.*

microbe, *n.* микро́б *m.*

microphone, *n.* микрофо́н *m.*

microscope, *n.* микроско́п *m.*

microscopic, *adj.* микроскопи́ческий.

mid, *adj.* сре́дний, средни́нный.

middle, *n.* середи́на *f.* **in the m.,** посреди́ *prep.* — *adj.* сре́дний **m.-aged,** *adj.* сре́дних лет.

midget, *n.* ка́рлик, лилипу́т *m.*

midnight, *n.* по́лночь *f.* — *adj.* полуно́чный.

midwife, *n.* акуше́рка *f.*

might, *n.* могу́щество *nt.*

mighty, *adj.* могу́щественный.

migraine, *n.* мигре́нь *f.*

migrate, *v.* переселя́ться *imp.*, пересели́ться *perf.*; мигри́ровать *imp.* & *perf.*

migration, *n.* переселе́ние *nt.*, мигра́ция *f.*

migratory, *adj.* перелётный.

mild, *adj.* уме́ренный, не́жный

mildew, *n.* пле́сень *f.*

mile, *n.* ми́ля *f.*

military, *adj.* во́инский, вое́нный.

milk, *n.* молоко́ *nt.* — *adj.* мле́чный. — *v.* дои́ть *imp.*, подои́ть *perf.* **-man,** *n.* разно́счик молока́. **-y,** *adj.* моло́чный.

mill, *n.* ме́льница *f.* — *v.* моло́ть *imp.*, смоло́ть *perf.*

millimeter, *n.* миллиме́тр *m.*

million, *n.* миллио́н *num.* **-aire,** *n.* миллионе́р *m.* **-th,** *adj.* миллио́нный,.

mimic, *n.* имита́тор, подража́тель *m.* — *v.* имити́ровать *imp.* & *perf.*

mind, *n.* ум, ра́зум *m.* — *v.t.* (*apply oneself to*) занима́ться *imp.*; (*object to*) возража́ть *imp.*, возрази́ть *perf.* **never m.,** ничего́. **-ful,** *adj.* по́мнящий, забо́тливый.

mine, *pron.* мой *m.*, моя́ *f.*, моё *nt.*, мои́ *pl.* — *n.* ша́хта

f.; (*explosive*) ми́на *f.* — *v.* (*mil.*) мини́ровать *imp.* & *perf.*

miner, *n.* горня́к, шахтёр *m.*

mineral, *n.* минера́л *m.* — *adj.* минера́льный.

mingle, *v.t.* сме́шивать *imp.*, смеша́ть *perf.* — *v. i.* сме́шиваться *imp.*, смеша́ться *perf.*

miniature, *n.* миниатю́ра *f.* — *adj.* миниатю́рный.

minimize, *v.* преуменьша́ть *imp.*, преуме́ньшить *perf.*

minimum, *n.* ми́нимум *m.* — *adj.* минима́льный.

mining, *n.* го́рное де́ло.

minister, *n.* мини́стр *m.*; (*eccles.*) свяще́нник *m.* — *v.* служи́ть *imp.*

ministry, *n.* министе́рство *nt.*, (*eccles.*) духове́нство *nt.*

mink, *n.* но́рка *f.*

minor, *n.* незначи́тельный; (*age*) мла́дший; (*mus.*) мино́рный. — *n.* несовершенноле́тний. (*mus.*) мино́р *m.*

minority, *n.* меньшинство́ *nt.*

mint, *n.* (*money*) моне́тный двор; (*plant*) мя́та *f.* — *v.* чека́нить *imp.*

minus, *prep.* без, ми́нус. — *adj.* отрица́тельный. — *n.* знак ми́нус.

minute, *adj.* (*small*) кро́шечный; (*time*) мину́тный. — *n.* мину́та *f.*

miracle, *n.* чу́до *nt.*

miraculous, *adj.* чудотво́рный, сверхъесте́ственный.

mirage, *n.* мира́ж *m.*

mirror, *n.* зе́ркало *nt.*

misbehave, *v.* ду́рно вести́ себя́.

miscellaneous, *adj.* разнообра́зный.

mischievous, *adj.* непослу́шный, озорно́й.

miser, *n.* скупе́ц *m.*

miserable, *adj.* жа́лкий, несча́стный.

misery, *n.* невзго́да *f.*; нищета́ *f.*

misfortune, *n.* несча́стье *nt.*

misgiving, *n.* опасе́ние *f.*, дурно́е предчу́вствие.

mishap, *n.* несча́стье *nt.*, неуда́ча *f.*

mislead, *v.* вводи́ть в заблужде́ние.

misplace, *v.* положи́ть не на ме́сто.

misprint, *n.* опеча́тка *f.*

mispronounce, *v.* произнести́ непра́вильно.

miss, *n.* (*young lady*) мисс *f. ind.*; (*failure*) про́мах *m.* — *v.* промахну́ться *perf.*; (*long for*) скуча́ть *imp.* **m. a train,** опозда́ть на по́езд.

missile, *n.* мета́тельный снаря́д.

missing, *adj.* отсу́тствующий; без ве́сти пропа́вший.

mission, *n.* ми́ссия *f.* **-ary,** *n.* миссионе́р *m.*

mist, *n.* тума́н *m.*

mistake, *n.* оши́бка *f.* **by m.,** по оши́бке. — *v.* приня́ть за (+ *acc.*) **to make a m.,** ошиби́ться *perf.*

mister, *n.* господи́н *m.*, ми́стер *m.*

mistreat, *v.* ду́рно обраща́ться

mistress, *n.* хозя́йка *f.*

mistrust, *v.* не доверя́ть *imp.* — *n.* недове́рие *nt.*

misty, *adj.* тума́нный; сму́тный

misunderstand, *v.* непра́вильно поня́ть.

misuse, *v.* злоупотребля́ть *imp.*, злоупотреби́ть *perf.* — *n.* злоупотребле́ние *nt.*

mitten, *n.* рукави́ца *f.*

mix, *v.t.* сме́шивать *imp.*, смеша́ть *perf.* — *v. i.* сме́шиваться *imp.*, смеша́ться *perf.* **-ture,** *n.* смесь *f.*

mix-up, *n.* пу́таница *f.*

moan, *n.* стон *m.* — *v.* стона́ть *imp.*

mob, *n.* толпа́ *f.*

mobilize, *v.* мобилизи́ровать *imp. & perf.*

mock, *v.* высме́ивать *imp.*

mode, *n.* (*manner*) о́браз де́йствия; спо́соб *m.*; (*fashion*) мо́да.

model, *n.* (*pattern*) моде́ль *f.*, образе́ц *m.* — *adj.* образцо́вый, приме́рный. — *v.*

(*shape*) модели́ровать *imp. & perf.*

moderate, *adj.* уме́ренный. — *v.* умеря́ть *imp.*, уме́рить *perf.*

moderation, *n.* уме́ренность *f.*

modern, *adj.* совреме́нный. **-ize,** *v.* модернзи́ровать *imp. & perf.*

modest, *adj.* скро́мный.

modesty, *n.* скро́мность *f.*

modify, *v.* видоизменя́ть *imp.*, видоизмени́ть *perf.*

modulate, *v.* модули́ровать *imp.*

moist, *adj.* сыро́й, вла́жный. **-en,** *v.* сма́чивать *imp.*, смочи́ть *perf.* **-ure,** *n.* вла́га *f.*, вла́жность *f.*

molar, *n.* коренно́й зуб.

molasses, *n.* па́тока *f.*

mold, *n.* фо́рма *f.*, шабло́н *m.*; (*fungus*) пле́сень *f.* — *v.* формова́ть *imp.*, сформова́ть *perf.*

moldy, *adj.* запле́сневелый.

mole, *n.* роди́нка *f.*; (*animal*) крот *m.*

molecule, *n.* моле́кула *f.*

molest, *v.* беспоко́ить *imp.*

moment, *n.* моме́нт *m.*; миг *m.* **-ary,** *adj.* момента́льный, мину́тный. **-ous,** *adj.* ва́жный.

monarch, *n.* мона́рх *m.*

monarchy, *n.* мона́рхия *f.*

monastery, *n.* монасты́рь *m.*

Monday, *n.* понеде́льник *m.*

monetary, *adj.* моне́тный, де́нежный.

money, *n.* де́ньги *pl.*

mongrel, *n.* ублю́док *m.* — *adj.* нечистокро́вный, сме́шанный

monk, *n.* мона́х *m.*

monkey, *n.* обезья́на *f.*

monologue, *n.* моноло́г *m.*

monopolize, *v.* монополизи́ровать *imp. & perf.*

monopoly, *n.* монопо́лия *f.*

monotonous, *adj.* моното́нный.

monster, *n.* уро́д *m.*

monstrous, *adj.* чудо́вищный, уро́дливый.

month, *n.* ме́сяц *m.* **-ly,** *adj.*

ежемéсячный. — adv. ежемéсячно.

monument, n. пáмятник, монумéнт m. **-al**, adj. монументáльный.

mood, n. настроéние nt.; (gram.) наклонéние nt. **-y**, adj. унылый.

moon, n. лунá f.

moor, n. вéресковая пýстошь. — v. пришвáртовывать imp., пришвартовáть perf.

moot point, спóрный вопрóс.

mop, n. швáбра f. — v. чистить швáброй

moral, adj. морáльный, нрáвственный. — n. морáль f.; (pl.) нрáвы pl. **-ity**, n. нрáвственное поведéние; нравоучéние nt.

morale, n. морáльное состояние.

morbid, adj. болéзненный, нездорóвый.

more, adj. бóльше. — n. бóльшее колúчество. — adv. бóльше, бóлее, ещё раз. **m. or less**, бóлее úли мéнее. **-over**, adv. сверх тогó, крóме тогó.

morgue, n. морг m.

morning, n. ýтро nt. **good m.**, дóброе ýтро. **in the m.**, ýтром.

morose, adj. угрюмый.

morphine, n. мóрфин m.

morsel, n. кусóчек m.

mortal, adj. смéртный, смертéльный. **-ity**, n. смéртность смертéльность f.

mortgage, n. ипотéка f., заклáдная f. — v. заклáдывать imp., заложить perf.

mosaic, n. мозáика f. — adj. мозáический.

Moscow, n. Москвá f.

Moses, n. (Bible) Моисéй m.

mosquito, n. москúт, комáр m.

moss, n. мох m.

most, adj. наибóльший. — n. наибóльшее колúчество. — adv. бóльше всегó. **at (the) m.**, сáмое бóльшее. **for the m. part**, бóльшей чáстью. **to make the m. of**, использовать наилýчшим óбразом. **-ly**, adv. по бóльшей чáсти; глáвным óбразом.

moth, n. моль f.

mother, n. мать f. **-hood**, n. матерúнство nt.

mother-in-law. n. (wife's mother) тёща f. (husband's mother) свекрóвь f.

motion, n. движéние nt., жест m. — v. покáзывать жéстом. **-less**, adj. неподвúжный.

motion picture, кинокартúна f., кинó nt., фильм m.

motivate, v. мотивúровать imp. & perf.

motive, n. мотúв m., побуждéние nt.

motor, n. мотóр m., двúгатель m. **-cycle**, n. мотоцúкл m. **-ist**, n. автомобилúст m.

motto, n. девúз, лóзунг m.

mound, n насыпь f.

mount, n. холм m., горá f. — v.t. вставлять imp., встáвить perf. — v.i. садúться на лóшадь.

mountain, n. горá f. **m. range**, хребéт m., горéц m.; (climber) альпинúст m. **-ous**, adj. горúстый.

mourn, v. оплáкивать imp. **-ful**, adj. печáльный. **-ing**, n. трáур m.

mouse, n. мышь f.

moustache, n. усы pl.

mouth, n. рот m.; (of river) ýстье nt.

move, n. ход m.; (abode) перемéна жилúща. — v. t. двúгать imp., двúнуть perf. — v. i. двúгаться imp., двúнуться perf.; (abode) переезжáть imp., переéхать perf. **-ment**, n. движéние nt.

moving, adj. движущийся, (fig.) трогáтельный.

mow, v. косúть imp., скосúть perf.

Mr., господúн m.

Mrs., госпожá f.

much, adj., adv. мнóго. **how m.**, скóлько. **so m.**, стóлько. **as m. as**, стóлько. . . скóлько.

mucous, adj. слúзистый.

mud, *n.* грязь *f.*

muddy, *adj.* грязный.

mug, *n.* кружка *f.*

mulatto, *n.* мулат *m.*, мулатка *f.*

mule, *n.* мул *m.*

multiple, *adj.* многократный.

multiplication, *n.* умножение *nt.*

multiplier, *n.* множитель *m.*

multiply, *v.t.* множить *imp.*, умножить *perf.* — *v.i.* увеличиваться *imp.*, увеличиться *perf.*; размножаться *imp.*, размножиться *perf.*

multitude, *n.* множество *nt.*

mumps, *n.* свинка *f.*

municipal, *adj.* муниципальный. -ity, *n.* муниципалитет *m.*

munificent, *adj.* щедрый.

munition, *n.* снаряжение *nt.*

mural, *adj.* стенной. — *n.* фреска *f.*

murder, *n.* убийство *nt.* — *v.* убивать *imp.*, убить *perf.* -er, *n.* убийца *m. & f.* (declined as *f.*).

murmur, *n.* журчание *nt.* — *v.* журчать *imp.*, шелестеть *perf.*

muscle, *n.* мускул *m.*

muscular, *adj.* мускульный, мускулистый.

muse, *n.* муза *f.* — *v.* размышлять *imp.*

museum, *n.* музей *m.*

mushroom, *n.* гриб *m.*

music, *n.* музыка *f.* -al, *adj.* музыкальный. — *n.* музыкальная комедия.

musician, *n.* музыкант *m.*

muslin, *n.* муслин *m.*

must, *v.* должен *m.*, должна *f.*, должно *nt.*, должны *pl.*

mustard, *n.* горчица *f.*

mute, *adj.* молчаливый; немой. — *n.* немой *m.*

mutilate, *v.* искажать *imp.*, исказить *perf.*

mutiny, *n.* мятеж *f.* — *v.* поднять мятеж.

mutter, *v.* бормотать *imp.*

mutton, *n.* баранина *f.*

mutual, *adj.* взаимный.

muzzle, *n.* намордник *m.* — *v.* заставить молчать.

my, *pron.* мой *m.*, моя *f.*, моё *nt.*, мои *pl.*

myriad, *n.* мириады *pl.*

myself, *pron.* сам *m.*, сама *f.*, само *nt.*; (refl.) себя. I m., я сам *m.*, я сама *f.*

mysterious, *adj.* таинственный.

mystery, *n.* таинство *nt.*, тайна *f.*

mystic, *adj.* мистический. — *n.* мистик *m.*

mystify, *v.* мистифицировать *imp. & perf*

myth, *n.* миф *m.* -ical, *adj.* мифический. -ology, *n.* мифология *f.*

N

nail, *n.* гвоздь *m.*; (finger) ноготь *m.* — *v.* прибивать *imp.*, прибить *perf.*

naïve, *adj.* наивный.

naked, *adj.* голый, нагой.

name, *n.* (first) имя *nt.* in the name of, во имя. — *v.* называть *imp*, назвать *perf.*; назначать *imp.*, назначить *perf.* -ly, *adv.* а именно.

nap, *n.* дремота *f.* to take a nap, вздремнуть *perf.*

naptha, *n.* керосин *m.*

napkin, *n.* салфетка *f.*

narcotic, *adj.* наркотический. — *n.* наркотическое средство.

narrate, *v.* рассказывать *imp.*, рассказать *perf.*

narrative, *adj.* повествовательный. — *n.* рассказ *m.*

narrow, *adj.* узкий, тесный.

nasal, *adj.* носовой. — *n.* (phon.) носовой звук.

nasty, *adj.* скве́рный, га́дкий.

Natalie, *n.* Ната́лия *f.*

nation, *n.* наро́д *m.*

national, *adj.* наро́дный, национа́льный. **-ism,** *n.* национали́зм *m.* **-ity,** *n.* наро́дность, национа́льность *f.* **-ization,** *n.* национализа́ция *f.* **-ize,** *v.* национализи́ровать *imp. & perf.*

native, *adj.* родно́й; тузе́мный. — *n.* уроже́нец, тузе́мец *m.*

natural, *adj.* есте́ственный, натура́льный. **-ize,** *v.* натурализова́ть *imp. & perf.* be naturalized, натурализова́ться *imp. & prrf.*

nature, *n.* приро́да *f.*; нату́ра *f.*

naughty, *adj.* непослу́шный.

nausea, *n.* тошнота́ *f.*

nauseous, *adj.* тошнотво́рный.

nautical, *adj.* морско́й, мореходный.

naval, *adj.* флотский.

navel, *n.* пуп, пупо́к *m.*

navigable, *adj.* судохо́дный.

navigate, *v.* управля́ть судно́м.

navigation, *n.* навига́ция *f.*

navigator, *n.* морепла́ватель *m.*; штурма́н *m.*

navy, *n.* вое́нно-морско́й флот *m.*

near, *adj.* бли́зкий; сосе́дний. — *adv.* бли́зко, недалеко́, о́коло. — *prep.* у, о́коло (& *gen.*) **-ly,** *adv.* почти́.

near-sighted, *adj.* близору́кий.

neat, *adj.* опря́тный. **-ness,** *n.* опря́тность *f.*

nebulous, *adj.* о́блачный, тума́нный.

necessarily, *adv.* необходи́мо.

necessary, *adj.* необходи́мый.

necessity, *n.* необходи́мость *f.*

neck, *n.* ше́я *f.* **-lace,** *n.* ожере́лье *nt.* **-tie,** *n.* га́лстук *m.*

need, *n.* нужда́ *f.* — *v.* нужда́ться *imp.*

needle, *n.* игла́, иго́лка *f.*

needless, *adj.* нену́жный.

negative, *adj.* отрица́тельный. — *n.* (*negation*) отрица́ние *nt.*

neglect, *n.* пренебреже́ние *nt.* — *v.* пренебрега́ть *imp.*

negligee, *n.* да́мский хала́т.

negligence, *n.* небре́жность *f.*

negligent, *adj.* небре́жный.

negligible, *adj.* незначи́тельный.

negotiate, *v.* догова́риваться *imp.,* договори́ться *perf.*

negotiation, *n.* перегово́ры *pl.*

Negro, *n.* негр *m.,* негритя́нка *f.* — *adj.* негритя́нский.

neighbor, *n.* сосе́д *m.,* сосе́дка *f.* **-hood,** *n.* сосе́дство *nt.*

neither, *adj.* ни тот ни друго́й. — *pron.* ни оди́н, никто́, никако́й. — *adv.* та́кже не. **neither . . . nor,** ни . . . ни.

neon, *n.* нео́н *m.* **n. light,** нео́новый свет.

nephew, *n.* племя́нник *m.*

nerve, *n.* нерв *m.*; (*impudence*) наха́льство *nt.*

nervous, *adj.* не́рвный.

nest, *n.* гнездо́ *nt.*

net, *adj.* не́тто. — *n.* сеть *f.* — *v.* приноси́ть чи́стый дохо́д.

Netherlands, The, *pl.* Нидерла́нды *pl.*

neurotic, *adj.* невроти́ческий.

neutral, *adj.* нейтра́льный. **-ity,** *n.* нейтралите́т *m.*

never, *adv.* никогда́.

nevertheless, *adv.* тем не ме́нее.

new, *adj.* но́вый.

news, *n.* но́вость *f.,* изве́стие *nt.* **-paper,** *n.* газе́та *f.* **-reel,** *n.* кино́ хро́ника *f.,* киножурна́л *m.*

New Zealand, Но́вая Зела́ндия

next, *adj.* сле́дующий, ближа́йший. — *adv.* зате́м, пото́м. **n. to,** ря́дом, о́коло

nice, *adj.* прия́тный, хоро́ший.

Nicholas, *n.* Никола́й *m.*

nickel, *n.* ни́кель *m.*

nickname, *n.* про́звище *nt.* — *v.* дава́ть про́звище.

nicotine, *n.* никоти́н *m.*

niece, *n.* племя́нница *f.*

Nigeria, *n.* Ниге́рия *f.*

night, *n.* ночь *f.* **at n.,** но́чью. **good n.,** споко́йной но́чи. **last n.,** вчера́ ве́чером. **and day,** днём и но́чью. **-gown,** *n.* ночна́я руба́шка. **-mare,** *n.* кошма́р *m.*

nightingale, *n.* соловей *m.*

nimble, *adj.* гибкий, проворный.

nine, *n.* девять *num.* девятка *f.*; (*colloq.*) — *adj.* девять *num.* -**teen,** *adj.*, *n.* девятнадцать *num.* -**ty,** *adj.*, *n.* девяносто *num.*

ninth, *n.* девятая; девятая часть.

nipple, *n.* соска *f.*; (*anat.*) сосок *m.*

nitrogen, *n.* азот *m.*

no, *adj.* никакой. — *adv.* нет.

Noah, *n.* (*Bible*) Ной *m.*

noble, *adj.* знатный, благородный. — *n.* дворянин *m.*

nobody, *pron.* никто. — *n.* ничтожество *nt.*

nocturnal, *adj.* ночной.

nod, *n.* кивок *m.* — *v.* кивать головой.

noise, *n.* шум *m.* -**less,** *adj.* бесшумный.

noisy, *adj.* шумный.

nominal, *adj.* номинальный, именной.

nominate, *v.* выставлять кандидатуру.

nomination, *n.* выставление кандидата.

nominee, *n.* кандидат *m.*

noncommittal, *adj.* уклончивый.

nondescript, *adj.* неопределённого вида.

none, *pron.* никто, ничто.

nonsense, *n.* вздор *m.*, пустяки *pl.*

nonstop, *adj.* безостановочный, беспосадочный.

noon, *n.* полдень *m.*

noose, *n.* петля *f.*, аркан *m.*

nor, *conj.* также не; ни.

normal, *adj.* нормальный, обычный.

north, *n.* север *m.* — *adv.* северу, на север.

northeast, *n.* северо-восток *m.* — *adv.* на северо-восток. -**ern,** *adj.* северо-восточный.

northern, *adj.* северный. -**er,** *n.* северянин *m.*, северянка *f.*

North Pole, Северный полюс.

northwest, *n.* северо-запад *m.*

— *adv.* на северо-запад. -**ern,** *adj.* северо-западный.

Norway, *n.* Норвегия *f.*

Norwegian, *adj.* норвежский. — *n.* норвежец *m.*, норвежка *f.*

nose, *n.* нос *m.*

nostalgia, *n.* ностальгия *f.*

nostril, *n.* ноздря *f.*

not, *adv.* не, нет. **not at all,** совсем не (нет).

notable, *adj.* выдающийся, значительный.

notation, *n.* нотация *f.*; система обозначения.

notch, *n.* выемка, зарубка *f.*

note, *n.* записка *f.*; (*mus.*) нота *f.* — *v.* замечать *imp.*, заметить *perf.*

notebook, *n.* записная книжка.

noteworthy, *adj.* заслуживающий внимания.

nothing, *pron.* ничто; ничего; (zero) нуль *m.*

notice, *n.* объявление *nt.* — *v.* замечать *imp.*, заметить *perf.* -**able,** *adj.* заметный.

notify, *v.* уведомлять *imp.*, уведомить *perf.*

notion, *n.* понятие, мнение *nt.*

notorious, *adj.* пресловутый.

noun, *n.* имя существительное

nourish, *v.* питать *imp.* -**ment,** *n.* питание *nt.*, пища *f.*

novel, *adj.* новый. — *n.* роман *m.* -**ist,** *n.* романист *m.*, писатель *m.* -**ty,** *n.* новизна *f.*

November, *n.* ноябрь *m.* — *adj.* ноябрьский.

novice, *n.* новичок *m.*

novocaine, *n.* новокаин *m.*

now, *adv.* теперь; тотчас же.

nowhere, *adv.* (*dir.*) никуда; (*loc.*) нигде.

nucleus, *n.* ядро *nt.*, ячейка *f.*

nude, *adj.* нагой. — *n.* обнажённая фигура.

nuisance, *n.* досада *f.*

nullify, *v.* аннулировать *imp. & perf.*

numb, *adj.* онемелый.

number, *n.* количество *nt.*, номер *m.*; (*gram.*) число *nt.* — *v.* нумеровать *imp. & perf.*

numerical, *adj.* числово́й, цифрово́й.

numerous, *adj.* многочи́сленный; *(many)* мно́гие *pl.*

nun, *n.* мона́хиня *f.*

nuptial, *adj.* бра́чный.

nuptials, *n.* сва́дьба *f.*

nurse, *n.* медици́нская сестра́; *(child's)* ня́ня *f.* — *v.* уха́живать за больны́м.

nurture, *v.* воспи́тывать *imp.*, пита́ть *imp.*

nut, *n.* оре́х *m.*; *(mach.)* га́йка *f.*

nutrition, *n.* пита́ние *nt.*

nutritious, *adj.* пита́тельный.

nylon, *n.* нейло́н *m.* — *adj.* нейло́новый.

nymph, *n.* ни́мфа *f.*

O

oak, *n.* дуб *m.* — *adj.* дубо́вый.

oar, *n.* весло́ *nt.*

oasis, *n.* оа́зис *m.*

oat, *n.* овёс *m.* — *adj.* овся́ный, овся́ной.

oath, *n.* кля́тва *f.*

oatmeal, *n.* овся́нка *f.*

obedience, *n.* послуша́ние *nt.*

obedient, *adj.* послу́шный.

obese, *adj.* ту́чный.

obey, *v.* слу́шаться *imp.*

obituary, *n.* некроло́г *m.*

object, *n.* цель *f.*; предме́т *m.*; *(gram.)* дополне́ние *nt.* — *v.* протестова́ть *imp.*, возража́ть *imp.*, возрази́ть *perf.*

objection, *n.* возраже́ние *nt.* -**able,** *adj.* вызыва́ющий возраже́ние.

objective, *adj.* объекти́вный. — *n.* стремле́ние *nt.*, цель *f.*

obligation, *n.* обяза́тельство *nt.*

obligatory, *adj.* обяза́тельный.

oblige, *v.* обя́зывать *imp.*, обяза́ть *perf.*; заставля́ть *imp.*, заста́вить *perf.*

oblique, *adj.* косо́й; ко́свенный.

obliterate, *v.* стира́ть *imp.*, стере́ть *perf.*

oblivion, *n.* забве́ние *nt.*

oblong, *adj.* продолгова́тый.

obnoxious, *adj.* проти́вный.

obscene, *adj.* неприли́чный, непристо́йный.

obscenity, *n.* непристо́йность *f.*

obscure, *adj.* мра́чный; ту́-
склый. — *v.* затмева́ть *imp.*, затми́ть *perf.*

observance, *n.* соблюде́ние *nt.*; обря́д *m.*

observant, *adj.* наблюда́тельный.

observation, *n.* наблюде́ние *nt.*; замеча́ние *nt.*

observatory, *n.* обсервато́рия *f.*

observe, *v.* наблюда́ть *imp.*

observer, *n.* наблюда́тель *m.*

obsession, *n.* наважде́ние *nt.*; ма́ния *f.*

obsolete, *adj.* устаре́лый.

obstacle, *n.* препя́тствие *nt.*

obstinate, *adj.* упря́мый.

obstetrician, *n.* акушёр *m.*, акуше́рка *f.*

obstruct, *v.* препя́тствовать *imp.*; загражда́ть *imp.*, загради́ть *perf.* -**ion,** *n.* препя́тствие *nt.*; обстру́кция *f.*

obtain, *v.* получа́ть *imp.*, получи́ть *perf.*; добыва́ть *imp.*, добы́ть *perf.*

obtuse, *adj.* тупо́й.

obvious, *adj.* очеви́дный.

occasion, *n.* слу́чай *m.*, возмо́жность *f.* -**al,** *adj.* случа́йный; случа́ющийся вре́мя от вре́мени. -**ally,** *adv.* иногда́, и́зредка.

occupant, *n.* оккупа́нт *m.*; занима́ющий ме́сто.

occupation, *n.* заня́тие *nt.*, до́лжность *f.*

occupy, *v.* занима́ть *imp.*, заня́ть *perf.*

occur, v. случа́ться imp., случи́ться perf.

occurrence, n. собы́тие nt.

ocean, n. океа́н m.

o'clock, час m. **ten o'clock**, де́сять часо́в.

octagon, n. восьмиуго́льник m.

octave, n. окта́ва f.

October, n. октя́брь m. — adj. октя́брьский.

octopus, n. осьмино́г m.

oculist, n. окули́ст m.

odd, adj. стра́нный, необы́чный; (number) нечётный.

odious, adj. отврати́тельный.

odor, n. за́пах m.; арома́т m.

of, prep. с, со; от (+ gen.); (about) о, об (+ prep.).

off, prep. с, со; от (+ gen.).

offend, v. обижа́ть imp., оби́деть perf. **-er**, n. оби́дчик m.; (law) престу́пник m.

offense, n. оби́да f.; (law) просту́пок m., преступле́ние nt.

offensive, adj. оби́дный; наступа́тельный. — n. наступле́ние nt.

offer, n. предложе́ние n. — v. предлага́ть imp., предложи́ть perf. **-ing**, n. предложе́ние nt.; же́ртва f.

offhand, adv. экспро́мтом, без подгото́вки. — adj. сде́ланный без подгото́вки; импровизи́рованный.

office, n. конто́ра f.

officer, n. офице́р m., должностно́е лицо́.

official, adj. официа́льный, служе́бный. — n. служе́бное лицо́.

officiate, v. исполня́ть обя́занности.

offspring, n. пото́мок, о́тпрыск m.

often, adv. ча́сто.

oil, n. ма́сло nt.; (petroleum) нефть f. — v. сма́зывать imp., сма́зать perf.

oily, adj. масляни́стый.

ointment, n. мазь f.; притира́ние nt.

old, adj. ста́рый. **old age**, ста́рость f., прекло́нные

го́ды. **old man**, стари́к m. **old woman**, стару́ха f.

old-fashioned, adj. старомо́дный.

Olga, n. О́льга f.

olive, n. оли́ва f.

omelet, n. омле́т m.

omen, n. предзнаменова́ние nt.

ominous, adj. злове́щий.

omission, n. про́пуск m.

omit, v. пропуска́ть imp., пропусти́ть perf.

omnipotent, adj. всемогу́щий.

on, prep. на (+ prep.); (onto) на (+ acc.); (about) о, об, обо (+ prep.) — adv. да́льше, вперёд.

once, adv. раз; одна́жды.

one, adj. оди́н n.; оди́н m.; едини́ца f. — pron. не́кто.

oneself, pron. себя́; сам, себе́.

onion, n. лук m.

only, adj. еди́нственный. — adv. то́лько, еди́нственно. **not only . . . but also**, не то́лько . . . но та́кже.

onward, adv. вперёд.

opaque, adj. непрозра́чный.

open, adj. откры́тый. — v.t. открыва́ть imp., откры́ть perf. — v. i. открыва́ться imp., откры́ться perf. **-ing**, n. отве́рстие nt.; (start) нача́ло nt. — adj. нача́льный, пе́рвый.

opera, n. о́пера f.

operate, v. управля́ть imp.; (surgery) опери́ровать imp. & perf.

operation, n. де́йствие nt., проце́сс m.; (surgery) опера́ция f.

operative, adj. де́йствующий, операти́вный; (surgery) операцио́нный.

operator, n. управля́ющий маши́ной.

operetta, n. опере́тта f.

opinion, n. мне́ние nt. **in my o.**, по-мо́ему.

opponent, n. проти́вник, оппоне́нт m.

opportunist, n. оппортуни́ст m.

opportunity, n. удобный случай.

oppose, v. сопротивляться imp,. противиться imp.

opposite, adj. противоположный. — prep. напротив; против (+ gen.) — n. противоположность f.

opposition, n. сопротивление nt.; оппозиция f.

oppress, v. притеснять imp,. угнетать imp.

oppression, n. притеснение nt. угнетение nt.

oppressive, adj. гнетущий.

optical, adj. зрительный, оптический.

optician, n. оптик m.

optics, n. оптика f.

optimism, n. оптимизм m.

optimistic, adj. оптимистический.

option, n. выбор m.

or, conj. или.

oral, adj. устный.

orange, n. апельсин m.; (color) оранжевый свет. — adj. оранжевый, апельсиновый.

oration, n. речь f.

orator, n. оратор m.

oratory, n. красноречие nt., риторика f.

orbit, n. орбита f.

orchard, n. сад m.

orchestra, n. оркестр m.; (theat.) партер m.

orchestrate, v. инструментировать, инструментовать imp. & perf.

orchestration, n. оркестровка f.

orchid, n. орхидея f.

ordeal, n. тяжёлое испытание.

order, n. порядок m.; (command) приказ m., распоряжение nt.; (business) заказ m. **in order to,** для того чтобы. — v. приказывать imp., приказать perf.; заказывать imp., заказать perf. **-ly,** adj. аккуратный, опрятный; методичный. — n. дежурный, санитар m.

ordinance, n. закон, декрет .m

ordinary, adj. обычный; простой.

ore, n. руда f.

organ, n. орган m.; (mus. орган m.

organdy, n. органди f. ind.

organic, adj. органический.

organism, n. организм m.

organist, n. органист m.

organization, n. организация f., устройство nt.

organize, v. организовать imp & perf.

orgasm, n. оргазм m.

orgy, n. оргия f.

orient, n. восток m. — v ориентировать imp. & perf -al, adj. восточный, азиатский. — n. (cap.) житель Востока.

orientation, n. ориентация f

origin, n. источник m., начало nt.; происхождение nt. **-al** adj. первоначальный, подлинный, оригинальный. — n. подлинник m. **-ity,** n подлинность f., оригинальность f.

ornament, n. украшение m орнамент m. — v. украшать imp., украсить perf. **-al,** adj декоративный, орнаментальный.

ornithology, n. орнитология f

orphan, n. сирота m. & f. **-age** n. приют для сирот.

orthodox, adj. ортодоксальный; (religion) православный.

ostentatious, adj. показной.

ostrich, n. страус m.

other, adj. другой, иной. — pron. другой.

otherwise, adv. иначе; в противном случае.

ought, v. должен бы m должна бы f., должно бы nt., должны бы pl.

ounce, n. унция f.

our, ours, adj. or pron. наш m наша f., наше nt., наши pl

ourselves, pron. себя, себе сами.

oust, v. вытеснять imp., вытеснить perf.

out, *adv.* из; вне, наружу; вон. be out, не быть до́ма. out of, *prep.* из, и́зо (+*gen.*)

outbreak, *n.* взрыв *m.*, вспы́шка *f.*

outcast, *n.* изгна́нник *m.*

outdoor, *adj.* находя́щийся на откры́том во́здухе.

outer, *adj.* вне́шний, нару́жный.

outfit, *n.* снаряже́ние *nt.*, экипиро́вка *f.* — *v.* снаряжа́ть *imp.*, снаряди́ть *perf.*; экипирова́ть *imp. & perf.*

outgrowth, *n.* отро́сток, о́тпрыск *m.*; результа́т *m.*

outing, *n.* экску́рсия *f.*

outlaw, *n.* изго́й, изгна́нник *m.*, челове́к вне зако́на. — *v.* объявля́ть вне зако́на.

outlet, *n.* вы́ход *m.*, (*business*) ры́нок сбы́та.

outline, *n.* очерта́ние *nt.*, эски́з, о́черк *m.* — *v.* наме́тить в о́бщих черта́х.

outlive, *v.* пережи́ть *perf.*

out-of-date, *adj.* старомо́дный, устаре́лый.

output, *n.* вы́пуск *m.*, производи́тельность, проду́кция *f.*

outrageous, *adj.* неи́стовый, оскорби́тельный.

outrun, *v.* перегоня́ть *imp.*, перегна́ть *perf.*

outside, *adj.* вне́шний, нару́жный. — *adv.* нару́жу, изви́не. — *n.* вне́шность *f.* — *prep.* вне, за преде́лами, за преде́лы.

outskirts, *n.* окра́ина *f.*, предме́стье *nt.*

outward, *adj.* нару́жный.

outwards, *adv.* нару́жу.

oval, *n.* ова́л *m.* — *adj.* ова́льный, яйцеви́дный.

ovary, *n.* яи́чник *m.*

ovation, *n.* ова́ция *f.*

oven, *n.* печь *f.*

over, *prep.* над, сверх, вы́ше; че́рез. — *adv.*, *designated in Russian by the prefixes*: пере-, вы-.

overcoat, *n.* пальто́ *nt. ind.*, шине́ль *f.*

overcome, *v.* превозмо́чь *perf.*

overdue, *adj.* запозда́лый, просро́ченный.

overflow, *n.* разли́в *m.*; избы́ток *m.* — *v.* перели́ться че́рез край.

overhaul, *v.* ремонти́ровать *imp. & perf.*

overhead, *adv.* над голово́й, наверху́.

overlook, *v.t.* просмотре́ть *perf.* — *v. i.* выходи́ть на.

overnight, *adv.* накану́не ве́чером.

overpower, *v.* переси́ливать *imp.*, пересили́ть *perf.*

overrule, *v.* аннули́ровать *imp. & perf.*, отверга́ть предложе́ние.

oversee, *v.* надзира́ть *imp.*

oversight, *n.* недосмо́тр *m.*

overtake, *v.* догна́ть *perf.*

overthrow, *n.* ниспроверже́ние *nt.* — *v.* сверга́ть *imp.*, све́ргнуть *perf.*

overtime, *n.* сверхуро́чное вре́мя. — *adj.* сверхуро́чный.

overture, *n.* увертю́ра *f.*

overturn, *v.t.* опроки́дывать *imp.*, опроки́нуть *perf.* — *v.i.* опроки́дываться *imp.*, опроки́нуться *perf.*

overwhelm, *v.* овладева́ть *imp.*, овладе́ть *perf.*; подавля́ть *imp.*, подави́ть *perf.* -ing, подавля́ющий.

overwork, *v.* переутомля́ться *imp.*, переутоми́ться *perf.* — *n.* переутомле́ние *nt.*

owe, *v.* быть в долгу́; быть обя́занным.

owing to, по причи́не, всле́дствие, благодаря́.

owl, *n.* сова́ *f.*

own, *adj.* со́бственный. — *v.* име́ть *imp.*, владе́ть *imp.* -er, *n.* владе́лец *m.*

ox, *n.* бык, вол *m.*

oxygen, *n.* кислоро́д *m.* — *adj.* кислоро́дный.

oyster, *n.* у́стрица *f.*

P

pace, *n.* шаг *m.* — *v.* шага́ть *imp.*

Pacific Ocean, Ти́хий океа́н.

pacify, *v.* успока́ивать *imp.*, успоко́ить *perf.*

pack, *n.* па́чка *f.*, тюк *m.* паке́т *m.*; (*cards*) коло́да *f.* — *v.* упако́вывать *imp.*, упакова́ть *perf.*; набива́ть *imp.*, наби́ть *perf.*

package, *n.* тюк *m.*; упако́вка *f.*

pact, *n.* пакт, догово́р *m.*

padlock, *n.* вися́чий замо́к.

paddle, *n.* гребо́к *m.*, гребля́ *f.* — *v.* грести́ весло́м.

pagan, *adj.* язы́ческий. — *n.* язы́чник *m.*

page, *n.* страни́ца *f.*

pail, *n.* ведро́ *nt.*

pain, *n.* боль *f.* **-ful**, *adj.* боле́зненный. **-less**, *adj.* безболе́зненный.

paint, *n.* кра́ска *f.* — *v.* писа́ть кра́сками; кра́сить *imp.* **-er**, *n.* маля́р *m.*; (*artist*) живопи́сец, худо́жник *m.* **-ing**, *n.* карти́на *f.*; (*act*) жи́вопись *f.*

pair, *n.* па́ра *f.* — *v.* спа́ривать *imp.*, спа́рить *perf.* **pair off**, разделя́ться на па́ры.

pajamas, *n.* пижа́ма *f.*

palace, *n.* дворе́ц *m.*

palate, *n.* нёбо *nt.*

pale, *adj.* бле́дный. **to turn p.**, бледне́ть *imp.*, побледне́ть *perf.*

pallid, *adj.* бле́дный.

palm, *n.* ладо́нь *f.* **p. tree**, па́льма *f.*

palpitate, *v.* пульси́ровать *imp.*

palpitation, *n.* бие́ние *nt.*, пульса́ция *f.*

pamper, *v.* балова́ть *imp.*

pamphlet, *n.* брошю́ра *f.*

pan, *n.* сковорода́ *f.*

pancake, *n.* блин *m.*

pane, *n.* око́нное стекло́.

panel, *n.* филёнка *f.*, пане́ль *f.*

pang, *n.* о́страя боль.

panic, *n.* па́ника *f.*

panicky. *adj.* пани́ческий.

panorama, *n.* панора́ма *f.*

pant, *v.* дыша́ть *imp.*

panther, *n.* панте́ра *f.*

pantomime, *n.* пантоми́ма *f.*

pantry, *n.* кладова́я *f.*

pants, *n.* брю́ки, кальсо́ны *pl.*

papal, *adj.* па́пский.

paper, *n.* бума́га *f.* — *adj.* бума́жный.

par, *n.* ра́венство *f.* **on a par with**, наравне́.

parachute, *n.* парашю́т *m.*

parade, *n.* пара́д *m.* — *v.* марширова́ть *imp.*

paradise, *n.* рай *m.*

paradox, *n.* парадо́кс *m.*

paragraph, *n.* пара́граф, абза́ц *m.*

parallel, *n.* паралле́ль *f.* — *adj.* паралле́льный. — *v.* уподобля́ть *imp.*, уподо́бить *perf.*

paralysis, *n.* парали́ч *m.*

paralyze, *v.* парализова́ть *imp.* & *perf.*

paraphrase, *v.* перефрази́ровать *imp.* & *perf.* — *n.* перефра́за *f.*, переска́з *m.*

parasite, *n.* парази́т *m.*

parasitic, *adj.* парази́тный, паразити́ческий.

parcel, *n.* паке́т, тюк *m.*

pardon, *n.* проще́ние, извине́ние *nt.* — *v.* проща́ть *imp.*, прости́ть *perf.*; извиня́ть *imp.*, извини́ть *perf.* **p. me!** извини́те!

pare, *v.* среза́ть *perf.*

parent, *n.* роди́тель *m.*

parenthesis, *n.* кру́глые ско́бки.

Paris, Пари́ж *m.* **-ian**, *adj.* пари́жский. — *n.* парижа́нин *m.*, парижа́нка *f.*

park, *n.* парк *m.* — *v.* ста́вить *imp.*

parley, *n.* совеща́ние *nt.*, перегово́ры *pl.*

parliament, *n.* парла́мент *m.* **-ary**, *adj.* парла́ментский, парламента́рный.

parlor, *n.* гости́ная *f.*

parody, *n.* паро́дия *f.* — *v.*

пароди́ровать *imp. & perf.*

parrot, *n.* попуга́й *m.*

parsimonious, *adj.* скупо́й.

parsley, *n.* петру́шка *f.*

part, *n.* часть *f.*; уча́стие *nt.*; (role) роль *f.* — *v. t.* разлуча́ть *imp.*, разлучи́ть *perf.* — *v.i.* разлуча́ться *imp.*, разлучи́ться *imp.* **p. with,** расстава́ться *imp.*, расста́ться *perf.*

partial, *adj.* части́чный.

participant, *n.* уча́стник *m.*

participate, *v.* уча́ствовать *imp.*

participation, *n.* уча́стие *nt.*

participle, *n.* прича́стие *nt.*

particle, *n.* части́ца *f.*

particular, *adj.* осо́бенный. — *n.* дета́ль, подро́бность *f.* **-ly,** *adv.* осо́бенно.

parting, *n.* расстава́ние *nt.*, разлу́ка *f.*

partisan, *adj.* партиза́нский. — *n.* партиза́н *m.*; сторо́нник *m.*

partition, *n.* расчлене́ние *nt.*

partly, *adv.* части́чно, о́тчасти.

partner, *n.* партнёр *m.*; компаньо́н *m.*

part of speech, (*gram.*) часть ре́чи.

party, *n.* ве́чер *m.*, вечери́нка *f.*; приём госте́й; (*political*) па́ртия *f.* — *adj.* парти́йный.

pass, *n.* прохо́д *m.*; про́пуск *m.*; (*cards*) пас *m.*; (*geog.*) уще́лье *nt.* — *v.* проходи́ть *imp.*, пройти́ *perf.*; (*exam*) сдава́ть *imp.*, сдать *perf.*; (*cards*) пасова́ть *imp. & perf.* **p. away,** сконча́ться *perf.*

passage, *n.* пое́здка *f.*, перее́зд *m.*; рейс *m.*; (*corridor*) прохо́д, коридо́р.

passenger, *n.* пассажи́р *m.* пассажи́рка *f.*

passer-by, *n.* прохо́жий *m.*

passion, *n.* страсть *f.* **-ate,** *adj.* стра́стный.

passive, *adj.* пасси́вный, ине́ртный; (*gram.*) страда́тельный.

passport, *n.* па́спорт *m.*

past, *adj.* про́шлый; (*gram.*)

проше́дший. — *n.* про́шлое *nt.* — *prep.* ми́мо (+ *gen.*); по́сле (+ *gen.*), за (+ *instr.*). — *adv.* ми́мо.

paste, *n.* кле́йстер, клей *m.* — *v.* скле́ивать *imp.*, скле́ить *perf.*

pasteurize, *v.* пастеризова́ть *imp. & perf.*

pastime, *n.* развлече́ние *nt.*

pastry, *n.* пече́нье, пиро́жное *nt.*

pasture, *n.* па́стбище *nt.*

pat, *n.* похло́пывание *nt.* — *v.* похло́пывать *imp.* **to stand pat,** не меня́ть свое́й пози́ции.

patch, *n.* запла́та *f.* — *v.* лата́ть *imp.*, залата́ть *perf.*

patent, *adj.* очеви́дный; патенто́ванный. — *n.* пате́нт *m.*, исключи́тельное пра́во. — *v.* патентова́ть *imp. & perf.*

patent leather, лакиро́ванная ко́жа.

paternal, *adj.* отцо́вский.

paternity, *n.* отцо́вство *nt.*

path, *n.* тропи́нка, доро́жка *f.*

pathetic, *adj.* патети́ческий.

pathology, *n.* патоло́гия *f.*

patience, *n.* терпе́ние *nt.*

patient, *adj.* терпели́вый. — *n.* больно́й *m.*, больна́я *f.*

patriot, *n.* патрио́т *m.* **-ic,** *adj.* патриоти́ческий. **-ism,** *n.* патриоти́зм *m.*

patrol, *n.* патру́ль *f.* — *v.* патрули́ровать *imp.*

patron, *n.* покрови́тель, патро́н *m.* **-ize,** *v.* покрови́тельствовать *imp.*

pattern, *n.* образе́ц *m.*, моде́ль *f.*

Paul, *n.* Па́вел *m.*

pauper, *n.* бедня́к, ни́щий *m.*

pause, *n.* па́уза, остано́вка *f.* — *v.* де́лать па́узу; остана́вливаться *imp.*, останови́ться *perf.*

pave, *v.* мости́ть *imp.*; устила́ть *imp.*, устла́ть *perf.*

pavement, *n.* мостова́я *f.*

pavilion, *n.* пала́тка *f.*, павильо́н *m.*

paw, *n.* ла́па *f.* — *v.* тро́гать ла́пой.

pawn, *n.* зало́г *m.*; (*chess*) пе́шка *f.* — *v.* отдава́ть в зало́г.

pay, *n.* (*payment*) пла́та *f.*; (*salary*) зарпла́та *f.*, жа́лованье *nt.* — *v.* плати́ть *imp.*, заплати́ть *perf.* **pay back**, отпла́чивать *imp.*, отплати́ть *perf.* **payment**, *n.* платёж *m.*

pea, *n.* горо́шина *f.*

peace, *n.* мир *m.* **-ful**, *adj.* ми́рный.

peach, *n.* пе́рсик *m.*

peacock, *n.* павли́н *m.*

peak, *n.* пик *m.*, верши́на *f.*

peanut, *n.* земляно́й оре́х.

pear, *n.* гру́ша *f.*

pearl, *n.* жемчу́жина *f.*

peasant, *n.* крестья́нин *m.*, крестья́нка *f.*

pebble, *n.* го́лыш *m.*

peck, *n.* уда́р клю́вом; (*measure*) пек *m.* — *v.* клева́ть *imp.*

peculiar, *adj.* осо́бый; стра́нный.

pedal, *n.* педа́ль *f.*

pedant, *n.* педа́нт *m.*

pedestal, *n.* пьедеста́л *m.*

pedestrian, *n.* пешехо́д *m.* — *adj.* пе́ший.

pediatrics, *n.* педиатри́я *f.*

pedigree, *n.* родосло́вная *f.*

peel, *n.* кожура́, ко́рка *f.* — *v.* очища́ть *imp.*, очи́стить *perf.*

peg, *n.* ко́лышек *m.*

pelt, *n.* шку́ра *f.* — *v.* забра́сывать *imp.*, заброса́ть *perf.*

pelvis, *n.* таз *m.*

pen, *n.* перо́ *nt.* **fountain pen**, авто́ру́чка *f.*

penalty, *n.* наказа́ние *nt.*

pencil, *n.* каранда́ш *m.* **in pencil**, карандашо́м.

pending, *adj.* ожида́емый. — *prep.* в ожида́нии.

penetrate, *v.* проника́ть *imp.*, прони́кнуть *perf.*

penetration, *n.* проница́тельность *f.*

penicillin, *n.* пеницилли́н *m.*

peninsula, *n.* полуо́стров *m.*

penis, *n.* полово́й член.

penitent, *n.* ка́ющийся гре́шник. — *adj.* ка́ющийся.

penknife, *n.* перочи́нный нож.

pension, *n.* пе́нсия *f.*

pensive, *adj.* заду́мчивый.

people, *n.* лю́ди *pl.*; (*nation*) наро́д *m.* — *v.* населя́ть *imp.*, насели́ть *perf.* не

pepper, *n.* пе́рец *m.*

per, *prep.* че́рез, посре́дством; в, на; по; с, за.

perceive, *v.* ощуща́ть *imp.*, ощути́ть *perf.*

percent, *adv.* проце́нт *m.* **-age**, *n.* проце́нт *m.*, проце́нтное отноше́ние.

perceptible, *adj.* ощути́мый, заме́тный.

perception, *n.* ощуще́ние *nt.*

perch, *n.* насе́ст *m.*; (*fish*) о́кунь *m.*

perennial, *adj.* многоле́тний; ве́чный.

perfect, *adj.* соверше́нный; (*complete*) по́лный. — *v.* соверше́нствовать *imp.*, усоверше́нствовать *perf.* **-ion**, *n.* соверше́нство *nt.* **-ive**, *n.* (*gram.*) соверше́нный вид.

perforation, *n.* просве́рливание *nt.*

perform, *v.* выполня́ть *imp.*, вы́полнить *perf.*; (*theat.*) исполня́ть *imp.*, испо́лнить *perf.* **-ance**, *n.* исполне́ние *nt.*; (*theat.*) представле́ние *nt.*

perfume, *n.* духи́ *pl.* — *v.* надуши́ть *perf.*

perhaps, *adv.* мо́жет быть.

peril, *n.* опа́сность *f.* **-ous**, *adj.* опа́сный.

period, *n.* пери́од *m.*, эпо́ха *f.*; (*punctuation*) то́чка *f.* **-ical**, *n.* периоди́ческий журна́л. — *adj.* периоди́ческий.

periphery, *n.* перифери́я *f.*

perish, *v.* погиба́ть *imp.*, поги́бнуть *perf.* **-able**, *adj.* скоропо́ртящийся.

perjury, *n.* клятвопреступле́ние *nt.*; лжесвиде́тельство *nt.*

permanent, *adj.* постоя́нный.

— n. (hair) завивка f., перманент m.

permeate, v. проникать imp., проникнуть perf.

permissible, adj. позволительный, допустимый.

permission, n. разрешение nt.

permit, n. разрешение nt. — v. разрешать imp., разрешить perf.

perpendicular, adj. перпендикулярный, отвесный. — n. перпендикуляр, отвес m.

perpetual, adj. вечный.

perplex, v. запутывать imp., запутать perf.

persecute, v. преследовать imp.

persecution, n. преследование nt.

perseverance, n. настойчивость f.

persist, v. упорствовать imp. **-ent**, adj. настойчивый.

person, n. особа, личность f.; (gram.) лицо nt.

personage, n. личность f.

personal, adj. личный, частный. **-ity**, n. личность, индивидуальность f., персонаж m.

personnel, n. персонал m., личный состав.

perspective, n. перспектива f. — adj. перспективный.

perspiration, n. пот m.

perspire, v. потеть imp.

persuade, v. убеждать imp., убедить perf.

persuasion, n. убеждение nt.

persuasive, adj. убедительный.

pertain, v. относиться imp.

pertinent, adj. подходящий; по существу.

pervade, v. проникать imp., проникнуть perf.

perverse, adj. порочный.

perversion, n. извращение nt.

pessimism, n. пессимизм m.

pestilence, n. мор m.

pet, n. любимец m., любимое животное. — v. ласкать imp.

petal, n. лепесток m.

Peter, n. Пётр m.

petition, n. петиция f. — v. обращаться с петицией.

petrify, v. окаменеть perf.

petroleum, n. нефть f.

petty, adj. маловажный, мелкий.

petulant, adj. раздражительный.

pew, n. скамья в церкви.

phantom, n. призрак, фантом m.

pharmacist, n. фармацевт m.

pharmacy, n. фармация f.; аптека f.

phase, n. фаза f.

pheasant, n. фазан m.

phenomenal, adj. феноменальный.

phenomenon, n. феномен m.

philantropy, n. филантропия f.

philately, n. филателия f.

philosopher, n. философ m.

philosophical, adj. философический.

philosophy, n. философия f.

phlegm, n. мокрота, слизь f.

phobia, n. невроз страха.

phonetic, adj. фонетический.

phonetics, n. фонетика f.

phonograph, n. граммофон, патефон m.

phosphorus, n. фосфор m.

photogenic, adj. фотогеничный.

photograph, n. фотография f., фотографический снимок. — v. фотографировать imp. & perf.

photography, n. фотография f. фотографирование nt.

phrase, n. фраза f., выражение nt. — v. выражать в словах.

physical, adj. физический.

physician, n. врач m.

physics, n. физика f.

physiology, n. физиология f

physiotherapy, n. физиотерапия f.

physique, n. телосложение nt.

pianist, n. пианист m., пианистка f.

piano, n. рояль m. **upright p.**, пианино.

pick, n. (choice) выбор m. —

v. (*choose*) выбира́ть *imp.*, вы́брать *perf.* **pick up,** поднима́ть *imp.*, подня́ть *perf.*

pickle, *n.* огуре́ц *m.* — *v.* маринова́ть *imp. & perf.*

pickpocket, *n.* вор-карма́нчик *m.*

picnic, *n.* пикни́к *m.*

picture, *n.* карти́на, карти́нка *f.* — *v.* вообража́ть *imp.*, вообрази́ть *perf.*

picturesque, *adj.* живопи́сный.

pie, *n.* сла́дкий пиро́г; торт *m.*

piece, *n.* кусо́к *m.*

pier, *n.* мол, волноре́з *m.*

pierce, *v.* пронза́ть *imp.*, пронзи́ть *perf.*

piety, *n.* набо́жность *f.*

pig, *n.* свинья́ *f.*

pigeon, *n.* го́лубь *m.*

pigment, *n.* пигме́нт *m.*

pile, *n.* ку́ча, гру́да *f.* — *v.* нагроможда́ть *imp.*, нагромозди́ть *perf.*

pilgrim, *n.* пало́мник *m.* **-age,** *n.* пало́мничество *nt.*

pill, *n.* пилю́ля *f.*

pillar, *n.* столб *m.*

pillow, *n.* поду́шка *f.* **-case,** *n.* на́волочка *f.*

pilot, *n.* пило́т, лётчик *m.* — *v.* пилоти́ровать *imp. & perf.*

pimple, *n.* пры́щик *m.*

pin, *n.* була́вка, шпи́лька *f.*; (*mach.*) па́лец, болт *m.* — *v.* прика́лывать *imp.*, приколо́ть *perf.*

pinch, *n.* щипо́к *m.* — *v.* щипа́ть *imp.*, щипну́ть *perf.*

pine, *n.* сосна́ *f.* — *v.* ча́хнуть *imp.*

pineapple, *n.* анана́с *m.*

pink, *adj.* ро́зовый. — *n.* ро́зовый цвет.

pinnacle, *n.* верши́на горы́; (*arch.*) шпиц *m.*, кульминацио́нный пункт.

pint, *n.* пи́нта *f.*

pioneer, *n.* пионе́р *m.*

pious, *adj.* набо́жный.

pipe, *n.* труба́, тру́бка *f.*; (*for smoking*) кури́тельная тру́бка *f.*

pirate, *n.* пира́т *m.*

pistol, *n.* пистоле́т *m.*

pit, *n.* я́ма *f.*; (*fruit*) ко́сточка *f.*

pitch, *n.* (*tar*) смола́ *f.*; (*ship*) ка́чка *f.*; (*mus.*) высота́ *f.* — *v.* подверга́ться киле́вой ка́чке. (*tent*) разбива́ть (ла́герь).

pitcher, *n.* кувши́н *m.*

pitiful, *adj.* жа́лкий.

pitiless, *adj.* безжа́лостный.

pity, *n.* жа́лость *f.*, сожале́ние *nt.* — *v.* жале́ть *imp.*, соболе́зновать *imp.*

pivot, *n.* сте́ржень *m.*, то́чка враще́ния — *v.* враща́ться вокру́г о́си.

placard, *n.* плака́т *m.*, афи́ша *f.*

placate, *v.* задо́брить *perf.*

place, *n.* ме́сто *nt.*; положе́ние *nt.* **take p.,** име́ть ме́сто. — *v.* ста́вить *imp.*, поста́вить *perf.*

placid, *adj.* споко́йный.

plagiarism, *n.* плагиа́т *m.*

plague, *n.* мор *m.*, чума́ *f.* — *v.* досажда́ть *imp.*, досади́ть *perf.*

plain, *adj.* просто́й. — *n.* равни́на *f.*, степи́ *pl.*

plaintiff, *n.* исте́ц *m.*, исти́ца *f.*

plan, *n.* план *m.*; прое́кт *m.* — *v.* замышля́ть *imp.*, замы́слить *perf.*

plane, *n.* самолёт *m.*; (*tool*) руба́нок *m.* — *v.* строга́ть *imp.*

planet, *n.* плане́та *f.*

planetarium, *n.* планета́рий *m.*

plank, *n.* доска́ *f.*

plant, *n.* расте́ние *nt.* — *v.* сажа́ть *imp.*, посади́ть *perf.*

plantation, *n.* планта́ция *f.*

planter, *n.* планта́тор *m.*

plasma, *n.* пла́зма *f.*

plaster, *n.* пла́стырь *m.*; (*wall*) гипс *m.* — *v.* штукату́рить *imp.*, оштукату́рить *perf.*

plastic, *adj.* пласти́ческий, пласти́чный.

plate, *n.* пласти́нка *f.*; (*dish*) таре́лка *f.* — *v.* накла́дывать *imp.*, наложи́ть *perf.* покрыва́ть *imp.*, покры́ть *perf.*

plateau, *n.* плоскогóрье *nt.*

platform, *n.* платфóрма *f.*

platinum, *n.* пла́тина *f.*

platitude, *n.* пóшлость *f.*

plausible, *adj.* вероя́тный, правдоподóбный.

play, *n.* игра́ *f.*; (*theat.*) пьéса *f.* — *v.* умоля́ть *imp.*, сыгра́ть *perf.* **-er**, *n.* игрóк *m.* **-ful**, *adj.* шутли́вый. **-wright**, *n.* драматýрг *m.*

plea, *n.* мольба́ *f.*

plead, *v.* умоля́ть *imp.* **p. a case**, защища́ть дéло.

pleasant, *adj.* прия́тный.

please, *v.* нра́виться *imp.*, понра́виться *perf.* — *adv.* пожа́луйста!

pleasure, *n.* удовóльствие *nt.*

pleat, *n.* скла́дка *f.* — *v.* дéлать скла́дки.

plebiscite, *n.* плебисци́т *m.*

pledge, *n.* залóг *m.*; зада́ток *m.*; (*promise*) обеща́ние *nt.* — *v.* закла́дывать *imp.*, заложи́ть *perf.*; руча́ться *imp.*

plentiful, *adj.* оби́льный.

plenty, *n.* изоби́лие *nt.*

pleurisy, *n.* плеври́т *m.*

pliable, pliant, *adj.* ги́бкий.

pliers, *n.* щи́пчики *pl.*; плоскогýбцы *pl.*

plight, *n.* затрудни́тельное положéние.

plot, *n.* уча́сток *m.*; (*fiction*) сюжéт *m.*, фа́була *f.* — *v.* замышля́ть *imp.*, замы́слить *perf.*

plow, *n.* плуг *m.* — *v.* паха́ть *imp.*

plug, *n.* заты́чка *f.*; прóбка *f.* — *v.* затыка́ть *imp.*, затка́ть *perf.*

plum, *n.* сли́ва *f.*

plumage, *n.* оперéние *nt.*

plumber, *n.* водопровóдчик *m.*

plumbing, *n.* водопровóдное дéло.

plump, *adj.* пýхлый, пóлный.

plunder, *n.* грабёж *f.* — *v.* гра́бить *imp.*, огра́бить *perf.*

plunge, *v.i.* погружáть *imp.*, погрузи́ть *perf.* — *v.i.*

погружа́ться *imp.*, погрузи́ться *perf.*

plural, *adj.* мнóжественный. — *n.* (*gram.*) мнóжественное числó.

plus, *prep.* плюс. — *n.* знак плюс.

pneumonia, *n.* воспалéние лёгких, пневмони́я *f.*

poached egg, яйцó-пашóт.

pocket, *n.* карма́н *m.* — *v.* прикарма́нивать *imp.*, прикарма́нить *perf.* **-book**, *n.* бума́жник *m.*; кошелёк *m.*

poem, *n.* поэ́ма *f.*, стихотворéние *nt.*

poet, *n.* поэ́т *m.* **-ic**, *adj.* поэти́ческий. **-ry**, *n.* поэ́зия *f.*

poignant, *adj.* éдкий, мучи́тельный.

point, *n.* тóчка *f.*; (*tip*) кóнчик *m.* **from a p. of view**, с тóчки зрéния. **that's not the p.**, дéло не в э́том. — *v.* пока́зывать *imp.*, указа́ть *perf.* **-ed**, *adj.* остроконéчный. **-less**, *adj.* бессмы́сленный, бесцéльный.

poison, *n.* яд *m.*, отра́ва *f.* — *v.* отравля́ть *imp.*, отрави́ть *perf.* **-ous**, *adj.* ядови́тый.

poke, *n.* толчóк *m.* — *v.* тыка́ть *imp.*, ты́кнуть *perf.*

Poland, *n.* Пóльша *f.*

polar, *adj.* поля́рный, пóлюсный.

pole, *n.* шест, столб *m.*; (*geog.*) пóлюс *m.*

Pole, *n.* поля́к *m.*, пóлька *f.*

police, *n.* поли́ция *f.* **-man**, *n.* полицéйский.

policy, *n.* поли́тика *f.*; (*insurance*) пóлис *m.*

polish), *n.* полирóвка *f.*; лоск *m.* — *v.* полирова́ть *imp.*; отполирова́ть *perf.*

Polish, *adj.* пóльский.

polite, *adj.* вéжливый. **-ness**, *n.* вéжливость *f.*

political, *adj.* полити́ческий.

politician, *n.* полити́ческий дéятель.

politics, *n.* поли́тика *f.*

poll, *n.* баллотиро́вка *f.*; *pl.* избира́тельный пункт.

pollen, *n.* пыльца́ *f.*

pollute, *v.* загрязня́ть *imp.,* загрязни́ть *perf.*

pollution, *n.* загрязне́ние *nt.*

polygamy, *n.* полига́мия *f.,* многобра́чие *nt.*

pomp, *n.* по́мпа, пы́шность *f.* **-ous,** *adj.* напы́щенный.

pond, *n.* пруд *m.*

ponder, *v.* обду́мывать *imp.,* обду́мать *perf.*

pony, *n.* по́ни *nt.* ind.

pool, *n.* лу́жа *f.*; бассе́йн *m.*

poor, *adj.* бе́дный. — *n.* беднота́ *f.,* бе́дные *pl.*

pope, *n.* па́па *m.*

popular, *adj.* популя́рный. **-ity,** *n.* популя́рность *f.*

population, *n.* населе́ние *nt.*

porcelain, *n.* фарфо́р *m.*

porch, *n.* вера́нда *f.*

pore, *n.* по́ра *f.*

pork, *n.* свини́на *f.*

porous, *adj.* по́ристый.

port, *n.* (city) портово́й го́род, порт *m.*; (of a ship) ле́вый борт; (wine) портве́йн *m.*

portable, *adj.* перено́сный, портати́вный.

porter, *n.* швейца́р, носи́льщик *m.*

portfolio, *n.* портфе́ль *m.,* па́пка *f.*

portion, *n.* часть *f.*; у́часть *f.*

portly, *adj.* оса́нистый.

portrait, *n.* портре́т *m.*

portray, *v.* изобража́ть *imp.,* изобрази́ть *perf.*

Portugal, *n.* Португа́лия *f.*

Portuguese, *adj.* португа́льский.

pose, *n.* по́за *f.* — *v.* пози́ровать *imp.* & *perf.*; ста́вить *imp.,* поста́вить *perf.* **p. as,** принима́ть по́зу.

position, *n.* положе́ние *nt.,* пози́ция *f.*; (rank) до́лжность *f.*

positive, *adj.* положи́тельный.

possess, *v.* владе́ть *imp.* **-ion,** *n.* владе́ние *nt.*; (pl.) иму́щество *nt.* **-ive,** *adj.* име́ю-

щий, владе́ющий; (gram.) притяжа́тельный.

possibility, *n.* возмо́жность *f.*

possible, *adj.* возмо́жный.

possibly, *adv.* возмо́жно; по возмо́жности.

post, *n.* столб *m.*; (mail) по́чта *f.* — *v.* выве́шивать *imp.,* вы́весить *perf.*; отправля́ть по по́чте. **-age,** *n.* почто́вая опла́та.

post card, *n.* откры́тка *f.*

poster, *n.* плака́т *m.,* афи́ша *f.*

posterior, *adj.* за́дний.

posterity, *n.* пото́мство *nt.,* пото́мки *pl.*

postman, *n.* почтальо́н *m.*

postmark, *n.* почто́вый штемпель.

post office, *n.* по́чта *f.,* почто́вое отделе́ние *nt.*

postpone, *v.* откла́дывать *imp.,* отложи́ть *perf.*; отсро́чивать *imp.,* отсро́чить *perf.*

postscript, *n.* постскри́птум *m.*

posture, *n.* по́за *f.* — *v.* пози́ровать *imp.* & *perf.*

pot, *n.* горшо́к, котело́к *m.*

potassium, *n.* ка́лий *m.*

potato, *n.* карто́фель *f.*

potent, *adj.* си́льный.

potential, *adj.* потенциа́льный. — *n.* потенциа́л *m.*

potion, *n.* до́за лека́рства.

pottery, *n.* гли́няные изде́лия.

pouch, *n.* мешо́к, мешо́чек *m.,* су́мка *f.*

poultry, *n.* дома́шняя пти́ца.

pound, *n.* фунт *m.* — *v.* толо́чь *imp.*

pour, *v.t.* лить *imp.* — *v.i.* ли́ться.

poverty, *n.* бе́дность *f.*

powder, *n.* порошо́к *m.* пу́дра *f.*; (gun) по́рох *m.* — *v.* пу́дрить *imp.*

power, *n.* си́ла, мощь *f.*; эне́ргия *f.* **-ful,** *adj.* си́льный, мо́щный. **-less,** *adj.* бесси́льный.

practical, *adj.* практи́ческий. **-ly,** *adv.* практи́чески; почти́.

practice, *n.* пра́ктика *f.*

prairie, *n.* пре́рия *f.*

praise, *n.* хвала́ *f.* — *v.* хва-

prank, *n.* шу́тка *f.*

pray, *v.* моли́ться *imp.* **-er**, *n.* моли́тва *f.*

preach, *v.* пропове́довать *imp.*

precarious, *adj.* риско́ванный, опа́сный.

precaution, *n.* предосторо́жность *f.*

precede, *v.* предше́ствовать *imp.*

precedent, *adj.* предше́ствующий. — *n.* прецеде́нт *m.*

precept, *n.* наставле́ние *nt.*

precious, *adj.* драгоце́нный.

precipice, *n.* про́пасть *f.*

precipitate, *v.* низверга́ть *imp.*, низве́ргнуть *perf.*

precise, *adj.* то́чный.

precision, *n.* то́чность *f.*; чёткость *f.*

precocious, *adj.* скороспе́лый.

predatory, *adj.* хи́щный.

predecessor, *n.* предше́ственник *m.*

predicament, *n.* затрудни́тельное положе́ние.

predicate, *n.* (*gram.*) сказу́емое *nt.*

predict, *v.* предска́зывать *imp.*, предсказа́ть *perf.*

predominant, *adj.* преоблада́ющий.

preface, *n.* предисло́вие *nt.*

prefer, *v.* предпочита́ть *imp.* **-able**, *adj.* предпочти́тельный. **-ence**, *n.* предпочте́ние *nt.*

prefix, *n.* пре́фикс *m.*, приста́вка *f.*

pregnancy, *n.* бере́менность *f.*

pregnant, *adj.* бере́менная.

prehistoric, *adj.* доистори́ческий.

prejudice, *n.* предубежде́ние *nt.*

preliminary, *adj.* предвари́тельный.

prelude, *n.* вступле́ние *nt.*; (*mus.*) прелю́дия *f.*

premature, *adj.* преждевре́менный.

premeditated, *adj.* преднаме́ренный.

premise, *n.* предпосы́лка *f.*;

(*pl. land*) помеще́ние *nt.*

premium, *n.* награ́да, пре́мия *f.*

premonition, *n.* предчу́вствие *nt.*

preparation, *n.* приготовле́ние *nt.*

preparatory, *adj.* подготови́тельный.

prepare, *v.t.* гото́вить *imp.*, пригото́вить *perf.* — *v.i.* гото́виться *imp.*, пригото́виться *perf.*

preponderant, *adj.* преоблада́ющий.

preposition, *n.* предло́г *m.* **-al**, *adj.* предло́жный.

preposterous, *adj.* абсу́рдный.

prescribe, *v.* предпи́сывать *imp.*, предписа́ть *perf.*; (*med.*) пропи́сывать *imp.*, прописа́ть *perf.*

prescription, *n.* предписа́ние *nt.*; (*med.*) реце́пт *m.*

presence, *n.* прису́тствие *nt.*

present, *adj.* прису́тствующий **to be p.**, прису́тствовать *imp.* — *n.* настоя́щее вре́мя; (*gift*) пода́рок *m.* — *v.* представля́ть *imp.*, предста́вить *perf.*; (*gift*) дари́ть *imp.*, подари́ть *perf.* **-able**, *adj.* прили́чный. **-ation**, *n.* представле́ние *nt.* **-ly**, *adv.* вско́ре, сейча́с.

preservative, *adj.* предохрани́тельный. — *n.* предохрани́тельное сре́дство.

preserve, *n.* храни́лище *nt.*; *pl.* (*jam*) варе́нье *nt.* — *v.* сохраня́ть *imp.*, сохрани́ть *perf.*; консерви́ровать *imp.* & *perf.*

preside, *v.* председа́тельствовать *imp.*

presidency, *n.* президе́нтство, председа́тельство *nt.*

president, *n.* президе́нт, председа́тель *m.*

press, *n.* пресс *m.*; (*printing*) печа́ть *f.*, (*newspapers, etc.*) пре́сса. — *v.* жать *imp.*; (*iron*) гла́дить *imp.*, погла́дить *perf.*

pressure, *n.* давле́ние *nt.*

prestige, *n.* прести́ж *m.*

presume, *v.* предполага́ть *imp.*, предположи́ть *perf.*

presumptuous, *adj.* самонаде́янный.

presuppose, *v.* предполага́ть *imp.*, предположи́ть *perf.*

pretend, *v.* претендова́ть *imp.*

pretense, *n.* предло́г *m.*

pretentious, *adj.* претенцио́зный.

pretext, *n.* предло́г *m.*, отгово́рка *f.*

pretty, *adj.* хоро́шенький. — *adv.* дово́льно, доста́точно.

prevail, *v.* преоблада́ть *imp.*

prevalent, *adj.* преоблада́ющий.

prevent, *v.* предохраня́ть *imp.*, предохрани́ть *perf.*; препя́тствовать *imp.* **-ion**, *n.* предохране́ние, предупрежде́ние *nt.* **-ive**, *adj.* предупреди́тельный.

preview, *n.* закры́тый просмо́тр.

previous, *adj.* предыду́щий. **-ly**, *adv.* зара́нее, предвари́тельно.

prey, *n.* добы́ча *f.* — *v.* гра́бить *imp.*

price, *n.* цена́ *f.* — *v.* назнача́ть це́ну; оце́нивать *imp.*, оцени́ть *perf.* **-less**, *adj.* бесце́нный.

prick, *n.* уко́л *m.* — *v.* коло́ть *imp.*, кольну́ть *perf.*

pride, *n.* го́рдость *f.*

priest, *n.* свяще́нник *m.*

prim, *adj.* чо́порный.

primary, *adj.* основно́й.

prime, *adj.* гла́вный, основно́й. — *n.* расцве́т *m.* — *v.* грунтова́ть *imp.*

primitive, *adj.* примити́вный.

principal, *adj.* гла́вный. — *n.* нача́льник, дире́ктор.

principle, *n.* при́нцип *m.*

print, *n.* печа́ть *f.*, шрифт *m.*; (*imprint*) отпеча́ток *m.*; (*art*) гравю́ра *f.* — *v.* печа́тать *imp.*, напеча́тать *perf.* **-ing**, *n.* печа́тание *nt.*

priority, *n.* приорите́т *m.*

prism, *n.* при́зма *f.*

prison, *n.* тюрьма́ *f.* **-er**, *n.*

заключённый *m.*; пле́нный *m.*

privacy, *n.* уедине́ние *nt.*

private, *adj.* ли́чный, ли́чный. — *n.* (*mil.*) рядово́й *m.* **in p.**, наедине́ *adv.*

privilege, *n.* привиле́гия *f.*

privileged, *adj.* привилегиро́ванный.

prize, *n.* приз *m.*, пре́мия *f.*, награ́да *f.* — *v.* высо́ко цени́ть.

probability, *n.* вероя́тность *f.*, правдоподо́бие *nt.*

probable, *adj.* правдоподо́бный, возмо́жный, вероя́тный.

probably, *adv.* вероя́тно.

probation, *n.* испыта́ние *nt.*

probe, *n.* зонд *m.* — *v.* зонди́ровать *imp.* & *perf.*

problem, *n.* зада́ча, пробле́ма *f.*

procedure, *n.* процеду́ра *f.*

proceed, *v.* продолжа́ть *imp.*; переходи́ть *imp.*, перейти́ *perf.*

process, *n.* проце́сс *m.*

procession, *n.* проце́ссия *f.*

proclaim, *v.* возглаша́ть *imp.*, возгласи́ть *perf.*

proclamation, *n.* провозглаше́ние *nt.*

procure, *v.* добыва́ть *imp.*, добы́ть *perf.*

prodigy, *n.* одарённый челове́к; чу́до-ребёнок *m.*

produce, *v.* производи́ть *imp.*, произвести́ *perf.*

product, *n.* проду́кт *m.*; результа́т *m.* **-ion**, *n.* произво́дство *nt.* **-ive**, *adj.* производи́тельный; плодоро́дный.

profane, *adj.* нечести́вый. — *v.* профани́ровать *imp.* & *perf.*

profanity, *n.* богоху́льство *nt.*; руга́тельство *nt.*

profess, *v.* откры́то признава́ть.

profession, *n.* профе́ссия *f.* **-al**, *adj.* профессиона́льный. — *n.* профессиона́л *m.*

professor, *n.* профе́ссор *m.*

proficiency, *n.* уме́ние *nt.*, о́пытность *f.*

proficient, *adj.* о́пытный, иску́сный.

profit, *n.* по́льза *f.*; при́быль *f.*, дохо́д *m.* — *v.* приноси́ть по́льзу. **-able,** *adj.* при́быльный.

profound, *adj.* глубо́кий.

profuse, *adj.* оби́льный.

prognosis, *n.* прогно́з *m.*

program, *n.* програ́мма *f.*

progress, *n.* прогре́сс *m.* — *v.* прогресси́ровать *imp.* & *perf.*; де́лать успе́хи. **-ive,** *adj.* прогресси́вный, поступа́тельный.

prohibit, *v.* запреща́ть *imp.*, запрети́ть *perf.* **-ion,** *n.* запреще́ние *nt.* **-ive,** *adj.* запрети́тельный.

project, *n.* прое́кт *m.* — *v.* проекти́ровать *imp.*, запроекти́ровать *perf.* **-ion,** *n.* прое́кция *f.*

prolific, *adj.* плодоро́дный, плодови́тый.

prologue, *n.* проло́г *m.*

prolong, *v.* продли́ть *perf.*

prominent, *adj.* выдаю́щийся.

promiscuity, *n.* неразбо́рчивость *f.*

promiscuous, *adj.* неразбо́рчивый.

promise, *n.* обеща́ние *nt.* — *v.* обеща́ть *imp.*

promote, *v.* продвига́ть *imp.*, продви́нуть *perf.*; (*raise*) повыша́ть *imp.*, повы́сить *perf.*

promotion, *n.* продвиже́ние *nt.*

prompt, *adj.* прово́рный. — *v.* побужда́ть *imp.*, побуди́ть *perf.*; (*theat.*) суфли́ровать *imp.*

pronoun, *n.* местоиме́ние *nt.*

pronounce, *v.* произноси́ть *imp.*, произнести́ *perf.*

pronunciation, *n.* произноше́ние *n.*

proof, *n.* доказа́тельство *nt.*

propaganda, *n.* пропага́нда *f.*

propagate, *v.* распространя́ть *imp.*, распространи́ть *perf.*

propel, *v.* приводи́ть в движе́ние.

propeller, *n.* пропе́ллер *m.*; дви́гатель *m.*

proper, *adj.* прили́чный, пра́вильный. **-ly,** *adv.* до́лжным о́бразом, как сле́дует.

property, *n.* иму́щество *nt.*, со́бственность *f.*; (*quality*) сво́йство *nt.*

prophecy, *n.* проро́чество *nt.*

prophesy, *v.* проро́чить *imp.*

prophet, *n.* проро́к *m.*

propitious, *adj.* благоприя́тный.

proponent, *n.* сторо́нник *m.*

proportion, *n.* пропо́рция *f.* **-ate,** *adj.* пропорциона́льный.

proposal, *n.* предложе́ние *nt.*

propose, *v.* де́лать предложе́ние.

proposition, *n.* предложе́ние *nt.*; (*math.*) теоре́ма *f.*

proprietor, *n.* со́бственник, владе́лец *m.*

propriety, *n.* присто́йность *f.*

prosaic, *adj.* прозаи́ческий.

prose, *n.* про́за *f.*

prosecute, *v.* пресле́довать суде́бным поря́дком.

prospect, *n.* ви́ды на бу́дущее. **-ive,** *adj.* ожида́емый: каса́ющийся бу́дущего.

prosper, *v.* преуспева́ть *imp.* **-ity,** *n.* благосостоя́ние *nt.* **-ous,** *adj.* процвета́ющий; успе́шный.

prostitute, *n.* проститу́тка *f.* — *v.* проституи́ровать *imp.* & *perf.*

prostrate, *adj.* распростёртый. — *v.* истоща́ть *imp.*, истощи́ть *perf.*

protect, *v.* охраня́ть *imp.*, охрани́ть *perf.* **-ion,** *n.* охра́на *f.* **-ive,** *adj.* предохрани́тельный. **-or,** *n.* защи́тник *m.*

protégé, *n.* протеже́ *m. ind.*

protein, *n.* протеи́н *m.*

protest, *n.* проте́ст *m.* — *v.* протестова́ть *imp.*

Protestant, *adj.* протеста́нтский. — *n.* протеста́нт *m.*

protocol, *n.* протоко́л *m.*

proton, *n.* прото́н *m.*

protrude, *v.* торча́ть *imp.*

proud, *adj.* го́рдый.

prove, *v.* дока́зывать *imp.*, доказа́ть *perf.*

proverb, *n.* посло́вица *f.*

provide, *v.* запаса́ть *imp.*, запасти́ *perf.*

provided, *conj.* в том слу́чае, е́сли.

providence, *n.* провиде́ние *nt.*

province, *n.* прови́нция, о́бласть *f.*

provincial, *adj.* провинциа́льный. — *n.* провинциа́л *m.*

provision, *n.* обеспе́чение *nt.*; (*stipulation*) усло́вие *nt.*; *pl.* (*supplies*) прови́зия *f.* — *v.* снабжа́ть продово́льствием.

provocation, *n.* провока́ция *f.*

provoke, *v.* провоци́ровать *imp.* & *perf.*

prowl, *v.* броди́ть *imp.*

proximity, *n.* бли́зость *f.*

proxy, *n.* дове́ренность *f.*, полномо́чие *nt.* **by p.,** по дове́ренности.

prudence, *n.* благоразу́мие *nt.*, рассчётливость *f.*

prudent, *adj.* благоразу́мный, расчётливый.

prune, *n.* черносли́в *m.*

psalm, *n.* псало́м *m.*

pseudonym, *n.* псевдони́м *m.*

psychiatrist, *n.* психиа́тр *m.*

psychiatry, *n.* психиатри́я *f.*

psychoanalysis, *n.* психоанали́з *m.*

psychological, *adj.* психологи́ческий.

psychology, *n.* психоло́гия *f.*

psychosis, *n.* психо́з *m.*

ptomaine, *n.* птома́ин *m.*

public, *adj.* публи́чный, обще́ственный. — *n.* пу́блика *f.*, наро́д *m.*

publication, *n.* опублико́вание *nt.*; изда́ние *nt.*

publicity, *n.* рекла́ма, гла́сность *f.*

publish, *v.* издава́ть *imp.*, изда́ть *perf.* опублико́вать *perf.* **-er,** *n.* изда́тель *m.*

pudding, *n.* пу́динг *m.*

puddle, *n.* лу́жа *f.*

puff, *n.* клуб *m.*; (*air, etc.*) дунове́ние *nt.* — *v.* пыхте́ть *imp.*

pull, *n.* тя́га *f.*, натяже́ние *nt.* — *v.* тяну́ть *imp.*, потяну́ть *perf.*; натя́гивать *imp.*, натяну́ть *perf.*

pulley, *n.* блок, воро́т *m.*

pulmonary, *adj.* лёгочный.

pulp, *n.* ма́сса, пу́льпа *f.*; (*of fruit*) мя́коть *f.*

pulpit, *n.* кафе́дра *f.*

pulsate, *v.* пульси́ровать *imp.*

pulse, *n.* пульс *m.*

pump, *n.* насо́с *m.*, водока́чка *f.* — *v.* кача́ть *imp.*

pumpkin, *n.* ты́ква *f.*

pun, *n.* каламбу́р *m.*, игра́ слов.

punch, *n.* уда́р кулако́м; (*mach.*) пробо́йник *m.* — *v.* ударя́ть кулако́м; (*mach.*) пробива́ть *imp.*, проби́ть *perf.*

punctual, *adj.* пунктуа́льный.

punctuate, *v.* ста́вить зна́ки препина́ния.

puncture, *n.* проко́л *m.* — *v.* прока́лывать *imp.*, проколо́ть *perf.*

punish, *v.* нака́зывать *imp.*, наказа́ть *perf.* **-ment,** *n.* наказа́ние *nt.*

puny, *adj.* сла́бый, ма́ленький.

pupil, *n.* учени́к *m.*, учени́ца *f.*; (*eye*) зрачо́к *m.*

puppet, *n.* марионе́тка *f.*

puppy, *n.* щено́к *m.*

purchase, *n.* поку́пка *f.* — *v.* покупа́ть *imp.*, купи́ть *perf.*

pure, *adj.* чи́стый.

purge, *v.* чи́стка *f.*

purify, *v.* очища́ть *imp.*, очи́стить *perf.*

puritanical, *adj.* пурита́нский.

purity, *n.* чистота́, непоро́чность *f.*

purple, *adj.* багря́ный, пурпу́рный. — *n.* багря́ный цвет, пурпу́рный цвет.

purport, *n.* смысл *m.*, значе́ние *nt.*; — *v.* подразумева́ть *imp.*

purpose, *n.* цель *f.* **for the p. of,** с це́лью. **-ly,** *adv.* наро́чно.

purse, *n.* кошелёк *m.*

pursue, *v.* гна́ться *imp.*

pursuit, *n.* пого́ня *f.*

push, *n.* толчо́к *m.* — *v.* прота́лкивать *imp.*, протолкну́ть *perf.*

put, *v.* класть *imp.*, положи́ть *perf.* **put aside,** отложи́ть в сто́рону. **put out a light,** погаси́ть свет.

putrid, *adj.* гнило́й.

puzzle, *n.* зага́дка, головоло́мка *f.* — *v.* ста́вить в тупи́к.

pyramid, *n.* пирами́да *f.*

Q

quack, *n.* кря́канье *nt.* — *v.* кря́кать *imp.*

quadrangle, *n.* четырёхуго́льник *m.*

quadruped, *adj.* четвероно́гий. — *n.* четвероно́гое *nt.*

quaint, *adj.* причу́дливый.

quake, *n.* дрожа́ние *nt.*; (*earth*) землетрясе́ние *nt.* — *v.* трясти́сь *imp.*

qualification, *n.* квалифика́ция *f.*; (*restriction*) ограниче́ние *nt.*, огово́рка *f.*

qualify, *v. t.* квалифици́ровать *imp.* — *v.i.* квалифици́роваться *imp.*

quality, *n.* ка́чество *nt.*

quandary, *n.* затрудне́ние *nt.*; затрудни́тельное положе́ние.

quantity, *n.* коли́чество *nt.*

quarantine, *n.* каранти́н *m.* — *v.* подве́ргнуть каранти́ну.

quarrel, *n.* ссо́ра *f.* — *v.* ссо́риться *imp.*

quarry, *n.* каменоло́мня *f.*; (*animal*) пресле́дуемый зверь.

quarter, *n.* че́тверть *f.*; *pl.* (*lodgings*) жили́ще *nt.* **a q. to one (two, three),** три че́тверти двена́дцатого (пе́рвого, второ́го). **-ly,** *adj.* трёхме́сячный. — *adv.* раз в три ме́сяца.

quartet, *n.* кварте́т *m.*

quartz, *n.* кварц *m.*

quaver, *v.* дрожа́ть *imp.*

queen, *n.* короле́ва *f.*; (*chess*) ферзь *f.*

queer, *adj.* стра́нный, чудакова́тый.

quench, *v.* гаси́ть *imp.*, погаси́ть *perf.*

query, *n.* вопро́с *m.* — *v.* спра́шивать *imp.*, спроси́ть *perf.*

quest, *n.* по́иски *pl.*

question, *n.* вопро́с *m.* **in q.,** о кото́ром идёт речь. **q. mark,** вопроси́тельный знак. — *v.* допра́шивать *imp.*, допроси́ть *perf.* **-able,** *adj.* сомни́тельный, подозри́тельный.

quick, *adj.* бы́стрый. **-en,** *v.* ускоря́ть *imp.*, уско́рить *perf.*

quiet, *adj.* споко́йный, ти́хий. — *n.* поко́й *m.*, тишина́ *f.* — *v.* успока́ивать *imp.*, успоко́ить *perf.*

quilt, *n.* одея́ло *nt.*

quinine, *n.* хини́н *m.*

quintet, *n.* квинте́т *m.*

quit, *v.* покида́ть *imp.*, поки́нуть *perf.*; броса́ть *imp.*, бро́сить *perf.*

quite, *adv.* совсе́м, вполне́. **not q.,** не совсе́м.

quiver, *n.* дрожь *f.*, тре́пет *m.* — *v.* дрожа́ть *imp.*

quorum, *n.* кво́рум *m.*

quota, *n.* кво́та, до́ля *f.*

quotation, *n.* цита́та *f.*; (*price*) расце́нка *f.* **q. marks,** кавы́чки *f. pl.*

quote, *n.* цита́та *f.* **quote ... unquote,** откры́ть кавы́чки ... закры́ть кавы́чки. — *v.* цити́ровать *imp.*, процити́ровать *perf.*; ссыла́ться *imp.*, сосла́ться *perf.*

R

rabbi, *n.* равви́н *m.*

rabbit, *n.* кро́лик *m.*

rabble, *n.* чернь *f.*

rabid, *adj.* бе́шеный.

rabies, *n.* водобоя́знь *f.*

race, *n.* го́нки *pl.*, бег *m.*; (*people*) ра́са *f.* — *v.* состяза́ться в ско́рости.

racial, *adj.* ра́совый.

racket, *n.* (*noise*) шум *m.*; (*tennis*) раке́тка *f.*

radar, *n.* рада́р, радиолока́тор *m.*

radiance, *n.* сия́ние *nt.*

radiant, *adj.* сия́ющий.

radiate, *v.* излуча́ть *imp.*

radiation, *n.* излуче́ние *nt.*

radiator, *n.* радиа́тор *m.*

radical, *adj.* радика́льный; коренно́й. — *n.* ко́рень *m.*

radio, *n.* ра́дио *nt. ind.*

radioactive, *adj.* радиоакти́вный.

radish, *n.* реди́ска *f.*

radium, *n.* ра́дий *m.*

radius, *n.* ра́диус *m.*

raft, *n.* плот *m.*

rag, *n.* тря́пка *f.*

rage, *n.* гнев *m.*, я́рость *f.* — *v.* беси́ться *imp.*

ragged, *adj.* обо́рванный.

raid, *n.* набе́г *m.*, налёт *m.* — *v.* де́лать обла́ву.

railroad, *n.* желе́зная доро́га.

rain, *n.* дождь *m.* — *v.*: **it is raining,** идёт дождь. **-bow,** *n.* ра́дуга *f.* **-coat,** *n.* непромока́емый плащ, непромока́емое пальто́.

rainy, *adj.* дождли́вый.

raise, *n.* подъём *m.*, повыше́ние *nt.* — *v.* поднима́ть *imp.*, подня́ть *perf.*

raisin, *n.* изю́м *m.*

ram, *n.* бара́н *m.*; (*tech.*) тара́н *m.*

ramble, *n.* прогу́лка *f.* — *v.* броди́ть *imp.*

ramp, *n.* укло́н, скат *m.*

ranch, *n.* фе́рма *f.*, ра́нчо *nt. ind.*

rancid, *adj.* прого́рклый.

random, *adj.* случа́йный. **at r.,** науга́д, наобу́м.

range, *n.* преде́л, разма́х *m.*

rank, *adj.* бу́йный; (*overgrown*) заро́сший. — *n.* (*row*) ряд *m.*; (*status*) зва́ние *nt.* — *v. t.* классифици́ровать *imp. & perf.* — *v. i.* классифици́роваться *imp. & perf.*

ransack, *v.* обы́скивать *imp.*, обыска́ть *perf.*

ransom, *n.* вы́куп *m.* — *v.* выкупа́ть *imp.*, вы́купить *perf.*

rap, *n.* стук *m.* — *v.* стуча́ть *imp.*

rapid, *adj.* бы́стрый, ско́рый.

rape, *n.* изнаси́лование *nt.* — *v.* наси́ловать *imp.*, изнаси́ловать *perf.*

rapture, *n.* восхище́ние, восто́рг *m.*

rare, *adj.* ре́дкий.

rarity, *n.* ре́дкость *f.*

rash, *adj.* необду́манный, безрассу́дный. — *n.* сыпь *f.*

raspberry, *n.* мали́на *f.*

rat, *n.* кры́са *f.*

rate, *n.* но́рма *f.*, ста́вка *f.*; сорт *m.* **r. of exchange,** валю́тный курс. — *v.* оце́нивать *imp.*, оцени́ть *perf.*

rather, *adv.* скоре́е, верне́е; предпочти́тельно; (*somewhat*) дово́льно.

ratification, *n.* ратифика́ция *f.*

ratify, *v.* ратифици́ровать *imp. & perf.*

ratio, *n.* пропо́рция *f.*, отноше́ние *nt.*

ration, *n.* паёк *m.* — *v.* норми́ровать *imp. & perf.*

rational, *adj.* рациона́льный. **-ize,** *v.* рационализи́ровать *imp. & perf.*

rattle, *n.* трескотня́ *f.*, треск *m.* — *v.* грохота́ть *imp.*, треща́ть *imp.*

ravage, *v.* опустоша́ть *imp.*, опустоши́ть *perf.*

rave, *v.* бре́дить *imp.*; неи́стовствовать *imp.*

ravel, *v.* запу́тывать *imp.*, запу́тать *perf.*

raven, *n.* во́рон *m.*

raw, adj. сырóй.

ray, n. луч m.

rayon, n. искýсственный шёлк; вискóза f.

razor, n. брúтва f.

reach, n. предéл досягáемости. **within reach,** в пределах достижúмости. — v. (attain) достигáть imp., достúгнуть perf.; доходúть imp., дойтú perf.

react, v. реагúровать imp. & perf.

reaction, n. реáкция f. **-ary,** adj. реакциóнный. — n. реакционéр m.

read, v. читáть imp., прочитáть perf. **-er,** n. читáтель m., читáтельница f.

readily, adv. охóтно, быстро; без трудá.

reading, n. чтéние nt.

ready, adj. готóвый.

real, adj. действúтельный. **-ist,** n. реалúст m. **-ity,** n. действúтельность f. **-ly,** adv. действúтельно.

realization, n. осознáние nt.; осуществлéние nt.

realize, v. t. осуществлять imp., осуществúть perf. — v. i. реализовáть imp. & perf.

realm, n. óбласть, сфéра f.

reap, v. жать imp., сжать perf.

rear, adj. зáдний. — n. тыл m. — v. воспúтывать imp., воспитáть perf.; вырáщивать imp., вырастить perf.

reason, n. рáзум, рассýдок m.; (cause) причúна f. — v. рассуждáть imp. **-able,** adj. благоразýмный; умéренный, приéмлемый.

reassure, v. заверять imp., завéрить perf.

rebel, n. повстáнец, бунтóвщик m. — v. восставáть imp. восстáть perf.

rebellion, n. восстáние nt.

rebellious, adj. бунтýющий.

rebuff, n. отпóр m. — v. давáть отпóр.

recall, v. вспоминáть imp., вспóмнить perf.

recapitulate, v. суммúровать

imp. & perf., резюмúровать imp. & perf.

recapitulation, n. суммúрование nt., резюмé nt. ind.

recede, v. отступáть imp., отступúть perf.

receipt, n. квитáнция f.; получéние nt.

receive, v. получáть imp., получúть perf.

receiver, n. получáтель m.; (telephone) телефóнная трýбка; (radio) приéмник m.

recent, adj. недáвний. **-ly,** adv. недáвно, в послéднее врéмя.

receptacle, n. вместúлище nt., приéмник m.

reception, n. приём m.; принятие nt.

receptive, adj. восприúмчивый.

recess, n. перерыв m.

recipe, n. рецéпт m.

recipient, n. получáтель m.

reciprocal, adj. взаúмный.

reciprocate, v. отплáчивать imp., отплатúть perf.; обмéниваться imp., обменúться perf.

recite, v. декламúровать imp. & perf.

reckless, adj. опромéтчивый.

reckon, v. считáть imp.

recline, v. откúдываться imp., откúнуться perf.

recognition, n. узнавáние nt.; (approval) одобрéние nt.

recognize, v. узнавáть imp., узнáть perf.

recollect, v. вспоминáть imp., вспóмнить perf.

recommend, v. рекомендовáть imp. & perf. **-ation,** n. рекомендáция f.

reconcile, v. примирять imp., примирúть perf.

reconsider, v. пересмáтривать imp., пересмотрéть perf.

reconstruct, v. перестрáивать imp., перестрóить perf.

record, n. зáпись f., протокóл m.; (mus.) граммофóнная (or патефóнная) пластúнка; (athl.) рекóрд m. — v.

запи́сывать *imp.*, записа́ть *perf.*

recount, *v.* пересчи́тывать *imp.*, пересчита́ть *perf.*; (*tell*) расска́зывать *imp.*, рассказа́ть *perf.*

recover, *v.* получи́ть обра́тно. — *v. i.* выздора́вливать *imp.*, вы́здороветь *perf.*

recovery, *n.* возвраще́ние *nt.*; (*health*) выздоровле́ние *nt.*

recruit, *v.* рекру́т *m.* — *v.* вербова́ть *imp.*, завербова́ть *perf.*

rectangle, *n.* прямоуго́льник *m.*

recuperate, *v.* выздора́вливать *imp.*, вы́здороветь *perf.*

recur, *v.* происходи́ть вновь.

red, *adj.* кра́сный. — *n.* кра́сный цвет.

redeem, *v.* выкупа́ть *imp.*, вы́купить *perf.*

redemption, *n.* вы́куп *m.*

reduce, *v.* уменьша́ть *imp.*, уме́ньшить *perf.*; сокраща́ть *imp.*, сократи́ть *perf.*

reduction, *n.* уменьше́ние *nt.*; сокраще́ние *nt.*

reed, *n.* тростни́к *m.*; (*mus.*) язычо́к *m.*

reef, *n.* риф *m.*

reel, *n.* шпу́лька, кату́шка *f.*; (*dance*) рил *m.* — *v.* кружи́ться *imp.*

refer, *v. t.* относи́ться. — *v. i.* ссыла́ться *imp.*, сосла́ться *perf.*

referee, *n.* судья́ *m.*

reference, *n.* ссы́лка *f.*

refill, *n.* пополне́ние *nt.* — *v.* наполня́ть вновь.

refine, *v.* рафини́ровать *imp. & perf.* **-ment,** *n.* утончё́нность *f.*

reflect, *v.* отража́ть *imp.* **-ion,** *n.* отраже́ние *nt.*

reform, *n.* рефо́рма *f.* — *v.* реформи́ровать *imp. & perf.*

refrain, *n.* припе́в, рефре́н *m.* — *v.* возде́рживаться *imp.*, воздержа́ться *perf.*

refresh, *v.* освежа́ть *imp.*, освежи́ть *perf.* **-ment,** *n.* подкрепле́ние *nt.*

refrigerator, *n.* холоди́льник, рефрижера́тор *m.*

refuge, *n.* убе́жище *nt.*

refugee, *n.* бе́женец *m.*

refund, *n.* возвраще́ние *nt.* — *v.* возмеща́ть *imp.*, возмести́ть *perf.*

refusal, *n.* отка́з *m.*

refuse, *n.* отбро́сы *pl.*, му́сор *m.* — *v.* отка́зывать *imp.*, отказа́ть *perf.*

refute, *v.* опроверга́ть *imp.*, опрове́ргнуть *perf.*

regain, *v.* получи́ть обра́тно.

regal, *adj.* короле́вский, ца́рский.

regard, *n.* взгляд *m.*; *pl.* (*greetings*) приве́т *m.* **with r. to,** относи́тельно. — *v.* смотре́ть на; относи́ться *imp.* **-less (of),** не обраща́я внима́ния (на); не взира́я (на).

regime, *n.* режи́м *m.*

region, *n.* райо́н *m.*, о́бласть *f.*; сфе́ра *f.*

register, *n.* рее́стр, журна́л *m.*; спи́сок *m.* **cash r.,** ка́ссовый аппара́т. — *v.t.* регистри́ровать *imp. & perf.* — *v.i.* регистри́роваться *imp. & perf.*

registration, *n.* регистра́ция, за́пись *f.*

regret, *n.* сожале́ние *nt.* — *v.* сожале́ть *imp.*

regular, *adj.* пра́вильный, регуля́рный. **-ity,** *n.* пра́вильность, регуля́рность *f.*

regulate, *v.* регули́ровать *imp. & perf.*

regulation, *n.* регули́рование *nt.*; (*rule*) пра́вило *nt.*, уста́в *m.*

rehabilitate, *v.* реабилити́ровать *imp. & perf.*

rehearse, *v.* репети́ровать *imp.*

reign, *n.* ца́рствование *nt.* — *v.* ца́рствовать *imp.*

reimburse, *v.* возмеща́ть *imp.*, возмести́ть *perf.*

rein, *n.* по́вод *m.*

reindeer, *n.* оле́нь *m.*

reinforce, *v.* уси́ливать *imp.*,

усилить *perf.* **-ment,** *n.* укрепление, усиление *nt.*

reiterate, *v.* повторять *imp.,* повторить *perf.*

reject, *v.* отвергать *imp.,* отвергнуть *perf.*

rejoice, *v.* радоваться *imp.*

relapse, *n.* рецидив *m.* — *v.* снова впасть *perf.*

relate, *v.* установить отношение; (*tell*) рассказывать *imp.,* рассказать *perf.*

relation, *n.* отношение *nt.* **in r. to,** в соотношении, относительно.

relative, *adj.* относительный, сравнительный. — *n.* родственник *m.,* родственница *f.*

relativity, *n.* относительность *f.*

relax, *v.t.* смягчать *imp.,* смягчить *perf.* — *v.i.* смягчаться *imp.,* смягчиться *perf.*

relay, *n.* смена *f.* — *v.* передавать *imp.,* передать *perf.*

release, *n.* освобождение *nt.;* (*issue*) выпуск *m.* — *v.* освобождать *imp.,* освободить *perf.;* выпускать *imp.,* выпустить *perf.*

relent, *v.* смягчаться *imp.,* смягчиться *perf.*

relevant, *adj.* относящийся к делу.

reliability, *n.* надёжность *f.*

reliable, *adj.* надёжный.

relic, *n.* пережиток *m.;* (*pl.*) мощи, реликвии *pl.*

relief, *n.* облегчение *nt.;* (*art*) рельеф *m.*

relieve, *v.* облегчать *imp.,* облегчить *perf.*

religion, *n.* религия *f.*

religious, *adj.* религиозный.

relinquish, *v.* сдавать *imp.,* сдать *perf.*

reluctant, *adj.* неохотный.

rely, *v.* полагаться *imp.*

remain, *v.* (*pl.*) остаток *m.,* — *v.* оставаться *imp.,* остаться *perf.* **-der,** *n.* остаток *m.*

remark, *n.* замечание *nt.* — замечать *imp.,* заметить *perf.* **-able,** *adj.* замечательный.

remedy, *n.* лекарство *nt.;* средство от болезни. — *v.* исправлять *imp.,* исправить *perf.*

remember, *v.* помнить *imp.*

remembrance, *n.* воспоминание *nt.*

remind, *v.* напоминать *imp.,* напомнить *perf.*

reminiscent, *adj.* вспоминающий.

remorse, *n.* угрызение совести

remote, *adj.* отдалённый.

removal, *n.* перемещение *nt.*

remove, *v.* передвигать *imp.,* передвинуть *perf.;* перемещать *imp.,* переместить *perf.*

renaissance, *n.* возрождение *nt.;* (*cap.*) эпоха Возрождения.

render, *v.* оказывать *imp.,* оказать *perf.;* воздавать *imp.,* воздать *perf.;* (*make*) делать *imp.,* сделать *perf.*

rendezvous, *n.* свидание *nt.*

rendition, *n.* изображение *nt.,* передача *f.*

renew, *v.* возобновлять *imp.,* возобновить *perf.* **-al,** *n.* возобновление *f.*

renounce, *v.* отказываться *imp.,* отказаться *perf.*

renovate, *v.* подновлять *imp.,* поднови́ть *perf.*

renown, *n.* слава, известность *f.*

rent, *n.* квартирная плата. — *v.* (*to*) сдавать в аренду; (*from*) брать в аренду.

repair, *n.* ремонт *m.* — *v.* ремонтировать *imp. & perf.*

repatriate, *v.* репатриировать *imp. & perf.*

repatriation, *v.* репатриация *f.*

repay, *v.* отплачивать *imp.,* отплатить *perf.*

repeat, *v.* повторять *imp.,* повторить *perf.*

repel, *v.* отражать *imp.,* отразить *perf.*

repent, *v.* раскаиваться *imp.,*

раска́яться *perf.* **-ance**, *n.* покая́ние, раска́яние *nt.*

repercussion, *n.* отраже́ние *nt.*, о́тзвук *m.*

repertoire, *n.* репертуа́р *m.*

repetition, *n.* повторе́ние *nt.*

replace, *v.* заменя́ть *imp.*, замени́ть *perf.*

replenish, *v.* пополня́ть *imp.*, попо́лнить *perf.*

reply, *n.* отве́т *m.* **in r. to**, в отве́т на. — *v.* отвеча́ть *imp.*, отве́тить *perf.*

report, *n.* отчёт *m.*, рапо́рт *m.* — *v.* сообща́ть *imp.*, сообщи́ть *perf.* **-er**, *n.* репортёр *m.*

repose, *n.* о́тдых *m.*, переды́шка *f.* — *v.* ложи́ться отдыха́ть.

represent, *v.* изобража́ть *imp.*, изобрази́ть *perf.*; представля́ть *imp.*, предста́вить *perf.* **-ation**, *n.* изображе́ние *nt.*; представле́ние *nt.* **-ative**, *adj.* характе́рный; показа́тельный. — *n.* представи́тель *m.*

repress, *v.* подавля́ть *imp.*, подави́ть *perf.*

reprimand, *n.* вы́говор *m.* — *v.* де́лать вы́говор.

reprisal, *n.* репресса́лия *f.*

reproach, *n.* упрёк, попрёк *m.* — *v.* упрека́ть *imp.*, упрекну́ть *perf.*

reproduce, *v.* воспроизводи́ть *imp.*, воспроизвести́ *perf.*

reproduction, *n.* воспроизведе́ние *nt.*

reprove, *v.* порица́ть *imp.*

republic, *n.* респу́блика *f.* **-an**, *adj.* республика́нский.

repudiation, *n.* отрица́ние, отрече́ние *nt.*

repulsive, *adj.* омерзи́тельный, отвраща́ющий.

reputation, *n.* репута́ция, сла́ва *f.*

request, *n.* про́сьба *f.* — *v.* проси́ть *imp.*, попроси́ть *perf.*

require, *v.* тре́бовать *imp.*, потре́бовать *perf.* **-ment**, *n.* тре́бование *nt.*

requisition, *n.* реквизи́ция *f.*

rescue, *n.* спасе́ние *nt.* — *v.* спаса́ть *imp.*, спасти́ *perf.*

research, *n.* иссле́дование *nt.* *adj.* иссле́довательский.

resemble, *v.* походи́ть *imp.*

resent, *v.* негодова́ть *imp.*

reservation, *n.* огово́рка *f.*; (*Indian*) резерва́ция *f.*

reserve, *n.* запа́с *m.*; (*restraint*) сде́ржанность *f.* — *v.* резерви́ровать *imp. & perf.*

reservoir, *n.* резервуа́р *m.*

reside, *v.* жить *imp.*; пребыва́ть *imp.*, пребы́ть *perf.*

residence, *n.* (*place*) местожи́тельство *nt.*; (*residing*) прожива́ние, пребыва́ние *nt.*

resident, *n.* постоя́нный жи́тель.

residue, *n.* оса́док *m.*; оста́ток *m.*

resign, *v.* уступа́ть *imp.*, уступи́ть *perf.*

resignation, *n.* отста́вка *f.*, отка́з *m.*; (*document*) заявле́ние об отста́вке.

resist, *v.* противостоя́ть *imp.*; отбива́ть *imp.*, отби́ть *perf.* **-ance**, *n.* сопротивле́ние *nt.*

resolute, *adj.* реши́тельный.

resolution, *n.* реше́ние *nt.*, резолю́ция *f.*

resolve, *v.* реша́ть(ся) *imp.*, реши́ть(ся) *perf.*

resonant, *adj.* звуча́щий, разда́ющийся.

resort, *n.* (*health*) куро́рт *m.*; (*recourse*) прибе́жище *nt.*, наде́жда *f.* — *v.* прибега́ть *imp.*, прибе́гнуть *perf.*

resound, *v.* звуча́ть *imp.*, прозвуча́ть *perf.*

resource, *n.* ресу́рсы, сре́дства, запа́сы *pl.* **natural resources**, есте́ственные бога́тства.

respect, *n.* уваже́ние, почте́ние *nt.*; (*reference*) отноше́ние *nt.* **with r. to**, что каса́ется; относи́тельно. — *v.* уважа́ть, почита́ть *imp.* **-able**, *adj.* почте́нный; заслу́живающий уваже́ния. **-ful**, *adj.* почти́тельный, вежливый. **-ive,** *adj.* соответственный.

respiration, *n.* дыхание *nt.*

respite, *n.* передышка *f.*

respond, *v.* отвечать *imp.,* ответить *perf.*

response, *n.* ответ *m.,* реакция *f.*

responsibility, *n.* ответственность *f.*

responsible, *adj.* ответственный.

responsive, *adj.* ответный, отзывчивый.

rest, *n.* отдых, покой *m.;* (*remainder*) остаток *m.,* остальные *pl.* — *v.* отдыхать *imp.,* отдохнуть *perf.*

restaurant, *n.* ресторан *m.*

restful, *adj.* успокоительный.

restitution, *n.* возвращение, восстановление *nt.*

restless, *adj.* беспокойный, неспокойный.

restoration, *n.* реставрация *f.*

restore, *v.* восстанавливать *imp.,* восстановить *perf.;* реставрировать *imp. & perf.*

restrain, *v.* сдерживать *imp.,* сдержать *perf.* **r. oneself,** сдерживаться *imp.,* сдержаться *perf.*

restraint, *n.* сдержанность *f.*

restrict, *v.* ограничивать *imp.,* ограничить *perf.*

result, *n.* результат *m.,* следствие *nt.* **as a result,** в результате. — *v.* следовать *imp.,* последовать *perf.*

resume, *v.* продолжать *imp.,* продолжить *perf.*

resurrection, *n.* воскресение *nt.*

retail, *n.* розничная продажа. *adv.* в розницу. — *v.* продавать в розницу.

retain, *v.* сохранять *imp.,* сохранить *perf.*

retaliate, *v.* отплачивать *imp.,* отплатить *perf.*

retard, *v.* задерживать *imp.,* задержать *perf.*

retention, *n.* удерживание, удержание *nt.*

reticent, *adj.* сдержанный, умалчивающий.

retire, *v.* уходить в отставку; (*sleep*) ложиться спать.

retreat, *n.* отступление *nt.;* (*haven*) убежище *nt.* — *v.* отступать *imp.,* отступить *perf.*

retribution, *n.* возмездие *nt.*

retrieve, *v.* взять обратно; снова найти.

return, *n.* возвращение. **in r. for,** взамен за. — *v. t.* возвращать *imp.,* возвратить *perf.* — *v. i.* возвращаться *imp.,* возвратиться *perf.*

reunion, *n.* воссоединение *nt.,* собрание *nt.*

reveal, *v.* выдавать *imp.,* выдать *perf.*

revelation, *n.* открытие, обнаружение *nt.*

revenge, *n.* мщение *nt.,* месть *f.* **get** *or* **take r.,** мстить *imp.,* отомстить *perf.*

revenue, *n.* доход *m.*

revere, *v.* почитать *imp.,* уважать *imp.*

reverence, *n.* почтение *nt.*

reverend, *adj.* почтенный; (*title*) преподобный.

reverse, *adj.* обратный. — *n.* противоположное *nt.,* обратное *nt.;* (*auto.*) обратный ход. — *v.* перевёртывать *imp.,* перевернуть *perf.*

revert, *v.* возвращаться *imp.,* возвратиться *perf.*

review, *n.* обзор *m.,* обозрение *nt.* — *v.* обозревать *imp.,* обозреть *perf.*

revise, *v.* перерабатывать *imp.,* переработать *perf.*

revision, *n.* ревизия *f.;* (*publishing*) исправленное издание.

revival, *n.* возрождение *nt.*

revive, *v. t.* возрождать *imp.,* возродить *perf.* — *v.i.* приходить в себя.

revoke, *v.* отменять *imp.,* отменить *perf.*

revolt, *n.* восстание *nt.* — *v.* восставать *imp.,* восстать *perf.*

revolution, *n.* революция *f.*

-ary, *adj.* революцио́нный. — *n.* революционе́р *m.*

revolve, *v.* верте́ться *imp.*

revolver, *n.* револьве́р *m.*

reward, *n.* награ́да *f.* — *v.* награжда́ть *imp.*, награди́ть *perf.*

rhetorical, *adj.* ритори́ческий.

rheumatism, *n.* ревмати́зм *m.*

rhinoceros, *n.* носоро́г *m.*

rhyme, *n.* ри́фма *f.* — *v.* рифмова́ть *imp.*

rhythm, *n.* ритм *m.* **-ical,** *adj.* ритми́ческий.

rib, *n.* ребро́ *nt.*

ribbon, *n.* ле́нта *f.*

rice, *n.* рис *m.*

rich, *adj.* бога́тый.

rid, *v.* избавля́ть *imp.*, изба́вить *perf.* **to get r. of,** избавля́ться *imp.*, изба́виться *perf.*

riddle, *n.* зага́дка *f.*

ride, *n.* прогу́лка *f.* — *v.* е́здить *imp. indet.*, е́хать *imp. det.*

ridge, *n.* гре́бень, хребе́т *m.*

ridicule, *n.* насме́шка *f.* — *v.* осме́ивать *imp.*, осмея́ть *perf.*

ridiculous, *adj.* смехотво́рный, смешно́й.

right, *adj.* пра́вый; ве́рный; пра́вильный. — *adv.* пра́вильно, ве́рно. — *n.* пра́во *nt.*; пра́вильность *f.*, справедли́вость *f.* (direction) пра́вая сторона́. **on or to the r.,** напра́во. — *v.* выпрямля́ть *imp.*, вы́прямить *perf.*; исправля́ть *imp.* испра́вить *perf.*

righteous, *adj.* пра́ведный, справедли́вый.

rigid, *adj.* жёсткий, непрекло́нный.

rigor, *n.* стро́гость, суро́вость *f.* **-ous,** *adj.* стро́гий, суро́вый.

rim, *n.* край, о́бод *m.*

ring, *n.* кольцо́ *nt.*, круг *m.*; (bell) звон *m.*, звуча́ние *nt.* — *v. t.* окружи́ть кольцо́м; звене́ть *imp.* — *v. i.* звони́ть *imp.*, позвони́ть *perf.*

rinse, *v.* полоска́ть *imp.*

riot, *n.* бунт *m.*, мяте́ж *m.* — v бунтова́ть *imp.*, принима́т уча́стие в бу́нте.

rip, *n.* разры́в, разре́з *m.* — *v.* рвать *imp.*; разрыва́ть *imp.* разорва́ть *perf.*

ripe, *adj.* спе́лый; зре́лый.

ripen, *v.* зреть *imp.*; созрева́т *imp.*, созре́ть *perf.*

rise, *n.* повыше́ние, возвы ше́ние *m.*; восхо́д *m.* — v поднима́ться *imp.*, подня́ть ся *perf.*; встава́ть *imp.* встать *perf.*; (sun) восходи́т *imp.*, взойти́ *perf.*

risk, *n.* риск *m.* — v. риско ва́ть *imp. & perf.*

risky, *adj.* опа́сный, риско́ ванный.

rite, *n.* церемо́ния *f.*

ritual, *adj.* ритуа́льный. — *n* ритуа́л *m.*

rival, *n.* сопе́рник *m.* **-ry,** со́перничество *nt.*

river, *n.* река́ *f.*

rivet, *n.* заклёпка *f.* — v заклёпывать *imp.*, заклепа́т *perf.*

road, *n.* доро́га *f.*, путь *m.*

roam, *v.* стра́нствовать *imp*

roar, *n.* рёв *m.* — *v.* реве́т *imp.*

roast, *n.* жарко́е, жа́реное *m* — *v. t.* жа́рить *imp.*, изжа́ рить *perf.*; — *v. i.* жа́рить *imp.*, изжа́риться *perf.*

rob, *v.* обкра́дывать *imp* обкра́сть *perf.*

robber, *n.* граби́тель *m.*

robbery, *n.* кра́жа, грабё *f.*

robe, *n.* ма́нтия *f.*

robin, *n.* малиновка *f.*

robust, *adj.* здоро́вый, кре́п кий.

rock, *n.* скала́ *f.*, утёс *m.* — *v.t.* (swing) кача́ть *imp* (shake) трясти́ *imp.*; кача́ть трясти́ *perf.* — *v.i.* кача́т *imp.*; трясти́сь *imp.*, за трясти́сь *perf.*

rocker, *n.* кача́лка *f.*, кре́сл кача́лка.

rocket, *n.* раке́та *f.*

rocky, adj. скали́стый, камени́стый.

Rocky Mountains, Скали́стые го́ры.

rod, n. жезл m.; брус m.; (branch) ро́зга f.

rodent, n. грызу́н m.

roguish, adj. жуликова́тый.

role, n. роль f.

roll, n. сви́ток, свёрток m.; (bread) бу́лочка f. — v.t. кати́ть imp. — v. i. кати́ться imp. **r. up,** ска́тывать imp., ската́ть perf.

Roman, adj. ри́мский. — n. римля́нин m., римля́нка f.

romance, n. рома́нтика f.; (love affair) любо́вный эпизо́д m.; (mus.) рома́нс m.; (lit.) рома́н m.

romantic, adj. романти́чный, романти́ческий.

roof, n. кры́ша f.

room, n. ко́мната, ка́мера f.; (space) ме́сто nt.

rooster, n. пету́х m.

root, n. ко́рень m. **to take r.,** укорени́ться perf.

rope, n. кана́т m., верёвка f.

rose, n. ро́за f. — adj. ро́зовый.

rosy, adj. ро́зовый; румя́ный.

rot, n. гние́ние nt., гниль f. — v. гнить imp., сгнить perf.

rotary, adj. ротацио́нный.

rotate, v. t. враща́ть imp. — v. i. враща́ться imp.

rotation, n. враще́ние nt.

rotten, adj. гнило́й, прогни́вший.

rouge, n. румя́на pl.

rough, adj. гру́бый, грубова́тый; косма́тый.

round, adj. кру́глый; кругово́й. — n. круг m., окру́жность f.; (boxing) ра́унд m. — v.t. округля́ть imp., округли́ть perf. — v. i. округля́ться imp., округли́ться perf.

rouse, v. буди́ть imp., разбуди́ть perf.; возбужда́ть imp., возбуди́ть perf.

rout, n. разгро́м m. — v. обраща́ть в бе́гство.

route, n. маршру́т m.; путь m.

routine, adj. определённый, шедло́нный. — n. рути́на f.

rove, v. стра́нствовать imp.

row, n. ряд m.; (uproar) шум, гвалт m. — v. грести́ imp.

rowboat, n. гребна́я ло́дка.

rowdy, adj. шу́мный, бу́йный.

royal, adj. короле́вский, ца́рский.

royalty, n. чле́ны короле́вской семьи́; (often pl.) (fee) а́вторский гонора́р m.

rub, n. тре́ние, натира́ние, расти́рание nt. — v.t. натира́ть imp., натере́ть perf. **r. off,** v.t. стира́ть imp., стере́ть perf. — v.i. стира́ться imp., стере́ться perf.

rubber, n. рези́на f., каучу́к m.; pl. (galoshes) гало́ши pl.

rubbish, n. му́сор m.

ruby, n. руби́н m.

rudder, n. руль m.

rude, adj. гру́бый. **-ness,** n. гру́бость f.

rudiments, n. нача́тки, зача́тки pl.

rue, v. сожале́ть imp.

ruffle, n. рябь f.; (trimming) обо́рка f. — v. ряби́ть imp., заряби́ть perf.; (dishevel) еро́шить imp.

rug, n. ковёр, ко́врик m.

rugged, adj. си́льный, кре́пкий.

ruin, n. ги́бель f.; (pl.) разва́лина f., руи́ны pl. — v. разруша́ть imp., разру́шить perf.

rule, n. пра́вило nt., уста́в m. **as a r.,** обы́чно, как пра́вило. — v. управля́ть imp.; пра́вить imp.

ruler, n. прави́тель m.; (measure) лине́йка f.

rum, n. ром m.

Rumania, n. Румы́ния f.

Rumanian, adj. румы́нский. — n. румы́н m., румы́нка f.

rumor, n. слух m., молва́ f.

run, n. бег, пробе́г m. **in the long run,** в коне́чном счёте. — v. бе́гать imp. indet., бежа́ть imp. det., побежа́ть *perf.* **run away,** убежа́ть *perf.* **run into,** нае́хать *perf.*

runner, *n.* бегу́н *m.;* (*sled*) по́лоз *m.*

running water, прото́чная вода́.

rupture, *n.* разло́м, проло́м, разры́в *m.;* (*med.*) гры́жа *f.* — *v.* прорыва́ть *imp.,* прорва́ть *perf.*

rural, *adj.* се́льский.

rush, *n.* стреми́тельное движе́ние; на́тиск *m.* — *v.* де́йствовать поспе́шно.

Russia, *n.* Росси́я *f.*

Russian, *adj.* ру́сский. — *n.* ру́сский *m.,* ру́сская *f.*

rust, *n.* ржа *f.* — *v.* ржа́веть *imp.,* поржа́веть *perf.*

rustic, *adj.* се́льский, дереве́нский.

rusty, *adj.* ржа́вый, заржа́вленный.

rut, *n.* колея́, борозда́ *f.;* (*tech.*) жёлоб *m.*

ruthless, *adj.* безжа́лостный.

rye, *n.* рожь *f.* — *adj.* ржано́й.

S

saber, *n.* са́бля *f.*

sable, *n.* со́боль *m.*

sabotage, *n.* сабота́ж *m.* — *v.* саботи́ровать *imp. & perf.*

sack, *n.* мешо́к *m.* — *v.* класть в мешо́к; (*dismiss*) уво́лить *perf.*

sacred, *adj.* свяще́нный, свято́й.

sacrifice, *n.* же́ртва *f.* — *v.* же́ртвовать *imp.,* поже́ртвовать *perf.*

sacrilege, *n.* святота́тство *nt.*

sacrilegious, *adj.* святота́тственный.

sad, *adj.* печа́льный, гру́стный. **-ness,** *n.* печа́ль *f.,* уны́ние *nt.*

saddle, *n.* седло́ *nt.* — *v.* седла́ть *imp.,* оседла́ть *perf.*

safe, *n.* несгора́емый шкаф *or* я́щик. — *adj.* безопа́сный, в безопа́сности. **-ty,** *n.* безопа́сность *f.*

safety pin, англи́йская була́вка.

sage, *n.* мудре́ц *m.* — *adj.* му́дрый.

sail, *n.* па́рус *m.* — *v.* пла́вать *imp.*

sailboat, *n.* па́русная шлю́пка.

sailor, *n.* матро́с *m.*

saint, *n.,* *adj.* свято́й.

sake, *n.:* **for the s. of,** ра́ди *m.*

salad, *n.* сала́т *m.*

salary, *n.* жа́лованье *nt.*

sale, *n.* прода́жа *f.* **on s.,** в прода́же.

salesman, *n.* продаве́ц, комиссионе́р *m.*

saliva, *n.* слюна́ *f.*

salmon, *n.* лосо́сь *m.*

salt, *adj.* солёный. — *n.* соль *f.* — *v.* соли́ть *imp.,* посоли́ть *perf.*

salute, *n.* приве́тствие *nt.,* салю́т *m.* — *v.* салютова́ть *imp. & perf.*

salvage, *v.* спасе́ние иму́щества. — *v.* спаса́ть *imp.,* спасти́ *perf.*

salvation, *n.* спасе́ние *nt.*

salve, *n.* целе́бная мазь; бальза́м *m.*

same, *pron.* тот са́мый *m.,* тот са́мая *f.,* тот са́мое *nt.,* тот са́мые *pl.* — *adj.* одно́ и то же; тот же са́мый.

sample, *n.* образе́ц *m.* — *v.* про́бовать *imp.,* попро́бовать *perf.*

sanction, *n.* са́нкция *f.,* одобре́ние *nt.* — *v.* санкциони́ровать *imp. & perf.*

sanctity, *n.* свя́тость *f.*

sanctuary, *n.* святи́лище *nt.;* убе́жище *nt.*

sand, *n.* песо́к *m.*

sandal, *n.* санда́лия *f.*

sandwich, *n.* са́ндвич, бутербро́д *m.*

sandy, *adj.* песо́чный, песча́ный.

sane, *adj.* здра́вый, здравомы́слящий.

sanity, *n.* здравомы́слие *nt.*

sanitary, *adj.* санита́рный, гигиени́ческий.

Santa Claus рожде́ственский дед, дед-моро́з *m.*

sap, *n.* сок *m.* — *v.* истоща́ть *imp.*, истощи́ть *perf.*

sapphire, *n.* сапфи́р *m.*

sarcasm, *n.* сарка́зм *m.*

sarcastic, *adj.* саркасти́ческий.

sardine, *n.* сарди́на *f.*

satellite, *n.* сателли́т, спу́тник *m.*

satin, *n.* атла́с *m.* — *adj.* атла́сный.

satire, *n.* сати́ра *f.*

satirical, *adj.* сатири́ческий.

satisfaction, *n.* удовлетворе́ние *nt.*

satisfactory, *adj.* удовлетвори́тельный.

satisfy, *v.* удовлетворя́ть *imp.*, удовлетвори́ть *perf.*

saturate, *v.* насыща́ть *imp.*, насы́тить *perf.*

Saturday, *n.* суббо́та *f.* — *adj.* суббо́тний.

sauce, *n.* со́ус *m.*

saucer, *n.* блю́дце *nt.*

sausage, *n.* колбаса́ *f.*

savage, *adj.* ди́кий, свире́пый. — *n.* дика́рь *m.*

save, *v.* спаса́ть *imp.*, спасти́ *perf.* — *prep.* за исключе́нием.

savings, *n.* сбереже́ния *pl.*

savior, *n.* спаси́тель.

saw, *n.* пила́ *f.* — *v.* пили́ть *imp.*

say, *v.* говори́ть *imp.*, сказа́ть *perf.* **-ing,** *n.* погово́рка *f.*

scald, *v.* ошпа́ривать *imp.*, ошпа́рить *perf.*

scale, *n.* ле́стница *f.*; (*fish*) чешуя́ *f.*; *pl.* (*for weighing*) весы́ *pl.* **on a large s.,** в большо́м масшта́бе. — *v.* лу́щить *imp.*; (*climb*) подни-ма́ться *imp.*, подня́ться *perf.*

scalp, *n.* ко́жа головы́; скальп *m.* — *v.* скальпи́ровать *imp.* & *perf.*

scan, *v.* сканди́ровать *imp.* & *perf.*

scandal, *n.* позо́р, сканда́л *m.*

scant, *adj.* ску́дный.

scar, *n.* шрам, рубе́ц *m.* — *v.* покры́ть рубца́ми.

scarce, *adj.* ску́дный, ре́дкий, недоста́точный. **-ly,** *adv.* едва́, едва́ ли.

scare, *v.* пуга́ть *imp.*, испуга́ть *perf.*

scarf, *n.* шарф *m.*

scarlet, *adj.* а́лый. — *n.* а́лый цвет.

scatter, *v.t.* разбра́сывать *imp.*, разброса́ть *perf.* — *v.i.* рассе́иваться *imp.*, рассе́яться *perf.*

scene, *n.* сце́на *f.*, ме́сто де́йствия; (*picture*) карти́на *f.*, пейза́ж *m.* **behind the scenes,** за кули́сами.

scenery, *n.* пейза́ж *m.*; (*theat.*) декора́ции *pl.*

scent, *n.* за́пах *m.*, духи́ *pl.*; (*sense*) чутьё *nt.*, нюх *m.* — *v.* чу́ять *imp.*, почу́ять *perf.*

schedule, *n.* расписа́ние *nt.*; спи́сок *m.*, пе́речень *m.*

scheme, *n.* план, прое́кт *m.*, програ́мма *f.* — *v.* замышля́ть *imp.*, замы́слить *perf.*

scholar, *n.* учёный *m.* **-ship,** *n.* (*stipend*) стипе́ндия *f.*; (*knowledge*) учёность *f.*

school, *n.* шко́ла *f.*; (*fish*) кося́к *m.* — *v.* шко́лить *imp.*

science, *n.* нау́ка *f.*

scientific, *adj.* нау́чный.

scientist, *n.* учёный *m.*

scissors, *n.* но́жницы *pl.*

scold, *v.* брани́ть *imp.*

scope, *n.* кругозо́р *m.*, сфе́ра *f.*

scorch, *v.* обжига́ть *imp.*, обже́чь *perf.*

score, *n.* ито́г *m.*; (*mus.*) партиту́ра *f.* **by a s. of,** со счётом; в тако́й отме́тки; (*mus.*) оркестрова́ть *imp.* & *perf.*

scorn, n. презре́ние nt. — v. презира́ть imp., презре́ть perf.

Scotch, n. (whiskey) шотла́ндское ви́ски.

Scottish, adj. шотла́ндский.

scour, v. чи́стить imp., почи́стить perf.

scout, n. разве́дчик m.; (boy scout) бойска́ут m.; v. производи́ть разве́дку.

scrambled eggs, яи́чница-болту́нья f.

scrap, n. клочо́к m.; скрап m.; (fight) дра́ка f. — v. отдава́ть на слом.

scrape, n. скрип m., шу́рканье nt. — v. t. скрести́ imp. — v. i. скрести́сь imp.

scratch, n. цара́пина f. — v. цара́пать imp., цара́пнуть perf.

scream, n. вопль, крик m. — v. вопи́ть imp.; крича́ть imp., кри́кнуть perf.

screen, n. заве́са f., засло́н m.; (movie) экра́н m.

screw, n. винт m. — v. приви́нчивать imp., привинти́ть perf. **-driver**, n. отвёртка f.

scrub, v. тере́ть imp.

scrupulous, adj. со́вестливый, скрупулёзный.

sculptor, n. ску́льптор m.

sculpture, n. скульпту́ра f., вая́ние nt. — v. вая́ть imp., извая́ть perf.

sea, n. мо́ре nt. **by sea**, мо́рским путём. **on sea**, на мо́ре.

seal, n. печа́ть f., клеймо́ nt.; (animal) тюле́нь m. — v. запеча́тывать imp., запеча́тать perf.

seam, n. шов m.

seaport, n. мо́рский порт.

search, n. по́иски pl. — v. иска́ть imp.

seasick, adj. страда́ющий от мо́рской боле́зни. **-ness**, n. морска́я боле́знь.

season, n. вре́мя го́да; сезо́н m. — v. приправля́ть imp., припра́вить imp.,

seat, n. стул m., ме́сто nt. — v. уса́живать imp., усади́ть perf. **be seated**, уса́живаться imp., усе́сться perf.

second, adj. второ́й. (time) секу́нда f.; (supporter) — помо́щник m., секунда́нт m.

secondary, adj. второстепе́нный, втори́чный.

second-hand, adj. поде́ржанный.

secondly, adv. во-вторы́х.

secret, n. та́йна f., секре́т m. — adj. та́йный, секре́тный.

secretary, n. секрета́рь m., секрета́рша f.

sect, n. се́кта f.

section, n. се́кция f., отде́л m.

secular, adj. мирско́й, све́тский.

secure, adj. споко́йный; надёжный, уве́ренный. — v. обеспе́чивать imp., обеспе́чить perf.; (get) достава́ть imp., доста́ть perf.

security, n. безопа́сность f., надёжность f.

sedative, adj. успока́ивающий. — n. успока́ивающее сре́дство.

seduce, v. соблазня́ть imp., соблазни́ть perf.

see, v. ви́деть imp. **see off**, провожа́ть imp., проводи́ть perf.

seed, n. се́мя, зерно́ nt. — v. се́ять imp., посе́ять perf.

seek, v. иска́ть imp.

seem, v. каза́ться imp.

segment, n. отре́зок m.; (math) сегме́нт m.

segregate, v. отделя́ть imp., отдели́ть perf.

seize, v. хвата́ть imp., схвати́ть perf.

seldom, adv. ре́дко.

select, adj. отбо́рный. — v. выбира́ть imp., вы́брать perf. **-ion**, n. вы́бор m. **-ive**, adj. отбо́рный.

self-confident, adj. самоуве́ренный.

self-conscious, adj. засте́нчивый, нело́вкий.

self-control, *n.* самооблада́ние *nt.*

selfish, *adj.* эгоисти́чный. **-ness**, *n.* эгои́зм *m.*

sell, *v.* продава́ть *imp.*, прода́ть *perf.*

semester, *n.* семе́стр *m.*

semi-annual, *adj.* полугодово́й.

semicircle, *n.* полукру́г *m.*

semicolon, *n.* то́чка с запято́й.

Semitic, *adj.* семити́ческий.

senate, *n.* сена́т *m.*

senator, *n.* сена́тор *m.*

send, *v.* посыла́ть *imp.*, посла́ть *perf.*

senile, *adj.* дря́хлый, ста́рческий.

senility, *n.* дря́хлость, ста́рость *f.*

senior, *adj.* ста́рший. **Sr.**, *n.* оте́ц.

sensation, *n.* ощуще́ние *nt.*, сенса́ция *f.* **-al**, *adj.* сенсацио́нный.

sense, *n.* чу́вство, ощуще́ние *nt.*, смысл *m.* — *v.* ощуща́ть *imp.*, чу́вствовать *imp.* **-less**, *adj.* бессмы́сленный.

sensible, *adj.* здравомы́слящий, разу́мный.

sensitive, *adj.* чувстви́тельный.

sensual, *adj.* чу́вственный, плотско́й.

sentence, *n.* (*gram.*) предложе́ние *nt.*; (*legal*) пригово́р *m.* — *v.* пригова́ривать *imp.*, приговори́ть *perf.*

sentiment, *n.* сенти́менты *pl.* **-al**, *adj.* сентимента́льный.

separate, *adj.* отде́льный. — *v. t.* отделя́ть *imp.*, отдели́ть *perf.* — *v. i.* отделя́ться *imp.*, отдели́ться *perf.*

separation, *n.* отделе́ние, разделе́ние, разлуче́ние *f.*

September, *n.* сентя́брь *m.* — *adj.* сентя́брьский.

sequence, *n.* после́довательность *f.*

Serbian, *n.* серб *m.*, се́рбка *f.* — *adj.* се́рбский.

serenade, *n.* серена́да *f.*

serene, *adj.* споко́йный, ти́хий.

sergeant, *n.* сержа́нт *m.*

serial, *adj.* сери́йный.

series, *n.* се́рия *f.*

serious, *adj.* серьёзный.

sermon, *n.* про́поведь *f.*

servant, *n.* слуга́ *m.*, служа́нка *f.*; служи́тель *m.*

serve, *v.* служи́ть *imp.*, послужи́ть *perf.*

service, *n.* слуга́ *f.* **at the s. of**, к услу́гам. **to be of s.**, быть поле́зным.

session, *n.* се́ссия *f.*, заседа́ние *nt.*

set, *n.* компле́кт, гарниту́р *m.*; (*tendency*) направле́ние *nt.*, тенде́нция *f.*; (*tennis*) сет *m.*; (*mach.*) ширина́ разво́да *f.*; (*theat.*) декора́ция *f.* — *v.* устана́вливать *imp.*, установи́ть *perf.*; (*sun*) заходи́ть *imp.*, зайти́ *perf.*

settle, *v.t.* устана́вливать *imp.*, установи́ть *perf.* — *v. i.* посели́ться *perf.*

settlement, *n.* (*colony*) поселе́ние *nt.*, коло́ния *f.*; (*payment*) упла́та *f.*, расчёт *m.*

settler, *n.* посе́ленец *m.*

seven, *n.* and *adj.* семь *num.* **-teen**, *n.*, *adj.* семна́дцать *num.* **-teenth**, *adj.* семна́дцатый. **-th**, *adj.* седьмо́й. **-tieth**, *adj.* семидеся́тый. **-ty**, *n.* adj. се́мьдесят *num.*

sever, *v.* перереза́ть *imp.*, перере́зать *perf.*; разъединя́ть *imp.*, разъедини́ть *perf.*

several, *adj.* не́сколько. — *n.* не́сколько, не́которое коли́чество.

severe, *adj.* стро́гий, суро́вый.

sew, *v.* шить *imp.*, сшить *perf.*

sewer, *n.* канализацио́нная труба́.

sewing machine, шве́йная маши́на.

sex, *n.* пол *m.* — *adj.* полово́й. **-ual**, *adj.* полово́й, сексуа́льный.

shabby, *adj.* потрёпанный, убо́гий.

shade, *n.* тень *f.* — *v.* заслоня́ть *imp.*, заслони́ть *perf.*; затеня́ть *imp.*, затени́ть *perf.*

shadow, *n.* тень *f.*

shady, *adj.* тени́стый; (*dubious*) сомни́тельный.

shaft, *n.* (*ray*) луч *m.*; (*column*) коло́нна *f.*, сте́ржень *m.*; (*mine*) ша́хта *f.*

shake, *v. t.* трясти́ *imp.* — трясти́сь *imp.* **s. hands,** пожа́ть ру́ки друг дру́гу.

shallow, *adj.* ме́лкий *f.*, (*fig.*) пове́рхностный.

shame, *n.* стыд *m.* — *v.* стыди́ть *imp.* **-ful,** *adj.* позо́рный, сканда́льный.

shampoo, *n.* шампу́нь *m.*; (*wash*) мытьё головы́.

shape, *n.* фо́рма *f.*, о́браз *m.* — *v.* придава́ть фо́рму.

share, *n.* до́ля, часть *f.*, уча́стие *n.*; (*stock*) а́кция *f.* — *v.* дели́ться *imp.*, подели́ться *perf.*

shark, *n.* аку́ла *f.*

sharp, *adj.* о́стрый. — *n.* (*mus.*) дие́з *m.* **-en,** *v.* заостря́ть *imp.*, заостри́ть *perf.*

shatter, *v. t.* разби́ть *perf.* — *v. i.* разби́ться *perf.*

shave, *n.* бритьё *nt.* — *v.t.* брить *imp.*, побри́ть *perf.* — *v.i.* бри́ться *imp.*, побри́ться *perf.*

shawl, *n.* шаль *f.*

she, *pron.* она́ *f.*

shears, *n.* но́жницы *pl.*

sheath, *n.* но́жны *pl.*; оболо́чка *f.*

shed, *n.* наве́с, сара́й *m.* — *v.* роня́ть *imp.*, урони́ть *perf.*

sheep, *n.* овца́ *f.*, бара́н *m.*

sheet, *n.* простыня́ *f.*; (*paper*) лист *m.*

shelf, *n.* по́лка *f.*

shell, *n.* скорлупа́, шелуха́ *f.*; (*sea*) ра́ковина *f.* — *v.* лущи́ть *imp.*

shellac, *n.* шелла́к *m.* — *v.* покрыва́ть шелла́ком.

shelter, *n.* прию́т, кров *m.* — *v.* дать прию́т; служи́ть убе́жищем.

shepherd, *n.* пасту́х *m.*

sherry, *n.* хе́рес *m.*

shield, *n.* щит *m.* — (*emblem*) значо́к *m.* — *v.* заслоня́ть *imp.*, заслони́ть *perf.*

shift, *n.* измене́ние, перемеще́ние *nt.*; (*work*) сме́на *f.* — *v.t.* перемеща́ть *imp.*, перемести́ть *perf.* — *v.i.* перемеща́ться *imp.*, перемести́ться *perf.*

shine, *n.* сия́ние *nt.*; блеск, гля́нец *m.* — *v. i.* сия́ть *imp.*; блесте́ть *imp.* — *v.t.* полирова́ть *imp. & perf.*; (*shoes*) чи́стить сапоги́.

shiny, *adj.* блестя́щий.

ship, *n.* кора́бль *m.*, су́дно *nt.*, парохо́д *m.* — *v.* отправля́ть *imp.*, отпра́вить *perf.* **-ment,** *n.* отпра́вка *f.*

shirt, *n.* руба́шка *f.*

shiver, *n.* дрожь *f.* — *v.* дрожа́ть *imp.*

shock, *n.* уда́р, толчо́к *m.*, потрясе́ние *nt.* — *v.* потряса́ть *imp.*, потрясти́ *perf.*

shoe, *n.* боти́нок *m.* **-lace,** *n.* шнуро́к для боти́нок. **-maker,** *n.* сапо́жник *m.*

shoot, *n.* (*bot.*) росто́к *m.* — *v.* стреля́ть *imp.*; (*wound*) застрели́ть *perf.*; (*execute*) расстреля́ть *perf.*

shop, *n.* ла́вка *f.*, магази́н *m.* — *v.* де́лать поку́пки.

shore, *n.* бе́рег *m.*

short, *adj.* коро́ткий, кра́ткий; (*stature*) ни́зкого ро́ста. **in s.,** вкра́тце. — *n.* (*pl.*) тру́сики *pl.* **-age,** *n.* недоста́ток *m.* **-en,** *v.* сокраща́ть *imp.*, сократи́ть *perf.* **-ly,** *adv.* вско́ре, незадо́лго.

shot, *n.* вы́стрел *m.*; (*marksman*) стрело́к *m.*; (*phot.*) фотосни́мок *m.*

shoulder, *n.* плечо́ *nt.* — *v.* брать на себя́.

shout, *n.* крик *m.* — *v.* крича́ть *imp.*, кри́кнуть *perf.*

shove, *n.* толчо́к *m.* — *v.* толка́ть *imp.*, толкну́ть *perf.*

shovel, *n.* лопа́та *f.* — *v.* сгреба́ть *imp.*, сгрести́ *perf.*

show, *n.* (*theat.*) зре́лище *nt.*, спекта́кль *m.*; (*movie*) киносеа́нс *m.*; (*display*) пока́з *m.*, вы́ставка *f.* — *v.* пока́зывать *imp.*, показа́ть *perf.*

shower, *n.* (rain) ли́вень *m.*; (bath) душева́я *f.*

shrewd, *adj.* у́мный, хи́трый.

shriek, *n.* крик, визг *m.* — *v.* пронзи́тельно кри́кнуть.

shrill, *adj.* пронзи́тельный.

shrimp, *n.* креве́тка *f.*

shrine, *n.* святы́ня *f.*

shrink, *v. t.* смо́рщивать *imp.*, смо́рщить *perf.* — *v.i.* смо́рщиваться *imp.*, смо́рщиться *perf.*

shroud, *n.* са́ван *m.*, пелена́ *f.*

shrub, *n.* куст, куста́рник *m.*

shudder, *n.* дрожь *f.*, содрога́ние *nt.* — *v.* вздра́гивать *imp.*, вздро́гнуть *perf.*

shun, *v.* избега́ть *imp.*, избе́гнуть *perf.*

shut, *v.* закрыва́ть *imp.*, закры́ть *perf.*; запира́ть *imp.* запере́ть *perf.* **s. up,** (*colloq.*) замолча́ть *perf.*

shutter, *n.* ста́вень *m.*, (*pl.*) жалюзи́ *pl. ind.*

shy, *adj.* пугли́вый, засте́нчивый.

Siberia, *n.* Сиби́рь *f.*

Siberian, *adj.* сиби́рский.

sick, *adj.* больно́й. **-ness,** *n.* боле́знь *f.*

side, *n.* сторона́ *f.*; бок *m.* **from s. to s.,** из стороны́ в сто́рону. — *v.* быть на чьей-либо стороне́.

sidewalk, *n.* тротуа́р *m.*

siege, *n.* оса́да *f.*

sieve, *n.* си́то *nt.*

sift, *v.* просе́ивать *imp.*, просе́ять *perf.*

sigh, *n.* вздох *m.* — *v.* вздыха́ть *imp.*, вздохну́ть *perf.*

sight, *n.* зре́ние *nt.* **at first s.,** с пе́рвого взгля́да. **within s.,** в преде́лах ви́димости. **-seeing,** *n.* осмо́тр достопримеча́тельностей.

sign, *n.* знак, си́мвол *m.*; вы́веска *f.* — *v.* подпи́сывать *imp.*, подписа́ть *perf.*

signal, *n.* сигна́л, знак *m.* — *v.* сигнализи́ровать *imp.* & *perf.*

signature, *n.* по́дпись *f.*

significance, *n.* значе́ние *nt.*, значи́тельность *f.*

significant, *adj.* значи́тельный, многозначи́тельный.

signify, *v.* означа́ть *imp.*

silence, *n.* молча́ние *nt.* — *v.* заста́вить замолча́ть.

silent, *adj.* безмо́лвный, молчали́вый.

silk, *n.* шёлк *m.*

silken, silky, *adj.* шёлковый.

sill, *n.* подоко́нник *m.*

silly, *adj.* глу́пый.

silver, *n.* серебро́ *nt.* — *adj.* сере́бряный. **-ware,** *n.* столо́вое серебро́.

similar, *adj.* подо́бный. **-ity,** *n.* схо́дство, подо́бие *nt.* **-ly,** *adv.* подо́бно, подо́бным о́бразом.

simple, *adj.* про́сто.

simplicity, *n.* простота́ *f.*

simplify, *v.* упроща́ть *imp.*, упрости́ть *perf.*

simply, *adv.* про́сто; простоду́шно.

simulate, *v.* симули́ровать *imp.* & *perf.*

simultaneous, *adj.* одновре́менный.

sin, *n.* грех *m.* — *v.* греши́ть *imp.*, согреши́ть *perf.*

since, *adv.* с тех пор. — *prep.* по́сле; с. — *conj.* с тех пор как.

sincere, *adj.* и́скренний.

sincerity, *n.* и́скренность *f.*

sinful, *adj.* гре́шный.

sing, *v.* петь *imp.*

singe, *v.* опаля́ть *imp.*, опали́ть *perf.*

singer, *n.* певе́ц *m.*, певи́ца *f.*

single, *adj.* оди́н, еди́нственный; (*unmarried*) холосто́й, одино́кий.

singular, *n.* (*gram.*) еди́нственное число́. — *adj.* исключи́тельный, необыча́йный.

sinister, *adj.* злове́щий.

sink, *n.* ра́ковина *f.*, сто́чная труба́. — *v.t.* затопля́ть *imp.*, затопи́ть *perf.* — *v. i.* тону́ть *imp.*, потону́ть *perf.*

sinner, *n.* гре́шник *m.*

sinus, *n.* па́зуха *f.*

sip, *n.* глото́к *m.* — *v.* прихлёбывать *imp.*

siphon, *n.* сифо́н *m.*

sir, *(title)* господи́н, сэр, суда́рь *m.*

siren, *n.* сире́на *f.*, сигна́л трево́ги.

sister, *n.* сестра́ *f.*

sister-in-law, *n. (brother's wife)* неве́стка *f.*, *(husband's sister)* золо́вка *f.*

sit, *v.* сиде́ть *imp.* sit down, сади́ться *imp.*, сесть *perf.*

site, *n.* местоположе́ние *nt.*

situate, *v.* располага́ть *imp.*, расположи́ть *perf.*

situated, *adj.* располо́женный.

situation, *n.* местоположе́ние *nt.;* положе́ние, состоя́ние *nt.*

six, *n., adj.* шесть *num.* **-teen**, *n., adj.* шестна́дцать *num.* **-teenth**, *adj.* шестна́дцатый. — *n.* шестна́дцатая часть. **-th**, *adj.* шесто́й. — *n.* шеста́я часть. **-tieth**, *adj.* шестидеся́тый. — *n.* шестидеся́тая часть. **-ty**, *n., adj.* шестьдеся́т *num.*

size, *n.* разме́р *m.*, величина́ *f.*

skate, *n.* конёк *m.* — *v.* ката́ться на конька́х.

skeleton, *n.* скеле́т, костя́к *m.*

skeptic, *n.* ске́птик *m.*, *adj.* скепти́ческий.

sketch, *n.* эски́з, набро́сок, о́черк *m.* — *v.* нарисова́ть эски́з.

ski, *v.* ходи́ть на лы́жах. — *n.* лы́жа *f.*

skid, *v.* скольже́ние колёс. — *v.* заноси́ть *imp.*, занести́ *perf.*

skill, *n.* иску́сство, мастерство́ *nt.*, ло́вкость *f.* **-ful**, *adj.* иску́сный, ло́вкий.

skin, *n.* ко́жа, шку́ра *f.* — *v.* сдира́ть ко́жу *or* шку́ру.

skip, *n.* прыжо́к, скачо́к *m.* — *v.* скака́ть *imp.*, пры́гать *imp.*

skirt, *n.* ю́бка *f.*

skull, *n.* че́реп *m.*

skunk, *n.* воню́чка *f.*, скунс *m.*

sky, *n.* не́бо *nt.*, небеса́ *pl.*

in the s., на не́бе. **-scraper**, *n.* небоскрёб *m.*

slab, *n.* плита́ *f.*

slacken, *v.* замедля́ть *imp.*, заме́длить *perf.*

slam, *n.* хло́панье *nt.; (cards)* шлем *m.* — *v.* хло́пнуть *perf.*

slander, *n.* клевета́ *f.* — *v.* клевета́ть *imp.*, наклевета́ть *perf.*

slang, *n.* жарго́н, сленг *m.*

slant, *n.* склон, укло́н *m.* — *v.* идти́ вкось.

slap, *n.* пощёчина *f.* — *v.* шлёпать *imp.*, шлёпнуть *perf.*

slash, *n.* разре́з *m.*, про́резь *f.* — *v.* разреза́ть *imp.*, разре́зать *perf.*

slaughter, *n.* резня́ *f.*, кровопроли́тие *nt.* — *v.* ре́зать *imp.*, сре́зать *perf.*

slave, *n.* раб, нево́льник *m.* — *adj.* ра́бский.

slavery, *n.* ра́бство *nt.*

Slav, *n.* славяни́н *m.*, славя́нка *f.* **-ic**, *adj.* славя́нский.

slay, *v.* убива́ть *imp.*, уби́ть *perf.*

sled, *n.* са́ни *pl.*

sleep, *n.* сон *m.* — *v.* спать *imp.*

sleepy, *adj.* со́нный.

sleet, *n.* дождь со сне́гом, крупа́ *f.*

sleeve, *n.* рука́в *m.*

sleigh, *n.* са́ни, сала́зки *pl.*

slender, *adj.* то́нкий, стро́йный.

slice, *n.* ло́мтик *m.* — *v.* ре́зать ло́мтиками.

slide, *v.* скользи́ть *imp.*

slight, *adj.* лёгкий, то́нкий, хру́пкий. — *n.* пренебреже́ние *nt.* — *v.* пренебрега́ть *imp.*, пренебре́чь *perf.*

slim, *adj.* стро́йный, то́нкий.

slime, *n.* слизь *f.*

sling, *n.* рога́тка *f.; (med.)* перевя́зь *f.*

slink, *v.* кра́сться *imp.*

slip, *n. (skid)* скольже́ние *nt.; (garment)* ни́жняя ю́бка *f.; (paper)* листо́к *m.* — *v.* скользи́ть *imp.*

slipper, *n.* ту́фля *f.*

slippery, *adj.* ско́льзкий.

slit, *n.* разре́з *m.*, щель *f.* — *v.* разреза́ть в длину́.

sliver, *n.* ще́пка, лучина́ *f.*

slogan, *n.* ло́зунг *m.*

slope, *n.* накло́н, склон, скат *m.* — *v.* име́ть накло́н.

sloppy, *adj.* небре́жный, неря́шливый.

slot, *n.* отве́рствие *nt.*, проре́з *m.*, щёлка *f.*

slovenly, *adj.* неря́шливый.

slow, *adj.* ме́дленный. to be s. (*timepiece*), отстава́ть *imp.* — v. s. down, замедля́ть *imp.*, заме́длить *perf.* -ly, *adv.* ме́дленно.

sluggish, *adj.* вя́лый, ине́ртный, медли́тельный.

slum, *n.* трущо́ба *f.*

slumber, *n.* дремо́та *f.*, сон *m.* — *v.* дрема́ть *imp.*, спать *imp.*

slush, *n.* сля́коть, грязь *f.*

sly, *adj.* хи́трый, лицеме́рный. on the sly, тайко́м *adv.*

smack, *n.* чмо́канье *m.*, зво́нкий шлепо́к. — *v.* чмо́кать *imp.*, чмо́кнуть *perf.*

small, *adj.* ма́ленький.

smallpox, *n.* о́спа *f.*

smart, *adj.* остроу́мный, ло́вкий. — *n.* испы́тывать жгу́чую боль.

smash, *v.* разби́ть вдре́безги.

smear, *n.* пятно́ *m.*, мазо́к *m.*; (*slander*) клевета́ *f.* — *v.* ма́зать *imp.*, па́чкать *imp.*

smell, *n.* за́пах *m.*; (*sense*) обоня́ние *nt.* — *v. t.* обоня́ть *imp.* — *v. i.* па́хнуть *imp.*

smile, *n.* улы́бка *f.* — *v.* улыба́ться *imp.*, улыбну́ться *perf.*

smock, *n.* хала́т *m.*

smoke, *n.* дым *m.* — *v.* дыми́ться *imp.*; (*tobacco*) кури́ть *imp.*; (*food*) копти́ть *imp.*, подверга́ть копче́нию.

smolder, *v.* тлеть *imp.*

smooth, *adj.* гла́дкий, ро́вный. — *v.* пригла́живать *imp.*, пригла́дить *perf.*

smother, *v.* души́ть *imp.*, задуши́ть *perf.*

smug, *adj.* самодово́льный, чо́порный.

smuggle, *v.* занима́ться контраба́ндой.

snack, *n.* заку́ска *f.*

snail, *n.* ули́тка *f.*

snake, *n.* змея́ *f.*

snap, *n.* треск *m.*, щёлканье *nt.* — *v.t.* щёлкать *imp.*, щёлкнуть *perf.* — *v.i.* защёлкиваться *imp.*, защёлкнуться *perf.*

snapshot, *n.* сни́мок *m.*

snare, *n.* лову́шка *f.* — *v.* пойма́ть в лову́шку.

snatch, *v.* хвата́ть *imp.*, схвати́ть *perf.*

sneak, *v.* кра́сться *imp.*

sneakers, *n.* та́почки, ту́фли *pl.*

sneer, *n.* усме́шка, насме́шка *f.* — *v.* насмеха́ться *imp.*

sneeze, *n.* чиха́нье *n.* — *v.* чиха́ть *imp.*, чихну́ть *perf.*

snob, *n.* сноб *m.*

snore, *n.* храп *m.* — *v.* храпе́ть *imp.*

snow, *n.* снег *m.* — *v.*: it is snowing, идёт снег.

snowstorm, *n.* мете́ль *f.*

snug, *adj.* ую́тный.

so, *adv.* так, таки́м о́бразом; насто́лько; (*also*) та́кже, то́же, и́ли so, приблизи́тельно. so that, что́бы, для того́ что́бы. — *conj.* (*consequently*) поэ́тому. — *pron.* так.

soak, *v.* прома́чивать *imp.*, промочи́ть *perf.*

soap, *n.* мы́ло *nt.* — *v.* намы́ливать *imp.*, намы́лить *perf.*

soar, *v.* пари́ть *imp.*

sob, *n.* рыда́ние *nt.* — *v.* рыда́ть *imp.*

sober, *adj.* тре́звый. — *v. t.* вытрезвля́ть *imp.*, вы́трезвить *perf.* — *v. i.* вытрезвля́ться *imp.*, вы́трезвиться *perf.*

soccer, *n.* футбо́л *m.*

sociable, *adj.* общи́тельный, дру́жеский.

social, *adj.* обще́ственный, **-ism**, *n.* социали́зм *m.* **-ist**, *n.* социали́ст *m.* — *adj.*

социалисти́ческий. **-istic**, *adj.* социалисти́ческий.

society, *n.* о́бщество *nt.*

sociology, *n.* социоло́гия *f.*

sock, *n.* носо́к *m.*; (*blow*) уда́р *m.* — *v.* уда́рить *perf.*

socket, *n.* (*mach.*) раструб, патру́бок *m.*; (*elec.*) патро́н *m.*

soda, *n.* со́довая вода́ *f.*; (*chem.*) со́да *f.*

sodium, *n.* на́трий *m.*

sofa, *n.* дива́н *m.*

soft, *adj.* мя́гкий.

soft-boiled egg, яйцо́ всмя́тку,

soften, *v.t.* смягча́ть *imp.*, смягчи́ть *perf.* — *v.i.* смягча́ться *imp.*, смягчи́ться *perf.*

soil, *n.* по́чва *f.* — *v.* па́чкать *imp.*, запа́чкать *perf.*

sojourn, *n.* пребыва́ние *nt.*

solace, *n.* утеше́ние *nt.* — *v.* утеша́ть *imp.*, уте́шить *perf.*

solar, *adj.* со́лнечный.

solder, *n.* припо́й *m.* — *v.* спа́ивать *imp.*, спая́ть *perf.*

soldier, *n.* солда́т *m.*

sole, *n.* еди́нственный. — *n.* (*foot*) подо́шва *f.*; (*shoe*) подмётка *f.*; (*fish*) морско́й язы́к. — *v.* ста́вить подмётку.

solemn, *adj.* торже́ственный.

solicit, *v.* выпра́шивать *imp.*, вы́просить *perf.*; проси́ть *imp.* **-ous**, *adj.* забо́тливый.

solid, *adj.* твёрдый, масси́вный; (*math.*) трёхме́рный, куби́ческий. **-ify**, *v.i.* твёрдеть *imp.* — *v.t.* де́лать твёрдым, **-ity**, *n.* твёрдость *f.*

solitary, *adj.* одино́кий.

solitude, *n.* одино́чество *nt.*

solo, *n.* со́ло *nt. ind.*, со́льный но́мер *m.* — *adj.* со́льный. **-ist**, *n.* соли́ст *m.*, соли́стка *f.*

soluble, *adj.* раствори́мый.

solution, *n.* реше́ние, разреше́ние *nt.*; (*liquid*) раство́р *m.*

solve, *v.* разреша́ть *imp.*, разреши́ть *perf.*

solvent, *n.* раствори́тель *m.* — *adj.* растворя́ющий.

somber, *adj.* угрю́мый.

some, *pron.* не́которые, одни́. — *adj.* не́кий, не́который; како́й-то, како́й-нибудь. — *adv.* (*somewhat*) не́сколько, отча́сти. **-body**, *pron.* кто́-то, кто́-нибудь. **-how**, *adv.* ка́к-то, ка́к-нибудь. **-thing**, *pron.* что́-то, не́что, что́-нибудь. **-time**, *adv.* когда́-нибудь. **-times**, *adv.* иногда́, по времена́м. **-what**, *adv.* отча́сти, немно́жко. **-where**, *adv.* (*loc.*) где́-то, где́-нибудь; (*dir.*) куда́-то, куда́-нибудь.

somersault, *n.* прыжо́к кувырко́м. — *v.* кувырка́ться *imp.*, кувыркну́ться *perf.*

son, *n.* сын *m.*

song, *n.* пе́сня *f.*

son-in-law, *n.* зять *m.*

soon, *adv.* ско́ро, вско́ре. **as s. as**, как то́лько. **as s. as possible**, как мо́жно быстре́е.

soot, *n.* са́жа *f.*

soothe, *v.* облегча́ть *imp.*, облегчи́ть *perf.*

soothing, *adj.* успокои́тельный.

sophisticated, *adj.* лишённый найвности, утончённый; лишённый простоты́.

sophomore, *n.* студе́нт-второку́рсник *m.*

soprano, *n.* сопра́но *nt. ind.*

sorcery, *n.* колдовство́, волшебство́ *nt.*

sordid, *adj.* гря́зный, по́длый.

sore, *n.* ра́на, я́зва *f.* — *adj.* боле́зненный, воспалённый; (*angry*) оби́женный.

sorrow, *n.* печа́ль *f.*, го́ре *nt.* **-ful**, *adj.* печа́льный.

sorry, *adj.* (*pitiful*) жа́лкий, несча́стный; (*sad*) гру́стный. **I'm s.**, винова́т; прости́те. **to be s.**, жале́ть *imp.*, пожале́ть *perf.*

sort, *n.* род, сорт, вид *m.* **sort of**, как бу́дто. — *v.* сортирова́ть *imp. & perf.*

soul, *n.* душа́ *f.*, дух *m.*

sound, *adj.* здоро́вый; логи́чный. — *n.* звук *m.*; (*geog.*) зонд *m.* — *v.t.* измеря́ть глубину́. — *v.i.* звуча́ть *imp.*, прозвуча́ть *perf.*; издава́ть звук. **-proof**, *adj.* звукоизоляцио́нный, звуконепроница́емый. — *n.* придава́ть звуконепроница́емость.

soup, *n.* суп *m.*

sour, *adj.* ки́слый.

source, *n.* исто́к *m.*, исто́чник *m.*

sour cream, смета́на *f.*

south, *n. m.* — *adj.* ю́жный. — *adv.* на юг, к ю́гу.

southeast, *n.* юго-восто́к *m.* — *adj.* юго-восто́чный. **-ern**, *adj.* юго-восто́чный.

southern, *adj.* ю́жный. **-er**, *n.* южа́нин *m.*, южа́нка *f.*

South Pole, Ю́жный по́люс.

southwest, *n.* юго-за́пад *m.* — *adj.* юго-за́падный. **-ern**, *adj.* юго-за́падный.

souvenir, *n.* сувени́р *m.*

sovereign, *n.* мона́рх *m.* — *adj.* сувере́нный, полновла́стный. **-ty**, *n.* суверените́т *m.*; верхо́вная власть *f.*

Soviet, *adj.* сове́тский. — *n.* сове́т *m.*

Soviet Union, Сове́тский Сою́з.

sow, *n.* (*hog*) свинья́ *f.* — *v.* се́ять *imp.*, посе́ять *perf.*

space, *n.* простра́нство *nt.*, расстоя́ние *nt.*; ме́сто *nt.* — *v.* расставля́ть с промежу́тками.

spacious, *adj.* п pосто́рный, обши́рный.

spade, *n.* лопа́та *f.*; (*cards*) пи́ки *pl.*

spaghetti, *n.* спаге́тти *nt. ind.*

Spain, *n.* Испа́ния *f.*

span, *n.* промежу́ток *m.*, расстоя́ние *nt.*, длина́ *f.* — *v.* перекрыва́ть *imp.*, перекры́ть *perf.*; соединя́ть берега́.

Spaniard, *n.* испа́нец *m.*, испа́нка *f.*

Spanish, *adj.* испа́нский.

spanking, *n.* трёпка *f.*

spar, *v.* бокси́ровать *imp. & perf.*

spare, *adj.* запасно́й, запас-

ный. — *v.* жале́ть *imp.*, пожале́ть *perf.*

spark, *n.* и́скра *f.*

sparkle, *n.* блеск *m.*, искре́ние *nt.* — *v.* и́скриться *imp.*; сверка́ть *imp.*

spark plug, запа́льная свеча́ *f.*

sparrow, *n.* воробе́й *m.*

sparse, *adj.* ре́дкий.

spasm, *n.* спа́зма *f.*

spasmodic, *adj.* спазмати́ческий, судоро́дный.

spatter, *v.* забры́згивать *imp.*, забры́згать *perf.*

speak, *v.* говори́ть *imp.* **-er**, *n.* говоря́щий *m.*; (*orator*) ора́тор *m.*

spear, *n.* копьё *nt.*

special, *adj.* специа́льный, осо́бый. **s. delivery**, сро́чная доста́вка. **-ist**, *n.* специали́ст *m.* **-ity**, *n.* специа́льность *f.*

species, *n.* вид, род *m.*, поро́да *f.*

specific, *adj.* осо́бенный, специфи́ческий.

specify, *v.* определя́ть *imp.*, определи́ть *perf.*; специфици́ровать *imp. & perf.*

specimen, *n.* образе́ц, экземпля́р *m.*

spectacle, *n.* спекта́кль *m.*, зре́лище *nt.*; *pl.* (*glasses*) очки́ *pl.*

spectacular, *adj.* импоза́нтный.

spectator, *n.* зри́тель *m.*

spectrum, *n.* спектр *m.*

speculate, *v.* разду́мывать *imp.*

speculation, *n.* размышле́ние *nt.*; спекуля́ция *f.*

speech, *n.* речь *f.*; (*language*) язы́к *m.* **-less**, *adj.* безмо́лвный, немо́й; онеме́лый.

speed, *n.* ско́рость, быстрота́ *f.* — *v.* спеши́ть *imp.* **-ometer**, *n.* спидо́метр *m.*

speedy, *adj.* бы́стрый, ско́рый.

spell, *n.* заклина́ние *nt.*, ча́ры *pl.*; (*time*) промежу́ток вре́мени. — *v.* произноси́ть по бу́квам.

spelling, *n.* правописа́ние *nt.*, орфогра́фия *f.*

spend, v. тра́тить *imp.*, истра́тить *perf.* -thrift. m. расточи́тель m.

sphere, n. сфе́ра f.; (shape) шар m.

spherical, adj. сфери́ческий.

spice, n. привкус m., при́месь f. — v. приправля́ть *imp.*, припра́вить *perf.*

spider, n. пау́к m.

spike, n. шип, гвоздь m.

spill, v. t. разлива́ть *imp.*, разли́ть *perf.* — v. i. разлива́ться *imp.*, разли́ться *perf.*

spin, v. t. крути́ть *imp.*, верте́ть *imp.* — v. i. крути́ться *imp.*, верте́ться *imp.*

spinach, n. шпина́т m.

spine, n. спинно́й хребе́т; (book) корешо́к m.

spinster, n. ста́рая де́ва.

spiral, adj. спира́льный. — n. спира́ль f.

spire, n. шпиц m.

spirit, n. дух m.

spiritual, adj. духо́вный. -ism, n. спиритуали́зм m.

spit, n. слюна́ f. — v. плева́ть *imp.*, плю́нуть *perf.*

spite, n. зло́ба, злость f. in s. of, несмотря́ на.

splash, n. бры́зги pl., бры́зганье nt. — v. бры́згать *imp.*, бры́знуть *perf.*

splendid, adj. великоле́пный, блестя́щий.

splendor, n. великоле́пие nt., блеск m.

splint, n. оско́лок m., щепа́ f.

splinter, n. оско́лок m., зано́за f. — v. t. раска́лывать *imp.*, расколо́ть *perf.* — v. i. раска́лываться *imp.*, расколо́ться *perf.*

split, n. раска́лывание nt., тре́щина, щель f. — v. t. расщепля́ть *imp.*, расщепи́ть *perf.* — v. i. расщепля́ться *imp.*, расщепи́ться *perf.*

spoil, n. pl. (booty) добы́ча f. — v. t. по́ртить *imp.*, испо́ртить *perf.* — v. i. по́ртиться *imp.*, испо́ртиться *perf.*

spoke, n. спи́ца f.

sponge, n. гу́бка f.

sponsor, n. попечи́тель, покрови́тель m. — v. субсиди́ровать *imp. & perf.*

spontaneous, adj. самопроизво́льный, спонта́нный.

spool, n. шпу́лька f.

spoon, n. ло́жка f.

sporadic, adj. спора́дический.

sport, n. спорт m., атле́тика f.

spot, n. пятно́ nt.; (place) ме́сто nt. — v. пятна́ть *imp.*; (detect) уви́деть *perf.*

spouse, n. супру́г m., супру́га f.

spout, n. но́сик m., ры́льце nt. — v. струи́ться *imp.*; ли́ться пото́ком.

sprain, n. растяже́ние свя́зок. — v. растяну́ть свя́зки.

sprawl, v. растяну́ться *perf.*

spray, n. бры́зги pl., водяна́я пыль. — v. обры́згивать *imp.*, обры́згать *perf.*

spread, n. распростране́ние nt.; протяже́ние nt. — v. t. простира́ть *imp.*, простере́ть *perf.* — v. i. простира́ться *imp.*, простере́ться *perf.*

spree, n. ша́лости pl., кутёж m.

sprightly, adj. оживлённый.

spring, n. пружи́на f.; (season) весна́ f.; (water) исто́чник m. in the s., весно́й. — v. вска́кивать *imp.*, вскочи́ть *perf.*

sprinkle, v. кропи́ть *imp.*, покропи́ть *perf.*

sprint, n. спринт m. — v. i. спринтова́ть *imp. & perf.*

sprout, v. пуска́ть ростки́.

spry, adj. живо́й, подви́жный.

spur, n. шпо́ра f.; (fig.) сти́мул m., побужде́ние nt. on the s. of the moment, экспро́мтом, сра́зу adv. — v. побужда́ть *imp.*, побуди́ть *perf.*

spurn, v. отверга́ть *imp.*, отве́ргнуть *perf.*

spurt, n. струя́ f. — v. бить струёй.

spy, n. шпио́н m. — v. шпио́нить *imp.*

squabble, *n.* ссóра, перебрáнка *f.* — *v.* вздóрить *imp.*, повздóрить *perf.*

squad, *n.* комáнда *f.*

squadron, *n.* эскадрóн *m.*

squall, *n.* шквал *m.*

squalor, *n.* запущенность, нищетá *f.*

squander, *v.* расточáть *imp.*, расточить *perf.*

square, *adj.* квадрáтный, прямоугóльный. — *n.* квадрáт, прямоугóльник *m.*

squat, *v.* сидéть на корточках.

squeak, *n.* скрип, писк *m.* — *v.* скрипéть *imp.*

squeamish, *adj.* подвéрженный тошнотé.

squeeze, *n.* сжáтие, пожáтие *nt.* — *v.* сжимáть *imp.*, сжать *perf.* ;(*fruit*) выжимáть *imp.*, выжать *perf.*

squirrel, *n.* бéлка *f.*

squirt, *n.* струя́ *f.*, шприц *m.* — *v.* пускáть струю́.

stab, *n.* удáр *m.* — *v.* вонзáть *imp.*, вонзить *perf.*

stability, *n.* стабильность *f.*

stabilize, *v.* стабилизировать *imp. & perf.*

stable, *n.* конюшня *f.* — *adj.* стóйкий, постоя́нный.

stack, *n.* стог *m.*, кýча *f.* — *v.* склáдывать в стог.

stadium, *n.* стадиóн *m.*

staff, *n.* (*stick*) посóх *m.*, пáлка *f.*; (*personnel*) служéбный персонáл. — *adj.* штáтный, штабнóй.

stag, *n.* олéнь-самéц *m.* — *adj.* холостя́цкий.

stage, *n.* (*platform*) пóдмости *pl.*, помóст *m.*, платфóрма *f.*; (*theat.*) сцéна, эстрáда *f.* — *v.* стáвить *imp.*, постáвить *perf.*; инсценировать *imp. & perf.*

stagger, *v. t.* поражáть *imp.*, поразить *perf.* — *v. i.* колебáться *imp.*, шатáться *perf.*

stagnant, *adj.* стоя́чий.

stagnate, *v.* застáиваться *imp.*, застоя́ться *perf.*

stain, *n.* пятнó *nt.* — *v.*

пятнáть *imp.*; пóртить *imp.*, испóртить *imp.*

stair, *n.* ступéнька *f.*; (*pl.*) лéстница *f.*, схóдни *pl.*

stake, *n.* кол, столб *m.*; (*bet*) стáвка *f.* — *v.* (*cards*) стáвить на кáрту.

stale, *adj.* несвéжий; чéрствый.

stalk, *n.* стéбель, черенóк *m.* — *v.* подкрáдываться *imp.*, подкрáсться *perf.*

stall, *n.* стóйло *nt.*, ларёк *m.* — *v. t.* останáвливать *imp.*, остановить *perf.*; задéрживать *imp.*, задержáть *perf.* — *v.i.* застревáть *imp.*, застря́ть *perf.*

stallion, *n.* жеребéц *m.*

stammer, *n.* заикáние *nt.* — *v.* заикáться *imp.*

stamp, *n.* штамп, штéмпель *m.*, печáть *f.*; (*postage*) почтóвая мáрка. — *v.* штамповáть *imp.*

stampede, *n*, паническое бéгство.

stand, *n.* останóвка *f.*; киóск *m.*; (*view*) взгляд *m.* — *v.* стоя́ть *imp.* **s. up**, вставáть *imp.*, встать *perf.*

standard, *n.* стандáрт *m.*, нóрма *f.* — *adj.* стандáртный. **-ize**, *v.* стандартизировать *imp. & perf.*

standing, *n.* положéние *nt.* — *adj.* стоя́щий; (*permanent*) постоя́нный.

star, *n.* звездá *f.* — *adj.* звёздный.

starch, *n.* крахмáл *m.* — *v.* крахмáлить *imp.*, накрахмáлить *perf.*

stare, *v.* смотрéть пристáльно.

stark, *adj.* абсолютный.

start, *n.* начáло *nt.*, старт *m.* — *v. t.* начинáть *imp.*, начáть *perf.* — *v. i.* начинáться *imp.*, начáться *perf.*

startle, *v.* испугáть *perf.*

starvation, *n.* гóлод *m.*, голодáние *nt.*

starve, *v.* голодáть *imp.*

state, *n.* (*condition*) состоя́ние, положéние *nt.*; (*government*) госуда́рство nt.; (USA) штат m. — adj. госуда́рственный. — v. сообща́ть impr., сообщи́ть perf.

statement, n. заявле́ние, сообще́ние nt.

statesman, n. госуда́рственный (or полити́ческий) де́ятель.

static, adj. стати́ческий, неподви́жный. — n. (radio) атмосфе́рные поме́хи.

station, n. ста́нция f., пункт m.

stationary, adj. неподви́жный.

stationery, n. канцеля́рские, принадле́жности, писчебума́жные принадле́жности f.

statistics, n. стати́стика f.

statue, n. ста́туя f.

stature, n. рост, стан m.

status, n. ста́тус m., положе́ние nt.

stay, n. пребыва́ние nt., остано́вка f. — v. остава́ться impr., оста́ться perf.

steady, adj. усто́йчивый; равноме́рный; неизме́нный. — v. остепени́ться perf.

steak, n. бифште́кс m.

steal, v. красть impr., укра́сть perf.

steam, n. пар m. — adj. парово́й. — v. i. выпуска́ть пар. — v. t. па́рить impr. -ship, n. парохо́д m.

steel, n. сталь f. — adj. стально́й.

steep, adj. круто́й.

steeple, n. шпиц m., (belfry) колоко́льня f.

steer, n. (ox) кастри́рованный бычо́к. — v. t. управля́ть impr. — v. i. направля́ться impr.

stem, n. ствол, сте́бель m.; (gram.) осно́ва f. s. from, происходи́ть impr., произойти́ perf.

stencil, n. шабло́н, трафаре́т m. — v. наноси́ть узо́р по трафаре́ту.

stenographer, n. стенографи́стка f.

stenography, n. стеногра́фия f.

step, n. шаг m.; (stair) ступе́нь, ступе́нька f. s. by s., шаг за ша́гом. — v. шага́ть impr.; ступа́ть impr., ступи́ть perf.

stepbrother, n. сво́дный брат.

stepfather, n. о́тчим m.

stepmother, n. ма́чеха f.

stepsister, n. сво́дная сестра́.

stereotype, n. стереоти́п m. — v. стереотипи́ровать impr. & perf.

sterile, adj. беспло́дный; стери́льный.

sterility, n. беспло́дность, стери́льность f.

sterilize, v, стерилизова́ть impr. & perf.

stern, n. корма́ f. — adj. стро́гий, суро́вый.

stethoscope, n. стетоско́п m.

stevedore, n. порто́вый гру́зчик.

stew, n. тушёное мя́со. — v. туши́ть impr. — v. i. туши́ться impr.

steward, n. официа́нт m. -ess, n. стюарде́сса f.

stick, n. па́лка f., трость f., трость f. — v. втыка́ть impr., воткну́ть perf. — v. i. ли́пнуть impr.

sticky, adj. ли́пкий, кле́йкий.

stiff, adj. туго́й, неги́бкий.

stigma, n. клеймо́ f., позо́р m., пятно́ nt.

still, adj. ти́хий, неподви́жный. — v. успока́ивать impr., успоко́ить perf. -ness, n. тишина́ f., безмо́лвие nt.

stimulant, adj. возбужда́ющий. — n. возбужда́ющее сре́дство.

stimulate, v. побужда́ть impr., побуди́ть perf.

stimulus, n. стиму́л, побуди́тель m.

sting, n. жа́ло nt., уку́с m. — v. жа́лить impr., ужа́лить perf.

stingy, adj. скаре́дный, скупо́й.

stipulate, v. обусло́вливать impr., обусло́вить perf.

stir, n. шевеле́ние nt. — v. t. разме́шивать impr., размешать *perf.* (*move*) возбужда́ть *imp.*, возбуди́ть *perf.* — *v. i.* дви́гаться *imp.*, дви́нуться *perf.*

stitch, *n.* стежо́к *m.*; шов *m.* — *v.* шить *imp.*, сшить *perf.*

stock, *n.* (*supply*) запа́с, инвента́рь *m.*; (*share*) а́кция *f.* **in s.,** на скла́де; в нали́чии. — *v.* име́ть в нали́чии (в прода́же). **s. exchange,** *n.* фо́ндовая би́ржа.

stocking, *n.* чуло́к *m.*

stodgy, *adj.* тяжелове́сный.

stoical, *adj.* стои́ческий.

stole, *n.* (*far*) мехова́я наки́дка

stomach, *n.* желу́док *m.*

stone, *n.* ка́мень *m.*

stool, *n.* табуре́тка, скаме́ечка *f.*

stoop, *v.* наклоня́ться *imp.*, наклони́ться *perf.*; (*fig.*) унижа́ться *imp.*, уни́зиться *perf.*

stop, *n.* остано́вка *f.*; (*pause*) па́уза *f.*, переры́в *m.* — *v. t.* остана́вливать *imp.*, останови́ть *perf.* — *v. i.* остана́вливаться *imp.*, останови́ться *perf.*

storage, *n.* хране́ние *nt.*; храни́лище *nt.*, склад *m.*

store, *n.* магази́н *m.*, ла́вка *f.*; (*warehouse*) склад, (*supply*) запа́с *m.* — *v.* запаса́ть *imp.*, запасти́ *perf.*; отдава́ть на хране́ние.

stork, *n.* а́ист *m.*

storm, *n.* бу́ря, гроза́ *f.*

stormy, *adj.* бу́рный.

story, *n.* (*floor*) эта́ж *m.*; (*lit.*) расска́з *m.*, нове́лла *f.*; анекдо́т *m.*

stout, *adj.* по́лный, ту́чный.

stove, *n.* печь, пе́чка *f.*

straight, *adj.* прямо́й. — *adv.* пря́мо. **-en,** *v. t.* выпрямля́ть *imp.*, вы́прямить *perf.* — *v. i.* выпрямля́ться *imp.*, вы́прямиться *perf.* **-forward,** *adj.* прямо́й, че́стный, открове́нный.

strain, *n.* натяже́ние, напряже́ние *nt.*; (*stock*) поро́да *f.* — *v.* натя́гивать *imp.*, натя́-

strainer, *n.* си́то *nt.*

strait, *n.* проли́в *m.*; *pl.* (*difficult situation*) затрудни́тельное положе́ние.

strand, *n.* (*string*) прядь *f.*; (*shore*) бе́рег *m.* — *v.* посади́ть на мель.

strange, *adj.* стра́нный; чужо́й.

stranger, *n.* незнако́мец *m.*

strangle, *v. t.* задуши́ть *perf.* — *v. i.* задыха́ться *imp.*, задохну́ться *perf.*

strap, *n.* реме́нь, ремешо́к *m.* — *v.* стя́гивать ремнём.

stratagem, *n.* уло́вка *f.*

strategic, *adj.* стратеги́ческий.

strategy, *n.* страте́гия *f.*

stratosphere, *n.* стратосфе́ра *f.*

straw, *n.* соло́ма *f.* — *adj.* соло́менный.

strawberry, *n.* земляни́ка *f.*

stray, *adj.* заблуди́вшийся. — *v.* заблуди́ться *perf.*

streak, *n.* поло́ска, жи́лка, прожи́лка *f.* — *v.* проводи́ть полосы.

stream, *n.* пото́к *m.*, струя́ *f.* — *v.* течь *imp.*; струи́ться *imp.*

street, *n.* у́лица *f.* **across the s.,** напро́тив. **in the s.,** на у́лице — *adj.* у́личный. **-car,** *n.* трамва́й *m.*

strength, *n.* си́ла *f.* **-en,** *v. t.* уси́ливать *imp.*, уси́лить *perf.* — *v. i.* уси́ливать *imp.*, уси́литься *perf.*

strenuous, *adj.* тре́бующий уси́лий; энерги́чный.

stress, *n.* напряже́ние *nt.*; (*gram.*) ударе́ние *nt.* — *v.* подчёркивать *imp.*, подчеркну́ть *perf.*; (*gram.*) ста́вить ударе́ние.

stretch, *v. t.* растя́гивать *imp.*, растяну́ть *perf.* — *v. i.* растя́гиваться *imp.*, растяну́ться *perf.* **v.** вытя́гивание, растя́гивание, удлине́ние, преувеличе́ние. **at one s.,** подря́д, без переры́ва. **-er,** *n.* носи́лки *pl.*

strew, *v.* разбра́сывать *imp.,* разбро́сать *perf.*

strict, *adj.* стро́гий.

stride, *n.* шаг, большо́й шаг *m.*; (*pl., fig.*) успе́хи *pl.* — *v.* шага́ть *imp.*; перешагну́ть *perf.*

strife, *n.* раздо́р, спор *m.*

strike, *n.* (*labor*) забасто́вка *f.*; (*blow*) уда́р *m.*; — *v. t.* ударя́ть *imp.,* уда́рить *perf.* — *v. i.* (*labor*) забастова́ть *perf.*

string, *n.* верёвка, ни́тка *f.*; (*mus.*) струна́ *f.*; (*row*) ряд *m.*

string bean, *n.* ло́мкая фасо́ль *f.*

strip, *n.* полоса́, ле́нта, поло́ска *f.* — *v.* сдира́ть *imp.,* содра́ть *perf.*

stripe, *n.* полоса́ *f.*; наши́вка *f.*

strive, *v.* стара́ться *imp.*; стреми́ться *imp.*

stroke, *n.* уда́р *m.*; (*pen, brush, etc.*) штрих *m.*; (*med.*) уда́р, парали́ч *m.* — *v.* гла́дить *imp.*; зада́вать такт.

stroll, *n.* прогу́лка *f.* — *v.* прогу́ливаться *imp.,* прогуля́ться *perf.*

strong, *adj.* си́льный; кре́пкий

-hold, *n.* кре́пость, тверды́ня *f.*

structure, *n.* структу́ра *f.*

struggle, *n.* борьба́ *f.* — *v.* боро́ться *imp.*

stub, *n.* пень *m.*; обло́мок *m.*; (*cigarette*) оку́рок *m.* — *v.* споткну́ться *perf.*

stubborn, *adj.* упо́рный.

student, *n.* студе́нт *m.,* студе́нтка *f.* — *adj.* студе́нческий.

studio, *n.* ателье́ *nt. ind.*; мастерска́я *f.*

studious, *adj.* приле́жный, усе́рдный.

study, *n.* изуче́ние, иссле́дование *nt.*; (*science*) нау́ка *f.* — *v.* изуча́ть *imp.,* изучи́ть *perf.*

stuff, *n.* материа́л *m.,* вещество́ *nt.* — *v.* набива́ть *imp.,* наби́ть *perf.*-**ing,** *n.* наби́вка *f.*

stumble, *v.* спотыка́ться *imp.,* споткну́ться *perf.*

stump, *n.* пень, обру́бок *m.*

stun, *v.* ошеломля́ть *imp.,* ошеломи́ть *perf.*

stunt, *n.* шту́ка *f.,* трюк, фо́кус *m.* — *v.* пока́зывать фо́кусы.

stupendous, *adj.* изуми́тельный.

stupid, *adj.* глу́пый, тупо́й. **-ity,** *n.* глу́пость, ту́пость *f.*

stupor, *n.* остолбене́ние *nt.*

sturdy, *adj.* сто́йкий, твёрдый.

stutter, *v.* заика́ние *nt.* — *v.* заика́ться *imp.*

sty, *n.* ячме́нь *m.*

style, *n.* стиль, слог *m.*; мане́ра, мо́да *f.,* фасо́н *m.*

stylish, *adj.* мо́дный; шика́рный.

subconscious, *adj.* подсозна́тельный.

subdue, *v.* покоря́ть *imp.,* покори́ть *perf.*

subject, *n.* те́ма *f.,* сюже́т *m.*; (*of study*) предме́т *m.*; (*political*) по́дданый *m.*; (*gram.*) подлежа́щее *nt. adj.* подвла́стный, подлежа́щий, подчинённый. — *v.* подверга́ть *imp.,* подве́ргнуть *perf.*

subjugate, *v.* подчиня́ть *imp.,* подчини́ть *perf.*

subjunctive (*gram.*) сослага́тельное наклоне́ние *n.*

sublet, *v.* переда́ть в субаре́нду.

sublimate, *v.* возвыша́ть *imp.,* возвы́сить *perf.*

sublime, *adj.* возвы́шенный, грандио́зный.

submarine, *n.* подво́дная ло́дка. — *adj.* подво́дный.

submerge, *v. t.* погружа́ть *imp.* погрузи́ть *perf.* — *v. i.* погружа́ться *imp.,* погрузи́ться *perf.*

submission, *n.* подчине́ние *nt.,* поко́рность *f.*

submit, *v.* представля́ть *imp.,* предста́вить *perf.*

subnormal, *adj.* ни́же норма́льного.

subordinate, *adj.* второстепе́нный, ни́зший. — *n.* подчинённый. — v. подчиня́ть imp., подчини́ть perf.

subscribe, v. подпи́сываться imp., подписа́ться perf.

subscription, n. подпи́сывание nt.; подпи́ска f.

subsequent, adj. после́дующий -ly, adv. впосле́дствии.

subside, v. па́дать imp., упа́сть perf.; убыва́ть imp., убы́ть perf.

subsidy, n. субси́дия f.

substance, n. вещество́ nt., су́щность f.

substantial, adj.* существенный.

substitute, n. замести́тель m. — v. заменя́ть imp., замени́ть perf.; замеща́ть imp., замести́ть perf.

substitution, n. заме́на f., замеще́ние nt.

subterfuge, n. уве́ртка, отгово́рка f.

subtle, adj. то́нкий, утончённый.

subtract, v. вы́читать perf.

subtraction, n. вы́читание nt.

suburb, n. при́город m. — adj. пригородный.

subversive, adj. подрывно́й.

subway, n. метрополите́н m., метро́ nt. ind. (colloq.)

succeed, v. преуспева́ть imp., преуспе́ть perf.

success, n. успе́х m., уда́ча f. -ful, adj. успе́шный.

succession, n. после́довательность f.

successive, adj. после́дующий, после́довательный.

successor, n. насле́дник m.

succumb, v. уступа́ть imp., уступи́ть perf.

such, adj. тако́й. — pron. таково́й.

suck, v. соса́ть imp.

suction, n. соса́ние, вса́сывание nt.

sudden, adj. внеза́пный. -ly, adv. вдруг, внеза́пно.

suds, n. мы́льная пе́на (or вода́).

sue, v. пресле́довать суде́бный поря́дком.

suffer, v. страда́ть imp., пострада́ть perf.

suffice, v. хвата́ть imp., хвати́ть perf.

sufficient, adj. доста́точный. -ly, adv. доста́точно, дово́льно.

suffix, n. су́ффикс m.

suffocate, v. задыха́ться imp., задохну́ться perf.

sugar, n. са́хар m. — adj. са́харный.

suggest, v. предлага́ть imp., предложи́ть perf. -ion, n. предложе́ние nt.

suicide, n. самоуби́йство nt.; (person) самоуби́йца m. to commit s., поко́нчить с собо́й.

suit, n. костю́м m.; (cards) масть f.; (law) проце́сс m. — v. i. удовлетворя́ть тре́бованиям. -able, adj. подходя́щий, соотве́тствующий. -case, n. ручно́й чемода́нчик.

suite, n. компле́кт, гарниту́р m.

suitor, n. проси́тель, покло́нник m.

sum, n. су́мма f., коли́чество nt., ито́г m. — v.: sum up, подводи́ть ито́г.

summarize, v. подводи́ть ито́г.

summary, n. кра́ткое изложе́ние.

summer, n. ле́то nt. in the s., ле́том.

summon, v. вызыва́ть imp., вы́звать perf. — n. (pl.) вы́зов m.

sun, n. со́лнце nt. in the s., на со́лнце. — v. гре́ться на со́лнце. -burn, n. зага́р m. -burned, adj. загоре́лый. -rise, n. восхо́д со́лнца. -set, n. захо́д со́лнца; зака́т m. -shine, n. со́лнечный свет.

Sunday, n. воскресе́нье nt. — adj. воскре́сный.

sunny, adj. со́лнечный.

superb, adj. великоле́пный, прекра́сный.

superficial, adj. пове́рхностный.

superfluous, adj. изли́шний.

superintendent, n. заведующий, управляющий.

superior, adj. высший, старший. — n. старший, начальник m. -ity, n. превосходство старшинство nt.

superlative, adj. величайший, высочайший, превосходный.

supernatural, adj. сверхъестественный.

superscript, n. надстрочный знак.

supersede, v. смещать imp., сместить perf.

superstition, n. суеверие nt.

superstitious, adj. суеверный.

supervise, v. надзирать imp.

supper, n. ужин m. at s., за ужином.

supplement, n. дополнение, приложение nt. — v. пополнять imp., пополнить perf.

supply, n. снабжение nt., запас m. s. and demand, спрос и предложение. — v. снабжать imp., снабдить perf.; доставлять imp., доставить perf.

support, n. поддержка f.; подставка, подпорка f. — v. поддерживать imp., поддержать perf.

suppose, v. предполагать imp., предположить perf. supposing that, допустим (or предположим) что.

suppress, v. подавлять imp., подавить perf. -ion, n. подавление nt.

supreme, adj. верховный, высший.

sure, adj. верный, несомненный. to make s., убедиться perf. — adv. конечно, действительно. -ly, adv. несомненно, конечно, наверно.

surf, n. буруны pl., прибой m.

surface, n. поверхность f.

surgeon, n. хирург m.

surgery, n. хирургия f.

surmise, n. предположение nt., догадка f. — v. подозревать imp., подозреть perf.

surname, n. фамилия f.

surpass, v. превышать imp., превысить perf.; перегонять imp., перегнать perf.

surplus, n. излишек m. — adj. излишний.

surprise, n. удивление nt.; неожиданность f., сюрприз m. by s., сюрпризом adv. — v. удивлять imp., удивить perf.

surrender, n. сдача, капитуляция f. — v.t. сдавать imp., сдать perf. — v. i. сдаваться imp., сдаться perf.

surround, v. окружать imp., окружить perf.

survey, n. обозрение nt., осмотр m.; (land) межевание nt., промер m. — v. обозревать imp., обозреть perf.; (land) межевать imp.

survival, n. выживание nt.; пережиток m.

survive, v. пережить perf.; остаться в живых.

susceptible, adj. восприимчивый.

suspect, v. подозревать imp., подозреть perf.

suspend, v. вешать imp., повесить perf.; приостанавливать imp., приостановить perf.

suspense, n. ожидание nt., нерешительность f.

suspension, n. вешание nt.; приостановка f.

suspicion, n. подозрение nt.

suspicious, adj. подозрительный.

sustain, v. поддерживать imp., поддержать perf.; испытывать imp., испытать perf.

swallow, n. глоток m.; (bird) ласточка f. — v. глотать imp.

swamp, n. болото nt. — v. (overwhelm) засыпать imp., засыпать perf.

swan, n. лебедь m.

swap, n. обмен m. — v. обмениваться imp., обменяться perf.

swarm, n. рой m.

sway, n. качание, колебание

nt. — *v.* кача́ться *imp.*; колеба́ться *imp.*; (*fig.*) повлия́ть *perf.*

swear, *v.* кля́сться *imp.*, покля́сться *perf.*; присяга́ть *imp.*, присягну́ть *perf.*

sweat, *n.* пот *m.* — *v.* поте́ть *imp.*

sweater, *n.* сви́тер *m.*

Swede, *n.* швед *m.*, шве́дка *f.*

Sweden, *n.* Шве́ция *f.*

Swedish, *adj.* шве́дский.

sweep, *v.* мести́ *imp.*; смета́ть *imp.*, смести́ *perf.*

sweet, *adj.* сла́дкий. **-heart**, *n.* возлю́бленный *m.*, возлю́бленная *f.* **-ness**, *n.* сла́дкость *f.*

swell, *n.* вы́пуклость *f.*, о́пухоль *f.*; (*sea*) зыбь *f.* — *v.* надува́ться *imp.*, наду́ться *perf.*; набуха́ть *imp.*, набу́хнуть *perf.*

swift, *adj.* ско́рый, бы́стрый. **-ness**, *n.* ско́рость, быстрота́ *f.*

swim, *v.* пла́вать *imp. indet.*, плыть *imp. det.*, поплы́ть *perf.*

swimmer, *n.* плове́ц *m.*, пловчи́ха *f.*

swimming, *n.* пла́вание *nt.* **s. pool**, бассе́йн для пла́вания.

swine, *n.* свинья́ *f.*; (*person*) наха́л *m.*

swing, *n.* каче́ли *pl.* — *v. t.* кача́ть *imp.*; колеба́ть *imp.* — *v. i.* кача́ться *imp.*; колеба́ться *imp.*

swirl, *n.* воро́нки *pl.*; круже́ние *nt.* — *v. t.* кружи́ть *imp.* — *v. i.* кружи́ться *imp.*

Swiss, *adj.* швейца́рский.

switch, *n.* прут, хлыст *m.*; (*elec.*) выключа́тель, переключа́тель, *m.* — *v.* переключа́ть *imp.*, переключи́ть *perf.* **-board**, *n.* распредели́тельный щит.

Switzerland, *n.* Швейца́рия *f.*

sword, *n.* са́бля *f.*

syllabic, *adj.* слогово́й, силлаби́ческий.

syllable, *n.* слог *m.*

symbol, *n.* си́мвол *m.*, эмбле́ма *f.*

sympathetic, *adj.* сочу́вственный; симпати́чный.

sympathy, *n.* сочу́вствие *nt.*; симпа́тия *f.*

symphonic, *adj.* симфони́ческий.

symphony, *n.* симфо́ния *f.*

symptom, *n.* симпто́м *m.*

synchronize, *v.* синхронизи́ровать *imp. & perf.*

syndicate, *n.* синдика́т *m.*

synonym, *n.* сино́ним *m.* **-ous**, *adj.* синоними́ческий.

syntax, *n.* синта́ксис *m.*

synthetic, *adj.* синтети́ческий, иску́сственный.

syringe, *n.* шприц *m.*

syrup, *n.* сиро́п *m.*, па́тока *f.*

system, *n.* систе́ма *f.*, органи́зм *m.* **-atic**, *adj.* системати́ческий.

T

table, *n.* стол *m.*; (*math.*) табли́ца *f.*, расписа́ние *nt.*

tablespoon, *n.* столо́вая ло́жка *f.*

tablet, *n.* доще́чка *f.*; (*med.*) табле́тка *f.*

tack, *n.* гвозди́к *m.*

tact, *n.* такт *m.*, такти́чность *f.*

tag, *n.* этике́тка *f.*

tail, *n.* хвост *m.*

tailor, *n.* портно́й *m.*

take, *v.* брать *imp.*, взять *perf.* **t. off**, снима́ть *imp.*, снять *perf.*; (*aviation*) взлете́ть *perf.* **t. out**, вынима́ть *imp.*, вы́нуть *perf.*

tale, *n.* расска́з *m.*, по́весть *f.*

talent, *n.* тала́нт *m.* **-ed**, *adj.* одарённый, тала́нтливый.

talk, *n.* разгово́р *m.*, бесе́да *f.* — *v.* говори́ть *imp.*; разгова́ривать *imp.* **-ative,** *adj.* болтли́вый.

tall, *adj.* высо́кий.

tame, *adj.* приручённый. — *v.* прируча́ть *imp.*, приручи́ть *perf.*

tan, *adj.* рыжева́то-кори́чневый свет; зага́р *m.* — *v. t.* дуби́ть *imp.*, вы́дубить *perf.* — *v. i.* загора́ть *imp.*, загоре́ть *perf.*

tangible, *adj.* осяза́емый, материа́льный.

tangle, *n.* пу́таница *f.*, сплете́ние *nt.* — *v. t.* запу́тывать *imp.*, запу́тать *perf.* — *v. i.* запу́тываться *imp.*, запу́таться *perf.*

tank, *n.* цисте́рна *f.*, бак *m.*; (*mil.*) танк *m.*

tape, *n.* тесьма́, ле́нточка *f.* — *v.* свя́зывать тесьмо́й *nt.*; (*record*) запи́сывать на плёнку.

tar, *n.* смола́ *f.*; дёготь *f.* — *v.* смоли́ть *imp.*; ма́зать дёгтем.

target, *n.* цель *f.*; мише́нь *f.*

tarnish, *v.* тускне́ть *imp.*, потускне́ть *perf.*

tart, *n.* пиро́г, торт *m.* — *adj.* те́рпкий, ки́слый, е́дкий.

task, *n.* зада́ча *f.*, зада́ние *nt.*

taste, *n.* вкус *m.* — *v. t.* про́бовать на вкус; чу́вствовать вкус — *v. i.* име́ть вкус.

tasty, *adj.* вку́сный.

taut, *adj.* упру́гий, подтя́нутый.

tavern, *n.* таве́рна *f.*

tax, *n.* нало́г *m.* — *v.* облага́ть нало́гом; такси́ровать *imp.* & *perf.*

taxi, *n.* такси́ *nt. ind.* **taxi driver,** води́тель такси́.

tea, *n.* чай *m.*

teach, *v.* учи́ть *imp.*; обуча́ть *imp.*, обучи́ть *perf.* **-er.** *n.* учи́тель *m.*, учи́тельница *f.*

team, *n.* кома́нда *f.*

tear, *n.* проре́з *m.*, дыра́ *f.*; (*eye*) слеза́ *f.* — *v. t.* рвать

tease, *v.* дразни́ть *imp.*

teaspoon, *n.* ча́йная ло́жка.

technical, *adj.* техни́ческий.

technique, *n.* те́хника *f.*

tedious, *adj.* ску́чный.

telegram, *n.* телегра́мма *f.*

telegraph, *n.* телегра́ф *m.* — *v.* телеграфи́ровать *imp.* & *perf.*

telephone, *n.* телефо́н *m.* — *v.* телефони́ровать *imp.* & *perf.*; позвони́ть по телефо́ну. **t. operator,** телефони́стка *f.*

telescope, *n.* телеско́п *m.*

television, *n.* телеви́дение *nt.* — *adj.* телевизио́нный. **t. set,** телеви́зор *m.*

tell, (*v.*) сказа́ть *perf.*; (*narrate*) расска́зывать *imp.*, рассказа́ть *perf.*

temper, *n.* настрое́ние *nt.*; (*anger*) раздраже́ние *nt.*, гнев *m.* — *v.* умеря́ть *imp.*, уме́рить *perf.*

temperament, *n.* темпера́мент *m.* **-al,** *adj.* темпера́ментный.

temperance, *n.* сде́ржанность, уме́ренность *f.*

temperate, *adj.* уме́ренный.

temperature, *n.* температу́ра *f.*

tempest, *n.* бу́ря *f.*

temple, *n.* храм *m.*; (*forehead*) висо́к *m.*

temporary, *adj.* вре́менный.

tempt, *v.* искуша́ть *imp.*, искуси́ть *perf.* **-ation,** *n.* искуше́ние *nt.*

ten, *n.*, *adj.* де́сять *num.*

tenant, *n.* нанима́тель, аренда́тор *m.*

tend, *v.* уха́живать *imp.* **t. to,** направля́ться *imp.*, клони́ться *imp.* **-ency,** *n.* накло́нность *f.*

tender, *adj.* не́жный, чувстви́тельный. **-ness,** *n.* не́жность *f.*

tennis, *n.* те́ннис *m.*

tenor, *n.* те́нор *m.* — *adj.* те́норовый.

tense, *adj.* натя́нутый, напряжённый. — *n.* вре́мя *nt.*

tent, *n.* пала́тка *f.,* шатёр *m.*

tenth, *adj.* деся́тый.

term, *n.* срок *m.;* (*name*) те́рмин *m.* — *v.* называ́ть *imp.,* назва́ть *perf.*

terminal, *n.* коне́чная ста́нция.

terrace, *n.* терра́са, вера́нда *f.*

terrible, *adj.* ужа́сный.

territory, *n.* террито́рия *f.*

terror, *n.* страх, у́жас *m.*

test, *n.* испыта́ние *nt.* — *v.* подверга́ть испыта́нию.

testament, *n.* заве́т *m.;* (*law*) завеща́ние *nt.*

testify, *v.* свиде́тельствовать *imp.*

testimony, *n.* свиде́тельство, доказа́тельство *nt.*

text, *n.* текст *m.,* те́ма *f.*

textile, *adj.* тексти́льный. — *n.* тексти́ль *m.,* тексти́льное изде́лие.

texture, *n.* строе́ние *nt.,* ткань *f.,* скла́дка *f.*

than, *conj.* чем.

thank, *v.* благодари́ть *imp.,* поблагодари́ть *perf.* **t. you,** спаси́бо. **thanks to,** благодаря́. **-ful,** *adj.* благода́рный.

that, *pron.,* *adj.* тот *m.,* та *f.,* то *nt.* — *adv.* так; до тако́й сте́пени. — *conj.* что; что́бы.

the, *def. art.,* *no equivalent in Russian.* the . . . the, чем . . . тем.

theater, *n.* теа́тр *m.*

theft, *n.* воровство́ *nt.,* кра́жа *f.*

their, *pron.* их; свой *m.,* своя́ *f.,* своё *nt.,* свои́ *pl.*

theirs, *pron.* их.

theme, *n.* те́ма *f.,* предме́т *m.;* (*mus.*) те́ма *f.*

themselves, *pron.* себя́, себе́; са́ми.

then, *adv.* тогда́; пото́м.

thence, *adv.* отту́да; отсю́да; с того́ вре́мени.

Theodore, *n.* Теодо́р *m.*

theology, *n.* богосло́вие *nt.*

theoretical, *adj.* теорети́ческий

theory, *n.* тео́рия *f.*

there, *adv.* (*loc.*) там; (*dir.*) туда́. **t. is, t. are,** есть; име́ется; име́ются.

therefore, *adv.* поэ́тому.

thermometer, *n.* гра́дусник, термо́метр *m.*

they, *pron.* они́.

thick, *adj.* густо́й. **-en,** *v.* t. сгуща́ть *imp.,* сгусти́ть *perf.;* — *v. i.* сгуща́ться *imp.,* сгусти́ться *perf.*

thief, *n.* вор *m.*

thigh, *n.* бедро́ *nt.*

thimble, *n.* напёрсток *m.*

thin, *adj.* то́нкий. — **t. out,** проре́живать *imp.,* прореди́ть *perf.*

thing, *n.* вещь *f.,* предме́т *m.*

think, *v.* ду́мать *imp.,* поду́мать *perf.* **-er,** *n.* мысли́тель *m.*

third, *adj.* тре́тий (тре́тья *f.,* тре́тье *nt.*).

thirst, *n.* жа́жда *f.*

thirsty, *adj.* томи́мый жа́ждой. **be t.,** хоте́ть пить.

thirteen, *n.,* *adj.* трина́дцать *num.* **-th,** *adj.* трина́дцатый.

thirty, *n.,* *adj.* три́дцать *num.*

this, *adj.* э́тот *m.,* э́та *f.,* э́то *nt.,* э́ти *pl.* — *pron.* э́то.

thorough, *adj.* соверше́нный; зако́нченный. **-ly,** *adv.* вполне́, соверше́нно.

though, *adv.* тем не ме́нее; одна́ко. — *conj.* хотя́; несмотря́ на.

thought, *n.* мысль *f.,* мышле́ние *nt.* **-ful,** *adj.* заду́мчивый; глубокомы́сленный.

thousand, *n.,* *adj.* ты́сяча. *num.*

thread, *n.* ни́тка, нить *f.;* (*of screw*) ход *m.*

threat, *n.* угро́за *f.* **-en,** *v.* грози́ть *imp.,* угрожа́ть *imp.*

three, *n.,* *adj.* три *num.*

thrift, *n.* бережли́вость, эконо́мность *f.*

thrill, *n.* волне́ние *nt.,* тре́пет *m.,* сенса́ция *f.* — *v.* испы́тывать тре́пет; взволнова́ться *imp.*

thrive, *v.* преуспева́ть *imp.,* преуспе́ть *perf.*

throat, *n.* го́рло *nt.*

throne, *n.* трон, престо́л *m.*

through, *prep.* че́рез (+ *acc.*),

сквозь (+ *acc.*), по (+ *dat.*). — *adv.* наскво́зь, соверше́нно. — *adj.* беспереса́дочный, прямо́й. **-out**, *adv.* повсю́ду; во всех отноше́ниях. — *prep.* че́рез; по всему́.

throw, *n.* бросо́к *m.* — *v.* броса́ть *imp.*, бро́сить *perf.* **t. away**, отбра́сывать *imp.*, отбро́сить *perf.* **t. out**, выбра́сывать *imp.*, вы́бросить *perf.*

thumb, *n.* большо́й па́лец *m.*

thunder, *n.* гром *m.* — *v.* греме́ть *imp.* **-storm**, *n.* гроза́ *f.*

Thursday, *n.* четве́рг *m.*

thus, *adv.* так, таки́м о́бразом, поэ́тому; до тако́й сте́пени.

ticket, *n.* биле́т.

tickle, *n.* щекота́ние *nt.*, щеко́тка *f.* — *v.* щекота́ть *imp.*, пощекота́ть *perf.*

ticklish, *adj.* щекотли́вый.

tide, *n.* морско́й прили́в и отли́в, *v.* по́лная вода́. **low t.**, ма́лая вода́.

tidy, *adj.* опря́тный.

tie, *n.* (*bond*) связь *f.*; (*pl.*) у́зы *pl.*; (*necktie*) га́лстук *m.*; (*equal score*) ничья́ *f.* — *v.* завя́зывать *imp.*, завяза́ть *perf.*

tier, *n.* я́рус *m.*

tiger, *n.* тигр *m.*

tight, *adj.* пло́тный; сжа́тый; туго́й; (*stingy*) скупо́й. **-en**, *v.* сжима́ть *imp.*, сжать *perf.*

tile, *n.* черепи́ца *f.*; ка́фель *m.*

till, *n.* ка́сса *f.* — *v.* паха́ть *imp.* — *prep.* до; не ра́ньше.

timber, *n.* бревно́ *nt.*, брус *m.*, лесоматериа́лы *pl.*

time, *n.* вре́мя *nt.*; раз *m.* **a long t.**, до́лго; давно́. **on time** (*punctual*), во́время *adv.* **for the first t.**, в пе́рвый раз. **from t. to t.**, вре́мя от вре́мени. **what t. is it?** кото́рый час? **-ly**, *adj.* своевре́менный.

timid, *adj.* засте́нчивый. **-ity**, *n.* засте́нчивость *f.*

tin, *n.* о́лово *m.*

tiny, *adj.* кро́шечный, о́чень ма́ленький.

tip, *n.* ко́нчик *m.*; (*gratuity*) чаевы́е *pl.* — *v. t.* (*tilt*) наклоня́ть *imp.*, наклони́ть *perf.*; (*gratuity*) дава́ть «на чай». — *v. i.* (*tilt*) наклоня́ться *imp.*, наклони́ться *perf.*

tire, *n.* ши́на *f.* — *v.* устава́ть *imp.*, уста́ть *perf.*

tired, *adj.* уста́лый.

tiptoe, *v.* ходи́ть на цы́почках. — *n.* **on tiptoes**, на цы́почках.

title, *n.* загла́вие, назва́ние *nt.* — *n.* называ́ть *imp.*, назва́ть *perf.*; дава́ть загла́вие.

to, *prep.* к (& *dat.*), в, на (+ *acc.*); (*until*) до (+ *gen.*). **to and fro**, взад и вперёд.

toast, *n.* гре́нок *m.*; (*drink*) тост *m.* — *v.* жа́рить *imp.*; поджа́ривать *imp.*, поджа́рить *perf.*; (*drink*) пить тост за.

tobacco, *n.* таба́к *m.*

today, *adv.* сего́дня. — *n.* сего́дняшний день.

toe, *n.* па́лец на ноге́.

together, *adv.* вме́сте.

toil, *n.* труд *m.*, рабо́та *f.* — *v.* труди́ться *imp.*

toilet, *n.* туале́т *m.*; убо́рная *f.* **t. tissue**, туале́тная бума́га.

token, *n.* знак *m.*, пода́рок на па́мять.

tolerance, *n.* терпи́мость *f.*

tolerant, *adj.* терпи́мый.

tolerate, *v.* терпе́ть *tp.*

tomato, *n.* помидо́р *m.*

tomb, *n.* моги́ла *f.*, надгро́бный па́мятник. **-stone**, *n.* моги́льный ка́мень.

tomorrow, *adv.* за́втра. — *n.* за́втрашний день. **the day after it.**, послеза́втра.

ton, *n.* то́нна *f.*

tone, *n.* тон *m.*

tongue, *n.* язы́к *m.*

tonic, *n.* тонизи́рующее сре́дство.

tonight, *adv.* сего́дня ве́чером; сего́дня но́чью.

tonsil, *n.* миндалеви́дная железа́.

too, adv. сли́шком; (also) та́кже, то́же. t. much, сли́шком мно́го.

tool, n. ору́дие *n.*; рабо́чий инструме́нт; стано́к *m.*

tooth, n. зуб *m.* **-ache,** n. зубна́я боль. **-brush,** n. зубна́я щётка. **-paste,** n. зубна́я па́ста *f.* **-pick,** n. зубочи́стка *f.*

top, n. верши́на *f.*, верх *m.* **from t. to bottom,** све́рху до́низу. — adj. ве́рхний. — v. превосходи́ть *imp.*, превзойти́ *perf.*

topic, n. те́ма *f.*, предме́т *m.*

torch, n. фа́кел *m.*

torment, n. муче́ние *nt.*, му́ка *f.* — v. му́чить *imp.*

torrent, n. ли́вень *m.*

torture, n. пы́тка *f.* — v. пыта́ть *imp.*; му́чить *imp.*

toss, v. броса́ть *imp.*, бро́сить *perf.*; мета́ть *imp.*, метну́ть *perf.*

total, adj. совоку́пный, тота́льный. — n. су́мма *f.*, ито́г *m.*

totalitarian, adj. тоталита́рный, тота́льный.

touch, n. прикоснове́ние, соприкоснове́ние *nt.* — v. каса́ть *imp.*, косну́ть *perf.*; тро́гать *imp.*, тро́нуть *perf.*

tough, adj. жёсткий; сто́йкий; (difficult) тру́дный.

tour, n. путеше́ствие *nt.*, пое́здка *f.* — v. соверша́ть путеше́ствие. **-ist,** n. тури́ст *m.*, тури́стка *f.*

tournament, n. турни́р *m.*

tow, n. букси́р *m.*, бурси́ровка *f.*, бечева́ *f.* — v. букси́ровать *imp.* & *perf.*

toward, prep. к; по направле́нию к; по отноше́нию к (+ dat.).

towel, n. полоте́нце *nt.*

tower, n. ба́шня *f.*

town, n. го́род, городо́к *m.*

toy, n. игру́шка *f.* — v. игра́ть *imp.*; забавля́ться *imp.*

trace, n. след *m.* — v. следи́ть *imp.*, вы́следить *perf.*, проследи́ть *imp.*

track, n. след *m.*; доро́га, доро́жка *f.*; лыжня́ *f.*; (athl.) бегова́я доро́жка. — v. следи́ть *imp.*

tract, n. тракт *m.*; (pamphlet) брошю́ра *f.*

tractor, n. тра́ктор *m.*

trade, n. торго́вля *f.* — v. торгова́ть *imp.*

tradition, n. тради́ция *f.* **-al** adj. традицио́нный.

traffic, n. движе́ние *nt.*

tragedy, n. траге́дия *f.*

tragic, adj. траги́ческий.

trail, n. след *m.*, тропа́ *f.* — v. i. идти́ по́ следу. — v. i. (drag) волочи́ться *imp.*

train, n. по́езд *m.* **by train,** по́ездом. — v. i. трениро́вать *imp.* — v. i. трениро́ваться *imp.* **-ing,** n. воспита́ние, обуче́ние *nt.*

traitor, n. преда́тель, изме́нник *m.*

tranquil, adj. споко́йный. **-ity,** n. споко́йствие *nt.*

transaction, n. де́ло *nt.*

transfer, n. перено́с *m.*, переме́щение *nt.* — v. переноси́ть *imp.*, перенести́ *perf.*; переме́ща́ть *imp.*, перемести́ть *perf.*

transform, v. превраща́ть *imp.*, преврати́ть *perf.* **-ation,** n. превраще́ние *nt.*

transfusion, n. перелива́ние *nt.*

transition, n. перехо́д *m.*, переме́щение *nt.*

translate, v. переводи́ть *imp.*, перевести́ *perf.*

translation, n. перево́д *m.*

transmit, v. передава́ть *imp.*, переда́ть *perf.*

transparent, adj. прозра́чный.

transport, n. тра́нспорт *m.*, перево́зка *f.* — v. перевози́ть *imp.*, перевезти́ *perf.* **-ation,** n. тра́нспортные сре́дства.

trap, n. лову́шка *f.* — v. лови́ть в лову́шки; зама́нивать *imp.*, замани́ть *perf.*

trash, n. отбро́сы *pl.*, хлам *m.*

trauma, n. тра́вма *f.*

travel, n. путеше́ствие *nt.* —

v. путеше́ствовать *imp.* -er, *n.* путеше́ственник *m.*

tray, *n.* подно́с *m.*

tread, *n.* обод *m.*; похо́дка *f.* — *v.* ступа́ть *imp.*; шага́ть *imp.*

treason, *n.* изме́на *f.*

treasure, *n.* сокро́вище *nt.*

treasurer, *n.* казначе́й *m.*; храни́тель *m.*

treasury, *n.* госуда́рственное казначе́йство *nt.* — *adj.* казначе́йский.

treat, *v.* обходи́ться *imp.*, обойти́сь *perf.*; (*med.*) лечи́ть *imp.* -ment, *n.* обраще́ние *nt.*; (*med.*) лече́ние *nt.*, ухо́д *m.*

treaty, *n.* догово́р *m.*

tree, *n.* де́рево *nt.*

tremble, *v.* дрожа́ть *imp.*

tremendous, *adj.* огро́мный.

trend, *n.* направле́ние *nt.*, тенде́нция *f.*

trespass, *v.* наруши́ть грани́цу.

trial, *n.* испыта́ние *nt.*, о́пыт *m.*, про́ба *f.*; (*legal*) суде́бный проце́сс *m.*

triangle, *n.* треуго́льник *m.*

triangular, *adj.* треуго́льный.

tribulation, *n.* несча́стье *nt.*

tributary, *n.* прито́к *m.*

tribute, *n.* дань *f.*

trick, *n.* обма́н *m.*, уло́вка *f.*; (*at cards*) взя́тка *f.* — *v.* обма́нывать *imp.*, обману́ть *perf.*

trigger, *n.* куро́к *m.*, крючо́к *m.*

trim, *adj.* опря́тный, наря́дный. — *v.* подреза́ть *imp.*, подре́зать *perf.*; (*hair*) подстрига́ть *imp.*, подстри́чь *perf.*

trinket, *n.* безделу́шка *f.*

trip, *n.* путеше́ствие *nt.*, пое́здка *f.* — *v. t.* опроки́нуть *perf.* — *v. i.* опроки́нуться *perf.*

triple, *adj.* тройно́й, утро́енный. — *v. t.* утра́ивать *imp.*, утро́ить *perf.* — *v. i.* утра́иваться *imp.*, утро́иться *perf.*

trite, *adj.* бана́льный, изби́тый.

triumph, *n.* триу́мф *m.* — *v.*

победи́ть *perf.* -ant, *adj.* победоно́сный.

trivial, *adj.* тривиа́льный, незначи́тельный.

troop, *n.* отря́д *m.*

trophy, *n.* трофе́й *m.*, добы́ча *f.*

tropical, *adj.* тропи́ческий.

tropics, *n.* тро́пики *pl.*

trot, *n.* рысь *f.* — *v.* идти́ ры́сью.

trouble, *n.* забо́ты, хло́поты *pl.*, затрудне́ние *nt.* — *v. t.* затрудня́ть *imp.*, затрудни́ть *perf.* — *v. i.* затрудня́ться *imp.*, затрудни́ться *perf.* -some, *adj.* причиня́ющий беспоко́йствие; тру́дный.

trough, *n.* коры́то *nt.*

trousers, *n.* брю́ки, штаны́ *pl.*

trout, *n.* форе́ль *f.*

truce, *n.* переми́рие *nt.*

truck, *n.* грузово́й автомоби́ль; грузови́к *m.*

true, *adj.* ве́рный, пра́вильный, правди́вый.

trump, *n.* ко́зырь *m.* — *adj.* козырно́й. — *v.* козыря́ть *imp.*, козырну́ть *perf.*

trumpet, *n.* труба́ *f.*

trunk, *n.* чемода́н *m.*; (*of a tree*) ствол *m.*

trust, *n.* дове́рие *nt.*, ве́ра *f.* — *v.* доверя́ть *imp.*, дове́рить, *perf.* -worthy, *adj.* заслу́живающий дове́рия.

truth, *n.* пра́вда, и́стина *f.* -ful, *adj.* ве́рный, пра́вильный, правди́вый.

try, *n.* попы́тка *f.* — *v.* про́бовать *imp.*, попро́бовать *perf.*; (*law*) суди́ть *imp.* **try on,** примеря́ть *imp.*, приме́рить *perf.*

tub, *n.* ка́дка, ба́дья *f.*; (*bath*) ва́нна *f.*

tube, *n.* труба́, тру́бка *f.*

tuberculosis, *n.* туберкулёз *m.*

Tuesday, *n.* вто́рник *m.*

tug, *n.* рыво́к *m.*; (*boat*) букси́рное су́дно. — *v.* дёргать *imp.*, дёрнуть *perf.*; букси́ровать *imp. & perf.*

tuition, *n.* пла́та за обуче́ние *f.*

tumble, *n.* паде́ние *nt.*: (*somer-*

sault) кувырка́нье *nt.* — *v.* па́дать *imp.*, упа́сть *perf.*; *(acrobatics)* кувырка́ться *imp.*

tumult, *n.* сумато́ха *f.*, шум *m.*

tune, *n.* мело́дия *f.*, моти́в *m.* — *v.* настра́ивать *imp.*, настро́ить *perf.*

tunnel, *n.* тунне́ль *m.*

turf, *n.* дёрн *m.*

Turk, *n.* ту́рок *m.*, турча́нка *f.*

Turkey, *n.* Ту́рция *f.*

Turkish, *adj.* туре́цкий.

turmoil, *n.* сумато́ха *f.*, беспоря́док *m.*

turn, *n.* оборо́т, поворо́т *m.*; изги́б *m.*; о́чередь *f.* — *v.* обраща́ть *imp.*, обрати́ть *perf.* — *v. i.* обраща́ться *imp.*, обрати́ться *perf.* t. **around,** обёртываться *imp.*, обёрну́ться *perf.* t. **on,** включа́ть *imp.*, включи́ть *perf.* t. **off,** выключа́ть *imp.*, вы́ключить *perf.*

turnip, *n.* ре́па *f.*

turtle, *n.* черепа́ха *f.*

tutor, *n.* репети́тор *m.* — *v.* дава́ть ча́стные уро́ки.

twelfth, *adj.* двена́дцатый.

twelve, *n.*, *adj.* двена́дцать *num.*

twentieth, *adj.* двадца́тый.

twenty, *n.*, *adj.* два́дцать *num.*

twice, *adv.* два́жды.

twig, *n.* ве́точка *f.*

twilight, *n.* су́мерки *pl.*

twin, *n.* близне́ц *m.* (*pl.* близнецы́).

twine, *n.* бечёвка *f.*, шпага́т *m.*

twinkle, *v.* мерца́ть *imp.*; сверка́ть *imp.*

twist, *v.* крути́ть *imp.*; сучи́ть *imp.*

two, *n.*, *adj.* два *num., m., nt.*; две *num., f.*

type, *n.* тип, род, класс *m.*; *(print)* шрифт *m.* — *v.* писа́ть на маши́нке. **-writer,** *n.* пи́шущая маши́нка.

typical, *adj.* типи́чный.

typist, *n.* машини́стка *f.*

tyranny, *n.* тира́ния *f.*

tyrant, *n.* тира́н, де́спот *m.*

U

udder, *n.* вы́мя *nt.* (*pl.* вы́мени).

ugly, *adj.* безобра́зный.

Ukraine, *n.* Украи́на *f.*

Ukrainian, *adj.* украи́нский. — *n.* украи́нец *m.*, украи́нка *f.*

ulcer, *n.* я́зва *f.*

ulterior, *adj.* скры́тый.

ultimate, *adj.* оконча́тельный.

umbrella, *n.* зо́нтик *m.*

umpire, *n.* судья́ *m.*

unable, *adj.* неспосо́бный.

unanimous, *adj.* единогла́сный, единоду́шный.

uncertain, *adj.* неуве́ренный.

uncle, *n.* дя́дя *m.* (*declined as f.*).

unconscious, *adj.* бессозна́тельный.

uncover, *v.* открыва́ть *imp.*, откры́ть *perf.*

under, *prep.* под. — *adv.* ни́же, вниз; внизу́.

underestimate, *v.* недооце́нивать *imp.*, недооцени́ть *perf.*

undergo, *v.* подверга́ться *imp.*, подве́ргнуться *perf.*

underground, *adj.* подзе́мный.

underline, *v.* подчёркивать *imp.*, подчеркну́ть *perf.*

underneath, *adv.* вниз, внизу́; ни́же. — *prep.* под (+ *instr.*).

undershirt, *n.* ни́жняя руба́шка.

understand, *v.* понима́ть *imp.*, поня́ть *perf.*; подразумева́ть *imp.*

undertake, *v.* предпринима́ть *imp.*, предприня́ть *perf.*

underwear, *n.* ни́жнее бельё.

undo, *v.* уничтожа́ть сде́ланное.

undress, *v. t.* раздева́ть *imp.*, разде́ть *perf.* — *v. i.* раздева́ться *imp.*, разде́ться *perf.*

uneasy, *adj.* обеспокоеный, встревоженный.

uneven, *adj.* неровный; нечётный.

unexpected, *adj.* неожиданный, непредвиденный.

unfair, *adj.* несправедливый.

unfit, неподходящий, негодный.

unfold, *v.* раскрывать *imp.*, раскрыть *perf.*

unforgettable, *adj.* незабываемый.

unfortunate, *adj.* несчастный.

unhappy, *adj.* несчастливый.

uniform, *adj.* единообразный. — *n.* форма *f.*

unify, *v.* объединять *imp.*, объединить *perf.*; унифицировать *imp. & perf.*

union, *n.* союз *m.*

Union of Soviet Socialist Republics, Союз Советских Социалистических Республик.

unique, *adj.* уникальный, единственный в своём роде.

unit, *n.* единица *f.*

unite, *v. t.* соединять *imp.*, соединить *perf.* — *v. i.* соединяться *imp.*, соединиться *perf.*

United States of America, Соединённые Штаты Америки.

unity, *n.* единство *nt.*

universal, *adj.* универсальный, всеобщий, всемирный.

universe, *n.* вселенная *f.*; мир *m.*

university, *n.* университет *m.* — *adj.* университетский.

unless, *conj.* если не.

unlike, *adj.* непохожий; не такой, как. -**ly,** *adj.* неправдоподобный, маловероятный.

unload, *v.* разгружать *imp.*, разгрузить *perf.*

unlock, *v.* отпирать *imp.*, отпереть *perf.*; открывать *imp.*, открыть *perf.*

untie, *v.* развязывать *imp.*, развязать *perf.*

until, *prep.* до (+ *gen.*); не раньше.

unusual, *adj.* необыкновенный.

up, *adv.* наверху; выше. — *prep.* вверх по; по направлению к; вдоль по.

uphold, *v.* поддерживать *imp.*, поддержать *perf.*

upholster, *v.* обивать *imp.*, обить *perf.*

upon, see on.

upper, *adj.* верхний; высший.

uproar, *n.* шум *m.*, волнение *nt.*

upset, *n.* опрокидывание *nt.* — *v.* опрокидывать *imp.*, опрокинуть *perf.*

upside down, вверх дном.

upward, *adv.* вверх; (*more*) больше.

Ural Mountains, Уральские горы.

urge, *n.* побуждение *nt.* — *v.* подстрекать *imp.*, подстрекнуть *perf.*

urgency, *n.* необходимость, крайность *f.*

urgent, *adj.* срочный, настоятельный, крайне необходимый.

USA, США.

use, *n.* употребление *nt.* — *v.* употреблять *imp.*, употребить *perf.* -**ful,** *adj.* полезный. -**less,** *adj.* бесполезный.

usher, *n.* билетёр *m.*

USSR, СССР.

usual, *adj.* обычный, обыкновенный. **as u.,** как обычно.

utensil, *n.* посуда, утварь *f.*

utmost, *adj.* крайний, величайший.

utter, *adj.* совершенный. — *v.* выражать *imp.*, выразить *perf.*; высказывать *imp.*, высказать *perf.* -**ance,** *n.* высказывание *nt.*

V

vacancy, *n.* вака́нсия *f.*; пустота́ *f.*

vacant, *adj.* вака́нтный.

vacation, *n.* кани́кулы *pl.*, о́тпуск *m.*

vaccinate, *v.* де́лать приви́вку.

vacuum, *n.* безвозду́шное простра́нство. **v. cleaner,** пылесо́с *m.*

vagina, *n.* влага́лище *nt.*

vagrant, *adj.* стра́нствующий.

vague, *adj.* неопределённый, нея́сный.

vain, *adj.* тщесла́вный, тще́тный. **in v.,** напра́сно, тще́тно *adv.*

valiant, *adj.* до́блестный.

valid, *adj.* име́ющий си́лу, действи́тельный.

valley, *n.* доли́на *f.*

valor, *n.* до́блесть *f.*

valuable, *adj.* це́нный.

value, *n.* сто́имость, це́нность *f.* — *v.* цени́ть *imp.*; оце́нивать *imp.*, оцени́ть *perf.*

vanish, *v.* исчеза́ть *imp.*, исче́знуть *perf.*

vanity, *n.* тщесла́вие *nt.*

vanquish, *v.* побежда́ть *imp.*, победи́ть *perf.*; покоря́ть *imp.*, покори́ть *perf.*

vapor, *n.* пар *m.*

variation, *n.* измене́ние *nt.*; переме́на *f.*; (*mus.*) вариа́ция *f.*

variety, *n.* разнообра́зие *nt.*

various, *adj.* разли́чный.

varnish, *n.* лак *m.* — *v.* лакирова́ть *imp. & perf.*

vary, *v. t.* изменя́ть *imp.*, измени́ть *perf.* — *v. i.* изменя́ться *imp.*, измени́ться *perf.*

vase, *n.* ва́за *f.*

vast, *adj.* обши́рный, огро́мный.

vat, *n.* чан *m.*; бак *m.*

vault, *n.* свод *m.*; подва́л *m.*; склеп *m.*

vegetable, *n.* о́вощ *m.* — *adj.* расти́тельный.

vehement, *adj.* неи́стовый.

vehicle, *n.* перево́зочное сре́дство.

veil, *n.* покрыва́ло *nt.*; вуа́ль *f.* — *v.* скрыва́ть *imp.*, скрыть *perf.*

vein, *n.* ве́на, жи́ла *f.*

velocity, *n.* ско́рость *f.*

velvet, *n.* ба́рхат *m.* — *adj.* ба́рхатный.

vengeance, *n.* месть *f.*, мще́ние *nt.*

vent, *n.* отве́рстие *nt.*

ventilate, *v.* прове́тривать *imp.*, прове́трить *perf.*

ventilation, *n.* прове́тривание *nt.*

venture, *n.* риско́ванное предприя́тие.

Vera, *n.* Ве́ра *f.*

verb, *n.* глаго́л *m.* **-al,** *adj.* у́стный; (*gram.*) глаго́льный.

verdict, *n* верди́кт *m.*, реше́ние *nt.*

verge, *n.* край *m.*

verify, *v.* проверя́ть *imp.*, прове́рить *perf.*

versatile, *adj.* многосторо́нний.

verse, *n.* (*of a poem, etc.*) строфа́ *f.*, стих *m.*; (*poetry*) стихи́ *pl.*

version, *n.* ве́рсия *f.*, вариа́нт *m.*

vertical, *adj.* вертика́льный.

very, *adv.* о́чень.

vessel, *n.* сосу́д *m.*; (*ship*) судно́ *nt.*

vest, *n.* жиле́т *m.*

veteran, *n.* ветера́н *m.*

veto, *n.* ве́то *nt. indecl.* — *v.* налага́ть ве́то.

vex, *v.* раздража́ть *imp.*, раздражи́ть *perf.*

via, *prep.* че́рез.

vibrate, *v.* вибри́ровать *imp. & perf.*

vibration, *n.* вибра́ция *f.*

vice, *n.* поро́к *m.*

vicinity, *n.* окре́стности *pl.*

vicious, *adj.* поро́чный; злой.

victim, *n.* же́ртва *f.*

victor, *n.* победи́тель *m.*

victorious, *adj.* победоно́сный.

victory, *n.* побе́да *f.*

view, *n.* вид *m.*, по́ле зре́ния. **in v. of,** в виду́. — *v.* осма́тривать *imp.*; рассма́тривать *imp.*

vigil, *n.* бо́дрствование *nt.* **-ant,** *adj.* бди́тельный.

vigor, *n.* эне́ргия, си́ла *f.* **-ous,** *adj.* энерги́чный, си́льный.

vile, *adj.* по́длый.

village, *n.* дере́вня *f.*, село́ *nt.*

villain, *n.* него́дяй, злоде́й *m.*

Vincent, *n.* Вике́нтий *m.*

vindicate, *v.* опра́вдывать *imp.* оправда́ть *perf.*

vine, *n.* виногра́дная лоза́ *f.*; ползу́чее расте́ние.

vinegar, *n.* у́ксус *m.*

vintage, *n.* урожа́й (виногра́да).

violate, *v.* наруша́ть *imp.*; нару́шить *perf.*

violation, *n.* наруше́ние *nt.*

violence, *n.* наси́лие, неи́стовство.

violent, *adj.* неи́стовый; наси́льственный.

violin, *n.* скри́пка *f.* **-ist,** *n.* скрипа́ч *m.*, скрипа́чка *f.*

virgin, *n.* де́ва *f.* — *adj.* де́вичый, де́вственный.

virile, *adj.* возмужа́лый, мужско́й, му́жественный.

virtual, *adj.* действи́тельный, факти́ческий. — *adv.* факти́чески; в су́щности.

virtue, *n.* доброде́тель *f.*

virtuous, *adj.* доброде́тельный.

virus, *n.* ви́рус *m.*

visa, *n.* ви́за *f.*

visible, *adj.* ви́димый, я́вный, очеви́дный.

vision, *n.* зре́ние *nt.*, проница́тельность *f.*

visit, *n.* посеще́ние *nt.*, визи́т *m.* — *v.* посеща́ть *imp.*, посети́ть *perf.* **-or,** *n.* посети́-

тель *m.*; (*guest*) гость *m.*

visual, *adj.* зри́тельный, нагля́дный.

vital, *adj.* жи́зненный. **-ity,** *n.* жи́зненность *f.*

vitamin, *n.* витами́н *m.*

vivacious, *adj.* оживлённый, живо́й.

vivacity, *n.* оживлённость, жи́вость *f.*

vivid, *adj.* я́сный; пы́лкий.

vocabulary, *n.* слова́рь *m.*; запа́с слов; ле́ксика *f.*

vocal, *adj.* голосово́й, вока́льный. **v. chords,** голосовы́е свя́зки.

vogue, *n.* мо́да *f.*

voice, *n.* го́лос *m.* — *v.* выража́ть *imp.*, вы́разить *perf.*

void, *adj.* неэффекти́вный; пусто́й. — *n.* пустота́ *f.* — *v. i.* (*empty*) опорожня́ть *imp.*, опорожни́ть *perf.* — *v. t.* (*nullify*) де́лать неде́йствительным.

volume, *n.* ёмкость *f.*; (*book*) том *m.*

voluminous, *adj.* многото́мный; объёмистый.

voluntary, *adj.* доброво́льный.

volunteer, *n.* доброво́лец *m.* — *v.* вы́зваться доброво́льно.

vomit, *v.* страда́ть рвото́й.

vote, *n.* голосова́ние *nt.*; го́лос *m.* — *v.* голосова́ть *imp. & perf.*

voter, *n.* избира́тель *m.*

vow, *n.* кля́тва *f.* — *v.* кля́ться *perf.*

vowel, *n.* гла́сный *m.*, гла́сный звук.

voyage, *n.* пла́вание *nt.*, морско́е путеше́ствие.

vulgar, *adj.* гру́бый, вульга́рный. **-ity,** *n.* вульга́рность *f.*

vulnerable, *adj.* уязви́мый, рани́мый.

W

wade, v. переходи́ть вброд.

wag, v. маха́ть imp., махну́ть perf.

wages, n. зарабо́тная пла́та.

wagon, n. коля́ска, теле́жка, пово́зка f.

wail, n. вопль m. — v. вопи́ть imp.

waist, n. та́лия f.

wait, n. ожида́ние nt. — v. ждать imp., подожда́ть perf. **w. on,** прислу́живать imp. **-er,** n. официа́нт m. **-ress,** n. официа́нтка f.

wake, v. t. буди́ть imp., разбуди́ть perf. — v. i. просыпа́ться imp., просну́ться perf.

walk, n. прогу́лка f.; ходьба́ f. — v. ходи́ть imp. indet., идти́ imp. det.

wall, n. стена́ f.

wallet, n. бума́жник m.

walnut, n. гре́цкий оре́х.

waltz, n. вальс m. — v. вальси́ровать imp.

wander, v. броди́ть imp.; стра́нствовать imp.

want, n. (desire) жела́ние nt., жа́жда f.; (need) потре́бность f.; (lack) недоста́ток m. — v. хоте́ть imp.; жела́ть imp.; (lack) недостава́ть imp., недоста́ть perf.

war, n. война́ f.

ward, n. (hospital) пала́та f.; (prison) ка́мера f.; (political) райо́н m.

wardrobe, n. гардеро́б m.; (checkroom) гардеро́бная f.

wares, n. изде́лия pl.

warm, adj. тёплый; горя́чий. — v. t. согрева́ть imp., согре́ть perf. — v. i. согрева́ться imp., согре́ться perf. **-th,** n. тепло́ nt.; (fig.) серде́чность f.

warn, v. предостерега́ть imp., предостере́чь perf.

warp, v. t. коро́бить imp., покоро́бить perf. — v. i. коро́биться imp., покоро́биться perf.

warrant, v. служи́ть оправда́нием.

Warsaw, n. Варша́ва f.

wash, v. t. мыть imp., вы́мыть perf. — v. i. мы́ться imp., вы́мыться perf.

washing machine, стира́льная маши́на.

wasp, n. оса́ f.

waste, n. у́быль f., уще́рб, убы́ток m., изли́шняя тра́та. — v. расточа́ть imp., расточи́ть perf.; (time) теря́ть imp., потеря́ть perf.

watch, n. стра́жа f., дозо́р m.; (timepiece) часы́ pl. — v. наблюда́ть imp.; следи́ть imp. **w. out,** остерега́ться imp. **-ful,** adj. бди́тельный. **-man,** n. сто́рож m.

water, n. вода́ f. — v. сма́чивать imp., смочи́ть perf.; полива́ть imp., поли́ть perf.; (animals) пои́ть imp., напои́ть perf. **-fall,** n. водопа́д m. **-proof,** adj. непромока́емый, водонепроница́емый. — v. де́лать непромока́емым, водонепроница́емым.

wave, n. маха́ние nt.; (sea) волна́ f. — v. t. маха́ть imp.; разма́хивать perf. — v. i. развева́ться imp.

wax, n. воск m. — v. вощи́ть imp.

way, n. путь, доро́га f. **by the way,** ме́жду про́чим. **on the way,** по доро́ге; по пути́.

we, pron. мы.

weak, adj. сла́бый. **-en,** v. t. ослабля́ть imp., осла́бить perf. — v. i. ослабева́ть imp., ослабе́ть perf. **-ness,** n. сла́бость f.

wealth, n. бога́тство nt.

wealthy, adj. бога́тый.

weapon, n. ору́жие nt.

wear, n. ноше́ние nt.; изно́с m. — v. носи́ть imp. — v. i. носи́ться imp. **w. out,**

изна́шивать *imp.*, износи́ть *perf.*

weary, *adj.* уста́вший, утомлённый.

weather, *n.* пого́да *f.*

weave, *v.* ткать *imp.*, сотка́ть *perf.*

weaver, *n.* ткач *m.*, ткачи́ха *f.*

web, *n.* ткань *f.*; (*spider*) паути́на *f.*

wedding, *n.* сва́дьба *f.*

wedge, *n.* клин *m.*

Wednesday, *n.* среда́ *f.*

weed, *n.* со́рная трава́; сорня́к *m.* — *v.* вычища́ть *imp.*, вы́чистить *perf.*

week, *n.* неде́ля *f.* **-day**, *n.* бу́дний день. **-end**, *n.* вре́мя о́тдыха с суббо́ты до понеде́льника. **-ly**, *adj.* еженеде́льный. — *adv.* еженеде́льно. — *n.* еженеде́льник *m.*

weep, *v.* пла́кать *imp.*

weigh, *v. t.* взве́шивать *imp.*, взве́сить *perf.* — *v. i.* ве́сить *imp.*

weight, *n.* вес *m.*; (*athl.*) штáнга *f.*

welcome, *adj.* жела́нный.

you 're w.! пожа́луйста! — *n.* приве́тствие *nt.* — *v.* приве́тствовать *imp.*

welfare, *n.* благосостоя́ние *nt.*

well, *adj.* хоро́ший; здоро́вый. — *adv.* хорошо́; как сле́дует. — *n.* родни́к, коло́дец *m.*

well-being, *n.* благополу́чие *nt.*

well-known, *adj.* изве́стный.

west, *n.* за́пад *m.* — *adj.* за́падный. — *adv.* к за́паду; на за́пад. **-ern**, *adj.* за́падный. **-ward**, *adj.* напра́вленный к за́паду. — *adv.* на за́пад.

wet, *adj.* мо́крый, вла́жный. **to get wet**, промока́ть *imp.*, промо́кнуть *perf.* — *v.* сма́чивать *imp.*, смочи́ть *perf.*

whale, *n.* кит *m.*

what, *pron.* како́й; что. **-ever**, *adj.* любо́й; како́й бы ни. — *pron.* всё что; что бы ни.

wheat, *n.* пшени́ца *f.*

wheel, *n.* колесо́, колёсико *nt.*

when, *adv.*, *conj.* когда́. **-ever**, *conj.* когда́ же.

where, *adv.* (*dir.*) куда́; (*loc.*) где. — *conj.* туда́; туда́ куда́; туда́ где; где. **-ever**, *adv.* где бы ни; куда́ бы ни.

whether, *conj.* ли.

which, *pron.* кото́рый; како́й; кто. **-ever**, *pron.* како́й; како́й бы ни.

while, *n.* вре́мя *nt.* **a long w.**, до́лго *adv.* **a short w.**, недо́лго *adv.* **for a w.**, на вре́мя. **once in a w.**, вре́мя от вре́мени.

whip, *n.* кнут, хлыст *m.* — *v.* хлеста́ть *imp.*; (*food*) сбива́ть *imp.*, сбить *perf.*

whirl, *v. t.* верте́ть *imp.*, кружи́ть *imp.* — *v. i.* верте́ться *imp.*; кружи́ться *imp.* **-pool**, *n.* водоворо́т *m.* **-wind**, *n.* вихрь *m.*

whiskers, *n.* бакенба́рды *pl.*

whiskey, *n.* ви́ски *nt. ind.*

whisper, *n.* шёпот *m.* **in a w.**, шёпотом *adv.* — *v.* шепта́ть *imp.*, шепну́ть *perf.*

whistle, *n.* свист *m.*; (*instrument*) свисто́к *m.* — *v.* свисте́ть, свиста́ть *imp.*, сви́стнуть *perf.*

white, *adj.* бе́лый. — *n.* бе́лый свет; белизна́ *f.*; (*of egg*) бело́к *m.*

who, *pron.* кто; кото́рый. **-ever**, *pron.* кто бы ни; кото́рый бы ни.

whole, *adj.* це́лый; весь. — *n.* це́лое *nt.*; ито́г *m.* **on the w.**, в о́бщем.

wholesale, *n.* опто́вая торго́вля. — *adj.* опто́вый. — *adv.* опто́м.

wholesome, *adj.* здоро́вый; благотво́рный.

wholly, *adv.* по́лностью, целико́м.

whose, *pron.* чей *m.*, чья *f.*, чьё *nt.*, чьи *pl.*

why, *adv.* почему́.

wicked, *adj.* злой, гре́шный.

-ness, *n.* злобность *f.,* злой поступок.

wide, *adj.* широкий. — *adv.* широко.

widen, *v. t.* расширять *imp.,* расширить *perf.* — *v. i.* расширяться *imp.,* расшириться *perf.*

widespread, *adj.* широко распространённый.

widow, *n.* вдова *f.*   **-er,** *n.* вдовец *m.*

width, *n.* ширина, широта *f.*

wield, *v.* владеть *imp.*

wife, *n.* жена *f.*

wig, *n.* парик *m.*

wild, *adj.* дикий.

wilderness, *n.* дикая местность.

will, *n.* воля *f.,* сила воли. *(legal)* завещание *nt.* — *v.* заставлять *imp.,* заставить *perf.;* *(legal)* завещать *imp.* & *perf.* **-ing,** *adj.* готовый. — *adv.* охотно.

wilt, *v.* вянуть *imp.,* завянуть *perf.*

win, *v.* выигрывать *imp.,* выиграть *perf.*

wind, *n.* ветер *m.; v. t. (coil)* извивать *imp.,* извить *perf.; (watch)* заводить *imp.,* завести *perf.* — *v. i.* извиваться *imp.,* извиться *perf.*

window, *n.* окно *nt.*

windy, *adj.* ветреный.

wine, *n.* вино *nt.* — *adj.* винный.

wing, *n.* крыло *nt.; (theat.)* кулисы *pl.*

wink, *n.* моргание *nt.,* миг *m.* — *v.* моргать *imp.,* моргнуть *perf.*

winner, *n.* победитель *m.*

winter, *n.* зима *f.* **in the w.,** зимой.

wipe, *v.* вытирать *imp.,* вытереть *perf.* **w. out,** стирать *imp.,* стереть *perf.*

wire, *n.* проволока *f.,* провод *m.* — *v.* монтировать проводá.

wisdom, *n.* мудрость *f.*

wise, *adj.* мудрый.

wish, *n.* желание, пожелание *nt.* — *v.* желать *imp.,* пожелать *perf.*

wit, *n.* ум, разум *m.;* остроумие *f.*

witch, *n.* ведьма *f.*

with, *prep.* с, со (+ *instr.*).

withdraw, *v. t.* отдёргивать *imp.,* отдёрнуть *perf.* — *v. i.* удаляться *imp.,* удалиться *perf.*

wither, *v.* сохнуть *imp.;* блёкнуть *imp.,* поблёкнуть *perf.*

withhold, *v.* удерживать *imp.,* удержать *perf.*

within, *adv.* внутри. — *prep.* в, в пределах внутри.

without, *adv.* вне, снаружи. — *prep.* без, безо (+ *gen.*).

witness, *n.* свидетель *m.* — *v.* быть свидетелем.

witty, *adj.* остроумный.

wizard, *n.* чародей *m.*

woe, *n.* горе *nt.*

wolf, *n.* волк *m.*

woman, *n.* женщина *f.*

womb, *n.* матка *f.*

wonder, *n.* удивление, изумление *nt.* **no wonder,** неудивительно. — *v.* удивляться *imp.* **-ful,** *adj.* замечательный.

woo, *v.* ухаживать *imp.*

wood, *n.* лес *m.;* дерево *nt.; (for fire)* дрова *pl.* **-en,** *adj.* деревянный.

wool, *n.* шерсть *f.* **-en,** *adj.* шерстяной.

word, *n.* слово *nt.* **w. for w.,** слово в слово. **in a w.,** одним словом. — *v.* выражать словами.

work, *n.* работа *f.; (creation)* произведение, сочинение *nt.; (toil)* труд *m.* — *v.* работать *imp.* **-er,** *n.* рабочий *m.*

world, *n.* мир *m.* — *adj.* мировой. **-ly,** *adj.* мирской.

world-wide, *adj.* всемирный.

worm, *n.* червяк *m.,* червь *f.*

worry, *n.* забота *f.* — *v.* беспокоиться *imp.*

worse, *adj.* худший. **to become w.,** ухудшаться *imp.,* ухудшиться *perf.* — *adv.* хуже.

worship, *n.* поклоне́ние *nt.* — *v.* поклоня́ться *imp.*

worst, *adj.* наиху́дший. — *adv.* ху́же всего́.

worth, *n.* сто́имость, це́нность *f.* — *adj.* сто́ящий. **-less,** *adj.* ничего́ не сто́ящий.

worthy, *adj.* досто́йный, заслу́живающий.

wound, *n.* ра́на *f.,* ране́ние *nt.* — *v.* ра́нить *imp. & perf.*

wrap, *v.* завёртывать *imp.,* заверну́ть *perf.*

wrapping, *n.* обёртка *f.*

wrath, *n.* гнев *m.*

wreath, *n.* вено́к *m.,* гирля́нда *f.*

wreck, *n.* круше́ние *nt.,* ава́рия *f.* — *v.* разруша́ть *imp.,* разру́шить *perf.*

wrench, *n.* га́ечный ключ.

wrestle, *v.* боро́ться *imp.*

wrestling, *n.* борьба́ *f.*

wretched, *adj.* жа́лкий.

wring, *v.* скру́чивать *imp.,* скрути́ть *perf.*

wrinkle, *n.* морщи́на *f.* — *v.* мо́рщить *imp.,* смо́рщить *perf.*

wrist, *n.* запя́стье *nt.* — *adj.* нару́чный.

write, *v.* писа́ть *imp.,* написа́ть *perf.* **w. down,** запи́сывать *imp.,* записа́ть *perf.*

writer, *n.* писа́тель, а́втор *m.*

wrong, *adj.* непра́вильный, оши́бочный; не тот. — *adv.* непра́вильно, неве́рно. — *n.* непра́вда, непра́вильность, оши́бочность. — *v.* вреди́ть *imp.,* повреди́ть *perf.*

X

x-ray, *n.* рентге́новы лучи́; рентге́новский сни́мок. — *adj.* рентге́новский. — *n.* просве́чивать рентге́новыми луча́ми.

xylophone, *n.* ксилофо́н *m.*

Y

yacht, *n.* я́хта *f.*

yard, *n.* двор *m.;* (*measure*) ярд *m.*

yawn, *n.* зево́та *f.* — *v.* зева́ть *imp.,* зевну́ть *perf.*

year, *n.* год *m.* **last y.** в про́шлом году́. **next y.,** на бу́дущий год. **this y.,** в э́том году́, в ны́нешнем году́. **-ly,** *adj.* ежего́дный.

yearn, *v.* тоскова́ть *imp.* **-ing,** *n.* тоска́ *f.*

yeast, *n.* дро́жжи *pl.*

yell, *n.* пронзи́тельный крик. — *v.* крича́ть *imp.,* кри́кнуть *perf.*

yellow, *adj.* жёлтый. — *n.* жёлтый цвет; желтизна́ *f.* **-ish,** *adj.* желтова́тый. **-ness,** *n.* желтизна́ *f.*

yelp, *n.* лай *m.* — *v.* ла́ять *imp.*

yes, *adv.* да.

yesterday, *adv.* вчера́. **the day before y.,** позавчера́; тре́тьего дня. — *n.* вчера́шний день.

yet, *adv.* ещё; всё ещё. — *conj.* одна́ко.

yield, *v,* дава́ть *imp.,* дать *perf.;* (*surrender*) уступа́ть *imp.,* уступи́ть *perf.*

yoke, *n.* я́рмо, и́го *nt.*

yolk, *n.* желто́к *m.*

yonder, *adj.* вон тот. — *adv.* вон там.

you, *pron.* ты; вы.

young, *adj.* молодо́й. **-ster,** *n.* ма́льчик, ю́ноша *m.*

your, *adj.* твой; ваш.

youth, *n.* ю́ность, мо́лодость

f.; (*man*) ю́ношь. *m.*; (*coll.*)
молодёж *f.* **-ful,** *adj.* ю́но-
шеский.

Yugoslav, *adj.* югосла́вский.
Yugoslavia, *n.* Югосла́вия *f.*

Z

zeal, *n.* усе́рдие, рве́ние *nt.*
-ous, *adj.* усе́рдный.
zebra, *n.* зе́бра *f.*
zero, *n.* нуль *m.*
zinc, *n.* цинк *m.* — *adj.*
ци́нковый.
zipper, *n.* застёжка-мо́лния *f.*

zone, *n.* зо́на *f.*, (*geog.*) по́яс *m.*
zoo, *n.* зоопа́рк (*abbr. of*
зоологи́ческий парк) *m.*,
зооса́д (*abbr. of* зоологи́-
ческий сад) *m.*, звери́нец *m.*
zoology, *n.* зооло́гия *f.*

Cardinal		Ordinal	*(declined as adjectives)*
1	оди́н *m.*, одна́ *f.*, одно́ *nt.*	1st	пе́рвый
2	два *m.*+*nt.*, две *f.*	2nd	второ́й
3	три	3rd	тре́тий, *(f. -ья, nt. -ье)*
4	четы́ре	4th	четвёртый
5	пять	5th	пя́тый
6	шесть	6th	шесто́й
7	семь	7th	седьмо́й
8	во́семь	8th	восьмо́й
9	де́вять	9th	девя́тый
10	де́сять	10th	деся́тый
11	оди́ннадцать	11th	оди́ннадцатый
12	двена́дцать	12th	двена́дцатый
13	трина́дцать	13th	трина́дцатый
14	четы́рнадцать	14th	четы́рнадцатый
15	пятна́дцать	15th	пятна́дцатый
16	шестна́дцать	16th	шестна́дцатый
17	семна́дцать	17th	семна́дцатый
18	восемна́дцать	18th	восемна́дцатый
19	девятна́дцать	19th	девятна́дцатый
20	два́дцать	20th	двадца́тый
21	два́дцать оди́н (одна́, одно́)	21st	два́дцать пе́рвый
30	три́дцать	30th	тридца́тый
32	три́дцать два (две)	32nd	три́дцать второ́й
40	со́рок	40th	сороково́й
43	со́рок три	43rd	со́рок тре́тий
50	пятьдеся́т	50th	пятидеся́тый
54	пятьдеся́т четы́ре	54th	пятьдеся́т четвёртый
60	шестьдеся́т	60th	шестидеся́тый
65	шестьдеся́т пять	65th	шестьдеся́т пя́тый
70	семьдеся́т	70th	семидеся́тый
76	семьдеся́т шесть	76th	семьдеся́т шесто́й
80	во́семьдесят	80th	восьмидеся́тый